A HISTORY OF MODERN GERMANY 1871 to Present

Second Edition

DIETRICH ORLOW
Boston University

PRENTICE HALL, Englewood Cliffs, New Jersey 07632

Library of Congress Cataloging-in-Publication Data

Orlow, Dietrich.
    A history of modern Germany : 1871 to present / Dietrich Orlow. --
2nd ed.
        p.   cm.
    Includes bibliographical references and index.
    ISBN 0-13-388505-4
    1. Germany--History--1871-   I. Title.
DD220.067 1991
943.08--dc20   90-39035
                                                            CIP

Editorial/production supervision
  and interior design: Bayani Mendoza de Leon
Cover design: Lundgren Graphics, Ltd.
Manufacturing buyers: Debbie Kesar/Marianne Gloriande
Map preparation: *Eliza McClennen,* Boston University Geography Department
Illustration credits: Hans Dollinger, ed. *Lachen Streng Verboten!* (Munich: Südwestverlag, 1972);
  Friedrich Arnold, ed. *Anschläge* (Ebenhausen: Langewiesche-Brandt, 1972);
  Maurice Richards, ed. *Posters of the First World War* (New York: Walker and Co., 1968).

© 1991, 1987 by Prentice-Hall, Inc.
A Division of Simon & Schuster
Englewood Cliffs, New Jersey 07632

Printed in the United States of America
10 9 8 7 6 5 4 3 2 1

ISBN 0-13-388505-4

Prentice-Hall International (UK) Limited, *London*
Prentice-Hall of Australia Pty. Limited, *Sydney*
Prentice-Hall Canada Inc., *Toronto*
Prentice-Hall Hispanoamericana, S.A., *Mexico*
Prentice-Hall of India Private Limited, *New Delhi*
Prentice-Hall of Japan, Inc., *Tokyo*
Simon & Schuster Asia Pte. Ltd., *Singapore*
Editora Prentice-Hall do Brasil, Ltda., *Rio de Janeiro*

CONTENTS

6

FOOL'S GOLD: THE WEIMAR REPUBLIC, 1924–1930

7

FROM AUTHORITARIANISM TO TOTALITARIANISM, 1930–1938

8

CONQUEST, DEATH, AND DEFEAT, 1938–1945

9

"CONDOMINIUM OF THE ALLIED POWERS," 1945–1949

MAPS

PREFACE

The present condition of Germany seemed to contradict the title of this book. For the last forty years Germany has been not one country, but two: West Germany, formally the Federal Republic of Germany, and East Germany, the German Democratic Republic. At first glance they seemed to have little in common. West Germany is a liberal democracy representing values of political and cultural pluralism and modified free enterprise. East Germany until very recently was a communist state whose leaders attempted to create a society founded on the principles of Marxism-Leninism. The two nations are integrated into opposing power blocs. West Germany is a friend of the United States and a member of the NATO alliance; East Germany is the Soviet Union's most important European ally and a member of the Warsaw Pact. For most of their history relations between the two Germanys have been strained.

Yet, as if to illustrate that nothing in history is permanent, as this second edition of *A History of Modern Germany* goes to press, the era of the two Germanys, too, seems to be coming to an end. When this text first appeared, four years ago, there seemed little likelihood that East and West Germany would be reunited. But the dramatic events of 1989 now make a united Germany a virtual certainty. In a few short months the East German Communist regime fell from power, the hated Berlin Wall crumbled, and the East German people in a genuinely free election voted for reunification with the West.

Ironically, as a divided nation the two German states achieved much of what the German people sought in vain when they were last a united country: a long period of political stability, economic prosperity, and peace with their neighbors. Equally paradoxically, despite the existence of two German states, interest in the two countries' joint history seems to increase. The reason is easy to see: The division of the country was the result of the course of German history in the years from 1871 to the end of World War II in 1945. For almost three quarters of a century German history was synonymous with "the German problem," a shorthand way of indicating that Germany was an unstable and unpredictable factor in modern European history. In domestic affairs the country was unable to achieve a political and social consensus. A revolution, several coup attempts, and four constitutions gave the country political systems that ranged from monarchical authoritarianism to liberal democracy and Nazi totalitarianism, but no lasting stability. Closely related to political and social upheavals, the German economy experienced alternate periods of boom and bust. Twice in modern times the country reached the brink of economic and fiscal collapse.

Domestic upheavals in turn were related to repeated attempts by Germany's leaders to change the balance of power in Europe and the rest of the world. Having achieved national unity by a victorious war, the German leaders repeatedly attempted to use international aggression to provide the nation with domestic stability, economic prosperity, and respect abroad. The pattern culminated with Adolf Hitler's deliberate unleashing of World War II to realize his vast ambitions. The Nazi dictator and his associates intended to establish permanently Germany's predominant role in the world. At the end of World War II, bombed cities, millions of dead and refugees, and a divided nation subject to the whims of the victors remained to represent the consequences of hubris.

Yet modern German history is more than Prusso-German authoritarianism, the Nazi dictatorship, military aggression, and the Holocaust. This account of the country's path from national unification in 1871 to the present division into two nations attempts to present the alternative aspects as well. Long-standing, if often submerged, traditions of political, cultural, and economic liberalism as well as left-wing radicalism existed side by side with authoritarian and regressive strains. Their surprisingly swift and strong establishment as societal values after World War II happened in large part because for many years these components in the German societal makeup, although not dominant, had been struggling for viability and recognition.

This is not a narrative history in the traditional sense. Many events have been omitted in order to keep the text "problem-oriented." I have tried to retain the central focus on the dynamics in German society that led to both the volatility and unpredictability in the country's domestic policies and foreign relations, and to its impressive achievements.

It is a pleasant duty to acknowledge the help that this book has received from a number of colleagues and friends. Werner T. Angress, Jeffrey Diefendorf, Werner Jochmann, Jean Leventhal, David Morgan, Arnold Offner, and Norman Naimark all took the trouble to read portions of the manuscript. I would like to thank them for their valuable comments and suggestions. I am grateful to Ann-Marie Devlin who spent long hours over a copying machine and to Eliza McClennen of the Boston University Geography Department for drawing the maps.

Thank you also to those who reviewed the manuscript of the first edition: Rudy Koshar, University of Southern California; Richard Breitman, American University at Chevy Chase, MD; and David A. Hackett, University of Texas at El Paso. The revised edition has also benefited from the comments of several colleagues who used the first edition in their courses and were kind enough to point out some factual errors and unclear interpretations in the earlier work.

In a very real sense this has been a family project. My daughter, my parents, and especially my wife, Maria, were all instrumental in bringing the book to a conclusion. Any shortcomings that remain are, of course, my own responsibility.

Dietrich Orlow
Chestnut Hill, MA
Gmunden, Austria

CHAPTER 1

THE QUEST FOR UNITY, 1815–1871

At the beginning of the nineteenth century the territories that would eventually become "Germany" bore resemblance to neither the German Empire of 1871 nor to the East and West German republics familiar to us today. In 1815 Germany was little more than "a geographic expression," as a contemporary statesman put it.

Then as now, the German Confederation, the geographic expression's formal name, occupied the bulk of the Central European plain, that large expanse of flatland stretching from the North Sea in the west to the Russian marshes in the east. On paper the German Confederation encompassed far more territory than is claimed by either West or East Germany today. Included were all of present-day Austria and Luxembourg, the Dutch province of Limburg, and parts of Denmark, Poland, Italy, and Czechoslovakia.

For Germans it has been a historical fact of life that the topography of their lands provides no real physical barriers either within the country or on the northern, eastern, or western frontiers of the territory, making travel—but also expansion and invasion—easy. Only in the south are there any mountains to speak of. Four major rivers—the Rhine, the Weser, the Elbe, and the Danube—dissect the plain, facilitate internal commerce, and provide access to international trade routes. The first three rivers are fully navigable for much of their course and empty into the North Sea, thus giving Germany ready access to the Atlantic trading routes. The Danube is commercially less useful. Not only is it a difficult river to navigate, but it empties into the Black Sea, a closed body of water in Eastern Europe.

The balance sheet of economic resources is similarly mixed. Generally speaking, the quality of Germany's agricultural land is considerably better west of the Elbe than in

1

Germany
1816-1866

the eastern regions. Traditionally, much of East Elbia was extensively rather than intensively cultivated, with rye, potatoes, and sugar beets the prevailing crops; the areas west of the river lent themselves to dairy and truck farming. Along the steep slopes of the Rhine and Mosel Rivers winemaking has been a tradition since Roman times.

As for the raw materials needed for a modern industrial society, Germany possesses only coal in abundance; there are virtually inexhaustible supplies of this resource in the Ruhr Valley and parts of Saxony and Silesia. The country has few iron ore reserves and virtually no oil deposits. Bauxite, copper, and uranium deposits are negligible.

At the beginning of the century these

limitations on industrial resources were of little concern since the German territories were still backwaters of economic development. In some areas—notably the Rhineland, Saxony, and Silesia—there were pockets of vigorous commercial and early industrial activity, but taken as a whole the German territories were in the "premodern" stage of economic development. Most Germans lived either in rural areas or small towns. The largest German city in 1800, Cologne, had a population of only fifty thousand, while such present-day metropolises as Berlin and Munich were little more than medium-sized towns with populations of twenty thousand and thirty-five thousand, respectively.

The population as a whole was small. In 1815 some 15 million people lived in what is now East and West Germany. (Today the population is about 80 million.) After declining in the wake of the Thirty Years' War (1618–1648), beginning around 1750 the population grew rapidly especially in the areas east of the Elbe River.

The primary reasons were better agricultural methods allowing a greater abundance of foodstuffs, improved hygienic techniques that resulted in a noticeable decline in the infant mortality rate, and the abolition of serfdom at the beginning of the nineteenth century.

The flavor of German society in 1815 very much reflected its rural and preindustrial character. Germany was essentially a country of peasants and small townspeople in the west and latifundia in the East. There was little large-scale manufacturing and no modern industry worthy of the name, although the extensive use of "putting out" in some sectors of the economy provided entrepreneurial skills that would be useful when industrialization seriously developed. ("Putting out" referred to the practice of dividing the manufacturing process among several, geographically disparate individuals; it was the nineteenth-century equivalent of today's "out-sourcing.") At the beginning of the nineteenth century, then, German society was slow-paced with few means of rapid communication or transportation; the first German railroad did not appear until 1836.

In its values, too, early nineteenth-century German society was more reminiscent of the past than of the future to come. The legacy of the body of ideas known as the German Enlightenment, an intellectual movement that differed in a number of ways from the better-known French variety, was pervasive among the educated and administrative classes. The German Enlightenment was never as iconoclastic or anticlerical as the parallel movement on the other side of the Rhine. Rather, German Enlightenment thinkers showed a singular propensity for accepting secular rationalism without attacking the traditional religious beliefs. In turn, the established Lutheran and Calvinist churches took over much of the Enlightenment mentality. In some of the southern German states and especially in Austria during the reign of Joseph II, the secular authorities did attempt to reduce the power and influence of the Catholic Church, but even before the Napoleonic Wars there had been a significant backlash against forced secularization.

German Enlightenment also lacked many of the characteristics of political radicalism. Instead, the German thinkers felt that the societal reforms, which they advocated as enthusiastically as intellectuals in other countries, could be accomplished most effectively not in opposition to the established authorities, but through the organs of the state. Many of the most vocal supporters of this "bureaucratic Enlightenment" could be found among the civil servants of the numerous principalities that dotted the German landscape. A symbiotic corollary to "bureaucratic Enlightenment" was the so-called "enlightened despotism" of some princes. (By no means were all rulers enlightened despots; many were simply despots.) Ideally, under this twin doctrine the ruler and his bureaucrats would set out to modernize German society not from the bottom up, but from the top down.

Perhaps the best example of combined bureaucratic and despotic Enlightenment was the publication in 1794 of the Prussian Code of General Laws (*Preussisches Allgemeines Landrecht*). Contrary to what the name implied, the Code was not really a compendium of laws. Rather, it represented the ideas of the Prussian king, Frederick the Great (he died in 1786 but much of the compilation was completed before his death), and his advisors on enlightened constitutionalism. With the Code they hoped to institutionalize a golden mean between individual freedoms and social responsibility and obligations. As a result, the Code put a great deal of emphasis not only on the rights and obligations of individual Prussians, but also on the rights and obligations of the socioeconomic groups to which they belonged, such as municipal corporations, guilds, and bodies of the nobility. From our vantage point the Code was probably an attempt to square the circle: The king and his advisors wanted to free the individual from the shackles of societal control, while at the same time forcing him (women's rights were not yet an issue) to remain an integral part of various collective entities.

At the same time the entire document was very much in the tradition of enlightened despotism: It came in the form of a series of royal decrees rather than as a result of deliberations by a freely elected constitutional convention.

THE BIEDERMEIER IDYLL, 1815–1848

For some ten years Napoleon and the French influenced much of Germany. Their legacy was mixed as they sought to bring the Germans into the mainstream of Gallic modernism. There was much release of energy—patriotic, social, economic—that resulted in a dynamic and changing society. At the same time there was also the fact that French military occupation and Napoleon's wars were a burden on Germany. By 1815 most Germans associated the French ideas of liberalism and modernization with constant warfare, economic dislocation, and forced requisition. At least for a time, the Germans were not resentful when their post-Napoleonic leaders pushed the country back into provincialism. The upheavals of the Napoleonic era were followed by the surface serenity and placidity of the Biedermeier era.

Originally the name for a style of post-Rococo furniture, the term Biedermeier conjures up the image of a slow-moving, self-satisfied, unheroic age that placed great store on polite forms and proper dress. It was an elegant age, dominated by the twilight years of Goethe, the lilting music of Schubert and Hummel, and the gentle comedies of the Austrian writer Johann Nestroy. There was a perceptible shift in the ideas and ideals of the Enlightenment. The goals of rationality and moral self-improvement through education (the elusive German concept of *Bildung*, about which more in a moment) remained valid for many in the upper and middle classes of Germany, but the focus shifted from the society to the individual. It was symptomatic of the era that between 1806 and 1826 no less than three multivolume standard encyclopedias made their appearance, while the impetus for reform legislation became progressively weaker. In a clear reaction to the anticlerical tendencies of the Enlightenment and to the French Revolution, the Biedermeier era was also characterized both by religious revivals among Protestants and a new emphasis upon popular religion among Catholics.

In general, Biedermeier society distrusted centralized authority, concentrating instead on preserving the autonomy of towns and estates. In our modern sense of the word it was a largely apolitical time, beginning a tradition that was to plague the evolution of German politics until quite recently. As the German historian Thomas Nipperdey has pointed out, unlike French and British parties in the nineteenth century, German political organizations tended to reject the view that they were pressure groups representing legitimate but specific interests in the society. They saw themselves as spokespeople for universal world views—*Weltanschauungen*—and denied their role in the decision-making process as primarily philosophical, not political.

Yet it would be misleading to suggest that the Biedermeier era was simply a slower-paced, inward-looking continuation of the eighteenth century, an era without dynamism or conflicts. Far from it. Below the surface of serenity the modern impulses provided by the Napoleonic era continued—but there also lurked irrationalism. It is symptomatic that it was during this time that magnetism as a universal cure for diseases enjoyed its greatest popularity, and the years 1815–1819 saw a number of anti-Semitic riots in various German towns. The latter especially showed decidedly antimodern tendencies in German society: The Enlightenment and the French Revolution had, after all, begun the process of legal emancipation for the Jews.

While most of society turned away from reforms, some political rules sought to strike a judicious balance between the desire to return to the old ways and the obvious inability to ignore the changes of the Napoleonic era. Their first task was the reorganization of the German territories. Until 1806 Germany had been divided into some three hundred large and small states, loosely organized in a fictitious entity called the Holy Roman Empire of the German Nation. With a stroke of his pen Napoleon had abolished this empire and substantially rearranged the boundaries of the German principalities. At the Congress of Vienna (1814–15) the Great Powers, under the leadership of Prince Clemens von Metternich, the chancellor of the Austrian empire proceeded to revise Napoleon's revision. What emerged was the German Confederation, composed of some thirty-five principalities and free cities. Among this group only five states could on their own exercise major influence in the Confederation's affairs: the three Southern states of Baden, Württemberg, and Bavaria; and the two largest entities in the confederation, Prussia and Austria. Prussia especially benefited from the territorial rearrangement of the German states after 1815. She added the populous regions along the Rhine in western Germany, as well as a portion of Saxony to her earlier East Elbian holdings, thereby becoming the largest, wealthiest, and most populous member of the Confederation outside of Austria.

As its name indicated, the German Confederation was a loose confederation of states rather than a federal union. The Confederation's executive entity and legislature was the same body of men, the Diet, an assembly of ambassadors appointed by the governments of the individual states. It met in Frankfurt, but had few powers. There was no federal judiciary system, no national army or currency. Commerce and industry were hampered by a crazy-quilt pattern of custom barriers.

From 1815 to 1848 the dominant figure in Germany's political life was Clemens von Metternich. The Austrian chancellor, a Rhenish nobleman by birth, was an eighteenth-century rationalist whose faith in reason and modernity had been destroyed by the experience of the French Revolution. By 1815 he had become convinced that such nightmare experiences as the Revolution and its aftermath inevitably resulted when rights of political power were extended to groups in society not qualified to exercise such privileges. In his view this meant virtually everyone except the landed nobility and the states' administrators.

But Metternich could not halt the clock, much less turn it back. German society continued to evolve, paradoxically propelled forward by the very group upon which the chancellor relied to freeze the settlement of 1815 into place. In fact, the legacy of the Napoleonic era was considerably stronger than Metternich acknowledged. In the annexed Rhineland, for example, the new Prussian administrators did not repeal the Napoleonic codes introduced by the French. Enlightened bureaucrats, many of them nobles, continued the fiscal, military, educational, and social reforms begun in response to the defeat of Prussia by Napoleon in 1806. Prussia abolished serfdom, modernized the tax structure somewhat, and expanded the system of universal education.

Southern Germany arrived at the same result by a somewhat different route. Bavaria, which had become Germany's third largest state (after Austria and Prussia) in 1815, continued a variety of administrative and legal measures begun during the Napoleonic era in order to consolidate the state's territorial gains. (Much of what is today recognized as typical Bavarian folklore was introduced into Bavaria as state-sponsored custom in the early nineteenth century.) Beyond that, the legacy of French influence had stimulated the rise of popular political movements in southern Germany demanding written state constitutions and popularly elected legislatures. At first glance it would seem that these states were developing along lines quite dissimilar to the more authoritarian patterns of Prussia. But the impression is deceiving. The rulers of the southern states did permit the election of popular assemblies, but their members were elected on the basis of highly restricted suffrage requirements. In addition, most of the representatives were civil servants in the employ of the state governments. The concerns of the southern legislatures closely paralleled those of the ministerial reformers in northern Germany: Municipal self-government, the tax structure, debates on the elimination of guild restrictions, the conversion of the peasants' feudal dues into quit rents, and the emancipation of the Jews occupied legislative and executive bureaucrats alike.

The Napoleonic experience, then, in a number of ways had left a more "unified" Germany; the Germans had not only similar problems in most areas of the country, but they were also looking at similar solutions.

STIRRINGS OF DISSATISFACTION: NATIONALISM, ROMANTICISM, AND LIBERALISM

As we saw, initially most Germans welcomed the serenity of the Biedermeier era. At first vocal opposition to the Vienna Settlement that followed Napoleon's rule in Central Europe was restricted primarily to the small number of university students (at the beginning of the nineteenth century less than 2 percent of Germany's college-age youth attended institutions of higher learning), but as the Metternich system became ever more repressive, resentment against it spread to other segments of the society as well.

Early critics focused their attacks on the failure of the Vienna Settlement to advance the cause of German nationalism. The concept of nationalism is among the most important but also one of the most volatile legacies of the eighteenth century. On the surface the ideals and aims of nationalism were simple enough: A people sharing a common language and culture should have the right to live in a territory surrounded by a single set of borders and governed by values and leaders in accord with the people's culture and ethnicity. These goals were fairly easily realized in such areas as Great Britain that possessed natural boundaries and a relatively homogeneous population. National unification was far more complicated in Central Europe, where for centuries political boundaries had had little relationship to linguistic, religious, or cultural divisions. A large number of Swiss certainly shared the German language and culture, but they had no desire to be included in any German national state. Similarly the Austrians were also German in language and culture, but for generations their political fate had been linked to a large number of non-Germans within the context of the Habsburg Empire. (The Habsburgs were the ruling family of the Austro-Hungarian Empire. For this reason historians use the terms Austrian, Austro-Hungarian, and Habsburg empire interchangeably.)

Even in its "pure" form nationalism was a difficult concept to put into practice, and its adherents complicated matters even further by linking nationalism and romanticism. In fact, nationalism was in one sense a child of romanticism. The latter was originally a literary movement that emphasized, among other things, the importance of collective cultural experiences in the life of peoples. Under the influence of romanticism nationalism postulated that the collective past experience of a people was a guide for its future path: Each nation had a historic destiny that could be recognized through the study of history. German romantic nationalists became fascinated with the Middle Ages and the imagined glories of the German past. They saw the now defunct Holy Roman Empire not only as the symbol of a glorious past, but also as the promise of an even greater future: A resurrected, nationally unified Germany would once again occupy all or most of the territory of the Holy Roman Empire. In projecting the past onto the future, German nationalists tended to ignore a major flaw in their dreams: German unification in its "historic" dimensions could only be accomplished by denying the equally valid "historic" destinies of the non-German peoples residing in Central Europe. Moreover, the "historic" glory of the Holy Roman Empire included long-term religious conflicts. Unlike England where a common religion formed part of the basis of national identification, in Germany the Reformation had left the country religiously divided with roughly two-thirds of the population Protestant and one-third Catholic.

It would be wrong to suggest that the cry for national unification in Germany was strong enough to drown out all other loyalties. Nationalism was primarily a phenomenon of the urban and educated sectors of the population, and at this time Germany was still an overwhelmingly rural society. Moreover, despite some passionate attacks on "particularism"—which meant both local and regional loyalties—at the beginning of the century most Germans remained genuinely attached to their individual states. Still, as the urban middle classes especially became dissatisfied with the Metternich system, they increasingly felt national unification would cure the shortcomings of the post-Napoleonic settlement.

We have already noted that the Austrian chancellor distrusted all popular political stirrings as inevitable precursors of revolution. Again and again he urged the members of the Confederation to impose tight controls on all political activities in the German *Länder,* or states. At first some of the states with liberal governments resisted the call for repression, but in 1819 a terrorist attack permitted Metternich to have his way. The chancellor used the murder of the conservative playwright August von Kotzebue (who was also a political agent of Metternich and the Russian czar), by a deranged student to convince the Diet that a widespread conspiracy existed to undermine the stability of the Confederation. Meeting in the Bohemian resort town of Karlsbad (now Karlovy Vary in Czechoslovakia) the Diet passed the so-called Karlsbad Decrees. They imposed press censorship, restricted academic freedom in the universities, and suspended most civil liberties throughout the German states.

The system of repression had the effect of spreading dissatisfaction from a relatively small number of students and intellectuals to a sizable and growing proportion of the German middle class. By 1830 the outbreak of new revolutionary upheavals in Paris led to parallel demonstrations in several German states, and two years later a festival staged to celebrate both the glories of the German nation and to protest the authoritarian repression of German political life drew thousands to the town of Hambach in Hessen. In 1837 a protest by seven members of the faculty of the University of Göttingen in the state of Hanover against the king's suspension of the relatively liberal state constitution became a national *cause célèbre*. Nevertheless, the growing waves of dissatisfaction did not inundate the Metternich system as a whole until economic problems were added to the complaints about political and national shortcomings.

ECONOMIC AND SOCIAL LIFE, 1815–1848

At the beginning of the nineteenth century there were few hints that three generations later Germany would become a predominantly urbanized and industrialized society. Agriculture, the means of livelihood for the vast majority of the population, used traditional production methods, relying almost exclusively upon manual labor and beasts of burden as sources of energy. True, for those with prescient eyes, the appearance of the first steamships on the Rhine in the 1820s augured the dawn of the new age. Most Germans, however, experienced modernity first in the form of administrative regulations, rather than changes in production methods. Although Metternich had attempted to freeze in place an essentially premodern social system, the continuing dynamics of Enlightenment administrative reforms increasingly undermined Germany's premodern economic and social structures. There was little doubt that reforms were needed. Even before the Napoleonic era the German states had outgrown the parameters of a premodern, estate-oriented society. Metternich's plans for Germany, however, envisioned a return to an economic system that was essentially self-contained and static. Peasants were to produce foodstuffs for the rural population and the towns that dotted the landscape. Both industry and trade were to be closely regulated by the state and various trade associations. The entire system postulated stable prices and population figures.

By the end of the Napoleonic era few of these assumptions held true. Despite the rapid strides in the commercialization of agriculture, the population explosion—especially in the rural areas—outstripped the ability of many regions to feed their inhabitants. Thousands were forced to leave the countryside, either to settle in neighboring cities and towns, or to leave Germany altogether and seek a new home overseas. At the same time, the success of the Industrial Revolution in Great Britain rendered obsolete the traditional mercantilist policies of the continental countries. The booming economy in England produced goods for export much more cheaply than could be done by the traditional, guild-dominated methods of manufacturing in Germany; despite the tariff barriers demanded by Germany's nascent manufacturing industries, British goods soon flooded the country. The success of Great Britain's economy also permitted that country to adopt a policy of free trade, thereby allowing imports of all kinds to flow freely into the British markets. Since British imports were growing rapidly along with the country's exports, the lure of this massive market quite naturally encouraged entrepreneurs in Germany (and other countries) to invest in manufacturing enterprises that were not subject to production limitations set by the traditional trade associations and to pressure the German state governments to repeal regulations that the entrepreneurs regarded as barriers to economic growth.

Ironically, the administrative measure that was to have the greatest impact in leading Germany into the liberal economic era, a customs union among most of the states of the Germanic Confederation, did not originate as an economic measure. The initial impetus came from civil servants in the Prussian Ministry of Finance, who in the true spirit of bureaucratic Enlightenment, were attempting to increase the rationalization and efficiency of the state's administration. The root of the inefficiency was Prussia's acquisition of new territories in Saxony and along the Rhine in 1815. Prussia's new lands in the west were physically separated from her traditional holdings in the east by a number of independent states, including the *Länder* of Hanover and Hessen. As goods were imported into the Prussian lands along the Rhine for shipment to the state's eastern areas, they had to traverse Hanover or Hessen, which levied duties on goods in transit. The Prussian authorities in turn imposed duties on goods whose final destination was one of the neighboring states.

Beginning in 1818 officials in the Prussian Ministry of Finance began working on plans to rationalize the system with a view toward reducing its cost and facilitating freer trade. Eventually their discussions resulted in proposals for a *Zollverein*, or customs union. Each member state was to levy an agreed-upon duty at the original port of entry, while all transit duties would be abolished. The revenues raised would then be allocated to the various member states according to a formula based upon the relative size of the member state's population.

The proposals for the *Zollverein* were models of administrative rationalization. Although originally addressed to Prussia's immediate neighbors, it was also obvious that such a union would have advantages for all of the Confederation's members since the transit problem concerned them as well. Still, implementation of the customs union was delayed by the states' fears of losing their political independence. This was especially true for the southern German states who traditionally distrusted Protestant Prussia and aligned themselves with Catholic Austria. The agreement did not go into effect until 1834, and even then the Austrian parts of the Confederation remained outside the *Zollverein*.

Austria would continue to present a special problem for German economic unity. The territories of the Austrian empire lay partly within the German Confederation and partly outside it. Guided by Metternich, Austria attempted to forge all of the Habsburg lands into a unified entity, and one way of achieving this was to create a single customs area for all of the Austrian territories, while erecting customs barriers at the external boundaries of the empire. Thus, the austrian lands included within the German Confederation would form a customs union with the areas under Habsburg control outside the Confederation, rather than be joined to any free-trade area within the Confederation itself. With this decision, the Austrians, although they did not realize it at the time, by default left the economic leadership of Germany to Prussia. The southern states of Baden, Württemberg, and Bavaria, located between Austria and Prussia, had no choice but to join the Prussian-sponsored *Zollverein* if they wanted to escape economic isolation. The Confederation's pattern of extreme decentralization was reversed in an important area of economic policymaking, and the Prussian currency, the *Thaler*, became the dominant German currency.

The macrocyclical development of the German economy in the nineteenth century involved the transformation from preindustrialism to industrial capitalism. The change began rather slowly, and the country as a whole did not reach the takeoff stage of industrial development until about 1842, some thirty years after peace had been restored in 1815. For example, gas lamps did not appear in German cities until 1829, and as late as 1836 only six kilometers of railroad track had been laid. (The first German train ran between Nuremberg and its suburb of Fürth.) One year later, there were only 423 steam engines in industrial or agricultural use in all of the German states.

At the same time, administrative policies and forms of economic organization laid the groundwork for what would become one of the fastest growing economies in the second half of the century. The significance of the *Zollverein* in facilitating the creation of a national market has already been noted. The same bureaucrats who made possible the tariff-free area were also responsible for the rationalization of the tax structure and the removal of some guild restrictions. By 1848 taxes in the German states, while neither fair nor progressive, were increasingly structured in such a way as to encourage and facilitate investment in new economic enterprises. In fact, their very regressiveness encouraged the investment of venture capital. Large sums could be speculated without fear of high taxation on the profits. Prussia and other states had also instituted *Gewerbefreiheit* (freedom to engage in trade), which eliminated the need to obtain permission from a guild or trade association before starting a business.

The pro-business climate, along with a growing population that provided a steadily increasing market for consumer goods, led to increasingly visible signs of industrialization by the 1840s. The six kilometers of railroad track in 1836 gave way to 550 kilometers four years later. The number of steam engines increased from 423 in 1837 to 1,139 in 1846. Even so, Germany remained a sellers' market. The needs of the economy far outstripped the capacity of German industry. Much of Germany's production of industrial goods was manufactured in small, often widely dispersed facilities with high overhead costs: The volume of imported finished products, primarily from Great Britain, remained high.

The development of the German economy in the first half of the century confirmed yet another generalization that economists have established to characterize the growth of industrialization and modernization in developing countries: Increases in productivity and changes in manufacturing methods stand in an asymmetrical relationship to changes in income distribution and marketing techniques. That is to say, the benefits of the new methods are not uniformly distributed throughout the society; for some time they remain restricted to those with large incomes. Many people at the bottom of the income scale may actually be temporarily worse off in a modernizing society than they had been in the premodern era.

Germany, like other countries undergoing rapid modernization, experienced the phenomenon of "pauperism." (The Germans took over the term from the British, who had experienced the same problem some years earlier.) The causes of pauperism were complex and more related to the population explosion than to changes in manufacturing methods, but since the phenomenon occurred at the time of the economic transition, contemporaries tended to blame industrialization for the problem. Most "paupers" were landless peasants who could no longer find work on the land. They drifted to the towns and cities where they became a more or less indigent subclass of unskilled labor straining the welfare budgets of their host towns. Until about 1850 the German economy was not sufficiently developed to absorb large numbers of these people as permanent industrial workers. Not all paupers, however, were unskilled labor. Another characteristic of early industrialization was the dislocation of some apprentices and journeymen. Unable to practice their craft in their home towns, they often moved to distant places in search of work, leaving family and friends behind.

In either case, pauperism presented German municipal and state authorities with severe problems. For the most part they responded with negative rather than positive measures: They attempted to export their pauper problem simply by restricting permission to settle within the boundaries of a town or *Land*. But such measures had no lasting effect on the problem itself, and bands of roving paupers became both a familiar sight and a volatile social problem in the German countryside. It is true, however, that both the Protestant and Catholic churches attempted to deal with the problem in a more positive manner. Particularly successful were the efforts of a Catholic priest, Father Kolping, who began a series of shelters to provide temporary housing and support for traveling apprentices and journeymen.

Pauperism was only one symptom of Germany's changing economic and social life. The growth of German capitalism also brought with it profound long-range social consequences. One was the mixing of Catholic and Protestant populations. Since the Thirty Years' War Germany had been rather rigidly divided into homogeneous Protestant and Catholic areas, but the economic developments of the 1830s and 1840s began what would become an accelerating process of confessional intermingling. Inhabitants from the rural areas of East Elbia (historians of demography have concluded that after 1840 East Elbia was unable to "absorb" further population increases) and western Germany, many of whom were Catholic and, in the east, ethnically Polish, moved to neighboring towns, which tended to be predominantly Protestant. Such migrations often brought with them problems of cultural and linguistic assimilation.

These developments forced the German states to make some fundamental economic policy decisions. The *Länder* had a number of models or combinations thereof available to them. One was economic liberalism, by now well-established in England, which essentially removed all state-imposed restrictions on economic activity, permitting market forces to regulate the growth and direction of the economy. A second model was an adaptation of the traditional mercantilistic and guild-oriented regulated economy. Under this scheme, which was typical of preindustrial Europe, the state either directly or indirectly through the guilds regulated and restricted occupational freedom and the activities of individual entrepreneurs. A third, and not very popular, choice was represented by the centralized and government-regulated state capitalist system of Bonapartist France.

With the benefit of hindsight the choice of economic liberalism may appear both natural and inevitable, although the victory of the free enterprise system did not come all at once, but proceeded by fits and starts. The guilds fought back with every means at their disposal, and from time to time won rearguard actions that delayed and sometimes reversed the erosion of their privileges. Ironically, while the political rulers of the German states were often genuinely sympathetic toward the plight of the artisans, they also felt that for both fiscal and economic reasons preindustrial economic policies could not be maintained.

Economic liberalism postulated that the obvious problems associated with economic change could most easily be solved by rapid growth of the economy. Expansion would be both cause and cure. The same developments that led to the changes in the traditional way of life would also be the most effective way of absorbing the dislocated part of the population into that new way of life. Beginning in 1846, however, at the time when industrial development was reaching the takeoff stage, faith in economic liberalism was dealt a setback. Germany was hit by a severe depression, creating the ingredients of an explosive sociopolitical situation that needed only a spark to set it off.

REVOLUTION AND COUNTERREVOLUTION, 1848–1851

For its contemporaries the Revolution of 1848 that brought down the entire Metternich system seemed to occur much like an earthquake, with little warning and devastating force. It is possible, however, to identify a number of portents that signaled that tensions in European society had reached the breaking point. Throughout the 1840s as economic liberalism advanced, political repression remained in force. By the end of the decade efforts by the governments of the German states to control and repress public opinion were becoming ludicrous and widely resented. Trials for sedition, control of intellectual life in the universities, and above all press censorship (publically demonstrated on a daily basis by large white spaces in the newspapers) characterized a system that had lost its credibility. Metternich, however, clung to conspiracy theories to explain the rampant dissatisfaction. His ubiquitous agents spent a great deal of time sniffing out "communist" circles and reporting on subversive literature.

Political dissatisfaction was aggravated by the serious economic problems that came to a head in the middle of the decade. In 1844 the weavers of Silesia, an economic group that was particularly hard hit by the importation of cheap English cloth and the spread of power looms, went on a rampage smashing machinery and attacking the houses of factory owners. The Prussian government sent troops to suppress the uprising. A short time later an outbreak of potato blight all but wiped out the harvests of the crop in 1846 and 1847, causing economic hardship among the peasants, and the rapid spread of diseases associated with starvation and malnutrition. In 1847 some eighty thousand people became ill with typhoid; sixteen thousand died of the disease.

Still, it is doubtful that these events in themselves would have unleashed nationwide outbreaks of revolutionary violence without the catalytic impact of news from Paris: The overthrow of the government of King Louis Philippe by the people of Paris in February of 1848 electrified the German lands. The first outbreaks of civil unrest in Germany occurred in areas that were culturally and geographically closest to France, that is, the Rhineland and Baden. From there the news of the Revolution spread rapidly throughout Germany and Austria.

Spearheading the violence in the early days of the Revolution were peasants who wanted relief from their immediate economic problems. Typically, they demanded tax abatement and the abolition of money payments due their former feudal masters. When the governments refused to grant these measures, roving bands took to burning tax files and, in some cases, residences of large landowners.

The spark of revolution in the countryside almost immediately ignited a series of protests and demonstrations in the cities and towns. Again, the unrest began in the west and southwest and spread north and eastward. In the urban areas the violence was led by artisans and especially unemployed journeymen. Like the peasants, they took drastic action to alleviate their immediate economic and social problems. In the first days of the Revolution they looted bread shops and attempted to destroy the factory machinery that they contended was putting independent artisans out of work. To prevent the further erosion of their standard of living they demanded restrictions on economic liberalism, opportunities for advanced training of artisans, reduced railroad fares for traveling journeymen, and the institutionalization of "codetermination" (*Mitbestimmung*) whereby masters and employees would jointly settle labor disputes.

The Revolution of 1848 was sparked by social unrest, but the accumulated dissatisfaction with the entire Vienna Settlement quickly led to demands for political reform and national unification as well. At first the seemingly universal support for the Revolution dissuaded the *ancien regime* from offering any resistance. The rulers readily agreed to the popular demands for removing units of the standing army from the urban areas. Hastily formed citizens' militias (on the model of the French National Guard) restored and kept order in the cities. In state after state the rulers and their governments also hastened to make personnel changes that they hoped would appease the wrought-up populace. By the end of March, conservative cabinets had resigned in virtually every German state, including Prussia and Austria, and had been replaced with ministers of a more liberal outlook. In addition, with a speed that was not usually characteristic of its deliberations, the Diet in early March 1848 voted a series of political reforms. The ambassadors repealed the repressive Karlsbad Decrees of 1819, scheduled free elections for a constitutional convention, and recognized the colors of black, red, and gold, which had become identified

A contemporary rendering of a clash between citizens and the army during the Revolution of 1848. The original caption reads, "The remarkable year of 1848. A new pictorial newspaper." (From a 1982 calendar)

with the liberal opposition against Metternich, as united Germany's national flag.

But the early victory of the Revolution was more apparent than real. To begin with, the new state governments were not all that different from their predecessors. While the new ministries had a different political outlook, like their reactionary predecessors, the liberal camp was led by civil servants, academics, and lawyers; "men of affairs"—businessmen, artisans, and farmers—were very much underrepresented in comparison to the population at large.

Still, the new executive leaders were liberals. The first item on their agenda was the formulation of written state and national constitutions that would embody what they saw as the foundations of a modern society: a catalogue of individual civil liberties, economic freedoms, and elected parliaments with considerable powers to enact legislation and control the state and national budgets. The demands did not include either the overthrow of the monarch or even that they be reduced to mere figureheads. Nor did most liberals advocate full-scale democracy;

they tended to favor property qualifications of some sort as a prerequisite for the right to vote and hold office. In essence, the political aims of the early liberal regimes were evolutionary rather than revolutionary. They hoped to use the popular unrest to eliminate the excesses of Metternich's system, but they had no intention of granting the radical socioeconomic demands voiced by some of the revolutionary leaders in the towns. Here lay the seeds of what was to become a decisive contradiction that would eventually lead to the failure of the Revolution.

The new leaders seriously underestimated the volatility of the social issues. Many liberal leaders remained convinced that what was needed were not handouts and relief programs, but the institutionalization of policy changes that would "modernize" Germany's economic and political system. The liberals also failed to consider that the ease of their initial victories had papered over the deep divisions in their own ranks. Basically, the reformers could be divided into two broad camps. They came to be identified as liberals and radicals, although a more accurate description would be moderate and less moderate liberals. (There were also a few genuine revolutionaries, including a handful of Marxists and some determined republicans, but their influence in 1848 was negligible. For a discussion of Marx' influence in German political thought, see pp. 40–41.) All liberals favored national unification, and most supported a constitutional monarchy headed by a hereditary emperor as the political form of the future united German Reich. The two major liberal groups disagreed primarily on the degree to which the "people" could be trusted to run their own affairs and on the role of the armed forces. The radicals had a deep distrust of professional standing armies and demanded that they be replaced by citizens' militias. In addition, the radicals favored less restrictive suffrage laws, a more complete separation of church and state, and more extensive parliamentary controls over the executive.

After a brief period of enthusiasm for the new order, many of the groups in German society who had expected immediate and concrete relief measures from the Revolution were disappointed. The peasants, who had started the unrest, benefited the most from the revolution. The liberal governments did accord them some tax relief and abolished many of the remaining statutory payments due the landowners. As a result the German peasants for the most part remained quiescent during the latter part of the Revolution. In sharp contrast, many artisans concluded that the policies of the liberal governments had actually made their situation worse. The artisans wanted the restoration of guild privileges and a regulated market in order to protect them from what they saw as the ruinous competition from factories and imports, while most liberals regarded guilds and trade restrictions as anachronistic features of an outmoded economic system.

Economic and social policies would continue to divide the revolutionaries, but there was unanimity on the desire for national unification. Regional loyalties did not disappear, but there was a nearly universal sense that the Revolution of 1848 could rectify the failures of the Vienna Settlement of 1815. Germany was to be a unified nation, preferably with a military victory to celebrate along the way. We have already noted that German nationalism was heavily influenced by romantic concepts of historic destiny. The vision of a new unified German Reich was based, as one author put it, on "historical fantasy structures." Three areas of dispute illustrated the difficulty of defining the legitimate borders of a unified Reich. The most important, clearly, was the question of the relationship of the Austrian empire to the German Reich, but there were also controversies over the future of the ethnic Poles in the state of Prussia, and the question of the two northern German provinces of Schleswig and Holstein.

The Austrian problem lay at the heart of the debate over the *grossdeutsch* (greater German) versus the *kleindeutsch* (lesser German) path to unification. The fact that the lands of the Austro-Hungarian Empire were partly inside and partly outside the Confederation constituted no problem for this loosely organized entity but if the hopes of the German nationalists for a unified Reich were to be realized, Austria's future had to be clarified. The German-speaking parts of the empire had to be clearly excluded or included. The proponents of the *grossdeutsch* solution favored including the Austrian parts of the Austro-Hungarian Empire within the boundaries of a unified German Reich, thereby splitting the Habsburg empire into two. In retrospect, this concept never had any real chance of success. It was opposed not only by the supporters of the *kleindeutsch* solution (more about this in a moment), but also by most opinion leaders in the Austrian empire. For example, the delegates to a Pan Slavic congress meeting in Prague in June 1848 passed a resolution reaffirming the need for an intact Habsburg Empire.

The Polish and Schleswig-Holstein issues involved a major dilemma for liberal German nationalists: how to reconcile the principle of the rights of self-determination for all peoples with the desire to create a German Reich with "historic" boundaries. Some liberals favored giving the Poles their own nation, but most of them unfortunately regarded the earlier destruction of the Polish nation by the partitions of Poland as "historically" justified. They rejected proposals that the new, unified, liberal Germany should give up any of the Polish lands acquired by Prussia and Austria in the course of the eighteenth century.

The Schleswig-Holstein controversy became one of the most intractable issues for European diplomacy and the indirect cause of two wars. In essence, the issues in the north German duchies revealed the difficulty of combining the principles of modern nationalism with the remnants of feudal traditions. Since the later Middle Ages the two duchies of Schleswig and Holstein had been governed as personal fiefs by the kings of Denmark. A treaty of 1460 also provided that the two provinces should remain "forever undivided." In the Vienna Settlement of 1815 the great powers decreed that the duchy of Holstein should become part of the German Confederation, while Schleswig would remain outside. However, both duchies were still fiefs of the Danish royal house; they were not part of Denmark. In 1848 Danish liberal nationalists, no less "historically" minded than their German counterparts, argued that the presence of a sizable Danish ethnic minority in the northern duchy justified changing the status of Schleswig: Instead of remaining a personal fief of the crown, the province should become an integral part of Denmark. German nationalists, bolstered by the indivisibility provision of the medieval treaty and the fact that a large majority of the population was German, insisted that both Holstein and Schleswig become part of any unified Germany.

The conflict erupted into the only war ever declared by the German Confederation. In 1848 German nationalists from all political camps discovered that the Schleswig-Holstein question was a crucible of national self-determination and that Danish ambitions would have to be thwarted by force of arms. (Cynics pointed out that Denmark appeared to be the only potential enemy that could be defeated by the weak German forces; the German navy in 1848 and 1849 consisted of some chartered freighters.)

It soon turned out, however, that even a war with Denmark was no simple matter. The Great Powers—notably France, Russia, and Great Britain—had a direct interest in all aspects of German unification since they recognized that any change in the territorial and political status quo in Central Europe would also significantly alter the international balance of power on the Continent. Among the Great Powers, Great Britain originally sympathized with the efforts to unify Germany under liberal auspices; Prince Albert of Saxe-Coburg, Queen Victoria's husband, especially supported the liberal cause. Expanding direct German control over Schleswig-Holstein, however, would alter the balance of power in both the North and Baltic Seas and would affect vital British interests. It should have come as no surprise to the liberals that German ambitions in the North turned England's sympathy for unification into something less than benevolent neutrality. The British Prime Minister Disraeli spoke exasperatedly of "that dreamy and dangerous nonsense called German nationality."

Still, it is not true, as later generations of German nationalists insisted, that German unification in 1848 was prevented by the opposition of the Great Powers. Far more significant were internal divisions among the revolutionary leaders on the constitutional makeup of the new Reich, and, above all, disagreements over the boundaries of the nation. We have already seen that the *grossdeutsch* faction wanted to incorporate part of the Austrian empire within the new Germany. The opposition, those favoring a *kleindeutsch* Germany, advocated boundaries that excluded all parts of the Habsburg realm. The conflict involved the very nature of German society. A German Reich with *grossdeutsch* boundaries would invariably have meant that Germany would be dominated by Austria and the Catholic states, while a *kleindeutsch* Germany meant Prussian hegemony and a Protestant majority. The liberals never resolved the *grossdeutsch-kleindeutsch* dilemma; the advancing counterrevolution rendered their passionate debates moot.

Though the German revolutionaries failed to achieve national unification, they could point with pride to some remarkable accomplishments at the state level. By the fall of 1848 constitutional conventions in all of the German *Länder* had given their states constitutions with a decidedly liberal and reformist character. They differed in many details, but they uniformly guaranteed civil liberties for all citizens (the Revolution of 1848, for example, completed the process of the legal emancipation of the Jews in Germany), limited the powers of the princes, assured the election of parliaments based upon relatively liberal suffrage laws, and removed many restrictions on freedom of economic activity.

The German constitutional convention, called the National or Frankfurt Assembly, was elected in May 1848. Most of the Assembly members were the same sort of men (there was no women's suffrage) who had risen to power in the states: "notables" and "men of substance and status"—lawyers, professors, civil servants who were well-known in their communities. In getting elected their personal reputations were often more important than their political views. In the Assembly there were no formal party caucuses, but only loose congregations of politically like-minded individuals. The caucuses that did organize were subject to frequent fluctuations in membership, and crossover voting was the rule rather than the exception.

During the debates at Frankfurt, which were often distinguished by a high level of sophistication and abstraction, two issues occupied most of the delegate's time: the size of the Reich and the rules for the election of a future German national parliament. The Assembly agreed without much controversy on a Bill of Rights. The delegates also voted to incorporate the principles of economic liberalism in the constitution.

On the *grossdeutsch-kleindeutsch* controversy a majority of the delegates originally favored the *grossdeutsch* solution. In the summer of 1848 the delegates elected an Austrian archduke as provisional head of state, and the issue was presumably settled in October 1848 when a majority of the Frankfurt Assembly voted to make Austria part of the German nation. But the vote was an empty gesture. By this time the Austrian conservatives, who categorically rejected any incorporation of Austrian territory within

Germany, had regained control of the Habsburg government. Recognizing the futility of their efforts, the delegates then turned to the *kleindeutsch* solution, eventually offering King Frederick William IV of Prussia the German imperial crown in the spring of 1849. The Prussian monarch contemptuously rejected a crown, offered, as he said, "by butchers and bakers" rather than his fellow princes.

Frederick William's contempt for the men of Frankfurt reflected the growing strength of the counterrevolutionary wave in the states that had left the Frankfurt Assembly a lame duck parliament. When the revolution broke out the conservative rulers had retreated and seemingly cooperated with the new liberal regimes. As the King of Württemberg pointed out, "I can't lead a cavalry charge against ideas." For the next few months the moderate liberal governments survived on this early credit line of support, but the old forces were not really swept from power. (Even at the height of liberal popularity, when the Frankfurt Assembly declared war over Schleswig-Holstein, its troops were Prussian units lent to the nation, as it were, by the Prussian king.) As the liberals failed to bring about either national unification or instant economic relief, there was a serious erosion of support for the new governments.

In the early fall of 1848 exasperated artisans and other urban groups began a new wave of demonstrations. The protesters called for relief measures for their immediate economic problems and the restoration of guild privileges to insure their future prosperity. When the state and national governments refused to meet these demands, dissatisfaction escalated to street violence and barricades. The much vaunted citizens' militias generally proved incapable of maintaining law and order, and the liberal governments had to call in units of the standing armies. In September, even the Frankfurt Assembly requested Prussian units to protect it from the anger of the citizens of Frankfurt. A little later, in October and November, a radical liberal alliance led by artisans, intellectuals, and university students actually took control of Vienna, forcing the moderate liberal cabinet to flee from the Austrian capital.

At the same time action by the liberals in the Assembly aggravated the situation. Almost simultaneously with the outbreak of new violence in Frankfurt in September 1848, a radical majority in the National Assembly voted against the armistice of Malmö, an agreement for the cessation of hostilities in northern Germany arranged through the good offices of Great Britain. The liberal radicals rejected the armistice because it did not satisfy all of the German nationalist demands; their decision seriously alienated British public opinion, isolating German liberalism from the only friend it had among the Great Powers.

The radicals also won a Pyrrhic victory on the suffrage issue. In order to secure the votes of some of the more radical members of the Assembly for the *kleindeutsch* solution, the moderates agreed to very democratic suffrage laws; the German national parliament was to be elected on the basis of universal male suffrage. Many more right-wing liberals, however (along with most conservatives), rejected a broad suffrage as excessively democratic.

The increasing evidence of antagonisms between moderates and radicals in the liberal camp, and the steady erosion of the support base for the revolution was watched with interest by the states' rulers and their conservative advisors. As they saw it, after only a few months in office reformist liberalism had reached a dead end. The moderates had no choice except to yield to "the rule of the mob and barbarism" or to cooperate with the forces of "authority and order."

The march of the counterrevolution began on the state level. Recognizing the weakness of the liberal regimes, the conservative rulers in state after state ordered troops back into the major urban centers. Sometimes the liberal cabinets asked for aid from the armed forces, sometimes not. In any case, they had no resources to prevent the implementation of the princes' decisions. By October, Prussian regiments had moved back from Potsdam to Berlin; in November Austrian forces commanded by the Bohemian general Prince Alfred von Windischgrätz subdued the radicals in Vienna. Secure in the knowledge of their military superiority, the German rulers then proceeded to shift the political center of gravity in the various state cabinets from moderate liberals to moderate conservatives. Simultaneously they denied the popularly elected assemblies the right to draft state constitutions, substituting instead documents by princely fiat.

Some reactionaries counseled the rulers to establish (or reestablish as the case might be) full-fledged autocracies, but the princes and their advisors at first tended to emphasize moderation and continuity. The new cabinets consisted of a mix of liberals and conservatives, with the liberals usually remaining in charge of economic policy. Even the new constitutions contained key provisions dear to liberals, such as a Bill of Rights, parliamentary control of the budget, and more liberal suffrage laws than had been in force before the revolution. Most of the conservative rulers were insistent only that the constitutions not contain provisions for ministerial responsibility, and that the parliaments have no influence over the command structure of the armies. In their own fashion the moderate conservatives even worked to advance the cause of national unification. The Prussian foreign minister, Joseph Maria von Radowitz, a Catholic moderate, urged the rulers to take the lead in creating a unified Reich through an alliance of the territorial princes.

The liberal forces put up little resistance to what amounted to their forced political eclipse. The reasons were complex. Certainly some liberal leaders were motivated by "fear of the mob" or they lacked civil courage. Many felt they had accomplished what they set out to do. Most liberals did not believe in radical political democracy anyway, and the new constitutions left intact what liberals felt had been some of their key revolutionary demands: civil rights, economic liberalism, parliamentary control of the budget. True, the failure of national unification was a severe disappointment, but since the moderate conservatives seemed to share the liberals' goal, perhaps all was not lost.

Then, too, the mood of German society was changing. There was a perceptible return to moderation and sobriety. Among Protestants the fundamentalist movement known as Pietism gained renewed popularity. The Pietists advocated spiritual renewal and individual self-cultivation instead of political upheaval. The tendency was even more pronounced among Catholics. Here a genuine revival movement was taking place, inadvertently fueled by the anticlericalism of the liberal regimes and, after the *grossdeutsch* solution to the national question proved unworkable, fear of Protestant domination. By October 1848 some 400 Pius Associations (named for the then reigning Pope Pius IX) with a total membership of 100,000 had been established in all parts of Catholic Germany. In at least some respects, then, the moderate conservatives who were returning to power could count upon the tacit support of many Germans.

Unfortunately, the moderate counterrevolution proved no more workable than the moderate revolution. At least some in the liberal camp were not content to vanish quietly from the scene. They attempted to rally support for continuing the revolution until democracy and unification with Germany's "historic" boundaries had been achieved. (Radical democrats were often also the most vociferous chauvinists.) In a number of German cities and towns violent clashes between regular troops and radical forces took place in the winter of 1848 and the spring of 1849. The confrontations reached a climax in the so-called second revolution in Baden in March and April 1849. Some radical leaders, backed by numerous elements in the Baden Citizens' Militia, made a last-ditch military effort to establish a German republic. The rulers of Baden and Württemberg requested the help of Prussian troops in dealing with the insurgents. This phase of the counterrevolution was not moderate, but a reign of terror. The military leaders staged numerous court martials which sentenced dozens of revolutionary leaders to death. In the course of the reestablishment of conservative rule in southwest Germany almost one-twentieth of the population, some eighty thousand persons, were forced to leave Baden. Most emigrated to America.

The experience of the abortive second revolution persuaded the German rulers that those who had counseled a moderate counterrevolution seriously underestimated the dangers of radicalism. As a result, Germany experienced another turn of the counterrevolutionary screw. In some of the states where popularly elected assemblies were still in session, pressure from the monarchs forced them to leave the capital cities (where they might rally potential supporters in their defense) and meet in provincial towns such as Kremsier (Austria) and Brandenburg (Prussia). The royal constitutions promulgated in the late fall of 1848 were substantially revised to curtail the powers of parliament and restrict meaningful political rights to the propertied few. The counterrevolutionary Schwarzenberg regime in Austria simply suspended the liberal constitution until the government had decided a time was propitious to put it into effect. As it turned out, that moment never came. Prussia did not go this far, but in May 1849 the relatively liberal suffrage provisions in the constitution were replaced with what was to become the infamous three-class system of voting.

The three-class system—which applied only to state and local elections in Prussia and not to national contests—was in effect until 1918, and remained as the primary obstacle to democratic reforms in what was to become Germany's largest state. For election purposes Prussian voters, that is, males twenty-five years of age and older, were divided into three classes with membership in each determined by the amount of *direct* taxes they paid. Direct taxes really meant property taxes; Prussia did not levy an income tax at this time. (Moreover, direct taxes in Prussia were not high, since the state's tax system, like that of most European countries at this time, relied heavily upon indirect levies, which fell disproportionately upon the less well-to-do segments of society.) Those voters contributing one-third of an electoral district's tax revenue, regardless of the number of people involved, voted in the first class and had the right to elect one-third of the delegates in parliament allotted to that district. (There were no single member districts in Prussia.) The second class consisted of those contributing the next one-third of the district's revenue from direct taxes, while the last class was composed of voters whose taxes made up the last one-third of the tax income as well as all voters who paid no direct taxes at all. The result was an extreme form of political discrimination: The relatively small number of voters in the first class and the much larger number of voters in the second and especially the third class were represented by the same number of parliamentary delegates. In practice the system resulted in a massive skewing of political power in favor of the rural and urban wealthy—as it was meant to do. In many of the East Elbian election districts the three class system of voting meant that the landowner voted in the first class, the schoolmaster and pastor in the second, and all of the landowner's sharecroppers in the third. The political result was an unfair advantage for conservative candidates for the state legislature during the next seventy years. As a rule conservative candidates (especially in the rural areas of Prussia) received not only the votes of those casting ballots in the first and second classes, but even those voting in the third class often had little choice except to support conservative candidates. Until 1918 there were no secret ballots in Prussian state elections, and fear of economic reprisals by landowners kept many sharecroppers from voting for opponents of Prussian authoritarianism. The long-term effects of the system may be gauged from the returns for the 1913 state election: The conservative parties received about 17 percent of the popular vote, and almost 50 percent of the seats in parliament; the Social Democrats received 28 percent of the popular vote and 2 percent of the parliamentary seats.

At first glance the Revolution of 1848 appears to have been a complete failure. By the end of 1849 all the German states were again subjugated to the authority of their conservative rulers. Many liberal and democratic statesmen were forced into exile, dismissed from office, or relentlessly prosecuted in the courts. German national unification was delayed for another twenty years, and when it came the liberals were restricted to playing a minor role. Even in the area of socioeconomic policy, there was some evidence that the clock had turned back. The Prussian commercial code (*Gewerbeordnung*) of 1849 gave the guilds a new lease on life; many of the artisans' and journeymen's demands were incorporated in the new code. The failure of the 1848 Revolution seemed to confirm the thesis of Germany's "special path" (*Sonderweg*) of historical evolution in the nineteenth century: Unlike Great Britain and France, countries that were becoming progressively modern and democratic societies, Germany embarked upon a road that would eventually lead to the horrors of the Nazi era.

In recent years a number of researchers, notably David Blackbourne and Geoffrey Eley, have raised serious questions about the validity of the *Sonderweg* thesis. They question the extent to which the clock was really turned back by the return of the conservatives. The era of constitutions, which Metternich had fought so hard to prevent, remained firmly established in Germany. The major German states kept written constitutions, providing for popu-larly elected parliaments, although the power of these assemblies to pass legislation and control the executive varied greatly from *Land* to *Land*. The peasants remained free of their manorial burdens. The relentless progress of economic liberalism was not seriously affected by the counterrevolution. The year 1848 marked no watershed in the socioeconomic development of Germany. The German states had not only entered the takeoff stage of industrial development, but the new state governments, for all their professed concern for the old ways of artisan manufacturing, also encouraged economic modernization by a variety of catalytic decisions. The Prussian *Gewerbeordnung* was progressively watered down in subsequent years.

Finally, in a development that is less easily subject to empirical measurement, the counterrevolution did not arrest the continuing "bourgeoisification" of German society. Despite their political failures, the self-confidence and self-consciousness of the middle classes increased unabated. German society after the restoration of conservative power provided for more equality and civil liberties than had been true of the years before the Revolution. The counterrevolution did not reverse the trend toward legal equality, one of the major principles of the bourgeois revolutionary movement. The conservatives did not reverse such innovations as trial by jury, nor did they repeal the laws providing for the legal emancipation of Jews and other minorities. Legal equality for German Jews certainly did not eliminate anti-Semitism from German society (indeed, in some ways it may have stimulated it), but it is significant that none of the restorationist regimes stopped the process of granting equal civil rights to all Germans. Even the Prussian army was not immune to "bourgeoisification." After 1848 its officers were prohibited from using the familiar *Du* (which at that time was generally employed for animals and children) when addressing enlisted men.

THE LOST DECADE OF THE 1850s

The time between 1850 and the first of the so-called "Wars of Unification" in 1864 tends to be somewhat neglected in accounts of modern German history. These years lack the drama of the domestic upheavals and the rousing military action that marked the forties and sixties. The only era in which the 1850s seem decisive was in the field of foreign affairs. The Crimean War (1853–1856) (see a later discussion, pp. 27–28) shook the foundations of Austria's predominant position in Germany.

Actually, the picture of the 1850s as a Rip Van Winkle time is misleading. The period between 1850 and 1864 decisively influenced the future evolution of Germany in a number of ways. It laid the foundation for the *kleindeutsch* path to unification, secured the victory of political conservatism, and brought about the final triumph of economic liberalism. These were the years in which Germany made major strides in her evolution from a primarily agricultural society to one increasingly dominated by industry and manufacturing. Except for a recession in 1856–1857 the economy was booming. There was readily available capital to invest in Germany (and more found its way there from the 1848–1849 California gold rush), while the likelihood of tremendous profits resulted in an unprecedented speculative fever. State governments did their part by encouraging economic development. In the 1850s many of the German *Länder* created new ministries to promote the spread of industrialization in their territories. New laws facilitated the establishment of corporations with limited liability and speculative banks. The educational infrastructure for modernization was expanded; a network of technical colleges and schools spread across the states, and the German universities became models of modern research institutions.

Most of the capital investment went into railroad construction. By the end of the 1850s the major trunklines in what was to become the German Reich were completed. As in the United States, the phenomenal pace of railroad construction was made possible not only by the ready availability of domestic and foreign capital, but by a ready supply of laborers in search of work. (Many of the paupers of the 1840s now found work on the railroads.) The German states aided the construction either directly by floating state bonds or indirectly by underwriting private investments with loan guarantees.

The growing transportation network, which also included the construction of better roads and inland shipping facilities, made possible the growth of modern industry. Retracing the progress of the industrial revolution in England, Germany's modern economic growth was also based upon the traditional pillars of textiles, iron, and steel. The largest concentration of iron and steel enterprises developed in Western Prussia, around the Ruhr River and parts of Westphalia and the Rhineland, where abundant deposits of coal and significant findings of iron ore led to the rapid rise of such firms as Krupp and Thyssen. The growth of these corporations and others that were to become giants in the field was in turn closely linked to the railroad construction, which required enormous amounts of steel for rails and rolling stock.

The steam engine became increasingly commonplace throughout German manufacturing. One major customer was the textile industry, which relied for its raw materials primarily upon cheap imports of cotton. (In 1859 the German *Länder* imported seven times as much cotton from the United States as in 1825.) The vastly increased manufacture of cotton cloth in turn required the development of chemical dyes (since organic dyes could not be produced in sufficient quantity), and that laid the foundation for the growth of the German chemical industry, particularly after it was discovered that aniline dyes could be easily extracted from coal tar. These years also saw the appearance of new construction materials, especially Portland cement and structural iron. They replaced the traditional building materials of stone and wood and made it possible to construct industrial buildings on a much larger scale than before.

Even agriculture moved with an accelerated pace into the modern age. Particularly on the larger holdings the mechanization of agricultural production methods made significant progress. Justus Liebig had invented artificial fertilizer in the 1840s and during the next decade its use became more widespread, resulting in significantly higher crop yields. The bigger harvests in turn made it economical to employ mechanical aids on the larger farms, notably steam-powered plows and milk separators. These developments also meant, however, that agriculture was becoming increasingly subject to the vagaries of the capital market, a trend that was to affect particularly landowners in the East Elbian areas. In the 1850s the Junkers—the term refers to the traditional leaders of Prussia, the landowning nobles of Pomerania and East Prussia—began to mortgage their lands heavily to invest in farm machinery in an effort to compensate for poor growing conditions and the decline of cheap manpower. (Many of the landless peasants preferred to seek work in industry.)

At the same time consumers benefited. Canning factories increased the availability of foodstuffs throughout the year. After 1850 there was a noticeable increase in meat consumption. Generally, the standard of living rose, especially among middle class Germans. Taxes and public expenditures remained low, while the discretionary income of the middle classes increased; they tended to spend their money on clothes, furniture, education, and travel.

Not surprisingly, the growing wealth and societal significance of the German middle classes in general and the industrial entrepreneurs in particular had profound effects upon the self-image of these groups. They developed a new sense of self-confidence and self-righteousness. Ernest Bramsted is quite right when he speaks of the German middle classes' "aspiring collective consciousness" in the decade of the 1850s. The growth of a distinctly bourgeois mentality in the Germany of the 1850s is often neglected since the bourgeoisie's political power was mostly restricted to local affairs. Statewide political organizations which had been active during the Revolution either dissolved themselves or became social clubs that limited their activities to promoting aesthetic self-cultivation. Prominent intellectuals—Arthur Schopenhauer is perhaps the best known—turned away from any belief in human collectivity and advocated individual escapism. As for the rising businessmen, many of them equated individual success with serving the common good.

Along with being industrialized, Germany was also becoming urbanized. Especially in the Rhine-Ruhr area, an ever greater proportion of the population lived in what were rapidly becoming modern urban concentrations. The growth of cities in turn facilitated the development of a new collective consciousness, partly by making possible the large-scale production of books and magazines. These found a ready public, particularly since the counterrevolutionary regimes did not reinstitute Metternich's heavy-handed censorship measures. The state governments attempted to guide education at all levels by controlling teacher appointments and curriculum content, but there was little effort to censor reading material available to the general public.

Novels and family-oriented periodicals were the primary vehicles for raising middle class consciousness. These literary products fit in well with an age that saw remarkable improvements in education among the middle classes. As we saw, in midcentury the German educational system, responding to the needs of the economy, was rapidly diversifying, particularly in the area of technical education. At the end of the 1850s a new type of high school, the *Realgymnasium*, was accorded equal legal status alongside the old *Gymnasium*. The new schools' curricula put more emphasis on the study of the natural sciences, while the traditional *Gymnasia* emphasized humanistic subjects and ancient languages. By the 1860s the fierce opposition of the traditional humanistic universities to "realistic education" had been overcome, and the German states established the first technical universities.

Gustav Freytag and Wilhelm Raabe were by far the most popular novelists, while one magazine, the *Gartenlaube* ("The Garden Cottage") dominated its market. Freytag and Raabe wrote true *Bildungsromane*, works of fiction that sought to educate as well as entertain. Freytag felt his works should "improve" the reader. In other words, for Freytag and his fellow middle-class authors literature served to teach and transmit values. The middle-class values mirrored in their works were not difficult to discern. They included three "antis"—anticlericalism, opposition to aristocratic pretentiousness, and antimaterialism—and two positive goals— the work ethic and nationalism. It will be readily appreciated that these were traditional liberal values, albeit now cast in the form of fictional plots rather than political tracts. (The political dimension of fiction is even more noticeable in the works of a man like Friedrich Spielhagen, whose novels center on the experiences and conflicts of the 1848 Revolution.)

In Freytag's and Raabe's novels, such as *Soll und Haben* ("Debit and Credit") (1855) and *Der Hungerpastor* ("The Starving Parson") (1864), anticlericalism and opposition to the aristocracy go hand in hand. The clergy, and particularly the Catholic clergy, is described as backward, preventing the victory of modern positivist doctrines. The clergy in turn is closely linked to the aristocracy, since the clerics support the nobility's pretensions that birth and heritage are entitled to special rights and considerations. The middle-class authors deny the legitimacy of privileges attached to birth alone, contrasting over and over again the uneducated boorish aristocrat, who clings to his anachronistic seigneurial rights, with the honest middle-class merchant, who through hard work and education has attained an "aristocracy of learning." Yet novels do not advocate overthrowing the aristocracy. Instead, a number of popular novels achieve a happy end of sorts as the aristocrat recognizes the folly of his ways and appreciates the values of the middle classes; the new outlook is often symbolized by his marriage to an educated and individually noble middle-class woman.

At first glance, it seems surprising to find a section of society that was riding the crest of economic development critical of materialism. As these authors portray the value of antimaterialism, however, the opposition is not toward money-making and material success per se, but toward "mere" materialism. Economic success must be accompanied by a corresponding gain in education and refinement. (The dangers of mere materialism seemed particularly obvious during the wave of speculation that gripped Germany in the mid-1850s.) The authors tend to stress—somewhat artificially—the difference between the "creative" and "rapacious" use of capital. It was unfortunate for the later evolution of German history that the popular mid-nineteenth-century writers identified the negative aspects of materialism not only with individuals, but more generally with one group in society, the Jews. To make their point, the authors invented a type of Jew—usually an unassimilated, recent immigrant from Poland or Russia—on whom they then projected the negative attributes of materialism. Repeatedly in these novels, the opportunistic rise to fame and wealth of this type of Jew was contrasted with the judicious and moral path of the honest German merchant who refused to employ amoral and dishonest methods in attempting to make his way in the world.

The negative descriptions of the hunger for money and success reflected not only dislike of some Jews, but they were also symptoms of anxiety about the modern age among writers and readers. There is considerable hidden nostalgia in these novels, and it is noteworthy that the positive character is far more often a merchant or professional than an industrial entrepreneur. In other words, anti-Semitism was also a shorthand way of personalizing the fears of the future which many middle-class readers felt.

The consciousness-raising aspects of middle-class writing are even more apparent in the periodical literature of the decade. As noted above, the *Gartenlaube* was by far the most successful of the family-oriented magazines. Beginning with a modest run of 5,000 in 1853, ten years later, it had reached a circulation figure of 157,000. The magazine appeared weekly as a judicious mix of serialized fiction, uplifting moralistic essays, and practical hints for housewives. It was specifically designed to be read aloud in the family circle, and thus contained nothing that might not be suitable for children's ears. Its fiction was written for a less educated audience than the novels of Freytag or Raabe, and the didacticism was a bit more heavy-handed. The *Gartenlaube* specialized in the novels of an otherwise obscure author who wrote under the pseudonym of E. Marlitt. (The author's real name was Eugenie John. She was for some years the paid companion of the Princess of Schwarzburg-Sonderhausen.) The plots of her novels, all of which appeared in serialized form in the *Gartenlaube*, typically revolved around life in a country Protestant parsonage, a forest ranger's lodge, or the village mill. Invariably, the simple existence of these people was contrasted with the empty life of luxury in the manor house on the hill. And equally invariably, the young aristocrat eventually saw the errors of the ways of the upper class after coming in contact with the simple middle-class family.

The middle classes, who often sympathized with political liberalism, developed a sense of self-confidence and self-righteousness, but this had little effect on their ability to influence political decision-making processes at the state and national levels. In contrast, the landed aristocracy and political conservatives, who exercised real power, seemed singularly inept at winning the hearts and minds of the people. True, the counterrevolutionaries were not unaware of mass media forces. *Daheim* ("At Home") was intended as a conservative counterpart to the *Gartenlaube*, and the founders of the Berlin *Kreuzzeitung* (literally "Cross Newspaper"; the name derived from the Prussian Iron Cross that formed part of its masthead) hoped that their publication would become a national mass circulation journal advocating conservative causes. But the efforts were qualitatively and quantitatively disappointing. *Daheim*'s circulation was always far less than the figures for its liberal rival, the *Gartenlaube*. More important, however, an attitude of siege and defensiveness continued to permeate conservative writings. Despite their rout of the liberal forces in 1850, the new rulers saw themselves surrounded by conspiracies.

As the decade wore on, conservatives turned increasingly to political repression and control of the public school curriculum to influence public opinion. Instead of attempting to convert the reading public to modern conservatism, the counterrevolutionaries borrowed from the Metternich book and instituted repressive measures to prevent a new rise of liberalism. In 1854 the Diet at Frankfurt passed an ordinance permitting the state governments to dissolve any social and political association that the state cabinets regarded as inimical to the rulers' interests. By the end of the decade, the spirit of bureaucratic Enlightenment was all but dead. Reform projects ranging from eliminating the last remnants of feudal obligations in the countryside to increasing rights of self-government in the municipalities—the cities were often strongholds of liberal political influence—were rescinded or shelved. Reactionary rulers and their restless middle-class subjects appeared once again to be on a collision course.

Seemingly at the last moment, the looming showdown was prevented by a change of sovereigns in Germany's second largest state, Prussia. As it turned out, the brief New Era (as the period from 1858 to 1860 would be called) was a severe disappointment to the middle classes, but for a few months the cooperation (if not fusion) of evolutionary liberalism and modern conservatism seemed a real possibility.

By 1858 it had become clear that Frederick William IV's state of mental health rendered him unfit to govern. He suffered from manic depression and paranoia and had to be permanently institutionalized. In September of that year the king's younger brother, Prince William, became regent. Two years later, Frederick William IV died, and William replaced his brother on the Prussian throne as King William I. The new ruler was something of an enigma to his contemporaries. During the Revolution of 1848 he had earned the reputation of a Prussian hard-liner. He had been the "grapeshot prince" who repeatedly urged his brother to use force against demonstrators. These qualities endeared him to the conservatives, but the new ruler of Prussia also believed in modernization and new ideas. His wife, Princess Augusta of Weimar, was sympathetic to liberal causes and through her William made the acquaintance of a number of progressive publicists and businessmen.

The regent's first actions seemed indeed to inaugurate a New Era. He appointed a cabinet of moderate liberals (mostly men who belonged to the queen's circle) to replace the clerical and reactionary ministers whom his brother had favored in the last years of his reign. As a result of Prussian initiatives, the Diet at Frankfurt rescinded the 1854 decree prohibiting liberal political organizations. Almost immediately political liberalism sprang to life again. Symptomatic was the appearance, shortly after the regent came to power, of a new journal, the *Preussische Jahrbücher* ("Prussian Yearbooks"). The editors specifically announced that the periodical was to be a vehicle of rejuvenated political liberalism.

All in vain. The New Era ended almost before it began when executive and legislative bodies quickly deadlocked over proposed reforms in the one policy area in which the king had a very personal interest: the army. William, who as a younger son had not expected to become king, had concentrated his interests on military affairs. He recognized that warfare was rapidly changing in the second half of the nineteenth century. Along with his closest military advisors, Minister of War Albrecht von Roon and Chief of Staff Helmuth von Moltke, William was convinced the Prussian defense establishment needed a thorough overhaul. He was not alone. In fact, there was general agreement that the Prussian army of the 1850s was a poor fighting force. Its size and organization had not essentially changed since 1815, and each major mobilization since then revealed glaring inadequacies in everything from logistics to training programs. Since the reforms of Napoleonic times the Prussian army had been divided into three parts: troops on active duty, the reserves, and militia units called the *Landwehr* (National Guard). The last was to become the focus of controversy. For many liberals the *Landwehr* represented the ideal of a citizens' army which had been instrumental in liberating Germany from the Napoleonic yoke. The Prussian military establishment, however, looked upon the *Landwehr* as a group of overaged civilians trying to play soldiers and regain their lost youth. The king and his advisors also remembered that during the counterrevolution of 1850–1851 some of the Prussian *Landwehr* units had refused to obey orders when asked to move against revolutionary disturbances. As far as the king and his cabinet were concerned, by 1860 the *Landwehr* was a militarily useless and politically suspect anachronism.

The conflict between the king and the revitalized Prussian parliament originated as a disagreement over the technical details of army reforms and escalated into a full-scale constitutional crisis. At the heart of the debate was the future role of the army in Prussian and German society. The king and the officer corps looked upon the army as an instrument of executive policy subject solely to the will of its royal commander-in-chief. In contrast, the liberal opposition focused on the preservation of the *Landwehr* as an instrument for diluting the reactionary character of the armed forces of Prussia and emphasized parliament's role in controlling the army through the legislature's power over the budget.

The test of wills between the king and the Prussian parliament lasted from 1859 to 1866. An impasse was reached when the king insisted upon his executive privilege to effect the necessary army reforms, while parliament was equally adamant that it had the constitutional right to refuse the appropriations needed to fund the government's reform plans. Even under the restrictive rules of Prussia's three-class system of elections, the voters overwhelmingly agreed with the liberals; by 1862 the Prussian parliament was solidly controlled by the opposition. (Incidentally, the political shift reflected the rapid accumulation of wealth and property in the hands of the middle class during the boom years of the 1850s.) The continuing conflict could have led to any number of scenarios, from a new revolution to the abdication of the king in favor of his reputedly more liberal son, but whatever the outcome, by 1862 the government decided that there existed what German constitutional lawyers then and later defined as a *Verfassungsnotstand* (state of constitutional emergency).

This concept, which we will encounter several times more in the course of modern German history, derived from the logical concepts of Roman law, which in Germany (as in the rest of the Continent) formed the basis of legal and constitutional thinking. Roman law held that a logical absurdity could not be legally sanctioned. Consequently, the government's lawyers argued, since the legislature's refusal to pass the budget made it technically impossible to govern the state, the legislature was guilty of creating an absurdity: Without government there was anarchy, and anarchy was absurd. Needless to say, the liberals disagreed with this interpretation of the Constitution; but in September 1862 the king had found a prime minister, Otto von Bismarck (more about him in a moment), who accepted the argument that a state of constitutional emergency existed and that the government had the right to put the king's program into effect regardless of parliament's wishes. At the end of that year what had started out as a New Era of goodwill under William I had turned into open conflict between the forces who favored more power for parliament and those who insisted upon maintaining the royal prerogatives intact.

All this looked familiar; it was 1846 and 1847 all over again. But there was no repeat of the Revolution of 1848. There are a number of reasons for this. For one thing, the economic and social conditions were quite different. The agricultural depression was missing, and industry and commerce had fully recovered from a slight downturn in 1856–1857. There certainly was not the problem of pauperism that loomed so large in all accounts of the pre-March 1848 era. Then, too, both conservative and liberal ideas had changed considerably in the last fifteen years. Constitutionalism and the existence of an elected parliament were no longer issues. Few conservatives objected to written constitutions and parliamentary elections as a matter of principle; most merely wanted to restrict the legislatures' powers. The liberals disagreed, but they also remembered the revolutionary spirals of 1848–1849. They protested loudly against high-handed actions by the executive, but it is also clear from their writings during the Prussian constitutional conflict that the doctrine of the *Verfassungsnotstand* did not fall on completely deaf ears in the liberal camp.

GERMAN UNIFICATION AND THE EUROPEAN BALANCE OF POWER

For the generation of Germans that experienced the unification of the country in 1871, nineteenth-century German history was dominated by the quest for national unity. The issue loomed so large in the Germans' minds that all other developments were significant only insofar as they either hastened or delayed this achievement. We now know that this was a highly distorted view. There was no red thread toward unification running through the century, and in fact there were long stretches during which the national issue was out of the limelight. The 1850s was certainly one such decade.

Still, unification inched forward, less by design than through changes in the international balance of power and the atmosphere of the times. The nineteenth century was the age of nationalism par excellence. Country after country either achieved national unification or at least discovered that it had a national identity. Greece revolted against the Ottoman Empire and gained independence in 1830; the Poles staged repeated (and unsuccessful) uprisings against their Russian overlords. All of this left the Germans in a difficult position. They had memories of a great imperial past and hopes for a united future, but they saw themselves left behind in the struggle for nationhood.

At the same time nationalist movements in southern and southeastern Europe threatened the viability of the Habsburg Empire. Hungarians, Italians, Czechs, Croats, and others resented their domination by the Habsburgs. The Austrians' dilemma reached a crisis stage during the Crimean War, a conflict that did not involve Germany, but which did more to facilitate German national unification than any other single event.

The Crimean War pitted Russia against France and Great Britain. (In the course of the conflict the Italian kingdom of Piedmont also joined the Western powers.) The war was one of those European conflicts whose ostensible origins had little to do with its actual significance. Basically, the war involved Russia's ambitions in the Balkan Peninsula and the eastern Mediterranean and France's and Great Britain's efforts to prevent Russian hegemony in this part of Europe. Austria was caught in the middle. Her Mediterranean ambitions at this time were limited to the Adriatic (Austria had a naval base at Trieste), but she was vitally interested in preventing Russia from filling the power vacuum created by the decline of the Ottoman Empire in the Balkans.

Austria was anxious to annoy neither the Western powers nor Russia, but she was equally compelled to assert her great power status. To escape her dilemma, Austria decided to impose a settlement on the belligerents: She hoped to tip the balance by threatening to join the war with her own forces on the side which refused her good offers to act as honest broker. Unfortunately for Austria the scheme was a bluff; Austria was militarily too weak to make good her threat of decisive intervention. The Austrian minister of war was quoted as saying, "May God support our army, because our finances can't." To compensate for her weakness, Austria appealed to the other states of the German Confederation, notably Prussia, to support the Habsburg Empire militarily and diplomatically.

This may be a good place to introduce the name of Otto von Bismarck, the man who was to dominate the last twenty-five years of nineteenth-century German history. Born in 1815, Bismarck came from an ancient Pomeranian Junker family (he liked to boast that his ancestors had been in Prussia longer than the royal family, the Hohenzollerns), although his mother was the daughter of a Bremen merchant. Bismarck received a conventional administrative law education. He attended some notably liberal universities, like Göttingen, but there is little evidence that any of his teachers, conservative or liberal, made much of an impact on the young man. After graduation he joined the Prussian civil service, but soon resigned, finding the work simply too boring. For a few years he managed his Pomeranian estates (which his father had mismanaged almost to the point of bankruptcy), and it was here that he experienced the Revolution of 1848.

Bismarck wholeheartedly disapproved of the Revolution; at one point he offered to arm his peasants with pitchforks to subdue the "revolutionary mob" in Berlin. It was no surprise, then, that after the counterrevolution Bismarck was identified by the conservatives as a young man to be watched. In 1851 he was appointed chief Prussian delegate to the Diet at Frankfurt. Although he had no diplomatic experience, he seemed ideally suited to the task. The ambassadors were not meant to make policy, but merely to follow the instructions of their home governments. Bismarck certainly supported the conservative, restorationist regime in Prussia, and he had also indicated that he did not feel it was Prussia's place to challenge Austria's restored *primus inter pares* role in the German Confederation.

All went well until the outbreak of the Crimean War. When Austria brought its proposal to the Diet to mobilize the troops of the German Confederation in support of the Habsburgs' self-serving mediation role in the conflict, Bismarck urged his government to reject the Austrian demand. He argued then and later that neither Prussia nor the other non-Austrian German states had vital interests in the Balkans. He readily conceded that Austria did, but this did not mean that the Habsburg Empire should expect Prussia and the other German states to risk war in support of what were purely Austrian interests.

Bismarck recognized that particularly for Prussia, the Crimean War was a no-win situation; any involvement would alienate either the Russians or the Western powers. Bismarck's advice eventually prevailed,

largely because the king's advisors in Berlin were badly split between those who wanted Prussia to support the Russians, and the liberals, who hoped Prussia would align herself with England and France. Given the deadlock, doing nothing, which Bismarck proposed, was a natural compromise.

With Prussia leading the opposition, the troops of the German Confederation were in fact never mobilized. As a result, Austria's clever scenario failed completely. At the end of the Crimean War her international position was far worse than it had been when the conflict began. Russia resented Austria's ingratitude. (Czar Nicholas I had sent Russian troops to Hungary in 1849 to help the Austrians defeat the Hungarian Revolution.) France and England, equally annoyed at Austria's lack of action, were instrumental in helping Italy achieve national unification, a development that threatened Austria's possessions in northern Italy.

Bismarck was not in Frankfurt to experience the full triumph of his policy. In 1858 he was sent as Prussian ambassador to Russia and in 1862 to France. It was here that the king's request to become prime minister reached him. Bismarck readily accepted, assuring William that he could carry forward the royal program without either yielding to parliament or provoking another revolution. As it turned out, Bismarck was right on both counts, and when, a few years later, he also led the way to national unification, he had earned the reputation of being a political genius. Actually, the prime minister's reputation for prescience was undeserved. In retrospect, it is clear that when he assumed office, Bismarck had no long-range program either for domestic success or for achieving national unification.

As far as domestic policy was concerned, the new prime minister relied upon the loyalty of the reorganized Prussian army to carry him through. As he explained in his famous "blood and iron" speech to the Prussian legislature's Ways and Means Committee in October 1862, in politics power counts more than votes. The legislators fumed at this revelation, but they also recognized that they had little alternative but to accept Bismarck's dictum. From all the available evidence, Bismarck was perfectly content to continue in this manner, that is, governing Prussia by administrative fiat, while the impotent opposition occupied the legislature's time with meaningless debates and votes of no confidence.

A new ingredient was injected into what both sides had expected to be a long and bitter deadlock when the Schleswig-Holstein question once again stirred national passions. In 1863 the Danish parliament had approved a new constitution. It was a decidedly liberal and nationalistic document which, among other provisions, declared the province of Schleswig to be an integral part of Denmark. German nationalists immediately demanded that this article be struck from the Danish constitution. After much impassioned oratory and frantic conferences among the Great Powers, war broke out, pitting Denmark against the troops of Austria and Prussia. It was a strange conflict. Neither Austria nor Prussia had any real interest in fighting Denmark; both were engaging in hostilities for domestic political reasons: The Confederation's two leading states were determined to prevent Schleswig-Holstein from becoming a stronghold of liberalism, whether under Danish or German auspices.

As was to be expected, the war in 1864 was a one-sided affair. The Danes were quickly defeated, and the Great Powers, led by England, arranged a new settlement for the two provinces. The Danish crown lost all of Schleswig-Holstein; the two provinces became the personal property of the emperor of Austria and the king of Prussia. The two monarchs in turn agreed to administer their spoils so that Austria would govern the northern province of Schleswig, while Prussia was in charge of Holstein. The arrangement ran into problems almost immediately. The emperor of Austria was anxious to be relieved of the burden of administrating a territory almost a thousand miles from the nearest Austrian border. Prussia, on the other hand, was in no hurry to change the treaty provisions; Holstein after all bordered on Prussia.

For the next two years, from 1864 to 1866, Prussia and Austria behaved a little like boxers seeking a good sparring position in the ring. Austria sponsored a number of federal reforms plans at the Diet. They included the creation of a new state of Schleswig-Holstein and the election of a national parliament. The Habsburgs also attempted to isolate Prussia by persuading at least the southern German states to join the Austrian protective tariff system. Prussia countered by negotiating a commercial treaty with France, which significantly enlarged the *Zollverein*'s free trade area. Both states paid lip service to the ideal of German unification, although Bismarck always made it clear that from his point of view there was no contradiction between Germany's national interests and Prussia's particular interests.

In 1866 the war of nerves and diplomacy turned into a shooting conflict. Again the military action was short and decisive. Using the resources of its reorganized and modernized army and relying upon its efficient railroad system, Prussia swept through Austria's north German allies and then defeated the Austrians in a single encounter, the Battle of Sadowa. In the subsequent peace settlement, Prussia established its hegemony in all of Germany north of the Main River. In rearranging the map of northern Germany Prussia severely punished all of those states which had openly sided with Austria: the Kingdom of Hanover, parts of Hessen, and the free city of Frankfurt all became part of Prussia. The new superstate, along with a few smaller territories that had had the foresight to side with Prussia in the war, formed the North German Confederation. The German Confederation was dissolved and the medium-sized southern German states were now entirely on their own. Austria lost no territory, but she had to agree to Prussia's annexation of Schleswig-Holstein, and, more important, she lost her predominant position in German affairs.

THE TRIUMPH OF *KLEINDEUTSCHLAND*

The North German Confederation is remembered chiefly for two reasons. One was that it was barely established when, less than five years later, it was replaced by the German Reich. The other remarkable event associated with the North German Confederation was the apparent capitulation of the Prussian liberals to Bismarck and the Prussian Junkers. Over the years historians have seen the first as evidence that Bismarck, who is regarded as the sort of *deus ex machina* of all major decisions in Germany after 1862, from the outset regarded the North German Confederation as a temporary entity, soon to be replaced by a unified Germany. The second seems to provide evidence of the liberals' spinelessness and their lack of commitment to strengthening parliament in the Prussian political system. At first glance it certainly does appear that Bismarck was the undisputed victor in the international conflicts of the 1860s. Four years after Bismarck had become prime minister, Prussia dominated all of northern Germany, while most Prussian liberals, far from objecting to his triumph, hastened to pass a so-called Indemnity Bill in the Prussian legislature that retroactively gave parliamentary approval to the government's unsanctioned activities since 1862.

Actually, Bismarck neither intended the North German Confederation as a short-lived governmental structure nor was the defeat of the liberals as one-sided as it appeared. It must be kept in mind that Bismarck in 1866 had no particular interest in German unification. He limited his ambitions to securing what he felt was Prussia's rightful place in German and European affairs. The North German Confederation admirably fitted this scenario: Prussia dominated all of northern Germany. Austria was

effectively excluded from playing a major role in German affairs, and the southern German states were not sufficiently strong to challenge Prussia's preeminence. In effect, the North German Confederation represented the triumph of Prussian counterrevolutionary conservatism in the heartland of Germany. Bismarck and his king had reason to be content with the outcome of their policies.

That left the liberals. Politically, they were defeated. Had not the dreams of 1848 died in the Austro-Prussian War, and been ignominiously buried with the Indemnity Bill of 1866? In a sense yes, but looked at in another way, the reformers realized a number of their long-term aims with the establishment of the North German Confederation. The new governmental entity had a popularly elected parliament with powers to control the Confederation's taxes and budgets. Indeed, the North German Confederation went further than most liberals had been willing to go in 1848. The Confederation's parliament was elected on the basis of universal male suffrage, at the time the most democratic manner of choosing parliamentary representatives. True, parliament's power existed more on paper than in practice. It had no control over the executive. (The Confederation had only one executive office anyway, that of chancellor.) It exercised control over the Confederation's budget, but that was largely meaningless, since only about 5 percent of all public money outlays were included in this budget. The real power of the purse lay with state and local authorities, and the legislature of Prussia—the Confederation's largest and dominant member—continued to be elected by the three-class system of voting.

In 1866 the liberals sacrificed political gains for achievements in the areas of trade and economic policy. The North German Confederation combined the advantages of the *Zollverein* with the benefits of a single commercial code for the Confederation's states, thereby greatly facilitating the establishment of banking and industrial opera-

Germany
1866-1918

tions. The new commercial code even pleased the embryonic workers' organizations by removing the old Confederation's prohibition on labor unions. At the same time the Prussian and Confederation leaders remained solidly committed to a policy of free trade. Symptomatic of this decision was the appointment of Rudolf Delbrück, a liberal and fanatic free trader, as chief of

staff in the Confederation's executive office. For the next dozen years Delbrück remained the dominant figure in determining German economic policy.

The North German Confederation, then, was a genuine if somewhat unequal compromise. Bismarck and the Junkers achieved Prussian hegemony in northern Germany that assured their predominance over political liberalism and parliamentarism. The liberals obtained a democratically elected, albeit largely impotent, parliament and the illusion that national unification was a step closer. Above all, however, the Confederation removed the last legal and institutional barriers to Germany's rapid economic modernization.

Unforeseen changes in the international balance of power shortened the life of the North German Confederation. An explosive mix of dynastic politics, rampant nationalism, and the hard-fisted interests of the Great Powers led, in 1870, to yet another European war. In a sense the chain of events began with some untidy ends left by the Austro-Prussian War. France, and particularly its emperor, Napoleon III, had hoped to use diplomatic pressure to impose a settlement on the German powers. The swift Prussian victory prevented Napoleon's diplomatic intervention, and for the next four years the French emperor, already beset by serious domestic problems, sought frantically to regain popularity at home by providing evidence of a diplomatic triumph abroad. Adroitly, Bismarck thwarted Napoleon's ambitions in Luxembourg and Belgium, until, by 1870 only the Spanish question remained to provide at least a negative French triumph.

The succession to the Spanish throne was almost as involved as the Schleswig-Holstein question; it, too, provided massive opportunities for the intervention of the Great Powers. After a series of juntas and regents proved unable to provide political stability for the country, the leaders of the various Spanish factions agreed to go outside Spain for a new ruler. Their eventual choice was Leopold von Hohenzollern-Sigmaringen, a member of the Catholic branch of the Prussian royal family. The prince was not in direct line of succession to the Prussian throne, but he was a nephew of King William I, and France was understandably concerned about the prospect of installing a Hohenzollern prince on the Spanish throne. Napoleon formally objected to Leopold's

becoming king of Spain, and the prince did indeed withdraw his candidacy. The crisis seemed to be settled until both Napoleon and Bismarck for reasons of domestic politics decided to use the issue to inflame French and German public opinion. Bismarck proved to be far better in this game of nerves and public relations. France declared war on the North German Confederation in July 1870, at a time when the French military was in no way prepared for a major conflict.

The Franco-Prussian War was not only the longest of the three "wars of unification"; it also had the most far-reaching and in many ways the most unfortunate results. The defeat of France led to Napoleon's abdication and the establishment of the French Third Republic. Under the terms of the Treaty of Frankfurt, which ended the conflict, France lost the provinces of Alsace and Lorraine, and she had to pay a large indemnity to the victorious Germans.

The founding of the German empire was directly associated with victory in the Franco-Prussian War, but the manner in which Germany was unified proved to be a major liability for future Franco-German relations and the development of democracy in Germany. The Franco-Prussian War was a war of nations. On both sides of the Rhine nationalistic passions were raised to a fever pitch. After France had declared war on the North German Confederation, the southern German states, who were not members of the Confederation and therefore technically not parties to the conflict, were immediately pressured by public opinion in their territories to join Prussia and her allies in declaring war on France. The concept of the "hereditary enmity" between Germany and France (a term that had been invented by French and German newspapers in the 1840s) was given a new lease on life. Even more tragically, the achievement of German unity became associated with the idea of a military victory over the neighboring nation. Staging the ceremony that proclaimed the founding of the German Reich in the Hall

A view of German unification by the French cartoonist Daumier. The Prussian Wolf, dressed as a shepherd, looks over his flock of sheep, the other German states. (Source: *Lachen*, p. 93.)

of Mirrors at the Palace of Versailles on January 18, 1871 provided a poignant reminder for both peoples. (Incidentally, there was a parliamentary and "democratic" side to unification as well. In December 1870, in a ceremony curiously reminiscent of 1849, the president of the parliament of the North German Confederation, Eduard von Simson, asked the Prussian king in the name of parliament to accept the imperial crown. This time the monarch agreed.)

But fears for the future certainly did not concern the Germans at the beginning of 1871. Seemingly all that mattered was that the nation had finally been united. After the initial triumph over Napoleon's armies, the southern German states joined with the North German Confederation in forming what became known as the Second German Reich. More precisely, the rulers of the southern lands negotiated with the king of Prussia and his allies to establish a union of princes that bore the name German Reich. (The term "Second Reich" was used to indicate that Bismarck's creation was the historic successor to the First or Holy Roman Empire. Napoleon I had dissolved the Holy Roman Reich in 1806.) Here lay a major difference between the Reich of 1871 and anything envisioned at Frankfurt in 1848: The new Reich was the work of Bismarck and the princes; the German people had little part in determining the terms of its establishment. The German princes agreed that the king of Prussia and his heirs should be hereditary German emperors. In addition, Prussia's territorial gains of 1866 remained intact; the south did not challenge Prussian political and territorial hegemony in northern Germany. In a very real sense the new Reich represented the ultimate triumph not just of the advocates of *Kleindeutschland*, but of the forces of the Prussian counterrevolution.

CONCLUSION

Two major threads run through the tumultuous course of nineteenth century German history. One is the peculiarly unsynchronized development of German society. In 1871 Germany was a society that had many of the attributes we tend to associate with modernism: rapid industrialization and urbanization, increasing levels of technology and education, economic structures assuring capital formation and the effective marketing and production of goods. At the same time, politically Germany in 1871 was characterized by premodern contours. The domination of the united Reich by the forces of the Prussian counterrevolution meant that the basic decision-making powers in the empire were in the hands of men who were proudly and stubbornly opposed to the forces of parliamentarism and democratic responsibility. They feared revolution and the rule of the people. They remained convinced that military power and unencumbered executive authority were the keys to societal stability.

A second dominant characteristic was the persistence of German federalism and particularism. Despite all the clamor for national unification and the celebration of becoming a single people, the German *Länder* were surprisingly alive and well even in 1871. In addition to Prussia, Bavaria was particularly successful in securing some special privileges. The state kept the right to maintain her own armed forces, postal, and railroad systems. In addition, the agreements provided that only a Bavarian could be chairman of the Foreign Affairs Committee in the national parliament. All of the German states also had the right to maintain embassies in foreign capitals. In a sense these examples of extreme federalism are still more evidence of Germany's warped modernization patterns in the nineteenth century. The trend toward national and economic unification stood in marked contrast to the evidence of political backwardness and fragmentation. It was clearly the task of the leaders of the new German Reich to align these asymmetrical patterns in order to facilitate Germany's path toward full modernization.

CHAPTER 2

THE FOUNDERS' GENERATION, 1871–1890

Contemporaries and historians have interpreted the significance of the events of 1871 in startlingly different ways. For most Germans the founding of the empire was evidence that providence had singled them and Germany out for special blessings. The military triumph over France, the annexation of Alsace-Lorraine, and 5 billion French francs (about 4 billion marks) in French reparations—here was clear evidence that God stood on the side of the Germans. As if to underscore the connection, the German victory and unity celebrations were permeated virtually everywhere by a tasteless amalgamation of chauvinism and religiosity. Even the liberals seemed to have been converted to unabashed militaristic nationalism. The *Gartenlaube*, that flagship of German liberal periodicals in the 1850s, developed an increasingly nationalistic and monarchist orientation after the empire had been established.

Later historians emphasized that unification was not the solution to the problems and tensions that beset Germany before and after 1871. They used such phrases as "crude materialism and shallow complacency" or "cultural despair" to characterize the new Reich. More recent writings treat the *Gründerjahre* (the term "founding years" is the label historians have given to the time span from the establishment of the empire in 1871 to Bismarck's retirement in 1890) as a time in which German society should be looked upon as a "patient" beset by serious ailments. The reasons for the contrasting views are not difficult to discern. Contemporaries looked back upon a divisive past and consequently saw unification as the beginning of a great future. With the benefit of hindsight, later historians analyzed the faults of the Second Empire as forebodings of the disasters that would follow.

Actually, that all was not well with Germany was apparent even to some prescient contemporaries. German unification came at a time when all of Western Europe was undergoing fundamental changes. By the 1870s the disintegration of traditional values was already well underway. Technological innovations brought rapid changes in all aspects of economic and social life. Politically, the growing industrial proletariat felt increasingly alienated. It was naive to believe, as most in the founders' generation did, that unification alone provided Germany with a magic key to cope successfully with the larger dilemmas affecting all of Western society. Political unification certainly did not eliminate economic difficulties. After a two-year boom, the bubble burst in mid-1873. For the next twenty years the Reich, despite some ups and downs in the economic indicators, was subjected to what was essentially a generation-long depression. The macroeconomic downturn was so shattering to the dreams of the founders' generation that some historians have seen it as the factor that dominated Germany's economic, political, and cultural life in the years from 1873 to the end of the Bismarck era in 1890.

The founders' generation, while celebrating the present, seemed strangely insecure of its future. These years are permeated with a wholly irrational fear of revolution and anarchy, with the agents of upheaval successively identified as French, Catholics, and socialists. Among intellectuals and artists a sense of pessimism about the future of man abounded. Friedrich Nietzsche, perhaps the most famous critic of the German society in the *Gründerjahre*, wrote bitingly about the foibles of his generation. His targets included everything from false religious fervor to the self-satisfied smugness of the German bourgeoisie. Similarly, Richard Wagner's operas, for all their surface nationalism, end in the *Götterdämmerung*, the destruction of the world of gods and humans. The Viennese poet Hugo von Hoffmannsthal was not entirely facetious when he noted that the men and

women of the 1860s and 1870s had left his own generation, that of the early twentieth century, two legacies: pretty furniture and hypersensitive nerves.

To be sure, gloom and doom did not replace joy and triumph. If the problems were real, so was the ability of the founders' generation to sublimate and escape them. A favorite device was to celebrate the glories of history. Professional historians did their part, but the country was also flooded with historical novels and romances—the latter often little burdened by any real knowledge of the facts. There seemed to be an insatiable market for highly fanciful treatments of every conceivable historic era from the Egyptians to the recent wars of unification. Life among the Germanic tribes and adventures located in the Middle Ages found a particularly appreciative reading public. Common to all was a "glittering national pride." Many a democrat who had played a prominent part in the events of 1848 now wrote a historical romance assuring readers that earlier longings had been fulfilled by the recent victory of Prussian arms. But while national synthesis replaced the earlier fictional accounts of conflicts among the Germans, nationality conflicts continued unabated in the stories of Germans and Poles in eastern Germany. Here a happy synthesis of German and Slavic cultures was not permitted to take place; German civilization had to triumph. The desire for reliving imagined past glories was not restricted to literature. Like her European neighbors, German builders exhibited a peculiar inability to find an architectural style to express the functional changes brought about by the Industrial Revolution. All over Germany (and the rest of the Continent) builders erected railroad stations that looked like pseudo-Gothic cathedrals and post offices that resembled Renaissance palaces.

Historical fiction and incongruous architecture were relatively harmless ways of denying the problems of the present. The consequences of the phenomenon that Gerhard Ritter has called "the militarization of the bourgeoisie" were far more serious. The phrase referred both to the actual power position of the military under the new constitution of 1871 and to the excessive awe in which the German middle classes held the military. Many Germans of the founders' generation were willing to accept military values and behavior patterns as models for civilian society as well. Emotional dependence on the military expressed itself not only in such outward signs as excessive respect for uniforms, but above all through the transference of military forms of etiquette and thinking to essentially civilian organizations and activities. Teachers attempted to model themselves after drill sergeants, and middle-aged businessmen proudly displayed their reserve officer's commissions. In effect, the militarization of the bourgeoisie meant the acceptance by the German middle classes of the military's position at the apex of German society. The dictum was epitomized by the writings of the historian Heinrich von Treitschke. A former liberal, Treitschke beginning in 1879 published a multivolume *History of Germany in the Nineteenth Century*, setting out to prove that in the final analysis military power alone determined a nation's destiny.

Even more disastrous for the future of the country was yet another manner of escaping the problems of modernity, anti-Semitism. Here, too, Treitschke served as an example. Like other intellectuals in Germany and elsewhere he identified the alienating and negative aspects of modern industrialism with the influence of Jews in society. The anti-Semitism of the founders' generation was linked to the earlier sentiments of Freytag and Raabe, two authors who retained their popularity after 1871. (In the 1880s, for example, Raabe's *Der Hungerpastor* became a standard high school text.) However, the anti-Semitism of the founders' generation also borrowed heavily and ominously from the pseudoracial theories first introduced in France by the writings of Count Gobineau. While the Jewish characters in Freytag's and Raabe's novels

tended to be identified as recent immigrants whose personalities improved with assimilation, the new anti-Semitism attributed Jewish "evils" to the ethnic makeup of the Jewish people. For these writers the only solution to the "Jewish problem" was to reverse the progress of Jewish legal emancipation and immigration. Still, it should be pointed out that German anti-Semitism at this time was neither unique in Europe (at the beginning of the 1880s the *Alliance anti-semitique universelle* was founded in Paris), nor particularly pervasive or virulent. In fact, German literary critics chided Austrian literature for its excessive concerns with the "Jewish question." Nevertheless, by the early 1880s anti-Semitism was more than a purely literary manifestation. A privately circulated petition demanding the curtailment of the Jews' legal rights obtained 250,000 signatures.

As the depression continued and the social problems associated with it became increasingly difficult to ignore, there was a brief period during the 1880s when it appeared that a more realistic mentality would replace the escapism that was characteristic of so much of the founders' generation. There were some serious attempts to liberate the middle classes from their emotional dependence upon the military and to persuade them to face realistically the problems of their own generation. In novels and musical compositions, specifically bourgeois forms and values emerged. A naturalist and realist style, largely borrowed from Zola and other French writers, found its way into German literature. Instead of finding their heroes in the past, writers looked at the problems of their own time: rampant industrialization, urban slums, and the destruction of lives through inhuman conditions in the workplace. Authors like Theodor Fontane wrote brilliant, sympathetic, and moving descriptions of the fast-paced, pulsating life in the Reich capital. In music Johannes Brahms created compositions with a somber and specifically bourgeois character. Realism and naturalism even served as a counterweight to the militarization of society, for, insofar as the naturalist authors were optimistic about the future of their society, they celebrated science rather than military power as the answer to its problems.

Unfortunately, as we will see in more detail later, the bourgeois revolt, if that is what it can be called, did not lead to any fundamental changes in the prevailing mood of German society. Fear of a Marxist revolution led most Germans to seek refuge once again in emotional and political association with militarism and nationalism. At the end of the *Gründerjahre* German society was no closer to facing its problems realistically or solving them than it had been twenty years earlier.

THE FABRIC OF SOCIETY: ECONOMIC AND POLITICAL POWER STRUCTURES

In 1871 Germany was a society in the midst of rapid transition. The country of some 41 million inhabitants was on the threshold of changing from a primarily agricultural society to one dominated by industry and manufacturing. When the Reich was founded about 50 percent of the workforce was still employed in agriculture. Ten years later the relationship had fundamentally changed: more Germans worked in industrial or manufacturing jobs than on the land. Changes in the relative value of landed and liquid wealth accompanied the shift in employment patterns. Real property, at least in the form of agricultural holdings, decreased in relative worth, while liquid and industrial assets became more important.

During the next thirty years the modernization of Germany acquired a dynamic of its own. By 1907 three out of every four German workers were employed in industry. Most of them were blue-collar employees, but as industrial production became increasingly linked to higher technology, the number of white-collar workers grew rapidly as well. Less than 2 percent of the workforce in 1882, white-collar workers in 1907 comprised more than 6 percent of all German employees. In other words, within one generation, German society had assumed the social profile characteristic of highly developed capitalist societies.

Industrialization and modernization went hand-in-hand with urbanization and internal immigration. There was a steady stream of Germans moving from east to west, swelling the population of industrial centers in central Germany and those along the Ruhr and Rhine Rivers. It was not difficult to see the reason. Whatever the hardships of industrial labor, they were preferable to the bleak future facing a landless peasant on the estates of East Elbia. (In the East the emigrants were replaced by increasing numbers of Polish migrant farm laborers.)

Modernization had its effect on the spectrum of German political parties as well. The traditional Conservative and Liberal parties were joined by new organizations formed to address the conditions and problems associated with modernization and unification, notably a Catholic party and groups representing industrial labor.

For the German Conservatives modernization meant being confronted with the increasing irrelevance of their political ideas. Traditionally, Prussian conservatism—and that was the dominant form of this political philosophy in Germany—had preferred Prussian particularism to German nationalism, favored agriculture over industry, and praised hierarchically determined responsibilities instead of individual freedoms. Conservatives had also insisted that political authoritarianism based on the union of throne, altar, and army, should prevail over popular elections and parliamentarism. The world of 1871 hardly fit the Conservatives' ideal. The unified Reich (dominated by Prussia, to be sure) had a government that espoused economic liberalism, and a national constitution which contained provisions for the election of a lower house of the national parliament (the

Reichstag) on the basis of universal male suffrage.

Under the impact of the new situation the Conservatives split into two groups: German Conservatives and Free Conservatives. The leaders of both parties continued to come from the ranks of the landed East Elbian aristocracy, and the two groups were united in their unflinching defense of the authoritarian system established in Prussia after 1851. They differed in their attitude toward the new Reich. While the German Conservatives emphasized the need to preserve the old ways untainted by the innovations of modernism, the Free Conservatives wholeheartedly endorsed national unification and industrialization as means of strengthening the power of Prussian conservatism in all of Germany.

Under the rules of universal male suffrage, the conservatives were at a decided disadvantage. (In Prussia, of course, the retention of the three-class system of voting assured them a dominant political position.) Traditionally, conservative voting strength came from the rural areas of Germany: Peasants and estate owners, Protestant clergy, and the inhabitants of small towns formed the heart of the conservative constituency. As Germany became increasingly industrialized, this support base was eroded through natural attrition. The rural population steadily declined; larger urban concentrations absorbed many small towns. The result was a precipitous decline of the conservatives' parliamentary strength in the national parliament. By 1912 only about one in ten German voters cast his ballot for one of the conservative parties.

The liberals also went separate ways. They split over the issue of the Indemnity Bill of 1866. (See an earlier discussion, p 30.) The right-wing liberals, who gave themselves the name National Liberals, were willing to forgive Bismarck his high-handed and unconstitutional actions after he became Prussian Prime Minister in 1862; they wholeheartedly endorsed his engineering of the North German Confederation and after unification worked closely with the imperial chancellor and the German Conservatives in forging the new Reich. The left-wing liberals, or Progressives, were less forgiving of Bismarck's contempt of parliament; in the new national legislature they continued to press for increased parliamentary rights. Nevertheless, the estranged brothers drew closer together after unification: The Progressives supported national union under Bismarckian auspices as enthusiastically as their right-wing colleagues, and the divided liberals held similar views on a number of other issues as well. Until 1878 both liberal parties were unequivocally committed to major tenets of liberalism, including free trade, anticlericalism, and, with some variations in emphasis, civil liberties.

The two liberal parties appealed to many of the same voters, mostly various segments of the middle classes. The National Liberals were particularly strong among the upper bourgeoisie, especially the new "barons of industry." The Progressives, on the other hand, did well among the ranks of the traditional *Mittelstand* and owners of family farms. (*Mittelstand* is one of those difficult to translate German words. In one sense it simply means middle class, but especially when used with modifiers such as "traditional" or "old" it refers primarily to occupational groups that existed before the advent of modern industrialization: the professions, small manufacturers, retailers, and independent artisans.) Neither received much worker support, but only the Progressives were fitfully concerned about liberalism's lack of appeal among the industrial proletariat.

A shift in government policy in the late 1870s, away from free trade and in favor of protective tariffs (see a later section, pp. 50–51) resulted in yet another liberal split. The Progressives unanimously rejected the new direction, but a majority of the National Liberal Party went along with the government's about-face. A minority among the National Liberals, however, regarded tariffs as a betrayal of a sacred liberal principle and seceded from the party. This group, which included a number of national liberal leaders, formed several new political organizations that eventually merged with the Progressives.

When Germany was unified along *kleindeutsch* lines, Catholics not only became a permanent religious minority in the country, but they confronted a rising tide of anticlericalism and anti-Catholicism from the liberal and Marxist parties. One result of these concerns was the creation, in 1870, of the Center Party. (The name derived from its position in the center of the parliamentary seating chart.) Under the skilled leadership of Ludwig Windthorst, the last minister of justice of the Kingdom of Hanover before it was annexed by Prussia, the Center Party quickly established itself as an effective political voice for German Catholics. From the beginning, the party assumed an essentially defensive stance. It defined its primary task as safeguarding Catholic rights, particularly in the areas of education and public financial support for Church institutions.

For virtually the entire span of its political life, the Center Party limited its appeal for members and voters to Catholics. It saw all German Catholics, from industrial laborers to landed magnates, threatened by a sea of Protestants and anticlericals and wanted to rally the entire Catholic constituency to what its leaders called the "Center Tower." It is true that from time to time there were voices within the party that advocated transforming the group into a political organization that appealed to both Protestants and Catholics, but such proposals were always quickly silenced by the party's leadership. As a political voice of Catholicism, the clergy welcomed the establishment of the Center Party, but the hierarchy never controlled the group. Windthorst early on determined that there was to be cooperation, but not subordination. The Center Party remained at all times a Catholic lay organization with its own program and leadership.

The Center Party did not succeed in becoming the party of all Catholics, however. On the average, somewhere between 50 and 60 percent of those Catholics who voted cast their ballots for the Center Party. The percentage was highest among middle- and upper-class voters and in rural areas, lowest among industrial workers. Still, over the years these voting percentages also remained remarkably stable, so that the party's leaders could count on roughly the same number of parliamentary seats after every national election.

If stability was the primary characteristic of the Center Party, explosive growth epitomized the development of the Social Democratic Party (SPD). This political group had been formed in 1875 by the merger of two earlier organizations, the General German Workers' Association (*Allgemeiner Deutscher Arbeiterverein*), founded in 1852, and the Social Democratic Party established in 1869. Although both groups saw themselves as representatives of the nascent industrial proletariat, originally the two organizations had quite dissimilar views on the political future of this segment of German society. Ferdinand Lassalle, the founder of the Workers' Association, favored *kleindeutsch* nationalism and cooperation with the state authorities in order to curtail the power of individual capitalists, while the Social Democrats followed Karl Marx in rejecting narrow nationalism and identifying the bourgeois state as the handmaiden of capitalist domination. According to this view, only a political revolution could liberate the proletariat from the oppression of both.

In the new party, Marxist leaders and ideas predominated. (Lassalle himself had in the meantime been killed in a duel over a love affair.) The party was committed to an ideology of revolution on the basis of class struggle and dialectical materialism. It contended the interests of labor and capital were irreconcilable, and capitalism, the dominant form of socioeconomic organization in the nineteenth century, would eventually be replaced by the ultimate and highest form of human society, socialism (and beyond that communism) in which common ownership of the means of production would replace private, capitalist control. The instrument that would achieve the transition from capitalism to socialism was an act of revolution by the industrial proletariat. In preparation for this revolution the workers had to organize themselves politically in the Social Democratic Party and economically through labor unions. Theoretically, the two labor organizations complemented each other: While the party prepared the proletariat for the political future, the unions sought to bring about material improvements in the present.

The German socialists identified nationalism as part of the bourgeois "superstructure" of a capitalist society. As a result the SPD refused to join in the rejoicing over national unification and instead saw itself as a separate social organism within the larger society. For the members of the socialist party, their organization represented the future world of socialism, while doomed capitalism dominated the bourgeois present.

The SPD was a class-specific organization. Many of its early leaders were middle-class intellectuals, but they had no interest in obtaining the votes and support of groups other than the industrial proletariat. In this aim they succeeded increasingly well. It is clear from the electoral returns that despite the party's anticlerical stance (the Marxists' also rejected organized religion as part of the superstructure of capitalism), a significant number of Protestant and Catholic industrial workers consistently supported the SPD rather than the Center Party or one of the conservative groups supported by the Protestant churches.

Catholic workers' support for an openly anticlerical party illustrated what was to become a growing problem for the SPD. Almost from the day of its founding the socialists' revolutionary rhetoric contrasted with their reformist behavior. As the SPD's appeal grew, it became increasingly clear that the party derived most of its mass support not from the promise of political revolution, but from its simultaneous advocacy of political and social reforms and its close association with the labor union movement. Since most unions advocated tactics of slow and steady improvements in wages and working conditions, the party's revolutionary rhetoric became increasingly remote from the members' day-to-day lives. At its congress in Gotha (1875) the party adopted a program that was closer to the principles Lassalle had enunciated earlier, but by 1891, under the impact of Marx' fierce criticism of the Gotha Program and Bismarck's Antisocialist Laws (see the discussion on pp. 53–54) the SPD's platform again followed the tenets of Marxist orthodoxy.

An overwhelming majority of German voters supported one of the four groupings discussed above, that is, the conservatives, the liberals, the Catholics, and the socialists. During the twenty years of the founders' generation the strongest parties were the National Liberals and the Center Party. The popular vote for the various conservative parties and the Progressives fluctuated considerably, but none of these parties was able to gain more than 20 percent of the total vote. Before 1890 the significance of the Social Democratic vote was primarily its rapid growth. At the beginning of the Bismarck era the Social Democrats had one representative in the national parliament; when the chancellor left office, the number had risen to thirty-five.

The constitutional structure of the Reich institutionalized what historians have called the Bismarck Compromise. It embodied three basic principles. To begin with, it maximized Bismarck's personal power. Second, it combined conservative authoritarian political ideas with liberal economic precepts. Finally, as a sort of corollary to the second principle, Bismarck was determined to exclude from political power in the future any political groups that had not been party to the original Compromise. This meant that the constitution of 1871 was to benefit primarily conservatives and liberals. Bismarck rejected as "unconstitutional" demands for a share of political power by groups that became politically significant after the Compromise had been established, notably Catholics and socialists. The constitution, in other words, did not provide for any post-1871 dynamics; it was designed to freeze the settlement of 1871 into permanence.

The constitution of 1871 was largely written by Bismarck and, with some changes, approved by the German princes. Its eventual adoption by the national parliament was pro forma. Under the terms of the document the German Reich became a hereditary monarchy with the imperial crown vested in the Prussian royal family. The king of Prussia was simultaneously German emperor. There was a national bicameral legislature, consisting of the *Reichstag* elected on the basis of universal male suffrage, and the *Bundesrat* (Federal Council), which was composed of delegates sent by the various state governments. Of the two houses, the Bundesrat was more powerful. Moreover, Prussia dominated the second chamber. The presiding officer of the Federal Council was always a Prussian government official, and the state controlled seventeen of the fifty-eight votes in the Bundesrat. (It should be noted that universal male suffrage applied only for election to the Reichstag. The states retained their own suffrage laws, which meant the three-class-system remained in force in Prussia.)

The powers of the popularly elected parliament were severely restricted. There was no provision for ministerial responsibility, so that the Reich chancellor and his cabinet served at the pleasure of the Emperor, not parliament. Moreover, all federal legislation had to be approved both by the Reichstag and the Bundesrat, which gave the Prussian state government a virtual veto power over national initiative. The Reichstag did have the power of the purse, but the federal budget, much like that of the North German Confederation, made up a very small part of the total public expenditures in the Reich.

At the time of its founding, the Second Reich had an embryonic national executive. In fact, originally there were only two cabinet offices, those of the Reich chancellor and foreign minister. Bismarck held both portfolios. Not until the later 1870s were additional cabinet-level offices created. There was also virtually no federal civil service. Federal legislation was commonly administered by the state bureaucracies, which meant in practice that the Prussian bureaucracy was in charge of implementing most Reich laws.

The German Constitution and the terms of the Bismarck Compromise placed major decision-making power in the hands of a small and sociopolitically homogeneous circle of men. An estimated twenty individuals made all major political decisions in the years from 1870 to 1890. This elite group, as well as their two hundred or so associates who headed the major administrative offices in the empire, came from essentially similar social backgrounds. They belonged to the landed aristocracy or, if not originally noble, were rewarded with a noble title in the course of their careers. They all went through roughly the same educational system and joined the same select group of fraternal organizations.

It has often been noted that the terms of the Bismarck Compromise were heavily influenced by the chancellor's experiences during the Prussian constitutional conflict. Nowhere was this more apparent than in the position of the military under the constitution of 1871. In times of peace there was no federal armed force, only the armies of the individual states. (In practice, except for Bavaria and Württemberg, most of the states' armed forces were integrated into the Prussian army structure.) The national parliament had no influence over the command structure or the composition of the officer corps in any of the units of the armed forces. The Reichstag's only means of influencing the composition of the armed forces came through its control of revenue outlays at the federal level. The Reichstag had to approve appropriations requested by the states' armed forces in order to carry out their federal defense duties. Once war had been declared (in the nineteenth century it was axiomatic that civilized nations did not fight wars without formal declarations) the state armies were federalized under the command of the emperor, who was, of course, the king of Prussia.

Parliament, then, was to have no substantive say in military affairs, but the Reich's leaders expected little resentment from the public at large. They hoped that after the victories of the Franco-Prussian War public opinion would agree that the army was entitled to special privileges, and for the most part they were right: The German military and particularly the Prussian army had reached an unprecedented level of prestige and popularity. In 1871 most Germans probably agreed with the assessment by the Prussian minister of war, General von Roon, that "an efficient army is the only conceivable protection against both the red and the black spectre [that is, international Marxism and Catholicism]. If you ruin the army, it is goodbye to Prussia's glory and Germany's greatness."

Constitutions are skeletons for the political and social life of a country. Ideally, the document should not only be well designed for the time during which it was written, but, perhaps even more important, it should allow for the possibility of amendments as political conditions change. Bismarck's constitution of 1871 failed on both counts. It was seriously flawed from the beginning, and it provided virtually no flexibility for the future. One glaring shortcoming was the fact that Bismarck had designed it specifically to ensure his own personal power. The document maximized power at the federal level in the hands of the chancellor and reduced the possibility for parties and parliament to challenge Bismarck's authority. The constitution, in other words, was not designed to permit political life to

evolve, but was a crutch to keep one individual in power. As we shall see, later in his career Bismarck became dissatisfied with his own creation. He suggested that the constitution needed to be rewritten to reduce the power of the emperor to dismiss the chancellor.

In attempting to freeze the conditions of 1871 into permanence, Bismarck acted like the proverbial king attempting to prevent high tide from flooding the beach. Actually, the inadequacies of the constitution became apparent very soon. To begin with, industrialization brought with it the need for expanded governmental structures at the federal level. True, between 1877 and the end of the decade, three new federal cabinet posts were created: the Ministry of the Interior, the Ministry of Justice, and the Treasury Department. However, all were headed in "personal union" by cabinet officers who chaired the analogous Prussian state ministries, so that the expansion of the federal bureaucracy did not diminish the influence of the states in federal affairs.

Bismarck was also concerned about military-civilian relations within the executive. Although for the most part Bismarck and the military agreed on major policy decisions, the chancellor recognized the military's ambitions for power aggrandizement and sought to contain them. While a number of prominent officers thought the military should make policy decisions independent of the chancellor's office, subject only to the dictates of the emperor, Bismarck insisted on the priority of the civilian executive. The chancellor vigorously opposed plans to create the office of federal minister of war, arguing the chancellor should remain the emperor's only constitutional advisor on all federal military policies.

Bismarck and the military quickly joined forces, however, when it came to minimizing the Reichstag's influence over military affairs. A conflict between parliament and the military emerged soon after the Reich was established. In 1874 the federal government introduced a so-called eternity bill (*Äternat*).

Under its provisions the Reichstag would have agreed to provide the military with appropriations at current levels of funding in perpetuity, provided the numerical strength of the armed forces remained unchanged. In effect, the Reichstag would have abdicated even the rudimentary controls over the military budget that the constitution allotted it. Even in the heady days of the early 1870s, the majority of the national parliament was unwilling to go this far. The government eventually had to settle for a "seven-year law" (*Septennat*), which gave the military a monetary free hand until 1881, but not in perpetuity.

The conflict of 1874 was symptomatic of what was perhaps the greatest problem with the Bismarck constitution of 1871. As noted above, it made no provisions for adapting to the shifting dynamics of German political life. Bismarck had agreed to a democratically elected national parliament largely because he felt the legislature itself could be ignored as a factor in the political decision-making process. It soon became clear to both Bismarck and his opponents, however, that parliament would play a crucial role in Germany's evolving political life. Bismarck himself early on recognized his "mistake" in agreeing to universal male suffrage as the method for electing the Reichstag and repeatedly considered proposals for amending the constitution to provide for a third federal legislative chamber. He hoped that a body composed of representatives elected from the membership of occupational and professional groups, a so-called economic parliament, would have a more conservative outlook than the popularly elected members of the *Reichstag*.

When these and other efforts at diluting the strength of the democratically elected national parliament failed, Bismarck increasingly resorted to other means to influence the domestic balance of power in his favor. He created artificial confrontations in which he attempted to rally the original supporters of the Bismarck Compromise against a succession of "enemies of the Reich."

THE KULTURKAMPF

One of the more bizarre episodes in German history was the *Kulturkampf*. (The term derives from the liberals' contention that this was a "battle for culture," against the forces of "clerical reaction.") There was no real cause for the altercation, which left much bitterness, but no victors. In one sense the *Kulturkampf* was a classic nineteenth-century conflict between church and state, with a European and even intrachurch dimension. The peculiar nature of the Bismarck Compromise, however, gave the struggle a political flavor not found in other European church-state conflicts.

Bismarck always maintained that the conflict was initiated by the Catholic Church, and in a way he was right. Faced with a rising tide of anticlerical modernism in the second half of the century, church leaders, including the aged Pope, Pius IX, felt it was necessary to reestablish church authority in the areas of doctrine and morals. As a result, the leaders hoped, the church would be able to provide more effective guidance as Catholics confronted the increasing errors and temptations of the secular world. This was one of the considerations which led to the promulgation of the dogma of papal infallibility at the first Vatican Council in 1870. According to this doctrine, when speaking *ex cathedra* ("from the podium [of St. Peter]") the Pope's rulings on matters of faith and morals were binding on all Catholics.

The theological validity of the doctrine was sharply debated both before and during the Council sessions, and among the leaders of the opposition to the new dogma were a number of German bishops and professors of Catholic theology. They opposed the majority view partly on theological grounds, but also because they felt it concentrated too much church authority in the hands of "ultramontane" (literally, "beyond the mountains," that is, the Alps) officials, that is to say, the Vatican bureaucracy. After the Vatican Council had made its decision, however, virtually all German Catholic leaders accepted the new doctrine.

The promulgation of the papal infallibility dogma at about the same time Germany achieved her unification was coincidental; its potential implications for the future of the Reich were not. While this was not a primary reason for its adoption, the dogma of papal infallibility was part of the defensive arsenal with which Catholics hoped to protect the church against inundation by hostile Protestant and anticlerical forces. In Germany itself the founding on the Center Party in December 1870 represented another such mechanism, although there was no direct link between the dogma and the establishment of the German Catholic political organization.

Bismarck, however, was convinced there was such a link. He contended that through the infallibility dogma and in cooperation with the leaders of the Center Party, the Pope was attempting to undermine the political balance of power established in the Bismarck Compromise of 1871. Consequently, the German Catholics, or at least those who supported the Center Party, were acting against the interests of the Reich; they had become "Reich enemies." Since German Catholics welcomed national unification no less enthusiastically than other Germans, it is difficult to see evidence of a Catholic conspiracy against Bismarck's handiwork. In fact, there was none. In his fear of a challenge to the Compromise, the chancellor was confusing potentiality with actuality. It was true that in 1871 Catholics constituted a potentially volatile minority in the country. The Reich's Catholic population was composed of three ethnic groups: Germans along the Rhine, in southern Germany, and in Silesia; Poles in East Elbia and, increasingly, the industrial west; and, after unification, the French of Alsace-Lorraine. Understandably, the Poles and the French were not enthusiastic about their

inclusion in the German Empire, and Bismarck was not totally wrong in expecting them to use religion for nationalistic and political purposes. But as far as the German Catholics were concerned, Bismarck had Prussian rather than Reich worries. He profoundly distrusted and disliked the Center Party's national leader, Ludwig Windhorst. In turn, Windhorst left no doubt about his own bitterness over the annexation of Hanover by Prussia.

The potential problem was compounded by the close intertwining of church and state in nineteenth-century Germany. Separation of church and state existed neither in theory nor practice. Public schools were segregated along religious lines; religious instruction was part of the compulsory curriculum. Professors of theology were state civil servants, just like other university teaching personnel. The states, or technically the princes, had a say in ecclesiastical appointments. Finally, both the Protestant and Catholic churches were supported by public taxes and subsidies.

Bismarck accused the Reich's Catholics of attempting to form a state within a state; they were disloyal subjects of the Emperor. Their vehicle for accomplishing their aims was the Center Party and Bismarck's ire focused on this organization. His answer to the imaginary danger was simple: The Pope had created the Center Party, and it was up to the Pope and the ecclesiastical authorities to control and prevent the party from organizing Germany's Catholics as a political pressure group. This view of the situation was profoundly naive. It completely misjudged the nature of the Center Party. The party was a grassroots organization of the laity over which the German bishops, much less the Pope, had only very limited influence. Consequently, even if the Pope had wanted to control the German party, it is doubtful that he could have done so, particularly since the infallibility dogma did not cover political decisions.

Germany's leadership, however, interpreted the Pope's unwillingness to act (what

Bismarck had in mind was an order dissolving the Center Party) as resistance, which would have to be broken. The battlegrounds for the coming *Kulturkampf* were typical of conflicts between church and state in nineteenth-century Europe: a series of laws designed to increase secular control over what the church regarded as its own sphere of influence. Most of the legislation came at the state level, since under the German federal system educational and ecclesiastical matters were subject to state rather than federal control.

As the largest state, Prussia led the way. Under the leadership of the radical and anticlerical minister of education, Adalbert Falk, the state legislature passed a package of legislation that became known as the May Laws of 1872. They stipulated the appointment of lay inspectors for public schools, provided for compulsory civil marriage (in addition to, not as a substitute for, a church ceremony), and instituted state supervision of seminaries and monastic orders. (It should be noted that these laws applied to the Protestant churches as well. They tended, however, to be rather unevenly enforced.) A short time later the Reichstag passed a law expelling all members of the Jesuit Order from Germany. All of these measures had the enthusiastic support of the liberals.

The reaction of the Papacy and Germany's Catholics was strong, and from Bismarck's point of view, completely counterproductive. In one of the last acts before his death, Pope Pius IX in May 1875 declared the entire package of *Kulturkampf* laws invalid and morally not binding on Catholics. The state responded by expelling some priests and bishops from their parishes and sees, leaving a large number of vacancies in the hierarchy. Eventually in 1878 Prussia cut off all financial subsidies (but not the regular income from church taxes) to the Catholic Church. Catholics neither deserted their church, nor did they cease their support of the Center Party. Rather, the discriminatory legislation forged a closer

alliance between laity, political organization, and clergy. Symptomatic of this development was the increase of the Center Party vote. The party obtained fifty-eight seats in the Reichstag elections of 1871, before the *Kulturkampf* began in earnest, but in the 1874 contest, after the May Laws had been in effect for two years, the figure rose to ninety-one. It stayed at this level, with only minor fluctuations, until the end of the empire.

Still, as the decade of the seventies wore on, both Bismarck and the church authorities concluded that it was in the interest of both to end the animosity. A turning point came with the death of Pius IX in June 1878. Partly because of his own bitter personal experiences with the Italian liberals, Pius IX had come to regard the anticlericalism of the liberals as the primary danger facing the Catholic faith. His successor, Leo XIII, was less concerned with liberalism and more worried about the challenge from the emerging Marxist organizations. As a result, he was anxious to end the altercation with Bismarck and the German liberals in order to concentrate the Church's defensive efforts in Germany on combating the influence of Marxism among Catholics. Bismarck, too, was concerned about the rising Marxist tide. The Reich government was understandably anxious to avoid domestic divisions in a time of growing strife. Finally, the Protestant churches were growing uneasy over the blatant anticlericalism of many proponents of the *Kulturkampf*.

Confidential negotiations between representatives of the German and Prussian governments and the papacy to end the *Kulturkampf* began in 1876. Three years later the parties reached an agreement. With the exception of the ban on Jesuits and the law on civil marriage, the government agreed to either rescind or no longer enforce all of the anti-Catholic measures. These were clear victories for the German Catholics, but the chancellor came away satisfied as well. The agreement with the papacy permitted Bismarck to claim that he was not defeated by a domestic opponent, but had reached an accord with a foreign power, the Holy See. Formally, the Bismarck Compromise remained intact; the German Catholics had not been able to break the political power monopoly of the liberals and conservatives. For this reason the *Kulturkampf* left a lasting and bitter legacy. Although the Center Party eventually became one of the government's parliamentary supports, Germany's Catholics continued to feel that they were second-class citizens, never quite accepted by the Protestant majority. As late as 1918 personnel records of the Prussian civil service were replete with judgments like "although a Catholic, he is a quite decent fellow." At the end of the 1870s Catholics had ceased being "enemies of the Reich," but they never quite became the empire's friends.

ECONOMIC AND SOCIAL DEVELOPMENTS

Between 1871 and 1890 the German economy went through wildly fluctuating boom and bust periods. The founders' years began with a brief "hyper-boom." Germany's political unification came during a long period of upswing that had begun in the 1850s. The already bullish economy received a concentrated infusion of investment capital from the French reparations. France paid off her debts within two years, and in Germany the rapid influx of money set off a wave of speculative fever that touched virtually all sectors of the economy.

By the end of 1872 there were clear signs that the economy was becoming overheated and in mid-1873 the speculative bubble burst. Numerous banks and businesses failed, and unemployment soared. For the next twenty years, despite some ups and downs, the German economy did not again achieve the impressive growth rates of the early 1870s. The depression was particularly severe in 1877–1878. That low was followed by a modest upturn and a new plateau in

the mid-1880s, but then came another recession which reached its nadir toward the end of the founders' years. Not until the mid-1890s did the economic indicators return to the levels of 1872.

While the economy did not attain the dizzy heights of 1872 until almost a generation later, German society as a whole in the next ten years moved relentlessly toward economic modernization and urbanization. The population of the country grew steadily as death rates dropped, emigration from Germany slowed, and immigration by foreigners to Germany increased. In the mid-1880s, when the economy experienced one of its brief upturns, Germany became a country of net immigration. Foreign workers, primarily from Italy and Russian Poland, poured into the country. At the same time, the number of people moving from the eastern areas of Germany to the industrialized west reached unprecedented levels. By 1890 internal immigration had reached levels three times as high as the figures for individuals emigrating permanently from Germany.

The occupational profile of the country was also changing rapidly. The population continued to grow, and while agricultural employment remained essentially stable, the number of persons employed in industry almost doubled. Industrialization created thousands of new factory jobs, but the modernization of the German economy also established numerous white-collar and skilled blue-collar positions. These seem to have been filled primarily with the children of first generation industrial workers, lower-level civil servants, and noncommissioned officers.

Both Marxist analysts and small businessmen's associations postulated that with increasing industrialization independent artisans and small businessmen as a class would disappear. Thousands, so the propaganda of the trade associations claimed, lost their livelihood and had no choice but to seek a wage position in industry. In fact, industrialization did not mean the disappearance of the German *Mittelstand.* The economy demanded new craft skills, and the total number of independent artisans and small businessmen actually increased. At the same time, positions opened up as well in the technical government services. The increasingly complicated economy required a diversification of technical officials (such as, mining and building code inspectors, health inspectors, railroad officials) at all levels of government.

German society was in the midst of social and physical flux, but its class relations remained highly stratified. Germans were divided by both status and income into lower, middle, and upper levels. Like other European industrialized societies in the last quarter of the nineteenth century, German society was characterized by a very small upper class, a somewhat larger middle level, and a sizable lower class. The prevailing income and tax structure produced extremely wide variations in the standard of living between the well-to-do and the poor. A large percentage of the population continued to live near subsistence level, while the upper-middle and upper classes could easily afford luxuries. It is also true, however, that the standard of living for most Germans, with the notable exception of the East Elbian landless proletariat, was rising fairly steadily. In other words, while the relative gap between rich and poor remained vast, the standard of living for both was rising.

A few typical prices and wages from the decade of the 1870s may illustrate the reality of stratification. In 1876 a machinist living in Munich earned about 270 marks a year, an elementary school teacher about 1,600, and a lawyer with his own practice 34,000 marks. The variations in standards of living became even more pronounced because of the prevailing price patterns. Generally speaking, basic foodstuffs were very expensive, particularly in comparison to what we would regard as luxury items. Thus, a loaf of bread cost 36 pfennigs (there were 100 pfennigs in a mark), which meant that the

machinist would have to work about one-third of a day for this basic necessity of life. A pound of butter was 1.10 marks, requiring one and one-third day's labor from the machinist. (As a result, butter consumption among the lower classes was low; they relied on lard as their primary source of fat.) In contrast, a pound of caviar cost 1.50 marks, so that this item, which we would clearly consider a luxury, made a very small dent in the budget of the well-to-do lawyer. In practice, the price and wage patterns meant that those at the lower end of the socioeconomic scale spent almost all of their earnings on the necessities; they had virtually no discretionary income. In contrast, the well-to-do could afford a wide variety of luxuries without actually regarding such expenditures as extravagant. The society, then, was characterized by vast gulfs not just in income levels, but in attitudes toward money and expenditures as well.

For a number of enterprising entrepreneurs, the boom of 1871–1873 provided the opportunity to make sizable fortunes. The level of investment activity in these two years can be gauged from the increase in the money supply: Despite negligible inflationary pressures, between 1871 and 1873 the German money supply increased by more than 50 percent. The ready availability of capital in the form of the French reparation payments had a multiplier effect that reverberated throughout the economy. In accord with classic economic theory, direct investment in high-growth industries, such as export-oriented and manufacturing enterprises, indirectly stimulated equivalent activity in services and products not specifically related to the original investment target.

The boom also marked the last chapter in the long cooperation between Bismarck and the liberals. Under the guidance of Rudolf Delbrück in the Reich chancellery and his liberal allies in the Prussian state cabinet, the Reich and Prussian governments continued a policy of free trade and minimal governmental intervention in the market place. At the beginning of the *Gründerjahre* there was still widespread support for the classic doctrines of economic liberalism in the business sector. Free trade was obviously beneficial to Germany's export-oriented enterprises. These included the chemical, textile, and nascent electrical industries. Agricultural interests, too, continued to favor free trade during the boom years. At the beginning of the 1870s Germany was still exporting sizable quantities of agricultural products to Great Britain. Moreover, duty-free importation of iron products kept prices for farm implements low. Competition from America and Russia was not yet a major threat. Finally, even those industries that traditionally relied upon domestic rather than foreign markets for their sales, such as iron and steel firms, benefited from the boom because of the rapidly expanding home market.

In addition to accelerating the modernization of the German economy, the hyperboom of 1871–1873 also inaugurated profound changes in the German banking and capital investment system. Before unification, the German banking community had been characterized by a large number of local private banks. The availability of tremendous amounts of capital for investment made possible the modern forms of German banking. So-called universal banks established branches throughout the country and handled all financial transactions from checking and savings accounts to stocks and bonds and mutual funds. Moreover, since the Reich government channeled the French reparation payments into the economy primarily through financial institutions located in Berlin (much of it went through the hands of Bismarck's personal friend, the banker Gerson Bleichröder) the banks in the Reich capital assumed a dominant position in the German economy. By the end of the decade Berlin had become both the political capital of the Reich and its banking center.

The crisis of 1873 accelerated the trend toward centralization in Germany's banking system. In the fall the crash of the Viennese stock market led to difficulties for a number of German financial institutions. Far more serious, however, was the collapse of the Jay Cooke Bank in New York; many German private banks held obligations from the New York firm in their portfolios. During the next few years, as many of the smaller private banks were forced out of business, four major universal banks emerged as controlling forces in the German banking and investment community: the Deutsche Bank, the Dresdner Bank, the Darmstädter Bank (this was later to become the present-day Commerzbank), and the Industrie- und Handelsbank. It was symptomatic of Berlin's emergence as a banking center since 1871 that two of the four, the Deutsche Bank and the Industrie- und Handelsbank, were headquartered in Berlin. Both were typical products of the boom years; neither had been in existence before 1871.

By the mid-1870s the crisis had affected all sectors of the economy. The overall impact of the depression may be gauged by the precipitous fall of prices and wages: between 1873 and 1878 wages fell between 50 percent and 70 percent and prices between 50 percent and 60 percent. At the same time, in part because of technological improvements in the production processes, the output of goods did not decrease proportionately, so that a constant surplus of unsold products delayed the onset of recovery. This phenomenon, the existence of a large volume of unsold goods, led in the second half of the decade to a passionate debate over one of the kingpins of German economic policies, the system of free trade.

While the crisis depressed the entire economy, some sectors obviously suffered more than others. Among those particularly adversely affected were agriculture, iron and steel, and textiles. As we saw, before the depression German agriculture had supported the free trade policies of the government. However, the situation changed abruptly in 1875–1876 with the collapse of international grain prices. The recovery of

American agriculture from the ravages of the Civil War and increased worldwide production depressed prices, all but eliminating the higher-priced German products from competition on the international market. To make matters worse, Germany's growing urbanization forced her, much as had been true of England forty years earlier, to import grain, and under the policy of free trade cheap food imports could enter the country without restriction. German agriculture feared it would be shut out even from its home market. By the mid-1870s German farmers were clamoring for a protective tariff.

Agriculture was actually the third link in a chain of economic interests demanding massive changes in Germany's traditional economic policies. The first sector of the economy that had called for protection was the iron and steel industry. With the onset of the depression its products were increasingly unable to prevail over foreign competition, and heavy industry formed a lobbying organization, the *Verband Deutscher Eisen- und Stahlindustrieller* (Association of German Iron and Steel Industrialists), which worked both publicly and behind the scenes for a protective tariff. Its arguments were in part strategic (without a viable heavy industry, Germany in times of war would be dependent upon imports from potential enemies) and partly economic and social. The spokesmen for heavy industry claimed that without protective tariffs they would be unable to pay their workers a living wage.

Another sector of the economy joining the cries for protectionism was the textile industry. Its membership in the protectionist front added not only numbers, but also geographic diversification. The supporters of lobbying efforts for heavy industry and agriculture came primarily from Prussia, while the Reich's textile works tended to be located in southern and central Germany. The textile manufacturers, handicapped by the technologically backward state of their facilities and the decentralized nature of their business, were unable to compete with cheaper imports from England and America. Like their colleagues in heavy industry, the textile manufacturers claimed that excessive foreign competition prevented them from paying higher wages to their workers. To coordinate their lobbying efforts the textile and iron and steel manufacturers joined in 1876 to create yet another and larger lobbying organization, the *Zentralverband Deutscher Industrieller* (Central Association of German Industrialists).

By 1878 the protectionists had mobilized sufficient support to overcome the fierce opposition of the export-oriented industries, the major German seaports, such as Hamburg and Bremen, and the Prussian Ministry of Commerce. (Especially the ministry had been staffed with enthusiastic free traders ever since the days of the North German Confederation.) By the end of the decade, Germany had joined the growing list of European countries abandoning free trade. (After 1880 Great Britain was virtually alone among the European countries in continuing a policy of complete free trade.) The Reich instituted relatively modest tariffs on iron and steel and textiles and somewhat higher levies on agricultural products.

The shift to protectionism had ramifications far beyond the field of economic policy. The decision to institute tariffs also brought about a profound political reorientation. One analyst has called it "the equivalent of re-founding the Reich." It involved a major shift in the focus of power within the framework of the Bismarck Compromise. Instead of working together primarily with both liberal parties, the chancellor now forged an alliance between the conservatives, the National Liberals, and to a lesser extent, the Center Party. This became possible because many of the landowners and industrialists who demanded tariffs aligned themselves politically with the conservative, National Liberal, or the Center Party camps.

The change in economic policy of 1878–1879 determined the economic and political priorities for the next ten years. The tariff decision facilitated the union of the Junkers, with their interests in large-scale agriculture, and the industrial barons who dominated heavy industry. Bismarck also turned away from the liberals in the Prussian ministries, with whom he had cooperated both during the *Kulturkampf* and in instituting the policies of free trade, and began replacing a number of prominent liberal officials with more conservative bureaucrats. During the latter years of the founders' generation Germany was well on its way toward assimilating the industrial interests into the basic power structure of the conservative counterrevolution. The only major factor left out of the new politicoeconomic equation was labor, which grew in both numbers and organizational strength in direct proportion to the advancing industrialization of the country. To deal with this problem Bismarck and his new partners once again invoked the concept of the "enemies of the Reich."

SOCIAL LEGISLATION AND ANTISOCIALIST LAWS

Social and labor policies were another example of the persistently asymmetrical patterns of modernization in Germany. At the end of the 1870s the Reich instituted what was to become the model for all systems of social legislation. Simultaneously, however, it began a full-scale attempt to suppress the political organizations of those who were likely to benefit from the social legislation. True, to some extent political repression and social concern sprang from the same ideological sources. A number of religious and political leaders were genuinely appalled by the social consequences of rapid industrialization, but, like Bismarck, they also worried about the stability of the Reich if industrial labor gained significant political or economic power. Political tactics during the tariff debates entered into the equation. At least some of the industrialists favoring protective tariffs felt that by advocating

some social legislation to benefit their employees, they could gain the support of labor organizations and social reformers for their primary goal, tariff legislation. From the employers' point of view labor support for protective tariffs had an added benefit: it undercut the organizing efforts of the Marxist SPD, part of whose political platform was free trade.

What emerged from this dual effort to alleviate the workers' worst suffering while suppressing their efforts to gain political power was a strange set of allies. Some of the genuine social reformers were also political anti-Semites. This was particularly true of Adolf Stöcker, a Protestant minister who was later to become imperial court chaplain. Stöcker, who had close ties to the German Conservative Party, was convinced that Jews were primarily responsible both for the excesses of rampant industrialism and the revolutionary doctrines and efforts of Marxism. He hoped that social reforms would lead the workers away from supporting Marxism and draw them toward conservatism and the Protestant churches. Other proponents of anti-Marxism, however, showed little interest in social reforms and concentrated on finding ways to use police power and the courts to destroy the workers' economic and political organizations.

In the first decade after the founding of the Reich the groups that would eventually arouse so much concern among Germany's leaders played a very minor role in German social and political life. To be sure, the boom years of 1871–1873 spurred the growth and militancy of the labor movement. Six years after the founding of the empire, the SPD vote had risen from 100,000 to 493,000, but the party's twelve seats in the Reichstag hardly made it a significant power bloc in German politics. The same was true of the socialist labor unions. It is estimated that among some 5 million industrial workers in 1875 only about 25,000 were organized in unions affiliated with Marxist organizations. By 1877–1878 the number had grown to

47,000, but then the membership declined sharply during the hard times of the 1880s. In the early seventies there had been an increase of strikes to gain higher wages and better working conditions, although even during the boom years few of these work actions involved more than a thousand workers. With the onset of the depression the strike wave soon dissipated. Nevertheless, in the government and among many employers with their traditional *Herr im Hause* (lord of the manor) attitude, the memories of a militant labor movement lingered.

For Bismarck and his allies, then, the Marxists constituted a real, if embryonic, threat on three fronts. Marxism was a movement whose revolutionary ideology did not preclude collective violence in the eventual overthrow of capitalism, although the socialists resolutely rejected the use of individual terror or assassination. The Social Democrat Party's 1875 program proclaimed that the organization would work for the overthrow of capitalism by all "lawful means." The SPD also proudly maintained ties to workers' organizations in other countries, proclaiming the need for all proletarians to cooperate in their struggle against capitalism. Partly because of this, Germany's governmental leaders tended to lump all socialist thinkers together, assuming that the writings of one were representative of all. The chancellor and some of his advisors regarded Germany's nascent political labor organizations as part of an international terrorist conspiracy whose aim was to foment a Marxist and anarchist revolution so as to destroy the European political and economic fabric of society. Finally, Bismarck had never forgiven the German socialist leaders for their *grossdeutsch* stand during the years of unification. The two most prominent German socialist leaders, Wilhelm Liebknecht and August Bebel, had bitterly opposed Bismarck's military road to unity, favoring instead a united Germany that was not dominated by Prussian authoritarianism.

By 1875 German socialism and the empire's leaders were on a collision course. Bismarck inaugurated a program of administrative repression, which systematically sought to prevent socialists and socialist ideas from entering the officer corps and the ranks of the civil service. (The latter, of course, included public school teachers and university professors.) In a stock phrase much used in socialist campaign oratory, this was the era in which a Social Democrat could not even become a night watchman in a German government building. Bismarck also began thinking seriously about banning the German socialist party altogether. In the spring of 1878 the government introduced legislation in the Reichstag (laws against political parties had to be introduced at the federal level, since most parties were organized throughout the Reich), but the bill failed to pass. Both the liberals and the Center Party refused to back such a blatant attempt at political repression.

The government's desire for persecution and parliament's concern for constitutional liberties hung in uneasy balance for a few months until two assassination attempts on the emperor tipped the scales in favor of the government. On May 11, 1878, an unsuccessful attempt was made on the life of the then seventy-eight-year-old emperor, a much venerated and genuinely popular figure. The monarch was not hurt, but there was an outcry of indignation; Bismarck immediately blamed the socialists for the crime, although even the government prosecutors could find no link between the assassin and any organized political group.

Unfortunately, less than a month later a second assassination attempt was almost successful. This time a physician with anarchist leanings, Dr. Nobiling, shot the emperor as he was riding in an open carriage through a Berlin park and seriously wounded the monarch. Nobiling was clearly mentally unbalanced. In fact, the Prussian Ministry of the Interior proposed that the physician be sent to an asylum for the criminally insane rather than stand trial. Bismarck, however, persisted in his linkage theory, citing that at one time Nobiling had attended a socialist meeting as proof that the assassination attempt was part of an SPD-controlled terrorist campaign. The government dissolved parliament and called for new elections. Since the last Reichstag had just been elected a year earlier, it was obvious that the chancellor hoped the voters' sympathy for the severely wounded emperor would result in a Reichstag majority favorable to the government's repressive aims.

Bismarck had judged the mood of the German electorate well. After a brief campaign characterized by near mass-hysteria, the voters elected a national parliament whose majority agreed with Bismarck that the German socialists were a threat to the stability of German society. After only two days of debate, the new Reichstag passed the Antisocialist Laws. The legislation forced the socialist party and its affiliated unions to disband. Also prohibited was any printed matter or meetings that in the opinion of the police advocated socialist doctrines. The penalties for violation were jail sentences and fines, as well as "internal exile," which meant that the police could keep anyone convicted of "socialist crimes" from residing in the town in which he had committed his offense. There was only one part of the legislation package which even this Reichstag refused to approve. Bismarck had wanted the parliament to expel its socialist members and preclude the voters from casting ballots for SPD candidates in future elections. Here the majority of the Reichstag felt that the fundamental right of parliament to determine its own membership was at stake, and that part of the legislation was voted down. The remainder of the package, however, passed, initially for three years. The Antisocialist Laws were periodically renewed until 1890, although the Reichstag majorities voting for the laws grew progressively smaller.

In the short run, Bismarck had scored a major political triumph; in 1878 public opinion was clearly on his side. At the same time, the Antisocialist Laws politically ostracized the fastest growing segment of German society. For the remainder of the Bismarck years the SPD remained an outlawed organization subject to constant harassment by local police officials. As in the case of the *Kulturkampf*, the repression did not destroy the organization. On the contrary, while the Antisocialist Laws were in effect, the SPD's strength increased continuously. Twelve years after the repressive laws were put on the books, the party's dozen deputies in the Reichstag of 1877 had grown to thirty-five. The effect of the Antisocialist Laws of 1878 was paradoxical: On the one hand they provided evidence for those within the socialist movement who argued that the liberation of the working class could never come in cooperation with the elite of the empire, but only through its complete overthrow. At the same time, however, the laws led the SPD to focus its political activities on parliamentary elections, since parliamentary campaigning and getting elected was the only form of political agitation not prohibited by the legislation.

Social reform legislation was a corollary to the Antisocialist Laws, although, significantly, repression preceded reform. Germany embarked upon government-sponsored social reforms at the beginning of the 1880s. There was little doubt that help was needed. The depression was nearing its climax, and times were particularly bad for industrial workers. Pleas for social activism from both Protestant and Catholic clerics increased. Adolf Stöcker founded the Christian Social Movement to give organizational force to his views, and in Catholic circles the Archbishop of Mainz, Emmanuel von Ketteler, developed a full-fledged social gospel program. Catholic thinking was a not insignificant factor as far as Bismarck was concerned. In the waning days of the *Kulturkampf*, paying at least lip-service to Catholic doctrines on social reform would clearly facilitate a rapprochement with the Center Party.

The road to reform was also opened by the apparent success of the Antisocialist Laws. For some two years after the repressive measures went into effect, a "graveyard silence" descended over the socialist movement. Its leaders decided on an appeasement strategy, in the vain hope that strict adherence to the letter of the Antisocialist Laws would persuade the authorities to administer the repressive acts in a more lenient manner. Instead of organizing an underground political movement, the SPD's leadership in 1880 decided to concentrate instead on supporting union activity in unprohibited, nonsocialist labor organizations.

The first indication of governmental interest in social reform legislation came in 1881 as part of a speech from the throne by the emperor. The monarch spoke of his concern for the sufferings of industrial laborers and endorsed the principle of social legislation. At the same time, in accord with Bismarck's strategy, he stressed that social reforms would be an effective antisocialist strategy: Workers would recognize the government's concern for their welfare and turn away from the Marxist doctrine of revolution. For a variety of reasons ranging from political opportunism to genuine social concern, the emperor's initiative was widely supported in the Reichstag. During the final vote only the German Conservatives opposed the government bills; even the Free Conservatives voted for the measures.

Between 1883 and 1889 the government introduced three major pieces of reform legislation. Together they were the beginnings of a "social net" designed to catch those hurt by economic developments through no fault of their own. The first bill inaugurated a national health insurance scheme. Through a system of employer and employee contributions the beginnings of a comprehensive health care system were created. A year later, in 1884, national accident insurance provided aid for workers hurt on the job. Finally, as a sort of capstone, in 1889 Germany's system of social security

was established. Under the provisions of the law an initially relatively small number of workers was guaranteed a very modest pension upon reaching the retirement age of sixty-five.

The Antisocialist Laws and the social reform legislation were meant to work in tandem, and in a sense they did, although hardly in the manner expected by the government. The social legislation in no way achieved its avowed aim of persuading the German proletariat to abandon Marxism. By 1890 the SPD's vote had grown to 1.4 million compared to 493,000 twelve years earlier. The increase was all the more impressive since it came during a time of increasingly severe administration of the Antisocialist Laws. The campaign of repression against labor organizations reached a climax of sorts in 1886, during the so-called Puttkammer era. Robert von Puttkammer, an archconservative Prussian minister of the interior who symbolized the reactionary regime of Bismarck's last years, even attempted, unsuccessfully, to eliminate by administrative fiat labor's right to strike. In more subtle ways, however, the social legislation did affect the workers' views of imperial Germany's society. While all members of the Social Democratic Party and its affiliated unions worked to defeat the Antisocialist legislation, the social reforms called forth a different reaction. Especially toward the end of the 1880s, some leaders in the SPD and even more in the unions argued that the reforms demonstrated that improvements in the workers' lot could come through further changes within the capitalist system rather than by relying primarily on the hope of political revolution. In introducing his repressive measures against the socialists Bismarck had hailed the legislation as the solution to the Marxist "problem." In a sense the reverse was true: Not the Antisocialist Laws, but the reform legislation had changed the nature of the German Marxist movement.

A cartoon from a September 1878 issue of the British magazine *Punch*.
The reference is to the Anti-Socialist Laws. Bismarck is trying to stuff
socialism back into the box. (Source: *Lachen*, p. 115.)

FOREIGN RELATIONS

While Bismarck's reputation as the architect of German domestic stability has become increasingly tarnished, the years since 1871 have done little to diminish the Iron Chancellor's prestige in the area of foreign policy. Here he has retained his reputation as a statesman who almost singlehandedly established an international balance of power that kept peace among the European great powers for more than forty years. In fact, our contemporary terminology on international relations is permeated with words and concepts invented by Bismarck. Terms like *Realpolitik* and "honest broker" have entered our language as commonplace, and a number of modern-day statesmen have consciously modeled their policies upon those of the Iron Chancellor. Bismarck's feat of maintaining a *pax teutonica* in Europe for forty-four years seems all the more remarkable since in Bismarck's era resorting to war was still considered a legitimate way to achieve foreign policy aims. Without the experience of two world wars and the prospect of nuclear holocaust to haunt them, the thought of military action to settle disputes was in no way abhorrent to European decision makers.

Before turning to a more detailed discussion of Germany's foreign relations in the *Gründerzeit*, the problem of priorities in Bismarck's foreign policies needs to be addressed. Were the chancellor's foreign policy aims dictated by the Reich's geopolitical position or was the conduct of Germany's foreign relations designed primarily to maintain authoritarianism at home? Bismarck himself and most German historians writing before 1945 tended to support a "priority of foreign policy" (*Primat der Aussenpolitik*) thesis. Confronted by France's desire for revenge, the Reich had no choice but to maintain a large military establishment and to secure France's diplomatic isolation. At the same time, the constant foreign threat prevented Germany from undertaking major domestic political reforms

(such as political democratization) since this would endanger domestic stability and weaken the Reich's military preparedness.

After the collapse of the empire in 1918, a school of younger historians, led by Eckhart Kehr, increasingly questioned Bismarck's claim that his foreign policy was dictated by the givens of Germany's geopolitical position. This, they contended, was a myth deliberately fabricated by Bismarck and his supporters to mislead the German public. The new school of interpretation argued that in reality a "priority of domestic concerns" (*Primat der Innenpolitik*) determined Germany's foreign policy. In order to preserve political authoritarianism in Germany and prevent democratization, Bismarck invented a military threat from France and allied the new Reich to Austria and Russia, the countries with the most reactionary domestic systems among the European great powers. At the end of World War II, a new generation of historians, now led by Hans Ulrich Wehler, rediscovered the writings of Kehr and others (which had been largely ignored after World War I, and suppressed by the Nazis), and buttressed them with new documentation.

Most contemporary historians accept many of the positions of the "domestic priorities" school. There is no doubt that Germany's unique geographic position in Central Europe had profound repercussions for the conduct of her international relations. But it is equally true that the conduct of Germany's foreign policy was closely linked to strengthening the Bismarck Compromise at home. Bismarck's basic foreign policy goals were designed to help preserve the authoritarian system at home, and his shift in foreign allies, as we shall see, was often little more than a reflection of changing political partnerships at home.

Bismarck never tired of elucidating the idea that under his leadership Germany's foreign policy was based upon a set of quite simple and unchanging principles. One was the idea that Germany had no territorial ambitions beyond those achieved in 1871;

the Reich was a "saturated" state. Second, the military victories of 1871 had given Germany the right to exercise hegemony in Central Europe, that is to say, she would not tolerate a second major power on the central European plain. Third, Bismarck (quite wrongly) rated conservative and monarchical regimes as inherently more stable factors in international relations than democratic and republican states. Consequently, he sought to create alliances among the three conservative empires of Germany, Austria-Hungary, and Russia, while isolating France as the least stable and most volatile among the Great Powers. Bismarck's only exception to the "democratic equals unstable" rule was Great Britain, which the chancellor did regard as a constant element of stability in the international balance of power. Bismarck's three axioms led him to conclude that Germany should cooperate with Austria and Russia to preserve authoritarianism on the Continent while working together with England to isolate France. Germany herself, as the most stable, saturated, and powerful nation on the Continent was uniquely qualified to play the role of "honest broker," mediating disputes among the Great Powers and preserving peace among them.

Bismarck's assumptions contained a fundamental flaw. The chancellor was convinced the rearrangement of the international balance of power in 1871 had created an essentially static and permanent set of relationships that could be frozen into perpetuity. The chancellor refused to recognize that domestic pressures in Germany and the other Great Powers regarding the conduct of their foreign relations would result in constantly changing balances among the great nations of Europe.

Bismarck's choice of allies to preserve the stability of the European balance of power illustrated the error of his assumption. The two countries that Bismarck regarded as the Reich's most reliable partners, Austria and Russia, were countries in domestic turmoil. Consequently, rather than being bastions of stability, their domestic difficulties led them to pursue aggressive and risky foreign policies. From Bismarck's point of view it was particularly unfortunate that Austria and Russia could achieve their foreign policy aims only at the expense of each other. This meant that for the most part they did not cooperate with Bismarck to stabilize the post-1871 balance of power, but sought his support to change it to their own advantage.

Bismarck was more fortunate in the choice of his primary Western ally, Great Britain. Not only was England genuinely interested in stabilizing the post-1871 international balance of power, but the relative absence of domestic tensions in Great Britain meant that the conduct of her foreign policy was singularly stable and predictable. As a result, Anglo-German relations were for the most part harmonious, until, beginning in the 1880s, Bismarck's own response to domestic pressures in Germany led to a cooling. As we saw, to forge his new domestic alliance with the conservatives, Bismarck agreed to endorse their demand for tariffs. In addition, the chancellor heeded their call for imperial possessions. However, Germany's quest for colonies negated what Bismarck himself regarded as the keystone of his balance of power system: Germany's self-defined territorial saturation. Inevitably, the fundamental change in positions led to questions in Great Britain about the Reich's future role in world affairs. Would Germany be content with her function as a Continental power, or would she become England's rival in extra-European affairs? The Chancellor himself recognized the pitfalls of imperialism and was reluctant to pursue colonial ventures. Nevertheless, for purely domestic reasons, the Reich in 1884 began its unfortunate career as a colonial power.

The decision of 1884 was symbolic of the increasing intertwining of domestic and foreign policy in the second half of the *Gründerjahre*. After 1878 the evolution of Germany's domestic relations increasingly influenced the conduct of the Reich's foreign policy. To be sure, even earlier the *Kultur-kampf* and Bismarck's alliance with the Liberals had created some tensions with Austria, a country which traditionally relied upon the Catholic Church as one of the pillars of domestic stability for its multinational empire. The end of the *Kulturkampf* improved relations between the Hohenzollerns and the Habsburgs. Bismarck's endorsement of the principle of protective tariffs improved the climate still further, since Austria-Hungary had always opposed a free trade policy. On the other hand, Bismarck's support of tariffs on agricultural products had profound repercussions for Russo-German relations. After 1879 Russian grain exports were increasingly excluded from the German market. In their anger the Russians were quick to remind Bismarck that they had potential alliance partners outside the conservative empires: There was always France.

Bismarck's failure to recognize the seriousness of the rivalry between Austria and Russia and his determination to maintain the domestic terms of the Compromise of 1871 resulted in a foreign policy that was by no means free from elements of instability and inconsistency. However, the chancellor's strategic errors were balanced by his tactical skills in negotiating a series of multilateral alliances and bilateral treaties. In fact, these tactical skills for a long time preserved his reputation as a master of *Realpolitik* and the controlling agent of the European balance of power. The construction of Bismarck's alliance system began, logically enough, with what the chancellor hoped would be the bedrock of the post-1871 balance of power: agreements of friendship and cooperation among the three conservative empires. Two years after the founding of the Reich, the Three Emperors Alliance was signed among the rulers of Austria, Germany, and Russia. It was the embodiment of Bismarck's belief in the viability of the monarchical principle in the conduct of foreign relations: The alliance

was a personal agreement between the individual monarchs.

The irreconcilable differences between Austria and Russia over the future of southeastern Europe soon turned partnership into mutual antagonism and suspicion. Russia supported the territorial and political ambitions of the Slavic nations in the Balkans against the Ottoman Empire, while Austria regarded Pan-Slavism as a threat to the stability of the Habsburg realms. Germany was caught in the middle. She herself had no direct interest in southeastern Europe (Bismarck had said repeatedly that the Balkans were not worth the bones of a single Pomeranian grenadier), but the chronic and growing Austro-Russian tensions made the Reich's self-defined role as the arbitrator of the post-1871 balance of power in Europe increasingly difficult.

This became apparent as early as 1875, during what Bismarck called the "war is in sight" crisis. The potential war he referred to was one between France and Germany, with Russia at least diplomatically ranged on the side of France. Actually, Bismarck wildly exaggerated the dangers of a diplomatic and military realignment in Europe at this time. The occasion for Bismarck's melodramatic outburst was Russia's frustration with the Three Emperors Alliance. Only two years after the solemn signing of this agreement, the Russian foreign minister went so far as to indicate publicly that better relations between the Czar and France were not out of the question. Although no concrete agreements followed these musings, Bismarck became exceedingly nervous: He had clearly failed in his quest to create a new balance of power on the basis of the long-term cooperation of the conservative empires.

Relations among the three emperors grew even worse with the outbreak of actual hostilities in the Balkans. In 1875 and 1878 Bulgaria went to war with the Ottoman Empire. During the conflict Russia openly supported the Bulgarians, while Austria and Great Britain gave diplomatic backing to the

Turks. Once again, Germany was caught in the middle, although Bismarck was also presented with a perfect opportunity to exercise his self-chosen role as honest broker. In the summer of 1878 the chancellor invited all interested parties to an international conference, the Congress of Berlin. The chancellor hoped that the Congress under his leadership would be able to settle the Turkish-Bulgarian conflict and create a new and stable order in southeastern Europe. However, he found it very difficult to play the part of honest broker. Austria and Russia were too far apart on most issues. In addition, the Congress of Berlin coincided with Bismarck's shift in domestic allies and the end of his coalition with the liberals. Although this issue was not directly connected to the debates over the fate of southeastern Europe, the Russians were understandably annoyed with Germany's endorsement of agricultural tariffs and consequently distrustful of Bismarck's self-proclaimed role as "honest broker."

Without admitting that his own actions were instrumental in destroying the original premise of the Three Emperors Alliance, after the Congress of Berlin Bismarck ended his tightrope walk between Russia and Austria and instead began to forge a closer bond between Germany and Austria. The result was the Dual Alliance of 1879. In this treaty Germany agreed to aid the Habsburg monarchy militarily and diplomatically if Russia attacked Austria.

Although the Dual Alliance was a defensive pact—if Austria went on the attack Germany obligated herself only to observe benevolent neutrality toward the Austrians—the treaty was not universally popular in Germany. To overcome some residual opposition among the conservatives to the Dual Alliance (many of whom wanted both tariffs and to preserve Germany's special relationship with Russia), the diplomatic treaty with Austria was supplemented by a new trade agreement between Austria and Germany that provided for a mutually advantageous protective tariff system.

Three years later the Dual Alliance was expanded to include Italy. Bismarck's aim in this Triple Alliance was to encourage the Italians to pursue their imperialist ambitions in Africa, where they would clash with France, rather than press for political and territorial demands in southeastern Europe, where Italy's aims would run counter to Austria's.

The permanently stabilizing effect that Bismarck had hoped would be provided by the Dual and Triple Alliances lasted less than five years. Italy remained an uneasy partner in the Triple Alliance and certainly did not give up her Adriatic ambitions. More significantly, domestic developments in Germany disturbed the Reich's traditionally good relations with Great Britain. Bismarck's new partnership with industrialists and Junkers tied him to forces that looked upon England as a commercial and imperialist rival. By the end of the 1880s the Reich felt it necessary once again to adjust her alliances. In 1887 Bismarck, never a modest man, negotiated a new agreement, the Reinsurance Treaty, with Russia that the chancellor regarded as a stroke of genius, but which his critics tended to see as a move just short of deliberate deception and duplicity.

Crises in the Balkans and France provided the immediate impetus for the Reinsurance Treaty. In 1885 friction between Bulgaria and Russia pitted Austria against Russia, and two years later Bismarck suffered further "nightmares" about France. In 1887 it appeared that a conservative and *revanchiste* military leader, General Boulanger, would become president of the French Republic. In Germany the government asked for and obtained authorization to increase the strength of the army; the Reich staged military maneuvers in Alsace to alert France to Germany's military preparedness. For nervous minds, war was again just around the corner. Understandably, the last thing that Germany wanted in 1887 was a rapprochement between Russia and France.

The Reinsurance Treaty was a desperate effort to preclude such a possibility.

As was typical of most alliances in nineteenth century Europe, the Reinsurance Treaty was a secret accord whose terms were not announced either to the general public or to the members of parliament. The chain of events that led to the Reinsurance Treaty began with an initiative by the Russian foreign minister, Count Shuvalov, suggesting the renewal of formal treaty ties between Russia and Germany. Since Germany was already bound to Austria under the specific terms of the Dual Alliance, Bismarck proposed an accord in which Russia secretly promised to remain benevolently neutral if France attacked Germany in an "unprovoked" manner. As a quid pro quo, in a "top secret" clause Germany promised to remain benevolently neutral toward Russia if the Czarist government took action to change the status of the Dardanelles and Bosporus Straits, which meant increasing Russia's military presence at the eastern end of the Mediterranean.

At first glance, Bismarck had succeeded in squaring a diplomatic circle. Germany had now obtained promises of benevolent neutrality from Russia in case of a French attack. At the same time, her special relationship to Austria under the terms of the Dual Alliance remained in effect, since the Reinsurance Treaty covered only Russian actions in the Straits, not an attack on Austria. The impression that all was well among the three Eastern powers was confirmed a year later when the emperors of Austria, Russia, and Germany renewed their promise of mutual consultations on all matters of common interest in yet another treaty, a second Three Emperors' Alliance.

In reality, the Reinsurance Treaty was a hollow triumph, and the new Three Emperors' Alliance demonstrated the limitations of personal agreements among heads of state in the conduct of international relations. In the long run, the Reinsurance Treaty was not really viable; Germany could not undertake to support both Russian and Austrian aims in the Balkans. The Reich's promise to remain neutral as Russia moved on the Straits violated at least the spirit of her general promise to aid Austria's efforts in stopping Russian ambitions in southeastern Europe. Bismarck's explanation to the Austrians that the "top secret" clause of the Reinsurance Treaty would actually aid the Habsburgs' interests, since any Russian moves toward Constantinople would call forth fierce British opposition and consequently bring England closer to the partners in the Dual Alliance, was not very convincing.

As this explanation showed, in some sense Bismarck himself recognized the fatal flaw of his diplomatic strategy. The assumption that the conservative empires in East and Central Europe had compatible interests just because they were authoritarian systems was simply wrong. Within two years after the signing of the Reinsurance Treaty, Bismarck's entire system of alliances was in serious disarray. Germany's new Emperor, William II, refused to extend the Reinsurance Treaty when it came up for renewal in 1890. Russo-German relations deteriorated accordingly. More significantly, the new monarch, unlike his grandfather, was determined to expand Germany's role as an imperialist power, thereby setting the Reich on a diplomatic collision course with Great Britain. At the end of the *Gründerjahre*, then, Germany's foreign policy was at a crossroads. Far from having stabilized the international balance of power, the Reich's system of alliances was subject to severe stresses and weaknesses, and Germany's self-selected position as honest broker had lost much of its credibility.

THE END OF THE *GRÜNDERJAHRE* AND BISMARCK'S DISMISSAL

Twenty years after the empire had been established amid pomp and martial ceremonies at the Palace of Versailles, the founders' generation looked back with pride on the past, and seemingly, with confidence into the future. Rising economic indicators suggested that the long depression was nearing its end. By 1890 the German economy had reached a new stage in its development: Germany was now a major capital exporter. Domestic stability seemed assured; there certainly was no real danger of revolutionary upheavals to overthrow the Bismarck Compromise. And in the field of foreign policy Bismarck's triumph in resurrecting the Three Emperors' Alliance had apparently secured Germany's continued hegemonial position on the Continent.

And yet there was a prevailing sense that all was not well. The malaise had numerous manifestations. Brahms' and Bruckner's somber compositions reflected a sense of pessimism about the future, which could not be entirely dispelled by the simultaneous popularity of frothy Viennese operettas. In literature the turn of the decade saw the brief flowering of the German naturalist and realist schools. Typical was the novel *Effi Briest* by Theodor Fontane, published in 1895. The story is that of the tragic death of a young noblewoman, who, after committing a single, naive indiscretion, is crushed by the weight of societal prejudices and lack of compassion. Like much of German society the novel exudes a sense of being trapped without a way out. Politically, this feeling manifested itself through a precipitous rise in political anti-Semitism. A flurry of short-lived anti-Semitic parties gained notoriety and some popularity by linking the evils of modernization with the emancipation and influence of the country's Jews.

At the level of high decision making, concern about modernization took a different form. By the end of the decade it had become clear that the terms of the Bismarck Compromise needed major revision. The Antisocialist Laws had not banished the spectre of revolutionary Marxism; on the contrary, as the economy recovered, new members flocked to both the SPD and the unions. Parliament was increasingly unwilling to accept its lack of real power under the constitution, pressing instead for a greater say in running the affairs of the country.

We now know that in response to the obvious tensions Bismarck himself was contemplating redrafting the Compromise of 1871. There are indications that he hoped to invoke once again the doctrine of the "state of constitutional emergency." As a solution to the "emergency" he apparently envisioned either a military coup or, more likely, a renegotiation of the princes' compact that had led to the creation of the Reich in 1871. The latter scenario would have involved a decision by the states' rulers to dissolve the old agreement—that is to say, the constitution of 1871—and, without consulting parliament, draft a new accord. The rewritten constitution, so Bismarck felt, should significantly reduce the rudimentary powers of the Reichstag, while increasing the authority of the chancellor.

Even more than one hundred years later, it is difficult to tell how serious any of these plans for constitutional revisions were. Bismarck was a master of the art of disinformation; much of what emanated from his office was designed more to mislead than to inform. In the end, it did not matter; all of the chancellor's maneuvers came to naught because of a feature in the constitution of 1871 that Bismarck had originally included as the keystone of his own power: the special relationship of the chancellor and the emperor. When Bismarck became prime minister of Prussia in 1862 he regarded himself as the "loyal servant of William I." As far as he was concerned, that relationship did not change for the remainder of his career; he chose the same phrase as the inscription on his tombstone. However, in 1888, death brought an end to the special partnership: in March, William I died at the advanced age of ninety-one. He was succeeded by his son, Frederick III, then a man in his sixties. At the time of his succession to the throne, however, Frederick III was already dying of cancer of the throat.

His death occurred in June, so that 1888 became a three-emperor year. Within the space of four months Frederick III had been replaced by his thirty-two-year-old son, William II, the man who was to be the last German emperor.

As crown prince, Frederick III, and even more his wife, Princess Victoria, a daughter of Queen Victoria of Great Britain, had had reputations as friends of liberalism and political modernization. For years Bismarck had lived in fear of Frederick's accession to the throne. The chancellor's concerns proved groundless, since, understandably, Frederick made no personnel or policy changes during his brief reign.

The situation was entirely different with his son, William II. The new monarch was an energetic, arrogant, impulsive man determined not only to look like a head of state but also act the part. Within a few months after becoming emperor, he was confronted with both the necessity and opportunity for making decisions on two fundamental policy issues. One involved the renewal of the Reinsurance Treaty and the other the extension of the Antisocialist Laws. In both cases William did not hesitate to reach a decision, and both times his judgment was diametrically opposed to Bismarck's.

Like many experts in the Reich foreign ministry, William became convinced that in signing the Reinsurance Treaty, Germany had maneuvered herself into an impossible position with respect to her obligations to Austria under the Dual Alliance. Consequently, against Bismarck's advice, the emperor decided the Reinsurance Treaty should not be renewed when it lapsed in 1890.

A second conflict between the aged chancellor and the young monarch arose over the future of the Antisocialist Laws. The year 1890 was also the time for the triannual renewal of this repressive legislation. Here Bismarck, in line with his "constitutional emergency" plans, proposed not only a simple extension of the legislation originally passed in 1878, but a tightening of the screws that was a clear affront to the tradition of immunity from political prosecution for members of parliament. The government submitted a bill to the Reichstag that would have permitted the police to arrest all socialist members of the Reichstag as common criminals. The chancellor was fully aware that it would be impossible to obtain parliamentary backing for the entire package. A majority of the delegates was willing to extend the Antisocialist Laws in modified form, but that majority would not agree to emasculate the rights of members of the Reichstag. In retrospect it appears that a parliamentary defeat of the legislation was part of Bismarck's strategy. He apparently planned to dismiss the Reichstag after the Antisocialist Bill had been defeated and schedule new elections. If, as expected, the elections produced another antigovernment majority, a state of constitutional emergency could be declared, and the Reichstag permanently prorogued.

To his credit, the emperor was unwilling to go along with such an artificially induced constitutional crisis. He favored negotiating a compromise with the parliamentary majority in order to obtain support for a weakened version of the Antisocialist Laws. Bismarck decided to turn the conflict between himself and William into a contest of wills. He threatened to resign unless the emperor agreed to maintain a hard line on the Antisocialist Laws. (Incidentally, threatening to resign was nothing new for the chancellor. He had used threats of resignation with

One of the most famous cartoons of all times, "Dropping the Pilot," was a *Punch* comment on William II's dismissal of Bismarck. It appeared in an 1890 issue of *Punch*. (Source: *Lachen*, p. 123.)

good effect on a number of occasions during his career.) The young monarch not only disagreed with Bismarck on the substantive issue involved, but he called the chancellor's bluff. Determined in any case to escape the tutelage of the grand old man, he quickly accepted the chancellor's resignation. The *Gründerjahre* and the long era of Bismarck's domination of German affairs came to an abrupt end in June of 1890.

CHAPTER 3

WILHELMINIAN GERMANY, 1890–1914

The years from Bismarck's dismissal in 1890 to the outbreak of World War I in 1914 present a series of contrasting and contradictory images to the historian. Germany had achieved the "place in the sun" that the emperor, William II, demanded for his nation. However, while the country had finally "arrived," Wilhelminian Germany was a society that was divided against itself. The economy fluctuated between bust and boom. The outwardly secure authoritarian political climate hid vacillation and paralysis in the decision-making processes behind the scenes. Germany's foreign policy was erratic. Years of patient negotiations for stable alliances were negated by impetuous and heavy-handed actions by the emperor and other leaders.

The contradictions inherent in Wilhelminian society were perhaps most noticeable in the areas of culture and values. Pervasive militarism in the society reached its high-point. Led by the emperor, Germans from the aristocracy to the lower-middle class delighted in uniforms and the aping of officers' mannerisms. At the same time, the Victorian stodginess in dress and manners was challenged by thousands of young Germans, who donned simple clothing, joined hiking clubs, and longed for the romantic simplicities of life.

Historians generally agree that Germany's problems were related to the phenomenon of telescoped modernization. Social scientists use this term to characterize fundamental changes in a society that occur within the time span of twenty-five years or less. In other words, a single generation was subjected to changes of values and life style. Wilhelminian Germany certainly fit this picture. The country was undergoing very rapid economic and technological development. In 1890 about half of all Germans were still employed in agriculture; at the end of the decade, after the depression had run its course, an unprecedented industrial boom began; and by 1914 only one-third of the German workforce worked on the land. The population continued to move westward from rural to urban areas, drawn by the economic opportunities in industry. Between 1870 and 1914, 2 million Germans moved from the agricultural areas of East Elbia to settle in Berlin and the urban centers of western Germany.

Not surprisingly, along with the shift in occupation and locale came demands for greater political participation—but here the old ruling classes and their supporters balked. While they pursued policies that encouraged modernization in economic and social life, they rejected modernism in politics. Specifically, they sought to preserve the fundamentals of Prusso-German authoritarianism as embodied in the Bismarck Compromise. The emperor in many ways epitomized this attitude. On the one hand he was genuinely concerned about the social problems of industrial labor, yet when workers demanded more political power, William II called them "a mob not worthy of the name human."

Art and literature also reflected the contradictions of the age. Official art—the styles approved by the academies and the country's social and political leaders—favored philistine paintings and bombastic statues of military heroes. But increasing numbers of painters and sculptors, following the lead of their French colleagues, "seceded" from the officially approved styles. Instead of pseudorealism and sentimental romanticism, a new generation of artists favored cubism and impressionism. Similarly, Wilhelminian architecture was characterized by a decorative style that delighted in stucco sculptures at the most unlikely places on the outside of buildings; bric-a-brac and overstuffed furniture were hallmarks of interior decorating. Yet here too there were signs of revolt. A German form of art deco known as the *Jugendstil* increasingly dotted the urban landscape with lean forms and graceful lines. Developments in literature ran along parallel paths. Heroic novels, farces, and light revues found a ready audience, but so did thoughtful works highly critical of Wilhelminian society. Gerhard Hauptmann's dramas of social realism played to packed audiences, while Thomas Mann's early novels, with their erudite but telling criticism of nineteenth-century middle-class smugness, became bestsellers almost overnight.

Wilhelminian Germany, then, was a time of contradiction, conflict, innovation, and rapid change. Many Germans recognized that between 1890 and 1914 their society was at a crossroads, but most Germans wanted it both ways: modernization and traditionalism.

PARTIES, LOBBIES, AND PATRIOTIC ORGANIZATIONS

Some of the most bitterly fought controversies in Wilhelminian Germany involved issues of political reform and restructuring. Both the traditional parties and new forms of mass mobilization sought to influence public opinion inside and outside of parliament. Perceptible shifts in electoral strength led to much internal soul-searching among the four major German parliamentary groups, the conservatives, liberals, Catho-

A cartoonist's view of Prussian political life as seen by a supporter of the three-class-system of voting. Most of the voters—the third class—are looked upon as a dangerous mob, the second class is a neutral crowd, but the real "people" are military officers and the well-to-do. (Source: *Lachen*, p. 125.)

Der Pöbel

Die Menge

lics, and Social Democrats. Generally speaking, as the country became more urbanized and industrialized, the voters' allegiances shifted to the left of the political spectrum. Hardest hit were the conservatives. The two conservative parties continued to dominate in their traditional strongholds in East Elbia, and the three-class system of voting in Prussia assured their iron grip on the Reich's largest state. In the Reichstag elections, however, the conservatives steadily lost ground. By 1912 (the year of the last national election before the outbreak of World War I) the conservatives had been reduced to about 10 percent of the national popular vote. The German Conservative Party was represented by only forty-five delegates in the Reichstag (in 1890 the party still had seventy-three) while its more moderate cousin, the Free Conservatives, were reduced to fourteen instead of the twenty delegates they had in the 1890 Reichstag.

Unfortunately, in their efforts to halt the erosion of their popular support the conservative leaders increased the intransigence of their programs and the demagoguery of their campaigns. Attempting to undercut the competition from Stöcker's Christian Social Movement (see the discussion on p. 53) and a bevy of anti-Semitic parties that arose cometlike in the early 1890s, the German Conservatives in 1892 adopted a new manifesto, the Tivoli Program. In this program, the German Conservative Party embraced anti-Semitism, while rejecting parliamentarism and Social Democracy as incompatible with Germany's national interests or political character.

In one sense, the conservative tactic was successful. The anti-Semitic parties disappeared as quickly as they had risen. They reached their peak in the election of 1893, when they obtained 2.9 percent of the national vote and sent sixteen delegates to the Reichstag. Ten years later, when the long depression of the 1880s and 1890s had run its course, not a single candidate of the anti-Semitic parties was elected to the national parliament. But the price was high. With the Tivoli Program the German Conservatives gave anti-Semitism a new respectability. The demise of the anti-Semitic parties represented not the decline of anti-Semitism, but its diffusion into other and more effective forms of organization. Even so, the conservatives' demagogic tactics could not prevent the party's decline at the polls.

Liberalism, too, suffered from political stagnation. The two liberal parties, the right-of-center National Liberals and the left-of-center Progressives, together sent 118 delegates to the Reichstag in 1890; by 1912 that number had fallen to 87. The Progressives suffered a disproportionate share of the decline, while the National Liberal strength held steady at about 10 percent of the popular vote—still a far cry from the halcyon days of 1874 when the National Liberals alone had 152 members in the Reichstag. The National Liberals, Bismarck's former allies, were torn between rejoining the "cartel" of parties supporting the government and increasing the party's electoral popularity by presenting a viable alternative to the authoritarian status quo. They were unable to resolve the dilemma. Instead, two powerful factions within the same party increasingly went their own ways.

A growing dichotomy emerged between the party's Reichstag delegation and its colleagues in the Prussian Landtag. The dispute was not over foreign policy. All National Liberals enthusiastically supported such nationalistic causes as colonialism and navalism. In many areas National Liberals formed the backbone of such government-sponsored chauvinistic efforts as the Naval League (see the later discussion on pp. 73–74). But on domestic policy the National Liberals did not see eye to eye. In Prussia the National Liberals continued their alliance with the conservatives, rejecting any changes in the Prussian electoral system, but in the Reichstag a new generation of National Liberal leaders was increasingly dubious about tying the party's fortunes to the authoritarian system. A group of Reichstag delegates, which included the party's future chairman, a young lawyer from Saxony named Gustav Stresemann, organized themselves as Young Liberals in 1900 and urged the party's leadership to loosen National Liberalism's ties to the increasingly reactionary conservatives.

The Progressives were something of a mirror-image of the National Liberals. To begin with, the Progressives were hampered by a series of party splits that clearly hurt them at the polls. A united Progressive Party did not emerge again until 1910 and by that time intraparty sniping had eroded much of the left-wing liberals' strength. In addition, the Progressives were also divided on the future of German politics. Most of them favored increased powers for parliament, some major changes in the Prussian electoral system, and some were even willing to break the pariah barrier around the Social Democrats. In the election of 1912 a few Progressive Party organizations concluded electoral alliances with the SPD that committed Progressive and Social Democratic candidates not to oppose each other in runoff elections.

But there was another side to the Progressives as well. The left-wing liberals were also caught up in the mentality of imperialism and chauvinism. When the forces of authoritarianism made imperialism and chauvinism a test of political allegiance to the Reich, the Progressives readily joined in the chorus of support for the emperor's risky game of global brinkmanship. Like the National Liberals, the Progressives were enthusiastic supporters of naval armament and imperialist expansion. A prominent leader, Friedrich Naumann, who worked hard to integrate Social Democracy into the German political fabric, also did much to propagandize Germany's need for a sphere of influence in southeastern Europe.

Success among the German parties came to the Catholics and the Social Democrats. A major political asset of the Center Party after 1890 was the predictability of the size of its Reichstag delegation. In every national election during the Wilhelminian years the party obtained between 14 percent and 16 percent of the popular vote, which translated into a solid block of around 100 delegates in the Reichstag (some 20 percent of the total), so that the votes of the party were decisive on many issues that came before the national parliament. In addition, Catholic leaders found other means of stirring public opinion among their constituents. A large lay organization, the Popular Association for Catholic Germany (*Volksverein für das katholische Deutschland*), founded in 1890, mobilized Catholic public opinion on educational questions and issues of church autonomy. At the same time, a growing Catholic union movement drew support especially from miners and metal workers in western Germany.

Still, all was not harmonious in the Catholic camp either. Shifting population patterns affected Catholics even more than Protestants, and the Center Party's share of the total potential Catholic vote fell as Catholics moved from the countryside to the cities. Catholic urban workers often turned to the Social Democrats. The result was intensified debate over the Center Party's social and political goals. The party's national leaders were proud of their gradual acceptance by the Reich's Protestant authoritarian establishment and generally supported imperialism and the military. A growing minority, however, felt that the price of "governmentalism" was too high, because it tended to alienate the increasing number of left-wing Catholics and thus hurt the party at the polls. Some younger leaders in the party, such as Matthias Erzberger (in 1912 at age twenty-eight the youngest member of the Reichstag) and the future chancellor Joseph Wirth, urged their party to endorse social activism and the reform of Germany's authoritarian political structure.

Rapid changes in German society led to debates on other intraparty controversies as well. The decision to serve as the political voice only of German Catholics inevitably condemned the Center Party to permanent minority status among Germany's political parties. With little danger of a new *Kultur-kampf*, some of the party leaders demanded that the Center Party "leave the [Catholic] tower" (*Heraus aus dem Turm*), and become a party that would be attractive to both Catholic and Protestant voters. The Center Party's national leadership, however, resolutely rejected such a course as too risky.

While the bourgeois parties were concerned about declining popularity or stagnation, the Social Democrats went from triumph to triumph. In 1890 the party sent thirty-five delegates to the Reichstag. Twenty-two years later almost one-fourth of the members of the national parliament, 110 in all, were Social Democrats. And even this figure was not fully representative of the party's popularity among German voters. In 1912 every third German voter cast his ballot for the SPD, but failure to redraw the districts since 1871 and the legal requirement for runoff elections (if no party obtained a majority of the votes in the districts) kept the party's Reichstag strength disproportionately low.

The SPD's problems were not lack of success at the ballot box, but growing internal divisions over the future of the party's ideological and tactical direction. By 1895 both Marx and Engels had died, so that the party had to find its way without the guidance of its intellectual founders. The end of the depression and the lapse of the Antisocialist Laws presented the SPD with a paradox. On the one hand the number of Social Democratic voters and members and the strength of the socialist unions was growing rapidly. At the same time, the boom years after 1897 clearly signaled that the collapse of capitalism was not imminent. In essence, then, the SPD had to decide how to use its popular strength in the age of high capitalism.

The conflict over the party's relationship to capitalism would eventually lead to the split of German Marxism into Social Democrats and Communists, but that development was still some years away. The debate over the need to adapt Marx' predictions to fit the reality of conditions at the turn of the century began innocently enough with the publication in 1898 of a small volume entitled *Foundations of Socialism and the Tasks of Social Democracy*. The author was Eduard Bernstein, a forty-eight-year-old Social Democratic newspaper editor and former bank clerk. Bernstein, who was one of the executors of Engels' literary estate, intended to update Marxism, but in the process he gave some radically new interpretations to such accepted Marxist concepts as the class struggle and dialectical materialism. Nevertheless, Bernstein never abandoned his belief that socialism would eventually replace capitalism as a higher form of human societal organization.

The thrust of his argument was that the road to socialism would be evolutionary rather than revolutionary. Consequently, Bernstein urged the SPD to work for the improvement of the workers' lot within the context of capitalism and not expect an early demise of the hated system. The unions should press for improved wages and working conditions, and the party should work for reforms leading to greater political democracy. To this end, Bernstein urged the SPD to exploit the tactical possibilities of parliamentarism both by using the proletariat's voting strength and by forging alliances with the more reform-minded segments of the bourgeoisie.

Especially the leaders of the rapidly growing socialist unions welcomed Bernstein's analysis since it stressed the importance of labor's struggle on such bread-and-butter issues as better wages and shorter hours. But there was also fierce opposition to "revisionism," as Bernstein's proposals came to be called. Led by Rosa Luxemburg, a brilliant writer and for many years one of the most popular teachers at the SPD's training center for party functionaries, left-wing socialists disagreed with Bernstein on virtually every point. Luxemburg and others argued that the advent of imperialism demonstrated capitalism was reaching its highest but also final phase, so that Social Democrats should be preparing the proletariat not for coexisting with capitalism, but for the revolution which was coming sooner rather than later. Instead of concentrating on bread-and-butter issues (important as these might be in the short run), the unions should plan for the general strike with which the workers would seize revolutionary power.

If carried to their logical conclusion, the disagreements between revisionists and antirevisionists would have split the party. Since this was an outcome both sides were anxious to avoid, most Social Democratic activists rallied around a third faction in the party. This group, called the centrists, included the SPD's long-time and much-respected national leader, August Bebel, as well as Karl Kautsky, the SPD's chief theoretician. (Kautsky wrote the theoretical sections of the party's official program, the Erfurt Program, Bernstein the parts on day-to-day tactics. As a result, the platform was a somewhat contradictory mix of Marxist revolutionary rhetoric and tactical suggestions for reforms within the context of capitalism.) The centrists argued that speculations about the future of capitalism should not deter the party from addressing its most pressing current concern: the need to forge a powerful working-class organization that would press forward Social Democracy's demands on both fronts, political and economic. The party organization itself thus became a primary goal. The ideological struggle between revisionists and their opponents continued to smolder, but it did not often surface into open conflict. One such occasion was the party's 1905 national congress. Here the left-wing radicals introduced a resolution putting the party on record as endorsing the concept of the political use of the general strike. The resolution was defeated, largely because the unions (who traditionally sent a large bloc of delegates to the SPD's national congresses) opposed it. Until World War I the SPD stayed ideologically on the fence. The official party platform remained the Erfurt Program of 1891.

The activities of the parties by no means exhausted the scope of politics. Efforts to organize public opinion outside the parameters of the parties were particularly important during the reign of William II. In fact, the 1890s might well be described as the decade of the mass lobbies. Dissatisfied with the effectiveness of the political parties, which, with the exception of the SPD, mostly lay dormant except when activated at election time, economic and social interest groups established lobbying organizations designed to persuade both the parties and the government to institute reforms and redress their grievances.

The influence of these extraparliamentary pressure organizations on the evolution of the German political scene is difficult to assess. Some historians contend that groups like the Agrarian League and the Naval League (see the later discussion on pp. 72 and 73–74) were instrumental in preventing further political modernization in Germany at a crucial time. Other analysts caution against overestimating the popularity and influence of the nationalist organizations, pointing out that far more Germans joined the SPD than even the most successful of the nationalist organizations, the Naval League. As usual, the truth lies somewhere in between. While the extraparliamentary organizations did not determine the shape of the government's policies, they did mobilize middle- and upper-class public opinion around certain emotion-laden issues, such as imperialism and navalism.

Lobbying efforts, of course, are a familiar phenomenon of all modern societies, but the extraparliamentary organizations of Wilhelminian Germany were unique in a significant way: Most of these groups identified their causes with the preservation of the political status quo in Germany, and they effectively severed whatever embryonic ties existed between the advocates of reform among the left wings of the liberal and Center parties and the right wing of the Social Democrats. As a result, the activities of the extraparliamentary lobbying groups widened the gap between those who wanted to preserve Prusso-German authoritarianism and the political opposition that worked for internal reform.

The prototype of a successful extraparliamentary mass mobilization effort was the Agrarian League (*Bund der Landwirte*, BdL). Founded in 1893, the Agrarian League lobbied against the liberal agricultural tariff policies of the Caprivi government (see the later discussion on pp. 81–82). The BdL was initiated and led by East Elbian landowners, but the appeal for tariff protection sparked an immediate response from farmers all over Germany, and the Agrarian League quickly grew into a large organization. By 1914 it had some 300,000 members. In its effective multimedia public relations campaign the BdL argued for higher tariffs and against political reforms. The *Bund der Landwirte* was officially a nonpartisan organization, but—not surprisingly in view of its political stand—it maintained close ties to the leadership of the conservative parties. It also succeeded in placing its friends in important government positions.

The BdL attempted to strengthen further its political influence by forming an alliance with another economic interest group, the Central Association of German Industrialists (*Centralverband Deutscher Industrieller* or CdI). When it became clear that even after the depression ended, heavy industry would remain a fairly stagnant part of the economy, the leaders of Germany's heavy industry also continued to oppose the Reich's free trade policy and insisted on permanent protection from foreign imports. By the end of the Wilhelminian years, cooperation between conservative farmers and the leaders of heavy industry was well established. United by a demand for tariff protection and anxious to reduce the power of liberalism and the Social Democrats in Germany, the BdL and the CdI sought to affect public opinion against constitutional reform and in favor of an assertive policy of imperialism.

Unlike agriculture, where the *Bund der Landwirte* dominated lobbying efforts, German industry did not speak with a single voice. The divergent interests of heavy industry, export-oriented industry, and small businessmen made it increasingly impossible to agree on a common economic or political line. Unlike heavy industry, Germany's rapidly growing electrical, chemical, and banking interests did not need to fear foreign competition. On the contrary, they benefited from a policy of free trade that facilitated exports. In addition, they were opposed to agricultural tariffs that would increase consumer prices and consequently the price of labor, which was a major cost factor in industries employing a large number of skilled workers. Politically, these growth-oriented industries wanted to modify those parts of the authoritarian system that permitted the stagnant agricultural and heavy industry segments of the economy to retain a disproportionately large share of political power. In 1909 leading representatives of Germany's major banks joined leaders of the electrical and chemical industries to form the Hansa Association (*Hansabund*). Like the Agrarian League and the CdI, the *Hansabund* had both economic and political aims. It supported a policy of relatively free trade and demanded at least some modifications of the Prussian three-class system of voting. Some members of the *Hansabund* even initiated modest efforts to integrate the moderate forces among the Social Democrats into Germany's social and political fabric.

The most strident linkage of politics and economics came in the decade before the outbreak of World War I. In 1904, frightened by the growing membership of the socialist unions and the SPD's electoral successes, the Agarian League, the CdI, and the Association of Small Businessmen (*Mittelstandsvereinigung*) united to launch yet another public relations effort, the National Association against Social Democracy (*Reichsverband gegen die Sozialdemokratie*). Nine years later, the same groups attempted to create a new, all-encompassing bourgeois political organization, something called the Cartel of Producing Estates (*Kartell der schaffenden Stände*). The cartel's program consisted of demands to reduce the power of the *Reichstag* and to place restrictions on the activities of labor unions. The group demanded right-to-work laws, a continuation of the prohibition on nationwide collective bargaining agreements, and a new set of antisocialist measures.

Much of the businessmen's lobbying activities was a response to the changing power dynamics in the marketplace resulting from the growing strength of Germany's unions. During the boom years organized labor increased rapidly in membership and militancy. Between 1890 and 1914 German union membership as a whole grew from 357,000 to 2.5 million—an almost sevenfold increase in twenty-four years. The largest gains were registered by the socialist unions: 278,000 members in 1890, 2.1 million in 1914. The socialist unions also improved their organizational structure. In 1890 they formed a new umbrella organization, the General Commission (*Generalkommission*). It was designed to improve coordination and cooperation among the various craft unions, which had been virtually autonomous until then. Catholic and liberal unions did not join the General Commission, but employers derived little comfort from this. As the experience during a number of bitter strikes showed, workers from all three wings of the union movement often cooperated in forcing concessions from the employers.

The various business lobbying groups differed on many political and economic issues, but they were united in their support of Germany's imperialist ventures. As we shall see (in the discussion on pp. 93–94), the Reich's authoritarian leaders eagerly used the widespread enthusiasm for acquiring colonies and naval armaments to neutralize demands for political and constitutional changes and create instead a common front of support for the government's policies.

The enthusiasm for imperialism resulted in large part from the success of the most influential supraeconomic lobbying groups in Wilhelminian Germany, the Colonial Association (*Kolonialverein*) and especially the Naval League (*Flottenverein*). Founded in 1897, the Naval League was a truly "modern" lobbying group. While traditional militarism had directed veneration toward the Prussian army, the Naval League lobbied for a branch of the armed forces that had an all-German rather than Prussian focus. The Naval League also gave expression to some specifically Wilhelminian values. It was an open celebration of Germany's quest for a "place in the sun": As a major imperial and industrial power, the Reich needed a strong navy to protect her overseas trade and colonial possessions. Celebrating the navy also fit in well with rapid industrialization, since the navy would epitomize the superiority of German technology and industry.

The initiative for the establishment of the Naval League came from the government itself. From the beginning, the driving force behind the organization was the state secretary (that is, minister) for naval affairs, Admiral Alfred Tirpitz. The admiral was a keen observer of the phenomenon of modern nationalism. Tirpitz was convinced that the navy could become the rallying point that would rekindle the sense of patriotism that he felt had been declining sadly since 1871. Enthusiasm for the navy would unite the nation behind the government's policies and generate pressure on the Reichstag to pass the naval construction bills that Tirpitz submitted at regular intervals to the national parliament. The admiral was one of the first to recognize the importance of the military-industrial complex in modern society. Although the League sought both individual and corporate memberships, it was financed primarily by corporate contributions.

Once launched, the organization became a rapid success. Within a few years it had a membership of more than 100,000. With its official sponsorship, the Naval League became part of the social and club scene in many communities. High school teachers served as secretaries of numerous local chapters. The League maintained an ambitious public relations program, ranging from public lectures by naval officers on their travels to providing slanted teaching materials for use in the public schools.

The Naval League was not the only extraparliamentary organization to plow the fertile field of nationalist agitation. Influential behind the scenes was the Pan German Association (*Alldeutscher Verein*). The guiding spirit of the Pan Germans was a former official in the Prussian ministry of justice, Heinrich Class. In 1894 Class, using a pseudonym, wrote a pamphlet with the provocative title, *Wenn ich der Kaiser wär'* ("If I Were the Emperor") in which he urged William II to reduce democracy and "Jewish influences" at home and press for greater German power abroad. The Pan Germans demanded that the Reich be more aggressive in gaining overseas territory, but they also wanted Germany to annex the German-speaking parts of Austria-Hungary. But such public efforts were not the essence of the Pan Germans' activities. Class emphasized working in secret to influence the views of the Reich's industrial, military, and political leaders. He had a tendency to overestimate his own persuasiveness, and the Pan German program never became German government policy—but a number of the emperor's personal advisors and leaders to the conservative parties were sympathetic to the Pan Germans' basic program, including its strident anti-Semitism.

POLITICAL ISSUES AND PERSONALITIES

Politics in Wilhelminian Germany, as in any other modern society, was a product of organizations, issues, and personalities. The members of the Reich and Prussian cabinets, the chiefs of the Prussian general staff, the leading administrators of the state governments, and some key personal advisors of the emperor constituted the Reich's oligar-chy of decision makers. It was a small group; as we saw, one historian has estimated that at any one time some twenty men determined the fortunes of the empire. It was also a politically and socially homogeneous circle, with shared family and educational experiences. Almost all the leading men in the empire possessed title of nobility, although few were Junkers in the strict sense of the word. For the most part the chancellors, military chiefs of staff, and cabinet ministers came from families that had their roots west of the Elbe or even outside of Germany. As a group, the German oligarchy of leaders, with their rural heritage, narrow social perspective, traditional education, and conservative political outlook, was not qualified to lead the country into the twentieth century.

Titular and symbolic head of this small group of decision makers was the man who gave the era its name, Emperor William II (Kaiser Wilhelm). Like the times in which he lived, William was a study in contrasts. Born with a physical disability that left him essentially without the use of his left arm, he was an overachiever whose personality traits were, at one and the same time, weakness of character, arrogance, intolerance, charm, quick-wittedness, and lack of perseverance. He was a man who needed constant reinforcement. Bismarck described William as someone "who wanted to have a birthday party every day of his life."

Although unsure of his opinions and anxious for popular and peer approval, the emperor insisted he was a leader who made his way undeterred by considerations of popularity or politics. It will come as no surprise that he selected friends and associates who were sycophants rather than honest advisors. They included such men as the romantic and sentimental aristocrat Phillip von Eulenburg; a mediocre general, Count Alfred von Waldersee; and a reactionary industrialist, Baron Carl Ferdinand von Stumm-Halberg. But there was also another side to the emperor. Among the monarch's long-time friends was Albert Ballin, the

Jewish head of a successful shipping firm, the Hamburg-America Line, and a man of unquestioned personal integrity.

Under the terms of the Bismarckian constitution the emperor presided over a three-layered executive structure. In addition to privy councils on military and civilian affairs, he appointed the Reich chancellor and federal ministers, as well as, in his capacity as King of Prussia, that state's prime minister and the other members of the Prussian cabinet. (With the exception of a few months, all the Wilhelminian chancellors also served as Prussian prime ministers.) Constitutionally, none of these appointments were subject to parliamentary approval, although the Reich and Prussian cabinets had to deal with their respective legislatures in order to get their budgets approved. In practice, the Reichstag's role as partner of the executive was expanding throughout the Wilhelminian years. Unwilling to countenance massive public disapproval, the Reich executive worked hard to obtain a parliamentary coalition on most major issues. It was not easy, however, to find government leaders who worked well within the strictures of this system of "parliamentary authoritarianism." Chancellors were typically required to maintain good relations with the conservative majority in the Prussian Landtag, but also work well with the increasingly left-leaning Reichstag, while at the same time constantly nursing the emperor's inflated ego. In fact, few men could do this for any length of time. The contradictory requirements help explain the succession of relatively short-term chancellors during the Wilhelminian years.

From 1890 to 1894 the chancellor was Leopold von Caprivi, a professional soldier who, to everyone's surprise, turned out to be a natural political talent. In contrast to his immediate predecessor, Caprivi, at fifty-nine, was virtually a young man at the time of his appointment. But Caprivi fell afoul of conservative opposition to his economic policies (see the discussion on pp. 80–81), and after four years he was succeeded by a seventy-five-year-old Bavarian aristocrat, Chlodwig von Hohenlohe-Shillingfürst. The chancellor's advanced age made it difficult for him to carry the burdens of office. In addition, Hohenlohe was unfamiliar with Reich and Prussian issues. His earlier career had been spent in Bavarian politics, and before going to Berlin he had been governor of Alsace-Lorraine. Originally the emperor and his advisor Phillip von Eulenburg had intended that the aged Hohenlohe should serve as transition leader until they could turn to Bernhard von Bülow, the man they regarded as Caprivi's ideal successor. The Hohenlohe era lasted rather longer than anticipated, largely because the chancellor refused to resign, and the emperor was not willing to face the political crisis that an outright dismissal would have caused.

In 1900 William II exclaimed "Bernhard has arrived, and I know all is well." In fact, all was not well for very long. The new chancellor, Bernhard von Bülow, was fifty-one years old and in the prime of life. He also had charming manners, a facility for languages, and an extraordinary ability to feed William with subservient memoranda. But he had spent all of his professional career in the German diplomatic service and had no experience in dealing with either parliament or domestic politics. When in 1906 Bülow proved incapable of preventing parliamentary investigations into some scandals in the Reich executive office (see discussion on pp. 82–83), the emperor turned against his erstwhile favorite and his facile charm.

For his last chancellor before World War I William turned to the epitome of an able but colorless Prussian bureaucrat, Theobald von Bethmann Hollweg. Bethmann Hollweg was fifty-five at the time of his appointment. He had spent his entire career in the Prussian civil service, rising to the post of minister of the interior in 1906. In contrast to Bülow, he was an able administrator and familiar with domestic issues, but Bethmann Hollweg had no foreign policy experience—a serious handicap at a time of rising international tensions.

Given the importance of the military in Wilhelminian Germany, the chief of staff of the Prussian army enjoyed a position of great influence and power. Here, too, practices during the Wilhelminian era contrasted sharply with those of the *Gründerjahre*. In 1890 the incumbent, General Helmuth von Moltke, was a very old man; he had been chief of staff since the Prussian constitutional crisis of the 1860s. In 1890 William replaced Moltke with a personal favorite, the fifty-nine-year-old General von Waldersee. The contrast between the two men was striking—and not just in terms of age. Unlike the brilliant Moltke, Waldersee was by all accounts a mediocre military talent. Moreover, while Moltke was taciturn and aloof, Waldersee enjoyed political intrigue and playing host to lavish parties at his Berlin home. (The latter would have been impossible on the modest salary of a Prussian officer, but Waldersee had had the foresight to marry an American heiress.)

Unfortunately for Waldersee, his social graces could not compensate for his lack of military capabilities. After only two years in office, he was replaced as chief of staff, although William continued to seek Waldersee's advice on political matters; the general remained a member of the emperor's personal entourage. Waldersee's successor came from the Moltke mold. General Hans von Schlieffen, fifty-nine years old in 1892, was a distinguished strategist with a long record of staff appointments behind him. Unlike Waldersee, Schlieffen felt politics and the military should not mix, or, more precisely, he assumed political considerations should at all times be subordinated to military plans and strategies.

Schlieffen retired in 1906, and the emperor, no doubt hoping that history would repeat itself, selected another Moltke as the next chief of staff. The "younger" Helmuth von Moltke (he was fifty-eight at the time of his appointment), was the namesake and nephew of the "great" Moltke. Unfortunately, he had inherited only the name, not the skills of his uncle. Another mediocre talent, he failed completely when his leadership was tested during World War I. Within a year after the outbreak of the conflict, Moltke resigned his post.

Running through the length of the Wilhelminian years were a number of specific political controversies, all of them concerned with a fundamental problem: the redistribution of political power as the Reich made the transition from a rural, traditional society to one dominated by industrial and urban life styles. To be sure, the issue was seldom stated so crassly. Instead, the debates over the basic problem of power tended to appear as high-minded discussions of political philosophy and values.

To begin with, there was the "federal problem," or to be more exact, the relationship between the Reich and its largest state, Prussia. Twenty years before, Bismarck had created a united Reich dominated by Prussia, and Prussia in turn was the political domain of the East Elbian Junkers. By 1890 it was clear that the Junkers were headed for economic decline and political isolation. Should this group continue to dominate Prussia, and, if so, should Prussia continue to exercise hegemony over the affairs of the Reich? The Junkers' own answer to this legitimate question was a resounding "yes," but that hardly settled the issue.

In this struggle for control of state and Reich, the Prussian ruling classes were not without political assets. The emperor agreed with their contention that Prussian authoritarianism was the key to the Reich's past and future greatness. As king of Prussia, William appointed well-known conservatives to a number of key Prussian positions. Ernst von Köller, the minister of the interior from 1894 to 1895, became hated for his reactionary appointment policies in the Prussian civil service and for his efforts to resurrect the laws against the socialists. Similarly, the state's prime minister from 1892 to 1894, Botho von Eulenburg, a cousin of Phillip's, sought to preserve the conservatives' power monopoly in Prussia; he single-handedly sabotaged efforts to achieve

Two leading political adversaries of the Wilhelminian years: August
Bebel (left), the fiery leader of the SPD, and Bernhard von Bülow (right),
the suave and elegant Reich chancellor. (Source: *Lachen*, p. 146.)

greater cooperation with the Catholic Center Party. The Prussian ministry of agriculture became a virtual branch office of the Agrarian League. The minister for most of the 1890s, Baron Ernst von Hammerstein-Loxten, as well as his successor Freiherr von Schorlemer-Lieser, had been active in the BdL before their appointments to the cabinet. The increasingly close ties between the Junkers and heavy industry were reflected in the appointment of the Prussian minister

of trade, Ludwig Brefeld, a man with good connections to the Central Association of Industrialists.

But Prussian internal politics were only one side of the federal issue. There was also the interaction of the Reich and Prussia. In spite of his boast that he would go his own way, undeterred by shifts of public opinion, William knew that he could not isolate Prussia from the political pressures of the Reichstag nor, in the long run, continue to impose

Prussia's authoritarian ways on the Reich as a whole. Köller's plans for a new set of antisocialist laws in Prussia were shelved, for example, when it became clear that a majority of the Reichstag was opposed. As the fulcrum of the German political spectrum continued to move left in the next twenty-four years, Prussia became politically more and more isolated, and relations between the state's ruling circles and the rest of the country grew increasingly strained. Unfortunately, this development also intensified the determination of Prussia's political leaders to maintain their control over the state at all costs.

A number of issues were involved in the Reich-Prussian relationship, but after 1890 the political debate centered largely on reforms of the Prussian electoral system as the key to changing Prusso-German authoritarianism. For good reason. The three-class system of voting that continued to be the law in Prussia enabled the Junkers and their allies to control politics in three-fifths of the Reich; if the rules of universal male suffrage, under which the Reichstag was elected, prevailed in Prussia as well, the Conservatives' domination of Prussia would end. By 1900 polarization on the electoral issue was virtually complete. Progressives and Social Democrats as well as some National Liberals and Center Party leaders demanded major reforms in Prussia. In contrast, Conservatives, most National Liberal leaders, Center Party leaders, and spokesmen for the Agrarian League and heavy industry insisted that the Prussian electoral system should be left unchanged. Indeed, they claimed that the real problem was universal male suffrage as practiced in national elections. They demanded property qualifications as a condition for the right to vote in all state and national elections, or—a plan Bismarck had also toyed with—a parliament that would be composed of representatives selected by economic interest groups and that would take the place of the Reichstag.

Most of the time the emperor and his advisors recognized that the clock of political modernization could not be held back. They tried to thread their way cautiously— too cautiously—between the intransigence of the Prussian Conservatives and the demands for change by most other Germans. As Prussian prime ministers, both Bülow and Bethmann Hollweg introduced reform bills in the Prussian Landtag that would have led to modest liberalizations of the Prussian electoral system. The proposals did not envision the abolition of the three-class system, but they would have mitigated some of the glaring discrepancies between the popular vote and parliamentary representation under the system established in 1851. All was in vain. Until 1918 the majority of the Prussian legislature, composed of the Conservatives and most National Liberal and Center Party representatives, consistently voted down all efforts to realize electoral reforms. William in turn was not willing to use his powers as king to impose his will upon the Prussian Conservatives. As a result, the gap between the politically dominant groups in the state and public opinion in Germany as a whole continued to grow. By 1914 the state that had united Germany was increasingly isolated from its own creation.

The unwillingness of William and his ministers to loosen the Conservatives' and National Liberals' control of Prussia was one of the factors that complicated relations between the Reich executive and the popularly elected Reichstag. Another was the problem of obtaining parliamentary backing for government policies. Both the emperor and the chancellors sought to obtain the support of the majority of the Reichstag on most issues. There were two ways of achieving this goal: The government had to work either with "floating majorities" for each specific bill that it wanted passed, or it could attempt to create a long-term alliance of parties that supported the executive because it agreed with the government's basic policy aims. From the Reich cabinet's point of view the latter was certainly preferable since it promised long-range stability in the relations between executive and legislature. But there was a major difficulty: The growing strength of the SPD and the left-wing of the Center Party steadily decreased the size of the delegate block that endorsed the authoritarian status quo as a matter of political philosophy.

Nevertheless, the Reich governments attempted to create long-term parliamentary coalitions, although they did not use this term. They spoke of "a cartel of parties." Major disagreements emerged, however, over the membership of such a political cartel. The driving force behind one particular form of cartel, called the *Sammlungspolitik* ("collection policy"), was the Prussian minister of finance from 1890 to 1901, Johannes von Miquel. The minister, an old National Liberal turned conservative, consistently advocated a resurrection of the coalition of Conservatives and National Liberals with which Bismarck had governed after 1878. Such a combination could be expected to support protective tariffs, imperialism, and a strong navy—and forcefully oppose reform in Prussia.

Miquel's scenario contained a major flaw, however: The Conservative-National Liberal alliance represented only a minority—and a declining one at that—of the Reichstag votes. For this reason, astute politicians like Caprivi rejected Miquel's *Sammlungspolitik* unless it included the Center Party and preferably the Progressives as well. Such a coalition would still support imperialism, but its endorsement of other issues on the conservative agenda was less certain. The Progressives opposed protective tariffs. The Progressives also demanded constitutional reforms, and the Center Party refused to join the cartel if the government insisted on reinstituting repressive laws against either Catholics or socialists.

Caprivi was willing to pay a high price for Progressive and Center Party cooperation, but the conservatives were not. When the chancellor in 1892 introduced restoration of church control of the public elementary schools as a gesture of goodwill toward the Center Party, the conservatives protested against the bill's implications for the "nationality struggle" in the east. Church control of elementary schools would have meant that in East Elbian regions with a predominantly Polish population, Polish Catholic priests would have been in charge of the Prussian public schools. The conservatives' opposition to the school bill was a major factor in Caprivi's decision to resign as Prussian prime minister, and the controversy also demonstrated the difficulty of "collecting" a politically viable cartel.

Hohenlohe and his successors recognized the futility of reviving the coalition of 1878. Increasingly, the Reich government relied upon the Center party as one of the groups in the Reichstag that supported the cabinet's general policies. In fact, Bülow made the Center Party the pivot of his Reichstag coalition. As a result, the Reich cabinet could expect solid majorities for its policies of imperialism and some support for protective tariffs, but not for plans to turn back the constitutional clock. On the contrary, the growing strength of the Center Party's left wing was reflected in 1906 and again in 1908 when the Catholics took the initiative in pushing through the Reichstag hearings on governmental abuses that seriously embarrassed the Reich executive. Bülow's angry attempt to rebuild the cartel of 1878 through gerrymandering and a media blitz in the election of 1907 had no lasting effect.

Bethmann Hollweg learned from his predecessor's errors. He abandoned the Conservative-National Liberal alliance at the Reich level and attempted instead to forge a coalition of all bourgeois parties. But this coalition was also a house divided against itself. The bourgeois groups were in full agreement only on a need for a strong defense and imperial activism. On most domestic issues the views of the Progressives, the Conservatives, and parts of the Center Party were often diametrically opposed.

By 1914 the attempts to "collect a cartel"

had largely failed. Or, more precisely, they had succeeded only in the areas of defense and imperialism. This is the essence of what has become known as the primacy of domestic politics in Germany's foreign affairs: The conduct of the Reich's global politics was to a large extent an attempt by the Reich's decision makers to maintain support for the country's domestic authoritarianism. Since the emperor and the ruling oligarchy were unwilling to countenance a political opening to the left, the chancellors felt they had no choice but to use an aggressive and activist foreign policy as a basis for preserving domestic stability.

As we saw, the attempt to establish a stable coalition among the bourgeois parties failed largely because the potential members of such a political alliance held contradictory views on a variety of long-standing domestic issues. One of these was Prussian electoral reform. Another was the linkage between social reform and renewed repression of the Social Democrats. Soon after coming to the throne William II, who regarded himself as a modern if patriarchal ruler, inaugurated what he called a New Course in social policy. Under this catchword the government proposed (and the Reichstag passed) improvements in the system of state arbitration tribunals, factory safety inspections, and laws governing the maximum number of work hours for women and children.

But the New Course had a political purpose as well. Like his grandfather, William expected that improvements in the lives of workers would lead them to abandon their allegiance to the Social Democrats. When it again became clear that industrial labor could not be bought off with kindness, the emperor ordered the Reich cabinet to submit a new series of antisubversion bills to the Reichstag. It was a futile effort. A majority of the national parliament voted down all such proposals until the government finally gave up the quest in 1899.

Stymied by the Reichstag's majority on the antisubversion laws, some of William's advisors, including Phillip von Eulenburg, toyed with the idea of forcing a change in the Reich constitution to give the emperor greater control over parliament. William was flattered by such scenarios, but he also recognized the political impracticality of any Bonapartist coup. Not only was the vast majority of public opinion opposed to a rewriting of the Reich constitution, but so too were the emperor's fellow rulers in the German states.

As was to be expected in a rapidly changing society, tax reform was another major domestic controversy. Like many industrializing countries, Germany had a problem of private wealth and public poverty. The states' operations were financed by property taxes and the income from state-run commercial enterprises, with the bulk of Prussia's revenues before World War I coming from the profits of the state railroad. In contrast, the federal government and the localities had no adequate tax base to pay for their growing obligations. Specifically earmarked for the federal government were only the incomes from tariffs, some consumers' taxes, and users' fees. The situation was even worse at the local level. The cost of constructing sewers, streets, and public transportation systems for the rapidly growing urban centers during the 1890s far outstripped the income from the municipalities' traditional tax base of levies on local commercial activities. The result was budgetary poverty at the Reich and local levels, while the states produced large budgetary surpluses. Since 1871 the *Länder*, through their representatives in the *Bundesrat*, had voted biannual subsidies to the Reich. Quite aside from the anomaly of having the Reich come hat-in-hand to its subdivisions every two years, these *Matrikularbeiträge* (literally, "inscription contributions"), as they were called, brought no relief at all for the cities.

By 1890 few in or out of government questioned that Germany's tax system needed an overhaul, but the financial and political implications of any reform package suggested aroused bitter controversy. Many German states still had electoral systems that linked the political weight of a voter's ballot to the amount of taxes he paid. This was especially true for Prussia, the state that made up three-fifths of the Reich. Consequently, any major shifts in the forms and amounts of taxation would involve changes in the class allocation of voters and bring with it alterations in the political balance of power.

Leopold von Caprivi's tax reform bill focused on the problem of the municipalities. Under the government's proposals the cities would benefit from a progressive income tax, rising to a maximum of 4 percent on annual income of 100,000 marks or more. Caprivi also suggested as part of his tax reform package that in Prussia the division of voters into electoral classes should be undertaken at the precinct rather than the district level. Under this scheme, relatively wealthy voters in poorer precincts would be classified in one of the first two classes, rather than the third class. Conversely, voters of moderate income in wealthy areas would be classified as voters in the last class.

Not surprisingly, the Prussian conservatives protested against the political implications of Caprivi's proposals. As a result, while the tax reforms were eventually adopted, they brought no changes in the Prussian electoral system. The allocation of voters into classes remained at the district level, leading to an increasingly glaring discrepancy between the popular vote and political representation in the Landtag, and consequently widening political polarization in the state.

The flow of governmental revenues during the boom years after 1897 carried Germany through the years of Hohenlohe's chancellorship, but Bülow was again confronted with a financial crisis. This time the problem was at the Reich level. Expenditures for the naval buildup and the rising costs of federal social welfare programs had raised the Reich's public debt by 1907 to 5 billion marks. For an age which regarded debts in any amount as a blight on public finances, this was a matter that could not be ignored.

Since tax reform inevitably endangered the cohesion of Bülow's fragile "bloc" of supporters composed of conservatives, National Liberals, and Catholics, the chancellor waited as long as possible before tackling the problem of tax reform. By 1908, however, it was clear that to balance the federal budget the Reich would need an additional 500 million marks annually in income for a number of years. To make good the shortfall, Bülow proposed 300 million marks from increased *Matrikularbeiträge*, an additional 100 million in the form of new consumer and indirect taxes, and finally, 100 million from the proceeds of a new Reich inheritance tax. The Reichstag passed the first two parts of the package, but Conservatives and Catholics (the latter in retaliation for Bülow's attacks on the Center Party during the 1907 election) combined to defeat the proposed inheritance tax. The resulting damage to Bülow's political reputation was a major factor in his eventual dismissal a year later.

Closely related to taxes was another perennial issue in German domestic politics: tariffs. When Caprivi assumed office agricultural prices had been rising for some years, and the chancellor felt that Germany's tariff structure should reflect what was expected to be a lengthy period of price stability. At the time most German farmers agreed. As a result, they raised only minimal objections to a series of twelve-year trade treaties which the Caprivi government negotiated with Germany's major international trading partners between 1890 and 1892. The treaties provided for low tariff rates for both agricultural and industrial imports.

Neither the Reich's farmers nor Caprivi foresaw the collapse of the international grain market in 1893. Newly organized in the Agrarian League, Germany's farmers clamored for renegotiation of the Caprivi treaties to protect them from cheap agricultural imports from America and Russia. The farmers failed to raise the Reich's tariffs (particularly since the terms of the Caprivi treaties continued to benefit the rapidly growing export industry), but they did obtain relief in the form of export subsidies. Moreover, the landowners' unhappiness was instrumental in forcing Caprivi's resignation less than a year later.

The tariff issue came to a head during Bülow's administration, when the Caprivi treaties expired. In 1902, Germany's tariff situation had become exceedingly complicated. A growing percentage of the Reich's wealth came from the exports of Germany's manufacturing industries, particularly chemicals and electrical products. At the same time, the significance of agriculture in the national economy was steadily decreasing. From a national point of view, then, tariffs that protected farmers, but endangered the flow of German exports abroad made no economic sense. But, as always, there was the political dimension. As we saw, the German farming community was dominated by East Elbian landowners, who were also the backbone of Prusso-German authoritarianism.

Confronted with a clear dilemma, Bülow equivocated. The chancellor was fully aware that Germany's exports were by now the lifeblood of the economy, but he also felt he had to appease the agricultural lobby. Consequently, the new tariff treaties his government negotiated provided for somewhat increased rates on agricultural and industrial imports, and they had a much shorter running time than Caprivi's; but Bülow also made sure that the rates were not so high as to provoke retaliation by Germany's trading partners against the growing volume of the Reich's industrial exports. Instead of getting all the tariff protection it wanted, agriculture was temporarily bought off by increased export subsidies and cheaper credit.

Taxes and tariffs involved conflicting economic interests; repeated clashes between the government and the Reichstag over the question of executive privilege and the role of the emperor as commander-in-chief of the Reich navy and the Prussian armed forces concerned the even more fundamental question of the evolution of the Reich constitution.

At first glance, the battles over executive privilege often concerned seemingly esoteric items. One was the Prussian code of military justice. Traditionally, the military establishments of Prussia and the other German states conducted court martials in secret, with the accused neither present nor able to respond to the charges. By 1896 most German states had changed their codes of military justice to give the accused the right to be present at his own trial. Prussia, however, lagged behind, and the emperor made reform of the code a major issue of executive privilege. He announced melodramatically that he owed it to his ancestors to maintain the Prussian system of military justice unchanged. It is indicative of the changing balance of power in German politics, however, that in the face of opposition from a majority of the Reichstag, William and his military advisors yielded. By the beginning of World War I, Prussia, too, had a reformed code of military justice.

An issue of executive privilege involving parliament's power of the purse came to a head in 1906. For this fiscal year the Reich government asked the Reichstag for a supplemental appropriation of 24 million marks in order to pay for unexpected expenses incurred in putting down a tribal rebellion in the German colony of South-West Africa (present-day Namibia). Prodded by the energetic young Center Party delegate Matthias Erzberger, parliament voted to hold hearings on abuses in Germany's colonial administration before appropriating the funds. The emperor objected strongly, claiming that such a step interfered with his powers as commander-in-chief of the armed forces, but the Reichstag did not yield. In fact, the hearings seriously embarrassed the German colonial office. Erzberger and his colleagues exposed a cesspool of corruption in the administration of Germany's African colonies.

If the emperor needed additional evidence that the military's claim to be a law unto itself was increasingly out of step with the mood of the country, it was provided by a celebrated incident involving military-civilian relations in the town of Zabern (Saverne) in Alsace in the fall of 1913. Here the commander of the local garrison, a lieutenant, without consulting the civilian authorities, had ordered force to be used against a group of French demonstrators. A number of demonstrators were illegally arrested and some maltreated and wounded. This time it was the crown prince (also named William) who inflamed public opinion. He dispatched a public telegram to the lieutenant in Zabern congratulating him upon his forceful action, but in a subsequent debate a majority of the Reichstag protested the military's (and indirectly the crown prince's) high-handedness.

The crown prince was not the only member of the royal family whose personal intrusion into the processes of shaping policy repeatedly caused constitutional crises. The emperor, too, became the center of controversy. The most celebrated incident was the *Daily Telegraph* affair of 1908. William, in a misguided effort to take a personal hand in improving relations between Great Britain and Germany, told the Berlin correspondent of the London newspaper *Daily Telegraph* that during the war between Great Britain and the Boers of South Africa, he, William, had stood firmly on the side of the British—although he knew that most Germans regarded the Boers as the underdog and England as the bully in the conflict. After it was published, the *Daily Telegraph* interview led to a Reichstag debate during which the emperor's "personal rule" was attacked from all sides. Every political group, including the Conservatives, demanded that the emperor be more circumspect in the future. The parliamentary outcry did not really abate until William in a published letter to Bülow promised that in the future he would refrain from further

efforts at personal policy making without consulting his constitutional advisors.

The imperial family's actions were symptoms rather than causes of the severe political and constitutional crisis in which Germany found herself on the eve of World War I. Chancellor Bethmann Hollweg, who had a perceptive eye for the domestic political situation, recognized that the political polarization in the country could only be bridged by meaningful reforms that would lead to greater parliamentarization and democratization. He noted that staging "chauvinistic elections" was by 1913 counterproductive. Beating the patriotic drums would not, in the long run, halt the decline of the Conservatives' and National Liberals' share of the popular vote. Other decision makers agreed with the chancellor's assessment, but unlike Bethmann Hollweg they were not willing to accept his corollary and endorse a policy of domestic political reform.

ECONOMIC DEVELOPMENTS

The dominant themes in Wilhelminian economic life were an accelerated pace of industrialization and a period of sustained prosperity. The years from the end of the depression until the outbreak of World War I were a period of growth interrupted only by two brief recessions in 1901–1902 and 1908–1909. The times were good for most segments of the population. Although life for many was hard and the gulf between rich and poor did not narrow, in the absence of significant inflationary pressures the standard of living for the majority of Germans increased markedly.

Prosperity was a byproduct of the Reich's continuing industrialization. In the period between 1885 and 1889, 30 percent of the workforce was employed in industrial or manufacturing jobs; by 1910–1913 the figure had risen to over 50 percent. Conversely, the agricultural segment of the workforce declined from 46 percent to 35 percent in the same time period. In line with this development, agriculture's contribution to the gross national product fell from 37 percent in the time span 1885–1889 to 25 percent at the end of the Wilhelminian years.

Contemporary observers recognized that capitalism came to permeate all facets of German life. The economist Werner Sombart described the purpose of a new journal for research in the social sciences which he founded in 1903 as the "historical and theoretical analysis of the cultural significance of capitalism." High capitalism also meant managerial capitalism. The industrial sector of the economy in particular was now largely controlled by what were essentially professional managers. The economic historian Hans Jaeger has provided us with a "group profile" of Wilhelminian executives. Often of humble background, they were proud of their accomplishments and thoroughly comfortable with the conventions of morality, decency, and authority prevalent in the late Victorian age. Strong personalities, they expected obedient employees, wives, and children, although in their own eyes they were caring business leaders, fathers, and husbands. The ideal of the *Bildungsbürger* celebrated earlier by Freytag and Raabe held little attraction for them. Their interests were largely confined to their businesses. By their own lights the managers were also apolitical. "Naturally" they were "nationalists," "patriots," and "anti-Marxists," but politics as such, they claimed, interested them only insofar as it affected their businesses.

These executives were managers of what was now the typical form of large-scale enterprise in Germany: the limited liability corporation. Close ties existed between major banks and industrial corporations because most stock certificates issued by German corporations were held as part of bank-owned portfolios. Yet another characteristic of German high capitalism was the growing number of industrial cartels and trusts. Firms in various branches—notably iron and steel—created both vertical (control of the manufacturing process from raw materials to final product) and horizontal (marketing and pricing agreements) trusts in order to stabilize prices and maximize profits. Such developments were actually encouraged by the country's political leaders. There was no antitrust legislation in Wilhelminian Germany, but there were close organizational and personal links between private enterprise and the Reich and state governments. Some historians have labeled the relationship between state and business "organized capitalism" and have suggested that political and economic leaders cooperated to control the economy, but newer evidence suggests that the influence exerted by the cartels and trusts on the economy as a whole was quite limited.

Industrialization and a rising standard of living encouraged further population growth and mobility. Germany's population grew from about 48 million in 1890 to slightly over 60 million twenty years later. Interestingly, the increase occurred while birth rates were declining. The growth was due instead to longer life expectancy that resulted from the welfare policies introduced since the 1880s, as well as improvements in hygiene and health care. Emigration declined, but the internal population movement continued undiminished. The primary migration pattern was still from east to west, leading to problems of urban crowding in the cities of the west and shortages of cheap agricultural labor on the estates of East Elbia.

Internal immigration was facilitated by the completion of Germany's national rail network. In 1879 a number of private companies operating in Prussia and the adjoining states had been merged into the Prussian-Hessian State Railroads. The new system served all of Germany, except for areas of Württemberg and Bavaria; both of these southern German states retained their own railroad systems. For both economic and strategic reasons the Prussian-Hessian State Railroads focused on rapid east-west connections. Trunk lines linked the industrial areas of western Germany to the seaports of Rotterdam, Bremen, and Hamburg, as well as the agricultural regions east of the Elbe. These same lines were equally capable of carrying fast-running troop trains from the French and Belgian frontiers to East Prussia and Silesia, enabling the rapid movement of troops in case the Reich's nightmare of a two-front war became a reality.

Virtually all Germans enthusiastically supported the development of railroads, but the construction of canals aroused bitter controversy. Ever since the 1850s economists and industrialists had advocated building a network of canals linking the Elbe, Weser, and Ems rivers in the west to Berlin and the Oder River in the east. Such a canal system would supplement the railroads and make the shipment of bulky goods such as coal and grains more economical. The heart of the proposed system was the *Mittellandkanal*, a waterway that was intended to connect the industrial areas of the Rhineland and Westphalia with the seaports of Bremen and Hamburg. Although the project had the enthusiastic endorsement of transportation experts and the emperor, it was never realized. The East Elbian agrarians, who dominated the Prussian Landtag, saw the canal network not as a boon, but as a threat to their economic future. They argued that the network of internal waterways might facilitate the shipment of their products to the west, but especially the *Mittellandkanal* would increase competition from foreign grain imports by significantly reducing shipping costs from the ports of entry to consumers in the west. In addition, they argued that construction of the canal itself would aggravate the labor problem in the east, since thousands of agricultural laborers would undoubtedly prefer work on the canal to laboring on Junker estates.

The agrarians managed to prevent the construction of the *Mittellandkanal*, but their efforts did not seriously delay the rapid expansion of German industry. By the end of the Wilhelminian years industrial patterns that are still apparent in present-day Germany had been well established. Heavy industry was concentrated along the Rhine-Ruhr Valley. Cities like Essen, Duisburg, Hamm, and Düsseldorf became major metropolises; firms like Krupp, Thyssen, and Gutehoffnungshütte became household words. The rapidly expanding chemical industry, whose explosive growth was based primarily on the chemistry of coal tar and analine dyes, settled somewhat further south along the shores of the Main. This branch of the economy was also already dominated by firms that are still giants of the industry: Hoechst, Bayer, BASF. In central Germany, the rich deposits of brown coal became the basis of a concentration of medium-sized manufacturing firms, specializing in textiles, machinery, and building products. Somewhat later, the region around Halle and Merseburg developed into a major center for the refining of petroleum products and the manufacture of cement.

Another growth sector in the German economy, the electrical industry, found its home in Berlin. This branch was also dominated by large-scale firms, notably Siemens and the Allgemeine Elektrizitäts-Gesellschaft. In the seaports of Hamburg and Bremen processing industries for imported raw materials like coffee, cocoa, and tobacco were established. Germany also built a sizable merchant fleet. Originally, the primary business of the two largest firms, the Hamburg-America Line in Hamburg and the Norddeutscher Lloyd in Bremen, had been to carry immigrants to America, but with the decline in emigration and a corresponding growth in the volume of German exports, they emphasized worldwide shipping and passenger service instead.

The most visible sign of Germany's exploding economy was the volume of the country's trade. The Reich's exports between 1889 and 1910 increased by 181 percent, from 825 million marks to 1.5 billion annually. These figures were considerably greater than the comparable percentages for Great Britain (105 percent), the United States (156 percent), and France (88 percent). Despite the impressive export statistics, Germany's imports, mostly in the form of raw materials and agricultural goods, increased even faster. The scissors were closed by another feature characteristic of high capitalism, the growing volume of German investment abroad. By 1910 Germany was no longer a net capital importer, but a sizable capital exporter. The country's firms and banks held investments of some 35 billion marks abroad, earning annual returns of 1.8 billion marks.

Investment at home and abroad, of course, strengthened the role of the banks in the economy. The trend toward concentration of financial power in the hands of the three big "D" banks—Deutsche Bank, Dresdner Bank, and Darmstädter Bank—continued; on the eve of World War I they controlled some 65 percent of all stock in German corporations. These banks were also the major conduit for German investment abroad, and they dominated the stock market. As we saw earlier, Germany's "full-service" banks traditionally acted as their own brokerage houses, and by the beginning of the century the German stock markets were essentially mechanisms for the banks to buy and sell stocks from the portfolios they controlled. Independent investors played only a minor part in stock market transactions.

The climate for business in Wilhelminian Germany was certainly favorable. A basically unregulated marketplace provided unprecedented opportunities for expansion and profits. Nevertheless, businessmen complained bitterly about what they saw as the growing welfare state. They attacked the whole concept of *Sozialpolitik* (social policy)—which included everything from government inspectors who reported violations of the occupational safety laws to old age pensions—as unwarranted interference by the state with the system of free enterprise.

Still, there is little doubt that businessmen fared well in the years before World War I. The condition of labor under high capitalism is less clear. Before the end of World War I a self-serving conservative historiography portrayed workers as increasingly prosperous and content with their lives. Their sense of well-being was disturbed only by the activities of socialist agitators. During the 1920s and especially since World War II a revisionist school has concentrated on doing empirical research into the real living conditions of Germany's industrial labor. Their conclusions often paint a bleak picture of economic exploitation and social misery. Weekly hours were long (fifty-seven was the average in 1914) and wages, by today's standards, low. The average annual wage (adjusted for inflation) in 1913 was 1,163 marks, as compared to 5,675 marks in 1959. Dark and dank housing in urban slums and poor nutrition led to the spread of such diseases as tuberculosis and rickets. Social problems like petty crime, alcoholism, and intrafamily violence were prevalent.

But there was another side to the picture as well. Labor did benefit from the boom of the Wilhelminian years. Real wages were rising fairly constantly for most German workers; the average annual wage, which was 1,163 marks in 1913, had been 711 marks in 1890. As union membership grew, so did labor militancy and the number of industrial workers covered by collective bargaining agreements. The figure reached 2 million in 1913, 18.5 percent of the total industrial workforce. (For comparison, the figure for the United States in 1989 was 17 percent.) Living conditions for the industrial proletariat, then, while still harsh and bitter for many, were also significantly better and more hopeful in 1914 than they had been when the Wilhelminian years began.

Present-day historians have centered their attention on growth of large-scale enterprises and organized labor during these years, but the contemporary discussion of economic developments seemed far more concerned about the future of a third component, the *Mittelstand*. Actually, this segment of society was by now composed of two rather distinct groups, the old and new *Mittelstand*, with the new *Mittelstand* (see the earlier discussion on this group, p. 39) growing far more rapidly than the old. The *Mittelstand* propagandists, however, focused almost entirely upon the old "middle estate." They saw independent artisans, members of the professions, retailers, owners of apartment houses—in fact, small businessmen of all kinds—threatened by the rise of big business and big labor.

Like the agrarians and the industrialists, members of the old *Mittelstand* organized a lobby to press their case. But the *Mittelstand's* public relations efforts were seriously hampered by the group's inability to agree on the best way to insure the future prosperity of Germany's small businessmen and artisans. There were those who longed for the utopian past of guild restrictions and legal limitations on the growth of big business. Others recognized the futility of turning back the clock. They argued that the future of the *Mittelstand* was at the side of big business in that industrialization would provide new opportunities for small businessmen as well as large corporations. (Incidentally, the second group was right: The number of independent artisans and small businessmen was significantly higher in 1914 than in 1890.) Unable to reach a compromise, spokesmen for the old *Mittelstand* concentrated their venom on the one enemy on which they could agree: the Social Democrats. Convinced that unionization of their employees raised labor costs to levels that drove many small businessmen into bankruptcy, they endorsed right-to-work laws and the aims of the National Association Against Social Democracy. On the eve of World War I the *Mittelstand* lobby was firmly allied to the political Right.

Despite the general level of prosperity in Wilhelminian Germany, there was at least one glaring weakness in the economy: agriculture in general and East Elbian agriculture in particular. The full extent of the structural problems in the east did not become apparent until the end of World War I, but acute observers recognized the signs of the structural agricultural crisis long before then. As early as 1900, the industrialist Siemens pointed to the heavy debt burden of East Elbian agriculture as a serious mortgage on the future. The causes of the problems were not difficult to identify. In anticipation of continuing high agricultural prices, the East Elbian agrarians had borrowed heavily to finance machinery and speculate in land. But, as we saw, beginning in 1892 prices on the international market fell precipitously. German agriculture was driven not only from the world markets, but undersold on the home market as well. (U.S. grain imports to Germany, for example, increased from 406 million tons in 1890 to 1.2 billion in 1906.)

The agrarians refused to recognize their problems as a structural crisis; they insisted instead that the issue was one of unfair competition. But the BdL's demand for protective tariffs did not address the root of the problem. As a result, the structural crisis of East Elbian agriculture was not significantly eased during the Wilhelminian era, and within a few years the foundation of the Junkers' economic strength would collapse under the weight of its accumulated debt.

Overall, the years from 1890 to 1914 brought the German economy to the stage of high capitalism. Rapid industrialization meant opportunities for expansion and profit, and despite hardships for the laboring classes, the standard of living for all those connected with industrialization rose. Fears of a *Mittelstand* in demise were greatly exaggerated; small business flourished as suppliers and spinoffs of industrialization. The only really weak sector was East Elbian agriculture, an increasingly less significant sector of the economy. Nevertheless, the agricultural sector had a disproportionately large impact on the country because of the political influence that its spokesmen wielded.

LITERATURE, ART, AND SOCIETY

The strains and stresses of modernization characterized the era's cultural and social life as well. Wilhelminian Germany exhibited two distinct, although overlapping, mentalities. The "establishment," that is to say, the men—and Germany, like all of Western society at this time, was dominated by males—who gave official or social sanction to the accepted values and art forms, were proud of their accomplishments and secure in their values. This group of social and political leaders also had few doubts about the wisdom of the dicta it sought to transmit to future generations through a rigid educational system. In fact, critics of the establishment focused their attacks on Germany's high school teachers, the *Oberlehrer*, as symbols of the system's sclerosis and arrogance. Perhaps the most famous such portrayal was in Heinrich Mann's novel *Professor Unrath*, the book that later became the basis for the movie *The Blue Angel* with Marlene Dietrich.

The established culture of the age was a closed and static system, in which sentimentality, militarism, narcissism, literary hero-worship (centered mostly around Goethe and Schiller), and uncritical acceptance of vulgarized versions of Wagner's and Nietzsche's messages predominated. As we noted earlier, pseudomilitary forms dominated social life in much of Wilhelminian society. High school teachers proudly displayed their military decorations in class every January 18, the day commemorating the founding of the empire in 1871, and the bourgeois man had "arrived" when he obtained his reserve officer's commission.

Much in the established cultural norms was contradictory and paradoxical. Many Germans had lost faith in the religious message of Christianity. Revealed truths were replaced by the presumed certainty of scientific and technological knowledge. At the same time, the establishment insisted that the churches remain the moral arbiters of society. Consequently, the major religious bodies became increasingly identified with the values of the establishment; they became social and cultural rather than religious institutions.

The Wilhelminian cultural establishment was *arriviste*, bourgeois, and aristocratic. It was questioned and opposed by at least two other sets of cultural and social values, one raised within the establishment's own ranks, the other outside its class parameters. Social Democratic organizations, of course, proudly rejected the establishment's norms as outgrowths of capitalist decadence. They contrasted official Wilhelminian culture with a class-conscious "proletarian" culture, an effort that always remained more potential than actual. Looking back it is clear that despite their social and cultural isolation within Wilhelminian society, even socialist workers accepted a good deal of the establishment's value system.

A more serious threat to the official culture came not through class antagonism, but from a generational conflict in the ranks of the Wilhelminian bourgeoisie. Not surprisingly, criticism of the establishment by the younger generation focused on the schools and the family. What would eventually become organized as the Youth Movement objected specifically to the rigidity of the school curriculum, patriarchal dominance in the family, the prevailing repression of sexuality and bodily freedom, and more generally what these critics called the "materialism" of the society. A favorite figure in Youth Movement fiction was the young, idealistic hero who, as a result of societal pressures, turns into a crass materialist.

The Youth Movement was never a monolithic, tightly knit organization. What came to be called a movement was originally little more than a vague feeling of dissatisfaction with the prevailing norms of society. Even those who decided to organize themselves did so in numerous small groups that were only very loosely coordinated at the national level. The revolt of Wilhelminian youth began innocently enough with the efforts of a university student from the Berlin suburb of Spandau, Karl Fischer. He was determined to provide an antidote to what he saw as the deadening effects of the German educational system. In 1901 he founded an organization he called the *Wandervögel*. (Literally, "hiking birds," but "backpackers" is probably a better translation.) The purpose was to encourage peer group interaction and physical activity in the form of weekend camping trips to the countryside in the Mark Brandenburg surrounding Berlin. From the beginning the *Wandervögel* preached and practiced what they regarded as antimaterialistic and antihierarchical values. On their hikes they emphasized an informal life style that stressed comfortable clothing, natural foods, and youthful equality. (The *Wandervögel* routinely used the *Du* rather than the *Sie* form of address.)

The *Wandervögel* movement spread rapidly throughout Germany; within a few years there were hundreds of local clubs in all parts of the Reich. Even more than Fischer's ideas, the appearance of a book of songs, *Der Zupfgeigenhansl* ("The Guitarist's Companion"), late in 1908 spurred growth of the movement. The collector and arranger of this edition of folksongs—which, incidentally, did a great deal to rekindle interest in German folk traditions—was Hans Breuer, a friend of Karl Fischer's. The songs had a practical purpose as musical accompaniment on the hikes, but the tunes were also intended to reduce the popularity among German teenagers of the popular but sentimental and banal rags and polkas of the day. The *Zupfgeigenhansl* became an immediate bestseller. Within seven years of its initial publication the book had gone through twenty-six editions.

The *Wandervögel* were both part of and forerunner of the actual Youth Movement. The latter, however, had a far broader purpose than the earlier organization. The Youth Movement intended to organize the "young," which were defined as sixteen- to thirty-five-year-olds, to change the basic values of the Wilhelminian establishment. Unfortunately, the Youth Movement's ideals themselves were not free of either contradictions or dangerous prejudices. The movement rejected materialism, but embraced nationalism as the highest form of idealism. Many, though not all, of the groups endorsed anti-Semitism, personifying Jews as the embodiment of materialism. The rejection of materialism also covered Marxism and Marxists, further widening the gulf between bourgeois and proletarian youth groups. The Youth Movement stressed democracy and equality in its own ranks, but regarded parliamentary democracy as interest-group politics without an idealistic purpose. Many in the movement were sharply critical of the pervasive militarism in Wilhelminian society, yet their intense, if "idealistic" nationalism did not make them immune to the siren calls of the same Wilhelminian imperialism and militarism.

The Youth Movement reached the pinnacle of its organized visibility in October 1913, when thousands assembled at a national festival on the mountain peak of the Hohen Meissner, in Hessen. This celebration of the German nation was deliberately intended to present a peaceful and spontaneous contrast to the militaristic and bombastic official commemoration of the hundredth anniversary of the Battle of Leipzig, staged at the same time. Yet the Hohen Meissner festival also revealed the limitations of the youth revolt. Those making the trek to the mountain peak were overwhelmingly male, middle class, and Protestant. The Youth Movement had no answer for the class or religious divisions in Wilhelminian Germany. Moreover, the movement's vision of the future was an idealized, utopian view of the past: a romanticized Germany made beautiful by the patina of age. Finally, it was bitterly ironic that many of the thousands who proclaimed their love of peace on the Hohen Meissner less than a year later enthusiastically rushed off to war.

The youth revolt did not achieve its aim of major reforms of the educational system before the War, but its ideas were rapidly disseminated in a society in which mass media in the modern sense—with the exception of the electronic variety—had become commonplace vehicles for the distribution of art, literature, and information. The trend toward ever wider proliferation of newspapers and periodicals accelerated. Aside from newspapers, whose circulation was helped by the advent of photojournalism, products targeted for specific audiences, especially women's magazines, became successful as leisure time among the middle and upper classes increased.

In line with the broad attacks on the values of the establishment, it was a golden age for political satire and muckraking journalism. The weekly *Simplizissimus*, published in Munich and edited by the publicist Th.Th. Heine, was one of the most widely circulated satirical periodicals. No person or institution in authority was spared in its biting and clever drawings. Maximilian Harden's *Zukunft* was a muckraking periodical that combined the features of investigative journalism with the sensationalism of a tabloid. Harden's exploits led to both increased circulation for his journal and a number of short-term jail sentences for the editor after convictions for libel and *lesé majesté*. His most famous case came in 1906 when Harden published a series of articles accusing the emperor's personal friend Phillip von Eulenburg of homosexuality. (At this time homosexuality even among consenting adults was, of course, a criminal offense.) Eulenburg sued for libel, but died before the case was finally decided. Far less lurid, though equally significant, were several journals of opinion, literary criticism, and fiction targeted for an audience of intellectuals. Especially notable among these was *Hochland*, which soon became the most influential journal among educated Catholics, and the *Deutsche Rundschau*, which performed much the same service for an audience of Protestant intellectuals.

Both "highbrow" and mass consumption literature flourished. It was the great age of the novel. In 1890, 1,731 works of fiction were published; by 1909 the figure had reached 4,297, an increase of 148 percent. To be sure, much of this production was what the Germans called *Trivialliteratur*, but

the themes of both serous literature and the "trivial" variety reflected the battle between the values of the establishment and the forces of reformism. Stories with a regional focus remained popular, although novels about foreign travel and adventures located in exotic colonial areas sold even better. Not incidentally, the latter also fit in well with the propaganda of the Naval League. As would be expected in an age of increasing technology, science fiction novels found a ready audience, but so did fiction with mystical and occult themes. Much of the *Trivialliteratur* consisted of books that were forerunners of today's "Modern Romances." Mostly written by women authors, many appeared first in serialized form in women's magazines. By far the most popular were the stories of aristocratic social life by Marie von Ebner-Eschenbach.

Above all, however, playwrights and authors put the city, its problems, and throbbing life at the center of their works. Indeed, by 1910 literary critics were already complaining that German literature was in danger of becoming monopolized by big city themes. Many of the novels were not so much celebrations of urban life as warnings against the city's unhealthy influence. Some authors like Theodor Fontane described the entirety of urban life of Berlin in loving if critical detail, but many others populated their books with prostitutes, vagabonds, and other victims of urban conditions. Most authors were pessimistic about the future of the bourgeoisie and its materialistic values. Heinrich Mann, one of the most noted German novelists during this time, wrote bitter satires of the dehumanizing effect that industry and money had upon society. Les strident in tone, but no more optimistic about the future of traditional bourgeois values, was Heinrich Mann's younger brother Thomas. His novel *Buddenbrooks*, published in 1901 when the author was twenty-six years old, became an immediate bestseller and firmly established Thomas Mann's reputation as a major literary talent. *Buddenbrooks* is at one and the same time a celebration of the traditional German middle class, its family-oriented and humanistic values, and the story of the inevitable decline of these values. Using the experience of his own upbringing in the city of Lübeck, Mann traces the history of one north German family from the 1830s to the beginning of the twentieth century. By the end of the novel the reader, if not the remaining Buddenbrooks, realize that the old bourgeois values celebrated by Freytag cannot survive the challenge of alienation, industrialization, and rampant materialism. Among dramatists there was only one towering figure, Gerhart Hauptmann. In a series of plays, such as *Die Weber* ("The Weavers"), he used naturalist techniques to depict the human tragedies that followed in the wake of industrialism and materialism.

Particularly evocative of some authors' antiestablishment stand were two other themes, sexual repression and dehumanization in the military. Frank Wedekind was the best known of a group of writers specializing in "student tragedies": stories in which the young protagonists die because society refuses to acknowledge their awakening sexuality. Similarly blunt in their criticism of establishment values were works about the brutality and mindlessness of German military training and the arrogance of the Prussian officer corps.

Unlike the print media, painting, sculpture, and architecture traditionally did not arouse mass interest. Perhaps precisely for this reason, the conflict between old and new values in art was not muted, but erupted into bitter, if contained, controversy. Wilhelminian "official" art, that is, the styles that received private and governmental commissions, was dominated by heroic and sentimental realism. An abundance of stern portraits, battle scenes, idealized rural landscapes, and equestrian statues filled the museums and city squares. As one wag has put it, this was the taste of an age that had no taste. It was certainly the taste of William II, himself something of an amateur drawing talent.

"Official" art, however, was rejected by a growing number of mostly younger painters and sculptors. Increasingly, French impressionism and, somewhat later, expressionism, influenced Germany's artists. In 1894 a group of painters in Munich refused to accept the decisions of the Academy of Art as to which pieces should be displayed in the officially sanctioned annual show. They "seceded" from the Academy and decided to exhibit the rejected works on their own. A few years later a similar revolt wracked the Berlin art world. Incidentally, as if to demonstrate that aesthetic and chronological youthfulness need not coincide, the secessionists in Berlin were led by the dean of German painters, the fifty-year-old Max Liebermann.

The secessionists initiated the triumph of impressionism and expressionism in German art; a short time later the "rebel" Max Liebermann was awarded an honorary doctorate from the thoroughly establishment University of Berlin. The new aesthetic brought a fundamental change in both styles and themes. There was no place for sentimentality or pseudorealism. Impressionist painters took as their subjects the play of light in nature and scenes from urban and rural bourgeois life; singularly absent were pictures of battles and conventional portraits. In contrast to impressionism, which as Gerhart Masur has pointed out, "lacked any note of social protest," German expressionism, led by groups of painters such as "The Bridge" in Dresden and "Blue Rider" in Munich, delighted in shocking the establishment by portraying the seamy side of life or by deliberately offending the prevailing moral codes.

"Secession" in architecture was more difficult to achieve. The means needed to finance architectural projects were obviously considerably greater than those required for completing a painting, and most major buildings were commissioned by agencies that approved of the official Wilhelminian styles: a heavy-handed grandiosity overladen with useless decoration. The streets of Berlin became impressive but oppressive facades reflecting the desire for grandeur in the capital. The overall effect was not pleasing. Unlike the Ringstrasse in Vienna, Berlin did not grow as an organic whole. Instead, each major new construction project tried to be impressive on its own.

Still, the prevailing prosperity brought about a building boom, and here and there new visions became apparent. Even some "official" architecture, like the *Museuminsel*, the cluster of buildings in Berlin that housed the major museums in the capital, achieved a pleasing neoclassical effect. More important, toward the end of the 1890s the *Jugendstil* was making inroads into both architecture and interior decorating. Lean, uncluttered buildings that combined gracefulness with functionality were making their appearance in German cities. As was true of the visual arts, in architecture, too, the age of modernism had arrived.

There are striking parallels between political and cultural developments during the Wilhelminian years. Culturally, too, the old and the new vied with each other. In art, literature, and social life new values of openness, spontaneity, and free expression existed side by side and in competition with the rigidity and pseudoheroism of Prusso-German authoritarianism. By 1914, the outcome of the struggle was not yet determined, but clearly the new and young were gaining the upper hand.

FOREIGN RELATIONS

At the end of 1913, Curt Riezler, a friend and advisor of Chancellor Bethmann Hollweg, noted "the danger of war in our time is greatest from those countries where a weak government is confronted with a strong nationalistic movement." Riezler, who was thinking of Austria and Russia rather than Germany when he made these remarks, also accurately described Germany's foreign relations dilemma. The leaders of the Reich, knowing that support for their authoritarian system was waning, hoped to rally public opinion in support of an aggressive foreign policy in order to stabilize the domestic situation. Unfortunately, the empire's decision makers did not recognize themselves in Riezler's mirror. On the contrary, they were convinced that Germany would not only remain stable domestically, but that the Reich was in a favorable position to manipulate the international balance of power as well. They cited a number of reasons—all wrong as it turned out—for their optimistic assessment.

Ever since the end of the Napoleonic Wars, it had been an axiom of European diplomacy that the position of Great Britain was the key to the balance of power. During most of the nineteenth century, except for the Crimean War, England had stayed out of Continental entanglements and remained in "splendid isolation." There were increasing signs, however, that isolation was becoming counterproductive for Great Britain and that the country would have to conclude alliances with one or more Continental powers in order to safeguard her overseas empire. The German leaders, and that meant especially Bülow, the man who shaped the Reich's foreign policy for more than a decade after 1897, were convinced that in view of England's rivalries with Russia and France, Great Britain had no choice but to ally herself with Germany. Consequently, they argued, the Reich was in a buyer's position and could exact a high price for accommodating Great Britain. Strategic confidence supplemented Germany's diplomatic illusions. The Reich's military leaders were convinced that the strategic concept known as the Schlieffen Plan (see the discussion on pp. 102–04) provided a fail-safe method for winning any military confrontation with Russia and France. In addition, Bismarck's nightmare of a two-front military conflict seemed to be less of a threat than it had been earlier. The Russo-Japanese War of 1904–1905 had demonstrated Russia's military weakness, and the Revolution of 1905 her domestic instability.

All of this reasoning was faulty, although admittedly there was an element of verisimilitude about it. Great Britain did have a sincere desire for an alliance with Germany, and, as World War I would reveal, the Russian empire was a tottering colossus. Nevertheless, the reasoning of the Reich's decision makers contained a fundamental flaw. For England, Germany's desirable position as a diplomatic partner was based upon a continuation of Bismarck's view of the German empire as a saturated power. That assumption, however, ran counter to the imperialist ambitions of the Wilhelminian leaders. Consequently, Germany's role in the balance of power was changing radically. The state secretary in the foreign ministry, von Oerenthal, put it well when he noted that Germany's global ambitions changed her diplomatic position from that of a bride to that of a suitor. Tragically, Wilhelminian Germany failed to recognize her changed circumstances. In the decade before the outbreak of World War I the Reich's foreign policy grew increasingly erratic, eventually resulting in Germany's virtual isolation in the concert of powers.

The key to Germany's problems was her unwillingness to restrict her role as a great power to the Continent. That decision in turn was linked to the Reich's leaders' encouragement of an imperialist mentality as a major element in their efforts to prevent progressive constitutional reforms. True, imperialism and navalism were hardly German inventions. In fact, the popularizer of navalism was an American, Admiral Albert Thayer Mahan. The impact of his book *The Influence of Sea Power on History*, which was published in 1895, was as great as the author's historical reasoning was dubious. Being a navy man, Mahan argued that history demonstrated that civilizations based on seapower were superior to those that relied on land forces. As a result, Mahan forecast a glorious future for Great Britain and the United States, while he was pessimistic about countries like Russia.

For both the public and the leaders in Germany (as well as other Western societies) navalism and imperialism went hand in hand with another popular theory, that of Social Darwinism. This doctrine was essentially a vulgarization and distortion of Charles Darwin's theory of evolution. While Darwin argued that nature determined the survival of the fittest through random selection, Social Darwinists linked the struggle among nations and individuals to the need for deliberate decisions that aided nations and individuals to survive as the "fittest." In its most blatant form Social Darwinism justified both laissez-faire capitalism and imperialism. As far as Germany was concerned, the ideas associated with imperialism, navalism, and Social Darwinism convinced the country's leaders that the Reich had a mission as a global rather than merely a Continental power. To take her place among the "fittest" of nations Germany required both a navy and an overseas empire.

In a sense, Germany's global ambitions were formally announced in a speech by the emperor on January 18, 1896. In his address commemorating the founding of the empire, traditionally a high point of patriotic fervor in Germany, William II signaled that under his leadership the Reich would demand to be consulted when it came to deciding the fate of both Europe and the rest of the world. Germany, like England and France, would intensify her efforts to obtain overseas colonial possessions.

The concrete results of Germany's global policy fell far short of her aspirations. Before the Reich was stripped of all her colonial possessions at the end of World War I, the German flag flew in the Pacific over some islands (the Marshall Islands and the Bismarck Archipelago) and Kiachow off the coast of China. In Africa a portion of the Cameroons (now part of the Republic of the Congo), German South-West Africa (now Namibia), and German East Africa (now Tanzania) were controlled by the Reich. The German colonies were of little strategic value and singularly unattractive

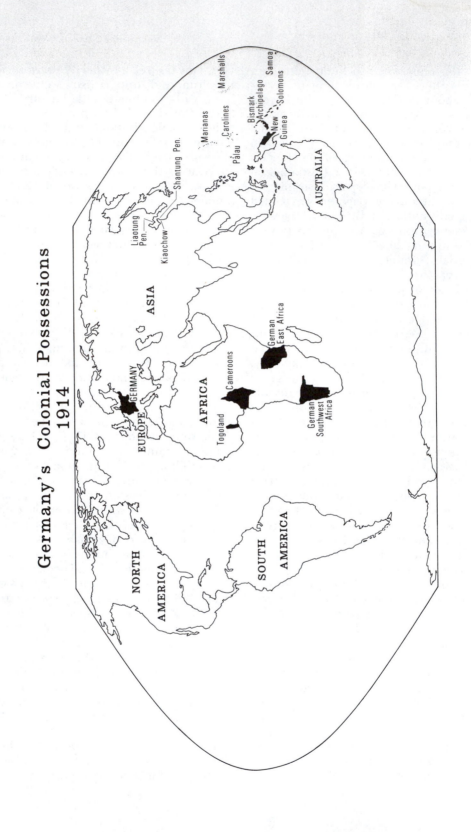

Germany's Colonial Possessions
1914

EUROPE

GERMANY

ASIA

Liaotung Pen.

Kiaochow

Shantung Pen.

Marianas

Carolines

Pálau

Marshalls

Bismark Archipelago

New Guinea

Samoa

Solomons

AUSTRALIA

AFRICA

Togoland

Cameroons

German East Africa

German Southwest Africa

NORTH AMERICA

SOUTH AMERICA

to German settlers. Far from being economic assets, their administration required constant subsidies from the Reich treasury. As for Germany's membership in the global club of imperialist nations, the Reich never achieved more than associate status. Western imperialism continued to be dominated by the British and French, as well as, after 1898, the Americans.

Still, in terms of domestic politics the colonies proved to be a major asset. Along with the growing volume of Germany's trade they were used to justify a major change in the Reich's military policy. In 1897 Admiral Alfred von Tirpitz, the Reich secretary of the navy, proclaimed the need to construct what he called a "deterrent fleet" (*Risiko-flotte*). Until then Germany's minuscule navy had consisted of some coastal defense vessels, but Tirpitz claimed that the Reich's role as a global power required a fleet that was strong enough so that no other naval power (and that meant essentially the British) would risk attacking it. Specifically, the admiral, backed by the emperor, proposed that the Reichstag appropriate funds to build a force of fifty destroyers for coastal defense, and nineteen "ships of the line." The latter category included battleships and their support vessels. The construction program was to extend over the next twenty-five years, and, according to the government, would require no additional outlays of money: Revenues obtained from the sustained growth of the German economy (1897 marked the end of the depression) would be sufficient to finance the construction of the fleet.

Tirpitz' proposals, which were vigorously endorsed by the newly established Naval League, aroused massive enthusiasm among most middle-class Germans, although the illusion that the navy could be built without additional burdens on the Reich treasury lasted only three years. Nevertheless, the supporters of navalism felt sufficiently sure of continuing public enthusiasm for their course that they proposed an augmented construction program in 1900. Arguing that both Great Britain's recent diplomatic defeat of France (in 1898 France had yielded to England in Africa, freeing the way for British control of Egypt and the Sudan) and the United States' victory in the Spanish-American War demonstrated the decisive importance of naval power, Tirpitz and the government proposed increasing the German deterrent fleet to forty "ships of the line." Even the navy's leaders no longer contended that sustained economic growth would be sufficient for the expanded construction program. Instead, the fleet was to be financed through bonds, in other words, an increase of the Reich debt. The outlay was now portrayed as an investment in Germany's future, since the fleet would protect the nation's merchant fleet and the growing volume of the Reich's overseas trade.

Within six years the construction of a new class of battleships by the British navy, the *Dreadnought* class, had rendered all previous naval construction plans obsolete. Despite the immense costs involved in pursuing the dream of a German deterrent fleet under the changed conditions, the Reich's leaders and a majority of the Reichstag decided to meet the British "challenge." After 1906 Germany, too, began to build *Dreadnoughts*. That decision did not diminish England's naval superiority, but it did significantly increase Germany's national debt. More important, the growing financial sacrifices for the navy made the fleet construction program an increasingly important factor in maintaining the domestic balance of power. As long as politicians could be found who agreed with the judgment by one of Tirpitz' subordinates that "everything in Germany including the constitution would have only one purpose: to serve the needs of the navy," the Reich's leaders would be tempted to use navalism to stabilize the domestic situation regardless of the international consequences.

Incidentally, it was indicative of the emotional mystique of navalism that public opinion and the Reichstag were far more critical of increases in the land forces. When the Caprivi government proposed raising the peacetime strength by 84,000 men, an increase that corresponded to the growth of the population, the Reichstag refused to vote appropriations for more than 59,000 men. It was not until 1913, in the face of changes that increased the de facto strength of the French army, that the German land forces were significantly augmented.

The fleet building program (and even more the rhetoric that accompanied it) provided a background cacophony that insistently disturbed the harmony of Germany's diplomatic relations. As noted above, Germany wanted good relations with Great Britain. Unfortunately the Reich demanded a diplomatic price from England that the island nation was not willing to pay: The Germans insisted not only on their recognition as a major imperial power, but also on tying any Anglo-German treaty to British support of Austro-German ambitions for attaining hegemony in central and southeastern Europe.

Negotiations between Germany and Great Britain began in 1898; they continued intermittently until 1912. At times the negotiators seemed to come close to an agreement, but eventually both sides admitted the failure of the Anglo-German talks. The main difficulty was the Reich's stubborn insistence that Germany continued to operate from a position of strength, while in reality a series of alliances and agreements among the other Great Powers produced major shifts in the balance of power that undermined Germany's initially strong position.

Partly as a reaction to the Reich's failure to renew the Reinsurance Treaty (see the earlier section, pp. 60 and 62), the French and the Russians in 1894 concluded a mutual defense alliance. Frustrated by the unproductive Anglo-German negotiations, Great Britain, too, eventually turned elsewhere for allies. The result was a series of agreements between England and Japan (1902), France (1904), and Russia (1907).

By the end of the decade Germany was diplomatically all but isolated; only Austria-Hungary, a country beset by increasing domestic problems, could be counted as a firm ally. Italy, the third partner in the Triple Alliance of 1881, made no secret of the fact that she was growing disenchanted with the Austro-German camp and drifting closer to France.

In the face of the front of Great Powers diplomatically aligned against her, German foreign policy after 1904 became increasingly erratic and frantic. In repeated efforts to weaken Anglo-French and Anglo-Russian ties, the Reich between 1905 and 1913 attempted to exploit the diplomatic crises that periodically resulted from the emergence of power vacuums as "the sick man of Europe," the Ottoman Empire, declined.

In 1905 the first Moroccan crisis began as a test of wills between France and Germany, but it quickly turned into an Anglo-German crisis as well. France, which had long pursued economic interests in Morocco, at the end of the century moved to establish a formal protectorate over the area. Germany, suddenly discovering her interest in the rights of self-determination for the weak Sultan of Morocco, protested France's unilateral moves and called for an international conference to determine the fate of Morocco. The other great powers agreed, but the meeting became a diplomatic defeat for Germany. With the exception of Austria, all of the Great Powers supported France. The Reich's position was certainly not helped by the dilettantish efforts of William II. He attempted (and failed) to weaken Russia's ties to France by personally negotiating a treaty of alliance with Czar Nicholas II of Russia.

Despite the earlier setbacks, during a second Moroccan crisis six years later, Germany again attempted to force international intervention. This time the Reich government even dispatched a naval vessel to the port of Agadir to underscore the Reich's concern for the fate of Morocco. Diplomatically, the result was another defeat for

William. At a second conference the German and Austro-Hungarian Empires were again isolated, although as a face-saving gesture Germany was awarded part of the Cameroons in Africa.

In the meantime, the focus of crisis management efforts by the concert of powers had shifted to southeastern Europe. In 1908 Russia and Austria agreed to end Turkey's nominal control of the province of Bosnia-Hercegovina (in what is now Yugoslavia) and Austria annexed the territory. Russia's prize in the bargain was to have been increased rights of passage for her naval forces through the Straits of Constantinople, but here Great Britain objected strongly. Three years later, a Turkish-Italian War seemed to signal the final demise of the Ottoman Empire. Not only did Turkey lose further territory in North Africa, but also her military weakness put the control of what remained of her European possessions in doubt. This was of considerable interest to Germany, whose growing investments in the Ottoman Empire (especially in connection with a "Berlin to Baghdad" railroad project) gave the Reich a vital interest in preserving the territorial integrity of the Ottoman Empire. Turkey's Balkan neighbors, on the other hand, had no interest in preserving the Ottoman Empire. A series of so-called Balkan Wars in 1912–1913 pitted Greece, Serbia, Bulgaria, Rumania, and Montenegro first against the Turks and then against each other, with Russia and Austria attempting to manipulate rival alliance systems behind the scenes.

Acting on behalf of the concert of powers, the ambassadors of the Great Powers in London, including the German emissary Prince Lichnovsky, met under the chairmanship of the British foreign minister Lord Grey, and eventually restored temporary peace in the Balkans. Nevertheless, Germany's diplomatic position on the eve of World War I remained precarious. From the Reich's point of view the balance sheet of Wilhelminian foreign relations was not favorable. Largely isolated in the concert of powers, Germany had little to show for her global ambitions except the ruins of failed efforts and persistent illusions.

GERMANY ON THE EVE OF WORLD WAR I

William II celebrated his silver jubilee as emperor in 1913. As was to be expected, the occasion was marked by great pomp and circumstance and in many ways it accurately reflected the mood of both the nation and its leader. The standard of living of most Germans was rising, the economy strong and expanding. Germans took pride in their country's technological and scientific accomplishments. Even the path toward nonviolent political modernization seemed to have been cleared. The election of 1912 had demonstrated the strength of the forces that favored convergence rather than increasing polarization. The extreme Right and Left were losing strength among the voters; most Germans clearly supported the moderate Center and Left. On the right side of the spectrum conservatism was reduced to a permanent and small minority. On the left side there were clear signs that the ostracism (both self-imposed and inflicted from the outside) of the Marxists was coming to an end. Votes by the SPD in support of budgets submitted by "bourgeois" governments in some southern German states, which broke a long-standing taboo in the party, represented a major victory for the revisionists in the SPD.

But there was another side to the picture. Optimism, pride, and consensus existed side by side with pessimism, alienation, and polarization. The late nineteenth century marked the final triumph of science, rationalism, and materialism, but there was also a growing feeling that something vital had been lost. As we saw, sometimes the reaction to the materialism of the Wilhelminian establishment took the form of a rebellion for modernity and self-proclaimed idealism. More often, the response was a sense of pessimism and fatalism. In Theodor Fontane's great novel *Der Stechlin*, a bittersweet account of the decline of the old Prussian ways, one of the characters reviews Prussia's past only to conclude that as far as the present was concerned, "the eagle has no spark left."

The signs of sociopolitical convergence, too, were not unambiguous. True, by 1913 William and his advisors had given up any thought of a coup from above to halt the erosion of political authoritarianism at the Reich level. At the same time, the failure of efforts to reform the three-class system of voting in Prussia demonstrated that the forces opposed to political modernization in Germany were fortifying their Prussian redoubt. The road to full modernization in Germany would certainly not be smooth.

The international scene also provided a set of contradictory indicators. On the positive side of the ledger was the restoration of the balance of power by the end of 1913. Although differences between the Great Powers persisted, the peace treaties imposed on the belligerents in the Balkan Wars and an Anglo-German agreement on economic spheres of influence in the Middle East just before the outbreak of World War I showed that the concert of powers was still capable of functioning well. Beginning in 1906 a flood of books appeared in Germany and other European countries attempting to prove that war was impossible and perpetual peace among the Great Powers inevitable. But again, there were countervailing tendencies. International conflicts and crises had clearly been on the rise in the last ten years, and there was increasing discussion of the "unthinkable": a military confrontation among the Great Powers. Helmuth von Moltke, the chief of staff of the Prussian army, remarked during a military appropriations debate that "eternal peace is a pipedream, and not a very pleasant one at that."

His sentiments were shared by many Germans and other Europeans. They convinced themselves that war promised an end to materialism and decadence. In 1912 the same year in which much pacifist literature appeared, a retired general, Friedrich von Bernhardi, wrote a bestseller, with the prophetic title *Deutschland und der nächste Krieg* ("Germany and the Next War") in which he described military conflict as not only inevitable, but as beneficial because it would end the age of materialism and selfishness, inaugurating a new era of heroism and self-sacrifice.

Most important, perhaps, were the signs that some groups in Germany longed for war as a way to stop Germany's political modernization. In 1913 the editor of the *Deutsche Arbeitgeberzeitung*, the organ of the country's employers' associations, decided a war was "the cure for [our] diseases." It is certainly true that the Reich's responsible leaders did not actively pursue policies in this direction, but when an occasion arose in which an unforeseen terrorist act presented them with the choice of dampening or heating up the conflict, they chose escalation. Their decision was motivated primarily by military and diplomatic considerations, but the German leaders were not unaware that war would mean a sense of release for many of their people and, more important, at least for a time unite the nation in support of an otherwise crumbling system of authoritarianism.

CHAPTER 4

THE FIRST WORLD WAR, 1914–1918

Few events have changed the course of human history as profoundly as World War I. Directly or indirectly the hostilities affected all Germans as well as most Europeans and Americans. By the time the war ended in November 1918 the old, arrogant, self-satisfied Germany and Europe had disappeared. Two revolutions in Russia ended the rule of the czars, while Austria-Hungary disintegrated into several new nation-states. In Germany Prusso-German authoritarianism was overthrown. William II abdicated and went into exile in Holland. He remained there until his death in 1940 and never visited Germany again. The country he led to war suffered an ignominious defeat.

The human costs of the war were no less staggering than the effects on the international balance of power. World War I was the first modern "total" war. Increasingly sophisticated (and destructive) armaments and mechanized warfare were not only very wasteful of human resources on the battlefield, but required mobilization of economic and human resources on the "home front" to an unprecedented degree. The results were enormous casualty figures and major societal dislocations. Germany suffered over 6 million dead, wounded, and missing soldiers. An additional 750,000 people are estimated to have died from war-related malnutrition and diseases.

In many ways the war broke up the solidified contours of Wilhelminian society. The massive influx of women into the workforce (replacing the increasing numbers of men sent to the front) substantially modified the Victorian image of womanhood: homebound and subject to the dictates of her father or husband. At the same time, liberalization and equality also had its price. Sharply increased venereal disease statistics reflected both changes in sexual mores and value disorientation.

THE OUTBREAK OF THE WAR

After World War I had ended, politicians and scholars on both sides of the Atlantic began a search that has continued until our own times for the persons or developments that had been "guilty" of starting the conflict. During the 1920s most Germans—but also many scholars in the Allied countries—supported the "revisionist" view that the German government had played only a minor part in the outbreak of the war.

Interest in the war-guilt issue waned as Europe was plunged into World War II. (There were no doubts about Nazi Germany's responsibility for unleashing that conflagration.) In 1961, however, the publication of a massive new study by the German historian Fritz Fischer reopened the debate. Fischer's book, *Germany's Aims in the First World War* (the German title of the work, *Der Griff nach der Weltmacht* ["The Grasp for World Power"] expressed the author's thesis even better) argued that an unholy alliance of Germany's military, industrial, and political leaders deliberately maneuvered the country into war in order to maintain the power of authoritarianism at home and extend German hegemony abroad.

Fischer's study aroused passionate controversy particularly among German historians. The author was severely criticized, but at least part of his thesis has stood the test of time. As we shall see, Germany's leaders were certainly not dragged into the conflict against their will, but saw the war as a domestic and foreign policy opportunity. But that leaves the question of Germany's actual war guilt. Fischer also contended that the imperial government and the Prussian general staff deliberately set out to wage war in 1914 in order to achieve aims laid out long beforehand. But here the evidence is less clear. Initially, it would appear, the "guilt" of Germany's political and military leaders, including the emperor, lay more in lacking judgment than in planning a conspiracy to wage war at all costs.

On June 28, 1914 the heir to the throne of the Austro-Hungarian Empire, Archduke Franz Ferdinand, was on an official visit to Bosnia-Hercegovina, a territory that Austria had formally annexed six years earlier. The itinerary of the archduke and his wife that day included an inspection of an army regiment and a reception by the mayor of Sarajevo, the capital of the province. As they were leaving the town hall, the royal couple, traveling in an open car, was assassinated by a young Bosnian, Gavrilo Prinčip.

This act of terrorism stood at the beginning of a chain of events that would eventually precipitate World War I, though initially few expected such an outcome. Political assassinations were regrettably common in late nineteenth and early twentieth century Europe. In 1881 Czar Alexander II was killed by a bomb Russian terrorists had placed under his carriage. A decade later, in 1892 Franz Ferdinand's aunt, Empress Elizabeth, was assassinated by an Italian anarchist. The motives of Prinčip and his six accomplices were also familiar then and now. The assassin and his fellow conspirators, young students and self-proclaimed intellectuals, belonged to an organization called Young Bosnia. The avowed aim of the group was to liberate Bosnia-Hercegovina from Austrian rule so that along with Serbia and other South Slav states it would become part of the nation of Yugoslavia.

The assassination became a crisis rather than just a tragedy, when the Great Powers, and particularly Austria, saw their vital interests threatened. Interrogations of Prinčip and his accomplices (all of the conspirators were quickly captured by Austrian police) convinced the Austrian authorities that Young Bosnia was far more than a club of misguided youths. The Austrian officials learned that the terrorists had been provided with weapons, passports, and safe conduct routes from Serbia into Bosnia by a secret Serbian terrorist and political organization, The Black Hand. It was also known that the leader of The Black Hand was the chief of the intelligence section of the Serbian general staff, Colonel Dragutin Dimitrijevič. From this information the Austrian authorities deduced—wrongly—that the Serbian government must have known of Prinčip's plans and that the assassination was in fact a case of state-sponsored terrorism.

Austria-Hungary refused to believe Serbia's protestations of shock and innocence; the Habsburg government was determined to strike back. The only question was how, or, more precisely, whether retaliation should take the form of diplomatic or military measures. For some years prior to 1914 a so-called war party in the Austro-Hungarian government had been advocating a preventive military strike against Serbia. This group, led by the chief of the Austro-Hungarian general staff, General Franz Count Conrad von Hötzendorff, was not only convinced that Serbia was actively undermining the stability of the Austro-Hungarian Empire, but that she was little more than a tool of Russia. Consequently, Hötzendorff and his allies argued that only Serbia's military defeat by Austria would convince Russia and Serbia to end their efforts at undermining the political and territorial integrity of the Austro-Hungarian Empire.

Until the assassination of the archduke, Hötzendorff and his supporters had been restrained by a "peace party" led by the Hungarian prime minister, Count Tizsa. This group countered Hötzendorff's offensive military strategy with warnings about an Austro-Russian conflict that would leave Austria isolated. (Under the terms of the Dual Alliance Germany was under no obligations to aid Austria in any offensive military operations.) After the murder at Sarajevo the "war party" repeated its arguments more forcefully. Tizsa agreed that Serbia would have to be punished in some way, but the "peace party" continued to oppose military operations, pointing out that there was no assurance that Germany would back such measures on Austria's part. Hötzendorff in turn proposed that the Austrians send a diplomatic mission to Berlin to determine the Reich's stand.

Austria's decision to involve the Germans was made on July 3. Two days later, a high-level Austrian delegation went to Berlin to request Germany's support for whatever Austria determined was necessary to "punish" Serbia. In submitting their case to the Germans, the Austrians did not indicate what specific action they had in mind, although military action was clearly not ruled out. William II met personally with the head of the Austrian delegation, Count Hoyos, and gave him assurances that the emperor and his government would back the Austrians in any actions they might take. Without consulting either the chancellor or the military chief of staff, William II had issued a blank check to the Austrians. (Chancellor Bethmann Hollweg was informed subsequently; the following day he amplified William's views in a conversation with the Austrian ambassador.)

There were a number of reasons for William's overtly hasty decision to sign the "blank check." The emperor was an impulsive man, inordinately proud of his ability to reach quick and "instinctively correct" judgments. The monarch also felt there should be no doubts that Germany would stand by her one remaining ally. Balance of power considerations entered into his decision. As noted above, both Austria and Germany were determined that Russia should not achieve hegemony in southeastern Europe and threaten Austria's and Germany's position in central Europe and the Ottoman Empire. Finally, there were the implications for domestic politics. When he promised his support William was clearly not contemplating a world war, but he also felt that a military triumph in a limited theater of operations would unify the nation and delay the growing demands for political modernization at home.

William's blank check enabled the "war party" in Austria to win its case for a "preventive" military strike against Serbia. As of July 7 Austria was determined upon military rather than diplomatic humiliation of her neighbor to the south. To be sure, the decision was kept secret from the other Great Powers (including Germany) for another two weeks. Not until July 23, when

Austria dispatched an ultimatum to Serbia, did the tragedy of Sarajevo become a full-scale international crisis. Although the Serbian answer to Austria's ultimatum was a model of accommodation (Serbia rejected only one of the ten demands made by Austria), the Viennese government determined that the Serbs' reply was unsatisfactory, and on July 28 Austria-Hungary declared war on Serbia.

Austria's move was not only a surprise to virtually everyone in Europe (William II, for one, had earlier expressed his opinion that the Viennese government would be satisfied with Serbia's apologetic reply to the Austrian ultimatum), but it changed the dimensions of the crisis entirely. The expected defeat of Serbia by Austria would have significantly altered the balance of power in the Balkans, something Russia was unwilling to accept. In response to Austria's declaration of war on Serbia, Russia put her troop contingents facing the Austrian border on alert. In addition, the Austro-Russian altercation led France to begin mobilizing her troops under the terms of the Franco-Russian alliance and led Germany to mobilize her troops under the agreement with Austria, the Dual Alliance. It was this aspect of the crisis, the mobilization timetables, that caused the Reich's military leaders to panic. In the midst of frantic last minute diplomatic efforts (mostly by Great Britain) in the final days of July to defuse what was now clearly the worst international crisis since the war scare of 1875, Moltke, the chief of the German general staff, telegraphed Hötzendorff asking his Austrian counterpart to ignore all further political and diplomatic attempts to delay military preparations and to begin immediate, full-scale mobilization.

The Austrian decision to declare war on Serbia and Moltke's precipitant action bypassing the political and diplomatic efforts to contain the rapidly growing crisis made a decisive struggle among the Great Powers inevitable. What had begun as a tragedy for the House of Habsburg and developed into a diplomatic crisis was about to become the first military confrontation since the Napoleonic Wars involving all of the Great Powers.

MILITARY DEVELOPMENTS

It is a truism among historians that military planners tend to assume that future wars, at least in strategic terms, will be variations on the themes of previous conflicts. As a result, strategic concepts for future conflicts tend to be implementations of lessons learned from the last war. The pattern certainly fit the German strategy in World War I; it was intended as an adaptation of the plans that had succeeded so well during the Franco-Prussian War of 1870–1871.

For land warfare Germany originally had only one strategic concept, the so-called Schlieffen Plan. Named for its originator, the chief of the Prussian general staff in the 1890s, General Alfred von Schlieffen, it was designed to meet the worst-case contingency of a two-front war in which Germany had to wage military operations simultaneously against the French in the west and the Russians in the east. It was well known that the Russians, who were hampered by an inadequate transportation system, required far longer to mobilize their troops than the Western powers and Germany. Consequently, Schlieffen's concept envisioned immediate and massive offensive operations against France, which would result in the defeat of Germany's western neighbor six weeks after war had been declared. Once France had been eliminated from the conflict, the Germans would move the bulk of their forces to the Eastern front just in time to face and defeat the lumbering Russians as they drew near the borders of East Prussia.

The Schlieffen Plan is still recognized as a bold and brilliant military concept. It used Germany's advantages in staff organization and speed of troop deployment to offset the Russians' superior numerical strength, while bold offensive moves were designed

Military Operations of W.W. I

Legend

- Extent of German Advances
- Russian Advances
- Stabilized Western Front, Dec. 1914
- The Hindenburg Line, 1917
- German Advances, 1918
- Front at the Armistice, Nov. 1918

Central Powers' Drives

Allied Drives

Areas of Submarine Warfare before declaration of unrestricted warfare, Jan. 1917

Labels

RUSSIA

GERMANY

AUSTRIA-HUNGARY

SWEDEN

DENMARK

NETHERLANDS

BELGIUM

FRANCE

SPAIN

SWITZERLAND

LUX

BALTIC SEA

NORTH SEA

Dvinsk

Memel

Königsberg

Danzig

Berlin

Hamburg

Bremen

Cologne

Munich

Frankfurt

Paris

Elbe

Weser R.

Main R.

Rhine R.

Danube R.

River

GERMANY

FRANCE

Somme

1914

1915

1916

1917

1918

Scale

0   50   100 Miles

0   100 Kms.

to outwit the French defensive strategists. France, for her part, also attempted to learn from the last war. French military planners interpreted the lessons of 1871 to mean that France needed to strengthen the defenses on her eastern border. As a result, the French after 1871 built a string of fortifications across the traditional invasion routes from Germany thereby effectively precluding a repetition of the German operations that had succeeded in 1871. To bypass the French defenses Schlieffen stipulated an alternate invasion route. Instead of confronting the French directly, the German armies would march through Belgium. The French armies, seeing themselves outflanked, would then have to withdraw major units from their original defensive positions, enabling the Germans to overrun the French fortifications. But the Schlieffen Plan's military advantage was also its political fatal flaw. In blithely contemplating marching through Belgium, Schlieffen and his successors felt that military considerations had to take priority over the serious political and diplomatic repercussions of violating Belgian neutrality: Since 1837 that country's neutrality had been guaranteed by all of the Great Powers, including Prussia and later Germany.

The declaration of war triggered the immediate implementation of the Schlieffen Plan; within three weeks some 2 million German soldiers were ready for battle. The German land forces were divided into eight armies. After mobilization seven advanced against France and Belgium, while one guarded the borders in the east. German troops did cross the Belgian frontier according to schedule, but contrary to German expectations, Belgium refused the Reich's request for unhindered passage. Instead, the Belgians put up stiff resistance, actually halting the German advance for a few days. Still, Belgium was obviously no military match for Germany. At the end of August the German armies advanced from Belgium into northern France, inflicting severe losses

on the weak French and British troops positioned there.

The German strategy soon ran into difficulties, however. The French were able to regroup and at the Battle of the Marne (September 1914) the German advance was halted—permanently, as it turned out. What had been planned as a war of swift movements in the west became a war of attrition. For the next three and a half years defensive operations were far more effective than offensive sallies. At the end of 1914 an elaborate system of trenches, stretching from the English Channel in the north to the Swiss border in the south, separated by no-man's land, dominated the strategic picture in the west. To be sure, there continued to be periodic limited offensives involving hundreds of thousands of men on both sides, but until mid-1918 these efforts were largely futile. Major innovations in weaponry, notably permanently mounted machine guns, enabled defenders to inflict heavy casualties. Offensive forces had no comparable weapons until the beginning of 1918 when tanks became operational on a large scale and tipped the balance in favor of the offensive.

Within two months after the start of the war, Germany's strategy for winning a two-front confrontation had failed. (The emperor's eldest son, Crown Prince William, admitted privately in November 1914, that Germany could not win the war.) One reason for this development was the unexpectedly early activation of the Eastern front. During the Battle of the Marne the Germans had to send two army corps (about 60,000 men) from the Western front to the Eastern front in order to deal with the surprisingly swift arrival of the Russians on the borders of East Prussia. Tactical mistakes by the commander in the Eastern front, General von Prittwitz, aggravated the situation. Almost in desperation in mid-August command of the Eastern front troops was transferred from Prittwitz to General Paul von Hindenburg. The new commander in turn selected General Erich Ludendorff as his chief of staff.

Hindenburg was the scion of an old-line Junker family. At age sixty-seven, he came out of retirement to assume command in the east. Ludendorff, some fifteen years Hindenburg's junior, was a far less popular and venerable figure. He did not belong to the nobility, nor had he served in one of the guard regiments which were the traditional grooming grounds for Prussian generals. In fact, Ludendorff had made his career in the quartermaster corps, traditionally the least prestigious branch of the military, but one which suited his own capabilities singularly well: Ludendorff's major strengths were organization and planning. The two men immediately demonstrated their military acumen in the Battle of Tannenberg. A brilliantly executed pincer movement managed to surround the invading Russians. In the resulting battle the Russians suffered more than 120,000 casualties and were forced to retreat more than 130 miles back into Russian territory. Hindenburg and Ludendorff had become instant heroes. William II talked of the team of "Wotan and Siegfried." Hindenburg, especially, came to personify Germany's determination to achieve victory.

Ironically, what had begun as a serious problem in the east promised, after the victory at Tannenberg, to become part of the solution to Germany's military dilemma. While operations in the west bogged down into trench warfare, the Eastern theater provided opportunities for large-scale offensive operations that could not only be converted into optimistic press reports, but eventually, in the spring of 1918, succeeded in forcing Russia to accept an ignominious peace treaty. For image and public relations purposes the victory at Tannenberg soon overshadowed the far more important defeat on the Marne.

While Hindenburg's and Ludendorff's stars were rising, the defeat on the Marne ended the military career of Helmuth von Moltke. In October 1915 he resigned as chief of staff. Moltke was succeeded by the Prussian minister of war, General Erich von Falkenhayn. The new chief of what was now called the supreme Command of the Armed Forces (*Oberste Heeresleitung*—OHL), knew that in spite of the optimistic press releases put out by the government's propaganda machine, the overall military situation was far from favorable. On the Western front the war of attrition produced heavy casualties, the blockade, which the British had imposed at the outbreak of the war, prevented needed imports from reaching Germany, and, as Napoleon had discovered a century earlier, large-scale operations on the Russian plain did not necessarily mean that Russia had been defeated.

As his answer to the impasse, Falkenhayn advocated what came to be known as the Verdun strategy. Specifically, the new chief of the OHL proposed a siege of the key French fortress of Verdun. Falkenhayn anticipated one of two outcomes: Either the Germans would capture the fortress, thereby decisively weakening the French defensive line, or the constant German pressure on the fortress would force the French to deploy a steady stream of defenders to the area, who would then become casualties of the constant German artillery barrages. Falkenhayn argued eloquently for his strategy, but he lost sight of the fact that at the beginning of 1916 the Reich did not have the military resources to maintain the steady and uninterrupted pressure on the fortress which would have been required to make Falkenhayn's Verdun strategy a success.

The attack upon the fortress system at Verdun began in February 1916. For the rest of the year the area was a constant battleground. Thousands of men lost their lives, but Germany did not gain the strategic advantage that Falkenhayn had predicted. To be sure, France's military commanders decided to defend Verdun at all costs (the fortress was never taken by the Germans) and the French suffered heavy casualties as a result, but the German losses were not significantly lower. In the meantime, Germany's overall strategic situation was steadily deteriorating. Italy's decision to join the war on the Allied side in the spring of 1915 had already put additional pressure upon the Austro-German southern flank. The blockade had increasingly severe repercussions for the German homefront. Like Moltke, Falkenhayn failed to produce a winning strategy. In fact, beginning in July 1916 the Germans were forced to send major reinforcements to the Somme front, where the Allies had begun an offensive that cost further thousands of lives on both sides. The Battle of the Somme lasted until November when winter and mud halted the operations. In August 1916 the emperor reluctantly accepted Falkenhayn's resignation as chief of the OHL. He was succeeded by the two military leaders who symbolized victory for most Germans, Hindenburg and Ludendorff.

The failure of the Verdun strategy was compounded by almost simultaneous setbacks suffered by the German navy. In strategic terms, the navy's primary responsibility during World War I was to break or at least loosen the British blockade. To accomplish its task the German navy relied upon blockade runners, the high seas fleet, and a new type of weapon, the submarine. Primitive by today's standards, virtually unarmed and with a cruising range that did not extend much beyond the English Channel, the German submarines were nevertheless eventually assigned a key role in the Reich's naval strategy.

In imposing their blockade, the British attempted to prevent virtually all imported materials from reaching Germany. At first the Germans were relatively unconcerned about the blockade (under the Schlieffen strategy the war should have been over before British naval measures could take effect), but as the conflict dragged on, the German war effort increasingly felt the adverse effects of Britain's naval superiority.

Germany's single effort to engage the British surface fleet came in May 1916, when the British and German fleets met almost accidentally off the coast of Norway. The outcome was a German tactical victory and a strategic defeat. The British suffered a loss of fourteen ships and 6,100 casualties, while the Germans lost only five ships and 2,500 men. At the same time, these figures were meaningless in strategic terms. As darkness fell on May 16, the remainder of the German high seas fleet returned to port, leaving the British naval hegemony (and the effectiveness of the blockade) intact.

From now on, Germany's efforts to break the British blockade and impose interdictions of her own were essentially reduced to attempting to establish a counterblockade by the use of submarine attacks on British shipping. However, this effort soon led to diplomatic complications, particularly with the United States. The rules for imposing a blockade had been laid down by international agreement in 1856, at a time when no power possessed submarines as part of its naval arsenal. Under the rules of 1856 a ship suspected of attempting to run a blockade could not be sunk until it had been stopped by a "shot across the bow," an inspection of its cargo had determined that it was carrying contraband of war, and provision had been made for rescuing the crew. World War I submarines were singularly unsuited for this sort of ritual. The early submarines were small vessels whose hulls could be easily pierced by naval gunnery or, for that matter, a machine gun mounted on the deck of a freighter. As a naval weapon, submarines were effective only if they could rely on stealth and fire their torpedoes without warning.

As a result of these considerations the German government claimed that the blockade rules of 1856 were impractical for twentieth-century warfare. The Reich contended that once an area had been defined as blockaded territory, submarines had the right to sink ships suspected of violating the blockade in the prohibited area without the usual warning. The United States—which so far had remained neutral in the war, but which was also Great Britain's major trading partner—vigorously protested Germany's announced disregard of the traditional blockade rules. Conflicts between the two powers over this issue surfaced repeatedly. The most famous incident was the sinking by a German submarine of the passenger liner *Lusitania* off the Irish coast in April 1915. The steamer was a British-owned and operated passenger ship that traveled regularly from New York to Liverpool and back. On this particular voyage, she carried about 1,900 passengers, including some Americans, and a load of munitions intended for the British army. The Germans justified the sinking by pointing to the munitions on board, while the Americans protested the loss of innocent life that followed the attack.

For the first two years of the war German submarine warfare was "restricted," that is to say, the Germans attempted to avoid attacks upon neutral and particularly American vessels. In the latter part of 1916, however, as the failure of the Verdun strategy became apparent, the Reich's military leaders turned to grasp at the straw of intensified submarine warfare in order to turn the tide of military fortune. In January 1917 the German government yielded to the pressure of the OHL and proclaimed a policy of unrestricted submarine warfare. The Reich declared the waters around the British Isles to be a war zone. Any ship, whether enemy or neutral, found within the zone would be presumed to be carrying contraband and consequently subject to attack without warning. The government knew that the new policy would in all likelihood bring the United States into the war on the side of the Allies, but the German military strategists regarded the political risks as acceptable. In their view unrestricted submarine warfare would succeed in bringing Great Britain to her knees before America's contribution to the war effort could become effective.

As had been true of the original Schlieffen Plan and the Verdun strategy, Germany's third attempt "to go for broke" also failed. To be sure, German submarines did sink a larger number of freighters bound for the United Kingdom, but unrestricted submarine warfare never came close to threatening the British economy or preventing U.S. troops and supplies from reaching Europe after America declared war on Germany on April 6, 1917. In the last year of the conflict, the United States significantly aided the Allied war effort with men and matériel.

By the end of 1917 Germany's military situation on the Western front was no more favorable than it had been three years earlier. At home things were far worse. Signs of deteriorating morale were becoming apparent throughout the fabric of German society. In addition, the Germans' only significant ally, Austria, had made it clear that she would not be able to survive another winter.

Recognizing that Germany was unable to force a decision in the west, the OHL increasingly pinned its hopes for a military reversal on developments in the east. In December 1916, Austrian and German troops inflicted a severe defeat on Russia's major Balkan ally, Rumania. A series of setbacks on the battlefront and two revolutions in the course of 1917 ended Russia's participation in World War I. Lenin (for whom the OHL had provided transportation from Switzerland to Russia) and the Bolsheviks came to power in November 1917. They were determined to conclude peace with Germany and Austria at any cost in order to safeguard the revolution in Russia and make preparations for its export to the rest of Europe. The result was the Treaty of Brest-Litovsk (March 1918) a decidedly one-sided pact by which Germany and Austria intended to secure their permanent control of eastern and southeastern Europe.

Victory in the east, of course, did not end the war, although the OHL had anticipated that by freeing major troop contingents in the east and exploiting Russia's resources, the Germans would be able to launch a new and final offensive in the west in the spring of 1918. Hindenburg and Ludendorff admitted that such an offensive would be very costly in both men and matériel—a casualty figure of 600,000 men was "precalculated"—but they argued that the eventual military gains would force the Allies to agree to peace on Germany's terms. Once again, the OHL was "going for broke." The Reich's military leaders knew that if the offensive did not succeed in ending the war, Germany would have no resources left to withstand an Allied counterattack.

The spring offensive began in March 1918 with a massive tank assault. For some days the Germans made impressive territorial gains, but soon lack of supplies and reserves slowed the forward momentum before any of the strategic goals could be reached. Instead, the Allies regrouped and began a counteroffensive. In July, the German defensive lines were pierced to a distance of some four miles. The breakthrough was the beginning of the end. On August 8, another Allied thrust on the Somme front led large numbers of German troops to flee in panic. Hindenburg and Ludendorff concluded that the Reich's military resources were now insufficient to stop an Allied invasion of German territory; on September 29, they advised the emperor to negotiate an armistice as quickly as possible. It went into effect on November 11, 1918.

Military historians have argued endlessly over the details of strategic decisions, personnel appointments, and missed opportunities among all of the belligerents in World War I, but they are generally agreed that the final outcome could have been predicted in September 1914. After the German defeat in the Battle of the Marne, time was increasingly on the side of the Allies. With only the relatively weak Austrians, Bulgarians, and Turks at her side, Germany did not have sufficient human or economic resources to defeat the powers arrayed against her. The Wilhelminian attempt to challenge the global balance of power was bound to end in military disaster.

DOMESTIC POLITICS: REFORM, REPRESSION, AND REVOLUTION

Germany's wartime leaders expected the war to eliminate domestic political division and for a time their expectations were fulfilled. When the emperor announced on August 4, 1914 that for the duration of the war a *Burgfrieden* ("peace in the castle") would end domestic conflicts and political divisions, most of his subjects enthusiastically welcomed the prospect of genuine national unity. At the beginning of the war virtually all Germans rallied behind the Reich's political and military leaders, convinced that Germany was fighting a just and legitimate war against a host of aggressors. In August 1914 most Germans were unreflective in their enthusiasm, although even then some spoke of their quiet determination to "accept the inevitable with [a] deep-seated sense of duty," as Theodor Wolff, the editor of Berlin's distinguished liberal newspaper, the *Berliner Tageblatt*, put it in his first wartime editorial.

The mood of August—epitomized by flower-draped soldiers singing lustily on their way to the front and railroad cars marked "to Paris" on their sides—was predicated on two premises: that the war would be both victorious and short, and that the Reich's leaders were committed to instituting domestic political reforms. Neither premise turned out to be true. As the war dragged on and the possibility of a negotiated peace—let alone victory—became increasingly remote, political differences not only reemerged, but became increasingly bitter. Politics in wartime Germany involved the interaction of four major institutions. To begin with, there were the Reich and Prussian executives, headed by the emperor. In 1914 both the Reich and Prussian cabinets were led by the man who had been chancellor since 1909, Theobald von Bethmann Hollweg. A second institution, the Reichstag, assumed an increasingly active role as the need for appropriations to finance the war effort forced the government to go to parliament frequently in order to obtain authorization to borrow money. Germany's military leaders constituted a third group in the country's political interaction process. Finally, as hardships at home and at the front increasingly polarized the country, new extraparliamentary pressure groups emerged on both the Right and Left of the political spectrum.

Bethmann Hollweg attempted to preserve national unity by pursuing what he called "the politics of the diagonal." By this the chancellor meant steering a course that lay "diagonally" between the demands of the conservatives, who insisted the war was being fought to maintain the status quo at home and increase the Reich's power abroad, and the "reformers," who argued that keeping up the national war effort required meaningful changes in the political structure to make it more accountable to the people. Bethmann Hollweg maintained his balancing act with considerable skill for almost three years, but, as we shall see, in the end, isolated and without support from any quarter, he had to admit failure.

Wartime politics focused on three major issues. One was the question of "war credits," which meant granting the government authority to issue bonds to finance the war. A second issue involved constitutional reforms that would change the Prussian electoral system and introduce ministerial responsibility for the Reich and Prussian cabinets. Finally, the formulation of Germany's war aims became an increasingly divisive issue.

Voting for war credits was a traumatic experience particularly for the Social Democrats. Until August 4, 1914 the SPD in the Reichstag had never voted for a defense appropriation. After an emotional caucus debate, the members of the SPD's Reichstag delegation were split, seventy-eight to fourteen, in favor of war credits. To preserve the appearance of unity, the party decided to cast its ballots unanimously for war credits. The party did so in the firm belief that not only was the Reich fighting a defensive

war, but that a victory for Germany's enemies, who included czarist Russia—for Socialists the most hated symbol of political repression—would mean a setback for the future of socialism in Europe.

Still, there were a number of Social Democratic delegates who even in August 1914 doubted the government's protestations of a purely defensive war effort. As the war dragged on, while the nature of German authoritarianism did not substantially change, the number of dissenters increased. A growing minority in the party either opposed voting for additional war credits altogether, or at the very least demanded immediate, concrete political reforms as the price of further votes for war credits. In December 1914 the divisions in the party became public when Karl Liebknecht, a leader of the party's left wing, broke party ranks and cast his vote in the Reichstag against a new government request for military appropriations.

In the course of the year 1915 signs of a split within the party became increasingly visible. At the beginning of 1915, a manifesto signed by more than a hundred party and union functionaries urged the party to reject all further war credits and to work for an immediate end to the war. At the end of the year twenty SPD Reichstag delegates openly voted against war credits. The government exacerbated tension and bitterness in the Social Democratic ranks still further by ordering the arrest in 1916 of Rosa Luxemburg for sedition and of Karl Liebknecht for high treason. Spearheaded by a group of left-wing labor leaders calling themselves Revolutionary Shop Stewards, 55,000 marched in Berlin to protest Liebknecht's court martial. (The socialist leader had in the meantime lost his parliamentary immunity because he was drafted into the army.)

By 1917 the conflict between those who wanted to end Social Democratic support of the war effort and those who argued for continued aid to the government in the expectation that cooperation would lead to reforms, could no longer be compromised. The dissidents formed a separate organization, the Independent Social Democratic Party of Germany (*Unabhängige Sozialdemokratische Partei Deutschlands—USPD*). As hardships at home increased and there seemed to be no end to the horrors at the front, more and more Social Democrats saw the USPD as the only alternative to resignation or continued collaboration with authoritarianism. Nevertheless, the founding of the USPD did not threaten the existence of the parent party. Most SPD activists and especially the rank and file of the socialist unions remained loyal to the SPD. The USPD's organizational strength was restricted to a few areas—notably Berlin, the port cities of Hamburg and Bremen, Saxony, and parts of the Rhine-Ruhr region. The USPD also suffered from excessive ideological diversity. Both Rosa Luxemburg and her long-time political opponent Eduard Bernstein were members of the party; they were united only by their joint opposition to a continuation of the war. Finally, the USPD was very loosely organized. Many of the USPD's leaders had long objected to what they regarded as excessive centralization and bureaucratization in the old party. Consequently, the USPD permitted various intraparty caucuses to have a great deal of organizational autonomy. The most important among these were the Revolutionary Shop Stewards and the Spartacus League. Founded at the beginning of 1916 and led by Luxemburg and Liebknecht, the Spartacus League argued that Germany had reached a protorevolutionary stage and urged workers to make active preparations for a violent revolution. This stand, however, was not shared by many of the USPD's national leaders who hoped to achieve a socialist revolution by nonviolent means.

One political reform on which the SPD and USPD were in full agreement was the demand for immediate changes in the Prussian electoral system. This issue also became the most important crucible of success for Bethmann Hollweg's politics of the diago-

nal. For the reformers changes in the Prussian electoral system were a litmus test of political modernization, just as the Prussian Conservatives regarded its preservation the cornerstone of authoritarianism. The chancellor attempted to follow a careful and slow course between these incompatibles, but his efforts were in vain. It required a great deal of persuasion on the part of Bethmann Hollweg (and the example of the February revolution in Russia) before the emperor agreed to announce publicly in the so-called Easter Message of 1917 that after the war he would propose changes in the Prussian electoral system to bring it more closely in line with the system of universal male suffrage used for Reichstag elections. But the Easter Message came far too late. By then the long months of delay had eroded virtually all of Bethmann Hollweg's credibility among the reformers. Moreover, the emperor's public pronouncement had no effect on the intransigence of the Prussian Conservatives and their allies. They continued to block all concrete reform proposals in the state legislature.

While the issue of Prussian electoral reforms had long dominated political discussions, the problem of ministerial responsibility was an issue born of the war experience. Before 1914 only the Social Democrats and, with some reservations, the Progressives had favored changing the Reich constitution to make the Reich government formally responsible to the Reichstag. But dissatisfaction with the government's handling of the war and growing distrust of the Reich leaders' ultimate war aims increased demands for legislative control of the executive among other parties as well. At the beginning of 1917 the parliamentary leaders of the Center Party, the right-wing Social Democrats, and the Progressives agreed to form a Multipartisan Committee (*Interfraktioneller Ausschuss*) to pressure the emperor and the Reich executive into recognizing an expanded role for the Reichstag majority in making national policy decisions. Representatives from the National Liberals eventually joined their colleagues on the Multipartisan Committee, so that by the end of the year only the Conservatives and the USPD stayed aloof. The former rejected any liberalization of the Bismarckian constitution, and the latter was convinced that reforms would merely perpetuate a capitalist system that needed to be swept away in its entirety.

The war aims issue became increasingly important in the face of rapidly declining morale at the front and at home. As the war continued, the reformist groups in the Reichstag insisted that parliament must be given a voice in formulating Germany's conditions for a negotiated peace. In all of the belligerent countries discussions of war aims involved two sets of political considerations. One was the determination by each country's leaders of the economic and territorial gains they felt would be necessary to insure the nation's self-determined place in the balance of power. This aspect of the process of formulating war aims meant give and take among the major economic, political, and military interest groups in the various warring nations. In addition, there was a second, mass psychological aspect to the problem. This concerned the relationship between sacrifices and hardships on the one hand, and "rewards" for the sacrifices on the other. It seemed axiomatic that the larger the deprivations endured at home, the more these sacrifices would have to be compensated by concrete territorial and economic gains at the end of the war. The industrialist Alfried von Krupp expressed this simplistic view well when he wrote to the chief of the emperor's privy council at the end of July 1915: "Germany must win a prize which makes worthwhile the blood shed by our sons and brothers."

But, as Krupp also recognized, that goal could be obtained only if "peace terms are dictated to our enemies." Here, as far as Germany was concerned, was the Achilles' heel of the quest for peace terms that correlated with the country's sacrifices. As the hardships continued, so did the list of war aims, but that equation also made a nego-

tiated peace increasingly remote. Only a clear military victory could break the vicious cycle, but, as more and more government leaders admitted privately, there was no real chance of winning the war militarily after November 1914.

Still, the Reich's leaders insisted on compiling long lists of unattainable and counterproductive war aims. The peace terms envisioned by Germany's decision makers would have involved a fundamental change in the European territorial, military, and economic balance of power. The "shopping list" really constituted an amalgamation of the territorial changes desired by the military to improve Germany's strategic position and demands by the Reich's industrialists to reduce Germany's dependence on imported raw materials, while improving her competitive role in international commerce.

In the west the military wanted to retain control of Belgium, including the naval bases on the English Channel. In addition, the generals also insisted on "rectifications" of the Franco-German border, so that, for example, the string of fortifications around Verdun would fall to Germany. The industrialists wanted to join the iron-rich French industrial area of Longwy-Briey with the coal-producing regions of the Ruhr to create a vast steelmaking basin. In the east the Germans were particularly interested in Russia's Polish and Baltic possessions. Poland was to become independent of Russia and linked to either Germany or Austria. In November 1916 Germany actually established an "independent" Kingdom of Poland, but this empty gesture fooled no one; the country remained under German occupation and control. As for Russia's Baltic provinces—the areas that are now the Lithuanian, Latvian, and Estonian Soviet Republics—the German war aims envisioned severing these areas from Russia and associating them as autonomous regions with the Reich. In southeastern Europe, the military leaders were uncharacteristically modest (this was, of course, the area of primary strategic interest to Austria-Hungary), but the industrialists and the diplomats demanded German economic hegemony in the Balkans and the Ottoman Empire.

Although mostly hidden from public view because of wartime censorship, the war aims issue occasioned bitter debates between "moderates" and "extremists" among the Reich's wartime leaders. From the perspective of Germany's enemies, the difference between the two groups may have been minimal, since both wanted to establish permanent German hegemony on the European Continent, but the varying views had major implications for the future evolution of German domestic politics.

The extremists, who included the leaders of the OHL, anticipated that the imposition of a "victory peace" upon the Allies would not only realize the Reich's military aims, but would also secure authoritarianism at home for the foreseeable future. The moderates, on the other hand, wanted to link domestic reforms with the territorial and economic war aims. Only such a linkage, they reasoned, would preserve national unity and maintain the morale necessary for continuing the war effort. In addition, the moderates, particularly as Germany's military position weakened, advocated a more flexible stand on such issues as the future of Belgium and the proclamation of the "independent" Kingdom of Poland.

Against the background of the relentlessly continuing war, debate over Germany's conditions for peace—even in the abbreviated form permitted by the censors—increasingly polarized the country. In response to the June 1915 manifesto by left-wing socialists advocating immediate and unconditional peace negotiations, 1,347 "celebrities," including almost 500 university professors and clergymen, published a countermanifesto. In contrast to the Social Democrats, the "celebrities" insisted that Germany would have to be guaranteed "political, military, and economic control of Belgium" as well as "large reparations" before agreeing to peace.

While the battle for public opinion took place in the pages of the press, the leaders of the OHL after August 1916 pressured Bethmann Hollweg and the emperor to commit themselves to a full set of maximal war aims. The chancellor warned against giving credence to Hindenburg's and Ludendorff's predictions of an early military breakthrough, and it was not until the spring of 1917, after the Russian March Revolution had significantly increased the chances for a military turnaround in the east, that the military succeeded in convincing the emperor to accept their terms for a "victory peace" and, not incidentally, withdraw his support from Bethmann Hollweg.

The circumstances surrounding Bethmann Hollweg's resignation in the summer of 1917 led to a major if unacknowledged constitutional crisis. Formally, of course, the chancellor served at the pleasure of the emperor, but in terms of practical politics he needed the support of a majority of the Reichstag if only to secure further votes for war credits. The OHL's interference in the constitutional balance of power completely ignored the political dimension of the chancellor's position. The issue was not so much support for Bethmann Hollweg—his failure to produce significant evidence of liberalization had also lost him the support of the reformers—as it was a disregard of the Reichstag in the process of choosing a successor to the hapless Bethmann Hollweg.

The leaders of the military considered Admiral Tirpitz and ex-chancellor Bülow for the position, but the emperor rejected both. Hindenburg and Ludendorff then insisted on the appointment of Georg Michaelis (until that time the deputy minister for agriculture in Prussia) as the new Reich chancellor. Michaelis was not a felicitous choice. He had no previous national political experience; indeed, his only qualifications for the job were the confidence of the OHL and a reputation as an able administrator of the food rationing system in Prussia. His lack of political experience was a serious handicap in dealing with a restive Reichstag. The reformist parties, who held a two-thirds majority in the national parliament, had not been consulted on his appointment.

The new chancellor's task was also made more difficult by the OHL's attempt to bypass the established political institutions and appeal directly to the "silent majority" of the German people, who, the military claimed, fully supported the OHL's aim to achieve victory at any price. Hindenburg and Ludendorff were convinced that their goals could be accomplished only if the civilian war effort were more effectively regimented than it had been in the first two years of the war. To this end, they proposed and the Reichstag in July 1916 passed the Patriotic Auxiliary Service Law. Under this legislation, the government, through a supercoordinating agency, the War Office, received wide-ranging authority to control wages, production levels, and prices, as well as restrict the free movement of labor. The legislation severely curtailed the bargaining rights of labor unions, but in line with the OHL's attempt to deal directly with economic interest groups, the law assigned the unions an institutional role in administering the legislation. Union representatives became ex officio members of various regional commissions that determined wage scales, worker mobility, and conditions of labor. The military leaders hoped that in return for these economic gains, the unions would forego their support of demands for political reform.

The OHL was not content just to interfere in the economy. Hindenburg and Ludendorff also wanted to mobilize public opinion in favor of the OHL's political aims and peace terms. A major vehicle for this propaganda effort was the Fatherland Party, which was founded with the OHL's blessing in September 1917. Led by one of Germany's minor territorial princes, Duke Johann Albrecht of Mecklenburg, and that former master of mass propaganda, Admiral von Tirpitz, the Fatherland Party had no parliamentary ambitions. Its sole purpose was to lobby that a "Hindenburg Peace" should be imposed on Germany's enemies,

while continuation of Wilhelminian authoritarianism should be maintained at home. The label "Hindenburg Peace" was symptomatic of yet another effort to bypass the regular constitutional channels of politics. The OHL openly encouraged a cult of personality around the figure of the aged field marshall. During the last two years of the war the German propaganda machine increasingly portrayed Hindenburg as the personification of the war effort and the guarantor of victory. His kindly and venerable face with the caption "let us help him do the job right" appeared on thousands of posters and millions of postcards.

Extraparliamentary activism was not limited to the supporters of authoritarianism and the Hindenburg Peace. Indeed, the deliberate efforts by the OHL and the political Right to ignore the growing signs of war weariness facilitated the organizing activities of the far Left. The first political strikes occurred in mid-1916, at the time of the Battle of Verdun. Despite the opposition of union leaders, a wave of political strikes—often organized by the USPD, the Revolutionary Shop Stewards, or the Spartacus League and encouraged by the revolutionary successes in Russia—enveloped the country during 1917 and 1918. The most dramatic evidence of the country's polarization was a major strike of munitions workers in Berlin in January 1918. In defiance of their union leaders, 120,000 workers staged a walkout lasting several days to demonstrate their support for peace and an immediate end to the Prussian three-class system of voting.

The increasing signs of domestic polarization were not lost upon the leaders of the Reichstag, who recognized that they might lose control of the situation in the streets. Spearheaded by the energetic, young Center Party Reichstag delegate Matthias Erzberger, the Social Democrats, the Center Party, and the Progressives introduced a joint resolution in the Reichstag in July 1917 calling for immediate peace negotiations on the basis of no reparations and no annexations. It passed easily.

The resolution was naive and impractical (by this time the Allies had no intention of returning to the status quo before the war), but the effort demonstrated the cooperation among the reformist parties, while revealing the isolation of the Conservatives and the ineptness of the new chancellor. (Incidentally, the peace resolution was one of the factors precipitating the founding of the Fatherland Party.) Michaelis, who used the debate on the peace resolution to make his maiden speech in parliament, gave ample evidence of his lack of political skills. Someone who regarded the Hindenburg Peace as a set of moderate terms was clearly out of touch with most of German public opinion, and his clumsy attempt to endorse the peace resolution "as I interpret it" (which he explained to the crown prince meant that the resolution enabled the government to conclude peace on any basis it wished) merely underscored his general untrustworthiness.

Michaelis' initial performance in the Reichstag did much to ensure an early end to his career as Reich chancellor. Less than three months after he came into office, even the OHL had to recognize his incompetence. His successor, Count Georg von Hertling, was a seventy-eight-year-old Bavarian conservative. Hertling was a Catholic and in earlier years had been an influential voice in the Center Party, so his appointment at least indirectly insured a closer relationship between the executive and a leading group among the reformers in the Reichstag. In addition, Hertling's appointment brought movement to the deadlocked political situation in Prussia. As a south German, Hertling was unfamiliar with Prussian affairs, and while he served as Prussian prime minister in name, the actual head of the Prussian cabinet after October 1917 was now the deputy prime minister, Robert Friedberg. Before he moved to the executive office, Friedberg had been the parliamentary leader of the National Liberal Party in the Prussian legislature.

Hertling came into office at a time of mounting evidence that the German political consensus was breaking down. In addition to the signs described earlier, political anti-Semitism had been on the rise for some time, and the OHL at least indirectly encouraged this particularly virulent form of political emotionalism. In 1916, responding to what the military said were complaints about the disproportionately large number of Jews serving in rear echelons, rather than at the front, the OHL commissioned an inquiry and then promptly refused to publish the results on the grounds that to do so would encourage further anti-Semitic sentiments. Needless to say, that announcement only led to more rumors and innuendoes. (The actual results of the survey, as Werner T. Angress has shown, revealed no significant differences in the military assignment of Jews and Gentiles.)

The new chancellor, then, knew that the time for domestic reforms was at hand. Having learned a lesson from the Michaelis fiasco, the emperor sounded out some Reichstag leaders on Hertling's appointment. Spokesmen for the reformers made it clear that the new chancellor would face a very hostile parliament unless he implemented reforms of the Prussian electoral system. The emperor, of course, had given such assurances in his Easter Message of 1917, but so far no concrete measures had followed his words. With the emperor's

An example of the cult of personality surrounding von Hindenburg. A poster urging the purchase of war bonds bears his picture and the caption, "The times are hard, but victory is assured." (Source: *Posters of the First World War*, p. 233.)

blessing both Hertling and Friedberg assured the Reichstag leaders that a bill significantly modifying the electoral system in Prussia would be introduced in the Prussian state legislature.

Hertling and Friedberg kept their word, but the measure was immediately voted down by a majority of the Prussian Landtag. The group of diehards included the Conservatives, about two-thirds of the National Liberals (who thereby rejected the stand of their former leader) and a substantial portion of the Center Party delegates. There the issue remained until the end of the war: a festering sore in German political life and a constant reminder of the failure of the reformers.

A final clash between old guard and reformers was postponed by Germany's military victories in the East. The defeat of Russia and Rumania permitted the military and the industrial interests to realize part of their maximal war aims in the Treaty of Brest-Litovsk. Under this Austro-German *Diktat* Russia lost some 1 million square kilometers of territory with a population of 50 million. In addition, Russia was deprived of over 90 percent of her coal mines, a third of her agricultural land, and virtually all of her known oil fields. Germany and Austria-Hungary extended their economic and military hegemony eastward from Königsberg and Cracow to Kiev. The Treaty of Brest-Litovsk rallied most Germans behind the banner of chauvinism for the last time. In the Reichstag the USPD opposed the agreement and the majority of Socialists abstained from voting, but all the bourgeois parties, including the Progressives and the Center Party, supported the treaty.

The Reichstag's reception of the Treaty of Brest-Litovsk convinced the Reich's political and military leaders that victories on the battlefield provided the most effective means of defusing demands for domestic reforms. Unfortunately for them the corollary to victory in the east, a successful offensive in the west, was unattainable. The failure of the Ludendorff offensive in the spring and summer of 1918 ushered in both Germany's military defeat and the collapse of the conservatives' domestic political strategy.

In mid-August the emperor for the first time privately acknowledged that the Reich would have to end the war. At the beginning of October, Ludendorff, now in a state of panic, dispatched his military aide, Colonel von dem Bussche, to inform the leaders of the Reichstag that armistice negotiations had to begin within forty-eight hours. The news sent shock waves through parliament; most of the political leaders had little inkling of how serious the military situation actually was. The military leaders, for their part, were unwilling to take responsibility for acknowledging the defeat. As a result, they now insisted on a step which until then they had strenuously resisted: They placed responsibility for ending the war and guiding Germany's political future in the hands of the Reichstag leaders, or, more precisely, the leaders of the reformist parties in parliament.

The reformers, in turn, used their newly won power not only to begin negotiating an armistice to end hostilities but also to implement the domestic reforms that they had been demanding since before 1914. The consequence was a package of constitutional changes that transformed Germany from an authoritarian into a parliamentary monarchy much like Great Britain. The proposals were certainly not new ones in German politics, but their hasty implementation at the behest of the OHL and their association with the parallel acknowledgment of military defeat was not fortuitous. Moreover, in their rush to present results, the reformers left many constitutional problems unresolved. For example, the October reforms did not eliminate the Reich-Prussian dualism. In addition, it was true that the emperor had promised the reformist parties he would agree to a parliamentary Reich cabinet as well as work to bring the Prussian electoral system in line with that of the Reich, but there was no indication what steps the monarch would take if the Prussian Landtag refused to follow along and instead continued to block reform legislation. Similarly, while the Reichstag obtained power to control the military in wartime, the peacetime relations between parliament and the military remained unclear. (In peacetime, it will be recalled, the national armed forces reverted back to their status as state, which meant largely Prussian, contingents.)

Still, on paper the reformers had succeeded in transforming the Reich into a constitutional monarchy. Some major personnel changes also seemed to signal the beginning of the new era. In late October, Ludendorff was forced to resign. He was replaced by the former head of the War Office, General Groener. (See the later discussion, pp. 121 and 128–29.) To Ludendorff's surprise, Hindenburg did not join him in resigning, but stayed on as chief of the OHL. Hertling left his post as chancellor and Prussian prime minister. He was succeeded by a politically moderate aristocrat, Prince Max von Baden. The new chancellor, a cousin of the reigning duke of Baden, inaugurated Germany's first parliamentary Reich government. Max von Baden had close ties to the leaders of the Progressive Party, and he refused to take office until he had received a full vote of confidence from the majority parties in the Reichstag. Moreover, he insisted that delegates of all the reformist parties, including the right-wing Social Democrats, be represented in his cabinet.

There is no doubt that for most Germans the October reforms satisfied their demands for political change. All over the Reich rallies were organized with speakers from the reformist parties celebrating the democratization of Germany's political system. Only the conservatives on the Right and the radical Left rejected the constitutional changes.

The hopes for an orderly transition to political democracy were dashed by precipitous action on the part of the emperor. William and the leaders of the OHL had agreed to the October reforms in a moment of panic. When the emperor recognized the full impact of the constitutional changes he had approved, William quickly went back on his promise to work with the reformers. For a few days the monarch wavered between accepting his new role as figurehead of the Reich and marching into Berlin at the head of "a few loyal regiments" to undo the reforms he had just approved. Eventually, his authoritarian and irrational leanings won out. On November 4, rather than oversee the implementation of the constitutional changes and work with the Baden government to guide electoral reform through the Prussian Landtag, the emperor suddenly left Berlin and travelled to the OHL's headquarters in Spa, Belgium. There was no military necessity for this step; it was an impetuous gesture to demonstrate that William II still identified himself with "his" generals rather than the democratic politicians. In all likelihood, his flight from Berlin and his association with the most authoritarian part of the old regime also ensured that the emperor himself was swept away when the entire Prusso-German authoritarian system collapsed less than a week later.

WAR AND SOCIETY

Like her enemies, Germany entered the age of twentieth-century global warfare woefully unprepared. World War I was the first "total war" in which victory depended as much on a country's economic and social resources as upon the military skills of her armies at the battlefront. Germany's military strategists were justly famous for their general staff work, but in planning for the eventuality of war they had completely neglected the economic and social implications of a drawn-out conflict among the Great Powers. Anticipating a short war, all of the military's plans assumed that the outcome of the conflict would be determined by one or two decisive battles.

As far as German life on the homefront

was concerned, the most important neglected factors in this scenario were the cumulative and debilitating effects of the British blockade, the lack of mechanisms to manage the war economy during the first two years of the conflict, and the pressures of inflation.

The blockade and the constantly increasing demands of the military quickly brought on an economy of chronic shortages. The primary victims both in terms of reduced supplies and higher prices were consumers, since in wartime the needs of the military always came first.

The economy of scarcity as such put pressure on the social consensus, but even more important for the breakdown of morale at home was the uneven impact upon the various sectors of German society. Some groups were hit particularly hard, while others, at least in relative terms, actually benefited from the situation. The defense-related sectors of the economy understandably did best. The military decided that production was more important than cost-consciousness, and manufacturers of war matériel were essentially able to charge whatever prices they wished. This resulted in vast profits for this sector of the economy (with no meaningful taxation to skim off the excess profits), but labor in defense industries indirectly benefited as well. For the first three years of the war, manufacturers outbid each other for the services of skilled laborers in frantic efforts to obtain lucrative army contracts.

In contrast, sectors of the economy oriented primarily toward the civilian market bore the brunt of the hardships. Farmers were one of the first sectors of the economy to be subjected to tight price controls. In an effort not to alienate consumers in the cities, the government early in the war decided that prices for basic foods should remain low regardless of market conditions. With some justification, farmers claimed that the government-set prices were considerably below production costs; fertilizer, animal feed, and farm machinery were obtainable

(if at all) only at price levels vastly above those of prewar times. The consequence was a ubiquitous black market in foodstuffs, fueled, ironically, in part by the decision to encourage the production of war matériel regardless of price considerations. Purchasing agents of defense industries routinely paid inflated prices for agricultural goods on the black market to provide additional supplies for their workers as hiring incentives or fringe benefits. Such practices in turn caused further problems for the farmers by reducing the supply of farm labor. Farmers constantly complained about the shortage of labor, contending that high wages paid in war-related industries led many agricultural workers to seek jobs there.

Manufacturers of consumer goods were hurt in two ways: First, they were increasingly unable to obtain raw materials. Either they could not compete with the defense industries on the open market, or, after centralized allocation agencies were established (see p. 121) their requests were always assigned a lower priority than those of war matériel manufacturers. In addition, they could generally not afford to pay the wages offered by defense industries, since the government, again with an eye toward maintaining low prices for such consumer goods as were available. The labor problem was aggravated as casualties mounted, and the military dipped ever deeper into Germany's reserves of draft-age men. While war-related industries could often get their labor exempted from the draft, applications from manufacturers of civilian goods were generally turned down. As was true of food, a thriving black market in consumer goods was the inevitable result of these conditions.

Finally, there was the service and retirees sector of the economy. Civil servants (who in Germany included teachers at all levels of education), professionals, old-age pensioners, and most white-collar workers had little bargaining power in the scramble for benefits in the economy of scarcity. For the most part living on fixed or even declining incomes (upper-level civil servants actually suffered significant salary cuts), they were largely excluded from participating in the black market economy. For most Germans, then, the war at home meant shortages of food, poor health conditions, housing in chronic need of repair, and a general deterioration in the quality of life.

Food was undoubtedly the greatest problem. Before the war Germany imported large amounts of agricultural products, including grains, animal feeds, meat, dairy products, as well as such items as coffee, cocoa, and tea. Most of the imports came from overseas areas, notably the United States, Canada, Australia, and Latin America. Once war was declared, German trade with all these areas virtually stopped; the British blockade effectively prevented overseas goods from reaching the Reich. Before 1914 Germany had imported large amounts of Russian grain and meat. The war also disrupted this trade. For most of the war, then, Germany could import agricultural goods only from Holland and the Scandinavian countries (these nations remained neutral), but even here the British exerted constant pressure in order to reduce the level of exports to the Reich.

Although the discovery of artificial nitrates by the chemist Fritz Haber eased the fertilizer shortage, any illusions that Germany's own farmers could replace the lost imports were soon dashed. The effects of the blockade were felt almost immediately. In October 1914, faced with a shortage of grain, the government authorized the baking of "war bread," a product composed of a mixture of 80 percent flour and 20 percent potato starch. It was the beginning of what would soon be an all-pervasive *Ersatz* economy. (The term "Ersatz" actually came into both German and English usage at the time of World War I.) By the summer of 1917, 837 nonmeat substitutes for sausage and cold cuts had been patented.

The food situation grew more severe with each year of the war. Far worse than the often only tasteless *Ersatz* products was the growing lack of actual food commodities. The shortages culminated in the so-called turnip winter of 1916–1917. By this time the long-time staples of the German diet, grain and potatoes, were in very short supply. The only available, relatively abundant substitute was turnips, or more precisely, rutabagas, and even these were rationed. The official weekly rations for an adult living in Berlin in January and February, 1917 consisted of between two and six pounds of turnips (or, if available, two pounds of bread), less than two ounces of butter, and one ounce of margarine. In August of that year, when the new harvest had come in, the weekly allotment had only increased to five pounds of potatoes, one half pound of meat, and three-quarters of a pound of sugar.

The economy of shortages changed and destroyed the country's prewar social infrastructure. The shortage of male labor meant a vast influx of women into the workforce, particularly in industry and the service sector. Food shortages brought on malnutrition-related diseases, such as tuberculosis, rickets, dysentery, and typhoid fever. The unaccustomed presence of many women outside the home changed sexual mores and increased the incidence of venereal disease. At the same time, housing and transportation facilities deteriorated through delayed maintenance, while rents, despite government efforts to control them, skyrocketed as landlords attempted to keep up with inflation.

The reality of the hardships contrasted sharply with the government's upbeat and simplistic propaganda about conditions on the homefront. Official statements praised the German inventive spirit for producing ingenious *Ersatz* products of every kind and claimed in February 1917 (at the height of the turnip winter) that the various shortages had no measurable effect upon public health. The people knew better. By 1917 "lack of enthusiasm" (to use the term employed by a government report) among the poorer classes had turned to despair and revolt. Official admonitions not to dwell on the hardships at home when writing to the soldiers at the front had little effect. The rising number of strikes were an indication of the growing frustration with the economic and political conditions.

However, not all of the German people went in a straight line from enthusiasm to alienation to despair and revolution. A far truer picture would reveal the increasing polarization of the society. For almost the entire duration of the conflict, there were many, especially among the upper and middle classes, who continued to believe the war was necessary and perhaps even morally uplifting. If strikes and grumbling on food lines were indications of disillusionment, much wartime literature was "pro-war." Most of the genre was, as one postwar literary critic has said, "not worthy of the greatness of the subject." The books, full of soldiers' humor and vulgarity, presented a world of black and white contrasts, in which noble-minded officers (in these novels the heroes are almost invariably officers) are fighting selflessly to defend their homeland and Western civilization against the onslaught of Russian, French, Belgian, and British barbarians.

Above the level of *Trivialliteratur* two themes dominated wartime literature. One was the myth of the *Fronterlebnis*, the experience of being at the front. Veterans, such as Ernst Jünger in his book *In Stahlgewittern* ("The Storm of Steel"), would later (the work was published in 1920) use their wartime experience to create the figure of the soldier *sui generis*. The war molded civilians from all walks of life into new human beings standing apart from and in a sense above the day-to-day cares of peacetime Germany. The experience of the front and especially what Ernst von Salomon would later call the "high of battle," alienated the soldier from the old society and made him a harbinger of a new revolutionary morality and ideology.

The other theme was the conflict of civilizations. Jünger was by no means the only intellectual who professed to find a larger meaning in slaughter and conquest. The June 1915 "Manifesto of Celebrities," which was signed by many German professors, demonstrated that much of the intellectual establishment supported the OHL's aim of a victory peace. Gerhart Hauptmann, the naturalist playwright who had been highly critical of Wilhelminian society before the war, published a famous open letter to the French writer Romain Rolland in which he defended Germany's role in the war, including the invasion of Belgium. Perhaps the most famous instance of German intellectual chauvinism was the publication in 1918 of Thomas Mann's *Betrachtungen eines Unpolitischen* ("Observations of an Apolitical Man"). In this book-length essay, Mann, the bestselling author of *Buddenbrooks*, angrily contrasted the materialistic "civilization" of the British and French bourgeoisie with the German *Bürger's* ideal of "culture." While Western civilization produced peoples with a narrow materialist outlook, German culture formed an educated, idealistic citizen of the world.

For intellectuals, too, the year 1917 represented something of a watershed. For many a feeling of disillusionment set in. A typical example was Walter Flex' *Wanderer zwischen beiden Welten* ("Wanderer Between Two Worlds"), a book that was to become something of a youth cult novel in the 1920s. Published at the end of 1918, the novel is a memorial to the author's wartime friend who died in battle. It is also a heart-wrenching portrayal of a sensitive man's reaction to the horrors of war. A far more radical rejection of the values of wartime chauvinism was the Dada movement, a form of cultural nihilism. Launched in a Zurich cafe in the summer of 1916 (the founding ceremony was repeated in 1917 in Berlin), the Dada movement was less important for the artistic products it inspired than for the antiestablishment sentiments of its philosophy: "Dada means nothing. It is the significant nothing which has no meaning at all. We want to change the world with nothing, we want to alter poetry and painting with nothing, and we want to end the war with nothing."

For some time it appeared as if the Reich's leadership was oblivious to the turmoils that raged within German society. It was as if the government regarded war and society as largely separate entities. True, prodded by executives from the large Berlin electrical manufacturing firm, AEG, the Prussian ministry of war established a War Raw Materials Section (*Kriegsrohstoffabteilung*) at the beginning of the war. The AEG's chairman, Walther Rathenau, became its director. The new office was given authority to monitor and control the use of scarce raw materials. But as for other facets of economic and social life during the first two years of the conflict, other than building a propaganda apparatus and instituting food rationing, the German government made little effort to coordinate and manage the wartime economy. This situation did not change until Falkenhayn's failure at Verdun. Now a rapidly expanding war-management bureaucracy was built up. Numerous allocation boards handling everything from textiles to shoelaces issued vast amounts of paper in a largely vain attempt to ensure some fairness in the distribution of increasingly scarce supplies.

A new stage in mobilizing the resources of the homefront came with the so-called Hindenburg Program. When Hindenburg and Ludendorff took over leadership of the OHL in August 1916 they demanded a 100 percent increase in small arms ammunition and a 300 percent increase for artillery shells and machine guns by the spring of 1917. These goals, which were completely unrealistic, required extensive control of industrial production and the total mobilization of the German labor force, including persuading thousands of women to take on industrial jobs. Bethmann Hollweg, if not the OHL, recognized that the momentous shift in manufacturing priorities envisioned

by the Hindenburg Program would seriously endanger the frayed social and political consensus. In an attempt to give the mobilization effort the appearance of a consensual rather than a dictatorial decision, the government proposed the Patriotic Auxiliary Service Law and the establishment of a War Office. Headed by General Groener, the War Office, which had overall charge of the economic mobilization effort, was particularly instrumental in trying to give the war effort the appearance of a cooperative venture of the military, government officials, and representatives of industry and labor.

Consensual management of the war economy was a victim along with the politics of the diagonal in the cold coup of August 1917. Like Bethmann Hollweg, Groener was dismissed. The War Office itself was largely dismantled and its functions decentralized under the overall direction of the so-called deputy commanders. These commanding generals of the reserve forces in Germany's military districts, mostly officers unsuited for frontline commands because of old age or infirmities, tended to be particularly insensitive to the morale problems of the homefront. Their answers to strikes and demonstrations were usually a single-minded decision to draft strike leaders and send them to the front. Relations between the army and the reformist forces, including the labor unions, deteriorated accordingly. By the end of the war the military for most Germans was symbolized by the figure of the deputy commander, whose only answer to war-weariness was repression.

While Germany did attempt to develop mechanisms for managing a totally mobilized war economy, the problem of financing the conflict was ignored almost completely. This neglect was to haunt the country for years after the lost war. In addition to the horrors of physical destruction and death, World War I was also a totally unexpected financial burden for all of the belligerents. As far as Germany was concerned, the cost of conducting the war rose from roughly 36 million marks a day at the beginning of the war to 136 million per day at the end. Since the German national debt was already sizable in 1914, the government had no reserves with which to finance the conflict.

But government expenditures can be met in only two ways: taxes and credits. Taxes are unpopular, particularly in wartime, although ironically, the excess of money over goods that is characteristic of an economy of scarcity makes it economically sensible to raise taxes. All of the belligerents relied upon war bond drives and other forms of credit to finance a good deal of their war expenditures, but the Germans attempted to finance almost the entire war effort with credits. Part of the reason was unjustified confidence that the expenditures would be quickly recovered from the defeated enemies. (The example of the 5 billion marks in French reparations after the Franco-Prussian War of 1870–1871 came readily to mind.) Then, too, the government was encouraged by the enthusiasm with which the early war bond drives were received. During the first bond drive between August and October 1914 1.2 million Germans subscribed a total of 4.5 billion marks. Subsequent bond efforts were less successful, but the expectation that the government credit was good and the money would be repaid with interest remained strong.

The success of the bond drives and the expectation of victory led the government to spend with little regard for actual resources. The cost of the Hindenburg Program was particularly staggering. As noted above, the military had no hesitation in paying vastly inflated prices and permitting employers to pay very high wages in order to obtain the needed war materials. A balanced budget, an unbreachable article of faith before the war, became an illusion and Germany's public finances essentially operated in an Alice-in-Wonderland world. There were some efforts to cut wages and prices in early 1918, but by that time inflation had acquired an unstoppable dynamic

of its own. At the end of the war, the mark was worth about half of what it had been in 1914. The implications were particularly severe for many middle-class Germans who had anticipated that their retirement years would be financed largely from the proceeds of life-long savings and war bonds. The German financing of World War I, then, failed in every sense: It burdened the country with a vast debt, and, by eroding the value of the mark, dashed the hopes for financial security in old age of a whole generation of Germans.

CONCLUSION

In November 1918, the Reich's new leaders inherited a staggering legacy of destruction, despair, and uncertainty. The armed forces had suffered more than 6 million casualties, including 1.6 million war dead. At home malnutrition-related diseases brought massive increases in the death rate. Germany faced peace with an exhausted population, worn out industrial facilities, and a vast national debt. (The total cost of World War I for all belligerents is estimated at about 1 trillion marks [about 238 billion dollars] in 1914 prices; Germany's share of that sum was 175 billion [about 42 billion dollars].)

These "material" consequences of the war had grave implications for Germany's future, but in a sense, perhaps even more ominous were the less tangible social and political results of the conflict. In at least three ways World War I shattered important aspects of the implicit prewar national consensus.

One was the implied promise of continuing prosperity and upward social mobility. The war ended abruptly the sustained high growth rates that would later give the years before 1914 the glow of a "golden age." During the war, the standard of living as a whole not only declined rapidly, but the burden of the conflict was also very unevenly distributed among the various segments of the population. Some suffered far more than others.

Shattered, too, was the illusion that Germany was advancing toward greater political modernization. The emperor's announcement of a *Burgfrieden*, his Easter Message of 1917, and Bethmann-Hollweg's politics of the diagonal had all raised expectations that the Reich's political and military leaders would cooperate in the effort to reform Prusso-German authoritarianism. The OHL's "silent dictatorship," the emperor's shortsightedness, and the intransigence of the conservatives destroyed that hope. The enactment of the October reforms came about only because the OHL and the emperor acknowledged—briefly—that they had lost their gamble to preserve authoritarianism at home through military victories abroad. The constitutional changes of 1918 did not result from a national consensus, but from the bankruptcy of the old regime.

Finally, a third shattered consensus was the promise of the correlation between sacrifices and rewards. Like the inhabitants of all the belligerent countries, the Germans (encouraged by the OHL's relentlessly upbeat propaganda about the military situation) were fully convinced that the coming peace would somehow make the sacrifices during wartime "worthwhile." This part of the national consensus held as late as the spring of 1918 during the debate on the Treaty of Brest-Litovsk. A few months later that bubble, too, had burst. The reaction was anger, disbelief, and alienation. When the industrialist Walther Rathenau proposed in early October 1918 that Germany launch a *levée en masse* to transform defeat into victory on the Western front, there was no response.

In November 1918, Germany was an exhausted, deeply polarized nation in need of a new national consensus. What the ingredients of that new consensus would be was largely unclear. The Germans were united for the moment only in their desire for peace and their determination to maintain the Reich's territorial and political integrity.

CHAPTER 5

REVOLUTION, INFLATION, AND PUTSCHES
The Search for a New Consensus, 1918–1923

The armistice ending World War I took effect on November 11, 1918. Most Germans welcomed peace, although few anticipated the difficulties involved in the search for economic recovery, a new social and political consensus, and a secure place in the international balance of power. The failure to achieve these goals repeatedly brought the Reich to the brink of political and economic collapse before a temporary stability of sorts was reached in 1924.

REVOLUTION

We have already seen how the emperor's symbolic flight from Berlin dealt a serious blow to the implementation of the October reforms that might have achieved an orderly transition from authoritarianism to parliamentary democracy. His action undoubtedly sealed the fate of Prusso-German au-

thoritarianism, but, more important, it also undermined the credibility of the reformers. Like the Reichstag's leaders, most Germans had assumed that in instituting the October reforms the party leaders would work together with the emperor and his old advisors. When this proved impossible, the initial euphoria which virtually all Germans felt in October over the anticipated constitutional changes was quickly followed in November by a profound distrust of all existing authorities and institutions. The distrust was most widespread among the soldiers and sailors. At the beginning of November, following the example of their contemporaries in Russia, German army and navy units established a German version of the soviets, the soldiers' councils (*Soldatenräte*). (As was initially true of the Russian soviets as well, the German term "council" [*Rat*] referred to an institution, not a political ideology.) Originally, most of the coun-

124

cils were representative organs of the enlisted men, concerned not with larger political issues, but with better food rations, putting an end to arbitrary disciplinary measures, and preventing officers from sending units on useless suicide missions in the last days of the war.

The first soldiers' (or rather sailors') council was established on November 4 in the Baltic seaport of Kiel, headquarters of the German naval command. Throughout the war complaints about conditions on naval ships had been endemic. Sailors resented the harsh discipline and the pronounced and highly visible differences in living conditions and food rations between officers and men. The situation had already led to a major mutiny in 1917. At that time, the naval command had brutally suppressed the uprising: Twelve of the mutineers were sentenced to death, and two were actually executed.

The developments in Kiel in early November 1918 must be seen against this background. It was a matter of common knowledge that the armistice was only days away. At the same time, it was an ill-kept secret that the leaders of the navy planned to send the fleet on a last engagement against the British that would save "the honor of the navy." When the naval command issued orders to some units to prepare their ships for a "routine training mission," coal stokers on a number of vessels, suspecting they were being sent on the planned suicide mission, refused to obey the orders. Shipyard and dockworkers in Kiel went on strike in support of the mutineering sailors. Together with the sailors they elected representatives to form the Kiel workers' and soldiers' council.

Faced with widespread support for the strike and mutiny, the mayor of the city and the commanding admiral of the Baltic Naval Station agreed to cooperate with the workers' and soldiers' council. In addition, at the request of the sailors and workers two Reichstag delegates, Gustav Noske, the SPD's expert on military affairs, and Hugo Haase, the national chairman of the USPD arrived in Kiel on November 5. It was Noske who quickly took charge of the situation. Elected chairman of the workers' and soldiers' council, Noske persuaded the military and civilian chiefs of administration formally to recognize the authority of the councils. The result was a curious dual system of government. Orders from the military commander and regulations from the civilian authorities went into effect only after they had been approved and countersigned by the chairman of the workers' and soldiers' council. The two chains of command worked reasonably well together; the naval command abandoned the planned suicide sortie, while the council helped to prevent looting and restored at least a modicum of discipline to the ships.

The system of dual lines first established in Kiel quickly became the model for the institutionalization of revolutionary authority throughout most of Germany. News of the events in Kiel spread rapidly as sailors took advantage of the opportunity to leave their ships and go home. In the next few days workers' and soldiers' councils sprang up in the urban areas of western and central Germany. Here, too, the councils generally did not attempt to take the place of the regular administrations, but permitted the established civilian and military administrations to continue functioning under the general supervision of the councils.

A far more political use of the new institutions began with events in Munich, Bavaria. At the beginning of November the decidedly left-wing chairman of the USPD (also referred to as the Independent Socialists) in Bavaria, Kurt Eisner, sensed that conditions were ripe for the overthrow of political authoritarianism as such. Eisner used the occasion of an antiwar rally on November 7 to stage a demonstration demanding the abolition of the Bavarian monarchy. The regent yielded to the antigovernment sentiment and hastened to renounce this throne. Eisner proclaimed the establishment of the "Free State of Bavaria," which was to be governed by the leaders of the SPD and the USPD in association with the workers' and soldiers' councils until elections for a constitutional convention could be held.

The fall of the Wittelsbach dynasty, which had ruled Bavaria for more than a thousand years, sent political shock waves through the country. Throughout Germany the workers' and soldiers' councils recognized that the old regimes were virtually without popular support. In the next two days all of the territorial princes, with the exception of the emperor, abdicated, leaving their states' affairs in the hands of new provisional governments and the workers' and soldiers' councils. For the most part, the German revolution was a bloodless and very moderate upheaval. The princes were not physically harmed; several even received formal expressions of gratitude form the workers' and soldiers' councils for their past services to the state. In turn the old rulers routinely requested that the states' civil servants stay on the job and cooperate with the new authorities. The revolutionaries also made no attempt to alter the federal structure of Germany. In fact, one of the motivating factors for revolution in many of the *Länder* had been the desire to escape the wartime tutelage of the central government in Berlin.

Remarkably, throughout the first week of revolutions the Reich capital remained an island of seeming calm. As late as November 8, Berlin was quiet, with public services and transportation functioning normally. Even the stock market was in operation. Berlin's status as a white spot on the revolutionary map changed abruptly on November 9. On this cold and wet Saturday, thousands of Berlin workers demonstrated to demand an immediate armistice and the abdication of William II as emperor and king of Prussia. As had been true in Munich two days earlier, they met no resistance; on the contrary, soldiers and police readily fraternized with the demonstrators.

The Reich chancellor, Max von Baden, and his government had been urging William II for some days to abdicate in favor of one of his younger sons, but the emperor hesitated until it was too late. The chancellor, seeing the milling thousands almost literally outside his office window, felt he had to act on his own. He made two decisions: one largely symbolic and the other with far-reaching constitutional implications. On his own authority he announced the emperor's abdication. (William actually relinquished his imperial crown a few hours later, but he did not formally abdicate as king of Prussia until November 28.) At the same time Max von Baden asked the leader of the SPD (also referred to as the Majority Socialists), Friedrich Ebert, to succeed him as Reich chancellor.

Baden, of course, had no constitutional authority to name his own successor. Since the October reforms that power rested with the Reichstag, and on November 9 parliament was not in session. But Baden also recognized that the demonstrators were clearly not in the mood for discussing constitutional niceties. After a brief conference with the leaders of his party, Ebert accepted the chancellor's offer; just before noon on November 9 Germany had its first Social Democratic Reich chancellor.

Ebert and his colleagues in the SPD realized that their position would be extremely difficult without the cooperation of the USPD. The Berlin district of the SPD had traditionally been dominated by the left wing of the party, and after the split Berlin became one of the strongholds of the USPD. Indeed, key segments of the Berlin proletariat sympathized with the far-left Revolutionary Shop Stewards movement. For this reason, the SPD's leaders, immediately after accepting Baden's offer, proposed to the USPD that the two parties share power and positions equally in the new Reich government.

The SPD's proposal—completely unexpected—left the USPD in a quandary. Some left-wing radicals like Karl Liebknecht and Ernst Dämig (the latter was a major figure in the Revolutionary Shop Stewards movement) were passionately opposed to working together with the right-wing socialists. At the same time, many in the USPD also feared the chaos and anarchy that would result if the governmental infrastructure broke down completely. They worried that the mass starvation, civil war, and widespread random violence that followed the Bolshevik Revolution in Russia would be repeated in Germany. Similarly, the commitment by the German Marxists to preserving the Reich's national unity should not be underestimated. Like their colleagues in the SPD, many USPD members were, as one USPD local in East Prussia put it, "German to the marrow of our bones."

For these reasons a majority of the USPD's leadership voted to accept the SPD's offer to form a new provisional national government, the Council of People's Plenipotentiaries (CPP) or, in German, *Rat der Volksbeauftragten.* The CPP would be composed of six members, with the two parties' national leaders, Ebert and Haase, serving as cochairmen. The other four members were Emil Barth, the head of the Revolutionary Shop Stewards in Berlin; Wilhelm Dittmann, a moderate USPD leader; Otto Landsberg, one of the SPD's experts on constitutional questions; and Phillip Scheidemann, the leader of the SPD's Reichstag caucus. With the exception of Max von Baden the incumbent ministers of the old cabinet stayed in office. They were to act as "technical aides" of the CPP.

The provisional government faced both immediate and long-range policy decisions. The two socialist groups agreed that the most pressing need was the conclusion of an armistice to end the fighting, but on other issues they were sharply divided. The SPD, the Majority Socialists, insisted on early elections for a constitutional convention, while the USPD, the Independents, wanted to "secure the revolution" first. The USPD assigned structural reforms of the economy a high priority. The USPD members wanted to press ahead with nationalization of certain sectors of the economy, especially coal mining, banking, insurance, and parts of the steel industry. The SPD, citing Kurt Eisner's famous aphorism, "you can't socialize bankruptcy," argued that the economy would have to recover before the sectors of the economy that were "ripe" for such a step could be nationalized.

While the USPD leaders debated whether to join the SPD in a coalition government, the revolution in Berlin had developed a dynamic of its own. At about two o'clock in the afternoon Phillip Scheidemann, sensing that the crowds wanted evidence of concrete changes, announced the formal establishment of the "German Republic." Scheidemann had no constitutional authority to make his pronouncements, but neither did Karl Liebknecht, who, two hours later in another part of the city, proclaimed the founding of the "German Socialist Republic" in which "all legislative, all executive, all judicial power" would be in the hands of the workers' and soldiers' councils rather than the CPP.

Liebknecht's vision of the revolution's radical progress was ended by decisions of the Berlin workers' and soldiers' councils themselves on November 10. A citywide meeting of elected representatives from the local workers' and soldiers' councils gave the CPP a vote of confidence, although the three thousand, often unruly, representatives also demanded that the CPP take immediate steps to implement the "socialization" of the economy and the "democratization" of society. However, the delegates rejected a motion sponsored by the Spartacus League (and modeled after the famous Army Order No. 1 adopted by the Petrograd soviet) to give the workers' and soldiers' councils direct command over the police and military forces in Berlin.

With the decisions in Berlin on November 10 the first stage of the German revolution ended, and it became possible to assess how much of a revolution there had been. On the surface, the changes seemed profound. Dynasties that had ruled in Germany for centuries had been swept away. The new leaders of the national and state governments were socialists, sometimes allied with left-wing Progressives and Catholics. A completely new set of institutions—workers' and soldiers' councils—at least in theory was the final arbiter of decisions on public policy.

Yet much remained as before. The old civil service continued to function. The new authorities took pains to protect private property and prevent looting and arbitrary expropriations. The armed forces remained under the command structure of the old officer corps, despite the presence of elected soldiers' councils. Terms like "socialization" and "democratization" had made their way into the political jargon, but little had been done to implement concrete reforms. In essence, the upheavals of early November 1918 had swept away the prewar political structure. Germany could now move in a variety of directions, from following the Bolshevik example in Russia to building a Western-style pluralist society, but as yet it was entirely unclear which path the Reich would take.

In theory, the important decisions were to be left to the constitutional convention. Actually, a series of tactical arrangements and agreements by forces outside the governmental structure in the second half of November severely restricted the range of possible future decisions. The new rulers agreed to respect "the well-earned rights" of the civil servants, virtually precluding any large-scale purge of the old imperial officials.

In mid-November representatives of the unions and employers' organizations established a Central Cooperative Working Group (*Zentrale Arbeitsgemeinschaft*, ZAG), which concluded a national collective bargaining agreement covering most industrial workers. Labor won some major concessions, such as the eight-hour day, higher wages, and the promise that returning veterans would be rehired without loss of seniority. But the collective bargaining agreement also precluded the implementation of any governmental plans to significantly alter the structure of the economy without the approval of both labor and management.

A second agreement with equally far-reaching implications involved a tactical partnership between the CPP and the OHL. On November 10, General Groener, Ludendorff's successor in the OHL, contacted Friedrich Ebert and offered him a deal: In return for keeping the officer corps free from "political" (that is to say, parliamentary) interference and supporting efforts to limit the activities of the soldiers' councils, the OHL would assist the CPP in maintaining order at home and administer the demobilization of the troops at the front. Ebert, without consulting his colleagues in the CPP, readily agreed to what became known as the "Ebert-Groener Pact."

This agreement has been severely criticized. Ebert's decision to leave the foundation of Prusso-German authoritarianism as an autonomous force—"a state within the state"—seemed both counterproductive and unnecessary at a time when the army's prestige and self-confidence were at their lowest point in a century. With the benefit of hindsight it is easy to see the force of these arguments. Indeed, the SPD would later profoundly regret the Ebert-Groener Pact. Ebert, however, had his eye on a number of short-term problems. One was the necessary demobilization of the front-line troops. He knew that as part of the armistice agreement the Allies would insist all German troops leave French and Belgian soil within two weeks. That meant transporting 2 million war-weary, exhausted, and bitter soldiers back to the Reich. Ebert was convinced that moving that many people in good order could only be done with the help of the army's corps of staff officers. And it was true: Germany's retreat was not marred by the scenes of looting and pillaging that had characterized the Russian demobilization earlier in the year.

Ebert's second consideration was the problem of internal security, especially in Berlin. When Groener made his offer, the

CPP had already come to realize that there was no really reliable force in the capital that could protect the national government. The regular Berlin police force was in disarray, and the new—self-appointed—police chief a man who sympathized with the Spartacus League. There were numerous self-styled militias in the capital, but all of them tended to disappear whenever confronted with any real challenge. Groener's offer to dispatch some reliable troops to Berlin was tempting; Ebert could not know that the OHL's "trustworthy" force would turn out to be just as unreliable as all the others.

A third area in which the freedom of future decision making was severely curtailed was the federal structure of the Reich. For many years the Social Democrats had advocated the abolition of the German *Länder* and the establishment of a strong central government. Once in power, however, the socialist state governments became enthusiastic supporters of states' rights. The states' new leaders endorsed centralism as a long-range goal, but insisted the process of abolishing the states should not begin with their own *Land*. German particularism had come through the revolution alive and well.

In the meantime, the CPP had begun its work. The members agreed that although the terms of the armistice proposed by the Allies to end the hostilities were harsh, Germany had no choice but to sign the accord. The armistice agreement went into effect on November 11, 1918.

By far the most divisive issue for the members of the CPP and their respective parties was setting the date for electing delegates to the national constitutional convention. The SPD advanced tactical and ideological reasons for early elections. The party hoped that the voters, grateful for peace and democracy, would be more likely to vote for one of the socialist parties while the memories of injustices under the old regime were still fresh. The Majority Socialists, who rejected the concept of the dictatorship of the proletariat, also felt strongly that the German people as a whole

should elect the members of the constitutional convention. The USPD, on the other hand, contended that a period of education and measures to democratize especially the army and the civil service were needed before the voters could be entrusted with sanctioning the new order.

The members of the CPP agreed to leave the final decision on the election date to a national congress of workers' and soldiers' councils. Meeting in Berlin in mid-December 1918, the decision of the congress was a severe disappointment to the USPD; by heavy majorities the delegates endorsed the SPD's position on setting the date for national elections. Indeed, while the SPD members of the CPP had proposed a date in early February, the congress scheduled national elections for January 19, 1919.

Still, the national congress of workers' and soldiers' councils did not merely rubberstamp the positions of the right-wing Social Democrats on the CPP. The delegates were sharply critical of the government's relations with the OHL and adopted a series of resolutions, the so-called Hamburg Points, designed to curb the autonomy of the officer corps and enlarge the scope of activities of the soldiers' councils. The congress endorsed the collective-bargaining agreement negotiated earlier by the ZAG, but the delegates also voted to appoint a Socialization Commission and charged it with investigating the feasibility of nationalizing major sectors of the Germany economy.

Nevertheless, the congress' decision on the election date destroyed the basis of the tactical partnership between the USPD and the SPD. The Independent members of the provisional government resigned at the end of the year; they were replaced by three new SPD leaders, including Gustav Noske. But the left-wing socialists still faced a basic dilemma. Should they accept defeat and attempt to argue their case during the deliberations of the constitutional convention, or should they attempt to propel the revolution forward? Most of the USPD decided on the former course of action, but some of the party's more radical elements were determined to stage a "second revolution."

On December 30, 1918 the founding convention of the German Communist Party (*Kommunistische Partei Deutschlands,* KPD) met in Berlin. With the creation of the KPD the Spartacus League severed its ties to the USPD. Against the advice of Rosa Luxemburg and Karl Liebknecht a majority of the delegates voted to boycott the national elections and to join the Revolutionary Shop Stewards in staging a Bolshevik-style revolution instead. "Spartacus Week," as the radicals' uprising from January 5–12 came to be known, was both a misnomer and a pitiful and amateurish attempt at a revolution. Most of the action took place in Berlin, where some one thousand armed men, led by an unwieldy executive committee of fifty-three, attempted to overthrow the CPP. They had no chance of success. The uprising was quickly and bloodily put down by regular army troops and government-paid volunteer vigilante groups—all under the command of Gustav Noske. (The vigilante groups, the so-called *Freikorps,* were to play a major role in the counterrevolutionary uprisings of the early 1920s; they will be discussed in more detail later, pp. 147–50.) The only legacies of the "second revolution" were the imprinting of a lasting fear of "Marxism" among the German middle classes, and the growing embittered relations between the Majority Socialists and their former comrades, largely due to the brutality of the *Freikorps* units: One of the vigilante groups murdered Luxemburg and Liebknecht.

THE WEIMAR CONSTITUTION

The elections of delegates to the constitutional conventions (in addition to the national constitutional convention many of the states, including Prussia, also held state assemblies) were held under rules determined by the CPP. They provided for equal and universal suffrage for all Germans twenty years or older; for the first time women as well as men had the right to vote.

The introduction of a truly democratic voting system meant that no political party could rely on the effects of the Prussian three-class system of voting to assure it a disproportionate share of political power. The bourgeois parties especially hastened to present a new image as parties of the people. In fact, the word "people" itself (in German, *Volk*) suddenly became part of most middle-class party labels.

Democracy confronted the conservatives with particularly difficult challenges. Their role as an oligarchic leadership group had come to an abrupt end. The conservatives met the new challenge boldly. In November 1918 the three wings of the prewar movement, the German Conservatives, the Free Conservatives, and what was left of Stöcker's Christian Socialists, along with some smaller groups, formed a new organization, the German National People's Party (*Deutschnationale Volkspartei,* DNVP). While the new party continued to be led by the old conservative notables, it attempted to broaden its voting appeal to include white-collar workers, professionals, and businessmen. The party also expanded its geographic base to all sections of the country, although it remained strongest in Protestant north German areas.

In 1919, the DNVP presented an image of progressive conservatism to the voters. The party stood for the traditional bourgeois values of free enterprise, protection of private property, and Christian ethics. It rejected all experiments of "Marxist collectivism." Temporarily, the party muted its traditional anti-Semitism. But the DNVP's openness to the new times did not last long. Within a year the party was denouncing the Republic, democracy, parliamentarism, and Jews, while demanding a return to the rule of the Hohenzollerns.

The National Liberals emerged after the upheavals of 1918–1919 as the German People's Party (*Deutsche Volkspartei,* DVP). In

January 1919, however, the party was only a shadow of its former self. In most areas of Germany it had no real organization, and the membership was reduced to a few followers of the party's new chairman, Gustav Stresemann. As a result, the DVP faced a difficult campaign in the election of 1919, particularly since it was hard to distinguish the DVP from the DNVP. The new party's voting appeal was directed primarily toward the urban upper and middle classes. The DVP had particularly strong support among industrialists and business executives.

The DVP made a striking comeback in 1920. Middle-class voters, disappointed by the ineffectiveness of the progressives and the DNVP's support for the counterrevolutionary upheavals of March 1920 (see the discussion on pp. 149–50), turned instead to Stresemann's party. Unlike the conservatives, who refused to become reconciled to the republican form of government, the DVP leaders, including especially Stresemann himself, adopted a middle-of-the-road stance. They became *Vernunftrepublikaner.* By this they meant that while in their hearts they remained monarchists, for the foreseeable future political reason dictated that the Republic would have to be accepted as Germany's legitimate constitutional form.

For a brief span the old Progressives were the largest bourgeois party. The Progressives were the only group that incorporated their support of democracy into their new name; they became the German Democratic Party (Deutsche Demokratische Partei, DDP). Initially, the party was supported by virtually all of the old Progressives and most National Liberals. The Democrats appealed to a wide cross section of middle-class Germans, from industrialists and professionals to white-collar workers and farmers. The party was particularly attractive to liberal intellectuals. During the 1919 campaign the DDP portrayed itself as the party that could gain the trust of the SPD, while at the same time holding the radical tendencies of the SPD in check.

The DDP's political glory vanished as quickly as it came. The party was unable to assimilate its early massive voting support into an effective organization. The death of the party's venerated leader, Friedrich Naumann, in 1919 left it without either direction or a coherent program. After the spring of 1919 large numbers of disappointed voters and members deserted the DDP and turned to the DVP instead.

The Center Party had the fewest adjustments to make. It toyed briefly with a new name (in 1919 the party campaigned as the Christian People's Party [*Christliche Volkspartei*]), but the Catholic party quickly abandoned such efforts to be fashionable and reverted to its old name of Center Party. The party remained primarily a Catholic interest group, but its prewar leadership group of right-wing Catholics made way for men from the populist, left-wing faction of the party. The new leaders readily accepted democracy as the basis of Germany's constitutional system. They also emphasized the party's concern for industrial workers and improved social welfare programs. At the same time, the party did not neglect its concern for safeguarding Catholic interests, especially in the fields of public education and civil service appointments.

The dispute over war credits and other issues had shattered the already fragile unity of German Social Democracy. Until 1922 three separate and largely antagonistic socialist organizations competed for the votes of the German industrial proletariat. All three professed to be guided by Marxist ideology as a blueprint for transforming present-day capitalism into future socialism. The Majority Socialists remained the largest of the three Marxist parties. The SPD was dominated by right-wing leaders who saw the establishment of political democracy as the necessary (and sufficient) instrument for protecting the interests of Germany's industrial workers. The party remained equivocal about the future of the workers' and soldiers' councils. The SPD was willing to accord them a role as spokesmen for the workers' economic interests, but it rejected their institutionalization as a legislative or executive bodies.

The Independents, the USPD, regarded the SPD's vision of the road to socialism and genuine democracy solely through the ballot box as naive and contrary to Marxist principles. There was certainly something to this criticism, and in recent years the USPD's position has received much praise from historians. Even in 1919 and 1920 the Independents' vision of a "third way," avoiding the mistakes of the Majority Socialists and the brutality of the Bolsheviks, had considerable appeal. The USPD argued that as long as the capitalists controlled the "commanding heights" of the economy and public administration, the socialists' domination of the political institutions was meaningless. For this reason, these left-wing Social Democrats wanted to retain the workers' and soldiers' councils as vehicles of proletarian control to implement the structural changes in German society necessary to transform it from capitalism to socialism.

In the second half of 1919 and the first months of 1920 it appeared that many German workers shared the USPD's vision of proletarian democracy. The USPD experienced a veritable explosion of members and votes in the wake of the counterrevolutionary activities that culminated in the Kapp putsch of 1920 (see the discussion on pp. 149–52). Unfortunately for the party it was the illusionary glow of health in a political organism already in the process of disintegration. In October 1920 the party split over the question of affiliation with the Russian-dominated Communist (Third) International (Comintern). Most of the Independent leaders did not favor affiliation with the Comintern, but the bulk of the membership left the USPD and joined the Communist Party, the KPD. The remnant of the USPD eventually rejoined the SPD in 1922.

The Communist Party was the most radical of the three Marxist groups. The Communists were committed to Marxism-Leninism in that they regarded the Bolshevik revolution in Russia (and the Bolshevik par-

ty's role in these events) as the basic model for future proletarian revolutions. They resolutely rejected democracy in its bourgeois sense (one delegate at the KPD's founding convention noted "ten proletarian fists are worth ten thousand votes"), and proclaimed the need for the dictatorship of the proletariat, exercised through the KPD as the vanguard of the proletariat. The KPD remained a largely sectarian splinter group until the fall of 1920 when the disintegration of the USPD enabled it to become a genuine mass party.

The national elections of January 19, 1919, showed continuity of a trend that had been apparent before the war: the growing strength of the reformist groups. Voter participation was again high; 85 percent in the last Reichstag election in 1912, 83 percent in 1919. The share of the Social Democrats' vote rose from 34.8 percent in 1912, to 45 percent in 1919 (37.9 percent for the SPD, 7.6 percent for the USPD). The KPD, of course, did not run.) The DDP became the strongest bourgeois party. The Democrats (formerly Progressives) obtained 18.5 percent in 1919, compared to the Progressives' 7.7 percent in 1912. The Center Party, benefitting from increased voter participation among Catholics, also increased its popular vote somewhat, from 16.4 percent in 1912 to 19.7 percent in 1919. The National Liberals in the guise of the DVP obtained a mere 4.4 percent of the popular vote. Finally, it appeared that the conservatives' strength had reached an irreducible nucleus even before the war. The combined popular vote of the conservative parties in 1912 had been 9.2 percent; in 1919, despite the DNVP's reorganizing efforts, it remained almost steady, 10.3 percent. The most striking result of the election of 1919, then, was the vote of confidence given the reformist parties. The SPD, Center Party, and DDP together received 76 percent of the popular vote in 1919, a figure substantially higher than the 58.9 percent they had obtained in 1912.

The National Assembly (*Nationalversa-*

mmlung) that was to write Germany's new constitution met not in Berlin, but in Weimar, an inconspicuous but famous town in the state of Thuringia. The reason was partly symbolic: In the eighteenth and nineteenth centuries Weimar had been the residence of Germany's greatest poet, Johann Wolfgang von Goethe. In addition, Berlin was still experiencing some aftershocks of the "Spartacus Week," and it was felt that the delegates' physical safety might be endangered in the capital.

The National Assembly had a dual function. It was both a provisional Reich legislature and a constitutional convention. One of its first decisions was to legitimize the political changes that had occurred since November and to replace the makeshift CPP and what remained of the workers' and soldiers' councils with a Reich president and a national cabinet. Friedrich Ebert was overwhelmingly elected president by the Assembly, while the Majority Socialist Phillip Scheidemann became chancellor of a coalition cabinet composed of ministers from the SPD, the Center Party, and the DDP.

But the National Assembly's main task, clearly, was to write a new constitution. Two issues in particular aroused long and passionate debates. One was the nature of the Reich's future political structure, the other concerned revisions in Germany's federal structure. In December 1918 the CPP had asked Hugo Preuss, a distinguished scholar of constitutional law and a member of the DDP, to write a draft constitution for presentation to the constitutional convention. There was no doubt about Preuss' position on the two basic questions. His draft envisioned a full-scale parliamentary democracy, modeled upon those of France and Great Britain. Universal suffrage and proportional representation provided for a national parliament that was fully reflective of public opinion. The executive was subject to control by the popularly elected Reichstag; the Reich cabinet served only as long as it had the confidence of the national parliament. The National Assembly ac-

cepted this part of Preuss' draft constitution. The second chamber of the national legislature, the *Reichsrat*, was not popularly elected. As was true before 1919 its delegates were appointed by the state governments.

In later years, the Weimar constitution would be much criticized for the peculiar position which it accorded the Reich president. Preuss had in mind an essentially ceremonial figure, who would stand above party strife and be representative of all the people. For this reason he proposed a popularly elected president. The president's seven-year term was designed to ensure that he was in office longer than the members of the Reichstag, who had to be elected every four years. Preuss' draft limited the president's powers to little more than nominating the Reich chancellor, but the National Assembly went beyond this and wrote article 48 into the constitution. This gave the president the right to declare an emergency and govern the Reich or a *Land* for a limited time without parliamentary approval. The delegates to the national assembly had the "Spartacus Week" upheavals of 1918–1919 in mind when they included article 48 in the constitution, but in later years the posers of this article would be used to undermine the very democratic system it was meant to strengthen.

Preuss' draft also proposed far-reaching revisions of Germany's federal structure. To strengthen the powers of the federal government he proposed the division of the Prussian super state into a number of separate *Länder*. The delegates in the convention proved unsympathetic toward Preuss' ideas on federalism. Prussia remained intact. In fact, with the exception of merging three former miniprincipalities in central Germany into the state of Thuringia, there were no significant territorial changes among the German states during the fifteen-year span of the Weimar Republic.

The balance of power between the federal government and the states did, however, shift in favor of the Reich. The new constitution transferred control of the armed forces, the *Reichswehr*, to the national government and expanded the role of the federal judiciary. Above all, the Reich was no longer dependent upon the states to finance the federal government's day-to-day operations. Under the guidance of Matthias Erzberger, the minister of finance in the Scheidemann cabinet, the National Assembly voted to reverse the prewar pattern of revenue allocations. Most direct taxes, including personal and corporate income taxes, were now earmarked for the federal government, while the states were left with property taxes and some indirect sources of revenue. Erzberger's reforms reversed the system of the states' supporting the Reich through the *Matrikularbeiträge* (see an earlier discussion, p. 80–81). Under the Weimar constitution the federal government returned a portion of the income tax collected to the *Länder*.

The Weimar constitution reflected the thinking of the reformist forces in Wilhelminian Germany. It was not a revolutionary document. Instead, given the self-imposed limitations of Wilhelminian reformism, the Weimar constitution provided something for everyone. The right-wing of the SPD had long demanded a fully democratic voting system, and this goal was realized in the constitution's provisions for proportional representation. The Democrats were pleased by the constitution's strong emphasis upon parliamentary control of the executive and the safeguards for civil rights and private property. Finally, the Catholics were able to write provisions into the document that ensured a continued institutional role for the Catholic Church in public life and the de facto maintenance of parochial schools.

At the same time, adoption of the constitution also marked the beginnings of future conflicts. Like the Bismarck constitution of 1871 the document written by the National Assembly did not create a national political consensus. True, the Weimar constitution had the support of three out of

four German voters in 1919, but the remaining one-fourth, the political "outs," composed of the new and old Right, the National Liberals, the left-wing Socialists, and the Communists, objected not only to specific provisions of the constitution, but refused to acknowledge the validity of the work of Weimar.

The seemingly unbridgeable gap between the new "ins" and "outs" occasioned some bitter debates during the convention over what were essentially symbolic issues. The one arousing perhaps the most deepseated emotions was the choice of national colors. The conservatives favored retaining the old imperial colors of black, white, and red to symbolize Germany's past.glories, but for the Socialists, Democrats, and parts of the Center Party black, white, and red stood for the rule of Prussian authoritarianism. They voted for black, red, and gold, the colors of national and political liberation during the Revolution of 1848. The radical Left rejected both and proclaimed their allegiance to the red flag of socialism. The National Assembly eventually adopted black, red, and gold as the Republic's colors (with significant exceptions for shipping and the army), but the flag controversy was to mar Germany's political life throughout the Weimar years. The Republican forces tried valiantly to popularize the new colors, but the political Right disdained the national colors as "black, red, and yellow" and continued to march behind the old imperial flag.

The flag issue was symptomatic of the Republic's deeper problem of alienation. Almost from the moment of its founding some important groups in society identified the new regime with the loss of their privileged status and the end of the empire's glory. The segments included the officer corps, high-ranking civil servants, industrialists, members of the judiciary, and many among the educated middle classes, the *Bildungsbürgertum*. In what in retrospect turned out to have been a grave mistake, the political leaders of the Republic for the most part left the "rejectionists" in positions of influence. It was thought that the old officials and leaders would serve the new regime as loyally as they had the old, and would in time, become sincere Republicans as well. That decision contained a twofold error. During the next few years the old guard, with some laudable exceptions, did not rally to the Republic, but used its control of key positions to undermine the new order. The regime's failure to remove these opponents of democracy from power in turn created a second alienation problem: The Republic quickly lost much of the support of the forces on the Left who had been instrumental in overthrowing the authoritarianism of the empire.

THE TREATY OF VERSAILLES

One of the decisions facing the National Assembly was to accept or reject the terms of peace which the Allies presented to the Germans in May 1919. The debate not only polarized German public opinion, but also left a bitter legacy for the subsequent discussions of the new democratic constitution. The peace treaty between Germany and the victorious "Allied and Associated Powers" has become known as the Treaty of Versailles, from the place of its eventual signing, the Hall of Mirrors at the Palace of Versailles. The Allies' choice of locale was deliberate: The German Empire was to suffer its final humiliation in the same chamber in which it had celebrated its initial triumph in 1871. As was the case for the earlier Treaty of Brest-Litovsk, which the Germans and Austrians had imposed on the Russians, the Treaty of Versailles was a one-sided pact; it embodied the victors' visions of a new balance of power in Europe and the world.

The final terms were negotiated among the leaders of the major Allied nations, principally David Lloyd George for Great Britain, Georges Clemenceau for France, and Woodrow Wilson for the United States, rather than between the Allies and their former enemy. President Wilson returned to America in February 1919 and thereafter most of the work was done by Clemenceau and Lloyd George and their aides. In May, the finished draft was handed to the Germans for their comments. The Scheidemann government drafted a lengthy reply, objecting to almost every paragraph in the document, but the Allies rejected virtually all of the Germans' counterproposals, leaving the Reich government in June with only two choices: to accept the Allied terms or reject them and risk the beginning of a new war.

We should note the sense of naivité about the peace-making process that permeated virtually all sections of German public and governmental opinion. When the draft treaty was handed to the Reich government a feeling of shock, even betrayal, over the presumed severity of the terms was widespread and genuine. The conservatives and their allies suddenly recalled that Germany's armies had been "victorious" until they were "stabbed in the back" by the Revolution of 1918. The conservative spokesmen no longer remembered that it was the OHL which had acknowledged military defeat and forced Germany to the peace negotiations. The Germans expected far more generous terms than they received (or had given at Brest-Litovsk). The illusion was largely based upon the mistaken belief that the Allies would treat a democratic Germany more leniently than one still ruled by the Junkers and their associates. Germany's enemies, however, took a different view. Quite aside from the fact that some of the men prominent in the Republican government had until recently been staunch supporters of Germany's maximal war aims, the basic purpose of the treaty as far as the Allies were concerned was unrelated to the change of regimes in Germany. The Allies' avowed goal was to effect a change in the global balance of power that would prevent further aggression on the part of Germany, assure the payment of sufficient reparations from the Reich (and her partners in the war) to help the Allies' recoup their wartime expenses, and inaugurate a new sense of morality and justice in the conduct of international relations.

Chancellor Scheidemann spoke for the nation when he originally rejected the treaty with words that were to haunt him for the rest of his career, "What hand would not wither when it signed such a treaty?" Otto Braun, the Social Democratic prime minister of Prussia, had visions of resuming military resistance form the state's East Elbian redoubt, much as Prussia had done after her defeat by Napoleon a hundred years earlier, but such political grandstand plays were completely unrealistic. As the government learned from Germany's military leaders, the Reich did not have any military resources with which to resist an Allied invasion and consequently no choice but to accept the treaty.

Even so, the disagreements over whether to accept or reject the peace treaty led to the young Republic's first cabinet crisis. The DDP, hopelessly deadlocked on the issue, dropped out of the government, and Scheidemann resigned as chancellor. The new cabinet was a coalition of SPD and Center Party ministers, headed by Gustav Bauer, a Social Democratic union leader. Eventually a majority of the National Assembly voted for acceptance, but the margin for approval was narrow and the sense of outrage and bitterness pervasive throughout the house.

In the Treaty of Versailles the goal of changing Germany's role in the European balance of power was implemented primarily by reducing the Reich's territory and population, and by placing restrictions on her military strength. Germany lost about one-tenth of her prewar territory and population. In the case of many, though by no means all, of the territorial changes mandated by the treaty, the inhabitants of the areas in question were asked to vote whether they wanted to remain in the Reich or become citizens of a neighboring state. Most of the German territorial losses involved

areas in the east that had mixed or predominantly Polish populations. Parts of the former Prussian provinces east of the Oder were incorporated into the newly established Republic of Poland. Other boundary changes involved the loss of Alsace-Lorraine to France and smaller transfers of territory and populations to Denmark and Belgium. Although the territorial changes were often in accord with the wishes of the inhabitants, the new boundaries did at times create an odd patchwork of overlapping jurisdictions. The Province of East Prussia, for example, which had voted to remain German, was physically separated from the rest of the Reich by a large strip of Poland, the so-called Polish Corridor.

Ostensibly as a prelude to worldwide disarmament, but actually to reduce Germany's military power, the treaty put severe limitations on the size and quality of Germany's military establishment. The German army was to be reduced to a force of 100,000 men. (The prewar strength had been 750,000.) In addition, the Reich was forbidden to continue universal military service, build military airplanes or submarines, maintain naval ships larger than 10,000 tons, or possess offensive land weapons. Essentially, the military sections of the Treaty of Versailles were designed to give Germany an army that was no match for Allied forces, although it would be sufficiently strong to maintain order at home. The treaty also provided for Allied troops to remain in occupation of the left bank of the Rhine for fifteen years.

The economic provisions of the treaty were to become the most controversial part of the pact. The Allies wanted Germany to reimburse them for at least part of the staggering sum of 632 billion marks that the war is estimated to have cost them. To this end, they forced Germany to acknowledge the principle of reparations. The treaty did not actually specify a sum. Rather, in agreement to the terms of peace the Reich agreed to sign a promissory note for an as yet unspecified amount. Other economic

Germany After W.W. I

provisions were designed to give Allied businesses a competitive advantage over the Germans. The Reich, for example, could not impose tariffs on imports from the Allied countries until 1925. But there were also forms of petty harassment, such as prohibition of labeling German sparkling wines "champagne."

The most innovative feature of the Treaty of Versailles and its companion pacts with Germany's wartime partners was the strong emphasis on morality in the future conduct of international relations. The guiding spirit here was Woodrow Wilson. He hoped that the principle of self-determination would eliminate many of the nationality conflicts that had led to war in Europe in the past. As a corollary, the American president also insisted that the concept of the League of Nations, which he envisioned as a sort of permanent international parliament, be made an integral part of the peace treaties.

There is no doubt that the emphasis on morality in international affairs redressed a number of ancient wrongs. The implementation of the concept of self-determination made possible the reestablishment of an independent Poland after two hundred years of partition as well as the creation of Czechoslovakia and the union of the South Slav peoples in the state of Yugoslavia. Unfortunately, in practice the proclaimed ethical values in the Treaty of Versailles at times also bore a marked similarity to the old power politics. Strategic considerations dictated that the principle of self-determination be set aside in the case of Austria. The German-speaking population of the former Habsburg Empire voted to join the new German Republic, but the plebiscite was ignored by the Allies since they felt Germany's expansion in southeastern Europe would threaten the newly independent states in that region. From the German perspective even the League of Nations was part of the victors' alliance; the Reich did not become a member until 1926. (The United States never joined the League, but here the reason was self-imposed isolation, not ostracism.)

In German eyes the attempt to link the treaty's economic provisions with the Allies' professed concern for ethics in international relations seemed particularly hypocritical. The economic sections of the Treaty of Versailles were preceded by a short sentence that was to dominate discussion of the treaty throughout the 1920s: article 231. In this paragraph Germany recognized the Allies' moral right to impose reparations because the Reich had been solely responsible for unleashing World War I. Article 231 was the "war-guilt clause."

Since 1919 the Treaty of Versailles has had a curious historiography. The debate over the justification for article 231 began almost immediately after the Germans had grudgingly signed the treaty in June 1919

and eventually produced a sizable literary industry. Many German but also a number of other scholars wrote "revisionist" histories, arguing that the Reich and its partners were not solely responsible for the outbreak of the war. The publication of John Maynard Keynes' *The Economic Consequences of the Peace* in 1919 severely criticized the economic terms of the treaty. The British economist contended that by subjecting Germany to excessive hardships, the peace terms had destroyed the bases of prewar European prosperity. The Great Depression of the 1930s and the rise of Hitler seemed for a time to provide additional evidence for this argument. However, the disastrous consequences of appeasing Hitler and the experience of World War II did much to discredit the earlier revisionists. During the 1970s the treaty debate was rekindled by a new generation of scholars. Following Fritz Fischer this group of "re-revisionists" argued that there was an organic link between Hitler's and the OHL's war aims. Others took up this theme and contended that the Treaty of Versailles did not impose impossible terms. These scholars claimed that the Reich's insistence that Germany could not meet her financial obligations was a smokescreen invented by political leaders who became quite ingenious in using a variety of subterfuges to escape honoring the Reich's treaty obligations. The real victors of World War I in this view were not France and Great Britain, but Hitler and the Nazis. The Allies' leniency made possible the later rise of totalitarianism.

A balanced assessment of the Treaty of Versailles is difficult without agreement on the terms on which the issue ought to be discussed. On the one hand, it is true that the treaty failed to change permanently the balance of power in Europe; Germany rose again. On the other hand, the treaty provisions by not smoothing the path of the democratic Republic into the family of nations, indirectly aided the rise of its enemies. As far as the long-standing argument over the severity of the reparations is concerned, it is impossible to extract this issue from its political implications. There is no doubt that Germany had the ability to pay the sums demanded of her. But there were two difficulties. Politically, it was impossible for a succession of Reich governments to impose the additional burden of the reparations upon a country already suffering from severe problems of postwar economic readjustment. In addition, most Germans, including many well-meaning Republican leaders, were convinced that the primary object of the reparations was not to make Germany pay, but to ruin the Reich's economy as a prelude to destroying Germany's political and territorial integrity. As long as this (as it turned out, mistaken) view persisted, Germany would attempt to evade the peace terms imposed upon her.

ECONOMIC AND SOCIAL PROBLEMS

Four years of war had severely disrupted Germany's social fabric and left the economy with a host of short-term and long-term problems. Even a casual observer could not help but notice the evidence of malnutrition, run-down transportation and production facilities, and the general decline in public morality. Nor did the signing of the armistice end shortages and black market activities. For some weeks after the fighting had stopped, the Allies continued the blockade while they and the Germans argued over the Reich's ability to pay for needed imports in gold or hard currency. The blockade deadlock was eventually resolved, but the terms of the armistice themselves compounded Germany's economic difficulties. The Reich had to agree to turn over to the Allies significant stocks of trucks, production machinery, and railroad rolling stock in order to aid in the recovery of the devastated areas of France and Belgium. Similarly, much of Germany's shipping tonnage was transferred to Great Britain.

But by no means could all of Germany's

problems be blamed on the Allies. The end of the war brought a new sense of militancy to the workers of the country. Segments that had not benefited from the war economy wanted to catch up. Railroad workers, whose already low standard of living had rapidly eroded during the war, turned especially militant. Recognizing their strong bargaining position, the railroad workers and other groups of employees in the public sector staged a wave of authorized and wildcat strikes in the winter of 1918–1919 in order to press for immediate wage hikes.

However justified, higher wages also compounded the problem of inflation. Despite the later claims of the political Right, the revolution did not cause Germany's inflation. The erosion of currency values was common to all of the belligerents, but the problem was particularly acute in Germany. The imperial government had decided to finance the war almost entirely with credits. By the end of the war the German mark had lost roughly half of its prewar value. From a value of 4.2 to the dollar in July 1914 it fell to 8.9 in January 1919 on the international money markets. In 1918 the interest on the national debt was higher than the whole federal budget had been in 1913. In the long run, the erosion of the mark would reduce the value of savings and pensions, but for the moment most Germans felt the result primarily in the increased costs of imports and higher outlays for social services. To be sure, in a fully functioning international economy higher prices for imports would be offset by a competitive advantage for German exports, but for some years after the end of hostilities normal patterns of international trade were disrupted. In the meantime, the country had spent increasingly large sums to pay for imports of raw materials and agricultural goods and to meet the demands for higher wages and veterans' benefits.

The problems of the German economy were real, but much of the discussion about what caused them was not. The Reich's postwar decision makers tended to ignore the effects of long-term structural changes and their own misguided policies as reasons for Germany's difficulties. Instead, they blamed the effects on the peace treaty. It is true that Germany lost 13 percent of her prewar land area in Europe, 10 percent of her population, and that the Reich was stripped of all of her colonies—but most of the lost lands were located in the poorer agricultural areas of East Elbia, which had been regions of chronic economic difficulties for years. Similarly, the population losses for the most part involved unskilled farm labor rather than skilled industrial workers. Setting aside emotional and nationalistic arguments, the Allies had inadvertently enabled the Germans to write off some of their prewar problems. This was especially true of the overseas possessions. All of the chauvinistic hand-wringing about the loss of the colonies could not hide the fact that before the war the administration of the colonies had required constant subsidies from the Reich budget. In economic terms, the most serious effects of the peace treaty were the loss of 75 percent of Germany's prewar iron ore reserves and significant portion of her coal mining capacity in the areas of Silesia, Alsace-Lorraine, and the Saar.

While Germany's economic and political leaders heaped scorn upon the Treaty of Versailles, they cast a blind eye upon a number of economic and social harbingers of change that were largely unrelated to the peace terms. War and revolution had caused tremendous shifts in the relative wealth and status of various groups in the society. By 1918 segments that had enjoyed high status and relatively secure economic positions in 1914—such as officers, high-level civil servants, teachers, professionals, urban landlords, and pensioners—suffered hardships, while other groups benefited. Among the latter were some categories of blue- and white-collar workers and many large-scale industrialists. Under the provisions of the ZAG (see the earlier discussion on p. 128) most industrial workers and white-collar

technical and clerical employees, the so-called new *Mittelstand*, were now covered by a blanket collective bargaining agreement that provided for increased wages, preferential rehiring of veterans, and the realization of such long-term demands as the eight-hour day. In addition, the ZAG, the Weimar constitution, and eventually a National Law on Industrial Councils of February 1920 enlarged the scope of workers' participation in managerial decisions. Through elected industrial councils, which were required in all firms employing twenty or more persons, blue- and white-collar workers, through their union representatives, had a voice in decisions affecting safety and efficiency in the production process, as well as hiring, firing, and wage determinations. At least on paper German businessmen had lost some of their traditional rights as "lords of the manor."

At the same time, there were reciprocal benefits for the industrialists. We have already seen that the ZAG itself blocked any large-scale government intervention in the economy. The trend toward private cartel and trust agreements continued unabated; the lack of real competition in turn enabled the industrialists simply to pass on increased labor costs in the form of higher prices. Many industrialists were also not overly concerned about inflation. The devalued mark enabled them to pay off prewar debts at a fraction of their original cost; the larger enterprises in particular often had hard currency deposits outside of Germany, enabling them to avoid paying for imports of raw materials in marks.

For farmers and urban landlords war and revolution presented a mixed picture. Initially, large-scale farmers and house owners benefited from the effects of the inflation. For the first time in several generations most East Elbian estates and many apartment houses were debt free, their mortgages wiped out by inflation. This happy state of affairs did not last long, and in any case both groups still felt they had reason to complain. Farmers and landlords bitterly resented what they saw as unfair government measures to benefit urban consumers. Farmers rejected price controls on farm products; landlords railed against rent controls.

Changes in relative social standing did not alter the fact that the economy as a whole was experiencing severe difficulties. Industrial production, to take the most important indicator, had declined from an index figure of 98 in 1913 to 56 in 1918 and 37 in 1919. Business, labor and politicians all agreed that something needed to be done. The obvious answer to the problem was the successful transition to a peacetime economy and the restoration of the international economic order. There was also widespread agreement that massive infusions of investment capital were needed to rebuild the economic infrastructure. Creating a favorable climate to attract capital from German and foreign investors would require currency stability, and that in turn meant curbing the inflation and providing for political stability. Finally, in some sectors of the economy structural reforms were long overdue. The continuing growth of trusts and cartels, especially in heavy industry, decreased competition and innovation and led to inflated prices for consumers. In the farm sector, despite the momentary lifting of the debt burden, East Elbian agriculture was no more efficient after the war than it had been earlier.

Identifying the milestones on the road to recovery proved considerably easier than overcoming the practical and political obstacles that stood in the way. In fact, a number of politically astute decisions had economically counterproductive consequences. Guaranteeing veterans an immediate return to their old jobs defused a potentially volatile social problem, but it also saddled employers with unneeded labor and precluded necessary geographic and occupational shifts in the workforce. Similar objections could be raised against some of the immediate postwar wage settlements. The increased wage scales for public sector

employees, such as railroad workers, inflated government budgets at a time when they were already out of control. Until the fiscal year 1925 government budgets at all levels—federal, state, and local—showed annual and growing deficits. Chronic budget deficits in turn had an adverse effect on the German economy's ability to raise investment capital. Government borrowing not only competed for investment money along with the private sector, but the deficits fueled the inflation, which led to further political unrest and subsequent discouragement especially of foreign investment.

The Germans attempted to address their immediate postwar dilemma in two ways. One stood the test of time, although it had little immediate impact; the other had only disastrous short- and long-term consequences. The solution with long-term benefits involved a new revenue system: The National Assembly adopted a much needed restructuring of the Reich's system of taxation and revenue allocation. The National Finance Act of 1919, by shifting the bulk of taxation from property and consumer revenues to personal and corporate income taxes, created a more rational and less regressive system of taxation. Unfortunately, these changes in the tax structure did not significantly increase the amount of revenue gleaned from an impoverished country. Recognizing the desperate need for capital, the Reichsbank, the German equivalent of the Federal Reserve System, made what in retrospect was a disastrous move: It printed money in the hope that the economic recovery would mitigate the obviously inflationary consequences of this decision. Indeed, the bank authorized the printing of a great deal of money. In the period 1919 through 1921 the money in circulation increased each year by 50 percent over the previous year.

For reasons that were numerous and complex, economic recovery did not materialize. Certainly, Germany's political instability (see the discussion on p. 149) was a major factor. In addition, it proved difficult to restore the traditional trade patterns. Some partners and competitors, like the United States, had benefited from the wartime absence of the Germans on the international markets. Quite generally, Germany's trading partners protected their home markets with tariff legislation, and the Reich inadvertently encouraged such retaliation by shortsightedly engaging in large-scale dumping practices. The low value of the mark, of course, made German exports relatively cheap, but this advantage was more than offset by the rapidly rising cost of raw materials and foodstuffs upon which the German economy remained heavily dependent. The country's economic difficulties can be readily gauged by the mark's declining value relative to the dollar, the strongest postwar currency: From January 1919 to January 1922, the value of the mark fell from 8.9 to the dollar to 191.8.

The Germans certainly recognized the problem, but until the fall of 1923 they also largely ignored it. The primary reason was the ready availability of a scapegoat for inflation and economic difficulties: reparations. This aspect of the Versailles settlement turned out to be far more complex than it had appeared. Basically, the Allies intended the reparations imposed on Germany to be simple financial transactions to compensate the victors for some of their wartime expenses in the form of cash and goods. In practice, things were considerably more complicated. To begin with, there was disagreement among the Allies on which losses the payments should cover. They agreed that Germany should pay for the recovery of the areas in Belgium and France that had been devastated by war, and compensate the British for the loss of freighters sunk by submarines. Such a view of reparations was a fairly narrow and traditional one. But there were also those in the Allied countries who argued that reparations should encompass a much wider scope. Germany, for example, should be responsible for underwriting the pensions of Allied war veterans.

Then there was the question of the link between the German reparations and the inter-Allied war debt problem. The latter issue in turn had two major dimensions. Before and during the war France (and to a lesser extent Great Britain) had made large loans to czarist Russia. When the bolsheviks came to power these sums became bad debts; the new Russian government refused to accept responsibility for them. While the European Allies had loaned money to Russia, they had in turn borrowed heavily from the United States. The American government and banks insisted that these loans would have to be repaid with interest. The European Allies, however, found themselves in a difficult position. With the Russian loans lost, the German reparations remained the only readily accessible source of assets to generate both recovery in the Allied countries and enable them to meet their obligations to America. Incidentally, this was one reason the Allies pressed for German cash payments, while the Reich, anxious to keep its reserves of hard currency, preferred larger percentages of payments in kind.

In April 1921 the Allies presented Germany with a reparations bill of 132 billion gold marks (31.4 billion dollars) to be paid over a number of years in the form of both money and goods. The initial German reaction was to reject this sum as far too high and patently unjust. After another government crisis and the occupation by French troops of the city of Duisburg, however, the Reich government agreed to yield to the Allied dictum.

That decision began a no-win tug of war that lasted for the next two and one-half years and brought German society to the brink of disintegration. There was almost universal agreement among German labor, business, and government leaders that Germany's gross national product was simply not large enough to bear additional obligations of 132 billion gold marks. Moreover, the reparations bill itself accelerated the inflation rapidly out of control; in June 1922 the dollar stood at 350 marks, in October it had risen to 4,500.

The Allies, however, were less than sympathetic toward Germany's cries of poverty. There was clear evidence that while the German government might have been poor, the Germans were considerably more wealthy. That is to say, the Allies complained that the German government was something less than forceful in taxing the often sizable assets that remained in private hands. The French in particular suspected that the Germans were husbanding their resources in order to regain their military strength. Allied control teams reported that there seemed to be secret paramilitary groups all over Germany, often trained by regular army officers, with hidden caches of arms. (The Allied officers tended to overlook, however, that much of this activity was directed not against a foreign enemy, but constituted preparations for overthrowing Germany's democratic government.)

Although the Allies presented a united front toward Germany on the reparations issue, they differed on the best approach. Generally speaking, Belgium, France, and Italy formed a hawkish bloc, while Great Britain took a more dovish approach. The reason for England's differentiated attitude was not so much credence in Germany's claims of poverty as concern for the revival of international trade. Increasingly, Great Britain recognized that without German recovery there would be little hope of a return to Europe's prewar prosperity. The Germans, of course, were aware of England's disagreement with the other Allies and tended to harbor quite unrealistic hopes that England would "mediate" the dispute.

The Germans grasped at the British straw at least in part because they had so few other options. True, a few diehard armchair strategists envisioned a scenario in which Germany would simply refuse to honor her reparations obligations, but more responsible leaders recognized that this would have meant the rapid disintegration of the Reich. To demonstrate its earnestness on the reparations issue, the Reich government turned to something called the "fulfillment policy." This strategy was the brainchild of two men: Joseph Wirth, a left-wing Center Party leader who served as Reich chancellor from May 1921 to November 22, and his minister for recovery (and later foreign minister), Walther Rathenau.

The fulfillment policy was not mere subterfuge on the part of Rathenau and Wirth. These leaders were truly convinced that the country did not have the resources to continue reparations payments for any length of time. In his capacity as minister for recovery, Rathenau took the lead in attempts to negotiate a series of agreements with the French that would have converted some of Germany's cash payments into alternative forms of compensation, such as supplying German laborers for construction work in the devastated areas of France. The fulfillment policy was also a deliberate and dangerous gamble. Its supporters hoped an honest and committed effort on the part of the Germans to pay their bills for a time would convince those on the Allied side with a truly open mind that even with the best of intentions the reparations system was not workable.

The fulfillment policy did not succeed. In Germany inflation continued unabated. The mark fell from 4,500 to the dollar in October 1922 to 18,000 in January 1923. In part to escape its diplomatic isolation (see the discussion on p. 154) the Reich concluded a friendship pact with Soviet Russia. The Treaty of Rapallo (April 1922) contained a clause providing for the mutual cancellation of debts. In French eyes this was an attempt on the part of the Germans to set a precedent for escaping the Reich's obligations toward the Allies. Even more disastrous for the continuation of the fulfillment policy was Walther Rathenau's murder in June 1922 by extreme-Right terrorists.

The unequal struggle over reparations came to a head in the Ruhr crisis of 1923. Wirth had been succeeded by Wilhelm

Cuno, a Catholic shipping magnate with close ties to the right wing of the DVP and wide-ranging prewar connections to American and English shipping interests. In December 1922 the Germans were, once again, behind in their reparations payments. (At issue was a shipment of telegraph poles.) The right-of-center French government, headed by a Conservative, Raymond Poincaré, distrusted Germany's intentions and asked the reparations commission, a body consisting of representatives from France, Belgium, Italy, and Great Britain that monitored the reparations schedule, to declare the Reich in default of her treaty obligations. By a vote of three to one (the British representative cast the negative vote) the commission authorized France and Belgium to take punitive action. In early January the two countries moved a contingent of engineers, accompanied by a small military force, into previously unoccupied parts of the Ruhr region to oversee the operations of the coal mines in that area. Ostensibly, their purpose was to ensure that coal earmarked for France and Belgium was actually shipped.

There was something rather tragicomic about the coming test of wills. To begin with, by the time the Allied engineers (the delegation went by the acronym of Micum, *Mission interalliée pour la contrôle des usines et des mines*, Interallied Control Commission for Factories and Mines) arrived on the scene, there was not a great deal to supervise. Anticipating the vote of the reparations commission, the Germans had transferred the records of the German coal syndicate from Essen to Hamburg some days before the French and Belgians moved into the Ruhr. In addition, the Germans were convinced the real aim of the French as to sever the Ruhr area from the Reich and consequently destroy Germany's national unity. As far as Poincaré and the French government were concerned, this was not true and the Germans' misreading of French and Belgian intentions led to what in retrospect turned out to be a disastrous overreaction.

Recognizing the Reich's inability to oppose the Allied moves with military force, the German government resorted to a policy of passive resistance. This meant political and economic leaders in the Ruhr, with the full support of the Reich and Prussian governments, called upon the population of the occupied area to stage what amounted to a general strike. Less coal was mined in the months from January to September than in the first ten days of the year.

While passive resistance inconvenienced the occupiers, their difficulties were minor compared to those the Germans caused for themselves. The Cuno government supported the idle population of Germany's industrial heartland with federal cash grants-in-aid. In effect, passive resistance was financed by authorizing the indiscriminate printing of money. The result was to open the floodgates of uncontrolled inflation. Between early January and November 15, 1923, when inflation was finally brought under control, the German mark in relation to the U.S. dollar fell from an already unprecedented 18,000 to the dollar to an astronomical 4.2 trillion. The social and economic consequences of state-sponsored inflation were enormous and disastrous. Tax collections (and government budgets) became meaningless as money lost its value by the hour. Worse, lifetime savings vanished overnight, while economic life was reduced to barter.

Passive resistance was a game of chicken played with unequal resources and for the highest stakes. The Cuno government gambled that once passive resistance had demonstrated Germany's resolve, the French and Belgians would recognize the failure of their adventure in the Ruhr and reopen negotiations on the reparations question. And even if the French proved stubborn, surely the British would make them see the folly of their ways. Neither scenario came true. The French and Belgians showed no signs of weakening for nine long months, and while the British remained critical of hawkish policies, they were not about to abandon their wartime allies and back the Germans. In the meantime, the German situation was growing desperate. Inflation and the obvious lack of political leadership brought within sight the day in which the country would sink into chaos.

On September 23, the Germans called "chicken." The Cuno cabinet resigned, and a new "grand coalition" Reich government headed by Gustav Stresemann and composed of ministers from the DVP, the DDP, the SPD, and the center party announced the end of passive resistance. Simultaneously the government declared a state of emergency throughout the Reich to deal with the political and economic aftermath of the Reich's diplomatic capitulation.

Stresemann and his minister of finance, Hans Luther (who had no party affiliation), recognized that the end of passive resistance would have to be followed by immediate currency restabilization. Unlike their predecessors they succeeded. Drawing upon ideas that had been floated earlier, the Stresemann cabinet authorized the establishment of a new bank, the *Rentenbank* (Mortgage Bank). The new agency in turn issued certificates of credit (*Rentenmark*) that had the force of money. The certificates were backed by a mortgage on Germany's agricultural and industrial assets, which was assigned to the *Rentenbank*. In a sense, it was a psychological trick, since foreclosure of such a "mortgage" was unrealistic, but, partly because the evils of inflation had become so patently obvious, no one pointed out that the new currency was an emperor without clothes. On November 15, 1923 (ironically, it was the day on which the old marked reached its lowest exchange value of 4.2 trillion to the dollar) the new Rentenmark officially replaced the old mark; it was pegged at the prewar value to the dollar of 4.2.

Four years after the end of the war Germans surveyed the ruins of failed recovery policies. The assessment contained a few grounds for optimism. Problems brought on by the war had been compounded by runaway inflation. Severe social dislocation and further political polarization pursued each other in a vicious cycle of cause and effect. The seeming miracle of restabilizing the currency in the fall of 1923 was at best a first step toward revitalizing an economy that had for almost ten years lived beyond its means.

COUNTERREVOLUTION

The first four years of the Weimar Republic were extraordinarily unstable times, characterized by widespread political violence. A primary cause of the chronic political unrest was the unwillingness of many individuals and groups in the society to accept the new democratic and parliamentary constitutional system. They became part of the "counterrevolutionary" movement that sought to undo the "revolution" of November 1918. It mattered little to them that the upheavals of 1918 hardly deserved the name of revolution. The counterrevolutionaries were rebelling against an imagined present evil in order to restore either a mythical past or bring about a utopian future.

The mentality of counterrevolution had a number of sources. Many in the generation that fought in World War I had a sense that the reality of peace fell short of the promise of war. The conflict destroyed their faith in progress, rationality in human affairs, and the desirability of civilian comfort and security. Intellectuals among them agreed with the conclusion of Eckert von Sydow's book *The Culture of Decadence*, published in 1921, that periods of decadence and turmoil were also eras of heightened creativity.

Metaphysicians, of course, were relatively rare among the counterrevolutionaries. Most joined their ranks for more mundane reasons, although these, too, could be intellectualized. Complaints that the world of individual honor and courage had been replaced by union bosses, war profiteers,

A poster urging passive resistance during the Ruhr crisis. A tough German worker defies French soldiers. The caption reads, "No! You won't subdue me!" *(Source: Anschläge, no. 40.)*

and masses acting through their undisciplined weight of numbers could also be read as resentment, particularly among the ranks of younger officers, that the Republic had failed to provide them with peacetime positions they felt were commensurate with their service and sacrifices to the nation.

Ironically, the Republican government provided the organizational format with which the counterrevolutionaries would attempt to overthrow parliamentary democracy. At the end of 1918 and well into the next year the Republican state and federal cabinets authorized and financed the organization of volunteer military units, so-called *Freikorps* (Freecorps). The *Freikorps* were envisioned as a strictly stop-gap measure to supplement the inadequate regular armed forces in order to deal with the January 1919 "second revolution" and Polish encroachments in the east. The *Freikorps* ranged in size from a few hundred men to eight thousand; the leaders were for the most part junior- and middle-level officers of the old army. Eventually, the combined number of these vigilante forces reached some 280,000 men organized in two hundred *Freikorps*. The fighters were recruited from a quite narrow age and social spectrum. Members of the middle and upper-middle classes predominated, with high school and university students, military cadets, and sons of farmers particularly strongly represented. Blue-collar workers were noticeably underrepresented in the *Freikorps*.

Unfortunately, many members of the volunteer units, and particularly some of the groups' leaders, were not content to limit their political and military activism to short-term emergency service. With varying degrees of sincerity and sophistication a minority among them—their number is estimated to have been about 30,000—came to believe that their experiences in the war and their success in "saving Germany from Bolshevism" had lifted them to a higher stage of consciousness, that of political soldier. The prose writings of *Freikorps* leaders

are often confused, but two leitmotifs are contempt for the civilian pursuits of political compromise, career, and comfort, and calls for action to create, "the future century of other-directed totality," as Ernst von Salomon put it.

Some of these politicized soldiers were attracted to Germany's embryonic version of fascism. Especially in Bavaria a large number of *völkisch* political organizations sprang to life. (Translating the word *völkisch* into English has always represented something of a problem. Literally, it refers to "people" or "folk," but in political terms those who identified themselves as *völkisch* used the term with clear implications of racism and anti-Semitism.) Although one group, the Nazi Party (*Nationalsozialistische Deutsche Arbeiterpartei*—NSDAP), would eventually eclipse its rivals, it was originally only one of some forty *völkisch* counterrevolutionary organizations active in Munich in early 1919. Moreover, there was little to distinguish the various groups from each other. All professed an ideology that was essentially an amalgam of antis: They were all antidemocratic, anti-Marxist, antiparliamentary, and anti-Semitic. The last programmatic feature was a reflection of the fascists' conviction that there was an international Jewish conspiracy that was responsible not only for Germany's defeat in World War I, but also for Germany's own Revolution and all other left-wing revolutions.

The distinct minority of political soldiers among the *Freikorps* and the as yet lunatic fringe fascist groups would not have been strong enough to cast Germany into four years of unending revolutionary turmoil. This became possible only because of the support these elements received from parts of the mainstream conservative political forces and elements of the regular army. Support came in various forms: editorial, organizational, financial, and, especially in the case of the Reichswehr, weapons and training. The sympathizers supported the aims (if not always the means) of the counterrevolutionaries, because they, too, looked

A typical ad for the Freikorps. A Freikorps volunteer is holding back a predatory Polish eagle. The text reads: "Buddy, join [in the fight] against Bolshevism, the Polish danger, and hunger. Enroll immediately in the German Protection Division (31st Infantry Division, Lüttwitz Detachment)." The bottom of the ad bears the inscription, "with the approval of the Reich Minister of Defense Noske." (Source: *Anschläge*, no. 24.)

upon parliamentary democracy as the ruin of Germany. In addition, these circles were also convinced the country lived under the constant threat of a Bolshevik-style revolution.

Ironically, the Communists' own activities gave an air of verisimilitude to these irrational fears. We have already noted the attempt by Spartacus and the Revolutionary Shop Stewards to stage a "second revolution" in January 1919. A few weeks later Bavaria was thrown into turmoil after Kurt Eisner was murdered by a member of the extreme Rightist Thule Society. The eventual results were two Bavarian "soviet republics," one dominated by some anarchists in Munich, and the other by the Communists. The first lasted for a week, the second for two weeks before both were bloodily put down by *Freikorps* and regular army troops, but the brief experience left a lasting impression on many middle-class Bavarians.

The Communist threat did not seem to lessen after 1919. In the spring of 1920 left-wing socialists and Communists organized the "Red Army of the Ruhr." Again, with great cruelty regular army units and *Freikorps* put down the uprising. After the disintegration of the USPD, most Independents joined the Communist party, giving the KPD the status of a formidable mass organization. In the spring of 1921, Communists were responsible for more political violence; the "revolution" was now centered in the central German region of Halle-Merseburg. This time it required only regular Prussian police forces to restore order.

The Ruhr crisis of 1923 seemed to provide the "Bolsheviks" with yet more opportunities. The Communists had gained a political base of operations by joining coalition governments with the SPD in the central German states of Saxony and Thuringia, and the growing economic problems increased the appeal of left-wing extremism among blue-collar workers. Still, it was all bluff. In the fall of 1923 Saxony and Thuringia were taken over by a federal executor backed by Reichswehr troops. There was another outbreak of violence in October 1923 in the city of Hamburg, but this, too, was an ill-prepared, localized affair, staged at the behest of the KPD's Comintern masters. Order was quickly restored by the local police.

An even more powerful catalyst in providing support for counterrevolution from the Right were the myths and realities surrounding the Treaty of Versailles. The peace treaty formed a large component in the political mythology of the Right. Its spokesmen incessantly claimed not only that the pact was unjust, but that Germany's own democratic government was guilty of treason for agreeing to sign the onerous treaty. The *Freikorps* also opposed the Treaty of Versailles because under its provisions the Reich government was committed to disbanding their units by April 1920. At least some members of the vigilante groups were determined to overthrow the Republican government rather than accept the end of their pseudomilitary careers.

The politicized *Freikorps*, then, were united in their stand against Versailles, democracy, and dissolution. The first serious threat to the Republic from the Right came during the Kapp-Lüttwitz putsch ("putsch" can be translated as "coup") just before the April 1920 dissolution deadline. This episode—and it was little more than that— was named after the two principal activists in the drama, General Walther von Lüttwitz, the commander of the Reichswehr's Berlin district and Wolfgang Kapp, a frustrated politician and East Prussian agricultural expert. Lüttwitz was a simple-minded officer who was convinced a military dictatorship would solve all of Germany's problems; Kapp was something of a professional conspirator, who delighted in drawing up grandiose plans and inventing secret codes. Both men, and the bevy of DNVP and DVP politicians with whom they were in contact, relied upon one of the most politicized among the *Freikorps*, the Ehrhardt Brigade, to carry out the actual putsch.

This unit, named for its commander, the

former marine commandant Hermann Ehrhardt, was stationed at Döberitz, an army post in the Berlin district located only some twenty kilometers from the capital. In its politics the Ehrhardt Brigade clearly sympathized with extreme Rightist and *völkisch* ideas. In the early morning hours of March 13, 1920, the Brigade as well as some regular army units under Lüttwitz' command seized control of Berlin. There was no resistance from either the police or other Reichswehr troops; the army declared it would remain at "parade rest." Initially, the coup seemed to be an instant success. The Reich ministers hurriedly left the capital. Kapp appointed himself Reich chancellor and named Lüttwitz as minister of defense.

The Kapp-Lüttwitz putsch soon demonstrated, however, that far-Right conspirators were no less amateurs than their rivals on the extreme Left. In any case, the rule of Kapp and Lüttwitz was restricted to the city of Berlin and some areas in East Elbia. It was also marked by confusion, ineptitude, and effective countermeasures by those opposed to the putsch. A paralyzing general strike, called by all three branches of organized labor a few hours after the Ehrhardt Brigade had marched into the city, shut off utilities in Berlin and made travel all but impossible. The Reich and Prussian civil service refused to carry out the conspirators' orders. After five days the putsch collapsed; the coup's leaders took refuge in more hospital climates. The old government seemed to return almost as quickly as it had been overthrown. With a few new faces a cabinet of the Weimar coalition parties (SPD, DDP, and Center Party) was returned to power.

Despite its swift collapse, the Kapp-Lüttwitz putsch had important consequences for the future development of the counterrevolution in Germany. While the coup failed in northern Germany, it succeeded in Bavaria. The commander of the Munich Reichswehr district, General Otto von Lossow, forced the democratically elected Bavarian state government to resign. In its

place moved a "state commissioner" of the army's choosing, Gustav von Kahr. The new Bavarian leader was an old-line Catholic conservative whose major political goal was the restoration of the Bavarian monarchy. Since he saw the existence of the German Republic as an obstacle to realizing this plan (the Weimar constitution guaranteed a Republican form of government in all federal states) Kahr welcomed as allies the counterrevolutionary forces that were equally determined to overthrow democracy, albeit for different reasons. Under the state commissioner's rule Bavaria became a haven for extreme Right fugitives from justice. (Ehrhardt, for example, lived openly in Munich.) In addition, the Kahr Lossow regime welcomed the activities of Bavaria's numerous indigenous extreme rightist groups, including the fledgling Nazi Party.

Putsches were not the only means used by the extreme Right to destabilize democracy. Counterrevolutionary rightists also resorted to individual acts of terror. Both Matthias Erzberger, the former Reich minister of finance, and Walther Rathenau were murdered by assassins with clear ties to the extreme Right scene. However, the death of Rathenau, the popular Jewish Reich foreign minister, in June 1922 also spurred the Reich government to take effective countermeasures. Rathenau's friend, Chancellor Wirth, took advantage of the spontaneous outcry of revulsion against the right-wing terrorists and persuaded the Reichstag to pass the Law for the Protection of the Republic. The measure made it a crime to engage in antirepublican activities and set up a special federal court to try those violating the new statute.

Unfortunately, national legislation could do little to curtail the activities of the counterrevolutionaries in Bavaria. The Kahr regime argued that the Law for the Protection of the Republic violated Bavaria's states' rights, and, in any case the new federal court duplicated the work of the state's own People's Courts, which had been established in 1919 to try leftist revolutionaries. With the Ruhr crisis looming on the horizon, the Reich government was unwilling to risk a conflict over states' rights, so that in practical terms, Bavaria remained an exceedingly friendly environment for right-wing counterrevolutionary groups and plots.

The extreme Right welcomed the Ruhr crisis as a boon to its cause. During the period of passive resistance, the counterrevolutionaries engaged in acts of sabotage against the occupation forces and the minuscule pro-French separatist organizations in western Germany. Above all, however, they expected that the end of passive resistance would enable them to move against the Republican government, since they would now be able to claim that the democratic leaders had given in to the foreign enemy and failed to save Germany from imminent Communist revolution.

Their hopes remained unfulfilled. Contrary to what the extreme Right had expected, the Stresemann cabinet's swift declaration of a state of emergency preserved law and order in most parts of the Reich. Under the terms of the decree, responsibility for administering the state of emergency was in the hands of both the Reichswehr and the states' civilian authorities. In contrast to its behavior in 1920, the Reichswehr in 1923 remained actively loyal to the Weimar constitution—at least in the states outside of Bavaria.

These developments were not welcome news for the Bavarian conspirators. They had been actively planning the overthrow of the Republic throughout the spring and summer of 1923. The numerous *völkisch* parties mounted a massive propaganda campaign to mobilize public opinion against the democratic Reich government. Simultaneously, paramilitary organizations sent their members on training missions and field maneuvers. The expectation was that when the signal for the uprising came, various paramilitary organizations, units of the Reichswehr, and the Bavarian government would cooperate in deploying the counterrevolutionary forces on their march to Berlin. On paper, the whole operation was very much modeled upon Benito Mussolini's successful march on Rome a year earlier.

The political side of the planned Bavarian putsch for the first time focused widespread public attention on the leader of the Nazi Party, Adolf Hitler. The chairman of this small *völkisch* group was born on April 20, 1889, in the Austrian border town of Braunau. Orphaned as a teenager, Hitler had ambitions to become an artist but did poorly in school and eventually drifted to Vienna and later Munich. In 1914 Hitler volunteered for the German army and served with some distinction in a Bavarian regiment. The future Nazi leader was mustered out as a lance corporal in 1918, but he remained a civilian employee of the army. In this capacity he lectured in a political indoctrination program, which some officers organized for their soldiers to "immunize" them against leftist political ideas.

In addition to his duties as a military propagandist, Hitler was also responsible for reporting on the activities of the various *völkisch* groups in Munich and recommending to his military superiors those that warranted receiving subsidies from secret army funds. In the course of his observations of Munich's *völkisch* scene, Hitler became acquainted with the *Deutsche Arbeiterpartei* (German Workers' Party, DAP), a minuscule group that had been funded by a Munich toolmaker in the spring of 1919. Hitler joined the party, quickly becoming its chief of propaganda and leading speaker. In 1920 the party was renamed the National Socialist German Workers' Party (NSDAP), and in July 1921 Hitler became the real leader of the Nazi Party. Although he quit his job with the army, the Nazi leader continued to enjoy excellent relations with the Bavarian military.

Hitler's undeniable rhetorical talents quickly propelled him to the forefront of Munich's *völkisch* scene, and the Bavarian counterrevolutionary leaders selected him to coordinate the political and propagandistic preparations for the planned putsch. All seemed ready for the enterprise at the beginning of November 1923. However, at the last moment the counterrevolutionaries' conservative allies in Bavaria decided to withhold their support when the commander-in-chief of the Reichswehr, General Hans von Seeckt, indicated that he would not permit the army to cooperate with the putschists. Hitler and his associates, who included Ludendorff and Captain Ernst Röhm, the former commander of a key Reichswehr unit in Munich, felt betrayed by what they regarded as the cowardice of Kahr and his military allies. Hitler decided to stage the "National Revolution" without the conservatives' cooperation, although he still hoped that the state commissioner and Lossow would jump on the bandwagon once the popularity of the putschists' cause had been demonstrated.

The effort failed. After Hitler and some members of the NSDAP's own paramilitary unit, the Stormtroopers (*Sturmabteilung*, SA) literally crashed a rally organized by Kahr to explain his decision to delay the expected putsch, von Kahr and von Lossow briefly agreed to join Hitler, but within hours both renounced their decision. In addition, Seeckt, when informed of the events in Munich, ordered Lossow's arrest. Hitler and Ludendorff led a demonstration of thousands through the streets of Munich on the morning of November 9, 1923, but this last effort to demonstrate to the Reichswehr the counterrevolution's grassroots support failed when shots, probably fired by nervous police officers, caused panic and dispersed the crowd. Ludendorff was arrested immediately. The other conspirators, including Hitler, who was slightly injured in the melée, fled, but they were eventually rounded up and tried for treason before the Bavarian People's Court. The judges proved lenient. Recognizing the "patriotic motivation" of the defendants, they imposed extremely light punishments. Ludendorff was acquitted and Hitler sentenced to only five years in prison. The Nazi leader was

paroled after serving nine months of his sentence in a very comfortable apartment at the fortress of Landsberg.

In later years Hitler's "beer hall putsch" was to occupy a large place in Nazi mythology, but in reality, like the Kapp putsch, it was a dismal failure. Above all, it demonstrated the futility of attempting to overthrow the Republic by force. Why did the counterrevolution fail? One reason, clearly, was the ineptitude of the counterrevolutionaries themselves. The Kapp-Lüttwitz coup was badly organized, and the Hitler-Ludendorff putsch was a hastily developed alternative after the original premise proved unworkable. In addition, the Republic had some powerful supporters. The loyalty of the labor unions proved decisive in 1920; their activism was not needed in 1923. Most significant, however, was the attitude of many mainstream conservatives in the army and the civil service. Much as they desired the end of democracy, many recoiled when confronted with the choice of taking up arms against the Reich government and risking the danger of civil war. Hitler, who in 1923 had no qualms about such a step, complained eloquently bout the fickleness of the conservative establishment. The experience was a bitter lesson for him, but one from which he learned well.

FOREIGN RELATIONS

The Reich's defeat in World War I not only ended Germany's dream of becoming a decisive factor in the global balance of power, but also deprived the country of the hegemonial position in central Europe it had held since 1871. For the foreseeable future, the Reich would be an object of, rather than a partner in, the conduct of international relations.

In the months between the signing of the armistice and the announcement of the peace terms, German foreign policy was essentially limited to dampening the fires of dissatisfaction in the Reich's border areas and eliciting sympathy abroad for the new Germany's difficulties and aims. The effort was not without success. The various separatist and autonomist movements had little popular support, and it soon became clear that the Allies, too, had no interest in dismantling the Reich. Indeed, in the Baltic areas of Estonia, Latvia, Lithuania, and parts of northern Poland *Freikorps* and regular army units operated for some time with the tacit approval of the Allies. Their ostensible purpose was to prevent Bolshevik incursions into the region, but it was an open secret that the German government was equally concerned about the growth of Polish power.

The territorial losses imposed by the Treaty of Versailles were not as onerous as they might have been. True, Alsace-Lorraine was lost to the Reich, but the Allies did not permit Poland to extend her western borders to the Oder-Neisse line (the country's present border with East Germany), nor was a new Confederation of the Rhine constituted. In addition, as we saw, the Treaty of Versailles sought to ensure ethnically fair boundaries throughout eastern and southern Europe by providing for a number of plebiscites in areas of mixed population. The outcome was in several cases gratifying to the German cause. The bulk of East Prussia, a considerable portion of Silesia, and much of Schleswig voted to remain in Germany. In fact it could be argued that with two notable exceptions Germany's post-1918 boundaries reflected the true wishes of the populations concerned.

The exceptions were Silesia and Austria. In the first case the Allies, in partial violation of the results of the plebiscite, decreed that for economic reasons the bulk of coal-rich Upper Silesia should go to Poland. In the case of Austria the people had voted overwhelmingly to join the German Republic, but the Allies prohibited the union since they felt a reconstituted *grossdeutsche* Reich—albeit in truncated form—would endanger the new balance of power in southeastern Europe.

After the Reich had grudgingly agreed to sign the peace treaty, Germany's and France's roles in the dynamics of European power relations were essentially reversed from what they had been in 1871. As the new hegemonial power in Central Europe, it was now in France's interest to isolate Germany diplomatically. In the next few years France established an intricate system of alliances, the *cordon sanitaire* ("belt of safety"), between herself and the newly independent powers of eastern and southeastern Europe. France obligated herself to come to the aid of Poland, Rumania, Czechoslovakia, and Yugoslavia if the territorial or political integrity of these nations were threatened either by Germany or a power allied to the Reich. The latter provision was directed against both a resurrected Habsburg empire and the possibility of a Russo-German rapprochement.

Much as France had done after 1871, Germany sought to break out of the diplomatic isolation the Treaty of Versailles had imposed upon her. Realistically, there were only two paths open to accomplish this aim: One was reaching a *modus vivendi* with one or more of the Western Allies, and the other involved an arrangement with the other pariah in international relations, Soviet Russia. Both scenarios contained considerable risks. An agreement with the West would give additional impetus to the counterrevolutionary Right, since France in particular would not accept Germany back into the family of nations unless the Reich acknowledged that she was no longer a great power. An entente with Soviet Russia involved relations with a power whose avowed aim was the spread of revolution throughout the world.

The foreign policy of the early Republican governments toward the Western Allies was not notably successful. France remained distrustful of German intentions. A much heralded international conference at Genoa in April 1922, which was attended by Germany and her former enemies including the United States and Soviet Russia, failed to break the deadlock over the linkage of reparations and inter-Allied war debts. As we saw, the Ruhr crisis of 1923 was a severe economic and diplomatic defeat for Germany. The Reich's attempts to drive a wedge between England and France were unsuccessful; Great Britain remained firmly on the side of France.

At first glance, Russo-German relations took a more promising turn. Substantively, however, the results were rather less impressive. To begin with, the two powers had little to offer each other besides mutual commiseration as international outcasts. The Russian civil war had brought that country's economy to the brink of collapse, so that her role as a trading partner was negligible. The German government continued to be suspicious of the close relations between Soviet Russia and the German Communists. Nevertheless, increasing frustrations over her failure to achieve a *modus vivendi* with the Western Allies led Germany in 1922 to play the Russian card. The move was a reactive maneuver rather than a bold new initiative. Russian overtures suggesting the normalization of relations between the two countries had been forthcoming for some time. They culminated in the draft of a treaty which the Soviet foreign minister, G. V. Cicherin, presented to the Germans when he stopped in Berlin on his way to the Genoa Conference. After the failure of the Italian reparations conference the Wirth government, with the full approval of Reich President Ebert, authorized Rathenau to initial the Russo-German draft treaty.

The resulting Treaty of Rapallo (Rapallo is a suburb of Genoa) implied far more than it delivered. The agreement contained no secret clauses and its published terms were innocuous enough. Germany and Russia accorded each other diplomatic recognition, agreed to a mutual cancellation of debts, and resumed normal commercial relations. These provisions were significant, but they hardly changed the balance of power in Europe. The diplomatic impact of the Treaty of Rapallo was related to what the pact was rumored to contain, that is, a secret military alliance directed primarily against Poland. Such Russo-German cooperation clearly would have had implications for the strength of the *cordon sanitaire* and the viability of the Versailles system. In fact, the treaty contained no such provisions, but from the perspective of the Western Allies, and particularly France, the Treaty of Rapallo was yet more evidence that Germany was continuing her efforts to escape the consequences of her defeat in World War I. (Incidentally, France's distrust was not entirely unjustified. Even before the Rapallo Treaty the Red Army and the *Reichswehr* agreed to cooperate, and throughout the 1920s the *Reichswehr* used the Russian connection to develop military hardware prohibited to the Reichswehr under the terms of the Treaty of Versailles. The Germans also made use of training facilities in Russia.)

On balance, the treaty probably brought more disadvantages than advantages to the Reich. It undoubtedly increased France's distrust of Germany's foreign policy aims. France's desire to demonstrate her strength was one factor in her decision to occupy the Ruhr in early 1923. Domestically, the counterrevolutionary Right in Germany saw the Treaty of Rapallo as further evidence of the workings of the international Jewish conspiracy: The treaty was the result of an arrangement between the Reich's Jewish foreign minister and the "Jewish" leaders of Bolshevik Russia. This myth contributed to the assassination of Rathenau two months after he had signed the Treaty of Rapallo.

The foreign policy record of the Republic's first five years, then, was not impressive. Despite some sincere attempts to face realistically Germany's new position as a lesser power, successive Reich governments had not been able to achieve Germany's reintegration into the family of nations. A largely symbolic pact with a destitute and weak Soviet Russia was clearly no substitute for achieving this primary objective.

CONCLUSION

Looking back on the preceding five years, few Germans in late 1923 felt good about the immediate past or confident about the future. Politically, the period had been marked by almost constant internal strife. Partly as a result of the turmoil, the Republic was held in low esteem by many Germans. The elections of 1919 seemed to show the strength of the reformist parties—SPD, DDP, and the Center Party—but that support eroded quickly. The Reichstag election of June 1920 already showed evidence that the Weimar Republic was destined to be a "democracy without democrats" as the right-wing Social Democratic speaker of parliament, Paul Löbe, put it. The 1920 contest showed major gains for the forces of the Right, notably the DNVP and the DVP, and antiparliamentary groups on the Left, the USPD and the KPD. True, these statistics were somewhat deceptive. The shock of the Kapp putsch persuaded the DVP to leave the ranks of the intransigent parties; in 1923 the right-wing liberals joined the DDP, SPD, and Center Party in a grand coalition government which ended passive resistance in the Ruhr. On the left the USPD disintegrated, but the party's dissolution hardly strengthened the cause of parliamentary democracy. Most of the former USPD members joined the Communists. The *völkisch* forces suffered a setback with the failure of the Hitler-Ludendorff putsch, but the DNVP remained a hard-line antidemocratic party, whose popularity was growing rather than declining.

The country's political developments, of course, were linked to its economic problems. Germany emerged from the war burdened with a huge internal and external debt. The Reich was also increasingly unable to control its runaway inflation. At the end of 1923 the country managed to stabilize her currency, but all of the well-known structural problems still awaited solutions.

At the same time, the last five years had also demonstrated that while the Republic did not have a surfeit of enthusiastic supporters, most Germans rejected as well the available alternatives to parliamentary democracy. Repeated efforts by left-wing extremists to stage a "second revolution" failed dismally. But so did counterrevolutionary attempts by the extreme-Right, such as the Kapp Lüttwitz and the Ludendorff-Hitler putsches.

In the area of international relations, all of Germany's attempts to evade accepting the consequences of the Versailles system had failed. Stonewalling the reparation demands led to France's exacting "productive guarantees" in the form of occupying various German cities. The Rapallo Treaty was a factor in France's decision to occupy the Ruhr. As we saw, this crisis resulted in economic disaster and diplomatic humiliation for Germany.

The main tasks for the future, then, were twofold: to translate recognition that there was no viable alternative to the Republic into positive support for parliamentary democracy and to gain acceptance for the new Germany abroad. Reaching the first goal required a period of sustained prosperity, and a change in the country's mentality: The ideals of Western pluralism had to be endorsed by the country's intellectuals and permeate Germany's *Bildungsbürgertum*— much as Wilhelminian authoritarianism had done before the war. As far as foreign relations were concerned, Germany had to regain her membership in the international community, but that meant genuinely accepting her role as a second rate power. At the end of 1923 the prospects for realizing either or both aims did not appear favorable.

CHAPTER 6

FOOLS' GOLD:
The Weimar Republic,
1924–1930

The six years between the currency stabilization in 1924 and the resignation of the last parliamentary Reich cabinet in March 1930 were the "golden years" of the Weimar Republic. For many contemporaries this was a time of renewed optimism for the present and hope for the future. In politics, the strength of the antidemocratic extremists seemed to be ebbing. Some sectors of the economy were finally showing signs of genuine recovery. Germany's acknowledgement in the Treaty of Locarno (see the discussion on pp. 171–72) that she accepted the legitimacy of her 1918 western boundaries promised to inaugurate a period of goodwill between Germany and France. Membership in the League of Nations and the award of a permanent seat on the League's Council of Ten, the equivalent of the United Nations' Security Council, signaled that at least on paper the Reich had returned to Great Power status. Finally, the "golden

years" are indelibly associated with a time of remarkable productivity and brilliance in Germany's cultural and artistic life.

The apparent return of stability and prosperity understandably induced a sense of self-satisfaction among those who had brought about the new orders in 1918–1919. While they had been on the defensive for the preceding five years as the Republic staggered from crisis to crisis, they now took painfully naive pride in their accomplishments. In his account of the revolution of 1918, written years after the events, the right-wing Social Democratic leader and Reich chancellor Hermann Müller expressed concern that his readers would take the blessings of democracy for granted. Müller should have directed his concerns elsewhere. Two years after the publication of his book parliamentary democracy in Germany was no longer functioning; the Reich president, not the Reichstag, made and unmade Reich chancellors. A few months later, the Nazis—sworn enemies of democracy, but until then the butt of numerous political jokes—had become the second strongest party in the national parliament.

These developments were not simply the results of forces and events that emerged in the course of two years. Rather, there was another side to Weimar's golden years: Much of the glitter was fools' gold. Politically, the strength of the extremists declined, but it was only a temporary lull. Moreover, even when the extremists had little parliamentary representation, the moderate forces were never able to forge a permanent national Republican consensus that might have sustained parliamentary democracy when it was faced with the problems that loomed ahead. The economic disasters to come also cast their shadows in the "golden years." The German economy lived on borrowed time, and the brief years of prosperity hid chronic structural difficulties and pockets of perennial recession.

In international relations "the spirit of Locarno" was only one side of the picture. Simultaneously, the paramilitary Right continued to foment hatred against what it called the Reich's "hereditary enemy," France. The Reichswehr, for its part, continued its efforts to escape the disarmament provisions of the Treaty of Versailles by intensifying its clandestine cooperation with the Soviet Red Army. And Weimar culture was also a culture of alienation. Germany's intellectuals and artists excelled in a variety of media, but few used their talents to support the Republic and its values.

In essence, then, the "golden years" represented a brief hiatus before a period of new and worse crises. As we shall see, the years of optimism were cut short by tragic and unforeseen developments, notably the advent of the Great Depression and Germany's inability to deal with its economic, political, and social consequences.

POLITICS: THE SEARCH FOR THE ELUSIVE CONSENSUS

In the middle period of the Weimar years politics were characterized by a number of seemingly contradictory developments. The center of the political spectrum shifted to the right in national elections, but for the legislatures and governments in the major Länder the voters appeared to prefer a more leftward tilt. The parliamentary strength of the extreme Right declined to virtual insignificance, but paramilitary and extraparliamentary rightist groups continued to flourish.

In May 1924, Germany held its first Reichstag election since June 1920. As was to be expected, the results reflected the political backlash from the country's economic hard times. The parties of the moderate center—SPD, DDP, Center Party, and DVP—suffered substantial losses, while the extremists gained. The Communists received 3.7 million popular votes, and the Nazis, despite their leader's recent conviction for attempting to overthrow the government, obtained almost 2 million votes and sent twelve deputies to the Reichstag.

But the return of currency stability quickly eroded the electoral strength of the extremists. The national parliament elected in May proved incapable of choosing a stable government, and after a few months, in December, the voters were again called to the polls. This time they elected both a new Reichstag and Prussian Landtag. The new results were considerably more gratifying to the supporters of parliamentary democracy. The Nazis lost more than a million votes, most of them going to the DNVP. The Communist vote, too, declined by almost 1 million. Most of those deserting the KPD turned instead to the Social Democrats.

In the December elections the DNVP became the second largest party in the Reichstag, and the election of a new Reich president in the spring of 1925 seemed to confirm the return of the conservatives to national political prominence. At the end

The love feast at Locarno: Cupid in the person of the French foreign minister, Aristide Briand, kisses Gustav Stresemann, the German foreign minister. (Source: *Lachen*, p. 232.)

of February 1925 the Republic's first leader, Friedrich Ebert, had died. Under the provisions of the Weimar constitution a successful candidate initially had to obtain a majority of the votes cast to be elected. Such an outcome was highly unlikely, given the fragmented political scene in Germany. As a result, the constitution provided for a runoff election, and this time a plurality of votes sufficed for victory. Furthermore, in a strange attempt to assure as much freedom of choice as possible, the framers of the constitution did not limit the candidates in the runoff contest to those who had participated in the first round of balloting. Parties were free to nominate new candidates.

Not surprisingly, none of the candidates received the necessary majority in the first round, which was held in March. For the runoff contest the SPD, DDP, and Center Party agreed to put forth the chairman of the Center Party and current Reich chancellor, Wilhelm Marx, as their joint candidate. The DVP and DNVP had been expected to renominate their lackluster choice in the first contest, Karl Jarres, the mayor of Duisburg, but at the last moment they turned instead to the retired hero of World War I, Field Marshall Paul von Hindenburg. The seventy-six-year-old general did virtually no campaigning, but the old-line Junker and avowed monarchist narrowly won the election.

There were some fears that with the field marshall's election the counterrevolutionaries had accomplished peacefully what they had failed to do with violence in March 1920: turning back the clock to 1914. There is no doubt that many of those who had proposed him for the presidency hoped that once elected Hindenburg would pave the way for a military coup, the restoration of the monarchy, or both. Hindenburg, however, took his oath to the Republican constitution seriously, and until the constitutional crisis of 1930 he exercised the functions of his office in a constitutionally correct manner. In addition, the national leaders of the DNVP for a time made their peace with the Republic. During the next few years conservative leaders actually held ministerial posts in a number of right-of-center coalition governments.

Stability in the center of the political spectrum contrasted with divisiveness and strife among the extremists. Like other European Communist parties, the KPD was deeply affected by the struggle for power among the Russian Bolshevik leaders that followed Lenin's death in 1924. Ultra-left, centrist, and rightist factions purged each other with dizzying speed in response to the Comintern's and eventually Stalin's directives. Turnover among the membership was high. A semblance of stability did not return until the end of the decade when the Stalinization of the German Communist party was complete. In the meantime the KPD was no serious threat to the stability of the Reich.

The Nazis and other *völkische* groups were also experiencing organizational difficulties. After Hitler went to jail, the NSDAP disintegrated into a number of feuding fragments. Several of these merged with other *völkische* groups, turning to outsiders, such as General Ludendorff, for leadership. Hitler himself briefly attempted to control developments from inside his prison apartment, but he soon recognized the futility of the effort, and concentrated instead on writing the first volume of his autobiography, *Mein Kampf* ("My Struggle").

When the Nazi leader was paroled in February 1925, he immediately set to work rebuilding the shattered party. It was an uphill struggle. Most of the preputsch membership had dropped out of active politics, and others had joined alternative *völkische* groups. Hitler essentially had to organize a new party. For some years after 1925 his primary goal was not size but exclusivity. The NSDAP was a small, even insignificant group, but it was also very much Hitler's own party. "The Hitler Movement," as the Nazi party now increasingly subtitled itself, had no formal ties to other *völkische* groups, and Hitler refused to permit party members or Stormtroopers (the Stormtroopers were the paramilitary wing of the party) to hold simultaneous memberships in any other political or paramilitary groups. (Multiple memberships were common in the *völkische* camp.) Hitler also deftly destroyed Ludendorff's aura as a potential rival leader. He persuaded the general to run for president on the *völkische* ticket in 1925. Ludendorff received 200,000 votes out of 27 million cast and vanished into political oblivion.

While Hitler successfully guarded his political turf and the NSDAP was even able to absorb a number of rival *völkische* groups, during the "golden years" the Nazis remained a political fringe group. Efforts to wrest urban workers from their traditional allegiance to the Marxist parties or the Catholic Center Party met with little success. Although since 1925 the NSDAP had concentrated its organizing efforts in the urban areas of northern Germany, in the Reichstag elections of May 1928 the party did particularly poorly in these regions.

Supporters of the Republic were also encouraged by developments in some of Germany's major Länder. In Prussia the parties of the Weimar coalition—SPD, DDP, and Center Party—retained comfortable majorities in the legislature. Indeed, in Germany's largest state in 1928 well over 60 percent of the voters cast their ballots for one of the moderate groups. As a result, Prussia was spared the frequent government crises that characterized the national scene. Otto Braun, the leader of the state's SPD, served as chief executive continuously for almost twelve years, from 1920 to 1932.

Democracy also returned to Germany's second largest state, Bavaria. Heavily implicated in the preparations, if not the implementation, of Hitler's Beer Hall putsch, the Kahr regime was forced out of office after the coup failed. The state again became a political fief of the Bavarian People's Party (*Bayerische Volkspartei*, BVP), a staunchly Catholic and conservative, but parliamentary, group. It governed Bavaria for the remainder of the Republican years.

Right-of-center cabinets were the rule for the national executive. Short-lived coalitions stretching from the DDP on the left to the Center Party and sometimes the DNVP on the right provided most of the federal cabinets. The chancellor was almost invariably a man from the Catholic Center Party; Wilhelm Marx, the chairman of the Center Party, headed four Reich governments in the span of four years.

The elections held in May 1928 could be seen as additional evidence of the country's return to political stability. The big winner was the SPD, the staunchest pillar of democracy in Germany; the Social Democrats obtained almost 30 percent of the popular vote. Together the parties of the Weimar coalition almost reached a majority, 47 percent, and if the DVP were added the mandate for the moderate groups was a comfortable 56 percent of the popular vote. The big losers were the antidemocratic forces on the Right; the Nazis were reduced to an unimportant splinter group. The new Reichstag for the first time since 1923 elected a cabinet of the great coalition. Ministers from the SPD, DDP, DVP, and the Center Party formed a government under a right-wing Social Democratic chancellor, Hermann Müller.

Unfortunately the portents of continued stability were misleading. The election returns of 1928 also contained evidence that a true Republican consensus continued to be an elusive goal. To begin with, the strength of the Weimar coalition parties was very uneven. While the SPD regained much of its earlier popularity, the two liberal parties continued their downward trend. The DDP was badly hurt; its overall share of the popular vote fell to below 5 percent.

Equally ominous were the internal developments within the DNVP. Many of the party's provincial leaders and most of its rank and file members rejected the national leadership's decision to steer the party in the direction of political moderation. At the end of 1928 the moderate national leadership, headed by Count Kuno von Westarp, was forced out by an intraparty maneuver led by the industrialist and owner of a film and newspaper empire, Alfred Hugenberg. The new leader was a fanatical opponent of parliamentary democracy. He saw the DNVP's path to power at the side of the Nazis and other extreme rightists, rather than in cooperation with moderate bourgeois groups. Some of the DNVP moderates eventually formed their own—ineffective—splinter group, the Conservative People's Party.

The Republic was also weakened by the premature death of Gustav Stresemann, the leader of the DVP, the right liberals. Since 1920 Stresemann had almost single-handedly kept the DVP in the ranks of the moderate parties and after he died in August 1919, his successor, Eduard Dingeldey, had neither the charisma nor the will to continue Stresemann's course. Instead, the DVP veered sharply to the right, attempting to occupy a position on the political spectrum that the DNVP under Hugenberg had vacated.

Above all, however, the narrow span of agreement on substantive issues among the moderate democratic parties hindered the emergence of a Republican consensus. The basis for agreement on substantive issues among the pro-Republican groups was tenuous, to say the least. For example, a serious political furor arose in 1928 over defense appropriations. The specific controversy concerned the advisibility of building a so-called pocket battleship. The government of the great coalition agreed to a request by the navy to include appropriations for the ship in its 1928 budget proposal. Battle cruisers were permitted under the terms of the Treaty of Versailles, though their military usefulness was the subject of fierce debates among political and military experts. The Social Democratic Reich ministers and the Prussian government both opposed the appropriation, but the bourgeois ministers, who held a majority in the Reich cabinet, insisted on the naval appropriations. When the budget proposals were made public, the traditional grassroots distrust of the military erupted into a revolt of the SPD's rank-and-file members against the party's leadership. The dissatisfaction among the membership led the SPD to endorse the Communists' call for cosponsoring a national referendum against building the battle cruiser. The campaign, which was defeated at the polls, put the Social Democratic Reich ministers, including Chancellor Müller, into a highly embarrassing position: Their party insisted that as members of the Reichstag they vote against the budget proposals that they had endorsed as members of the Reich cabinet.

The open disagreement on major policy issues among the Republican parties undoubtedly contributed toward alienating large numbers of Germans from the parliamentary system as such. One disquieting symptom of this political malaise was the persistent presence of numerous paramilitary groups even during the Republic's golden years. They represented all political camps, but most of them supported the far Right.

Masquerading under the guise of veterans' organizations (actually, anyone, veteran or not, who liked to turn out on Sunday afternoons to demonstrate against the Republic could join) their members and leaders were contemptuous of democracy and convinced that Germany should not and need not accept the political consequences of the lost war. Instead, they hoped for the return of authoritarianism or the triumph of a "nationalist revolution." The largest and most influential of the ostensible veterans' groups was the "Steel Helmet—Association of Front Fighters" (*Stahlhelm—Bund der Frontsoldaten*. At one point the "Steel Helmet" had a membership of more than 5 million. It was also a thoroughly "respectable" organization; the Reich president himself was the *Stahlhelm*'s honorary national chairman. At the same time, the group's politics were the same as those of Hugenberg wing of the DNVP, and, like

Hugenberg, in later years the "Steel Helmet" joined forces with the Nazis.

The problem of alienation among the aging veterans could be explained by the residual effects of the war, but this was not true for the Republic's failure to win the allegiance of large numbers of Germany's high school and university students. The Weimar Republic was plagued by a chronic problem of right-wing political radicalism among its student population. Many students were active in the paramilitary groups, and as early as 1927 the German National Student Organization, following the example of its Austrian counterpart, voted to include a clause in its bylaws that would have excluded Jews from membership in the organization. The intervention of the Prussian minister of education prevented the vote from having any practical effect, but the resolution was symptomatic of the popularity of *völkische* ideas among the students. Long before the Nazis scored a major victory in national elections, Hitler's supporters dominated student governments in many of the German universities.

The emergence of a viable parliamentary democracy was also hindered by the proliferation of single-issue parties in the wake of the economic disasters of 1923. In some Reichstag elections voters filling out their ballot had to make their way through a list of twenty-six parties. To be sure, few of these groups were able to obtain the 60,000 votes needed to send a representative to the national parliament, although single-issue parties did receive more than 10 percent of the national vote in the 1928 and 1930 Reichstag elections. Most of these parties pressed for economic relief of specific interest groups. Typical was the largest and politically most successful of the single-issue parties, the Economics Party (*Wirtschaftspartei*, WiP), which gave itself the subtitle "Reich Party of the German *Mittelstand*." In fact, the Economics Party was little more than a lobbying group for real estate interests; the party was financed almost entirely by the Reich and Prussian Associations of Real Estate Developers. The WiP demanded an end to rent control, the abolition of subsidies for the construction of public housing, and lower property taxes. Since the democratic parties had voted for all of these social welfare measures, the WiP's leaders opposed parliamentary democracy and until the final years of the Republic tended to vote with the DNVP. The party's political success (the WiP became an effective vote-getter, receiving almost 1.4 million popular votes, 4.5 percent of the total in 1930), came at the expense of the left liberals, the traditional political voice of the urban middle classes.

Farmers, too, in increasing numbers deserted the traditional political parties in favor of single-issue organizations. As the crisis in agriculture foreshadowed the advent of the Great Depression (see the discussion on pp. 172–75 numerous peasant parties, many with a purely regional orientation, appeared on the political scene, all insisting that agriculture needed protection in the form of tariffs and cheap credit. Their combined strength cut significantly into the vote of the major parties, especially the already decimated Liberals. The DNVP was less severely affected since in east Germany the Agrarian League continued to maintain its close ties to the conservatives.

The balance sheet of political developments during the Republic's golden years, then, presented a decidedly mixed picture. It is true that ideological differences, for the most part, were carried out with political means; the Republic was secure from military coups or revolutionary violence. Moreover, there were indications that the moderate groups in the center of the political spectrum were gaining strength as the economy recovered and "normal" times returned. But allegiance to the democratic system had not yet laid down firm roots in much of German society, and even the pro-Republican groups remained divided on fundamental policy issues. Democracy in Germany needed time and continued prosperity to integrate many of those now distrustful of the Republican system. Unfortunately, as it turned out, parliamentary democracy in Germany had very little time in which to demonstrate that it was the better system.

ECONOMIC AND SOCIAL DEVELOPMENTS

The Ruhr crisis was not only a political watershed in the Weimar years, but an economic one as well. No recovery of the German economy was possible until confidence in the stability of the Reich's currency had returned. The creation of the Rentenmark in the fall of 1923 was an important first step toward this goal, but long-term stabilization was dependent upon reaching agreement on a complex set of political and economic issues. These included the rebuilding of the international credit system and Germany's recognition of the territorial and financial provisions of the Versailles settlement.

The Rentenmark was without any real metallic backing—the Reich had virtually no reserves of gold or silver—so that the actual foundation for a stable German monetary system would have to be hard currency reserves, especially U.S. dollars. Those could come only in the form of loan packages subscribed to by private investors in Germany and, more important, the United States. It was obvious, however, that the Reich would remain a poor credit risk so long as large and chronic deficits were the rule at every level of government and Germany continued to attempt to evade the financial obligation imposed upon her by the Versailles Treaty.

The importance of the link between domestic and international decisions was shown in the spring of 1924, by the simultaneous retirement of the Rentenmark, the introduction of a new, permanent national currency, the Reichsmark, and the negotiations of a new reparations agreement between Germany and her former enemies.

To demonstrate their seriousness of purpose, all levels of government in Germany made drastic budget cuts for the fiscal year 1924. For the first time since the end of the war, Germany's local, state, and federal governments presented balanced budgets to their respective legislatures. At the same time, the *Reichsbank*, under its new president, Hjalmar Schacht, severely restricted credit and kept interest rates high. (Throughout the remainder of the decade German interest rates were consistently higher than those of other major industrialized nations.)

These moves brought about immediate social and financial consequences. The budget balancing act was accomplished largely at the expense of state and federal employees. Since entitlement programs, such as the social security system, traditionally were self-carrying insurance schemes and not part of the annual budgets, personnel costs were the single largest item of both state and federal budgets. Hardest hit were blue- and white-collar workers and public school teachers (who, it will be recalled, were state employees in Germany) with little seniority. In Prussia, Germany's largest state, some 14,500 teachers were laid off between the end of 1923 and mid-1925, a development that severely aggravated an already serious unemployment problem among college-educated youth. Tenure rules protected the jobs of other civil servants, but even senior bureaucrats had to accept substantial pay cuts. On the other hand, the high interest rates and Germany's fiscal austerity program made the country attractive to foreign investors. Between 1924 and 1930 foreign creditors invested 20.5 billion Reichsmark ($4.9 billion) in the German economy.

Putting Germany's domestic fiscal house in order was one prerequisite for economic recovery, but it would remain a hollow gesture unless it were supplemented by an agreement on reparations. In the summer of 1924 a committee of fiscal experts from the Allied countries, led by Charles Dawes, the president of the First Bank of Chicago, submitted a new proposal to the Germans. The Dawes Plan did not alter the actual total of the reparations bill (it remained at 132 billion marks), but the scheme eased Germany's fiscal position in a number of significant ways. To begin with, the Allies arranged for an initial loan to Germany of 200 million dollars by a consortium of American banks in order to provide the Reich with much needed hard currency reserves. (The loan was secured by the assets of the German national railroad system.) The Reich's annual reparation payments were pegged at the modest sum of 2.5 billion Reichsmark. More important, under the Dawes Plan Germany's creditors abandoned the policies of "productive guarantees," that is to say, the occupation of German cities as a punishment for nonpayment. Instead, the Dawes Plan contained provisions designed to insure that the transfer of payments did not endanger the stability of the new Reichsmark. A reparations agent, the American banker Parker Gilbert, established an office in Berlin to oversee the transfer of payments and report to the Allies on German economic and fiscal policies.

Although the Dawes Plan was a decided improvement over the policies that had led to periodic confrontations in earlier years, many among the political Right rejected the new scheme because of the continued shackles on Germany's fiscal and economic sovereignty. Still, even the Right was not blind to the practical advantages. In August 1924, exactly half of the DNVP's Reichstag delegates voted with the government majority, thereby insuring the votes necessary to give approval to the Dawes Plan.

The Republican authorities had acted swiftly to create a stable currency, but, important as this was, it did not solve the problem of the aftermath of the ruinous inflation. Clearly, some equitable way had to be found to "re-valuate" long-standing commercial obligations, savings, and bonds that had been calculated in what were now worthless marks. Not surprisingly, this issue became a major political controversy. Pensioners, creditors, and holders of savings accounts wanted to protect their assets, while debtors insisted "a mark is a mark." After all, it was not their fault that the collapse of the currency had enabled them to pay off their obligations cheaply. In the end, the Reich Supreme Court and the Reichstag reached a conclusion that pleased neither side. Liquid assets were "re-valued" at 15 percent of their original worth, while real property retained its full value. Since this decision gave a relative advantage to owners of real property, a special tax, earmarked for the construction of public housing, was levied on house owners. Angered by what they saw as an unfair burden on their properties, real estate interests were instrumental in the establishment of yet another anti-Republican party, the Economics Party (WiP), discussed earlier.

A stable currency and a good credit rating were the foundations of Germany's economic recovery. A credit crisis of 1924 brought contractions in the economy, but in 1924–1925 a miniboom led to overheating and a severe, if brief, recession in 1925–1926. The next few years, however, were marked by steady, albeit uneven expansion. Aided by the flow of foreign investments, industrial production in 1928 rose to an index figure of 114 (Comparing favorably to 1913, when the figure was 100), while corporate profits increased from 5.1 percent of equity in 1924–1925 to 72. percent 1928–1929. But there was a darker side here as well. Domestic investment activity never regained the levels of 1913, and neither did exports. From 1910 to 1913 exports composed 17.5 percent of the German GNP; by 1925 to 1929, the figure was only 14.9 percent.

The boom also created and hid a number of important structural changes in the economy. In the industrial sector, the most noticeable development was the accelerated trend toward "rationalization," that is to say, the reorganization of the manufacturing process to save labor costs. Particularly in labor-intensive, export-oriented industries, machines increasingly replaced human labor. The result was a 25 percent increase in productivity, and a rise in real wages in some industries, but also a depressingly high rate of overall unemployment. From 1924 to 1929 unemployment never fell below 6.8 percent and during the recession of 1925–1927 it rose as high as 18 percent. The problem was particularly severe in some geographic areas like Saxony and in older industries like iron, steel, and coal mining. Here, labor-management relations were chronically acrimonious, as employers sought to cut wages, increase the work day, and replace skilled male workers with unskilled (often female) laborers. In 1928 a lockout in the steel industry, which affected 80 percent of the workforce, created a great deal of bitterness in the Ruhr area.

Large numbers of unemployed workers (incidentally, this was a problem that plagued other industrialized countries as well) were only one indication of profound changes in the structure of Germany's economic and social life. The role of government changed dramatically. It became increasingly common for government arbitrators to settle labor disputes. At the same time, the country's *Sozialpolitik*, that network of insurance schemes and legal safeguards designed to protect employees from hardships, was knitted considerably tighter. The most important addition was the introduction of compulsory unemployment insurance in 1927. In general, the portion of public expenditure devoted to welfare costs and social services exploded. Veterans' pensions and disability payments required large sums. In 1927 the federal government used its sizable surplus to restore a good part of the salary cuts for civil servants that had been enacted in 1923–1924. In the period 1925 to 1930, expenditures for public housing construction, largely financed by the receipts from the inflation-related tax on real property, were twice as high as those for defense. But the easy availability of credit tempted many cities and states to

float bond issues with which to finance a variety of improvements in their infrastructure. Overall, annual government expenditures for social services at all levels increased from 1.8 billion marks in 1910–1913 to 2.6 billion in 1925–1929.

Nevertheless, the recovery also left large pockets of structural distress. Agriculture remained a chronic trouble spot. Farm debt climbed from the equivalent of 3 billion Reichsmark in 1923 to 12 billion seven years later, while prices for agricultural products, after reaching a postwar high in 1926, continued to fall beginning in 1927. Although experts recommended cutbacks in planting, farmers for the most part attempted to increase production. To become more efficient they purchased expensive machinery, a decision that turned out to be counterproductive since it aggravated their indebtedness, while the augmented production depressed prices still further. Before long Germany's farmers were again demanding tariff protection.

The *Mittelstand*—small businessmen, retailers, independent professionals—also complained about continuing hardships. Spokesmen for these interest groups (and their political allies) described the "crisis of the *Mittelstand*" in vivid terms: Not only were their savings wiped out by the inflation, but the recovery passed them by as well. There is no doubt that some parts of the *Mittelstand* suffered relative deprivation in the redistribution of income during the Weimar years. Small businesses had a harder time obtaining credit than did large export-oriented industries, and many retail establishments were hurt by the growing competition from chain and department stores. Compared to the years just before the war the *Mittelstand*'s share of the GNP fell while that of labor and corporations rose. The real income of the traditional white-collar employees (retail clerks, secretaries, and so forth) declined, while the wages of blue-collar workers rose.

At the same time, the plight of the *Mittelstand* must not be exaggerated. For many small businesses and independent artisans the effect of the inflation had been cushioned by their ownership of real estate. During the second half of the decade the number of new businesses increased rapidly. Equally important, the members of the new *Mittelstand*, such as technically skilled white-collar workers, benefited from the rationalization measures in some industries. On balance, most members of the *Mittelstand* remained better off than many blue-collar workers and civil servants. In objective terms, then, the *Mittelstand*'s complaints were not justified. In reality, members of this group mourned the loss of status and relative standing in the society that they associated with the Wilhelminian era.

By the end of the decade, the German economy, despite some chronic problems, gave cause for continued optimism. Even the reparations did not seem to present a major difficulty. The annual payments consumed about 10 percent of the federal budget—not an exorbitant sum, particularly since most of the money derived from foreign loans. The absence of "reparations crises" and the expectation of continued prosperity led financial experts from the Reich and her creditors in June 1929 to agree on a new repayment plan. The Young Plan (named for the American banker who chaired the negotiations between Germany and the Allies) was a monument to economic hopes and illusions. The ink on the agreement was hardly dry when the collapse of the New York Stock Market ushered in the Great Depression, and with it an entirely different set of problems. Still, the Young Plan does illustrate what might have been. The new agreement set up a schedule of fifty-nine annual payments ranging from 1.6 to 2.4 billion Reichsmark ($381 to 571 million). In addition, all international controls on German economic life were removed, and the Allies agreed that the last French and Belgian troops would leave German soil in 1930.

The Young Plan did not cause the Depression, but when the effects of the economic down-turn were felt in Germany, the plan became an object of fierce political attacks. The anti-Republican forces concentrated their venom on the plan's long-term payment schedule: While millions of Germans suffered hardships, the Republican authorities had obligated themselves to continue reparations for another sixty years to pay for a war that few Germans felt personally responsible for either beginning or losing. Such attacks ignored the fact that overall Germany paid only a little over 10 billion marks in reparations in the years between 1924 and 1930.

Looking back from the depths of the Great Depression most Germans could see little good even in the "golden years," but we should remember that the second half of the decade produced important, and, on the whole, positive changes in German economic and social life. There were continuing structural problems—agriculture, young academics, depressed regions—but these years were also a time in which the GNP grew rapidly, much of German industry was modernized, and the construction of the "social net" continued.

WEIMAR CULTURE

The glitter of the Weimar era's golden years was particularly dazzling in the fields of art and literature. Moreover, while economic recovery and political stability proved to be short-lived, the patina of Weimar culture has endured. From architecture to films, from the novel to interior design, the Weimar years continue to influence our own times.

The artistic flowering during these years was not just the result of fortuitous circumstances. Convinced that a spiritual and cultural regeneration would provide a vehicle for Germany's return to greatness, the Republic's political leaders consciously set out to provide a fertile environment for the country's renaissance of culture. Symptomatic were the public expenditures for education and the arts: Until the Great Depression forced cutbacks, budgetary outlays for education and the arts at all levels of government were substantially higher than during the Wilhelminian years.

Still, money alone cannot create culture; art and literature are produced by artists and other creative talents. With important exceptions, Bismarckian and Wilhelminian Germany were not noted for either. Why then the cultural explosion during the Weimar years? Why were such an extraordinary number of outstanding talents singularly productive during a very brief time span? In part Weimar's glow derives from contrasting it with the cultural dark age that followed. Weimar culture ended abruptly when the Nazis came to power, ironically, just as many of the finest works, particularly in literature, were being produced. After 1933 many of the Weimar artists, now in foreign exile, their careers destroyed or at least interrupted, remembered the years before the Nazis as having had the quality of an artists' Camelot.

Such remembrances contained a good deal of subjective selectivity. Nevertheless, there was more to Weimar culture than false memory. The extraordinary flowering of artistic endeavors in Germany came about largely because of the interaction of three factors: the technical and stylistic originality of many of the works produced, the importance of Berlin as the center of cultural modernism, and the eclecticism of the German artistic scene.

During the 1920s Germany for the first time in modern history had a cultural capital. To be sure, artistic life in the provinces did not die out—then as now even moderately sized cities maintained municipal theaters and opera houses—but as a concept Weimar culture was to a large extent synonymous with the capital. As if by a magnet aspiring artists were drawn to Berlin; feared and famous critics on the city's daily newspapers determined the fate of books and theater productions. And, equally important, in Berlin there existed an audience for virtually any innovative concept, no matter how outrageous. The result was an intellectual and artistic hothouse atmosphere that provided a great deal of mutual support and encouragement, but also, it must be admitted, a sense of freneticism that at times encouraged a flaunting of deliberate decadence and sensationalism.

More than anything else, Weimar culture was a genuine multimedia phenomenon. The artists and writers of the 1920s were fortunate in that they worked at a time when new media and new mass audiences for artistic endeavors—notably the cinema—were becoming available. During the Weimar years films outgrew the status of novelties shown at carnivals and became a recognized art form suitable for mass audiences. Weimar artists took enthusiastically to the new medium. Germany was flooded with good and bad films, and actors and actresses became household words overnight. Marlene Dietrich achieved instant stardom in her first major film role, the wanton Lola in *The Blue Angel*. An early horror film, *The Cabinet of Dr. Caligari*, demonstrated the effectiveness of expressionism (see the discussion on p. 170) as a cinematic style. Moreover, the influence of Weimar filmmakers was not limited by the German borders. Many leading artists and directors during the 1930s found a new home in Hollywood when the Nazis ended the artistic freedom that had characterized the Republican years.

In addition, the experience of the war had done much to weaken the influence of established techniques and values in such traditional fields as painting, architecture, sculpture, music, and literature. The atonality of Arnold Schönberg and his students dominated "serious" music, while the influence of American jazz enriched popular music. The first German musical, *The Threepenny Opera*, with lyrics by Bertold Brecht and a score by Kurt Weill, was an instant hit when it was first performed in 1928. In painting and sculpture the sentimental realism of the Wilhelminian years was replaced by a variety of schools, ranging from neorealism to cubism. In literature expressionism and neorealism dominated.

For all its eclecticism Weimar artistic life was also remarkable for some attempts to fuse the various visual and handicraft art forms into a coherent statement that expressed both the functionality and aesthetic of modernism. That effort was particularly epitomized by a unique school, the *Bauhaus* (House for the Building Arts). It was founded in 1919 through the efforts of the architect Walter Gropius and a number of leading painters and craftsmen, including Wassily Kandinsky, Paul Klee, and Oskar Kokoschka. The *Bauhaus* attempted to create a teaching and work atmosphere in which the lines between functionality and aesthetics and those between art and craftsmanship were fluid. Furniture and buildings were to be no less works of art than paintings or pieces of sculptures. Without imposing any strictures on its associates, the *Bauhaus* faculty developed a style of design for furniture and interior decorating that remains a model of uncluttered leanness. Like so much else that was original in Weimar culture, the *Bauhaus* aroused the ire of the Nazis. They criticized the *Bauhaus* style as "degenerate" and "*unvölkisch*" and forced the school's closing in 1933.

Political didacticism reached high levels of sophistication during the Weimar years. Two media forms, investigative journalism and the political cabaret, attracted particularly outstanding contributors. Carl von Ossietsky, the editor of the journal *Die Weltbühne* ("The World Stage") succeeded in exposing many vestiges of authoritarianism in German politics (he earned the hatred of the far-Right by revealing some of the Reichswehr's secret rearmament activities) and attacking the philistinism of the Republican authorities. A frequent contributor to *Die Weltbühne* was Kurt Tucholsky, a brilliant satirist who ridiculed the German political and social establishment in numerous prose and poetry pieces. It should be noted that while Weimar's political authors justifiably

attacked many abuses, they also tended to hurt their own causes. At times seemingly unwilling to make a distinction between the shortcomings of the Republicans and those who worked actively to overthrow the Republic, they helped to undermine confidence in the democratic and parliamentary system.

The variety of cultural forms was immense, but this was not true of the themes and topics that inspired Weimar artists. Probably the most pervasive theme in literature was a profound sense of cultural pessimism: The end of Western and particularly German civilization was at hand. A typical representative of this mood was the historian Oswald Spengler. His two-volume work *The Decline of the West* (the first part was published in 1918, the second in 1922), attacked hedonism and materialism as the forces that were hastening the end of Western civilization. Authors of fiction echoed Spengler's theme of decay. Hermann Broch's novel trilogy *The Sleepwalkers* (published in 1931 and 1932) documented the disintegration of Wilhelminian values. While Broch emphasized the progressive emptiness of prewar society, Josef Roth's *Radetzkymarsch* (1932) provided a more sympathetic, seriocomic, and nostalgic view of the vanished Habsburg Empire. Thomas Mann's *The Magic Mountain* (1924) also exuded a sense of death and disease. Mann chose as the locale for his story a tuberculosis sanitarium in the Swiss Alps. Here, the hero, a young Hamburg engineer, surrounded by slowly dying fellow patients, is exposed to a variety of philosophical systems, none of which he regards as satisfactory explanations for the state of the world.

The authors' pessimism about the future of the West and Germany derived in large part from their conviction that alienation was the most prominent characteristic of modern society. Alienation came in a variety of forms. In Alfred Döblin's epic novel *Berlin Alexanderplatz* (1929) a "good man" who has run afoul of the law is destroyed by the cruelties of bourgeois society. The figure of the *Spiesser*, the self-satisfied, middle-class boor, often portrayed as a heartless war profiteer, became a staple of Weimar literature. On the political Left, authors like Bertold Brecht and Heinrich Mann, artists like George Grosz, and investigative journals like *Die Weltbühne* attributed the slaughter of World War I and the rampant materialism of Weimar Germany to the greed and insensitivity of capitalism and capitalists.

In contrast, artists sympathetic to the political Right identified the bourgeoisie with rationalism, modernism, and lack of *völkisch* consciousness. Hans Grimm's bestseller, *Volk ohne Raum* (*A People without Space*) celebrated the victory of the South African whites over an alien culture and a physically harsh environment. Möller van den Bruck's *Das Dritte Reich* (*The Third Reich*) looked to the future to overcome the distasteful modernism of his day, while Oswald Spengler called for a return to "Prussian socialism," which he identified with German society during the time of Frederick the Great.

More common than accounts of class or national alienation, however, were tales of fictional characters feeling individually isolated because they were unable to relate to the society around them. Often the struggle took on epic dimensions. In Robert Musil's *Der Mann ohne Eigenschaften* (*The Man Without Qualities*), published between 1930 and 1943, the hero attempts (and fails) to find a bridge between his own intellect and the consciousness and values of prewar Austro-German society. Undoubtedly, the most famous case of multiple alienation was Franz Kafka. Although he died young, at the age of 41 in 1924, the emotional intensity of his novels and short stories has made the adjective "Kafkaesque" a synonym for the state of total alienation, which the author himself felt keenly. As a son Kafka felt estranged from his father. As an author writing in German he was alienated from the Czech culture of his native city of Prague, yet as a Jew he also felt alienated from the German culture around him. For Kafka, as for many Weimar artists, existence was "base-less" and "context-less."

Not surprisingly, World War I had a major impact on German cultural life during the 1920s. Some artists celebrated the war as the crucible that transformed men into heroes for a new age. Ernst Jünger's wartime diaries, *In Stahlgewittern* (*The Storm of Steel*), published in 1920, were particularly influential in creating the myth of the *Fronterlebnis*. Ernst von Salomon's *Das Buch vom deutschen Freikorpskämpfer* (*The Book of the German Freikorps Veteran*), which appeared in 1938, carried the same theme forward to the revolutionary upheavals of 1918–1919.

While celebrations of the war experience were rushed into print soon after the conflict ended, the two most famous antiwar novels, Erich Maria Remarque's *Im Westen nichts Neues* (*All Quiet on the Western Front*) and Ludwig Renn's *Krieg* (*War*), were not published until a decade later. Then, however, both of these powerful statements on the senselessness and dehumanization of war became immediate bestsellers. Remarque's novel was also turned into a major film.

Value confusion as it related to youthful adjustment to adult life was another prevalent theme of Weimar culture. As Sigmund Freud's ideas found a wider audience, the problems of sexual awakening and relations between men and women became a prominent topic of artistic productions. Notable (amidst much titillating sensationalism) were the stories of Arnold Zweig, an author who was famous for his portraits of the female psyche, and Hermann Hesse's novels of youthful escapism to exotic places and states of mind.

In the early 1930s numerous authors used the Great Depression as a theme. Hans Fallada's 1932 novel *Kleiner Mann—was nun?* (*Little Man, What Now?*) became an instant bestseller; millions of copies in twenty languages were sold. Fallada's particular concern was the impact of the Great Depression on the *Stehkragenproletariat*, the lower-middle class white-collar workers. Unaccustomed to unemployment, and insecure in their status, the Depression crushed them psychologically even more than materially.

The themes of Weimar culture were to some extent universal ones, but the styles of the age had unique features. Undoubtedly, expressionism was the most important stylistic contribution of Weimar culture. Expressionism began as a prewar phenomenon (the term was first used in 1901), but it was not until World War I and its immediate aftermath that the style for a brief time came to dominate virtually all art forms. Expressionism was a revolt against rationalism. Its followers rejected artistic portrayals of empirical reality and sought instead to "express" an inner reality of emotion. Beginning and culmination of the artist's (and man's) liberation was the "expressionist scream," a primordial outcry against the present. As a consequence, artists and authors stressed pure emotion and their subjects' character makeup at the expense of plot development and representation.

In films, where expressionism was particularly important and its influence continued longer than in other media, the elements of the style resulted in characteristic visual shock treatments to create an emotional impact. Expressionist filmmakers were particularly fascinated by portraying human madness on the screen—both individual and in the form of mob hysteria.

Despite its wide-ranging influence, expressionism did not remain the dominant stylistic form for long. Most writers became frustrated by expressionism's lack of emphasis on plot and story. In drama, audiences found it hard to identify with generic characters like "father,' "son," "man," and "woman." In the second half of the 1920s, expressionism increasingly lost ground to neorealism and neosentimentalism. Neorealism, or "new objectivity" as it was known in Germany, brought renewed emphasis on empiricism in literature and functionality or abstraction in the visual arts. The *Bauhaus* effort was one example of successful mod-

ified modernism. In contrast, some of those rejecting modernism turned from expressionism to preindustrial forms and values. Often the result was unabashed sentimentalism and *völkisch* kitsch, but in one field, architecture, the controversy yielded very positive results. The 1920s saw a genuine renaissance of German architecture with buildings inspired by *Bauhaus* fictionalism standing next to edifices that frankly aimed at a romantic revival of earlier styles. In aesthetic terms, examples of both were highly successful.

Weimar culture, like all of German society during the golden years, was divided and poised at a crossroads. A variety of voices and forms clamored for attention. Unfortunately, eclecticism did not result in tolerance and pluralism so much as in politization and mutual distrust. As the society became destabilized with the onset of the Great Depression, the various schools of artists sought an exclusivity for their themes and styles that in the end undermined all of them, much as the Republic which had enabled them to flower was destroyed by Nazi totalitarianism.

FOREIGN RELATIONS

As was true of the economy and cultural life during the Republic's golden years, Germany's foreign relations took a turn for the better. Largely through the efforts of Gustav Stresemann, the Reich foreign minister from 1923 until his death in 1929, Germany emerged from her postwar diplomatic isolation and achieved a degree of reconciliation with her former enemies, notably France.

Although Stresemann's six-year tenure as foreign minister provided much needed continuity in this important post, he was never without critics. The German Nationalists, ironically Stresemann's coalition partners in the Reich cabinets of 1924 and 1927, especially bitterly attacked the foreign minister's efforts at Franco-German reconciliation, characterizing them as appeasement and a sellout. The foreign minister also had considerable difficulties with his own party, the DVP. Stresemann remained the uncontested national chairman of the right liberals, but the powerful right wing in the DVP consistently put pressure on the foreign minister to abandon his policies of reconciliation with the Western Allies and draw closer to the DNVP's position.

Stresemann's overall foreign policy aim was to "revise" the consequences of the Treaty of Versailles. Concretely, this meant ending Germany's diplomatic isolation, removing the remaining occupation troops from her territory, and eliminating the Allied Control Commission's monitoring of German disarmament. To this end Stresemann was willing to pay the "price of Locarno." The Locarno treaties were the keystone of Germany's foreign relations in the second half of the decade. At the suggestion of Lord D'Abernon, the British ambassador in Berlin, the German government at the beginning of 1925 proposed to Great Britain and France that the Reich would be willing to recognize the legitimacy of her western boundaries if the Allies agreed to a withdrawal of their occupation troops from German soil before the scheduled date of 1935 and readmitted Germany into the family of nations on an equal footing.

The British responded positively, but the French were less eager to take up the German offer. After waiting six months before replying, the French countered Stresemann's proposal with a demand that Germany also recognize the legitimacy of her eastern borders and that the entire treaty package be guaranteed by a mutual assistance pact among France, Great Britain, and Italy.

It took several months of negotiations in Locarno, Switzerland, between Stresemann, his French counterpart Aristide Briand, and their staffs, before the treaty package could be initialed in October 1925. Even then the "Eastern Locarno" proved unattainable. Not only were the Germans unwilling to recog-

nize the legitimacy of their 1918 boundary with Poland (although the Reich agreed to forego any use of force in attempting to change the boundaries there), but the British refused to accept any responsibility for guaranteeing the boundaries in the east. In the final treaty the Reich only agreed not to challenge her new boundaries in the west, and Great Britain and Italy in turn guaranteed the inviolability of these territorial changes. Germany was also accepted as a member of the League of Nations. The Allies for their part speeded up the removal of some of their occupation forces, and withdrew the Inter-Allied Control Commission, which had been monitoring the progress of German disarmament.

Although the Locarno agreements enabled Germany to break out of her diplomatic isolation and regain much of her sovereignty, the treaties became the subject of a bitter debate within Germany. After originally supporting the Locarno initiative (the DNVP was a member of the Reich cabinet when the negotiations began) conservatives and the *völkische* soon attacked Stresemann because he had failed to achieve the impossible: They demanded that he should have insisted on the return of Alsace-Lorraine to Germany and obtained from the Allies an agreement to rescind the war-guilt clause of the Versailles Treaty.

Although for Stresemann reconciliation with the Western powers was a primary goal of his foreign-policy aims, the foreign minister was careful to balance the agreement with the West by good relations with Soviet Russia. In April 1926, the Reich and Soviet Russia signed the Treaty of Berlin. In this agreement the two partners confirmed the terms of the Treaty of Rapallo and agreed that if either were attacked by a third power the other would remain neutral. (Unlike the Locarno pacts, the Treaty of Berlin was not controversial; all parties in the Reichstag voted for its ratification.) The Russians were also pleased that before taking her seat in the League of Nations, Germany had issued a declaration announcing that in her disarmed state she could not be expected to bear the full burden of any sanctions that might be imposed against the Soviet Union by the League. Finally, although the new agreement with the Soviet Union was silent on this point, good relations with Russia also made it possible for the Reichswehr to continue testing armaments forbidden Germany under the terms of the Versailles Treaty.

This last feature was an integral part of Stesemann's foreign-policy goals; the third pillar of his revisionist foreign policy was rearmament. To be sure, in contrast to the *revanchistes* of the radical Right, the foreign minister had no wish for a renewed armed conflict with France. He was convinced, however, that a true European balance of power was impossible if Germany remained defenseless. For this reason Stresemann not only supported all rearmament measures that were legal under the Treaty of Versailles, such as the construction of the pocket battleship, but he also approved of the Reichswehr's clandestine activities, including the ongoing cooperation with the Soviet Red Army.

Stresemann's foreign policy demonstrated both the usefulness and the limitations of the "spirit of Locarno." The treaty package did bring the Reich out of diplomatic isolation and began a process of removing some of the mutual suspicion between Germany and her former enemies. At the same time, the "spirit of Locarno" was not able to bring about an era of real peace based upon mutual trust. Neither the Allies nor the Germans could escape thinking in categories of national policies and national rivalries. A great deal of distrust remained among the "hereditary enemies." Stresemann wanted to use the Locarno agreements to regain Germany's Great Power status. The French in turn remained suspicious about the Germans' motives, and were consequently reluctant to give up their "productive guarantees." It was not until the Young Plan had been ratified in 1930 that the last French soldiers left Germany.

By that time, Stresemann had been dead for almost a year. In ill health for some years, he was finally worn down by the incessant attacks of his domestic political foes—both among the radical Right and in his own party. At the time of his death his foreign policy remained uneasily poised at a halfway point of reconciliation with Germany's former enemies.

THE COLLAPSE OF THE ECONOMY AND THE END OF PARLIAMENTARY DEMOCRACY

At first glance 1929 was in many ways the Republic's best year. Industrial production exceeded the prewar high set in 1913. The "spirit of Locarno" had returned Germany to international respectability, and the Young Plan promised a final and relatively painless settlement of the vexing reparations issue. Weimar Germany's Berlin-centered cultural and artistic life glittered and dazzled.

Actually, as we now know, Germany (and indeed all of Europe) stood at the edge of a precipice. The signs of optimism in the heady days of 1929 hid a host of unresolved problems that had been left in the wake of World War I. Germany's and Europe's economic growth lagged behind such "takeoff" areas as the United States. Despite the impressive recovery in the second half of the decade, Europe had lost its position as the pivot of the international economic system. Growth rates for the kingpin of prewar European prosperity, international trade, for the period 1913 to 1929 were only 25 percent of what they had been for the years 1880 to 1913.

Germany's chronic economic problems, especially the difficulties in agriculture and labor unrest, caused tensions in the grand coalition, but they remained manageable until the fall of 1929, when the financing of unemployment compensation caused a battle over principles among the coalition partners. When the German national system

A 1928 campaign poster of the Bavarian People's Party portrays the "golden years" of the Weimar Republic: In 1918 a Bolshevik arsonist stalked the land; in 1928 peace and prosperity have returned. (Source: *Anschläge*, no. 56.)

of unemployment compensation was established in 1927, it was intended to be a self-perpetuating insurance scheme financed by contributions from employees and employers. It worked well until the particularly severe winter of 1928–1929 when unexpectedly large numbers of unemployed had required subsidies from the Reich budget to keep the insurance fund solvent. The crisis seemed to be over when the economy picked up again in the summer of 1929, but less than a year later with the onset of the Great Depression the insurance system collapsed entirely. Disagreements over financing unemployment compensation led to the fall of the government in March 1930 and the Republic's final constitutional crisis.

Economic historians continue to debate the long- and short-range causes of the Great Depression, but there is little disagreement about its devastating impact. The seeming suddenness of the downturn, its rapid spread, its depth and duration created a political and social crisis from which no Western society was immune, but which reached disastrous dimensions in Germany.

The Depression caused interdependent fiscal, credit, and confidence crises that brought economic life to a virtual standstill and plunged Germany into a political and constitutional catastrophe. The fiscal impact came first, and it was linked to American investment in Germany. During the "golden years," American investors had channeled billions of dollars into the private and public sectors of the German economy. With the crash of the New York stock market in October 1929, that flow of capital came to an abrupt end. In fact, caught short by the market crash, American investors hastened to cash in many of their short- and medium-term obligations in Germany, leading to a massive flight of capital.

The first to be adversely affected by the shortage of foreign capital were the German cities. During the golden years numerous municipalities had floated bonds on the American money markets to finance improvements in their infrastructures. The rapid withdrawal of these obligations, coupled with decreasing tax receipts and increased expenditures for social services that resulted from the economic impact of the Great Depression, led to the bankruptcy of many cities. The municipal fiscal crisis in turn had repercussions for the states, since under German law the latter were responsible for the cities' debts.

The fiscal crisis in the public sector was both caused and compounded by a credit crisis in the private sector. Here, too, foreign and domestic investors abruptly withdrew their monies in the fall of 1929. The downward spiral continued with a crisis of confidence leading to precipitous declines in production and consumption, while business failures and unemployment simultaneously climbed to unprecedented levels.

The debate over unemployment was the immediate catalyst that added a political crisis to the country's economic woes. In the winter months of 1929–1930 unemployment, which had been a chronic irritant until then, was rapidly transformed into a national obsession. In 1929, 1.9 million (8.5 percent of the workforce) had been out of work; a year later the figure was 3.1 million (14.0 percent of the workforce). There was agreement that these figures represented a severe impact on the economy, but there was no consensus on how to deal with the problem. In the Reich cabinet a classic debate pitted the DVP as the party of business against the SPD as the spokesman for labor. Faced with the necessity of transferring funds from the Rich budget to keep the unemployment scheme solvent, the DVP insisted that the system had to be self-supporting. Only increased contributions or decreased benefits would restore investor confidence in the economy. The Social Democrats, on the other hand, were equally adamant that priority be given to the needs of the unemployed.

In March 1930, the Reich cabinet faced a decision on how to meet the rapidly growing deficits of the unemployment insurance program. The SPD ministers (and especially the secretary of labor, Rudolf Wissell) favored subsidies from general revenues, while the DVP demanded an increase in payroll deduction taxes of 0.25 percent for employers and employees. Unable to compromise on this issue, the Reich cabinet submitted its resignation. The differences seemed narrow on the surface (and indeed many SPD leaders criticized Wissell's obstinacy), but in reality the two sides were at odds over a fundamental issue: Labor felt that recovery should not be accomplished on the backs of those who suffered immediate hardship, while businessmen increasingly came to believe that the high cost of unemployment compensation and social services in general prevented an upturn in the economy.

The Müller cabinet was the last government of the Weimar era that was supported by a majority of the Reichstag. After March 1930 the fragile consensus of Republican forces was replaced by what Eberhard Jäckel has called the "mutual paralysis of forces." No combination of political and socioeconomic groups was strong enough to govern Germany under the rules of parliamentary democracy, but a number of them did have sufficient strength to block the coming to power of rival coalitions. The result of this constitutional impasse was the virtual paralysis of the political decision-making process. Political life in the last years of the Weimar Republic was characterized by increasing street violence of competing political armies and efforts by a variety of interest groups—from the army to industrial lobbies—to influence decisions through extraparliamentary means.

The paralysis of parliament elevated the Reich president to a position as supreme arbiter of the nation. For the next three years the president, rather than parliament, would determine the fate of chancellors, cabinets, and legislation to cope with the Great Depression. Unfortunately, the incumbent, Paul von Hindenburg, was singularly ill-equipped to shoulder the burdens that fell to him. Now eighty years old, Hindenburg's mental and physical powers were rapidly deteriorating. In addition, he had little knowledge of the complex economic and political problems facing the country. In fact, he was a virtual prisoner of the camarillas that surrounded him in the presidential palace and on his East Prussian estate. In Berlin, Hindenburg's personal advisors were for the most part conservative politicians, Reichswehr officers, and his son Oskar von Hindenburg, who was then a major in the army. Among the Reichswehr officers, General Kurt von Schleicher, the chief of the defense department's Political Bureau, played a key role in the president's entourage. In East Prussia, the president socialized with his Junker neighbors, most of whom supported Hugenberg's DNVP.

Hindenburg's, or rather his advisors', choice as chancellor to succeed Hermann Müller was Heinrich Brüning. At first glance Brüning seemed to bring a number of important assets to the job. He was a leading member of the Center Party, the political group that had supplied more Weimar chancellors than any other party. At age forty-five he was relatively young, energetic, and ambitious. For some years he had served with distinction as the chairman of the Reichstag's Ways and Means Committee, earning a well-deserved reputation as an expert on the intricacies of the federal budget.

But there was another side to Brüning. Like the president and his entourage Brüning had long-standing reservations about the democratic constitutional system and the revolution of 1918 that had brought it about. Brüning rejected continuing the coalition with the Social Democrats; he readily promised the president to appoint only members of the bourgeois parties to his cabinet. Above all, however, Brüning would work to weaken parliamentary democracy.

We now know that he favored the restoration of the monarchy and the return of at least a modified form of authoritarianism. The chancellor agreed with the conservatives surrounding the Reich president that the Weimar constitution would have to be amended so as to curtail severely the powers of the Reichstag. Brüning, then, promised to use the economic crisis to make fundamental changes in Germany's democratic constitutional system. It was this latter goal that made him acceptable to the president's advisors.

CHAPTER 7

FROM AUTHORITARIANISM TO TOTALITARIANISM, 1930–1938

Heinrich Brüning's appointment as Reich chancellor undoubtedly marked an important milestone in the course of German history. There is considerably less agreement, however, on the relationship between the advent of the "presidential regimes" and the coming to power of the Nazis in 1933. Did Brüning and his two presidential successors, Franz von Papen and Kurt von Schleicher, pave the way for Nazi totalitarianism, or were they the last barrier stemming the tide? Most historians tend to see Hitler's appointment as Reich chancellor, in January 1933, as a crucial watershed in modern German history, but in reality the change from the "New Conservatism" of the presidential governments to the totalitarianism of the Nazi regime, was fluid rather than abrupt. True, Hitler and the Nazis radicalized and brutalized the political practices of the New Conservatives, yet in the first five years of their rule they also continued many of the New Conservatives' constitutional, economic, and foreign policies. Both groups rejected parliamentary democracy as a political system. They were also united in their opposition to Stresemann's policy of international reconciliation and compromise; they placed more faith in diplomatic confrontation and bluff. Instead of free trade and priority for overseas exports, both groups pursued economic autarky—that is to say, national self-sufficiency—and regional trading systems. Not altogether surprisingly, a number of New Conservatives thought of the Nazis as their natural allies and, as we shall see, some among them were instrumental in helping Hitler come to power.

THE RULE OF THE NEW CONSERVATIVES

Parliamentary democracy ended in March 1930, when the systemic consensus among the major societal segments broke down permanently. For the next three years Germany was governed by forces that ruled virtually unchecked in the absence of parliamentary control: the civil service, the army, and, to a lesser extent, major business and agricultural groups. Politically, these forces subscribed to ideas that for want of a better name have been labeled "New Conservatism," while administratively they relied on the authority and charisma of the Reich president.

In the last years of the Weimar Republic the spectrum of German politics shifted considerably. Both liberal and traditional Conservative parties failed to retain a significant following among the German voters, and they all but disappeared from the political landscape. Political Catholicism and Marxism did much better in keeping the allegiance of their supporters, but their mutual antagonisms prevented effective cooperation among them. The Communists regarded the Social Democrats (SPD) as a "social fascist organization," and the leader of the Center Party elected in 1928, Monsignor Kaas, was determined that political Catholicism should become a right-wing nationalist movement opposed to cooperation with all forms of organized Marxism.

The failure of parliamentarism and the reality of political atomization quite naturally led to efforts to achieve systemic consensus outside the framework of political democracy. The most important of these plans were those advocated by the New Conservatives, the Nazis, and the Communists.

Despite impressive strength at the polls and in the streets, the Communists' hope for revolution and the dictatorship of the proletariat was doomed to failure. The expectations of the German Communist Party (KPD) that the Great Depression signaled the final collapse of capitalism in Germany was not only wishful thinking but politically counterproductive. The party's revolutionary rhetoric helped to strengthen the Nazis by persuading large numbers of Germans, especially among the middle classes and the well-to-do, that only Nazism could block the victory of Bolshevism in Germany. In addition, under the Comintern-dictated doctrine of "social fascism" (which was not dropped until 1935), the KPD concentrated its efforts upon weakening the Social Democrats, defined by the party's masters in Moscow as the real vanguard of fascism. The result was a paralyzing fraternal conflict among the German working classes that, in the final analysis, benefited only the Nazis in their quest for power.

The Nazis' road to unity and recovery was in some ways the mirror image of the Communist path; the Nazis agreed with the Communists that Germany could only choose between Nazism and communism. Both, therefore, sought to evoke an apocalyptic atmosphere, but in contrast to the Communist appeal to proletarian revolution, Hitler's movement promised to overcome class divisions and create a genuine "national community" with economic prosperity and national greatness. To achieve this goal, the Nazis demanded the destruction of democracy, the elimination from power of those forces that in their view had brought ruin to Germany—Jews, Marxists, democrats, and republicans—and their replacement by Adolf Hitler and his minions.

Among the practitioners of the "new politics" the New Conservatives had the least popular appeal. While the Communists and Nazis steadily increased their voting support as the Great Depression deepened, the electoral success of the New Conservatives remained miniscule. But this was of little concern to them; their aim of restoring authoritarianism to Germany depended on the support of the traditional, "natural" elites that had governed Germany before World War I. In addition, some New Conservatives were not opposed to cooperating with a force that had demonstrated its mass appeal: the Nazis. They saw no real contradictions between the goals of the Nazis and those of the New Conservatives. They were convinced that the Nazis, for all their rabble-rousing talents, needed the guidance of the old elites if they hoped to share in exercising political power.

The New Conservatives would eventually discover that in their relationship with the Nazis they were the tail rather than the dog; but for almost three years, from March 1930 to the end of January 1933, control of the Reich lay in the hands of the New Conservatives. Three presidential chancellors followed each other in quick succession. We have already met Heinrich Brüning, the right-wing Conservative Catholic who succeeded Hermann Müller. He was followed, in May 1932, by Franz von Papen, nominally another member of the Center Party. Papen was a Westphalian aristocrat and wealthy landowner who had been a cavalry officer and diplomat in World War I. His political views were those of an extreme conservative; since 1925 he had urged German Catholics to renounce cooperation with the Social Democrats in any form. Finally, for a brief two months in December 1932 and January 1933, the chancellor's office was occupied by the man who was in many ways a political father of New Conservatism, General Kurt von Schleicher. This master of intrigue was a major force behind the scenes in every one of the presidential cabinets. It was Schleicher who had recommended both Brüning and Papen to Hindenburg.

In time the three presidential chancellors became bitter personal enemies, but they shared a common outlook on Germany's political and social future. At the heart of their political strategy lay the conviction that the Depression and the political paralysis of the early 1930s presented Germany with massive social and economic problems, but also with unique opportunities to solve what they termed the country's "constitutional emergency" and its diplomatic impotence. The reality of political polarization and the threat of societal disintegration would, they felt, enable them to change Germany's constitutional structure from democracy to authoritarianism while simultaneously forcing the Allies to restore the Reich to the status of full equality in the concert of powers. The three presidential cabinets were determined to use the "constitutional emergency" in order to replace, in Brüning's words, a "senseless form of parliamentarism" with a "healthful, limited democracy." Concretely, the domestic plans of the New Conservatives involved a strengthened Reich executive, severe curtailments of the powers of the Reichstag, and reforms of Germany's federal structure to reduce the residual powers of the *Länder*. The key to realizing this reform program was the Reich president's unwavering support of "his" chancellor, unity among the "natural" elites, and the continuing paralysis of the political opposition, notably the Social Democrats and the labor unions.

At the same time, the presidential cabinets hoped that Germany's deflationary policies (see the following, pp. 181–82) would enable the Reich to throw off what they regarded as the last major burden of the Versailles system: the reparations payments. The belt-tightening measures they imposed were at least in part designed to convince the Allies that Germany simply had no resources with which to continue reparations payments. The New Conservatives, then, were not overly concerned about the country's economic problems; on the contrary, they actually expected the country's growing social misery to advance their long-range domestic and foreign policy goals.

By the time Heinrich Brüning moved into the chancellor's office the worrisome credit and investment crisis had become a major recession. It would continue to grow worse throughout Brüning's chancellorship; by the summer of 1931 the crisis had become a full-scale depression. Germany's industrial production decreased by 50 percent between 1927 and 1928 and 1932 to 1933; exports declined from 26.9 billion

An example of the cult of personality around Brüning. A 1930 Center Party campaign poster shows Communists and Nazis struggling in vain to overcome "Brüning, the last defense of liberty and order." Hitler is the man pictured at the extreme lower right-hand corner. (Source: *Anschläge*, no. 86.)

marks in 1929 to 10.4 billion in 1932. Despite the decline in production, there continued to be a surplus of unsold goods. Business failures and farm indebtedness multiplied dramatically, and that in turn caused massive liquidity problems for many banks, including some of the Reich's largest. In July 1931, the government was forced to declare a banking holiday for almost two weeks to prevent panic withdrawals.

These structural symptoms of economic dislocation were real enough, but the average German was more concerned with the immediate social consequences of the Depression: both actual and feared unemployment, and the decline in the standard of living. Unemployment was the most visible and immediate manifestation of economic difficulties. Lack of jobs had been a chronic problem for many even in the "good" years of the Weimar Republic, but during the Great Depression unemployment grew to catastrophic levels. In 1930 the official statistics registered 3.1 million without work. In the summer of 1932 that figure had risen to 6.2 million; one-third of the work force was without a job. The actual unemployed included mainly blue-collar workers and those just starting their careers. In most sectors of the economy there were very few entry-level jobs.

But the growing unemployment figures had an adverse effect even on those lucky enough to keep jobs. Repeated wage cuts and loss of benefits were a fact of life for virtually all members of the workforce. Moreover, white-collar workers, professionals, and management-level employees were particularly susceptible to a psychological "fear effect." Unlike blue-collar workers, for whom at least temporary layoffs were not an unfamiliar experience, the salaried segments of the workforce were unaccustomed to being laid off, and they associated unemployment not only with a decline in their standard of living but, worse, with a loss of status and reversal of upward mobility.

As we shall see, the presidential Reich cabinets seemed singularly blind to the social and economic consequences of the Depression. To be sure, they were aware of the rising misery index, but Brüning and his successors were also convinced that efforts to address the social problems directly (other than through charity and minimal welfare payments) were both economically and politically counterproductive. In agreement with most experts in Germany (and other industrialized nations) the New Conservatives regarded the Depression in economic terms as a "cleansing crisis" by which the market forces rejuvenated themselves after a period of imbalance caused by hyperactivity.

Remarkably, even politicians and union leaders politically opposed to the New Conservatives did not give their highest priority to finding jobs for the unemployed. Numerous organizations and individuals presented plans for "counter-cyclical" measures—mostly schemes for public works programs—but not until late 1931 and 1932, when the number of jobless was already above 5 million, did the German labor unions develop proposals for massive public works programs, and even then many union leaders remained skeptical about any program that raised the spectre of government deficits. Like the New Conservatives, they, too, regarded fiscal orthodoxy as an article of economic faith. As far as incentives for the private sector were concerned, it was not until the brief chancellorship of Kurt von Schleicher that a modest program of tax relief for employers who hired new workers was tried.

For the New Conservatives the principal role of government during the "cleansing crisis" was to prevent the erosion of the value of the German currency. They were convinced that only faith in the mark's stability would persuade private entrepreneurs to invest their money in the Reich's economy and thus start the cycle of economic recovery. In practice this meant a rigid policy of deflation. Regardless of the social consequences, public expenditures would not be allowed to outpace current tax receipts. (This was also the reason the Reichsbank and especially its president, Hans Luther, fiercely opposed any public works program that involved deficit financing.) Balanced budgets, of course, can be produced in only two ways: cutting costs or increasing revenue. The Germans did both. The reductions focused on civil servants' salaries (between 1930 and 1932 civil servants' wages were reduced by 20 percent) and unemployment and welfare payments. Still, with tax receipts steadily declining as the Great Depression grew worse, these measures were far from sufficient to balance the budget. The presidential governments (and, pressured by them, state and local authorities as well) increasingly resorted to raising taxes. Such revenue-enhancement measures—in retrospect, economically absurd policies that served to delay creating a favorable investment climate—ranged from income tax surcharges to a series of consumption taxes. The latter imposed levies on luxury items and alcoholic beverages, but also on such everyday necessities as sugar, salt, and meat. The most resented of the new taxes was actually a throwback to premodern times, a "head tax" levied on every adult German regardless of income. To keep German industry competitive in the shrinking world market, the government put pressure on the private sector to cut wages and prices. Both were to be cut by 10 percent but for prices the indexing began with the levels of December 1931, while the 10 percent wage reduction was based on the wage levels of 1927. (The government argued that between 1927 and 1931 wages had outpaced increases in productivity.)

The New Conservatives were considerably more successful in reaching their immediate foreign policy goals than in achieving their domestic aims. Following the lead of President Herbert Hoover when he declared a one-year moratorium on inter-Allied debts in 1931, Great Britain and France agreed to a suspension of the payments Germany owed them as well. The morato-

rium actually ended reparation payments permanently; Brüning and Papen could take credit for lifting the reparations burden from Germany.

At home, however, the domestic consequences of New Conservatism were far less fortuitous. The overall economic policies understandably annoyed labor, but more important was the disaffection of segments of the New Conservatives' constituencies among the "natural elites." As the government-imposed fiscal strictures affected their specific interests, spokesmen for these groups sought access to the Reich president, often bypassing the chancellor, in order to seek redress of what they regarded as unfair burdens.

This was true of the East Elbian and especially East Prussian landowners. Throughout the 1920s the chronically depressed agricultural areas of the east had benefited from an "Aid for the East" (*Osthilfe*) program, which provided cheap credit to East Elbian farmers and businessmen. Until 1930 the program was largely financed by federal money but administered by Prussian state agencies. The Prussian authorities applied fairly stringent criteria before applicants could qualify for subsidized loans. The state administrators were generally not willing to waste money on estates that were so heavily indebted as to be unsalvageable even with government credit.

The Depression vastly increased not only the need for subsidies, but also the number of farms threatened by bankruptcy. The Junker spokesmen for East Elbian agriculture appealed to Hindenburg—a fellow East Prussian landowner—to force a liberalization of the aid program. Brüning was aware of these concerns, and before becoming Reich chancellor he promised the Reich president he would take steps to ease the credit crisis in the East. He kept his promise by gradually pushing Prussian state agencies out of the administration of the *Osthilfe*. But even these measures were not enough to satisfy Hindenburg's friends and neighbors;

they denounced the chancellor as an "agrarian Bolshevik" who was trying to destroy the Junkers as a social class. Their criticism was echoed by the Agrarian League and the DNVP, both of whom grew increasingly strident in calling for Brüning's dismissal.

The first phase of the New Conservative era came to an abrupt end in the spring of 1932. Hindenburg's term of office as Reich president ended in April of that year, and Brüning had hoped that the major parties, including the Nazis and the DNVP, would agree to Hindenburg's reelection by acclamation. The moderate groups agreed, but the German Nationalist People's Party (DNVP), the Nazis, and the Communists refused. Eventually the DNVP nominated Theodor Duesterberg, the second-in-command of the *Stahlhelm*; Hitler became the Nazi Party's candidate; the Communists put up their own leader, Ernst Thälmann; and Brüning and the moderate Weimar parties (including the SPD) supported Hindenburg. After a bitter campaign the former field marshal was reelected, but the country he headed was more polarized than ever.

Soon after the presidential election, Hindenburg withdrew his support from Brüning. Kurt von Schleicher and other New Conservatives close to the president persuaded him that the Center Party chancellor, for all his good intentions, had been too accommodating to the forces of democracy and parliamentarism, especially the Social Democrats. Franz von Papen promised to have fewer scruples. His goals for constitutional reform were not significantly different from those of his predecessor, but his political tactics were far less subtle. While Brüning had at least adhered to the letter of the constitution and attempted to find a consensus in the Reichstag for his policies, Papen reveled in his near total lack of support in parliament; an overwhelming majority of the elected representatives of the German people opposed him and his government. Papen's continuation in office and the realization of his program were completely dependent on the Reich president and the men around him.

Papen moved quickly to translate the New Conservatives' ideas on constitutional "reforms" into practice. With the stroke of the Reich president's pen, the chancellor obtained the destruction of major parts of the German federal structure. State elections in April 1932 had produced a parliamentary deadlock in Prussia. The Landtag was unable to elect a new government, and under the terms of the Prussian constitution the old cabinet remained in office as a caretaker government. Both the New Conservatives and the Nazis had long regarded the Prussian cabinet, in which Social Democratic ministers headed key departments, as a major obstacle to their long-range plans. The Prussian government, for example, had been instrumental in persuading the Brüning cabinet to order the dissolution of the two primary causes of the escalating street violence, the Nazi Stormtroopers and the Communists' Red Frontfighters Association. Papen, soon after coming into office, revoked the ban on the Nazi Stormtroopers (the ban on the Communist paramilitary organization remained in force), permitting the Nazi thugs to resume their activities on Germany's streets. When the level of political violence predictably increased, Papen claimed that the Prussian government was unable to maintain law and order. On July 20, the Reich cabinet issued a presidential order placing the administration of Prussia under federal control, with Papen himself serving as Reich commissioner for Prussia. For the remainder of the year Papen and the Reich minister of the interior, Baron von Gayl, an old-line Hugenberg Conservative, worked diligently to carry out a purge of the Prussian civil service. Dozens of pro-republican administrators were dismissed or retired and replaced with men who sympathized with the New Conservatives.

Papen's decision to rescind the dissolution order against the Stormtroopers was a gesture of appeasement toward the Nazis. Like Brüning, Papen initially regarded Hitler's movement as an adjunct, not an enemy, of New Conservatism. For this reason the New Conservatives had not been unduly alarmed when, as a result of the national elections in September 1930, the Nazis became the second largest party in the Reichstag. Instead of the 12 deputies elected in 1928, there was now a sea of 107 brownshirts in the national parliament. The Nazis' attitude during the presidential election of 1932 eventually convinced Brüning that he could not deal with Hitler, but Papen was sure he could secure the goodwill of both the DNVP and Hitler's party. There were no difficulties with Hugenberg, the leader of the DNVP. The DNVP provided most of the ministers in Papen's "cabinet of barons" (so called because of the large number of aristocrats in the government) and the only real parliamentary support for the second presidential chancellor. Papen also had the support of most East Elbian land owners and a large section of the business community. As for the Nazis, Papen (and Schleicher) followed the same course that had led Brüning to disaster. Papen agreed to Hitler's demand for new national elections in July 1932, when the Great Depression had reached its full impact. The results were yet further losses for the moderate parties and the DNVP, while the Nazis more than doubled their representation in the Reichstag. They were now the largest party in parliament; their parliamentary leader, Hermann Göring, was elected speaker of the house.

In return for these political gifts, Papen and Schleicher thought they had Hitler's agreement to support, or at least tolerate, the New Conservative regime. Here they were very much mistaken. The Nazis were not willing to become Papen's junior partners. In August Hitler demanded that Hindenburg appoint the Nazi leader as chancellor with powers to run the country by decree—much as Brüning and Papen had been doing since 1930. On Papen's advice, the Reich president refused, and that decision ended, at least for a time, the honey-

moon between the new chancellor and the Nazis. In a desperate attempt to gain time, Papen called for new elections only four months after the July Reichstag had been elected. The results of the November 1932 contest brought significant losses for the Nazis, although the NSDAP (Nazis) remained the strongest party in the Reichstag. In view of what the New Conservatives called the continuing "constitutional emergency," that is to say, a Reichstag that refused to cooperate with the New Conservatives, Papen then asked the Reich president to suspend the constitution and establish a temporary military dictatorship.

Papen made his new "reform" proposal in November, but by that time the real power behind the last two New Conservative chancellors, Kurt von Schleicher, felt he had a better alternative. The general knew that Hindenburg would be reluctant to agree to the blatant destruction of the constitution which he had sworn to uphold. In addition, Schleicher argued that Papen's plan for a military dictatorship was both politically risky and unnecessary. The general felt he had found a way out of the constitutional impasse that would accomplish the basic goals of the New Conservatives without resorting to open dictatorship. Schleicher offered to head a Reich government that he claimed would, unlike his predecessor's, be able to work harmoniously with a majority of the Reichstag.

Kurt von Schleicher's brief tenure as chancellor revealed a third variant of the New Conservative scenario. The new chancellor was hardly a flaming democrat. Like Brüning and Papen, the general was disdainful of parties and parliamentary democracy. He differed from his immediate predecessors only in that he envisioned an extraparliamentary populist corollary to the basic authoritarian structure that he was convinced Germany needed. The core of Schleicher's plans—and little more is discernible even now since the general was given to great secrecy but little systematic thought—seems to have been to ally the forces of New Conservatism with big business, organized labor, and the left-wing of the Nazi Party. To secure the support of these groups, he offered the employers tax relief, the unions an expanded public works program, and the Nazis a share of governmental power; Gregor Strasser, the number-two figure in Hitler's party, would become vice-chancellor in Schleicher's cabinet.

Schleicher's scheme failed ignominiously and rapidly. Some spokesmen for the business community reacted positively, but most union leaders were unwilling to trust a political general who, in the past, had made no secret of his animosity toward organized labor and social democracy. As for the Nazis, Gregor Strasser was willing to go along with Schleicher's plans, but Hitler was not. Schleicher had hoped that Strasser would join the cabinet on his own, thereby pitting himself and his followers against Hitler, but instead the NSDAP's second-in-command resigned all of his party offices and went on an extended vacation to Italy. Before departing Germany, he left behind a message urging all those who sympathized with his views not to follow his own example, but to remain loyal to Adolf Hitler. By the end of December 1932 Schleicher, too, fell back on the proposal of a military dictatorship as the only way out of the constitutional impasse. Hindenburg still refused.

After almost three years in power, the balance sheet of New Conservatism was not impressive. The presidential chancellors had destroyed parliamentary democracy and a good part of the German federal structure, but they were unable to put into place constitutional changes that would restore authoritarianism permanently to the Reich. But all was not yet lost. Papen, who had by now recovered from the shock of his dismissal and betrayal by his old friend Kurt von Schleicher, had another plan for realizing the New Conservatives' political goals. He claimed the scheme would not violate the letter of the Weimar constitution, it would secure the Nazis' cooperation, and it would keep the New Conservatives in positions of real power.

THE NAZIS' RISE TO POWER

After he became chancellor in 1933, Adolf Hitler often included in his interminable speeches a section that came to be dubbed his "party history." Invariably lasting about half an hour, the party history expressed the *Führer's* conviction that providence had selected him, the unknown soldier of World War I, to overcome all obstacles and create first a powerful political movement and then the Third Reich.

Actually, Hitler's rise to power reflected more mundane factors at work. One of these was German history itself. The Nazis did not burst upon the German political scene without warning. They were the inheritors and beneficiaries of deep and ill-hidden strains of anti-Semitism, anti-modernism, and antiparliamentarism in German society. This was the fertile soil that had nurtured *völkisch* movements since the 1890s. The lost war and the disappointments many Germans felt with the lackluster performance of the Weimar Republic provided further nourishment. Still, with all these factors present, the Nazis received less than 3 percent of the popular vote in 1928.

It required the Depression to transform the National Socialists from a fringe group to a major political force. What might be called the secondary effects of the economic disaster—the paralysis of the parliamentary system, the government's seeming unwillingness to deal with the Depression, the rising strength of the Communist Party, and the attempt by the New Conservatives to use the situation for their own purposes—persuaded many Germans that only Hitler and his party provided hope for the future and an alternative to the triumph of Bolshevism. The Nazis scored their first success in the Prussian local elections of December 1929 and then, roughly paralleling the continuing downturn of the economic indicators, went from victory to victory until in the depths of the Depression 37 percent of the German electorate cast their ballots for Hitler's movement.

To make effective use of the influx of members and voters that the Depression brought to the party, the Nazis used a system of three parallel organizational levels, each with separate but complimentary functions. The party proper was divided into regional units called *Gaus*, headed by a *Gauleiter*. The *Gaus'* boundaries for the most part corresponded to the Reichstag electoral districts, and the primary function of the activists in the *Gaus* was to campaign and get out to vote.

A second organizational rung consisted of affiliates (*angeschlossene Verbände*) in which Nazi sympathizers (and party members) were organized according to economic and professional interest groups ranging from farmers to the "National Socialist Association of Munich Coal Dealers." Their purpose was to spread the Nazi influence among the various economic interest groups and, if possible, turn them into agencies of political support for the Nazi cause. The party was particularly effective in organizing farmers, retailers, and physicians.

Finally, there was the most visible element of the Nazi Party, the paramilitary groups, notably the Stormtroopers (*Sturmabteilung*, SA). (The organization that was later to become the dreaded symbol of the regime, the *Schutzstaffel*—[Protection Squad, SS]— was still in an embryonic stage of development.) During the last years of the Weimar Republic, the SA with a membership of about 400,000 at the end of 1932, was undoubtedly the most important part of the Nazis' political strategy. The Stormtroopers put up posters, protected the party's rallies from disturbances by political rivals, and terrorized opponents and innocent bystanders alike. The Stormtroopers effectively symbolized both of the Nazis' militancy and their brutality.

The Nazis' triple organizational structure and their eclectic and opportunistic pro-gram were well designed to reap political benefits from an atomized and fearful German electorate. In literally hundreds of rallies the Nazis practiced a typically fascist style of campaigning: masses of swastika flags and patriotic symbols, stern-looking uniformed guards, martial music, and histrionic speakers. At the same time, the omnipresent Stormtroopers, who were involved in almost daily brawls with Communists and other political opponents, impressed particularly the German middle and upper classes with their dedication to saving Germany from the—imaginary—imminent Bolshevik revolution. The Nazis were also sophisticated politicians; Hitler was the first modern political leader to make extensive use of the airplane during his campaigns.

The NSDAP's message in its rallies was always the same. The party's speakers insisted that Germany's political and economic problems had personified causes—Jews, "November criminals," Marxist—and that the only solution was the elimination from power of these evildoers and of the system of parliamentary democracy that, the Nazis claimed, had enabled these elements to come to power. Adolf Hitler and his party did not limit themselves to attacking the Weimar Republic. They also promised relief from want and fear to virtually every segment of German society. (The effectiveness of the Nazis' campaign message was inadvertently reinforced by the absence of ideas that would solve the real problems facing the country among the moderate Left and Right parties.) It did not seem to matter that some of the proposals were mutually contradictory, or that the party could show no realistic means of financing its various giveaway plans. The message repeated *ad nauseam* was that once the Nazis came to power, all of the difficulties would be automatically resolved.

For a time, these methods worked well. Desperate times produced desperate reactions. The spectacular Nazi successes in the September 1930 Reichstag elections (18 percent of the popular vote) were only a first step. In the next two years the Nazis increased their vote in almost every local, state, and national election. Eventually, more than three out of every ten voters cast their ballots for the Nazis, enabling the party to control a number of state and local governments.

The question as to who joined and voted for the Nazis has long fascinated historians. For some years, it was accepted as axiomatic that the Nazis obtained most of their support from the lower middle class, but newer studies have demonstrated that they made significant inroads into all segments of German society. Still, there were differences. Among the party's members and activists the lower middle class was heavily overrepresented relative to its share of the population. In contrast, blue-collar workers, particularly if they lived in large cities, were underrepresented. As far as the voters were concerned, Catholics cast fewer Nazi ballots than Protestants. Small-town and rural inhabitants were more likely to vote Nazi than those who lived in large cities. In terms of occupation and social class there was a positive correlation between income and status and the Nazi vote. That is to say, Nazi support was strongest among the well-to-do. What in Germany constituted the old *Mittelstand* (small businessmen, retailers, civil servants, and academics) cast the highest proportion of the Nazi vote.

The NSDAP's chauvinistic, anti-Marxist, antidemocratic, and anti-Semitic message generated massive popular support, and for that reason the New Conservatives were eager to use Hitler's movement for their own purposes. As a result, the Nazis and the New Conservatives joined forces in a number of antirepublican ventures. Supported with glowing editorial comments by Hugenberg's media empire, the Nazis and *Stahlhelm* in November 1929 launched an initiative campaign against the Young Plan. In August 1931, the Nazis and a variety of New Conservative groups met in Harzburg in the state of Brunswick (the *Land* Brunswick was by now under the control of a Nazi–New Conservative coalition government) to inaugurate the "National Opposition," or "Harzburg Front," promising to cooperate in destroying the Brüning government and parliamentary democracy.

Hitler was undoubtedly gratified both by the enthusiasm of the thousands who packed his rallies and by the interest that the leaders of Germany's "natural" elites took in his movement, but he also recognized the political limitations of his present situation. The NSDAP's New Conservative allies were quite content to permit the NSDAP its rallies and often violent street demonstrations, but they had no intention of yielding real power to the party. The Reich president twice—in August and November 1932—categorically refused to give Hitler dictatorial authority as the head of the Reich government.

The road to power through the ballot box presented similar obstacles. Without a clear majority at the polls, the Nazis—as the party's leader in Berlin and later Reich minister for propaganda, Joseph Goebbels, recognized—were in danger of "winning ourselves to death." In late fall 1932 it became obvious that the Nazis' popularity had crested. The noticeable decline of the party's popular vote in the November Reichstag elections was accelerated in the state and local contests that followed.

As it lost its momentum, the party developed serious organizational and financial problems. By the end of the year, it became difficult to maintain the party's cohesion. Especially the Stormtroopers were becoming restless and anxious to obtain the spoils of power. There had been a regional revolt in Berlin as early as March 1931, and extraordinary efforts on the part of Adolf Hitler were required to subdue the rebellious foot soldiers. Hindenburg's refusal to appoint the Nazi Führer chancellor on August 13, forced the SA to delay again the long expected "night of the long knives," during which the Stormtroopers would be able to take revenge on their political and

One of the most famous political posters of the Weimar era. A SPD prediction during the Reichstag election of July 1932: If the Nazis come to power, the workers of Germany will be crucified on the Swastika.
(Source: *Anschläge,* no. 77.)

personal opponents without worrying about the legal consequences.

Finances presented another pressing problem. Both contemporaries and some later scholars have argued that corporations and individual businessmen had supplied large sums to the NSDAP in the 1920s and especially after the party's impressive showing in the September 1930 elections. Actually, support from these sources did not represent a major factor in the Nazi Party's finances. The NSDAP for the most part financed its activities on a pay-as-you-go basis through membership dues and various money-making schemes. It is true, however, that as victory seemed in sight in 1932, the party had gone heavily into debt, and the political setbacks in the fall of that year made it difficult for the Nazis to repay these loans. For a variety of reasons, then, contemporary observers predicted that at the end of 1932 the NSDAP was on the verge of disintegration.

The party's political and financial difficulties persuaded Gregor Strasser—whose position as the NSDAP's chief of administration provided him with good insight into the party's true situation—to recommend that Hitler accept Schleicher's offer and permit him, Strasser, to join the general's cabinet as vice-chancellor. The Nazi leader, however, refused; he wanted all or nothing. From the vantage point of December 1932, it looked very much as though it would be the latter.

The Nazis' further decline was halted not by destiny, but by Franz von Papen and some of the other New Conservatives. The last phase of Hitler's rise to power is not the story of elemental forces in the electorate, but of backstage intrigues, blind ambition, and political naiveté among a small group of men. The ex-chancellor wanted revenge for Schleicher's cold coup, which had forced him out of office. Almost as soon as Papen cleared out his desk he began to send out feelers to Hitler and his associates. The efforts intensified in mid-December, as it became clear that Schleicher's scheme for securing the Nazis' cooperation had failed. By early January 1933, a series of secret meetings involving Papen, Hitler, and a number of go-betweens had worked out what amounted to a backstage deal for a new coalition. Hitler would become chancellor in a cabinet composed of Nazis and New Conservatives. Papen intended that he would be the real power in the government. For himself he reserved the post of vice-chancellor and Reich commissioner for Prussia. In addition, the New Conservatives would have a clear majority in the cabinet; there were to be only three Nazi ministers. Papen's scheme promised a squaring of the political circle. If Hitler agreed, the new cabinet would be able to obtain a vote of confidence in the Reichstag, and thus relieve the Reich president of the necessity of violating the letter of the constitution. At the same time, the proposed distribution of cabinet seats seemingly guaranteed New Conservative domination of the government.

There remained only two obstacles: securing the cooperation of the *Reichswehr* and persuading Hindenburg to accept the scheme. The first difficulty was resolved by selecting General Werner von Blomberg as the minister of defense in the new cabinet. Blomberg, a career officer and personal friend of the president's son, was known as a Nazi sympathizer. Hindenburg's approval for a cabinet headed by Hitler was a little more difficult to obtain. The president had a personal dislike for Hitler, and Schleicher had been arguing—quite correctly—that the Nazis had lost their momentum, so that all that was needed was to await their disintegration. Papen countered by pointing to the Nazis' recent success in the state elections in the minuscule *Land* of Lippe (with a total population of about 20,000), which Papen maintained showed the NSDAP was still a force that needed to be tamed. (Papen did not mention that the Nazis' success in the Lippe elections was the result of concentrating all of the party's resources on this agrarian backwater, or that the moderate parties had done proportionately much better than Hitler's movement.)

Papen's arguments won out over Schleicher's. Hindenburg agreed to appoint Hitler chancellor, and on January 30, 1933, the new Reich cabinet was ready to take the oath of office. In addition to Hitler as Reich chancellor there were only two other Nazi cabinet members: Hermann Göring served as Reich minister without portfolio and acting Prussian minister of the interior, while Wilhelm Frick, an old Bavarian associate of Hitler's from the days of the Beer Hall Putsch, became Reich minister of the interior. They were joined by what appeared to be a formidable array of prominent New Conservatives including—in addition to Papen—Hugenberg, who became Reich and Prussian minister of economics and agriculture, and, as Reich minister of labor, the head of the *Stahlhelm*, Franz Seldte. The rest of the cabinet consisted of civil servants with conservative leanings, some of them holdovers from the Brüning cabinet.

GLEICHSCHALTUNG: THE ESTABLISHMENT OF NAZI TOTALITARIANISM

Adolf Hitler was determined to subject the Reich to permanent and total Nazi control. Germany was to become the instrument with which he would accomplish his long-established domestic and foreign-policy goals. The Nazis, who were masters at creating bureaucratic euphemisms and doublespeak, termed the first step in process "synchronization," or *Gleichschaltung*. In essence, *Gleichschaltung* constituted a series of measures that prohibited all organized political activity other than that of the Nazi Party, established an increasingly efficient system of state-sponsored terror, converted the country's vestigial parliamentary democracy into Hitler's personal dictatorship, and attempted to infuse all traditionally nonpolitical activities with Nazi ideology.

For Hitler the *Gleichschaltung* was the means to larger and ultimate ends. His final goals were based on two *idées fixes* that he pursued single-mindedly in the face of all setbacks and contrary empirical evidence. The Nazi leader's *Weltanschauung*—spelled out in considerable detail long before 1933 in innumerable speeches, his autobiography, *Mein Kampf*, and a later unpublished manuscript (which was published after World War II under the title *Hitler's Second Book*)—rested on twin foundations: race and space. Hitler's "solution to the racial question" was the elimination of the Jews from Germany and Europe, although in 1933 it was not clear—perhaps not even to Hitler— if the means was to be forced emigration or physical extermination. There was no doubt, however, that "space" referred to the conquest of Russia and Eastern Europe to obtain the vast new *Lebensraum* (living space) that Hitler insisted Germany needed.

Ironically, the Nazis' *Gleichschaltung* was implemented largely by the New Conservatives who had originally intended that Hitler and the Nazis would play roles as junior partners in fulfilling the triumph of New Conservatism. The reason was that at least in the early stages of the *Gleichschaltung*, the New Conservative goals matched Hitler's own: destruction of democracy, rearmament, revision of the Versailles system, economic recovery. Initially, the two most important goals of the self-styled "government of national resurgence" were the attainment of a monopoly of political power for the "nationalist parties," and getting people back to work.

During the drive for power the Nazis' economic proposals had often been the object of derision by their opponents. Such ideas as abolishing interest in all banking transactions (one of the articles in the party's official 1920 program) were clearly ludicrous in a highly developed industrialized economy. During their many political campaigns Hitler and his associates did not hesitate to promise relief measures to virtually all segments of the economy: Farmers were assured that under Nazi rule tariffs would be sufficiently high to keep out foreign competition, while small retailers could expect legislation forcing department stores out of business. Once in power the radicalism soon softened. Neither interest rates nor department stores disappeared. In fact, for the most part, the chancellor during the first few months of 1933 left economic policies pretty much in the hands of his New Conservative minister of economics, Alfred Hugenberg, and the president of the Reichsbank. They in turn continued the price, wage, and currency controls that Brüning had begun and Papen and Schleicher continued.

Nevertheless, there was a noticeable shift in priorities and, after a few months, major personnel changes as well. In contrast to his predecessors, Hitler determined that the government's first priority was not to safeguard the value of the mark, but to reduce unemployment: The *Führer* insisted on government-sponsored public works programs. Simultaneously he launched an unprecedented arms buildup. Within a week after becoming Reich chancellor, Hitler announced to his cabinet that during the next four to five years the regime's top priority would be providing the armed forces with whatever they needed. There were no objections from his New Conservative allies: Defense appropriations, which had constituted 4 percent of all public outlays before 1933, rose to 50 percent by 1938. The most dramatic and visible link between the public works effort and rearmament was the construction of the system of strategic super highways, the *Autobahnen*. The emphasis on "getting things done" in turn contributed to the Nazis' undeniable popularity in the early years of the Third Reich. Here were leaders who seemingly did not let the country drift; they acted to lift Germany from the morass of economic turmoil. And the results were dramatic: The number of unemployed, which had stood at 6 million in January, 1933, fell to 4 million by the end of the year.

Public works and rearmament programs are quite costly. Fearful of the inflationary effect of spending money the government did not have, Hitler's predecessors had consistently refused to embark on the path of deficit financing. Here, too, the new administration broke with the practices of earlier cabinets. The Nazis had no patience with theories about orthodox public finance. The Reich chancellor immediately demanded that the Reichsbank advance the government funds with which to revitalize the economy and begin the rearmament program. Since the president of the Reichsbank, Hans Luther, was known as an extreme fiscal conservative, Hitler asked him to resign. (Luther became ambassador to the United States.) His successor was Hjalmar Schacht, former president of the Reichsbank whom the Republican government had dismissed early in 1930 when Schacht endorsed the Nazis' and New Conservatives' critique of the Young Plan. In September 1933 Hugenberg was maneuvered out of the cabinet. His successor as Reich economics minister was Kurt Schmitt, an insurance executive. The personnel change was more significant in Hugenberg's other position in the cabinet, that of minister of agriculture. Here his successor was R. Walther Darré, the NSDAP's specialist for agriculture. Darré became the fourth Nazi member of the cabinet.

In insisting on deficit financing, Hitler was not guided by any economic theories; he simply refused to let fiscal considerations stand in the way of his political goals. Schacht was concerned about fiscal policy, but, like John Maynard Keynes in England, he was also convinced that the German economy had so much unused capacity in 1933 that loosening the credit screws did not pose an inflationary danger. He agreed to advance the government an initial 600 million marks. They were followed in the next five years by an additional 12 billion marks. Especially in the first two years of the Nazi era the pump-priming funds were not given in outright grants, but channeled through what was formally a private cor-

A Nazi attempt to have Hitler ride on Hindenburg's coattails. The caption reads, ''The marshal and the corporal are struggling with us for peace and equality.'' (Source: *Anschläge*, no. 89.)

poration. Established in 1933, the Corporation for Metallurgical Research (known by its acronym as the Mefo Corporation) was a phantom business enterprise that awarded government contracts to various private companies, especially in the defense sector. The work contracted was paid for in advance by "Mefo credits," that is to say, bonds backed by the Mefo Corporation. The Mefo credits were guaranteed by the Reichsbank and could be exchanged for actual marks at any German bank.

While some New Conservatives may have been skeptical about deficit financing, the dissolution of the independent labor unions had their full approval. On May 2, 1933, the government dissolved all labor unions and seized their assets. In place of an independent labor movement the Nazis established the German Labor Front (*Deutsche Arbeitsfront*, DAF) The new organization became an affiliate of the Nazi Party. Membership was compulsory for both employees and employers, and the DAF had neither the right to strike nor the power to bargain collectively. The head of the new giant organization was Robert Ley, Gregor Strasser's successor as the NSDAP's chief of administration.

The governments' ongoing efforts toward autarky, the attainment of self-sufficiency in raw materials and foodstuffs, also continued earlier New Conservative policies. Like many Germans on the political Right, Hitler was convinced that the Allied blockade in World War I had been decisive in creating a seedbed for the revolutionary upheavals of 1918. Brüning and his successors had already raised tariffs on agricultural goods to protect Germany's farmers, but the Nazi regime went much further. The Law on Hereditary Landholding (*Reichserbhofgesetz*) and the establishment of the *Reichsnährstand* (Reich Food Estate) protected farmers against foreclosures, but also severely regimented them. They were prohibited from selling their land; to link "blood and soil" in the Third Reich farms had to be passed intact to a male heir.

Inaugurated in September 1933, the administration of the Reich Food Estate controlled agricultural prices, production quotas, and imports. The goal was to raise agricultural production by providing farmers with a closed market and stable prices.

The drive for autarky and the one-sided emphasis on rearmament changed the traditional equilibrium of the German economy, a development that, ironically, soon threatened the success of the rearmament program itself, As we saw, since the founding of the empire, German economic growth was fueled primarily by exporting finished goods and importing food and unprocessed raw materials. The Nazi (and New Conservative) economic policies resulted in a sharp decline of the country's exports and a corresponding loss of foreign-currency income to buy needed imports. It soon became clear that without exports, the Reich would not be able to pay for the import of raw materials and agricultural commodities indispensable for armaments production and feeding the country's industrial workers.

A scheme of Schacht's, the "New Plan," seemed to provide a solution for a time. Schacht, who replaced Schmitt as economics minister at the beginning of 1935, proposed that rather than trading on the open world market, Germany should orient her trade relations toward those nations willing to conclude bilateral agreements that would bypass the hard currency problem. The cost of exports and imports would be calculated in the two national currencies, rather than in an international medium of exchange like the U.S. dollar or British pound, and the accounts settled through "clearing agreements." Germany concluded a series of these bilateral agreements in the next few years but, since the United States and Great Britain refused to enter into international trade pacts on this basis, the Reich lost many of her traditional markets in North America and Western Europe. Instead, her trade was increasingly diverted toward eastern and southeastern Europe and South America.

The new plan prevented the collapse of Germany's international trade in the early Nazi years, but it could not keep pace with the needs of the rearmament program. By the beginning of 1936 the Reich faced a very severe hard currency crisis; at one point the Reichsbank had on deposit only 88 million marks in hard currency—enough to finance Germany's imports for only one week. But a more serious problem soon developed: Germany's lack of strategic raw materials threatened Hitler's rearmament plans. As noted before, with the exception of coal, the Reich had virtually no significant amounts of commercially viable mineral resources. Hitler, however, was determined to achieve autarky in this area as well.

In August, 1936, the *Führer* proposed that Germany develop a Four Year Plan—so named because it was to enable the Reich's army and economy to wage war within four years. He wrote a long memorandum that began by reiterating the inevitability of armed struggle against Bolsheviks and Jews, and concluded with the demand that top priority be given to making Germany self-sufficient in strategic food stuffs and raw materials. Under the administration of a vast new bureaucracy, headed by Hitler's long-time associate, Hermann Göring, the Four Year Plan began the development of marginal raw material resources in Germany (regardless of the prohibitive costs involved) and the manufacture of synthetic substitutes, such as artificial rubber and gasoline extracted from coal. The focus was on matériels needed for war, principally steel and fuel.

The financial implications of the Four Year Plan led to a break between Hitler and his wizard of economic recovery, Hjalmar Schacht. In the past, private industry had shown little interest in developing Germany's mineral resources because of the costs involved; it was far cheaper, for example, to import iron ore from Sweden than to mine Germany's own low-grade deposits in Lower Saxony. Under the Four Year Plan the huge costs involved would be borne by the government (eventually a new nationalized, state-owned conglomerate, the Reich Works "Hermann Göring" was set up for the purpose), and Schacht protested the inflationary consequences of this decision. When Hitler ignored his advice, Schacht at the end of 1936 resigned as head of the Reichsbank and as Reich economics minister. He was replaced by Walther Funk, a spineless former journalist who left economic decision making to Göring and the bureaucrats in the Four Year Plan administration. The Four Year Plan was not a success. At the beginning of World War II, Germany's dependence on imported raw materials and foodstuffs was not significantly different than it had been in 1936. When the Four Year Plan was launched its advocates claimed that Germany could save 464 million marks annually in hard currency spent on imports, but the actual figure in 1939 was closer to 150 million marks, and most of the improvement came not from reduced imports but from increased exports in 1937 and 1938 as the worldwide Great Depression abated.

During their campaigns the Nazis had promised an entirely new economic system, free of conflicts, efficient, self-sufficient, with special consideration for the needs of farmers and the *Mittelstand*. The reality bore little resemblance to the propaganda vision. Structurally, the Reich remained what it had been since the last quarter of the nineteenth century: a highly industrialized country dominated by large-scale enterprises. In fact, the Nazis' determination to rearm regardless of cost actually encouraged the further growth of cartels and pricing arrangements, especially in heavy industry. The importance of small businesses and retailers was often emphasized in Nazi propaganda, but in reality their position in the economy was no less difficult than before.

The Nazis also did not "cure" the Depression, although the combination of price, wage, and currency controls along with deficit financing and the public works program probably enabled Germany to come out of the depths of the Depression somewhat faster than was true of some other industrialized countries. There was a dramatic and rapid drop in the number of unemployed; in 1933 there were 4.8 million persons without a job, while three years later that figure had dropped to 1.6 million. By 1938 the German industrial index had risen to 125 from a base figure of 100 in 1929. Still, all of this did not amount to the "revolution" that Nazi propaganda continued to extol.

The real Nazi "revolution," as David Schoenbaum has pointed out, came in the area of politics and social relations, and even here the Nazis fell far short of their goals. One of their stated aims, for example, was the elimination of women from the labor force. A woman's natural place, the Nazis claimed, was in the home raising a family. In reality, however, the number of gainfully employed women rose from 4.2 million in 1933 to 5.2 million five years later.

Among the various social groups, labor suffered the most severe decline in rights and privileges, if not in standard of living. During the Weimar Republic, German workers had obtained a position of legal and financial security. Under the Nazis, as we saw, independent labor unions were eliminated outright on May 2, 1933. Their place was taken by the DAF and a variety of symbolic and cosmetic benefits. The "Strength through Joy" movement—vacations to foreign lands for a relative few, some physical improvements in the workplace for most—and similar propaganda efforts were certainly not equitable substitutes for the right of collective bargaining and protection from arbitrary dismissals. Nevertheless, the propaganda effect was not negligible. Many workers and their families were appreciative of the fact that the regime seemed concerned about humanizing the work environment. In addition, the wages of some highly skilled specialists rose to such an extent that in 1936 the government determined excessive wage increases were

creating inflationary pressures and decreed a wage freeze. Still, as a group, labor was undoubtedly worse off than during the "good" years of the Weimar Republic when workers enjoyed collective bargaining rights and a closely knit mesh of social legislation.

In sharp contrast to labor, large-scale industrialists, particularly those in heavy industry and armaments manufacture, were the real beneficiaries of the regime's policies. Iron and steel, portions of the chemical industry, and segments of what was then high technology (manufacturers of bomb sights, optics, and so forth) all gained at the expense of consumer industries. Farmers and some professionals also benefited, at least in economic terms, during the Nazi era. Although the basic problems of German agriculture were not addressed by the Nazis (German and European agriculture to this day suffers from inherent structural difficulties), farmers were undoubtedly better off than they had been during much of the Weimar and Depression eras. Protection against foreclosures and the establishment of a regulated market along with price subsidies enabled many farmers to hold on to their land. Benefits for professionals came mostly at the expense of some of their colleagues when the Nazis' political legislation prohibited political opponents and Jews from practicing law and medicine, or holding government jobs. (See the later discussion pp. 198–99).

Perhaps the most remarkable feature of the regime's economic policies was the relative absence of benefits for a group that had supported the Nazis' struggle for power in disproportionately large numbers, the commercial and retailing sector of the old *Mittelstand*. Although Nazi propaganda continued to praise the small businessman as the personification of the "honest" merchant, and contrasted him with the avaricious Jewish "peddler," when it came to actual practice, the government gave preference to large-scale businesses. As had been true of the controlled economy during World War I, small businesses simply could not compete with the giant corporations in either prices or wages. In addition, allocation of raw materials was consistently unfavorable to this segment of the economy.

The economic policies of the "government of national resurgence" were a key factor in the regime's early and genuine popularity. They were also the least specifically "Nazi" aspects of the government's policies. Except for the public works programs and the DAF, they constituted—albeit in accelerated form—a continuation of initiatives instituted earlier by the presidential cabinets. The characteristically Nazi features of the Third Reich appeared in the regime's attempts to transform Germany culturally and politically and in Hitler's foreign policy. Here both the Nazis' goals and tactics went far beyond the timid efforts of the New Conservatives to return the Reich to authoritarianism.

Quite literally, Germany's first experience with what Ernest Fraenkel has called the "dual state"—that peculiar parallelism of government-sanctioned Nazi Party activities and party-approved government acts—was a wave of random political terror early in 1933. One of Hermann Göring's first decisions as acting Prussian minister of the interior was to dismiss most of the incumbent chiefs of police in Germany's largest state. With few exceptions, they were replaced by high-ranking SA leaders who immediately deputized hundreds of Stormtroopers as auxiliary police, ostensibly to prevent Communist violence and insure that "law and order would be maintained" during the campaign for a new Reichstag, to be elected on March 5.

There were virtually no Marxist disturbances, but during and after the campaign the SA used its semiofficial status to settle old and new scores. The country was soon dotted with unofficial concentration camps in which the SA (and in some cases SS units) incarcerated and maltreated their political opponents. In Prussia alone between 25,000 and 30,000 persons were taken into "protective custody" in March and April 1933.

Other Stormtroopers roamed through the streets engaging in random acts of violence against the property of Jews and political opponents. The SA was determined to have its "revolution."

After a few months, the government put an end to this phase of more or less spontaneous violence by the Stormtroopers. At the beginning of June, Hitler announced the Nazi revolution would continue for a thousand years, so there was no need for rash actions. Under the leadership of Heinrich Himmler and Reinhard Heydrich, the head of the NSDAP's own espionage service (*Sicherheitsdienst* [SD]) the SS took the place of the Stormtroopers as the regime's primary instrument of terror. By 1936 the traditionally decentralized German police administration was nationalized and centralized, with Heinrich Himmler, who had begun his rise to power by seizing control of the Bavarian state police in 1933, appointed "head of the SS and chief of the German police," a position that left him only nominally subordinate to the Reich minister of the interior. The Nazis' terror apparatus included a national secret police (the infamous Gestapo), which replaced the states' political police units, and a regularized system of concentration camps that would eventually include the notorious extermination camps of World War II. The network of concentration camps initially included three large institutions—Dachau near Munich, Sachsenhausen near Berlin, and Buchenwald near Weimar—and several smaller camps. The camps were run by a special unit of the SS, the Death Head Formations, under the command of Theodor Eicke, and old-line Nazi and first commandant of Dachau. In 1937 the number of inmates was about 10,000, but the power of terror went far beyond the actual number imprisoned. Increasingly, the SS took justice into its own hands. Despite the efforts of some judges to preserve judicial autonomy, the Gestapo claimed the right to keep in "protective custody" even those who had been acquitted of all crimes by the regular courts.

The rise to power of Himmler and the SS was facilitated by a purge of the SA's leadership in mid-1934. The Stormtroopers, and especially their ambitious chief of staff (nominally Hitler was head of the SA), Ernst Röhm, were not content to be relegated to the position of an honorific Sunday afternoon marching society. Röhm in particular hoped to destroy the autonomy of the Reichswehr and drown the army in a "sea of brown-shirted militia."

From January 1933 to June 1934 conflicts among the army, the SS, portions of the government, and the Nazi Party leadership simmered under the surface. It is now clear that the SS and the Reichswehr cooperated in amassing evidence (much of it fabricated) that persuaded Hitler that Röhm and his associates were planning a putsch against the government and the NSDAP's civilian leadership. At the end of June 1934 Hitler ordered a purge of the Stormtroopers. Between June 30 and July 2, eighty-five prominent SA members, including Röhm and most the the SA's provincial leaders, were summarily shot without trial by SS execution squads. At the same time, the driving forces behind the purge, Göring, Goebbels, and Hitler's secretary Rudolf Hess (who was appointed deputy Führer for party operations in the summer of 1933), also decided on the death of some long-time political opponents who clearly had no connection to the SA or its possible ambitions. Gregor Strasser, Ernst von Kahr, Kurt von Schleicher and his wife, Papen's private secretary, and scores of others were all executed by SS killers.

The purge of the SA leaders was followed almost immediately by a less violent but equally significant turnover in the ranks of the NSDAP's administrators. About 20 percent of the party's functionaries who held office in January 1933 were dismissed in the summer and fall of 1934. Most of them were replaced by new party members, that is, those who had joined the NSDAP since January 1933.

Sadly, there were few protests from Hitler's New Conservative allies against the obvious violations of legal safeguards during and after the Röhm affair. (In a rare show of civil courage, Papen in a sense triggered the Röhm purge with a public speech in which he condemned the regime's many illegal acts.) In part, the reason for silence lay in the attitude of the army, an attitude which many New Conservatives shared. By destroying the SA, the Reichswehr felt it had eliminated the most "radical" element in the NSDAP. Hitler and the SS were seen as forces of moderation.

A seemingly important clue to Hitler's willingness to cooperate with the old elites was the treaty with the papacy, for which negotiations began early in 1933. (The concordat itself was signed in July). In return for a promise to stay out of politics and dissolve the Center Party, Germany's Catholics were permitted relatively free exercise of their religion and—a touchy subject throughout the Weimar years—the retention of segregated Catholic public schools. The price paid by the Catholic Church, however, was high: The concordat constituted at least tacit approval of the Nazis' dictatorship. In addition, the Nazis began to violate the terms of the agreement almost immediately, and we now know that one of Hitler's long-range goals was the destruction of both the Catholic and the Protestant churches.

The New Conservatives were also grateful to the Nazis for seemingly stopping the Bolshevik revolution before it could begin. Here the Nazis took advantage of a fortuitous incident. On February 28, 1933, the Reichstag building was set on fire. The government immediately announced that the fire had been set by the Communists as a signal to launch the Bolshevik revolution. Within hours the Reich president, citing the Communist menace, signed a decree authorizing the arrest of all members of the Communist Party as well as suspending civil liberties for the entire country. Today it is known that the Reichstag fire was not the work of the Communists. The arsonist was a deranged Dutch citizen, Martin van der Lubbe, who had no connection to the KPD. Historically, the importance of the incident was not the fire but its political consequences. The decree destroying civil liberties was supplemented by an Enabling Act, in March 1933, that gave the government power to rule by decree for the next four years. With the exception of the SPD all parties in the Reichstag voted for the law, thus ensuring the two-thirds majority needed for amending the constitution.

Political *Gleichschaltung* now moved into high gear. The decree of February 28 and the Enabling Act provided the legal authority for dissolving the Social Democratic Party soon after the KPD had been prohibited. A few months later, in July 1933, all parties except the NSDAP became illegal and the Nazi Party was declared the "foundation of national authority." Even the various nationalist but non-Nazi paramilitary groups were merged with their Nazi counterparts.

By the end of 1933, the NSDAP had achieved a monopoly on political power in Germany, but the Nazis were not content with the destruction of political pluralism and individual civil liberties. On the first anniversary of Hitler's appointment as Reich chancellor, German federalism was destroyed. Instead of autonomous *Länder* the German states were reduced to subunits of the central government. They were now headed by Reich plenipotentiaries, most of whom were Nazi Party *Gauleiters*. In their new positions as government officials the party's provincial leaders worked under the supervision of the Reich minister of the interior but, typical of the dual state, as *Gauleiters* they remained Hitler's direct subordinates.

The most important constitutional change, however, came after the death of the Reich president in August 1934. Hindenburg's demise had been expected for some time, and both Hitler and the New Conservatives had plans for the future. It was no secret that many of the New Conservatives hoped for a restoration of the monarchy after Hindenburg's death. Hitler, of course, had no intention of sharing power with an emperor. Instead he hastened to secure the support of the Reichswehr, potentially the most important autonomous power factor in the country, for his future plans. This objective was apparently one of Hitler's motives for staging the Röhm murders when he did. The scheme worked. Hitler's gift to the army in the form of rendering the Stormtroopers politically impotent persuaded most of the Reichswehr's leaders that their organizational future was secure under Hitler's leadership. They raised no objections when immediately after Hindenburg's death Hitler added the functions of the Reich president's office to his other duties. On the contrary, the army's relationship to Hitler was cemented by an oath of personal loyalty to the Nazi leader in his new capacity as Reich president. As of mid-1934 Hitler's power rested on the triple authority of his function as Reich president, Reich chancellor, and head of the Nazi Party.

Along with the political transformation of the country, the Nazis enacted measures designed to eliminate Jews and political opponents from playing any part in German public life. As early as April 1933, a euphemistically named "Law for the Reestablishment of a Professional Civil Service" provided for the dismissal of all political opponents and Jews from any civil service positions. The initial exemption for veterans of World War I was soon eliminated from the law. In quantitative terms, the subsequent purge of the civil service involved some 1 to 2 percent of Germany's public employees (between fifteen thousand and thirty thousand persons), but in the higher ranks of the civil service the percentage of those dismissed or demoted was as high as 12 percent.

At the same time, the most notorious Jew-baiter among the Nazi provincial leaders, Julius Streicher (the *Gauleiter* of Franconia), organized with Hitler's personal approval a nationwide anti-Jewish boycott that was accompanied by renewed violence against Jewish-owned property. Negative international reaction to Streicher's boycott—in the form of countermeasures against German exports in the United States and other foreign countries—as well as the SA's uncontrolled violence, soon brought an official end to the anti-Jewish boycott, but not to further anti-Semitic measures. The regime simply turned to legislation instead of party-sponsored "spontaneity." Meeting in a special session at the 1935 Nazi Party congress the thoroughly *gleichgeschaltete* Reichstag passed the Nuremberg Laws. This series of measures attempted to define "Jewishness" on the basis of a person's ancestry: Thus persons having one or more Jewish grandparents were categorized as Jewish or of "mixed race." Marriages between non-Jews and Jews were prohibited, and Jews lost their German citizenship; they became aliens in their own country.

These essentially negative measures destroyed all forms of pluralism in German society. They were also a prerequisite for what the Nazis saw as the positive building blocks toward the establishment of totalitarianism. Such "positive" steps included above all the politization of all cultural and artistic life. An important development in this respect was the establishment of the Reich Ministry of Propaganda and Public Enlightenment. Headed by Joseph Goebbels, the *Gauleiter* of Berlin and long-time propaganda chief of the NSDAP, the new ministry, staffed by a massive bureaucracy, made sure that nothing was published or exhibited that was not approved by the propaganda ministry. To ensure that unsuitable literature did not reach the eyes of the public in the future, the propaganda ministry and various party offices issued monthly lists of indexed and approved literary offerings. The German press was issued daily guidelines by the propaganda ministry complete with suggested editorials and instructions on how to treat various stories.

Long before they came to power, the Nazis had promised that under their rule German cultural and artistic life would experience a new burst of creativity. "Folk-related" and "race-conscious" arts and literature were to take the place of "Jewish decadence" and "liberal philistinism." The Nazis' cultural program, in short, was a revolt against modernism. As was true of most of their endeavors, the Nazis proved far more adept at destruction than creativity. The new era of cultural flowering began, appropriately enough, with black listings and book burnings. In May 1933, university students in various German towns, with the full approval of Goebbels and other leaders, staged an auto-da-fé in the capital and other cities during which they committed to the flames literary symbols of Germany's supposedly decadent Jewish and liberal past: books by Heinrich Heine and the Mann brothers, the plays of Bertolt Brecht, and the works of Sigmund Freud among many others. These authors were then officially banned in the Third Reich; their works disappeared from book stores and library shelves.

In the visual arts, too the focus of the regime's attacks was modernism. Painting and sculpture representing schools from expressionism to abstract art were defined as "degenerate" and removed from the walls of museums. The artists were forbidden to practice their craft. The equivalent of book burning for the visual arts was a traveling show entitled "Degenerate Art," which toured Germany under the sponsorship of the Nazi Party in 1935 and 1936. For this purpose the Nazis selected a number of modern—especially expressionist—paintings and sculptures and by clever use of lighting and labeling attempted to demonstrate the works' lack of artistic merit.

Through the Nazi purge of all forms of modernism German intellectual life suffered a tremendous bloodletting. Since university professors were civil servants, the

Law on the Restoration of a Professional Civil Service applied to them as well. About 1,600 Jewish and liberal university teachers were dismissed; many went into exile, especially to the United States. Nazi attempts to replace them with "racial scientists" or to have something called "German physics" replaced Einstein's "Jewish Theory of Relativity" were little more than laughable. After the 1933 Nobel Peace Prize was awarded to a well-known pacifist, Carl von Ossietsky (who was already in a concentration camp at the time), Germans were prohibited from accepting further Nobel prizes. Instead, the regime created the German National Prize, whose first recipient was the NSDAP's semi-official theoretician, Alfred Rosenberg.

Literature and art, too, suffered a precipitous decline. Many of Germany's best known authors—the Mann brothers, Bertolt Brecht, Alfred Döblin—were forced into exile. In their place moved *völkisch* hacks, who produced an endless stream of novels and short stories extolling the virtues of farm life and military combat. Hitler himself imposed his personal taste on the visual arts and architecture. In painting, Hitler preferred a sort of idealized realism, in which unrealistic but photographlike reproductions of rural idylls, battle scenes, and portraits of Nazi leaders predominated. Typical of the sculpture of the Third Reich were oversized, idealized, neoclassical nudes representing heroic abstractions ("The Army," "The Party," "Motherhood"). In Nazi architecture neoclassical bombast was also the rule. Under Hitler's watchful eye, the Führer's personal architect, Albert Speer, designed monumental structures intended to impress with their grandeur rather than please with their proportions. Only in the area of the cinema did productions of the Nazi era attain a technical quality that in some cases was greater than that of the Weimar years. This is not surprising, for film was particularly suited as a propaganda medium.

Propaganda and—literally—uniformity were the real essences of Nazi culture. From the attempt by the SS to create perfect physical specimens in its elite ranks (members of the SS had to submit themselves and their prospective brides to a "racial examination" before they could marry) to compulsory membership in the Hitler Youth after 1936 for all girls and boys over the age of ten, uniforms characterized the Nazis' projected image. The most impressive manifestation of the Nazis' self-projection was the NSDAP's national congresses, staged each September in Nuremberg. Here hundreds of thousands of Germans—all arrayed in a variety of uniforms—paraded before Hitler in an unending series of marches and ceremonies. Albert Speer designed massive neoclassical reviewing stands and arranged for special pyrotechnical effects. The purpose was to evoke the impression for both participants and observers of a unified nation subject to the total control of its godlike Führer.

FOREIGN RELATIONS

The foreign-policy aims and tactics of the Weimar parliamentary governments were distinctly different from those of the New Conservative and Nazi regimes that followed. All of the Reich cabinets after World War I attempted to "revise" the terms of the Versailles Treaty to improve Germany's relative position in the international community. The parliamentary foreign ministers, and that meant principally Gustav Stresemann, sought to realize their revisionist ambitions primarily (though not exclusively) through bilateral and multilateral agreements with Germany's former enemies. As we saw, these efforts culminated in the Treaty of Locarno and Germany's membership in the League of Nations. The foreign policy of the new presidential cabinets did not abruptly reverse Stresemann's tactics of accommodation, but there was a distinct change in atmosphere. Increasingly, the

"Spirit of Locarno" was replaced by confrontation and diplomatic bullying.

The presidential governments pursued three immediate foreign policy goals: reestablishing the Reich's freedom of diplomatic action, ending reparations, and securing Germany's right to parity in armaments. Eventually, they hoped to restore to Germany the hegemony she had enjoyed in central and southeast Europe before 1914.

The results of their efforts were mixed. Brüning's most spectacular bilateral initiative, the Austro-German customs union of August 1931, was a complete failure. France immediately used her financial leverage in Vienna to force Austria to withdraw its signature from the treaty. The New Conservatives did somewhat better in the area of armaments and reparations. In the fall of 1932 the International Disarmament Conference at Lausanne, Switzerland, recognized in principle Germany's right to equality in armaments. And, as we saw, the Hoover moratorium effectively ended the thorny reparations issue. Germany never resumed payments after 1932. On balance, the New Conservatives had a right to be pleased with their tactics. As Gerhard Weinberg has pointed out, in 1932, given the Soviet Union's relative weakness, Germany's position among the Great Powers did not compare unfavorably with that of 1914.

Some historians have interpreted Hitler's foreign-policy ambitions as a continuation of the goals of Germany's leaders during World War I and their New Conservative successors, but in reality there was an essential qualitative difference between the two sets of objectives. The Nazi dictator, almost from the moment he became chancellor, was not content to regain the boundaries of 1914, even if augmented with German control of Belgium and Holland. In line with his fixation on race and space, Hitler regarded such objectives as completely inadequate. He aimed at the military conquest of Eastern Europe and the Soviet Union, eventually to be followed by the establishment of German global hegemony. The

years of "moderate" goals from 1933 to 1938 resulted from purely tactical considerations. The Nazi leader wanted to preclude Allied moves against Germany while the Reich was still in the early stages of rearming, while at the same time he hoped to bring about by peaceful means territorial and political "revisions" of the Versailles settlement that would place the Reich in a more favorable position to wage war.

Still, this meant that the New Conservatives and Hitler initially agreed on tactics and interim goals. They differed only in their ultimate aims and these, even Hitler recognized, were some years off. For the moment, the new regime was served well by the old diplomats. (The common goals help explain, for example, why only one German ambassador, von Prittwitz in Washington, resigned his post in protest over Hitler's appointment as chancellor.) Even Hitler's views on Germany's friends and foes among the Great Powers were not all that different from those of the New Conservatives. For the Nazi leader the primary enemy was always Russia; there lay the vast expanses that Hitler insisted Germany was destined to conquer. Few of the New Conservatives shared Hitler's racial interpretation of history, but since Russia in 1933 meant the Soviet Union, the Führer's passionate anti-Bolshevism had their full approval.

Hitler and most New Conservatives also shared a deep-seated dislike of France. To be sure, for Hitler the humiliation of France was a mere sideshow compared to the ultimate battle with Soviet Russia, but he and the New Conservatives agreed that in the long run France remained an enemy power with which reconciliation was impossible. As far as Great Britain was concerned, Germany since 1918 had attempted to maintain good relations with England, primarily as a counterweight to France. Hitler continued this policy, although he remained ambivalent about the island nation. Hitler admired Britain's domestic stability and her ability to control a vast empire with limited human

An official portrait of Hitler at the height of his power. The caption reads, ''One People, one Reich, one Führer.'' (Source: *Anschläge*, no. 116.)

and material resources, but the Nazi leader despised British democracy and England's traditional policy of maintaining a balance of power on the Continent.

Neither Hitler nor the New Conservatives had shown much interest in the United States (except for the reparations issue) during the 1920s, although Hitler at times seemed convinced—based on the U.S. immigration laws then in force and the practice of segregation in the South—that America's ruling classes shared his concern about suppressing inferior races. After Franklin Delano Roosevelt's election as president and his open opposition to Nazism, Hitler abruptly changed his mind. He now claimed that America was increasingly dominated by Jews and blacks.

Italy was the only great power which Hitler consistently regarded as Germany's natural ally. This conclusion derived less from a rational assessment of the country's strength and interests than from unabashed admiration for Mussolini. To achieve a German-Italian alliance Hitler was even willing to violate his own dictum that all German-speaking minorities in Europe should be brought within the territorial boundaries of a Greater German Reich. As early as 1927 he agreed that the German-speaking population of the southern Tirol, an area that had been ceded to Italy in 1919, should remain under Italian control.

Historians tend to divide the Third Reich's foreign policy into two distinct periods, the years of "peaceful" revisionism from 1933 to 1938, and the following period from 1938 to 1945 in which Hitler turned to military aggression in pursuit of his goals. This distinction is useful as far as it goes, but we must remember that for the Nazi dictator his twelve-year rule constituted a continuum in which the "peaceful" years were diplomatic preparation for his ever-present, long-range strategic goals. In his speeches to government and military leaders, Hitler made no secret of his ultimate ambitions. Four days after he became Reich chancellor he addressed the leading generals of the Reichswehr on the need for rearmament, *Lebensraum*, and the conquest of Eastern Europe.

Still, for the first six years of Nazi Germany's history the crises were diplomatic rather than military. They followed a constant pattern. After articulating a particular territorial or political demand, there would be a delay after which Hitler in a surprise move seized the object of his ambitions. The Führer then invariably proceeded to calm the resultant furor among the other powers with a solemn announcement that this had been his last revisionist demand.

Since this pattern was repeated several times between 1933 and 1939 the question arises as to why the Allies and particularly France and Great Britain permitted Hitler to use this ploy successfully time after time. The answer lies in a number of factors, including the Western leaders' conviction that their military defenses were sufficient to defy and any real German aggression and Hitler's willingness to take large risks. Above all, however, the Nazi leader cleverly and rather more consistently than his parliamentary predecessors used two of the fundamental principles that were the basis of the Versailles treaty system, national self-determination and anti-Bolshevism, to justify his revisionist demands.

The "government of national resurgence" established its line of diplomatic activism early and forcefully. In October 1933, Germany withdrew from the League of Nations, the second major power to do so; Japan had abandoned the international body in May 1933. Hitler and his associates claimed that the principle of equality in armaments, which the Allies had conceded in 1932, had remained a paper declaration. The decision to leave the League of Nations was popular at home. Not just the New Conservatives in the army and the foreign ministry, but most Germans regarded the League as part of the hated Versailles system. The regime felt safe in scheduling a plebiscite on the decision to leave the League; the voters overwhelmingly endorsed the decision to withdraw from the international body.

The Nazis were particularly effective in using their image as champions of anti-Communism for diplomatic ends. Friction between Germany and Poland had been endemic during the Weimar years, but in February 1934 Hitler put German-Polish relations on a new footing by signing a ten-year nonaggression and friendship pact with Poland. The Nazis would violate the treaty with impunity five years later, but in 1934 the agreement solidly established the new government's anti-Communist credentials. In place of the traditional entente between Germany and Russia, the Nazis joined another fiercely anti-Russian power to guard Europe against Russian expansionism. Equally important, the treaty signaled to France that the much vaunted *cordon sanitaire* in Eastern Europe could be breached.

France's position was also weakened by the return of the Saar early in 1935. Under the Treaty of Versailles, it will be recalled, France was given the right to administer this territory for fifteen years. At the end of this period the inhabitants were to vote on their future status. Since the population was (and is) overwhelmingly German, it was not surprising that the people of the Saar voted by a heavy majority to rejoin the Reich.

The Nazis effectively employed even the countermeasures that the Allies took to halt the Reich's diplomatic offensive. At the beginning of 1935 France, clearly worried by the agreement between Germany and Poland and even more by the pace of German rearmament, signed a treaty of mutual assistance with the Soviet Union. Hitler responded quickly by using the agreement as justification for the reintroduction of universal military service, a measure that was a blatant violation of the Treaty of Versailles. The German argument was that the move was necessary to block the Bolsheviks' advance westward.

A few months later, the Franco-Soviet Pact again served as an excuse for a second, even more audacious move by Hitler. After much public controversy the French parliament ratified the Franco-Soviet Pact early in 1936. For the Nazis this development was a welcome chance to employ, for the first time, military means in attaining a foreign policy objective. Arguing that the ratification of the Franco-Soviet agreement threatened Germany's national security, the Reich government on the morning of March 13, 1936, dispatched troops into the demilitarized Left Bank of the Rhine, thereby violating both the Treaty of Versailles and the Treaty of Locarno. Initially, the French response was vigorous (eighteen divisions were put on full alert), but Hitler won his gamble. The French government appealed to Great Britain for joint action against Germany, but the British cabinet refused. England's Conservative prime minister, Stanley Baldwin, felt any military confrontation between Germany and the Western Allies would only benefit the Soviet Union. Since the French were unwilling to take action on their own, the Allies limited their response to a formal protest, and Hitler had triumphed. The reoccupation of the Rhineland was, moreover, a victory that was particularly impressive in the eyes of the New Conservatives. After all, previous German governments had negotiated for years just to get the French troops removed from German soil, while Hitler in the course of one Saturday morning reestablished German military sovereignty over the Reich's western borders.

By no means all of Hitler's initiatives were instant successes, however. One serious setback was the Nazis first crude attempt to annex Austria. In July 1934, the Austrian branch of the Nazi movement attempted to overthrow the pro-Italian government of Chancellor Dollfuss and pave the way for the annexation of Austria by Germany. Although the putsch was planned by the Austrian Nazi Party, the NSDAP's headquarters in Munch were fully cognizant of the sister party's plans. The insurgents succeeded in murdering the Austrian chancellor but not in toppling his regime. When Mussolini rushed troops to Italy's border with Austria to demonstrate his country's concern for Austria's independence, Hitler backed off immediately and made no attempt to challenge the Italian dictator. For another four years Austria retained her independence.

The initial reaction to Germany's unilateral reintroduction of universal military service appeared equally strong. Italy, France, and Great Britain—allies since 1915—responded by forming the Stresa Front and promising to act jointly in thwarting any further violation of the Versailles system. Coupled with the Franco-Soviet Pact and the Soviet Union's apparently growing willingness to join a collective security system against the Nazis, Hitler's ambitions seemed to be confronted with formidable obstacles.

But the barriers were without substance. What appeared on paper as a phalanx of diplomatic agreements arrayed against the Nazis was in fact little more than a collection of meaningless "statements of principle." The reason for the breakdown of collective security was simple: The partners did not trust each other. Italy, which had single-handedly stopped Hitler's attempt to annex Austria in mid-1934, increasingly veered toward Germany when Great Britain and Franco—half-heartedly—opposed Mussolini's ambitions in Ethiopia and his support of the Nationalist side in the Spanish Civil War. Germany, on the other hand, stood solidly behind Italy; by the fall of 1936 the Stresa Front had been replaced by the Rome-Berlin Axis. As for the Franco-Soviet Pact, it, too, had a major Achilles' heel. Even the French government that negotiated the agreement was less than enthusiastic about its alliance with the forces of international Bolshevism.

Above all, however, Great Britain developed growing doubts about the value of collective security. Hitler's claim that his ambition was only to fulfill the principle of national self-determination and that a strengthened Germany meant a stronger bulwark against the spread of Bolshevism found willing ears among the British government. Largely propagandistic actions on the party of Germany—like the 1936 summer Olympics in Berlin, and the signing of the Anti-Comintern Pact between Germany and Japan in the same year (Italy joined the pact in 1937)—also impressed the British. As early as the spring of 1935 Germany and Great Britain negotiated a bilateral agreement on naval armaments that permitted the Nazis substantially to exceed the limits set down in the Versailles Treaty. England's inaction during the Rhineland crisis was another symptom of her alienation from the principle of collective security. Hitler was undoubtedly gratified when the British foreign secretary, Lord Halifax, assured the German dictator in November 1937 that the British cabinet was convinced Hitler's actions against the German Communists had saved Western Europe from Bolshevism. Halifax also let it be known that there would be no objection on the part of his government to further territorial changes in Hitler's favor provided that they could be achieved by diplomacy rather than war. Hitler listened well: He had been given the green light for what was to become a year of crises in 1938. Appeasement, not collective security, triumphed.

CONCLUSION

Adolf Hitler was convinced it was his destiny to rule Germany and Europe, and, by the end of 1937, the dictator had traveled a considerable distance toward reaching his goal. The Nazis had established a totalitarian, "dual state" regime that controlled all aspects of public life from art to sports. An efficient terror machine assured that there was no organized opposition in the country.

In international affairs the balance sheet was clearly in Hitler's favor. Germany had regained her position as an equal among the Great Powers. Hitler managed to break up both the Locarno and Stresa fronts.

Germany's support of Mussolini's military activities against Ethiopia, and the Reich's and Italy's joint intervention on the Nationalists' side in the Spanish Civil War persuaded the Italian dictator to veer increasingly toward the German orbit. A state visit by Mussolini to Germany in September 1937 formally confirmed the Rome-Berlin Axis. Earlier, the Anglo-German naval agreement and Great Britain's inaction during the Rhineland crisis had revealed serious cracks in the Franco-British relationship.

Still, neither Hitler nor the Germans felt satisfied at the end of 1937. In fact, the regime was in the midst of a serious malaise. As far as the German people were concerned, the euphoria about the Third Reich had dissipated quickly. The early economic measures of the regime had given it genuine popularity among most Germans, but the reality of restrictions, terror, and repression turned enthusiasm into growing passivity and sullenness. In August 1934, only 84.6 percent of those voting in a plebiscite staged to approve Hitler's assuming the powers of the Reich presidency cast their ballots in favor; dictatorships are accustomed to affirmative voting in the 99th percentile. A few months later, DAF-sponsored national elections for factory shop stewards were so disastrous for the Nazis that the results were not published; we now know that despite immense pressure only 30 to 40 percent of the workers voted for the Nazi list of candidates. Even more ominous from the NSDAP's point of view, when the party permitted Germans to apply for membership in the Nazi Party again (the membership rolls had been closed since March 1933) the results were a severe disappointment: The number of those applying for party membership fell far short of expectations.

Hitler was fully aware of the impotent unrest among the people he ruled (the Gestapo had a quite efficient net of agents to report on the mood of the country), but he was dissatisfied for his own reasons as well. The German dictator was convinced both that his ultimate goals could be accomplished only with military force and that he alone could lead the Reich in this war of conquest. At the same time, he was sure he would die an early death. The realization that he would be fifty years old in April 1939 persuaded him that he needed to accelerate the pace of his actions, rather than remain content with his accomplishments.

This was the background for a meeting with his top military and diplomatic advisors that Hitler called on November 5, 1937. His select audience included the Reich's military chiefs, Blomberg, Fritsch, Göring, and Raeder, as well as the Reich foreign minister, Konstatin von Neurath. In the course of his interminable, four-hour long monologue, the Führer reiterated his view that race and space determined the fate of empires and peoples and that to fulfill her destiny Germany would have to undertake military operations in the near future.

The significance of this November 1937 conference did not lie in Hitler's general remarks, but in the concrete conclusions that he drew from his analysis of the world situation. His listeners were intimately familiar with the racist litany that he repeated yet again. However, while in the past the Reich's need for *Lebensraum* in Eastern Europe was foreseen as a more long-range aim, this time Hitler demanded immediate military preparations to enable Germany to annex Austria and conquer Czechoslovakia by "lightning-fast actions." Hitler dismissed the risks involved: The Western Allies were weak entities that would not seriously resist Germany's drive to the east and southeast.

After he had concluded his address, Hitler discovered to his dismay that while the Reich's military and diplomatic leaders did not object to the Nazi dictator's long-range goals, they had serious reservations about Hitler's assessment of the diplomatic and military risks involved. They did not share his view that the Western Allies would not resist continued German efforts to change the map of Europe. But objections of the military and civilian leaders did not shake Hitler's convictions. On the contrary, more than ever he was determined to move fast. On December 22, 1937, the general staff began preparing plans for "Case Green," the undertaking of military operations against Czechoslovakia. Equally important, Hitler recognized that to accomplish his goals he would have to part company with some of those New Conservatives who had served him so well during the first five years of his rule.

CHAPTER 8

CONQUEST, DEATH, AND DEFEAT, 1938–1945

In the brief time span covered by this chapter, the German Reich reached its pinnacles of power and territorial expansion, but the Germans also experienced unprecedented depths of defeat and despair. Announcing that "Germany will be a world power, or it will vanish," the Nazi dictator dropped the mask of peaceful revisionism and unleashed World War II. With the end of that conflict the second part of Hitler's prophecy had come true: For all practical purposes Germany was no more. In 1945 Germany, as Andreas Hillgruber has remarked, stood not at the level of 1939 or 1914, but—in terms of sociopolitical development—closer to 1815. Adolf Hitler's rule had set German history back 150 years.

Compressed into these momentous years are three interconnected themes. The first is the accelerated growth of totalitarianism and terror in Germany. The groups that had retained a measure of autonomy during

the first five years of the Third Reich increasingly became subject to further controls and infiltration. The process of Nazifying previously autonomous segments of the society and the expansion of Nazi rule to most of Europe during World War II presented new opportunities for terror and power aggrandizement, but also increased the already bitter rivalries among the various wings of the Nazi establishment.

The Nazis' drive to conquer all of Europe (and more) and their parallel attempt to physically exterminate Europe's Jews and other "inferior" races constitute a second theme. Hitler launched World War II for two reasons: He had long been convinced Germany needed to wage war in order to obtain *Lebensraum*, and he recognized that only German control of Europe would enable him to undertake the physical extermination of millions of people, most importantly the Jews of Europe. The Holocaust, then, was not incidental to the war effort, but a major theme and integral part of Hitler's war of conquest.

Finally, the disintegration of the Reich presents a third theme of this chapter. When Hitler realized that he had lost his gamble for world conquest, he unleashed a process of self-destruction that led to the disappearance of a united German nation.

FURTHER GROWTH OF THE NAZI FÜHRER STATE

The first five years of the Third Reich were characterized by an increasingly strained symbiotic relationship between the Nazi Party and its leaders on the one hand and the traditional German elites on the other. True, the Nazis and especially Hitler himself were clearly the dominant partners in this relationship. With the often enthusiastic cooperation of the old elites, the Nazi Party had destroyed democracy in Germany and secured a monopoly of political power. By 1938 no major societal interest group openly opposed the Nazis, but there were some segments that retained a measure of organizational autonomy. The most important among these were the diplomatic establishment (the Reich foreign minister, Konstantin von Neurath, had been in office since 1932), the *Wehrmacht*, portions of the civil service, the Catholic and Protestant churches, and the nation's business leaders.

At the beginning of 1938 Hitler and the Nazis were not particularly concerned about the last three groups on the list. It did not appear that the business leaders or the civil servants had either the means or the desire to challenge the Nazis' future plans. The churches remained an unknown factor in the long run, but for the immediate future Hitler was most concerned about the military and diplomatic leaders: The dictator recognized that the realization of his far-reaching plans needed the enthusiastic cooperation of the Reich's diplomatic establishment and of the leaders of Germany's

armed forces. Until now the members of both groups—with negligible exceptions—had backed Hitler's goals, but their lukewarm reception of Hitler's plans for war in November 1937 indicated to the Nazi leader that the symbiosis was coming to an end.

The opportunity for expanding Nazi control over the diplomatic and military establishments came unexpectedly in February 1938. Nazi Party organs had attempted to meddle in the conduct of the Reich's foreign policy since 1933, but their efforts had not been notably successful. Alfred Rosenberg, the NSDAP's self-styled theorist, established a "Foreign Political Office" with ties to various fascist groups outside of Germany, but these initiatives were hampered by Rosenberg's usual ineptitude and dilletantism. Considerably more important was the "Bureau Ribbentrop" that operated within the organizational framework of the Office of the Deputy Führer for Party Operations. Joachim von Ribbentrop was a relative newcomer to the party, having joined the NSDAP only in 1932. He also had no diplomatic experience. As an international wine dealer before the Nazis came to power Ribbentrop did, however, possess wide-ranging foreign contacts. With funds provided by the Nazi Party treasurer, Ribbentrop assembled a motley group of amateur diplomats that attempted to "Nazify" German foreign policy.

The regular foreign service officers complained bitterly about the unwanted competition, but Ribbentrop quickly gained the approval of the one man who counted. His successful handling of negotiations that led to the Anglo-German Naval Agreement of 1935 convinced Hitler that Ribbentrop was the Nazi Bismarck, with skills far superior to those of Germany's professional diplomats. It was no surprise, then, that Hitler appointed Ribbentrop as Reich foreign minister in February 1938, replacing the—from the Führer's point of view—no longer satisfactory Neurath.

At almost the same time, a string of fortuitous circumstances enabled the Nazis to purge the command structure of the armed forces. In this case the initiative came not from Hitler, but from Heinrich Himmler and Hermann Göring. Both held long-standing resentments against the traditional leaders of the *Wehrmacht*: Himmler felt the old-line Prussian officers were hampering the expansion of the SS, and Göring was convinced that they did not appreciate the importance of a large air force in modern warfare.

Fortunately for the two conspirators, personally damaging material seemed to be available against two of Germany's most important military leaders, General Werner von Blomberg, the Reich minister of defense since 1933, and the commander of the land forces, General Werner von Fritsch. Until now neither had given the Nazis any trouble. Blomberg had been an early, consistent, and enthusiastic supporter of Hitler's rearmament program, and Fritsch prided himself on being "just a soldier" who did not interfere in political decisions. Both men were alarmed, however, by Hitler's plans for what they regarded as risky and premature military adventures.

Under these circumstances, real and manufactured revelations of Blomberg's and Fritsch's personal misconduct came at an opportune time not only for Himmler and Göring, but for Hitler as well. Blomberg, a widower for some years, had remarried in 1937; Hitler and Göring had been witnesses at the ceremony. Blomberg's bride was then a secretary in his office, but a few months later Himmler produced evidence from police files that some years earlier the new Mrs. Blomberg had posed for pornographic pictures. Blomberg was quietly permitted to resign. Fritsch, on the other hand, was the victim of a deliberately organized frame-up. Reinhard Heydrich, the head of the SD, brought forward an individual who (falsely) swore that he had had homosexual relations with Fritsch. The frame-up was later exposed, and a court of honor exonerated the general, but by that time Fritsch had already been forced to resign from his post. Despite the verdict of the court of honor, Hitler refused to reinstate him.

In historical terms, the personal tragedy of the two officers was overshadowed by the organizational and personnel repercussions of the affairs. By 1938 the Nazification of the armed forces was advancing rapidly. The expansion of the officer corps since 1933 had already led to the appointment of many pro-Nazi officers in all branches of the *Wehrmacht*, and now Hitler took personal control of the armed forces. Hermann Göring, who held the position of air force commander among his many jobs, suggested himself as Blomberg's replacement as head of the Ministry of Defense, but the Führer rejected the proposal. Instead, Hitler abolished the ministry altogether and replaced it with the High Command of the Armed Forces (OKW), a structure potentially not unlike the U.S. Joint Chiefs of Staff. As head of the new agency Hitler did not select a distinguished officer, but a military cipher: Wilhelm Keitel was a thoroughly colorless and nondescript officer who, like Ribbentrop, had no ambitions except to carry out Hitler's wishes. In effect, then, the Nazi dictator became his own minister of defense. Keitel's chief of staff was Alfred Jodl, an able, but also thoroughly Nazified officer. Fritsch's replacement was equally symptomatic of the growing Nazi influence in the officer crops. As the new commander of the army Hitler selected Walther von Brauchitsch, an opponent of Göring, but also one of the earliest and most enthusiastic Nazi fellow-travelers among the *Wehrmacht* officers.

A few months later, the army's chief of staff, General Ludwig Beck, was also dismissed. Beck, who would later become one of the leaders of the military conspiracy against Hitler (details of this story will be covered in Chapter 9), had voiced political and tactical objections to the Führer's plans to invade Czechoslovakia. Beck's place was taken by Franz Halder, another officer in the Fritsch mold of "just a soldier."

The Nazification of the armed forces and especially Hitler's personal control of the military operations accelerated during the war itself. The dictator held the pliable commander of the army Brauchitsch responsible for the German defeat in the Battle of Moscow in December 1941. To the accompaniment of a great deal of propaganda fanfare, Hitler now took over day-to-day supervision of military operations, often deciding even minor tactical decisions at the regimental and company level. (For a discussion of the military operations in World War II, see the next section of this chapter, pp. 220–26.)

As the tide turned and the German setbacks multiplied, Hitler increasingly vented his frustrations on the officer corps. Especially, it was the army chiefs of staff who caught his ire: Between 1942 and 1945 four generals followed each other in brief succession. But tenure was barely more secure in less exposed positions. By the time World War II ended, Hitler had dismissed half of all officers who held the rank of general at the beginning of the war.

What little remained of the *Wehrmacht's* organizational autonomy was destroyed in 1944. When it became clear that the conspiracy against Hitler in July 1944 (see p. 240) involved a number of high-ranking officers, the Nazis conducted a full-scale purge of the armed forces. In addition to ordering the execution of dozens of officers and appointing Himmler commander of the reserve forces, Hitler insisted that all German army units be provided with so-called National Socialist Leadership Officers. Modeled on the political commissars in the Soviet army, their function was to motivate the soldiers in their charge with Nazi political fanaticism. Needless to say, at the end of 1944 with the German armies in full retreat on virtually every front, such desperate measures had no practical effect.

The erosion of autonomy in the military sphere had its counterpart in the progressive Nazification of the Reich's civilian administration. In the course of the war Hitler and the party leaders vastly expanded their control over the Reich's administrative apparatus and the processes of political decision making. In June 1942, during what was to be its final session in the Third Reich, the thoroughly Nazified Reichstag passed legislation giving Hitler full authority to issue laws as well as the power to dismiss civil servants, judges, and prosecutors who, in the Führer's opinion, "were not doing their duty."

As the fortunes of war turned against the Third Reich, Hitler increasingly delegated authority to the only men he felt he could fully trust, the *Gauleiters* of the Nazi Party. Most of these "old fighters" had been serving as chiefs of the *Länder* administrations since 1933, but in 1942 the Führer gave eighteen of them additional functions as "Reich Defense Commissioners." In this capacity they were the civilian counterparts of the commanding generals in the Reich's military districts, responsible for all aspects of the civilian administration. Other Gauleiters were entrusted by Hitler with far-reaching authority to administer large policy areas. The Gauleiter of Saxony, Fritz Sauckel, was given the task of securing foreign workers as replacements for the Germans who were drafted into the army in ever larger numbers. Sauckel began with material and propagandistic inducements but, when the results were unsatisfactory, he turned to terror and force. In the latter war years the Germans with the help of the collaborationist regimes in the occupied areas simply rounded up able bodies and transported them to the Reich. Joseph Goebbels, the Gauleiter of Berlin and Reich propaganda minister, reached the apex of his powers in 1943 when Hitler appointed him "Plenipotentiary for the Total War Effort," with authority to coordinate all civilian aspects of the German war effort.

The process of assigning additional spheres of power to certain party leaders had a dual effect: It created a jungle of overlapping jurisdictions that enabled Hitler to continue his long-time practice of playing his various underlings off against each other, and it produced some clear victors and losers among the various Nazi Party leaders and organizations. The most notable beneficiaries of the growth of the Nazi Führer state were an individual, Martin Bormann, and an organization, the SS. Since 1933 Bormann had been the chief of staff for Rudolf Hess, the deputy Führer for party operations. When Hess flew to England in May 1941 (see p. 224), Bormann made the most of the opportunity. Taking charge of the organization of the deputy Führer (now renamed the "Party Chancellery"), he remained physically close to Hitler at all times, and eventually served as a funnel through which all access to the dictator took place. Hitler trusted Bormann explicitly; the chief of the Party Chancellery became Hitler's alter ego, carrying out without question the Führer's wishes and commands.

Ironically, the SS rose in importance as the power of the Third Reich declined. Under the determined if pedantic leadership of Heinrich Himmler, the Nazi elite organization had always regarded itself as the true embodiment of Nazism, but the SS owed its rise to power more to its efficient management of terror than to Himmler's muddled racial endeavors, which included establishing institutions for the breeding of superior children.

The SS had begun to lay the groundwork for its expanded activities long before the war, but with the start of military operations the SS succeeded even further in merging party and state functions under its control. Only four weeks after World War II had begun, the SS's "Security Service" (SD) and the state political police (Gestapo) were combined into a single organization, the "Reich Security Main Office" headed by one of Himmler's most vicious subordinates, Reinhard Heydrich. During the war Heydrich and his successor—the former head of the Austrian SS, Ernst Kaltenbrunner—(Hey-

drich was assassinated by Czech resistance fighters in 1942) rapidly expanded their network of state-sponsored terror. Himmler, too, continued to amass additional state titles and functions. In August 1943, he became Reich minister of the interior, and thus nominal superior of all German civil servants. Finally, after the July 1944 assassination attempt on Hitler, the chief of the SS was appointed commander of the German army reserves.

Although few church leaders advocated open resistance to the Nazis, Hitler and most leaders of the NSDAP wanted to eliminate organized Christianity in German society. Especially in the early years of the Third Reich there had been repeated attempts by the *Gauleiters* to subordinate the churches in their provinces to direct Nazi control. But Hitler remained curiously apprehensive about challenging the autonomy of the churches, and particularly during the war he ordered the cessation of efforts to suppress the churches. The Führer feared a new *Kulturkampf* ("struggle for culture") might turn public opinion against the regime.

The moral power of the churches was demonstrated by their opposition to a program that had been assigned a high priority in the Nazi catalogue of racially motivated measures. In 1938 the Nazis had begun a program of killing mentally ill individuals who were kept in state institutions. These "mercy killings" were justified on the grounds that they would prevent hereditary genetic defects from perpetuating themselves in the German racial stock. Nevertheless, the killings were quietly abandoned when the Catholic archbishop of Münster, Count Galen, publicly protested the practice. Unfortunately, by the time Galen took to the pulpit some 80,000 mental patients had already been murdered.

The Nazis' soft glove approach toward the churches during World War II did not apply to Nazi-church relations in the occupied areas of Eastern Europe. In Nazi-occupied Poland many Catholic clerics were murdered as part of the effort to deprive the Poles of their intellectual and moral leaders. Similarly, in the German border area with Poland, the Warthegau, the Nazi *Gauleiter* Arthur Greiser had Hitler's full approval for his systematic campaigns of persecution against the clergy and practicing members of both Christian churches.

When the Third Reich collapsed in May 1945, Germany had been subjected—on paper at least—to a full-fledged totalitarian system in which virtually all power rested in the arbitrary hands of Adolf Hitler and his henchmen in the Nazi Party. The German wartime experience constitutes a case study in the transformation of a modern pluralist society into what Robert Koehl has called a neofeudal dictatorship without institutional safeguards for the rights of either individuals or groups.

TRIUMPH AND FALL

The Diplomacy of Appeasement

One of Hitler's unshakable *idées fixes* was to wage a war of conquest that would result in the subjection of the European continent to Nazi rule. The year 1938 marked an important watershed in the pursuit of Nazism's ultimate goals. During the first five years of the Third Reich the Nazi leaders had claimed that Germany wanted only to be treated as an equal among the world's Great Powers; the Reich merely sought a revision of the "unfair" portions of the Treaty of Versailles. At the beginning of 1938, however, the Nazis dropped the mask of peaceful revisionism. Instead, Hitler made it clear that he expected the other Great Powers to acquiesce to Germany's control of territories that lay beyond the Reich's boundaries of 1914. Some of these lands were, it is true, inhabited by German-speaking populations, and for a time Hitler justified his territorial ambitions by the doctrine of national self-determination. However, by the fall of 1938 even this pretense

had to be dropped. Hitler's aims were revealed in their stark reality: conquest and control, not fairness and international justice.

The Nazi leader used the occasion of his meeting with the Reich's military and civilian leaders in November 1937 to announce the start of a new phase in Nazi foreign policy. Hitler insisted Germany now needed to take advantage of her headstart in rearmament to begin a series of military operations before the French and British rearmament programs had a chance to catch up. Hitler also left no doubt about the progression of the Nazis' victims: Austria, then Czechoslovakia, and finally Poland and Russia. At the same time, the German dictator thought in global terms; he wanted to coordinate his conquest of Europe with Japanese expansions in Asia. German foreign policy gave up its traditional tilt toward China in favor of a political and military alliance with Japan.

Austria, the Nazis's first new territorial objective, was particularly well chosen to mark the transition from revisionism to conquest. The country was German in both language and culture, and at the end of the 1930s its political independence rested on increasingly precarious foundations. Since the unsuccessful Nazi putsch in July 1934, Austria had been ruled by an "Austro-fascist" regime led by Kurt von Schuschnigg. The Austrian leader's government relied on Mussolini to protect it from German aggression and on restrictions on the political freedom of its own people to prevent opposition at home. Both the Austrian Social Democrats and the Nazis were prohibited; the only party allowed in Austria was the government-sponsored Fatherland Front.

Unfortunately for Schuschnigg and his regime, the international and domestic situations underwent profound changes after 1934. The Italian dictator abandoned his concern for Austrian independence in favor of strengthening the Rome-Berlin Axis. In Austria itself, the contrast between the country's economic stagnation and the pace of

Germany's Expansion
1933- 1939

economic recovery in Germany led to a sizable increase in the support for the illegal Nazi movement, especially among younger Austrians.

Consequently, Hitler held two trump cards in his hands when he all but ordered Schuschnigg to come to the Führer's moun-

tain retreat at Berchtesgaden on the Austrian border. During their meeting the German leader insisted that Schuschnigg reorganize his cabinet by including some of the leaders of the outlawed Austrian Nazi Party.

Recognizing the weakness of his position, Schuschnigg did not reject the German demand outright, but he did attempt to counter Hitler's pressure with a public relations coup of his own. The Austrian government announced that it would stage a plebiscite on the question of Austria's independence on March 12, 1938. It was, to be sure, a rigged election. For example, the Austrian voting age was raised from 21 to 25 just for the plebiscite in order to keep the many younger Nazi sympathizers from casting ballots. Nevertheless, the outcome of the election would presumably not have supported the German Nazis' contention that the overwhelming majority of Austrians were longing to "come home to the Reich."

Hitler was determined to prevent the plebiscite from taking place. The German government reacted to Schuschnigg's announcement by demanding not just the withdrawal of the plebiscite, but Schuschnigg's resignation in favor of the leader of the Austrian Nazis, Arthur Seyss-Inquart. If the terms of the ultimatum were not accepted, Hitler threatened military action against his homeland.

After a frantic and futile effort to secure Mussolini's help, Schuschnigg resigned on the evening of March 11, 1938, yielding power to Seyss-Inquart. The new leader of Austria promptly asked that German troops be sent to Austria to help him "maintain law and order." On the morning of March 12, German units crossed the border; they were met with what appeared to be near-universal acclaim by the Austrian population. One day later, Hitler himself "came home." Hitler began a triumphant tour of the country that culminated in a rally staged in the square in front of the old imperial castle in Vienna. Here an audience of 100,000 cheering listeners heard Hitler "report before history" that his homeland had returned to the Reich.

For the Nazi dictator, the *Anschluss*, as the union of Austria and Germany is called, was a political, diplomatic, and even economic triumph. Politically, Hitler had created the Greater German Reich, a feat not even Bismarck could rival. In addition, a look at the map showed that German territory now surrounded Czechoslovakia like a vice. In economic terms, the Reich's chronic lack of hard currency was temporarily eased by the quite substantial Austrian hard currency reserves. Above all, however, Hitler had seemingly proved himself to be a master at international diplomacy. His "instincts" about the reaction of Great Britain and France turned out to be far more accurate than the fears of some of his advisors.

After World War I the Allies, especially France, had acted repeatedly to prevent what they saw as threats to Austria's independence, but in 1938 France and Great Britain limited their action to diplomatic protest notes and quickly accepted the *fait accompli* of Austria's annexation. Mussolini, another former champion of Austrian independence, simply washed his hands of the whole affair.

The Allies' surprising lack of vigorous reaction was a consequence of the policy of appeasement, the diplomatic strategy that the leaders of Great Britain and, to a lesser extent, France adopted in the hope that it would both respond to and contain Hitler's "revisionist" ambitions. We now know that appeasement was a completely counterproductive policy; it encouraged rather than contained Hitler's drive for power. Appeasement failed to preserve Austria's independence, and a few months later the Western Allies in the name of this misguided policy would present Czechoslovakia to Hitler on a silver platter as well. Why, then, did the foreign-policy leaders of Great Britain and France persist in holding on to what was clearly an unsuccessful diplomatic strategy?

The term *appeasement* will always be associated with the name of Neville Chamberlain, the British Conservative politician and prime minister who was the most enthusiastic advocate and practitioner of that policy. For Chamberlain appeasement was a way of accommodating Nazi Germany's "legitimate" desires for revision of the post–

World War I international balance of power without risking a military confrontation, while at the same time safeguarding Great Britain's and France's vital interests. The diplomatic strategy of appeasement was based upon two major premises, both, as should have been clear at the time, fundamentally false. One assumed that Hitler was as anxious to avoid a new world war as the leaders of the Allied countries, and the second postulated that the Nazi leader's desire for changes in the balance of power was motivated primarily by his opposition to the spread of Soviet communism. That is to say, the appeasers saw a fundamental union of values between themselves and Adolf Hitler. From this it followed that Nazi Germany—as Western civilization's major bulwark against Communist expansion—was justified in her demands for substantial revisions of the terms of the Versailles system.

Unfortunately, Hitler's interpretation of Nazi Germany's legitimate ambitions had nothing in common with those of his diplomatic partners and adversaries. To be sure, he was fundamentally opposed to Bolshevism and intended to subjugate Soviet Russia, but he planned that fate as well for France and most of Continental Europe. In view of his own ambitions the Nazi dictator looked upon the policy of appeasement not as an honest offer of compromise, but as a demonstration of the weakness of his adversaries. For Hitler appeasement was proof that democracy was a political system that produced leaders who were cowards and consequently wanted to avoid war at all costs.

The Czechoslovak crisis during the fall of 1938 demonstrated particularly well both the folly and the illusions associated with the policy of appeasement. After his triumphs in Austria Hitler lost no time in turning to his next victim, Czechoslovakia. At the end of May, he issued secret orders to draft plans for the "obliteration" of Czechoslovakia. Hitler intended to seize control of Germany's southeastern neigh-bor, although there was no "legitimate" justification for German rule in Czechoslovakia.

Both politically and economically Czechoslovakia was a success story among the various states that resulted from the breakup of the Austro-Hungarian empire. This new Central European nation, with its developed and well-balanced economy, was the only one among the successor states of the Habsburg Empire to establish and maintain a viable parliamentary democracy. Czechoslovakia even managed to defuse conflicts among its various ethnic minorities; the country was noteworthy for its enlightened policies on cultural pluralism. Although some 3 million Germans (known as Sudeten Germans because most of them lived in the area of the Sudeten Mountains) and thousands of Poles and Hungarians remained within the boundaries of Czechoslovakia, relations between them and the majority Czech and Slovak peoples were largely free of friction during the 1920s and early 1930s. This was particularly true for the Germans, Czechoslovakia's largest minority.

Unfortunately, the multinational harmony broke down with the advent of the Depression. Some of the areas with large German-speaking populations were particularly hard hit by the economic downturn. A government-sponsored policy that favored hiring Czechs for civil service jobs over minority peoples aggravated the situation. In the meantime, much as had been true in Austria, the seemingly rapid recovery of Germany itself under Nazi rule led to increased support for a pro-Nazi group, the Sudeten German Party (*Sudetendeutsche Partei*—SdP). Publicly, the SdP demanded increased political and cultural autonomy for the Sudeten Germans, but in reality the party and its leader, Konrad Henlein, worked for the annexation of the Sudeten areas by the German Reich.

At the end of March 1938, Hitler began using Henlein and his group to initiate a continuous diplomatic crisis between Ger-

David Low's accurate depiction of the results of appeasement: Using the "spineless leaders of democracy" as stepping stones, a nose-thumbing Hitler marches toward his ultimate goal. (Source: *Lachen*, p. 280.)

many and Czechoslovakia. The SdP was ordered to wage a campaign of violence accompanied by constantly escalating demands. The object was to put the Czechoslovak government on the defensive while enabling the German propaganda machine to create the myth that the Sudeten Germans were an oppressed people longing for union with the Reich. During the spring and summer of 1938 tensions mounted rapidly.

Initially, the Czechoslovak government refused Henlein's demands outright. The reason for the Czechoslovaks' courageous resistance in the face of a much stronger power lay in the fact that, on paper at least, the small country had some very powerful friends. In 1924 France and Czechoslovakia signed a military alliance that obligated France to come to Czechoslovakia's aid if

the latter were attacked by a foreign power. Czechoslovakia negotiated a similar agreement with Soviet Russia, although the Russians insisted on a clause that their commitments would come into effect only if France honored her obligations. Great Britain and Italy, however, were not directly committed to protecting Czechoslovakia, and they took the lead in initiating the diplomatic maneuvering that would eventually sacrifice Czechoslovakia's very existence on the altar of appeasement.

The Nazis used their national congress in early September 1938 to bring the tensions between Czechs and Germans to a frenzied climax. Characterizing the Czechoslovak government as a friend of Soviet communism, Hitler demanded that the Sudeten Germans be given the right of self-determination immediately. If the "oppressive" Czech regime remained unyielding, he would take matters into his own hands. The Czechoslovaks, relying on the promises of protection incorporated in their alliance system, made it clear that they would resist by force any German invasion. War seemed inevitable.

For Neville Chamberlain, the prospect of war in Central Europe was unthinkable. He remained convinced that such a conflict would only aid the cause of world communism. In mid-September he flew to Berchtesgaden to plead with the German dictator to restrain his use of military force a little longer; in the meantime Allied diplomats would attempt to find a diplomatic solution to the crisis. Hitler agreed that he could probably resist the pressure of German public opinion for action on his part for a few days longer. Chamberlain in turn praised Hitler's moderation and regarded his visit as a triumph of appeasement.

Chamberlain completely misjudged Hitler's character, for the Führer always looked upon concessions as a sign of weakness. Within days he announced that a plebiscite among the German minority in Czechoslovakia was not enough; the Sudeten area would have to be turned over to Germany without a vote. In addition, the Germans became solicitous of the Hungarian and Polish minorities. They, too, should be permitted to join their respective motherlands. Since the Czechs still remained unyielding, Europe again seemed poised on the brink of war.

Only Chamberlain had not lost hope. He went to Germany a second time to renew his pleas for a peaceful solution. After another week in which war hysteria mounted, his efforts appeared to be successful. The leaders of Germany, Italy, France, and Great Britain agreed to meet at a summit conference on September 29. The meeting was held, appropriately enough, at the *Führerbau*, part of the complex of buildings that formed the national headquarters of the Nazi Party in Munich. Without consulting either the Czechs or the Russians, the par-

ticipants accepted a "compromise" proposal offered by Mussolini as a diplomatic solution to the Sudeten crisis. The document was actually an Italian translation of Hitler's latest demands. By this "compromise" Czechoslovakia was forced to yield the Sudeten areas to Germany without a plebiscite. If the Czechoslovaks refused to accept the dictum of the Four Power Conference, France would refuse to honor her treaty obligations. If Czechoslovakia accepted the judgment, however, the Four Powers agreed to "guarantee" the territorial integrity of what remained of Czechoslovakia. It was a cynical sell-out to Nazi Germany, but Chamberlain returned home having achieved what he thought was "peace in our time."

Having gotten his way at Munich, Hitler initiated a dual course of action. The German government announced solemnly that the Reich had no further territorial ambitions anywhere in Europe. To give additional credence to this declaration, the German foreign minister Joachim von Ribbentrop at the beginning of December traveled to Paris and signed a joint declaration with France; the Reich again renounced any ambitions to regain Alsace-Lorraine. But at the same time, hidden from public view, Hitler issued orders to "take care of the rest of Czechoslovakia."

The second Czechoslovakian crisis came in March 1939. The Nazis pressured some right-wing Slovak political leaders to declare their independence from Czechoslovakia, thereby dismembering the country. Slovakia became an ostensibly independent country, although it was actually a satellite of Nazi Germany. As for the Czech part of the country, the Germans reduced it to a colony of the Reich. Threatening the Czechs with bombardment and military invasion, the Nazis blackmailed the Czech leaders into asking that their lands be placed under German "protection." What remained of Czechoslovakia became the Reich Protectorate of Bohemia and Moravia. The first Reich "protector" was Konstantin von Neurath, the man Hitler had dismissed as foreign minister in February 1938.

The Nazis' cynical destruction of Czechoslovakia five months after they had agreed to guarantee its continued existence brought a swift and ignominious end to the policy of appeasement. Instead of seeking to accommodate the Nazi dictator's further ambitions, Great Britain and France issued guarantees of support to Hitler's most likely next targets, Poland and Rumania.

The Nazi leader was not impressed. He regarded the guarantees as a bluff and proceeded to initiate the next crisis. Immediately after the dissolution of Czechoslovakia, Germany proposed bilateral talks on boundary rectifications to Poland. Compared with the destruction of Czechoslovakia the Germans' initial demands seemed almost modest: the autonomous city of Danzig (today Gdansk in Poland), which did have a largely German population, should be returned to the Reich and an extraterritorial road should be built through the Polish Corridor to facilitate access to the German exclave of East Prussia. In return, Hitler offered to extend the 1934 German-Polish nonaggression pact for another twenty-five years. The Germans also tried to lure the Poles with hints of the possibility of joint German-Polish moves against the Soviet Ukraine. The Polish leaders, with the fate of Czechoslovakia (in whose dismemberment they had participated) vividly before their eyes and emboldened by the Franco-British guarantee, resolutely refused to yield to the German demands.

Hitler was not overly concerned by the impasse. At the beginning of April he ordered plans for "Case White," an attack on Poland sometime after September 1, 1939. The Nazi leader's confidence came partly because his "infallible" advisor on foreign policy, Ribbentrop, assured the Führer that Great Britain would not go to war over Poland. In addition, Germany's diplomatic position seemed to be improving rapidly in the spring and summer of 1939. The conclusion of the Pact of Steel between Italy and the Reich in May bound the two fascist states to support each other in all endeavors. However, a far more dramatic shift in the balance of power was the conclusion of a nonaggression pact between Nazi Germany and the Soviet Union in August.

The Nazi-Soviet agreement was an alliance between two most unlikely partners. Hitler had made something of a career of anti-Bolshevism, and the Russian leader, Joseph Stalin, while distrustful of all of his Western neighbors, had in the past poured particular venom on Hitler and the Nazis. However, the policy of appeasement (and especially the Allies' behavior at the Munich Conference) revived Stalin's fears that the Western powers were encouraging Hitler to seek territorial and political gains at the expense of the Soviet Union. Hitler, too, for all his anticommunist bravado, saw an opportunity in the summer of 1939 to strike a tactical bargain with his fellow dictator and suggested bilateral talks. After some months of not very secret negotiations, Ribbentrop and his Soviet counterpart Molotov signed two agreements on August 23, 1939. One was a public document, a nonaggression pact, in which each partner promised to remain benevolently neutral toward the other in case of war with third countries. The benefits to Germany were obvious. Not only were the Nazis relieved of Bismarck's nightmare of a two-front war, but in case of conflict with the Western powers Germany could make use of the Russian land route to obtain needed imports from Asia and Russia herself, thereby undermining the effect of any British blockade.

Far more important in the short run, however, was the second agreement, a secret codicil that envisioned a fourth partition of Poland and a full-scale territorial rearrangement of Eastern Europe. Under the terms of this secret agreement, Russia essentially regained the lands she had lost in 1918. Germany agreed that the Soviet Union could seize control of the independent Baltic states of Lithuania, Estonia, and Latvia, the eastern parts of Poland, and Bessarabia. In

One of David Low's most famous cartoons. Hitler and Stalin meet across a dead Poland. Stalin inquires if he is indeed meeting the "bloody assassin of the working class" (as Soviet propaganda had titled Hitler before the Nazi-Soviet pact) and Hitler assumes he is correct in facing "the scum of humanity," as the Nazis had been fond of labeling the Soviet dictator. (Source: *Lachen*, p. 288.)

addition, the Germans acknowledged that Finland was part of the Soviet hegemonical orbit. In return, Russia agreed to German control of the remainder of Poland. In effect, then, Hitler was free to annex the bulk of Poland.

Military History of World War II

The Nazi-Soviet Pact effectively undercut the Anglo-French guarantees of Poland, and Hitler felt free to attack Germany's eastern neighbor with impunity. Ignoring Mussolini's lack of enthusiasm about a Europe-wide conflict and qualms by some of Nazi leaders, including Hermann Göring, the Führer ordered a full-scale attack on Poland beginning at dawn on September 1.

The Polish campaign introduced two new elements into warfare that were to become characteristic of Nazi operations in World War II. One was the strategy of the *Blitzkrieg* (lightning-fast war). Taking advantage of technical improvements in armaments, the Germans subjected Poland and subsequently other opponents to massive and coordinated attacks by waves of fighter

Military Operations of W.W. II
The German Offensives, 1939-1942

planes, massed tank assaults, and swiftly moving infantry. The Poles resisted valiantly, but ineffectively. Eighteen days after the war began Poland capitulated. But the Polish campaign, as would be true of the war in Russia later, was also a *Weltanschauungskrieg*, a clash of ideologies and values in which the Nazis' aim was not just military victory, but extermination and subjugation of an entire people.

After the German military operations in Poland had been concluded, and Soviet troops had moved into the parts of Eastern Poland assigned them by the Nazi-Soviet Pact, Poland disappeared from the map. The Germans annexed outright those parts of the country that had belonged to the

Reich before 1918 and converted the rest into a colonial entity called the "General Government" (*Generalgouvernement*). As governor-general, Hitler chose an old-time Nazi and his own personal legal counsel, Hans Frank.

The military operations against Poland testified to the effectiveness of the Nazi rearmament program, but Hitler's expectation that the Western Allies would now write off the East European state much as they had Czechoslovakia earlier, did not come true. Two days after Germany moved into Poland, both France and Great Britain declared war on the Reich. This move confronted Hitler with a genuine dilemma. Not only had his "instinct" betrayed him, but

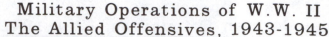

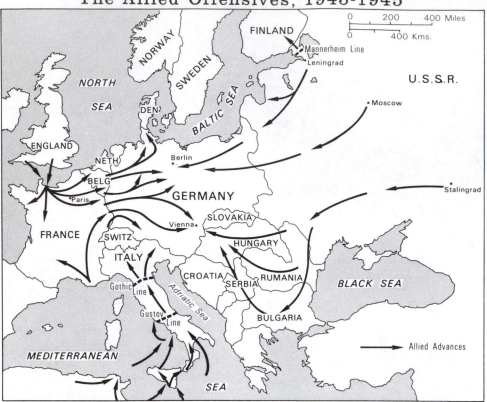

the Nazis had no strategic plans for military operations against the Western Allies. True, Hitler certainly envisioned a war with France at some time in the future, but in the fall of 1939 military plans had to be improvised. At first, the Nazi dictator attempted to revive the ploy that had succeeded so well in the past. On October 6, 1939, he repeated his longing for genuine peace and renounced any further conquests in Europe. But Great Britain and France had definitely abandoned the policy of appeasement. They ignored Hitler's "peace offer."

This forced Germany for the rest of the war essentially to improvise a strategy or, rather, a series of strategies. The result was

what Andreas Hillgruber has called the "global blitzkrieg." Concretely, Hitler determined that he would attempt to repeat the successful operations in Poland by similar lightning attacks on other continental targets, notably France in the West and later the Soviet Union in the East. (The fate of Great Britain remained unclear; Hitler continued to harbor hopes of a bilateral agreement with England that would temporarily divide the world into British and German spheres of influence.) In each case the campaigns were envisioned to last no more than a few weeks or at most months. There were no German plans for either a conflict of attrition or drawn-out defensive operations, because Hitler was convinced that each suc-

cessful blitzkrieg would be sufficient to persuade his remaining enemies to accept peace
on the Nazi dictator's terms.

Hitler's scenario also assigned roles to his
principal allies, Italy and Japan. Mussolini
was to conduct operations in the Mediterranean area, cutting the British supply lines
to India and the Far East. As for the Japanese, Hitler urged them to direct their military operations against British and Soviet
targets in Asia, and, once U.S. support for
Great Britain became obvious, American
objectives as well.

The strategy of the global blitzkreig had
no chance of success. It seriously underestimated the inherent weaknesses of the Axis
powers, including Germany. In addition,
there was no coordination between the Axis
partners. The Japanese, notably, had no
intention of having their strategic goals determined by the Nazis. Japan, rather than
attacking the Soviet Union, concluded a
neutrality pact with Russia in April 1941.
The island empire instead turned eastward
and challenged the United States directly
by bombarding the U.S. naval base at Pearl
Harbor (Hawaii) in December of the same
year. Italy's weakness became glaringly apparent in the fall of 1940. Mussolini staged
an unprovoked attack on Greece, but the
Italian troops were swiftly driven back into
Albania. The Italians had to be rescued by
the intervention of German units. It Italy
was unable to prevail over Greece, she was
clearly no match for British strength in the
Mediterranean and North Africa. Germany,
for her part, did little better. Despite Göring's boasts the Nazis failed to achieve air
superiority in the West during the Battle of
Britain. Later, the Third Reich's inability to
defeat the Soviet Union (see p. 225) in the
most important thrust of the global blitzkrieg sealed the fate of Nazi Germany.

But these developments lay in the future.
In the fall of 1939 Hitler was confronted
with the necessity of continuing the war in
the West. On October 9 he ordered the
OKW to submit plans that would result in
the "definitive military annihilation of the
Western powers." The German generals
feared another war of attrition on the Western front since defeating France or Great
Britain was clearly not the same as overrun-
ning Poland. (Virtually all of the high-level
German officers had, of course, served in
World War I.) The planners' qualms and
poor weather conditions delayed the attack
in the West until May 1940. Just prior to
this, the Germans had launched a successful
amphibious operation that led to Nazi control of Denmark and Norway. Outracing
the British, who had similar designs, the
Scandinavian operations assured that Swed-
ish iron ore would continue to reach German ports. (Sweden remained neutral
throughout the war.)

Like the North Sea operation, the blitzkrieg against France was a master stroke of
military maneuvering. The Germans by-
passed the massive French defensive positions, the Maginot Line, and attacked from
the north as Ludendorff had attempted to
do in the summer of 1918. This meant
violating Dutch and Belgian neutrality, but
Hitler was never one to concern himself
about international law and treaty obligations. This time, there would be no years of
trench warfare in the West. Six weeks after
the attack began, France suffered a humil-
iating defeat. Using the same railroad car
in which the Germans had had to acknowledge their defeat in 1918, the Nazis forced
France to sign an armistice that divided the
country into a northern zone under German
military occupation and an ostensibly independent southern zone. The latter was eventually governed by a collaborationist regime
led by the eighty-four-year-old French
"hero of Verdun," Marshal Phillipe Petain.

After the defeat of France the Nazis were
in virtual control of the Continent east of
the Russian borders, but contrary to Hitler's
expectations Great Britain still refused to
negotiate a peace treaty with the Third
Reich. On the contrary, Neville Chamberlain's replacement by Winston Churchill as
Great Britain's prime minister on May 10,
1940— the same day the Germans launched

their offensive on the Western front— signaled that England was more determined than ever to defeat the Nazis. Churchill had opposed the policy of appeasement, arguing—quite correctly—that dealing with Hitler was not possible. German aerial bombardment of England, including the destruction of many civilian targets, stiffened British resistance still further.

Defeated in the Battle of Britain, Hitler did not pursue his attacks on England. The Nazi dictator instead next turned his military machine against Russia. In July 1940, he ordered work to begin on plans for a full-scale attack on the Soviet Union in the spring of 1941. The Nazi leader apparently reasoned that Great Britain was unwilling to conclude peace despite her hopeless position, as Hitler saw it, because she expected that an eventual conflict between the Soviet Union and Germany would result in a stalemate enabling England to impose peace. The defeat of the Soviet Union in yet another blitzkrieg would demonstrate to the British that this scenario was unworkable. The result would be England's agreement to Hitler's plan for a global division of power between Germany and Great Britain.

Hitler's deluded hopes for global power sharing with Great Britain were apparently also involved in one of the more bizarre episodes of World War II, the flight of the deputy Führer for party operations, Rudolf Hess, to England in May 1941. Hess decided he would make a personal effort to persuade the British to come to terms with Hitler. He was as unsuccessful as his master. The British, after determining that he had no military secrets to reveal, interned the deputy Führer for the duration of the war, while the Germans declared Hess insane.

Any attack upon the Soviet Union would, of course, be a blatant violation of the Nazi-Soviet Pact, but Hitler insisted that the normal rules of international relations had no place in wars for *Lebensraum* and battles of *Weltanschauungen*. At the height of his power in the summer of 1940 Hitler felt that he no longer needed Stalin's friendship.

The Nazi dictator was returning to his original and most abiding ambition, the conquest of Eastern Europe. Moreover, talks involving Hitler, Ribbentrop, and Molotov in November 1940 revealed fundamental differences with the Russians over the future of the Soviet Union's hegemonical status in Europe. While Hitler, however insincerely, was tempting Russia with visions of conquest in the direction of Iran, Iraq, Afghanistan, and India, Molotov insisted that the Soviet Union was more concerned about the Balkans, the eastern end of the Mediterranean and the Baltic Sea—all areas that Hitler included in his definition of Germany's indispensable *Lebensraum*.

Since the fall of France, Stalin had been pursuing his own version of appeasement with Germany, so the Nazis' attack in June 1941, intended as yet another blitzkrieg operation, was completely unprovoked. A force of 3 million soldiers (153 infantry and 19 tank divisions) and 2,700 airplanes launched a three-pronged attack directed at Leningrad, Moscow, and Kiev. The strategy was designed to bring the Soviet Union to her knees after a campaign lasting no longer than four months.

The beginnings of "Plan Barbarossa" had been scheduled for May, but the Germans had to divert some units to subdue Yugoslavia first, and the actual attack on Russia did not start until June 22. Initially, the campaign seemed a repeat of earlier Nazi successes. The German troops advanced hundreds of miles a day. In a series of encirclement battles the *Wehrmacht* wiped out entire Russian armies and took thousands of prisoners each day. By July 4, 1941, Hitler was convinced the Soviet Union had been irrevocably defeated; the Führer was already thinking of new campaigns in India, Afghanistan and, closer to home, Switzerland and Sweden. Ironically, many Western military experts and political leaders agreed. The Atlantic Charter, Churchill's and Roosevelt's 1941 joint manifesto on the liberation of the oppressed peoples from the Nazi yoke, made no mention of the Soviet Union, seemingly accepting its defeat by the Nazis as a *fait accompli*.

Hitler and the experts were wrong. The Russian campaign began the downfall of the Third Reich; the Führer and his generals—like Napoleon earlier—had vastly underestimated the strength of the Russians. Not only were the Soviet armaments, especially the T-34 tank and Russian field artillery, far more effective than the Nazis anticipated, but German intelligence seriously underrated the Russians' overall manpower reserves. In August 1941 the chief of the army's general staff noted ruefully that the Soviets had about twice as many divisions as the Germans had reported.

The German advance began to slow in July, although the forward movement was still impressive. By December, it had come to a halt. Long logistical lines and effective harassing of German communications by a growing Soviet partisan movement seriously weakened the German position. The Nazis laid siege to Leningrad, but could not capture the city. Their situation was even more precarious in the central sector of the front. A brilliant Soviet counterattack during the Battle of Moscow at the beginning of December for the first time in the war put the Germans on the defensive. At the end of the year, it was clear that the strategy of the global blitzkrieg had failed.

By December 1941, World War II had become what Hitler had always sought to avoid, a war of attrition. There was little prospect of defeating the Soviet Union quickly, while in the west the Nazis faced a new adversary. After the Japanese had attacked Pearl Harbor, Germany immediately declared war on the United States. Hitler took this step partly to demonstrate support for the Japanese, but also because he was convinced that eventually he would have to battle the United States for global supremacy in any case.

There are indications that early in 1942 the Führer realized that rationally the Third Reich had little hope of winning the war. Hitler and the other Nazi leaders increasingly placed their faith in the fanaticism of the German soldier, which would somehow prevail over the Allies' manpower and material superiority. Equally unrealistic, Hitler expected the wartime alliance of the Soviet Union, Great Britain, and the United States to break up before the end of the conflict. Irrationally, Hitler still hoped for an Anglo-Nazi partnership. He was convinced Great Britain would object to an expanded U.S. role in Asia and turn to the Nazis for support against America. Above all (see below, pp. 231–32) at the beginning of 1942 the racial Manichaeanism of Hitler's vision of world conquest took priority. As the dream of carving out a conquered *Lebensraum* faded, the Nazis carried out Hitler's other priority, the systematic extermination of the Jews.

Stopped in the north of Russia, the Germans launched another major offensive in the summer of 1942. The objectives were the southeastern regions of Russia and especially the oil fields of Baku. In late July, Rostov fell, and Hitler ordered Army Group B to seize Stalingrad. The Battle of Stalingrad was the last large-scale Nazi offensive on the Eastern front and one of the costliest; between November 1942 and February of the following year the Germans lost more than 800,000 men. In strategic terms the Soviet victory at Stalingrad turned the tide of the war. The back of the Nazi war machine had been broken. Hitler reacted with a succession of futile "no retreat" and "scorched earth" orders by which he sought to delay the end and gain time for the Holocaust. Even during the Battle of Stalingrad transportation facilities for shipping Jews to the death camps had priority over those supplying troops on the Eastern front.

Heavy manpower losses (some 2 million men by the summer of 1943) coupled with inadequate reserves and the failure of German submarines to interdict Allied transatlantic supply lines enabled the Allies to take the initiative on all fronts. In the West the Allied landings in North Africa (November, 1942) and Sicily (July, 1943) ended the

German dream of cutting the British lifeline to India and, instead, established bridgeheads for an Allied counteroffensive on the European Continent. In May 1943 the last units of the German *Afrika Korps* under General Erwin Rommel, sent to aid the faltering Italians, surrendered to British forces commanded by Field Marshal Bernard Montgomery. Finally, the long awaited Allied landings on the French coast in June 1944 inaugurated the liberation of Western Europe and, at the end of the year, brought the war to Germany itself. Hitler's hope that recently developed "miracle weapons," the V-1 and the V-2 "rockets" (actually rocket-propelled drone bombs directed toward England from launching sites in northern Germany) had little effect on Allied operations. (The V stood for *Vergeltung*, the German word for "retaliation.") Far more effective were the constant nighttime and later daytime bombings of German cities by British and American air forces.

Whatever hope Hitler had of a falling-out among his enemies faded rapidly. In January 1943, the United States and Great Britain had announced the policy of "unconditional surrender," precluding a negotiated peace as an end to the war. Stalin, too, endorsed this policy, particularly after what were apparently tentative feelers for a separate peace between Germany and Russia were decisively rejected by Hitler in December 1942. (The long delays in the Anglo-American cross-Channel invasion had possibly revived Stalin's fears that the Western Allies were planning to deal with Hitler behind his back.)

The last German offensive operation was the Battle of the Bulge in late 1944 and early 1945. The unsuccessful operation had the objective of reconquering Antwerp to disrupt Allied supply lines and of dividing American and British troops in the West to delay their advance into Germany. After some initial ground advances, Allied air superiority and lack of fuel for the Germans' motorized elements quickly blunted the offensive. In retrospect, this concentration of resources in the West undoubtedly contributed to the collapse of the central part of the Eastern front, enabling the Russians to speed their final advance toward eastern Germany and the Elbe.

In the spring of 1945 World War II came to an end. For some weeks after the Battle of the Bulge, Hitler still sent phantom armies into battle, fantasized about new miracle weapons, and clung to the hope that the Allies would have a falling-out at the last moment. He briefly interpreted Roosevelt's death in April 1945 as such a turning point, but the dream of world conquest had ended. On April 30 after marrying his long-time mistress, Eva Braun, Hitler and his new wife committed suicide. Before he died, the dictator named Grand Admiral Karl Dönitz, the commander of the German submarine force and a Nazi fanatic for many years, to succeed him as Reich president. Joseph Goebbels was named Reich chancellor, while Himmler and Göring, both of whom had made contact with Allied authorities in the last days of the war, were dismissed for defeatism. (Dönitz accepted his appointment, but Goebbels and his entire family committed suicide shortly after Hitler took his own life.) Espousing his racial fanaticism to the end, Hitler left a political testament admonishing the German people above all to continue the struggle against "international Jewry."

On April 25, 1945, American and Russian troops joined up at Torgau on the Elbe. On May 7, the German forces on the Western front surrendered to the Allied commander-in-chief, General Dwight D. Eisenhower. And one day later General Wilhelm Keitel on behalf of the High Command of the Armed Forces signed papers of unconditional surrender at the headquarters of General Zhukov, the commander of the Russian forces, in Karlshorst just outside Berlin.

NAZI RULE IN EUROPE

The Nazis' goal of permanent mastery over Europe was always an illusion, but for almost four years much of continental Europe was under direct or indirect Nazi control. As was true of their military strategy, Hitler and his henchmen did not develop specific long-range plans for German rule in Europe before or during the conflict. Nevertheless, it is possible to delineate some *leitmotifs* in the hegemonical thinking of Hitler and various other Nazi leaders. Essentially, the Continent would have been divided into three categories of territories subject to varying degrees of German control. An engorged Greater German Reich constituted the planned core of Nazi Europe. In addition to the areas which Germany had already absorbed—Austria, Czechoslovakia, parts of Poland—Nazi planners were anxious to incorporate the remaining "Germanic" areas of Europe, such as Holland, Denmark, Norway, and the Dutch-speaking parts of Belgium. Second, particularly in western and southeastern Europe, the Nazis envisioned areas that would be dotted by German military bases and the presence of Nazi troops, but which would be accorded some rights of autonomy and ruled by indigenous collaborationist regimes. Finally, there were the vast areas of Eastern Europe and the Soviet Union. Under all Nazi scenarios these territories were listed as objects of pure colonial exploitation, without any rights of self-government.

Although most of the Nazi plans for the postwar future can only be reconstructed from Hitler's monologues (the so-called table talks) and the musings of other Nazi leaders, the fundamental differences between the German occupation policies in Western and Eastern Europe were apparent even during the war. Some areas in Western Europe, like Belgium and northern France, remained under military administration throughout the war. In the rest of France, as well as in Holland and Denmark, the Nazis for a time permitted apolitical or non-Nazi right-wing groups to administer the countries under German supervision rather than install the minuscule proto-Nazi groups that offered themselves as collaborators. In Norway, however, the Nazis appointed as leader of the government a man whose name became a synonym for treason, Vidkun Quisling, the head of the small Norwegian Nazi Party.

Although the German occupation was obviously never popular, initially some collaborationist and caretaker regimes in Western Europe were welcomed as a way of dealing with the reality of defeat after the failure of the previous governments. In the first months of Nazi rule resistance in western and southeastern Europe was relatively unimportant. Collaborators—using the word to include everyone who was willing to deal with the Nazis—far outnumbered resistance fighters.

The picture changed rapidly as the Nazis' true intentions became clear. Although Hitler had declared repeatedly (as late as five days before the outbreak of the war) that Germany had no designs on Alsace-Lorraine, the Reich forced the French to give up the two provinces as part of the armistice agreement. The Germans similarly annexed Luxembourg and a small section of Belgium. Moreover, the Nazis were not content simply to reincorporate these territories; they attempted a "cleansing" of the population by expelling thousands of people whom the Nazi racial experts judged to be "un-German."

Dislike of the Nazi occupation and the collaborationist regimes the Germans had installed in Western Europe increased rapidly when the Nazis inaugurated their three most disastrous policies, the Holocaust, the requisition of forced labor, and the large-scale execution of hostages. By the time the German troops had been driven out of Western Europe, both they and their collaborationist regimes had earned the hatred of the vast majority of the people of Western Europe.

Now resistance—until then largely limited to members of the outlawed Communist parties—increased rapidly as thousands of young men went underground rather than face deportation as forced labor to the Reich. (The Communists of Western Europe remained quiescent or even cooperated with the German occupation authorities during the period of the Nazi-Soviet Pact, but they spearheaded the resistance after the German attack on the Soviet Union.) Indiscriminate taking and execution of innocent hostages fueled the flames of resistance even further. In 1942 the Nazis murdered the entire male population of the Czech village of Lidice in retaliation for hiding the assassins of Reinhard Heydrich, the SS official who was then serving as "Reich Protector" of Bohemia and Moravia. Two years later in an equally infamous incident, the village of Oradour in France was wiped out to avenge the killing of two SS officers by French resistance fighters. As for the collaborationist regimes, they were indelibly tainted with the more or less willing participation in the reign of horrors that the Germans unleashed on all the occupied areas.

The question of collaboration or resistance, which constituted a major dilemma for many in Western Europe, never posed itself in the occupied areas of the East. In Poland and Russia the Nazis had no interest in cooperative governments; the sole goal was naked exploitation and repression. Here the Nazis planned (and began implementing) a form of colonial rule that would have forced Eastern Europe back into the Dark Ages.

The administration of occupied Russia quickly became a confused melee of overlapping jurisdictions. The Nazis established a ministry for the occupied eastern territories headed by the Nazi theoretician Alfred Rosenberg. (The new minister's sole qualifications were his background as a Russian-speaking Baltic German; he was born in Riga and had been a student in Moscow.) Territorially, occupied Russia was to be divided into four administrative zones, called Reich Commissariates: Moscow, Crimea, "Eastland" (the Nazis' collective name for the three Baltic countries of Lithuania, Latvia, and Estonia), and the Ukraine. Since the German armies were unable to conquer either Moscow or southern Russia, only the viceroys for "Eastland" and the Ukraine took up their positions. As administrator for "Eastland" Hitler chose Hinrich Lohse, the *Gauleiter* of Schleswig-Holstein, while Erich Koch, the *Gauleiter* of East Prussia reigned in the Ukraine.

What looked on paper like a rational chain of command for the occupied Russian zones was in fact administrative chaos. Although Lohse and Koch were technically Rosenberg's subordinates, both *Gauleiters* had direct access to Hitler and paid little attention to their nominal superior, who in any case maintained his well-deserved reputation as a weak administrator and incompetent infighter. In addition, neither the Reich commissioners nor the minister had any real authority over the SS, which had exclusive jurisdiction in the area of "security affairs" in Poland and Russia, a mandate that included everything from dealing with guerrilla warfare to the extermination campaigns against the Jews.

Neither Hitler nor Himmler, nor many of the *Wehrmacht* leaders, felt the rules of "civilized conflict" applied to occupied Russia and Poland. Instead, the reality of "racial war" justified systematic attempts physically to eliminate the native Slavic elites. Even before the actual attack on the Soviet Union the High Command issued an infamous "commissar order" to all *Wehrmacht* units. It authorized the troops to execute all captured "Bolshevik leaders and Red Army commissars" rather than send them to prisoner-of-war camps. Throughout the years of Nazi rule the *Einsatzgruppen* (Special Units) of the SS roamed the occupied areas

A biting comment on Nazi occupation policies. Meeting beneath a group of hanged hostages, Hitler asks Himmler, "Why don't they like us, Heinrich?" (Source: *Lachen*, p. 305.)

of Poland and the Soviet Union executing those whom the SS arbitrarily labeled as "Jews and Bolsheviks."

For the long-range future the Nazis had plans for a new *Drang nach Osten*. They intended to force much of the Slavic population of Russia to resettle east of the Ural Mountains. Those who remained in European Russia would be reduced to slavery in the service of the thousands of "Germanic" settlers—Germans, Dutch, Scandinavians—

who would populate what the Nazis regarded as the vast empty spaces in Eastern Europe.

In view of the Nazi practices during occupation, it was not surprising that German rule in Eastern Europe quickly developed into open warfare between ruler and oppressed. Even where German troops and officials had been welcomed as liberators from the Bolsheviks (this was especially true in the Baltic countries), the feelings of sympathy quickly turned to hatred as the reality of Nazi rule became apparent. The Russians were able to establish a large-scale partisan movement, whose effective guerrilla tactics did much to harass the German lines of supply throughout the war.

In the final analysis, then, Nazi rule in Europe demonstrated the same nihilism that characterized the regime's rule in Germany. In the end the Nazis brought nothing but subjugation, oppression, and terror to the peoples under their control. Paradoxically, while the Nazis' ability to occupy much of Europe was dependent on the Reich's military power, the Germans' occupation policies, especially in the East, helped to undermine the military strength of the regime.

THE HOLOCAUST

It is impossible to think of the history of the Third Reich and Nazi rule in Europe without at the same time mentioning the Holocaust. This systematic program of genocide was not an incidental aspect of the Nazis' drive for power but an essential part of their program. During the Holocaust the Germans and their collaborators in the occupied areas selected and murdered millions of people. The victims singled out for extermination included groups as diverse as Polish priests and Hungarian gypsies. But there was never any doubt that the Holocaust was directed primarily against Europe's Jews: Six million, about two-thirds of all Jews living in Europe in 1939, would eventually perish at the hands of the Nazis.

The Holocaust put into gruesome practice the racial Manichaeanism that Hitler had enunciated as early as 1919. Nazi measures against the Jews can be divided into two phases. During the first five years of the Third Reich the Nazis enacted a variety of measures designed to reverse the emancipation of Germany's Jews that had begun at the outset of the nineteenth century. Between 1933 and 1938, Jews were systematically subjected to a variety of discrimi-

natory measures: They were prevented from engaging in their chosen business or professional activities; the Nuremberg Laws of 1935 prohibited intermarriage between Germans and Jews; and the same laws deprived Jews of their German citizenship. The legal status of Jews became that of resident aliens in the Reich.

Paralleling the legal discriminatory acts were periodic outbreaks of violence, ranging from the nationwide boycott of Jewish stores in April 1933 to random harassment of individual Jews. Nevertheless after the April boycott anti-Semitism was, for the most part, more verbal than violent. When it served their purpose, the Nazis even temporarily rescinded some of the anti-Jewish measures. During the summer Olympic Games of 1936, when thousands of foreign tourists flocked to Germany, villages and towns were quietly ordered to take down their "no Jews allowed here" signs. The overall object of the Nazis' campaign against the Jews in this first phase was to force Germany's Jews to leave the country. It was not, however, a benign exodus. Jews who did leave Germany were required to leave most of their property and assets behind.

The beginning of the second part of the Nazis' campaign against the Jews was coupled with the aggressive phase of Nazi territorial expansion. The first public and very violent manifestation came in the fall of 1938. On November 7, Herszel Grynzpan, a young Polish Jew living in Paris, assassinated Ernst vom Rath, a diplomat attached to the German embassy in Paris. Grynzpan acted on his own; the Jewish community in France neither knew of his plans nor approved of the murder.

The Nazi leaders, however, pretended that Grynzpan's act of personal desperation was part of an international Jewish conspiracy. Hitler and his associates decided to stage a vicious nationwide pogrom. The result was the "Reich Night of Crystal" (*Reichskristallnacht*), a name that derived from the number of windows that were broken during the two days of violence. On the evening of November 9, Joseph Goebbels delivered a furious anti-Semitic tirade to Nazi Party and government leaders assembled in Munich for the annual commemoration of the unsuccessful 1923 Beer Hall Putsch. Immediately after the speech orders went out to Stormtroopers and other party units to begin attacks against Jews, their homes, businesses, and synagogues. At the same time the police were specifically instructed not to interfere as the pogrom took its course during the next two days.

By the time the violence ended, almost all of Germany's synagogues and some seven thousand Jewish homes and stores had been destroyed, mostly through fires set by the Nazi thugs. In addition, hundreds of Jews were taken into "protective custody." Many were physically maltreated, and scores died as a result of their injuries. To increase the economic impact of the pogrom on the Jewish community, the government ordered the insurance companies in the Reich to refuse any claims for damages incurred during the *Reichskristallnacht*. Finally, a 1 billion mark fine was levied on the Jewish community as punishment for having "provoked" the pogrom.

In the first years of the Third Reich much of the violence against Jews was committed by the Stormtroopers, but the "Night of Crystal" was their last major operation. Responsibility for the systematic killing during the actual Holocaust was in the hands of another party formation, the SS. In addition to Hitler three men—Heinrich Himmler, the national leader of the SS; Reinhard Heydrich, the man in charge of the Reich Security Main Office (*Reichssicherheitshauptamt*, RSHA); and Heydrich's successor, Ernst Kaltenbrunner—were primarily responsible for carrying out the Holocaust. Heydrich, a former naval officer who was dismissed from the German navy for violating the service's honor code, joined the SS in 1932. Himmler, who was already head of the SS at the time, quickly recognized Heydrich's cold-blooded administrative efficiency and placed the young ex-officer in

charge of the SS's system of political espionage. After the *Machtergreifung* (the Nazis' seizure of power) Heydrich's responsibilities expanded to include the whole range of the Nazis' terror activities. Kaltenbrunner, who headed the Austrian SS until the *Anschluss*, replaced Heydrich when Czech resistance fighters assassinated the chief of the RSHA in 1942.

Like Hitler, Heydrich, Himmler, and Kaltenbrunner were fanatic anti-Semites who believed firmly that World War II was a battle for global control between Jews and "Aryans." The physical extermination of Europe's Jews was an integral part of this *Weltanschauungskrieg*. Himmler took particular pride in the role of the SS in the extermination process. A few months before the end of the war, in August 1944, the head of the SS called the murder of millions of Jewish men, women, and children the group's "most historic deed."

Systematic planning for the Holocaust began in February 1939. Heydrich ordered the "Reich Central Office for Jewish Emigration," headed by another Austrian SS officer, Adolf Eichmann, to cease its concern with encouraging Jewish emigration and begin instead drawing up plans for the concentration and ghettoization of Europe's Jews. The Nazi attack on Poland inaugurated the extermination of that country's Jews. Behind the German lines roving SS execution squads (*Einsatzgruppen*) killed thousands of Jews, mostly intellectuals and individuals of some standing in the community. In addition, the Germans forced those of Poland's Jews who were not immediately killed to live in abominably overcrowded, sealed-off, and easily controlled ghettoes located in the *Generalgouvernement*, the German-occupied section of Poland.

Between July 1941 and January of the following year the machinery for the Holocaust was set in motion. On July 31, 1941, Göring in his capacity as chief of administration for the economic war effort instructed Heydrich to submit a coordinated plan for the "final solution" of the Jewish question, as the extermination of Jews and other undesirables living in all areas of Europe under German control was officially termed. Heydrich in turn assigned the tactical job of planning the deportation and concentration of Europe's Jews to Eichmann. Six months later, the chief of the RSHA presided over the Wannsee Conference, a meeting of representatives of various party and state agencies. The delegates to the conference agreed on the final modalities of the Holocaust: All of Europe's Jews were to be deported to areas of occupied Poland where their actual extermination would take place.

Between the beginning of 1942 and November 1944, when the advancing Red Army forced the closing of the killing centers, the Nazis sent millions of people to their deaths. The Holocaust began with the Jews of western and southeastern Europe. Here the collaborationist regimes had the responsibility for identifying their Jewish citizens and sending them to concentration camps before the Germans transported the victims to Poland. A variety of execution methods were used during the Holocaust ranging from mass shootings to the use of poison gas. Eventually, the Nazis decided on specifically designed extermination camps, the largest of which were Auschwitz and Treblinka. After some trial and error, they also determined that an insecticide, the gas Zyklon B, was the most "efficient" means of killing large numbers of people. In Auschwitz alone some 2 million Jews lost their lives.

Of the 6 million Jews killed during the Holocaust, by far the largest number—some 4 million—came from Russia and Poland. Nevertheless, the Jewish communities of virtually every country under Nazi occupation (with the exception of the small number of Danish Jews and the bulk of Bulgaria's Jewish population) were decimated. Roughly half of the 500,000 Jews living in Germany before Hitler came to power lost their lives in the Holocaust. Most of the others had emigrated, the bulk to the United States and what is now the state of Israel, before the systematic exterminations began. About 20,000 survived the war in hiding in Germany.

The Holocaust left not only millions of dead, but also numerous unanswered questions. The most basic and important of course was, How could it happen? The answer lies in a combination of factors: The long history of German anti-Semitism, the racial fanaticism of the SS, the available twentieth-century technology for mass killings are some of them. Did the German people know of the Holocaust? Officially the exterminations were classified "top secret," and the Nazis took considerable care to hide their gruesome activities. In addition, the killing centers were located in remote areas of the occupied East. Thousands of Germans knew of the Holocaust, nevertheless, and millions more probably guessed the truth. Why then was there no protest by the German people? It was wartime, and people were concerned with their own problems; the terror of the Gestapo did not abate until the end of the war; and, above all, it was easier to ignore the horror than take action against it.

While the "large" questions involve primarily issues of individual morality and group guilt, two factual queries have increasingly concerned historians in recent years. One is Hitler's personal involvement in the planning and implementation of the Holocaust, and the second concerns the question of Jewish resistance. As we saw, the planning apparatus was formally set in motion by an order from Göring to Heydrich. The absence of written documentation with Hitler's signature on it has led some historians to question whether the Führer actually ordered the Holocaust. The "revisionists" claim that the exterminations were, so to speak, implemented by Himmler and Heydrich behind Hitler's back.

The attempt to relieve Hitler of responsibility for the Holocaust is misguided and futile. As Gerald Fleming has convincingly demonstrated, Hitler's personal responsibility for the exterminations is well established even in the absence of written orders. The dictator often issued oral orders to his subordinates, and the men in charge of executing the Holocaust—Himmler, Heydrich, Kaltenbrunner, Eichmann—left no doubt that their orders had come directly from the Nazi leader. In addition, Hitler repeatedly referred to the Holocaust during his wartime "table talks," indicating that he was kept fully informed of the operations.

As for the question of why 6 million Jews permitted a few thousand SS troops to lead them to slaughter, there are two answers. First, the bulk of the victims were East European Jews, a people that traditionally coped with pogroms and other forms of anti-Semitism by bending with the wind. Most did not realize until it was too late that the Nazi Holocaust was not a pogrom, much less a relocation program, but a systematic effort at genocide. And second, there was considerably more Jewish resistance than the Nazis had anticipated or acknowledged. There were periodic revolts in the death camps, the largest taking place at Treblinka in the fall of 1943. But the most noteworthy instance of resistance was the uprising in April and May 1943 of the Warsaw ghetto. For two weeks the Jews of Warsaw, without heavy weapons or outside help, held out against superior German forces. The uprising could not save the Jews—of Warsaw or of Europe—but it lays to rest the myth that there was no Jewish resistance against the Holocaust.

ECONOMY AND SOCIETY

The Nazis set out to establish a "totalitarian" regime in Germany, and to a large extent they succeeded. Lack of political freedom, complete control over all forms of public life, and the ever-present fear of Gestapo terror constituted a yoke that bore heavily upon those who valued their political and intellectual liberty. This is the picture of Nazi Germany that many historians have

accepted, but recent scholarship has made it increasingly clear that there was another side to the Third Reich. For many Germans life under the Nazis was not all that different from what it had been before Hitler came to power. For the average, apolitical German—and this category included the vast bulk of the population—it was accommodation and conformity rather than a complete change of life style that was expected. Gestapo and party agents listened intently for signs of criticism in public places, but most Germans learned quickly to restrict their honest language to family members and trusted friends. Displaying a swastika flag on the many Nazi holidays and contributing money to the numerous party-sponsored collections was usually all that was necessary to show that one was a "good German." In a very real sense, the society continued to function because most Germans including many in the traditional elites—scientists, intellectuals, technocrats—did their jobs as they had done before. Even some opponents of the regime were permitted to live relatively unmolested for long periods of time once they agreed to refrain from political activity.

In particular the economy was subjected to relatively few restrictions. Despite currency controls, until the war much of the free market economy prevailed. Businessmen were free to make (and lose) money. During the peacetime phase of the Third Reich there was no commodity rationing in effect, and while workers lost many of their rights, notably that of collective bargaining, most could still change jobs without undue difficulties. At the same time a price-and-wage freeze introduced in 1938 helped control inflation. From 1936 to 1944 inflation was less than 2.9 percent per year.

As the regime moved into the aggressive phase of its plan of conquest there were some important changes in the management of the German economy. Hjalmar Schacht's dismissal as Reich economics minister in 1936 signaled a new emphasis on preparing Germany for war. Military officers occupied high-level positions in the organization of the Four Year Plan in ever larger numbers, pushing aside the civilian bureaucrats from the Reich ministry of economics.

Nevertheless, even with the outbreak of hostilities, by no means all of Germany's economic resources were allocated to the war effort. That decision was motivated primarily by political considerations. Hitler was convinced shortages at home had led to declining morale and eventually revolution during World War I. For this reason he was determined to prevent another "turnip winter" in Germany. In consequence, while there were certainly shortages on the home front during World War II, they were never as severe as they had been in the earlier conflict. Especially during the first two years of the war the regime was careful to cultivate the goodwill of industrial laborers with extra rations.

In strategic terms the decision to plan only for a short conflict completely misjudged the nature of World War II. As far as industrial production was concerned, the entire rearmament program of the 1930s was geared toward the strategy of "lightning operations." Employing the elements of surprise and, initially, superior munitions and logistical supplies, the Nazi planners anticipated that World War II would be a blitzkrieg affair rather than the drawn-out and ultimately disastrous struggle that World War I had been. But as we have seen, Hitler's scenario failed completely; by the beginning of 1942 (after the entry of the United States into the conflict) it was clear to competent observers that the Reich faced another war of attrition.

While the Nazis for a time dealt effectively with the problems that had plagued Germany's home front in World War I, they failed to give adequate attention to a new element in warfare, aerial bombardment of civilian populations. The Nazis had used massive bombings with devastating effect on Rotterdam and later on English cities in the Battle of Britain, but by 1942, partly because Hitler underestimated the Allies' capabilities

and refused to accelerate Germany's fighter plane program, the Allies achieved air superiority and turned the new strategy against the Germans. At first daytime and by mid-1943 nighttime bombings of German cities became daily occurrences. World War II, until the Allied invasion, was brought home to the Germans primarily in the form of increasingly destructive aerial bombardments. By the time the war ended, major urban centers like Cologne and Hamburg consisted of little more than rubble and hundreds of thousands of lives had been lost in the air raids.

After the German defeat in the Battle of Stalingrad (January–February 1943), it was clear even to insiders in the Nazi regime that the German economy and home front were not prepared for a drawn-out conflict. The Nazis introduced major organizational and lifestyle changes. In February 1942 the Four Year Plan and Hermann Göring lost their dominant position in the management of the economy. A new Ministry for War Production, headed by Hitler's architect Albert Speer, was established and given vast powers to coordinate all war-related economic production. Speer and his associates succeeded in increasing the production of war material to a remarkable extent. Aided by the fact that the Allies (like the Germans earlier) had for much of the war concentrated their attacks on civilian housing and had limited their bombings of specific industrial targets to one-time raids, Germany's industry achieved its highest output in September 1944, only a few months before the end of the war. The Reich's economic collapse began only in the late fall of 1944, when the Allies directed their attacks primarily against industrial production facilities. In the spring of 1945 the lack of fuel and Allied bombings of the German railroad network brought the Reich's war machinery to a final halt.

Speer accomplished his feat of increasing industrial production partly by returning much authority for economic decision making to the private sector, thereby eliminating much of the political interference by party and military officials. Equally important, however, was the regime's decision to use female workers and to use forced labor from the occupied areas of Eastern and Western Europe. At the beginning of World War II at least some foreign workers had been attracted by the relatively high German wages but, as the tide of war turned, Sauckel, the Reich commissioner for foreign labor, increasingly relied on terror to fill his and Speer's quotas for laborers. Concentration camp inmates, too, were forced in ever larger numbers to work in war-related industries. By the end of the war, 7 million laborers had been forced to work in the Reich.

The concept of "total war" on the home front was formally launched in February 1943. Goebbels addressed an audience hand-selected by the propaganda ministry in the Berlin *Sportpalast*, the scene of many of the minister's propaganda triumphs in the political campaigns before 1933. His speech culminated in the question, "Do you want total war?"—to which the audience screamed a predictable, "Yes!" The German populace saw this performance as part of the newsreels shown in movie theaters, complete with close-ups of recognizable media personalities.

The campaign of "total war" meant that guns now took definite precedence over butter. The civilian population had to get used to growing shortages of virtually all commodities. In addition, "total war" brought a massive buildup of the regime's terror presence. Anonymous denunciations were encouraged even more than before, and the Nazis introduced the death penalty for a whole series of minor infractions including the crime of being a "defeatist." By the end of the war, it is clear that whatever sympathies the regime had enjoyed among the Germans had largely dissipated. Life had become a daily struggle in the face of constant bombings, shortages, and fear of the regime's terror.

Still, the Nazi propagandists did not aban-don their efforts to replace lack of resources with fanaticism. In the fall of 1944 they ordered the creation of the "People's Storm" (*Volkssturm*), a paramilitary organization composed of all male Germans between the ages of sixteen and sixty. In the minds of the writers of propaganda brochures these units would become the *levée en masse* that would finally destroy the Allied armies as they crossed the German borders. The *Volkssturm* existed mostly in the minds of its creators. Few units were actually set up, and those that were organized tended to melt away before making contact with the enemy. They did not flee alone; most NSDAP leaders, including the Gauleiters, took flight, often when the Allied armies were still hundreds of miles away.

In macabre scenes worthy of a greater cause, Hitler spent the last weeks of the Third Reich in the bunker underneath the Reich chancellery in Berlin drafting phantom plans for the future. Hitler was particularly concerned with the architectural reconstruction of the three cities which he saw as the epitome of his regime: Berlin, the capital of the Greater German Reich; Munich, the home of the Nazi Party; and Linz in Upper Austria, the city in which Hitler had spent much of his youth and which he regarded as his home town. On the dictator's orders, Speer and other architects throughout the years of the Third Reich fashioned drawings and constructed scale models of mammoth pseudoclassical structures that were intended to demonstrate the grandeur of Hitler's vision. Until the end, the Führer took a regular and active interest in all this. He even insisted on seeing how the buildings would look as ruins; he wanted the remains to compare favorably with the Pyramids.

THE END OF THE THIRD REICH

Since the 1938 decision to "obliterate" Czechoslovakia, each stage of the Nazi march of conquest across Europe had begun with a "Führer directive," a document drafted by Hitler outlining the basic aim and strategy of the next campaign. The last of these directives came in November 1943. The contents involuntarily revealed how the tide had turned against Hitler and the Nazis. While the earlier directives demonstrated the acumen of Hitler's intuitive approach to balance-of-power politics and military strategy, the November 1943 document was based upon little more than illusion and wishful thinking. Hitler was fanatically determined to accomplish his goal of *Lebensraum* in the East. To this end he ordered preparations for new land offensives against Russia, and a new air offensive against Great Britain through the use of the rocketpropelled "V-bombs."

Hitler's directive was based upon a completely unrealistic assessment of Allied and German resources. The *Wehrmacht* could not stop the Allied invasion of France in June 1944, the V-weapons were more of an irritant than a threat to England, and on the Eastern front the Nazis were unable to prevent the Russian drive westward, much less launch new offensive operations of their own.

After the failure of the Battle of the Bulge Hitler's essential nihilism broke through entirely. In one of his last orders to his troops, the so-called Nero order of March 1945, he insisted that as the Allies entered Germany they should find only scorched earth, much as the Germans had left behind when they were forced to withdraw from the Soviet Union.

Actually, by the spring of 1945, Hitler's orders were obeyed instantly only in his suite of rooms in the bunker under the Reich chancellery. Not only did the Allies advance far too swiftly for the Germans to effect an orderly retreat, but the forces in German society that had been willing to support the Nazis for so long had finally begun to disengage themselves from the regime's headlong dash toward self-destruction. The leaders of Germany's industry, especially, had as early as the summer of 1943 started to make plans for Germany's

postwar and post-Nazi future. As the outcome of the war became increasingly obvious, Hitler's senseless orders for destruction were quietly sabotaged by Speer and other government ministers. Just before the end even some of the Nazi *Gauleiters* refused to carry out Hitler's scorched earth orders. As a result, when the war ended, Germany's industrial and economic potential was far less completely destroyed than either Hitler or the Allies believed. It was revealed after the war, for example, that only about 10 to 15 percent of the productive capacity of the Ruhr had been eliminated by either wartime bombing or by the destruction of the retreating German forces.

With Germany's unconditional surrender in May 1945 the Reich as a political entity ceased to exist. All levels of government and all administrative decisions were the responsibility of the Allied occupation forces. Hitler's designated successor, Admiral Dönitz, had retreated to Murwik, the naval base outside of Flensburg, where he maintained a shadowy existence as "Reich president" for about two weeks. But the Allies never recognized this "government," and at the end of May the "cabinet" was unceremoniously arrested by British forces.

Hitler and the Nazis left Germany a heavy and wholly negative legacy. Millions of Germans had died either at the front or during the air raids; millions more had become refugees when the Russian armies reached the eastern borders and pressed westward. The country's infrastructure was in shambles, Germany's cities were smoking ruins. More important (for the physical damage turned out to be less devastating than it appeared), the Holocaust attached a permanent weight of moral guilt to the German name. Finally, as Andreas Hillgruber has pointed out, Adolf Hitler's most lasting legacy to Germany was the destruction of the national unity for which Germans had strived since the beginning of the nineteenth century. Hitler had undone Bismarck's historic achievement. The "Germanys" were quite literally once again a geographic expression rather than a nation.

CHAPTER 9

"CONDOMINIUM OF THE ALLIED POWERS," 1945–1949

Hans Kelsen, one of the many academics whom the Nazis forced to leave Germany, coined the title phrase of this chapter when he taught at the University of California at Berkeley during World War II. He sought to describe Germany's unique constitutional position after the collapse of the Third Reich. The country was like a condominium. Each of the four occupying powers had separate apartments—their individual zones of occupation—but as owners they were also jointly responsible for maintaining the building as a whole. The original builders, however, had lost their proprietary rights.

As we shall see, in its pure form the Allied condominium phase of German history did not last long. Both the Allies and the Germans soon recognized that they were dealing with postwar realities far different from what they had expected. Only four years after the Reich's unconditional sur-

render, the former landlords began to take charge of their apartments again, although the Allies retained many rights in the building. Especially surprising was the rapid economic recovery and political transformation of what was to become West Germany. A country that, according to one American observer, looked like "the face of the moon" in 1945, four years later was on the threshold of an "economic miracle" and beginning to build a successful parliamentary democracy.

THE GERMAN RESISTANCE: STRENGTHS AND DELUSIONS

The German resistance movement tends to receive minimal attention. To some extent this is justified. The German resistance was clearly not effective in overthrowing the Nazis. Relative to the size of the population there were fewer resistance fighters in Germany than in other European countries, although both the Nazis and the Allies, for different reasons, tended to belittle what resistance there was in the Reich. In the thirty months between the beginning of 1943 and the end of the war, more than 11,000 Germans were executed for anti-Nazi activities, 5,000 in 1944 alone. The German resistance, of course, had some peculiar handicaps. While the resistance movements in other countries worked to liberate their nations from foreign domination, the German resistance had to work against its own national government. In addition, after 1939 German resistance fighters had to be active while the country was at war, so that their activities risked arousing another stab-in-the-back legend. (It will be recalled that during the Weimar years the extreme Right consistently—and falsely—portrayed the revolution of 1918 as a "stab-in-the-back" that led to Germany's defeat.)

Still, members of the resistance came from all segments of society and all political camps, although the bulk of the resisters came from the bottom and top layers of the social strata. The earliest—and also least effective—resistance came from the political Left. Nazi terror turned first against Communists and Social Democrats. The Communists especially suffered at the hands of the SA, the SS, and the Gestapo. The party's national leader, Ernst Thälmann, was arrested almost immediately after the Nazis came to power and later killed in a concentration camp. In fact, after the Nazis in 1943 broke up the largest Communist underground resistance organization, the "Red Orchestra" (*Rote Kapelle*), only a handful of German Communists survived the war in Germany either underground or in jails or concentration camps. The leaders of the German Communist movement after World War II for the most part came from the ranks of those who had spent the Nazi years in exile in the Soviet Union although, iron-ically, many of the exiles there became victims of the Stalinist purges.

In cooperation with the Russians, the German Communists in exile were also instrumental in organizing the *Nationalkomitee Freies Deutschland* (National Committee for a Free Germany, NKFD) among German prisoners of war captured on the Eastern front. The group's wartime success in persuading German soldiers on the Russian front to desert was minimal, but the NKFD was useful in organizing nationalist support for the Communist regime in the Soviet zone of occupation after 1945.

Many Social Democrat leaders also fled Germany. Unlike the Communists, most of them chose to spend their years of exile in Western countries, especially Great Britain, the Scandinavian countries, and the United States. Proportionately far more Social Democrats than Communists, however, stayed in Germany. A large number of SPD leaders survived the Third Reich in Germany. A few attempted to appease the Nazis, but most either ceased all political activities or spent the years of the Third Reich in Nazi prisons and concentration camps.

The bourgeois groups of the political Center and Right played a contradictory role in the German resistance story. In contrast to the Communists and Social Democrats, most middle-class Germans collaborated with the Nazis both before and after 1933. On the other hand, while resistance on the Right was much less widespread, some members of the old elite who were opposed to Nazism continued to occupy key positions in the government, the military, and the economy even after the *Gleichschaltung*. Those that did join the resistance were therefore in a much better position to make their anti-Nazi activities count.

Given their limited objectives, opposition by the organized religions was particularly effective. Hitler and the Nazis had immense respect for the moral influence of the churches; despite their hatred of Christianity the Nazis were anxious to avoid a new

Kulturkampf. But the churches also faced a dilemma. The Catholic Church had signed a formal treaty with the Nazis, the Concordat, which church leaders were determined to uphold. The Nazis violated the treaty with impunity, but it was not until Pope Pius XI's 1937 encyclical *Mit brennender Sorge* ("With Burning Concern") that Catholic opposition to the Nazi immoral activities received widespread support from the clergy. One spectacular instance of effective opposition was the protest by the Bishop of Münster, Count Galen, against the government's program of killing the mentally insane. As we saw, he succeeded in having these murders stopped.

The Protestant churches were institutionally and ideologically even less well prepared to resist governmental actions. German Protestantism had long been associated with Prussian authoritarianism and German nationalism. Here resistance originally arose not against Nazism as such, but as a reaction to the regime's attempt to interfere with the churches' theological teachings and administrative autonomy. Many church leaders' first experience with resistance came in 1933–1934; the Nazis attempted to destroy the independence of the individual state churches and impose a Nazi fellow-traveler as "Reich bishop" upon a centralized, national Protestant church, but massive opposition from the ranks of the Protestant clergy forced the Nazis to abandon their efforts. A number of Protestant pastors also rejected the "Aryan paragraph," which prohibited pastors of Jewish descent from serving as ministers in the churches. Led by a Berlin minister, Martin Niemöller, several thousand pastors and laity seceded from the established Protestantism and formed the "Confessional Church." In addition, a number of courageous Protestant theologians, like Dietrich Bonhoeffer, joined actively in the plot to overthrow the Nazis. The decision cost Bonhoeffer his life; he was executed at the beginning of 1945. Niemöller spent long years in a concentration camp.

High government officials and especially the military had the best opportunities to thwart Nazi aims and policies. But members of these groups also had a long tradition of opposition to democracy, and the leaders of the military enthusiastically applauded Hitler's rearmament program and his early foreign policy successes. Still, some of the most effective and spectacular resistance activities came from a small number of Germany's old elite. In addition to using their offices to save some victims of Nazi terror, government officials and military officers planned and implemented the plot against the regime that culminated in the July 1944 attempt to assassinate the dictator.

There were numerous loosely knit conspiratorial groups, but one, the "Kreisauer Circle," deserves particular mention. (The name derives from the estate of the Moltke family at Kreisau in Silesia that served as an out-of-the-way meeting place for the group's members.) The Kreisauer Circle consisted of a number of relatively young men, from left-wing Social Democrats like Julius Leber to dyed-in-the-wool conservatives, but the members of the Circle were not representative of their social and political groups. On the contrary, they tended to be intellectuals who became resisters precisely because they were outsiders. Virtually all leading members of the Kreisauer Circle were executed in the wake of the July 1944 plot against Hitler.

There was little opposition to Hitler among the military while the dictator seemed to be redrawing the map of Europe without risking war. After the Blomberg-Fritsch crisis and especially after the Munich Crisis, however, a few leading officers, like General Ludwig Beck, realized that Hitler's path would inevitably lead Germany into another world war. The German defeat at the Battle of Moscow convinced additional members of the officer corps that only the elimination of Hitler and the Nazi regime would save Germany from complete destruction.

The history of the German military and governmental resistance is punctuated with failed plans to overthrow the Nazi dictatorship. The conspirators—many of whom worked in the *Abwehr*, the *Wehrmacht*'s espionage and counterintelligence unit—were ready to move in late September 1938 when Neville Chamberlain's offer to take the lead in ending the Munich crisis thwarted their intentions. Later as various plans for a bloodless coup proved unworkable, the conspirators increasingly recognized that only Hitler's death would paralyze the Nazi power structure. Instrumental in persuading the conspirators of the necessity of killing Hitler was a young colonel, Claus Count von Stauffenberg, one of those involved in the Kreisauer Circle. Several attempts to assassinate the dictator failed, but on July 20, 1944, Stauffenberg was able to place a bomb under the table in the conference room at Hitler's East Prussian headquarters. The conspirators intended that immediately after Hitler's death, units of the reserve army would arrest leading party and SS functionaries, while a cabinet composed of members of the resistance, headed by General Ludwig Beck as temporary chief of state, would keep law and order and negotiate an end to the war. The plot failed completely. Hitler was only slightly wounded by the explosion, and the conspiracy quickly collapsed.

The Nazi regime took terrible revenge on its enemies. Stauffenberg, Beck, and their closest associates were killed immediately, and rigged trials before a "people's court" handed out a steady stream of death sentences in the weeks following the attempt on Hitler's life. Thousands of less prominent members of the resistance were simply seized by the Gestapo. A so-called kith and kin directive ordered that members of the extended families of the major conspirators—from second cousins to infant grandchildren—be put into concentration camps.

The failure of the July 1944 plot ended any real chance of overthrowing the Nazis from within, but in retrospect this may not have been altogether bad. Quite aside from the danger of a new "stab-in-the-back" leg-

end, for all their undoubted hatred of the Nazi dictatorship many leading members of the German resistance were singularly naive about the country's past and future. It was not that they had no plans. On the contrary, if anything there was a surfeit of plans and constitutional schemes. The difficulty was, rather, that many leaders of the resistance assumed that the "excessively" democratic Weimar constitution had permitted the Nazis to come to power. Although some, including Stauffenberg, recognized that Germany's future needed to be built on a democratic basis involving all segments of the population, several prominent leaders of the German resistance were convinced the country took the wrong path in 1918. For them the answer to Hitler was not a return to the parliamentary democracy of Weimar, but to "authoritarian democracy," a form of government which many in the military conspiracy and even some in the Kreisauer Circle naively associated with the enlightened despotism of the Hohenzollern kings and what Oswald Spengler had called "Prussian socialism."

The naivité about constitutional reconstruction was matched by illusion about the Reich's international standing after the defeat of the Nazis. Most planners in the resistance assumed that Germany would remain a major European power, and some even insisted that Austria should remain part of Germany. They did recognize that the countries of Eastern Europe (not to mention Western Europe) would become independent again, but many among the military opposition, who were scions of old noble families of Eastern Germany, remained convinced that the Reich should continue its "civilizing mission" in Poland and Russia in some form or other.

Many prominent members of the German resistance, then, refused to recognize that the Allies' demand for Germany's unconditional surrender marked their refusal to respect Germany's status as a Great Power in the future. Moreover the Allies, as we shall see, tended to identify—wrongly—

Prussianism and Nazism, so that they were unlikely to support the resistance's effort to return Germany to the days of Frederick the Great. Instead, the country's postwar future, insofar as it involved the Germans at all, would lie in the hands of the Weimar democratic leaders, most of whom had spent the years of the Third Reich in concentration camps.

ALLIED VISIONS AND PLANS, 1941–1945

While the planners in the German resistance continued to hope that after the fall of Nazism they would take charge of the Reich's future, the Allies shattered such naive beliefs with their announcement in February 1943 that they would not negotiate with any Reich government but would accept only a declaration of "unconditional surrender." The policy of unconditional surrender deprived the Germans of any recognized role in the country's immediate future, but it left unanswered a host of questions about the Allies' own ideas and approaches. Generally speaking, the Russians were most anxious to reach concrete decisions before the hostilities had ended. They offered suggestions for defining Germany's postwar boundaries as early as July 1941. The Soviets also favored the dismemberment of Germany so as to preclude the existence of a strong power in Central Europe. In principle, American and British planners, too, accepted dividing the Reich into three or more independent states as the most effective means of preventing a German colossus in Central Europe. At the same time, the U.S. president, Franklin Delano Roosevelt, was particularly reluctant to draw up concrete plans for the future of a country that, as he put it, "we have not yet conquered."

As the tide of the war turned, however, the Americans and the British, too, began to be concerned over the lack of concrete plans for Germany's postwar future. The Big Three agreed on the eradication of Nazism and were resolved that the Reich should not again be in a position to wage war upon her neighbors. On the other hand, the Western powers had to recognize that the total defeat of Germany would create a power vacuum in Central Europe that would bring with it far-reaching consequences. Almost by definition, a powerless and dismembered Germany would mean Russian hegemonial control in Central Europe. Indeed, some Western analysts expected that at the time of Germany's surrender the Red Army would have reached the Rhine in its westward push. The prospect of Russian domination in Germany was not particularly disturbing to those in the West who expected the wartime alliance of the Big Three to continue as a peacetime partnership, but others were less sanguine. As the Russians made their heavy-handed presence felt in Eastern Europe, Winston Churchill and the British especially grew increasingly reluctant to tolerate Soviet hegemony in Central Europe.

The Americans remained divided. Henry Morgenthau, Jr., the U.S. secretary of the treasury and the president's personal friend, argued that a complete power vacuum in Central Europe was the only answer to the "German problem." In contrast, Morgenthau's colleague in the cabinet, Secretary of War Henry Stimson (the War Department was not renamed the Department of Defense until 1947) and officials in the State Department insisted a united, economically strong Germany was needed if Europe was as a whole to recover and stand on its own feet.

By the end of 1944, when the Allied armies stood poised to carry the war into Germany proper, the Big Three had not yet made a determination of Germany's territorial and societal future. In response to a British suggestion, the Big Three had agreed in September 1943 that after the Third Reich had capitulated each of the Big Three would administer a zone of occupation. Largely to dilute Russian influence in

Germany, the British proposed that France should also be assigned a zone of occupation. Neither the Americans nor the Russians were enthusiastic, but it was eventually agreed to carve out a French territory from the previously established British and American zones. The zonal boundaries would follow established provincial and *Land* borders. In theory the basis of the zonal division was Germany's territorial status as of 1937. This meant that Austria and Czechoslovakia would, of course, regain their independence, but East Prussia, for example, remained technically part of Germany. Actually, the Allied leaders agreed in their summit conference at Teheran in the fall of 1943 to far-reaching territorial revision in Eastern Europe. In accord with this de facto agreement the Soviets at the beginning of 1945 had annexed the northern half of East Prussia, including the city of Königsberg. (It was renamed Kaliningrad.) The Russians also held on to eastern Poland (the parts of the country which the Soviet Union had claimed in the Nazi-Soviet Pact), while agreeing that Poland was to be compensated for her losses by German territories lying east of the Oder and Neisse rivers and the southern parts of East Prussia.

At least on the surface, there seemed to be considerable consensus among the Allies about the need to restructure German society. The Big Three and France agreed that after the war Germany needed to be subjected to the "four D's": demilitarization, decartellization, de-Nazification, and democratization. To be sure, here, too, agreement was more theoretical than substantive. The "four D's" were essentially negative goals, not a positive blueprint for Germany's political, economic, and social future. Democratization, for example, meant something entirely different to the Russians than it did to the Americans.

On the Western side the most comprehensive and, given its basic premise, also the most logical scheme for a fundamental reconstruction of German society was the one proposed in the fall of 1944 by Henry Morgenthau. The Morgenthau Plan, which its author entitled "Program to Prevent Germany from Starting a World War III," postulated that Hitler's rise to power was the logical consequence of German national character that had earlier produced Prussian authoritarianism and militarism. The U.S. secretary of the treasury argued that a powerful, industrialized Germany would inevitably attempt to wage war on her neighbors and the world. Only the country's territorial dismemberment and political and economic impotence would assure future peace. Concretely, the secretary proposed Germany's permanent occupation by Russia and other European countries (but not the United States) and the destruction of Germany's industrial power. The Reich's natural resources, such as the Ruhr coal mines, should be placed under permanent international control. Germany was to become "a country primarily agricultural and pastoral in character." To compensate for Germany's traditional role in the international economic order, Morgenthau proposed that the United States should underwrite the recovery of the Soviet Union and Great Britain with large loans.

The Morgenthau Plan was a radical solution to the "German problem"—assuming one agreed that there was a "German" as opposed to a "Nazi" problem. For a brief time the secretary of the treasury convinced Roosevelt and even Churchill of the effectiveness of his approach. The American president agreed instinctively with many of Morgenthau's assumptions, and he welcomed that under the Morgenthau Plan American troops would be able to come home soon after the war ended, leaving European affairs in the hands of the Europeans. The British prime minister was lured by the expectation that the total deindustrialization of Germany would eliminate Great Britain's traditional economic rival, and by the prospect of a large American loan for Great Britain's postwar reconstruction that Morgenthau had promised.

Churchill and Roosevelt gave tentative

approval to Morgenthau's proposals when they met in Quebec in October 1944 but, almost immediately, vigorous opposition to the plan arose among American and British officials. The U.S. secretary of state, Cordell Hull (whom Roosevelt had not taken along to Quebec), pointed out that the Morgenthau Plan would give the Russians continental hegemony, while Germany's "pastoralization" would permanently disrupt the international economic system. Churchill's advisors used similar arguments against such "planned chaos." A short time later, both Roosevelt and Churchill withdrew their approval of Morgenthau's proposals. As a result, when the first American and British troops crossed into Germany, neither occupying power had a comprehensive plan for dealing with its new responsibilities.

Compared with American and British ideas, Russian and French plans on how to treat Germany at the end of World War II were considerably more concrete. In addition to territorial changes, the Soviet Union was determined to extract from Germany reparations—in the form of goods and labor, not money—in order to rebuild the areas of Russia devastated by the Nazis' unprovoked attack. The Russians put the value of the reparations to which they were entitled at $10 billion. In addition, the Soviets insisted there was a causal link between capitalism and Nazism. Only structural reforms that deprived the big capitalists and landowners of their economic and political power would guarantee that Nazism would not return to Germany.

Like the Russians, the French gave top priority to making the Germans pay for the damage they had inflicted during the war. To this end the French were determined to use the resources of their zone for France's benefit. In addition, the French, too, demanded far-reaching territorial changes in Germany; both the Saar and the entire Rhineland were to be separated from Germany and remain under at least indirect French control. As for the problem of Nazism, French thinking linked this to German nationalism. France argued against the reestablishment of any central German governmental authority. In the words of the leader of the Free French, General Charles de Gaulle, there should be "no Reich [but] a return to the Germanys."

In February 1945 the leaders of the wartime alliance, Roosevelt, Churchill, and Stalin (de Gaulle was not invited) met at Yalta on the Black Sea for their last summit meeting before the unconditional surrender of the Third Reich. The Big Three refined their zonal arrangements by agreeing on the division of Berlin into four sectors of occupation, with the Russians guaranteeing Western access to the city. (The city of Berlin, of course, was located in the middle of the Soviet zone of occupation.) Specifically, three air corridors from the Western zones to the former Reich capital were established. Stalin raised the reparations issue and, while there was no formal agreement, the Western Allies did not object to the Russian figure of $20 billion, of which the Soviets were to receive $10 billion. German reparations would be in the form of capital goods, current agricultural and industrial production, and forced labor. Roosevelt and Churchill also took note of the de facto territorial changes in Eastern Germany, although final disposition of this issue was left for a later peace treaty. In reality what were to become the post–World War II boundaries had already been established. The Communist-dominated Polish government had seized the former German territories east of the Oder-Neisse rivers, and Poland had already begun to expel the ethnic Germans still remaining in the area.

As for Germany itself, the Big Three reiterated their determination to enforce the "four D's." They clarified the nature of military government in the occupied country. Issues involving Germany as a whole would be decided by the Allied Control Council meeting in Berlin and composed of representatives from the zonal commands, but the military governors retained virtually complete autonomy. Not only were they free to make whatever decisions they deemed necessary in their own zones, but each occupying power had the ability to paralyze the Allied Control Council since all decisions of this body had to be unanimous.

THE IMMEDIATE LEGACY OF THE THIRD REICH: THE REALITY OF "ZERO HOUR"

On June 5, 1945, the Allied military commanders took charge of a country that for all practical purposes had ceased to function as a viable society. Five years of bombing had left the German cities, in the words of one American observer, "endless rows of empty, burnt-out structural shells which reached into the sky like twisted fingers of a leper's hand." The housing shortage was especially acute in the larger cities: Fifty percent of the housing in Hamburg and 80 percent of that in Cologne had been destroyed. An equally serious problem was the breakdown of the transportation system. Concentrated tactical air attacks on the German rail system in the last months of the war destroyed some 10,000 locomotives and 112,000 freight cars and finally broke the back of Nazi resistance, but the bombings also left the country without a distribution system for its immediate civilian needs.

Ironically, the devastated country had to feed and house a far larger population than before the war. At the end of the war 7 million refugees had found their way to the three Western zones; despite wartime losses, the population of what was to become West Germany was 20 percent larger in 1945 than it had been in 1938. At the same time Germany had lost territory that before the war produced 25 percent of the country's food supply.

It was not a good omen for their future cooperation that the Allies began their joint responsibility for Germany with haggling over territory. There were no excessive delays in removing American forces from the parts of East Germany that they had occupied in the last days of the war, and the Russians withdrew from the Western sectors of Berlin without much difficulty; but a serious dispute arose between the Americans and the French over the final delineation of their respective zones. The French insisted on controlling Karlsruhe and Stuttgart, but the Americans remained adamant. It was not until July that these various territorial disputes had been settled and the military commanders took formal charge of their zones.

At the same time, the leaders of the Big Three (once again France was not invited) assembled at Potsdam, outside of Berlin, for another summit conference. There were several reasons for another exchange of views, now that Germany had finally capitulated. The Yalta Conference had left a number of issues unresolved. There had also been a change of leaders for two of the Big Three: Vice-President Harry S. Truman succeeded Franklin D. Roosevelt when the American president died on April 12, 1945, and in Great Britain when Winston Churchill's cabinet suffered a defeat at the polls while the Potsdam Conference was in session. The new Labour government in Great Britain was headed by Clement Atlee.

Some agenda items at the Potsdam Conference aroused little controversy. The Allies gave retroactive sanction to the de facto boundary changes in Eastern Europe and the expulsion of the ethnic Germans from this area. (The conference's admonition that the population transfers be effected "under humane conditions" had no practical effect.) The Big Three also reiterated their support for "four D's," and emphasized the need for reeducation of the Germans, which they defined as follows: "German education shall be so controlled as completely to eliminate Nazi and militarist doctrines and to make possible the successful development of democratic ideas."

It was a different story, however, when the Big Three turned to the reparations issue. The Russians proposed that they should receive half of the $20 billion in

Germany Since 1945

reparations that should be imposed on the Germans. The remainder of the sum would be divided among the Nazis' other European victims.

In addition, the Soviets demanded that reparation be the "first charge" on any German industrial or agricultural production. The Western Allies were concerned above all that the country should not become a financial burden on their own economies. As a result, they argued that the "first charge" on German production had to be relieving the Allies of the necessity of feeding and housing the German population. In the end the Big Three, while agreeing that at least for the time being Germany was to be treated as an "economic unit," allowed the zonal commanders to set their own reparations policies: Each occupying power was free to remove from its own zone whatever goods and services it identified as not necessary for Germany's future peacetime needs, crediting the value against the eventual reparations bill to be presented as part of a peace treaty. The Western Allies also acknowledged that the Soviets were entitled to receive 10 percent of the manufactured goods or industrial facilities that the Western commanders determined were not needed for the peacetime needs of their zones. Finally, in return for agricultural goods sent from the Russian zone to West Germany, the Soviets could expect another 15 percent of the current production from the Western zones.

The lack of agreed-upon occupation policies turned out to be of primary benefit to the Russians. Unlike the British and the Americans, the Soviets went into Germany with a specific plan of action. Even before hostilities had ceased the Russians established the Soviet Military Administration for Germany (usually known by its German acronym SMAD), headed by Marshal Georgij K. Zhukov, the Red Army's commander in Germany. Immediately after the German surrender, SMAD authorized what were essentially functional, cabinet-level German ministries for the Soviet zone. Each was headed by a non-Nazi civil servant, with a German exile-Communist as the number-two man (and real power behind the scenes). Two months after the end of the war, SMAD permitted the reorganization of German political life on a zone-wide basis. Four non-Nazi parties were allowed to set up political organizations: the Communists, the Social Democrats, the Liberals, and the Christian Democrats.

In the area of economic policies, the Russians immediately began a vigorous program of extracting reparations. Working from lists prepared in Moscow, Russian reparation teams roamed over the Soviet zone dismantling (and shipping to the Soviet Union) everything from scores of factories (such as the Zeiss optical works and Opel

car assembly plants) to thousands of bathtubs. The Russians also transferred large numbers of livestock and agricultural implements to the Soviet Union to replenish their depleted stocks. The immediate benefits to the Soviet Union were questionable. The program was conducted hastily and vastly overestimated the capacity of the Soviet economy to absorb the dismantled German material. Much valuable equipment rusted in open railroad cars that remained standing for months on sidings either in Germany or in the Soviet Union.

In striking contrast to the purposeful Soviet moves, the early occupation policies of the British and Americans appeared hesitant and even contradictory. The British did establish two central administrative offices, one for economic affairs and one for agriculture; both were headed by leading German anti-Nazis. They also instituted wide-ranging administrative reforms in their zone. In the place of the defunct Prussian administration (Prussia was formally abolished by the Allied Control Council in 1947), the British established three new administrative units—the present West German *Länder* of Schleswig-Holstein, Lower Saxony, and North Rhine-Westphalia. It was not until the beginning of 1946, however, that zone-wide German legislative institutions and political parties were again permitted.

American occupation policies were initially perhaps the most confusing. Part of the problem was the absence of a clear line of command. The Office of Military Government for the U.S. Zone (OMGUS) was headed by General Joseph T. McNarney, who had been Eisenhower's deputy. McNarney, however, had little interest in the job, and the key man in the OMGUS administration became General Lucius Clay, McNarney's deputy until 1947 and his successor after that date. Clay was a professional officer whose military career had been spent in the Army Corps of Engineers; he was sent to Germany because Roosevelt and later Truman felt his construction expertise would be useful in getting the U.S. zone functioning again.

The American administrators in Germany were also hampered by unclear policy directives from Washington. As American troops began their occupation duties, they were issued what were essentially contradictory sets of guidelines. One was the *Handbook for Military Government in Germany*, which showed the influence of planners at the State Department. It assigned first priority—aside from the "four D's"—to economic recovery so as to make the U.S. zone self-sufficient as rapidly as possible. But the *Handbook* was partially superseded by additional guidelines, JCS-1067, drafted under the auspices of the Joint Chiefs of Staff. JCS-1067 followed the basic line of the Morgenthau Plan and emphasized the negative goals of U.S. occupation policies. JCS-1067, for example, contained an absolute ban on "fraternization" between Americans and Germans. (It was not, for example, until November 1945 that fraternization with "very small children" was permitted.) There was no mention of economic recovery or political activity. Instead, JCS-1067 stressed the need for structural changes that would deprive the wealthy bourgeoisie and large landowners of economic and political power. In this sense JCS-1067 paralleled some of the Russian directives. Both sets of American guidelines called for the decentralization of German economic and political life.

For the first few months of the occupation, then, American commanders could essentially choose between a "soft" and a "hard" line. Some, like General George Patton, who served briefly as military governor in Bavaria, preferred the "soft" approach. He simply returned the pre-Nazi elite in Bavaria to power. Others attempted to apply the spirit and letter of JCS-1067.

In most areas of occupation policy the French were the odd-man-out among the Allies. They were as enthusiastic about political decentralization as the Americans but agreed with the Russians that extracting reparations from their zone had first priority. Since the French had not been invited to participate in the Potsdam Conference, they refused to accept the agreements reached there as binding upon them. The French rejected particularly treating the country as an economic unit. Instead, the French military commander, General Pierre Koenig, like the leader of the Free French, Charles de Gaulle, was determined that France should retain full control over "her" German territories. For this reason the French jealously guarded the veto power of each zonal commander on the Allied Control Council.

Early French occupation policies were a curious mixture of economic exploitation, the "four D's," and missionary zeal to bring the blessings of French civilization to the Germans. The zone was hermetically sealed off from the rest of Germany, but even within the French territories German officials had to use the military government as intermediary when corresponding with each other. French economic policies reminded many Germans of Poincaré's goals in the 1920s. The Saar became economically part of France, and in the first months after the war as much as 80 percent of the industrial production in the French zone was exported to France.

The French took the self-imposed task of reeducating the Germans very seriously. Censorship in the French zone was stricter than in the U.S. and British, but the French also sent dozens of teachers into their zone to rebuild the German school system, while touring French theatrical companies brought glimpses of French culture into Germany's bombed-out cities. One of the lasting and salutary legacies of the French occupation was the founding in 1947 of the University of Mainz. (The French looked upon it as a reopening, since the institution had operated briefly during the Napoleonic occupation of the Rhineland.)

The positive influence the French attached to French culture and civilization was also apparent in their early personnel appointments. The military government, for example, appointed Professor Carlo Schmid as the first postwar prime minister of Baden. To be sure, Schmid was a staunch anti-Nazi and Social Democrat, but more important was his marriage to a French woman, his ability to speak flawless French, and his reputation as a friend of France—which ironically he had earned when he served as a civilian employee with the German army of occupation in France after 1940.

It soon became apparent, then, that the Big Four had quite different ideas about their role as occupying powers in Germany. George Kennan, an especially perceptive American diplomat who had served in the U.S. embassy in Moscow during the war, noted as early as the summer of 1945 that it was "madness" to think that Germany could be governed in unison with the Soviet Union. In the following spring Winston Churchill had come to the same conclusion; in a March 1946 address delivered in Fulton, Missouri, Churchill spoke of the "Iron Curtain" with which the Soviet Union had divided Europe from the Baltic to the Mediterranean. As we saw, the French were determined to go their own way without much regard for what the other Allies were doing in Germany. Many questions about the former Reich's future remained unanswered, but one fact was clear; only a few months after their united efforts had defeated the Third Reich, the members of the Grand Alliance were unable to agree on a unified policy for the country that was now their joint responsibility.

REPARATIONS AND ECONOMIC RECOVERY

It was perhaps inevitable that discussions about reparations both during and after World War II had a sense of *déjà vu* about them. Once again, the European countries that had been devastated and exploited wanted the Germans to make good the

damage the Nazis had caused. The devastation was heavy in both East and West Europe, but there was little doubt that the Soviet Union had suffered most from the Nazis. Russia's wartime casualties were estimated at 20 million people, and the Nazis' scorched-earth policies had left much of the western Soviet Union an economic wasteland.

Most U.S. and British planners soon recognized, however, that the Russian approach to reparations would in effect force the Western Allies to subsidize the Russian claims. Since the American zone and particularly the British zone did not produce sufficient agricultural goods to feed their populations, agricultural goods would have to be imported, and exports of German-manufactured goods were the only available means by which the Germans could pay for such imports. Likewise, another Allied goal—the destruction of much of Germany's industrial base because it could be used in waging war—was counterproductive, since there would clearly not be enough manufacturing facilities to pay for both reparations and food imports.

The Potsdam agreements, such as they were, were made in the face of a major unknown: the real state of the German economy. Its state of health turned out to be a paradox. In the short run the German economy was worse off than had been anticipated, but in the long run the devastation turned out to be less severe than originally thought.

At the moment, of course, it was the immediate future that counted. And it looked bleak. Germany in late spring, 1945, bore little resemblance to a functioning economy. There was no currency. With the collapse of the government, the reichsmark had lost its value and credibility. American cigarettes quickly became the preferred medium of exchange, severely distorting the incentive to earn money. A typical example of the warped economy was the case of a coal miner who in 1946 earned a weekly wage of 60 marks. He also owned a chicken, which laid five eggs during the week. He ate one egg and traded the other four for twenty American cigarettes, which he sold for 160 marks on the black market. As a result, the chicken produced almost three times as much income as a week's work in the coal mines.

In addition, the transportation system had broken down almost completely. Millions of refugees and expellees aggravated the already catastrophic housing shortage. A number of reputable economists predicted that it would take a minimum of thirty years to rebuild Germany's cities. The final military operation of the war had prevented spring planting in many areas of the country, and the German diet was close to subsistence levels and often below in the cities. In the summer of 1945 the total amount of foodstuffs obtainable on ration coupons for each inhabitant of Hamburg (which was part of the British zone) amounted to a little more than a thousand calories per day.

The state of the economy presented the Germans and the occupying forces with massive problems, but the collapse also provided opportunities for structural modifications. Both the Allies and many in the German resistance were convinced the traditionally close link between business and the political elite in Germany had not been a healthy development. Non-Nazi Germans of all political persuasions wanted to implement rather massive structural changes in the economy. Concretely, many of the resistance groups envisioned the breakup of the cartels and their replacement by some form of nationalization, particularly in the areas of heavy industry and natural resources. As we saw, the Allies, too, had plans for the "decartellization" of German industry.

In the face of the devastated condition of the German economy, the Americans, the British, and many Germans in the Western zones rapidly abandoned any structural reform plans. Only the Russians pursued their structural goals with unrelenting vigor.

The Soviets were convinced that Nazism was essentially a political manifestation of "monopoly capitalism," and they set out systematically to destroy the economic power of "major capitalists" in the Russian zone. SMAD took over immediate control of all banks and their assets which, it will be recalled, in Germany traditionally included large stock portfolios. Simultaneously, individual bank accounts with a balance of more than 3,000 marks were confiscated and all private and public debts declared invalid. Much as the Bolsheviks had done in Russia in 1917, Soviet rule in East Germany started with a clean financial slate.

Next SMAD turned to the industrial sector of the economy. All manufacturing facilities were classified into one of three categories. List A consisted of "economically important" enterprises, in Marxist terms the "commanding heights" of the economy. These were immediately placed under SMAD's direct control and eventually became the backbone of collectivized industry in East Germany. List B consisted of "small and unimportant enterprises," and most of these were left in private hands. List C was composed of "ownerless" properties, which meant firms whose "Nazi" owners were deprived of their businesses for political reasons. In practice, the third category included all large-scale enterprises since the Russians saw no distinction between leading capitalists and leading Nazis. Enterprises in category C were either dismantled outright or became "Soviet corporations" (SAGs), which meant that they produced solely for export to the Soviet Union. By 1946 there were 213 SAGs in the Russian zone. Beginning in the fall of 1945, the Soviets also inaugurated a systematic land reform program. Starting with the province of Saxony, SMAD ordered the breakup and expropriation of all farms larger than three hundred acres. These properties were divided into smaller holdings and turned over to small farmers or landless peasants.

The economic effects of the Russian policies were mixed. The takeover of the banks and the cancellation of debts eliminated the inflation and doubts about currency revaluation that for a time hampered economic recovery in the West. More important, however, were the political consequences and severe economic dislocations that followed the structural reforms in the Russian zone. Almost overnight the traditional German economic elite was deprived of its power and property. By the beginning of 1946 the state controlled the "commanding heights" of the economy; free enterprise was restricted to relatively unimportant sectors. In June 1946 a Communist-sponsored plebiscite in Saxony—the Russians tended to hold plebiscites first in this province because it had the best-organized Communist Party—retroactively approved the expropriation without compensation of properties owned by "war criminals and active Nazis."

After being characterized by initial confusion, American economic policies were marked by growing pragmatism. Like the Russians, U.S. economic planners were initially determined to eliminate Germany's war-making potential. American officials drew up a list of 1,210 plants that were to be dismantled. But there was a problem. Some American planners, notably those sympathizing with the spirit of the Morgenthau Plan, wanted to reduce German industrial production permanently to between 70 and 75 percent of the 1936 level. Eliminating all 1,210 plants on the list would have been a major step toward reaching this goal. At the same time, it was a consistent American goal to make the U.S. zone as economically self-sufficient as possible, and economic self-sufficiency could only be achieved by exporting industrial goods in exchange for needed imports of food and raw materials. But that raised questions about the future of the dismantling program. Should a ball-bearing factory be dismantled because its products had been used in tanks, or permitted to start up again because its products could now be used in farm tractors?

In May 1946 a so-called Level of Industry Plan attempted to resolve the dichotomy. This document endorsed the goal of maintaining Germany's future industrial production at very low levels. Almost immediately the Level of Industry Plan was severely criticized both by the nascent German economic administration (see p. 251) and by American planners. The critics pointed out that in 1946 exports from the American zone were valued at $28 million, but imports, mostly in the form of food, fertilizer, and seeds, had a value of $300 million. In effect, the privilege of occupying a part of Germany cost the American taxpayers $272 million. The experience of the winter of 1946–1947 aggravated the problem. It was one of the coldest in decades. There was widespread suffering and malnutrition, and there would have been more except for massive aid from the Western Allies, especially the Americans. There was clearly no alternative to enlarging German industrial production if the Western zones were to avoid becoming a permanent ward of the United States and Great Britain.

The emerging Cold War and the decline in agricultural productivity in Eastern Germany made the goal of treating the four zones as an "economic unit" increasingly unrealistic. As a result, the Level of Industry Plan was essentially shelved and the dismantling program quietly abandoned. Of the 1,210 plants originally tagged for dismantling, only 24 had been disassembled by May 1946. At the same time, reacting to what OMGUS felt was French intransigence, Russian obstinacy, and British inefficiency in running their zones, the United States halted reparation transfers from the American zone. In 1947 a new review removed 523 from the theoretical list, and virtually none were actually dismantled after that date. In 1949 the entire dismantling program was formally abandoned.

Long before then American economic policy had undergone a fundamental change. The new direction was signaled in October 1946 in an address by the United States secretary of state, James F. Byrnes.

Speaking in Stuttgart, the secretary announced that in the face of Soviet intransigence the United States would not only retain her military presence in Germany but would also help the Germans in the Western zones get back on their economic and political feet. As in the case of the Russians, the American economic policies had political implications as well. With the decision to endorse German economic recovery, the United States also moved to put up barriers against major structural changes in the German economy of the American zone. Economic recovery essentially meant the preservation of a free market economy. When the voters of Hessen by a 70 percent majority ratified a state constitution providing for state control of major sectors in the economy, the American military governor ordered the offending part of the constitution suspended indefinitely. Similarly, the prime ministers of the four *Länder* in the American zone endorsed the principle of union representatives serving as ex officio members on the boards of directors of major enterprises (the technical term is "codetermination" or *Mitbestimmung*), but General Clay prohibited its implementation. Russian and American economic planning, then, had the effect of creating very dissimilar economic structures in East and West Germany.

British economic policies for the most part followed the American lead. Initially, the British had also drawn up an ambitious dismantling program, concentrating on the heavy industry of the Ruhr (part of the British zone), but economic realities soon forced changes. The British zone produced even fewer agricultural goods than the American, and it consequently became a heavy burden for the home government; between 1945 and 1948 the British had to pour £200 million sterling into their zone to pay for needed imports of foodstuffs and raw materials. Since England was experiencing severe economic problems at home, the British had little choice except to join the Americans in the decision to help German recovery. U.S. aid was crucial not only for economic recovery in England, but also for maintaining the British zone in Germany.

Until the summer of 1948, the French stubbornly pursued their own single-minded course of action. Despite a lack of economic cohesion in the territories they controlled, the French were determined to treat their zone as an integrated unit not linked to the rest of Germany. Within their zone the French made few structural changes. Instead, they concentrated on production for the French market.

By the summer of 1946 the economic unity envisioned for Germany at Potsdam was illusionary. In the face of Russian and French refusals to cooperate in treating Germany as a single economic unit, the Americans and the British felt compelled to coordinate economic policies for their two zones. The result was the establishment of the "Bizone" on January 1, 1947. The Bizone was not a political entity, but its establishment confirmed that a free market economy would prevail at least in the industrial heartland of West Germany. The new structure had administrative offices that closely resembled ministries, headed by a "director-in-chief." The latter office was occupied by Hermann Pünder, who had been chief of staff in the Reich chancellery when Heinrich Brüning was chancellor.

The decision to establish the Bizone was a response to the economic difficulties encountered in the British and American zones in 1945 and 1946, but the decision was politically confirmed, as it were, by the results of the Moscow Four Power Conference on Germany in March 1947. This foreign ministers' meeting revealed the chasm that divided the Allies' economic policies in Germany. The Russians accused the West of violating the Yalta Agreement on reparations. The West countered by disputing that such an agreement had been reached and accused the Russians of failing to supply the promised shipments of agricultural goods to the Western zones.

The Moscow Conference convinced

American policymakers in particular that the Soviet Union's economic policies were part of a larger plan to subject all of Germany, and indeed all of Europe, to Russian control. In response to this perceived threat to the West, the Americans announced two new policies. First they put forth the Truman Doctrine, which allocated U.S. economic and military aid to Greece and Turkey in order to help these countries prevail against the Communist danger. Second, and even more important, they introduced the Marshall Plan, a bold scheme launched in June 1947 under which the Americans offered to underwrite the economic recovery of Europe, including that of Germany. Under the European Recovery Program, as the Marshall Plan was formally known, the United States between 1948 and 1952 gave some $4 billion in economic aid to the countries of Western Europe. The Marshall Plan was instrumental in the recovery of Western Europe and West Germany, but American aid did not come without visible and invisible strings. The United States clearly wanted to support free enterprise in Europe. Moreover, given the strength of the American economy the Marshall Plan would establish the U.S. dollar as the dominant currency. Above all, as far as the Germans were concerned, the Marshall Plan meant that at least the economies of the three Western zones would become an integral part of the Western economic system. (Inclusion of the French zone was part of the price France had to pay for getting American aid.) There would be no unchecked "German colossus."

In a sense, the American aid program became another step toward the final division of Germany into separate Eastern and Western entities but, despite this potential drawback, sentiment for accepting the terms of the Marshall Plan both in West Germany and in Western Europe was overwhelmingly positive.

Long before the announcement of the Marshall Plan it was recognized that the Achilles' heel of any recovery plan in the Western zones was the absence of a stable currency. The controlled and centrally planned economy in the Russian zone could function with a currency that had neither metallic- nor hard-currency backing, but a resurgent free market economy would not flourish without a new and trustworthy currency. The Americans had reached this conclusion at the end of 1947, but it took another six months before a new currency, the *deutsche mark*, made its appearance in all three Western zones in June 1948. The new currency was valued at one deutsche mark to ten of the old reichsmark and was exchangeable on international currency markets at 4.2 deutsche marks to one U.S. dollar.

The Marshall Plan along with the currency reform set the stage for the West German "economic miracle," although in 1948 the prospects for an economic boom seemed rather more modest. The German economy was still an economy of shortages; everything from food to furniture was rationed, empty shelves had been the rule for years. The picture changed literally overnight, in large part as a result of an audacious decision by the man in charge of the economic administration for the Bizone, Ludwig Erhard. Without consulting the occupation authorities, Erhard combined the announcement of the currency reform on June 20, 1948, with the virtual elimination of all economic controls and forms of rationing. He realized that the certainty of American support for West German recovery and persistent rumors that the currency reform was imminent had already awakened the dormant productive capacities of the German economy. As a result, in June 1948 consumers with "real" money in their hands were met by stores stocked full of goods that had not been seen since before the war. West Germany became, as one British observer put it, "an economy in search of a state."

A poster extolling the benefits of the Marshall Plan. Against the backdrop calling attention to a construction site, the caption reads, ''We're making progress thanks to the Marshall Plan.'' (Source: *Anschläge*, no. 138.)

EXORCISING THE EVIL: DE-NAZIFICATION AND REEDUCATION

There was never any doubt among the Allies that de-Nazification—and its corollary reeducation—was the most important of the "four D's." Demilitarization, decartellization, and democratization remained illusionary as long as Nazism had not been eradicated from German society. Both the Allies and most anti-Nazi Germans also agreed that there were two aspects to de-Nazification: the punishment of individual Nazis for the crimes they had committed during the Third Reich, and the exorcising of fascist and protofascist attitudes from the German population and the country's institutions. The latter process had to involve a critical self-examination among the Germans themselves, including an in-depth look at the country's authoritarian heritage as a seedbed for Nazism. Signs of honest self-criticism came early. For example, the leaders of the Protestant churches publicly acknowledged in the summer of 1945 that their rejection of democratic traditions had indirectly helped Nazism to come to power.

The Allies decided as early as September 1943 that the punishment of the Nazi regime's major leaders would be their joint responsibility, while the de-Nazification of German society would be handled by the zonal commanders in accordance with instructions from their home governments. In addition, Nazi criminals who had committed crimes outside of Germany would be extradited and tried in the country in which they had committed their criminal acts.

There was little difficulty with the first part of this scenario. Beginning in November 1945, 24 civilian and military officials of the Nazi regime, including Göring, Ribbentrop, Hess, Speer, Keitel, and Streicher, were tried by the International Military Tribunal (IMT) in Nuremberg. (Hitler, Himmler, and Goebbels had committed suicide before they could be apprehended; Robert Ley, the head of the DAF, committed suicide in Nuremberg before the trial began. Martin Bormann, the NSDAP's general secretary after 1941, was tried and convicted in absentia. It was not yet known that he had died while trying to escape from Berlin in May 1945.) The accused were indicted for crimes against peace, war crimes, unleashing aggressive war, and crimes against humanity. The Allied powers provided both judges and prosecuting staffs, while the defendants were represented by German non-Nazi lawyers.

The trial lasted until the fall of 1946. At its conclusion, 11 of the remaining 22 accused (including Göring, Ribbentrop, Keitel, and Streicher) were sentenced to death and executed (Göring committed suicide before he was scheduled to be hanged); 8 received long prison sentences; and 3 were acquitted. The last group included Franz von Papen and Hjalmar Schacht.

Both the premise and the verdicts of the IMT provoked heated debates. The tribunal was accused of practicing "victors' justice." Then there was the claim that the court's moral authority was irrevocably compromised by the presence of Soviet judges on the bench. There were also some problems with the terms of the indictment, especially if the IMT was to serve a didactic function as part of the larger de-Nazification effort. The tribunal limited itself to trying the Nazi leaders for "international" crimes, so that political treason in Germany itself was left unpunished. As a result, men like Papen and Schacht, who, as we saw, had been instrumental in destroying democracy in the Weimar Republic, were acquitted.

There is some truth in all this, but it is difficult to fault the tribunal for either its procedures or its verdicts. Particularly the British chief justice attempted to be scrupulously fair to the defendants. Most important, however, those accused had really condemned themselves; the trial at Nuremberg for the first time revealed the full horror of the Nazis' reign of terror in Germany and Europe.

The IMT ended the Allies' joint de-

Nazification efforts. The remainder of the task was now in the hands of the zonal commanders. The Russian de-Nazification campaign was swift, radical, but, at least from a Western point of view, also unfair and simplistic. As we saw, the Soviets insisted on linking capitalism and Nazism. As a result, they concentrated their de-Nazification efforts on individuals who had occupied positions of economic or political influence in pre-1945 Germany. Under the Russian de-Nazification criteria, some 45,000 leading industrialists, landowners, military officers, civil servants, and Nazi Party officials were identified as active Nazis and punished. About a third of those accused were sent to labor camps in the Soviet Union; all lost their property and positions. The Soviet de-Nazification effort had the virtue of speed—the entire process was concluded by the beginning of 1948—and some obvious criminals were punished, but the Russians were also quick to brand as "fascists" anyone who opposed the Russian-sponsored transformation of the Soviet zone into a "people's democracy." Moreover, the Russian de-Nazification procedures could be easily exploited by opportunists. Former members of the Nazi Party or its affiliates who came from a working-class or lower-middle-class background could escape punishment with a simple declaration that false class consciousness had led them to join the Nazis. Cooperation with the Soviet authorities was also seen as evidence that the individual had been cleansed of Nazism.

The Western powers, on the other hand, erred on the side of excessive deliberation and overestimating the number of "Nazis" in Germany. Moreover, their procedures, too, were not free of opportunistic and quixotic considerations. For example, the French often overlooked the "brown past" of individuals who were willing to cooperate with the French occupation authorities, but at the same time they regarded all Germans over the age of twelve as a "lost generation" whose immersion in Nazism was so complete that it would take years of reeducation to eradicate it. For this reason, the French concentrated their de-Nazification campaign on the teaching profession. Half of all teachers in the French zone were dismissed by the military government.

The Americans launched the most conscientious, but in some ways also the most inconsistent, de-Nazification campaign. American military courts tried groups of defendants representing major SS officials, leading businesspersons, government officials, and members of the diplomatic establishment who had been involved in the Holocaust or the use of slave labor. However, the elimination of "average" Nazis from German society proved much more controversial. Stung by charges that the American army was coddling Nazis, in September 1945 OMGUS took a hard line. Law No. 8 ordered the internment of thousands of former Nazis. In addition, anyone who had been a member of the Nazi Party or one of its affiliates before 1937 was prohibited from continuing in his or her regular line of work. The new policy created a crisis in professional and governmental services. The Nazi *Gleichschaltung* had forced not only civil servants, but professionals like doctors and dentists, to join a Nazi Party affiliate in order to continue practicing. Under Law No. 8 these professionals were sent out to clear rubble from the streets.

The policy of "guilt by office holding and membership" was obviously unsatisfactory; at the end of 1945 the Americans had jailed 100,000 "dangerous Nazis." (For comparison, the numbers for the other zones were: 64,000 in the British, 19,000 in the French, and 67,000 in the Russian.) In an effort to speed up the de-Nazification process, and also return to the principle of individual guilt or innocence, the Americans in February 1946 inaugurated the "questionnaire phase" of the de-Nazification campaign. In a massive effort worthy of a greater cause, 12 million questionnaires were issued to all adults in the American zone asking for information on everything from noble titles of the individuals' grandparents to membership in political organizations. The answers on the questionnaire were used to classify the respondents into one of five categories: major offender, offender, lesser offender, fellow-traveler, and untainted. Only the last verdict meant that there would be no penalties. OMGUS estimated that after the questionnaires were processed, some 3 million persons would have to be tried before "hearing committees" staffed by anti-Nazi Germans.

The American effort was a well-meant attempt to eliminate Nazism from the American zone "root and branch," but in practice the campaign soon ran into massive difficulties. To begin with, processing millions of questionnaires was too formidable a task for the available personnel. The Americans complained that German de-Nazification tribunals were too lenient, while the Germans contended that the U.S. authorities failed to understand the nature of living and working under Nazi totalitarianism. More important, changes in the international climate distorted the original intent of the de-Nazification effort. While the hearing committees concentrated on processing the "lesser offender" and "untainted" categories, leaving the more serious classifications for more detailed examination at a later date, policy changes in 1947 and 1948 reduced the priority value of the de-Nazification effort. Many presumed major offenders and war profiteers did not have to go through the gauntlet of the de-Nazification procedures because they were suddenly needed as senior executives in the revitalized economy. There were bitter comments that while it was important in 1945 to have been a member of the VVN (the German letters standing for the Association of Victims of Nazism), it was far better in 1947 to be a WWN, a *wirtschaftlich wichtiger Nazi*—that is, an economically important Nazi.

In principle, British de-Nazification practices followed the American lead, although in practice the British military authorities generally showed more astuteness in rec-

ognizing that local officials and educators in particular had often held only nominal membership in one or more of the various Nazi organizations. Consequently, this category of officials was de-Nazified and restored to office rather early in the British zone. Still, there were some glaring errors. One of the more famous was the dismissal by the British of Konrad Adenauer as mayor of Cologne. Adenauer, whom the Nazis had forced out of office in 1933, had been restored to his mayoral post in April 1945 when the Americans captured the city. When the British moved in, the local commander regarded Adenauer as too conservative to be reliably anti-Nazi, and Adenauer was again dismissed. However, the brigadier's high-handed action was quickly reversed by his superiors.

De-Nazification was designed to eliminate an evil from German society; the measures grouped under the label "reeducation" were meant to put something positive in its place. Reforms in education and the media would ensure that in the future the German people would be saturated with "antifascist" values. The effort to rebuild the German education system faced formidable obstacles. Physical facilities were woefully inadequate. In major urban centers, like Cologne, 92 percent of all elementary schools had been destroyed by bombing. In rural areas damage was less severe, but here the influx of refugees had led to staggering increases in the school population. There were also problems with textbooks and teaching personnel. Virtually all teachers had been members of the Nazi Party or one of its affiliates, and many had held local offices in the party. Textbooks were largely unusable, since the Nazis had inculcated their racist thinking into all subjects.

There was no shortage of reform ideas, either, from the Germans or the Allies, but the two sides started from rather different premises. In fact differences of opinion over educational reforms became one of the first tests of wills between the occupying powers and the Germans' resurgent sense of autonomy. The Germans tended to regard the Nazi influence over the educational system as a perversion of the traditional ideals of German education, which they saw as either Catholic Christian humanism or the progressive ideas of secular reformism that were in vogue during the 1920s. As might be expected, educational conservatives dominated in the Catholic areas of the south, while in the north the reformers turned to ideas associated with the pre-1933 Prussian ministry of education. In fact, the last pre-Nazi Prussian minister of education, Adolf Grimme, became the first minister of education of the new *Land* Lower Saxony.

With the exception of the British, the Allies looked upon their own educational systems as models for the reforms that were needed in Germany. The British, to their credit, almost immediately cooperated with the German reformers. The question of textbooks was handled effectively by joint British-German committees, and the person responsible for education policy in the British military government, Sir Robert Birley, assured the German authorities as early as 1946 that the British would make no decisions that had not been approved by the responsible German officials. (The French eventually limited their reform efforts to bringing a significant number of German teachers to France for intensive retraining courses.)

The Americans were originally determined to take a much more direct hand in implementing structural reforms of the German school system. In 1946 a commission of U.S. experts, headed by the then president of the U.S. Council of Education, George F. Zook, recommended several fundamental changes. In essence, the Zook Report concluded that Germany would be better off with an American-type system of education. Specifically, the American experts wanted to abolish the *Gymnasium*, and replace it with twelve years of comprehensive schooling for all children. The Americans also advocated eliminating the segregation by religious affiliation in the German

public elementary schools. As for textbooks, the Americans wrote their own. Unfortunately, the results, to quote Sir Robert Birley, were "hardly readable."

The Zook Report ran into formidable and passionate opposition. Criticism centered on the proposals for a comprehensive twelve-year school system and the "secularization" of elementary schools. German anti-Nazi scholars pointed out that the American comprehensive school system was alien to such European democracies as France and Great Britain. Fierce opposition to abolishing the religion-segregated elementary school came from the Catholic church and the minister of education in Bavaria, Alois Hundhammer.

The American frontal assault on the traditional German education system was a failure. The major recommendations of the Zook Report were not implemented; the U.S. zone kept the German three-tiered school system, with textbooks and curricula reflecting the ideas of Christian Catholic humanism. The elementary schools were not secularized, although in practice the postwar population changes destroyed the religious homogeneity of southern Germany and transformed the public schools into multiconfessional institutions.

As had been true of their de-Nazification efforts, the Russians did not allow obstacles to stand in the way of what they felt were needed educational reforms. In 1946 SMAD ordered the abolition of the three-tiered school system. In its place a comprehensive twelve-year school program was established throughout the Soviet zone. The Russians also decreed changes in teacher education and textbooks, putting reliable German Communists in charge of implementing these reforms.

Like de-Nazification, reeducation succeeded in spite of itself. Except for the Soviet zone where cooperation between SMAD and the Communist-dominated German educational administration was intense and purposeful, the Allies had little success in transforming German education to bring it in line with their own national systems. The Allied pressures rather became catalysts that allowed the reform ideas of the Weimar era to be resurrected and finally implemented.

Immediately after the war, control of the mass media was important for both practical and political reasons. With a shortage of newsprint and transportation facilities, the radio became the military governments' primary means of communicating with the German population. As life returned to a semblance of normalcy, newspapers served as major vehicles for reeducation in the widest sense, that is, dissemination of the truth about the Nazis and the propagation of antifascist values.

Initially the Allied military governments took direct charge of the mass media. Radio stations were run by Allied personnel and each of the four occupying powers founded German-language newspapers. Of particular interest was the paper in the American zone, *Neue Zeitung* ("New Newspaper"). The paper was well-edited by Hans Habe, a Hungarian refugee who had lived for some years in Austria prior to the *Anschluss.*

Within a year after the war some German control of publishing and broadcasting was restored, although understandably each occupying power continued to supervise closely the rebirth of German mass media. Not surprisingly, here too, each of the Allies was convinced its own national system was best. As far as the radio was concerned the British proposed a German equivalent of the BBC, in other words, a politically autonomous public radio organization. The Americans preferred a decentralized, privately owned, and commercially financed radio system, while the French insisted upon a centralized but politically balanced system. The Russians set up a state-controlled monopoly. The Germans for their part wanted to go back to the Weimar model, a centralized but apolitical system financed by compulsory fees from listeners.

What emerged in the end was an amalgam of German and Allied ideas—at least in the West. The Germans rejected commercialization of their air waves, but accepted decentralization of the radio network. As for control of program content, the Germans adopted the BBC model of an autonomous board of governors, but, like the French, they insisted upon including political parties among the "balance of interests" that controlled the public radio stations.

In permitting the German press to start up again the four Allies also went their own ways. The Russians appeared to take the most liberal and permissive approach. Almost simultaneously with the publication of SMAD's own newspaper, the *Neue Rundschau* ("New Observer"), the Russians allowed "antifascist progressive forces" to publish newspapers. All of the newly legalized political parties took up the Russian offer, although for most the experience was frustrating. SMAD's allocation of newsprint favored the Communist press, and views critical of the Soviets or their Communist allies were routinely censored.

The Western Allies were less insistent upon political conformity. The French permitted the newly legalized political parties to maintain their own press organs, while the Americans and British preferred a nonpartisan press with editorials clearly separated from news stories. All of the Western Allies gave permission to publish newspapers on a case-by-case basis. "Licenses" were granted only to potential publishers who could demonstrate their democratic credentials to the military authorities.

The postwar German newspaper scene showed the least continuity with the Weimar years. Some of the editors and reporters returned to their desks, but the leading West German dailies after 1945—like *Die Welt* ("The World"), the *Frankfurter Zeitung* ("The Frankfurt Newspaper"), and the *Süddeutsche Zeitung* ("The South German Newspaper")—were all newly founded, often by journalistic novices like West Germany's long-time press czar, Axel Springer. This was an area in which the Allies' direct influence was most noticeable. Sixteen publishers who eventually obtained a newspaper license in the American zone had earlier worked on the editorial staff of the *Neue Zeitung*. The format of German papers changed too. After 1945 the press in the West was far less politicized and, in particular, the earlier habit of permeating news stories with a particular political slant disappeared. Owing largely to French influence, the *Feuilleton* ("art and culture") sections of the German provincial press became a more important part of the papers.

De-Nazification and reeducation were important factors in the reconstruction of the German society, but the actual results were hardly what the Allies originally set out to accomplish. In the West the Allied practices had the effect of resurrecting and strengthening the liberal and democratic traditions of the Weimar Republic, rather than creating a society modeled more decisively on Western examples. In the Soviet zone Russian policies laid the foundation for the transformation of this part of the country into a "people's democracy."

REVIVAL OF ADMINISTRATIVE, POLITICAL, AND CULTURAL LIFE

Immediately after the war much of Germany may have reminded observers of the surface of the moon, but the country was hardly devoid of life. As we saw, although an estimated 6 million Germans (including almost a quarter million Jews) died from war-related causes, by 1950, as a result of the influx of millions of refugees, Germany's population was larger than it had been before the war. The population transfers created not only major immediate problems, but had important long-range effects on the structure of German society as well. Population density and along with it industrialization and urbanization increased markedly, especially in Western Germany. The population became more heterogeneous. In 1950 one out of every four inhabitants in the Western zones had been born east of the Elbe. The refugees also transformed the religious mix of Germany. While the Soviet zone remained predominantly Protestant, in the West Catholics for the first time since the Reformation were no longer a minority. The population of the Western zones became almost evenly divided between Catholics and Protestants.

At the time of "zero hour"—the collapse of Nazi rule and the beginning of Allied occupation—both the Allied authorities and the Germans were primarily concerned with restoring a rudimentary level of service to the society, but the feeling was also widespread that there was in 1945 an unparalleled opportunity to "start over again" and create a new and better society. Unfortunately, it was almost impossible to coordinate the short-term goals with remaking the society. Although the Americans originally favored the root-and-branch approach of the Morgenthau Plan, they soon turned to old officials to run the new Germany. The military government appointed Fritz Schäffer, a prewar leader of the Catholic and conservative Bavarian People's Party, as the first postwar prime minister of Bavaria. Schäffer was certainly no Nazi sympathizer, but neither was he a fresh start. After a few months Schäffer was replaced with another new "old face"—Wilhelm Hoegner, before 1933 the chairman of the Bavarian Social Democrats.

Much earlier than their transatlantic cousins the British gave the Germans considerable autonomy in rebuilding their society. They recognized that there were many Germans who were as anxious to create a new democratic society as their conquerors. As a senior British official pointed out, it was hardly necessary to give elementary lessons in democracy to a man who had just spent the last ten years in a Nazi concentration camp for his democratic beliefs.

The French and the Russians undertook the most radical restructuring of their zones. The French program was simple: to maximize French control over all affairs of their zone and to delay the rebirth of autonomous

German societal institutions as long as possible. The Russians had no hesitation in putting Germans in charge of their zone, but they had to be "their" Germans. Unlike the Western Allies, who appointed German administrative officials on a case-by-case basis, the Soviets brought administrative and indoctrination teams with them. In April 1945, two groups of German Communists who had spent the war years in Russia were brought back to Germany by the Soviet Air Force. The more important of the two was headed by Walter Ulbricht, the prewar Communist leader of Berlin.

The Russians repeatedly assured the inhabitants of their zone that the Soviets did not intend to create a Soviet Germany. In a sense this was true. Their aim was not to achieve Stalinist socialism but a "people's democracy." Soviet theorists at the time defined such an entity as a society in which "the commanding heights of decision making" would be under the direct or indirect control of the Communists and SMAD, although ostensibly the society retained its pluralistic character and mixed economy. In remarks to a Communist Party meeting in 1946 Ulbricht expressed these goals in blunt terms: "Everything has to look democratic, but everything has to be controlled by us." The Russians succeeded in achieving their aim; by the summer of 1946 the Russian zone was a people's democracy in all but name.

Most postwar German leaders—with the obvious exception of the Communists—did not advocate a root-and-branch approach but, to stay with the metaphor for a moment, advocated pruning the tree to remove dead branches and alien growth. For the most part their ideal of a "new" society was an improved and corrected version of the Weimar Republic. In concrete terms, this meant that the basic principles on which the Weimar Republic had been founded would be accentuated in any post–World War II German society. Subject to varying degrees of control by the occupation powers, the Germans began rebuilding their political organizations in the summer and fall of 1945. Except for the discredited extreme right, whose renewed activity all of the Allies prohibited, the ideological spectrum was essentially the same as during the Weimar years.

Aided by a clear vision of Germany's postwar future and prodded by the Soviets, the Communists took the initiative in rearranging the organizational contours of the traditional German party scene. In the spring of 1946 they proposed the union (or better *re*union) of the Social Democrats and Communists under the leadership of the KPD. It is, of course, one thing to propose a political alliance and quite another to obtain the partner's agreement. To be sure, many Social Democratic leaders were anxious for working-class cooperation, but most rejected a merger of the two parties; the great majority of Social Democrats regarded the KPD as an undemocratic front organization for SMAD. In April 1946, massive pressure from SMAD succeeded in creating the Socialist Unity Party (*Sozialistische Einheitspartei*, SED) as a single successor organization to the SPD and the KPD in the Soviet zone, but the forced union was restricted to Soviet-occupied territory. In the absence of pressure from the Western Allies, the Social Democrats in the West rejected the merger, and the two parties remained separate organizations in those zones. In West Berlin, for example, 82 percent of the SPD's membership turned down the merger proposal when it was put to a vote. (The Russian authorities prohibited a similar plebiscite in East Berlin and the Soviet zone.)

The shotgun marriage of Social Democrats and Communists in the Russian zone put an end to the SPD's existence as an independent political party east of the Elbe, but in the Western zones the SPD was the first party to be reorganized. On April 18, 1945, eight days after British troops occupied the city of Hannover, Kurt Schumacher, the leader of the city's Social Democrats before 1933, presided over the SPD's first postwar meeting. He announced the rebirth of the Social Democratic Party in the British zone. Schumacher, who had spent ten years during the Third Reich in a concentration camp, quickly emerged as the SPD's unchallenged and charismatic leader. Like the Communists, the Social Democrats immediately presented a full-fledged program for reconstruction. Under Schumacher's leadership the SPD reiterated its belief in parliamentary democracy and democratic socialism. Schumacher was also adamant that the Reich's unity needed to be preserved, although his eventual goal was the integration of a socialist Germany in a democratic-socialist Europe.

Under Schumacher's direction the SPD became again what it had been in the latter 1920s: a Marxist, democratic, nationalist, working-class party. The SPD rejected the Communist doctrine of the dictatorship of the proletariat, but the party's essentially Marxist program did not smooth cooperation with the middle-class parties. The SPD's dealings with the occupation authorities were not much better. Schumacher was convinced that Germany's capitalists, aided and abetted by their compatriots in the Allied countries, had been responsible for the rise of Hitler. He liked to remind officials in the military governments that he and many of his fellow Social Democrats had been incarcerated in concentration camps at a time when the Allied leaders were still negotiating treaties with Hitler.

In contrast to Schumacher, whose leadership of the SPD remained unchallenged until his death in 1952, the dominant figure in the largest middle-class party had to overcome considerable obstacles before his position was generally recognized. The Christian Democratic Union (CDU) was a new organization that united parts of the old Catholic Center Party with elements of anti-Nazi Protestant conservatism. The new party was founded in the Soviet zone in June 1945 and, in the Western zones, in the fall of that year. Almost immediately two leaders and two strategies battled for CDU supremacy.

In the Soviet zone Jakob Kaiser, a former official in the Catholic Union movement, emerged as the CDU's leader. Kaiser did not sympathize with communism, but like the Communists, he did agree that the democratic parties should cooperate to form an antifascist-bloc. Kaiser was convinced only the preservation of the Grand Alliance would preserve Germany's national unity. A united, democratic Germany had to function as a "bridge" between the Russians and the Western Allies, preventing the breakup of the Allies. To this end, Kaiser was willing to go to a considerable distance in accommodating the Russian plans.

Kaiser's views were vigorously opposed by the man who was to become the leader of the CDU in the Western zones, Konrad Adenauer. The mayor of Cologne, 70 years old when elected chairman of the CDU in the British zone, had already been a major figure in Weimar politics in the 1920s. Adenauer argued that Kaiser's "bridge function" was an illusion since the Soviets had already decided against genuine democracy in their zone but planned to incorporate East Germany into the Soviet orbit. According to Adenauer, then, the CDU's task was to build democracy in the Western zones and to forge a strong link between Western Germany, Western Europe, and the United States. Programmatically, the CDU stood for federalism, individual freedoms, and at least initially also favored some nationalization of the economy. (Limited nationalization was dropped when Americans voiced their opposition.)

As had happened after World War I, middle-class politics in Bavaria went its own way. After an attempt to revive the Bavarian People's Party as the Bavarian Party (*Bayernpartei*, BP) failed, the dominant political force in the state became the Bavarian branch of the CDU, the Christian Social Union (*Christlich-Soziale Union*, CSU). In national politics the CSU formed a partnership with the CDU that has continued to this

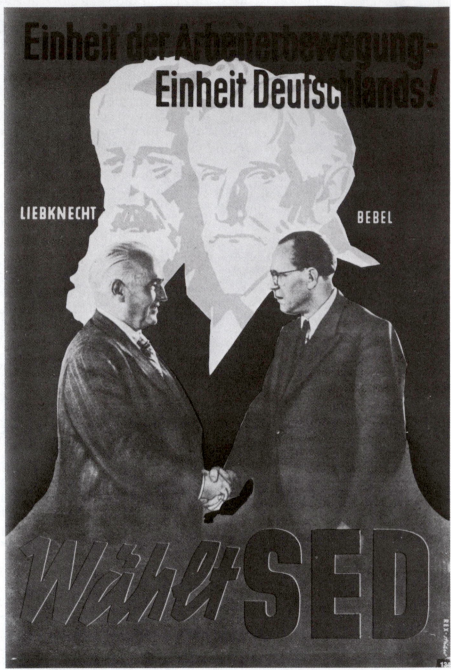

An early campaign poster of the SED. Beneath portraits of the nineteenth-century SPD leaders Wilhelm Liebknecht and August Bebel, Otto Grotewohl (SPD) and Wilhelm Pieck (KPD) are reuniting the German working class. The text reads, ''Unity of the workers' movement—unity of Germany.'' (Source: *Anschläge*, no. 134.)

day, but organizationally the Bavarian group has remained separate from the parent body. The CSU's activity is restricted to Bavaria; by agreement with the CDU the party does not attempt to organize supporters outside of the state.

The liberals, too, established themselves first in the Soviet zone. The party called itself the Liberal Democratic Party of Germany (*Liberaldemokratische Partei Deutschlands*, LDPD). The group had no choice but to steer the LDPD in the tradition of the Progressives and the DDP, since the Russians regarded right-wing liberalism as a fascist ally of monopoly capitalism. Nevertheless, the LDPD quickly ran into difficulties with SMAD. Its founders were forced to resign, and it was not until Otto Nuschke, a left-wing DDP delegate in the Prussian Landtag during the Weimar years, became the party's chairman that the Soviets judged the LDPD suitably "progressive." Nuschke led the LDPD to a position as bourgeois junior partner of the SED.

In the Western zones liberalism did not follow Nuschke's lead. Instead, the West German liberals succeeded in uniting their traditionally feuding left and right wings into a single party, the Free Democratic Party of Germany (*Freie Demokratische Partei Deutschlands*, FDP). Ideological divisions persisted under the organizational umbrella, however, and the FDP had considerable difficulty agreeing on a consistent program. The national liberal priorities of nationalism and unfettered free enterprise vied for supremacy with the civil libertarian, anti-clerical, and social welfare traditions of progressivism. There were also some practical organizational difficulties. In the West, liberalism was traditionally strongest in southwestern Germany. These areas, however, were mostly located in the French zone, and until the middle of 1948 the French authorities severely restricted travel between their zone and the rest of Germany.

Once parties were permitted to organize again in the summer and fall of 1945, political life in the Soviet and Western zones proceeded along increasingly divergent paths. Although the Soviets allowed zone-wide elections for a "German People's Congress for Unity and a Just Peace" as early as the fall of 1946, they also insisted that all "democratic" parties cooperate under the leadership of the SED. Candidates nominated for the Congress had to promise support for an antifascist-bloc strategy before they could be certified by SMAD. The actual elections were relatively free of direct Soviet interference, but by a variety of tactics SMAD assured that the Congress would be dominated by the SED.

The Western Allies followed a more cautious approach in allowing the resumption of organized political activity. Once the decision to let the Germans become politically active again had been made, however, the Western Allies, unlike the Russians, made no effort to control the emerging party spectrum, except for the obvious prohibition of the Nazis and their fellow-travelers. No restrictions were put on the KPD.

In line with their more cautious approach and in order to discourage a revival of German nationalism, the Western Allies sought to make local and state affairs the focal point of political activity. In 1946 the voters in each *Land* elected a state legislature that then drafted new state constitutions. To coordinate decisions at the zonal level the British and Americans institutionalized meetings of the states' prime ministers in the two zones under the name of States' Councils (*Länderräte*). With the establishment of the Bizone, the *Länderräte* of the two zones turned into a single body.

The Americans wanted to extend this confederative arrangement to all four zones. Secretary Byrnes in his September 1946 Stuttgart speech proposed that the prime ministers of the *Länder* meet as a "national council" in order to work out a German federal constitution. The proposal was rejected by the Russians, who argued that this was the proper task of the Soviet-sponsored Peoples' Congress, and by the French, who at this time still wanted to restrict German political activity to the local and state levels.

Along with renewed political life, there was also a rebirth of art and literature. But while post-1945 politics was grounded in the experiences (and missed opportunities) of the Revolution of 1918–1919 and the Weimar years, German writers and artists turned to new forms. For the past twelve years German cultural life had stagnated under the iron hand of the Nazis' blood-and-soil ideology, and artists and audiences alike after the war rejected taking up again the stale debates of the 1920s and 1930s.

There was an explosion of new literary magazines and sophisticated journals of opinion. Between 1945 and 1950 over 150 periodicals began publication and, although most folded after a few issues, some like the *Frankfurter Hefte* ("Frankfurt Notebooks") and *Der Monat* ("The Month") continue to enliven the literary scene. Audiences eagerly discovered the literature of the occupying powers; immediately after the war Thornton Wilder's *Our Town* was the most popular stage production in Germany.

New German dramas and novels were less predominant, but two stage productions—Carl Zuckmayer's *Des Teufels General* ("The Devil's General," 1946) and Wolfgang Borchert's *Draussen vor der Tür* ("On the Outside," 1947)—played to packed audiences. Zuckmayer had spent the Nazi years in exile in Vermont, and his play dealt with the problem of "inner emigration" and resistance among the German military. Borchert, a young veteran, attempted to address the emptiness and alienation felt by those who returned home to lost ideals and bombed-out cities.

Borchert's play illustrated one of the dominant themes of the post-1945 cultural revival, a profound pessimism about the future of civilization. World War II, "the picture of hell on earth," had ended the Age of Humanism. Modern people, most artists suggested could only seek refuge in religious revival, absurdity, nihilism, or a private world unconnected with larger

events. Totally absent was the celebration of the "front experience" that had characterized so much of the literature after World War I. There were war novels, like Theodor Plievier's *Stalingrad* (1945), but their emphasis was on the senseless horror of war, not its supposed heroism. Even Ernst Jünger, whose books had been instrumental in creating the myth of the "front experience" after World War I, abandoned his belief that war forged a "new man." His diary of the World War II, *Strahlungen* ("Rays") is a powerful statement of the author's recognition that his earlier ideals had become perverted and useless.

Except for the British, all of the Allies took active steps on their own to encourage the permeation of democratic values in German cultural life. (The British tended to rely more on Germany's own regenerative processes.) The Americans did not even wait for the war to end. Talented writers among the German prisoners of war in the United States were encouraged to contribute literary pieces to a camp magazine called *Der Ruf* ("The Call"), which the U.S. authorities distributed among the German POWs. Many of these authors would later become leaders of the West German literary establishment.

The Russians, too, made an effort to encourage "progressive" traditions among the writers and artists in their zone. In early July 1945 the "Cultural Association for the Democratic Renewal of Germany" (*Kulturbund zur demokratischen Erneuerung Deutschlands*) was founded as the umbrella organization for "cultural producers" in the Soviet zone. Although the guiding forces behind the *Kulturbund* were a group of Communist fellow-traveling authors, many of whom had belonged to the "Association of German Proletarian and Revolutionary Writers" during the 1920s, at first SMAD made no effort to politicize the association. Indeed, the group's journal *Aufbau* ("Construction") for a time became one of the liveliest literary journals in Germany. Its pages were open to a wide variety of authors and literary forms.

THE COLD WAR AND THE DIVISION OF GERMANY

The wartime agreements among the Allies were based on the assumption that joint and cooperative control by the Big Four of the defeated Reich would extend into the peacetime future. Within a year after Germany's unconditional surrender, however, the Cold War had destroyed the anti-Hitler alliance and pitted West against East. In Germany the Cold War led first to the breakdown of four-power cooperation, and later to the establishment of separate East and West German states.

The Cold War was not planned. As far as Germany was concerned, it came about because the Big Four increasingly recognized that their policy goals and priorities for the country were incompatible. The Russians insisted that reparations be given absolute priority in any Allied "German policy" and that "democratization" and capitalism were incompatible. The West was equally adamant that reparations should not take precedence over current production or economic recovery and that "democratization" should not be a synonym for Communist control and the destruction of political and cultural pluralism.

In the Russian zone the establishment of SAGs and the Saxon land reforms in 1946 signaled the Soviets' determination to go their own way. The SAGs—the abbreviation stood for *Sowjetische Aktiengesellschaft* or Soviet corporation—were enterprises located in the Soviet zone that were wholly owned by the Russians and whose entire production went to the Soviet Union. In the West the founding of the Bizone at the beginning of 1947 similarly indicated that the British and the Americans intended to assign German economic recovery a higher priority than reparations and structural reforms. Soviet aggression in southeastern Europe

and the U.S. responses in the form of the Marshall Plan and the Truman Doctrine further worsened the climate for four-power cooperation.

The London Conference of Big Four foreign ministers in December 1947 was a watershed in the developing East-West split over Germany. As a result of this meeting each side became convinced that the other was unwilling to compromise on Germany. Immediately after the failure of the London Conference the Russians moved to solidify control of their zone and their general sphere of influence in Eastern Europe. SMAD dismissed Jakob Kaiser, the chairman of the CDU in the Soviet zone, and under Kaiser's successors the party abandoned its quest for an independent policy and became instead one of the SED's junior partners. Two months later, a bloodless coup in Czechoslovakia brought the Communists to power in this Central European country. In April the Soviet authorities began harassing Allied and German traffic in and out of Berlin. True, simultaneously the Russians offered a comprehensive proposal for maintaining Four Power cooperation in Germany, but the West treated such gestures as mere propaganda.

Instead of chasing after the chimera of inter-Allied cooperation, the Western powers set about integrating their zones into the Western political and economic orbit. From February to June 1948 the Big Three Western Allies and the Benelux states of Belgium, Luxembourg, and the Netherlands met again in London. Prodded by the Americans, the delegates agreed that the three Western zones would be joined into a single economic unit and would participate fully in the European Recovery Program under the Marshall Plan. Most Germans regretted the deepening division among the Allies because they were anxious to preserve the unity of the Reich, but despite a wealth of conflicting ideas on how to prevent a falling out of the Grand Alliance, the practical influence of the Germans on the flow of events was minimal.

The Berlin blockade was both the most dramatic development in the growing division of Germany, and the event that convinced most Germans in the Western zones and West Berlin that they had no real alternative to becoming part of the Western camp. As with most conflicts in the accelerating Cold War, West and East attributed aggressive motives to each other. The Russians accused the West of using economic pressure to subvert Soviet control of the Russian zone, while the West was convinced that the Soviets were attempting to drive the Western Allies out of the former capital and incorporate all of Berlin into the Soviet zone.

The Berlin blockade was triggered by a dispute over the type of currency to be used in the city. Until June 1948 the legal tender used in the Soviet zone and all sectors of Berlin was the occupation money issued under the authority of SMAD. Since the city's economic hinterland was the Soviet zone, this arrangement made economic sense. But with the West German currency reform an entirely new situation arose. The introduction of the deutsche mark signaled the creation of two separate economic systems. The Western Allies had not originally intended to introduce the new currency in Berlin, but German economic administrators in the city and the Western zones pointed out that not distributing the deutsche mark in Berlin condemned the city to economic isolation and eventual incorporation into the Soviet zone. As a result, the Western Allies agreed to introduce the new mark in the parts of Berlin under their control. It became legal tender alongside the occupation currency of the Soviet zone.

Aware of the old adage that a hard currency would drive out soft money, the Russians saw the Western decision as a direct challenge to their control of East Germany and East Berlin. They also argued that by distributing the new currency in the Western sectors of the city, the Western Allies would effectively undermine Four-Power control of the former capital. On June 22, SMAD prohibited the distribution of the deutsche mark in all sectors of Berlin. The West in turn protested the Soviets' action and went ahead with the distribution of the new currency in the Western sectors. One day later, the Russians, citing the pretext of needed repairs to road, rail, and water networks, closed all land access to West Berlin from the Soviet zone and Western Germany. They also interdicted the shipment of all supplies from their zone to the city; Germany's former capital was subjected to a full-scale blockade.

In 1948 the city of Berlin had a population of roughly 4 million, of which 2.5 million lived in the Western sectors. Normally, almost all of the supplies of food, fuel, and other necessities for the inhabitants of all four sectors came from the surrounding Soviet zone. For this reason, the Russians undoubtedly calculated that the West had no choice except to yield to the Russian demands. Since it was well known that the leaders of the Western Allies were anxious to avoid a direct military confrontation, the Soviets felt they were in a position to dictate terms to the West. The Western Allies, however, again led by the Americans, used the inter-Allied agreements on access routes to practice a form of brinkmanship that would call the Russian bluff without resorting to military force. In November 1945 the Four Powers had agreed that the Western Allies could use their air corridors, one from each of the Western zones, to supply their forces in Berlin. The Western Allies now decided to use these corridors to airlift supplies not just to their troops, but to the entire population of the three Western sectors in the city.

The Russians, like the Western powers, were unwilling to mount a direct military challenge to their opponents, and the Berlin Airlift remains one of the most impressive examples of logistical support in modern times. Landing virtually nonstop in West Berlin, planes of the Western Allies by December 1948 were able to bring 4,500 tons of supplies to the city each day, and by the spring of the following year that figure had been increased to 8,000 tons. It became clear that despite tremendous hardships— electricity could be turned on only four hours each day—West Berlin could be supplied from the air indefinitely.

The Russians also recognized their defeat, and during the winter began signaling that they were anxious to end the blockade without losing diplomatic face. After months of behind-the-scenes negotiations the Soviets, in May 1949, lifted the blockade (officially, the needed repairs to transport networks had been completed) without having achieved any of their objectives. In terms of the Cold War the Berlin blockade was a clear Western victory.

The year-long confrontation over Berlin sealed the economic and political division of Germany and the city itself. Berlin developed into two separate administrative entities. The city was not yet physically divided, as it would be later, and in all four sectors the Allied commanders retained far-reaching control rights, but by June 1949 Germany's former capital had two separate municipal governments. In the three Western sectors the mayor and city council were freely elected, while in the Soviet sector a Communist city government was installed by SMAD. Even more important, the introduction of the deutsche mark as the only legal currency in the Western sectors at the end of the blockade meant that West Berlin would become an integral part of the West German and West European economic systems.

The ongoing Berlin blockade also provided the final catalyst needed to push the Western Allies and the Germans in the West to the realization that there would have to be separate political entities in East and West Germany. In view of the Russian attempt literally to starve out West Berlin, no major political group in the Western zones—with the exception of the Communists—held fast to the conviction that the illusion of national unity was worth the price

of Russian domination. Some political leaders continued to drag their feet but, by July 1948, most German leaders of the Western zones had accepted the position of the Allied military governors: that there was no alternative to a separate state in the Western zones. As Ernst Reuter, the Social Democratic mayor of West Berlin reminded his colleagues, "Germany is not being divided; it is already divided." It is also noteworthy that the fortitude of the West Berliners during the blockade did much to change the image of the Germans among the Western Allies. The Berliners' willingness to endure months of hardship to preserve their freedom in the face of Communist threats did much to wipe away the image of the "ugly Germans" and to replace it with the beginnings of a picture of "good, democratic Germans."

In July 1948 the state legislatures of the three Western zones elected delegates to a Parliamentary Council. Beginning in September 1948, to the accompaniment of the continuing blockade, the Parliamentary Council met in the Rhenish university town of Bonn and debated the terms of a West German constitution. It was completed and submitted for ratification to the state legislatures in the spring of the following year. The Russians and their Communist allies watched developments in West Germany with great interest. All along the Soviets were anxious to prevent the formation of a separate non-Communist West German state; indeed it seems clear that the blockade had been a last-ditch effort by the Soviets to prevent the creation of such an entity. Even when this strategy failed, the Russians did everything possible to put the onus for dividing Germany on the Western Allies and the West Germans. Only after the West German constitution had been ratified, was a newly elected (Third) Congress for Unity and a Just Peace charged with drafting an East German alternative constitution. Unlike the Parliamentary Council, the Third Congress was formally elected directly by the voters of the Soviet zone, but in reality the people had little choice in the matter. The ballots permitted only a "yes" or "no" vote on a list of antifascist-bloc candidates selected by SMAD and the SED.

CONCLUSION

By the middle of 1949, then, only four years after the "condominium of the Allies" had been established, the owners of the building had developed irreconcilable differences and divided their property. In one sense this development reversed the flow of German history in the last eighty years, but in other ways the two Germanys that emerged out of the Cold War continued separate but specifically German historic traditions.

In both East and West the new German societies attempted to revive and fulfill the promise of the post-1918 era. In the Soviet one SMAD and the SED intended to complete the socialist revolution that had failed in 1919. The new leaders of the West were also determined to avoid the mistakes of Weimar while holding fast to the ideal of the first republic: cultural pluralism; a socially responsible, free-market economy; and parliamentary democracy.

The Germans' selective dipping into their past was, of course, only part of the story of the country's division—and the lesser part at that. More important, as long as the Cold War lasted, both German states were part of the East-West confrontation—and subject to control and guidance by the Big Four. East and West Germany were founded as, and would remain for many years, objects of Cold War politics.

CHAPTER 10

THE FEDERAL REPUBLIC OF GERMANY, 1949–1990

The two states that emerged from the rubble of the Third Reich, the Federal Republic of Germany (FRG) and the German Democratic Republic (GDR), have been the most successful societies in modern German history. For almost forty years Germans on both sides of the Elbe have enjoyed unprecedented political stability, economic prosperity, and genuine international respect. The achievements of the Federal Republic have been particularly remarkable. West Germany is a democratic society with a high degree of political consent and a balanced federal and religious structure.

THE ADENAUER ERA, 1949–1963

Political Stability

In 1949 few West Germans would have predicted that the state they were reluctantly creating was in fact the beginning of a West German nation. The framers of the constitution constantly emphasized the provisional nature of their work. Nevertheless, they succeeded in writing a remarkably effective document.

West Germany's leaders faced a difficult task. They wanted to write a constitution that was in accord with Germany's own political traditions, but they also had to construct basic political guidelines that could obtain the approval of the Allied military governors. Fortunately the two sets of criteria were not incompatible, although the priorities of the Allies and the Germans differed. Both sides agreed that the new West German state should be a parliamentary democracy and that the new constitution should draw upon Germany's only other experience with parliamentary democracy, the Weimar constitution. The Allies assigned a high priority to redrawing the German state boundaries, while territorial reform ranked much lower on the German agenda. Understandably, the disagreements were sharpest on the sovereignty issue. The Allies wanted to retain far-reaching rights even after the constitution had gone into effect; the Germans were anxious to reduce as much as possible the residual powers of the occupation forces.

The Basic Law, as the Germans insisted on labeling the constitution to underscore its provisional character, was drafted by the Parliamentary Council. In this assembly the SPD and the CDU/CSU were each represented by twenty-seven delegates; the remaining twelve delegates were divided among five smaller parties, including the Liberals and the Communists. Eleven of the sixty-six delegates had sat in the state legislatures or the Reichstag during the Weimar Republic. The chairman of the CDU, Konrad Adenauer, was elected president of the Parliamentary Council, while Carlo Schmid, a recognized constitutional expert and leader of the SPD in southwest Germany, became chairman of the council's most important subdivision, the drafting committee.

The Parliamentary Council began its deliberations at the beginning of September 1948. Eight months later, in May 1949, it submitted the Basic Law for ratification to the state legislatures. The final document was in many ways an improved version of the Weimar constitution. Particularly apparent were three major changes. One concerned the election and powers of the head of state, the federal president. (Partly in response to Allied sensitivities, the Basic Law avoided using the word *Reich*. Instead, the delegates went back to the pre-1871 term *Bund* or federation.) Second, the framers of the Basic Law attempted to reduce the large number of cabinet crises that had been characteristic of the Weimar years. Finally, there was the problem of the second chamber of the national legislature. During the Weimar Republic the power of this *Länder*-controlled body had resulted in con-

stant friction between the states and the central government.

The Basic Law sought to provide correctives for all of these weaknesses in the Weimar constitution. The powers and stature of the federal president were significantly reduced. In contrast to the Weimar practice, where the Reich president had been something of an *Ersatzkaiser*, the West German counterpart is not elected by direct popular vote and his or her functions are largely limited to representative and ceremonial duties. The West German federal president has no emergency powers analogous to Article 48 of the Weimar constitution.

Undoubtedly the most important features of the new constitution concern the nature of relations between the federal executive and the legislature, and the election of the federal parliament. Like the Weimar Reichstag, the West German national parliament is elected at least every four years. However, unlike the system of extreme proportional representation that elected the Weimar Reichstag, the West German national parliament, or *Bundestag*, has members elected both by a system of proportional representation and by delegates chosen in single-member districts. One-half of the Bundestag members are elected in single-member districts (originally it was three-fifths), and the remainder are selected from "party lists" allocated on the basis of proportional representation. Equally important, subsequent election laws mandated a specific and, as it has turned out, very effective provision making it more difficult for splinter parties to gain representation in the national parliament. To gain a seat in the Bundestag the constitution provided that a party had to gain at least 5 percent of the popular vote in a state or a majority in at least one single-member district. (Since 1949 these provisions have been amended, raising the hurdles to 5 percent of the national total or a majority in three single-member districts.)

The delegates to the Parliamentary

Council also attempted to reduce the likelihood of cabinet crises. In a parliamentary democracy the legislature has both the power to elect and—through a vote of no confidence—to dismiss the cabinet. In the last years of the Weimar Republic cabinet crises had been frequent and long as Communists and Nazis combined their strength to overthrow one government after another. To prevent a repetition of this state of affairs, the Basic Law provides for a "constructive vote of no confidence." In practice this means that a vote of "no confidence" is not valid unless the opposition can demonstrate beforehand that it has agreed on the composition of a new cabinet to take the place of the one it seeks to dismiss.

The guarantees of civil liberties and individual rights in the Basic Law were also a modified version of the Weimar model. The new constitution lists the classic civil rights—such as freedom of speech and assembly—but remembering the Nazis' abuse of these rights, the Parliamentary Council coupled them with a specific prohibition against their use by any individual or organization to advocate anti-Semitism, racism, or the overthrow of the democratic form of government. The delegates rejected Social Democratic proposals to include a list of "socioeconomic rights"—such as the right to employment, and joint labor-management control of major corporations—in the Basic Law, but they did reaffirm the constitutional duty of public support for institutions like family and church. An important symbolic link to Germany's first attempt at democracy was the reinstitution of the colors black, red, and gold as the FRG's flag and the *Deutschlandlied* as its national anthem.

In line with German particularist traditions, but also at the insistence of the Allies, the Basic Law is quite solicitous of states' rights. As they had during the empire and the First Republic, the *Länder* retain a number of specific residual powers, especially control over public education at all levels. In addition, the state governments control the second chamber of the national legislature, the Federal Council (*Bundersrat*), whose members are not elected directly by popular vote but selected by the state legislatures. The second chamber has less direct influence over national legislation than the Bundestag, but the states can use this chamber to at least delay measures that they see as inimical to their interests.

An interesting innovation in German constitutional practice was the establishment of a Federal Constitutional Court (*Bundesverfassungsgericht*). This tribunal, clearly modeled on the U.S. Supreme Court, has original and final jurisdiction on all questions affecting the constitutionality of federal, state, and local legislation as well as administrative acts and international treaties.

The Parliamentary Council approved the Basic Law on May 8, 1949, by a vote of fifty to twelve. The negative ballots came from some of the smaller parties, including the KPD, and all members of the Bavarian delegation. The latter rejected the Basic Law because, in its view, the document did not go far enough in guaranteeing states' rights. Four days later, the three military governors gave their approval. The draft was then submitted to the state legislatures for ratification. With the exception of Bavaria, all of the German states voted for the Basic Law. In September 1949 the new Federal Republic of Germany elected its first national parliament.

At the same time, the Allies transformed their offices of military government into civilian high commissions. Both the Americans and the French replaced their military chiefs of administration with civilian officials. John J. McCloy, a New York banker and close associate of presidents Roosevelt and Truman, took the place of General Lucius Clay, the head of OMGUS. The French high commissioner was André François-Poncet, a career diplomat who had been France's ambassador to Berlin in the 1930s. The British retained General Robertson as high commissioner, but to underscore his new status the general retired from active army service.

The early West German political scene maintained its "traditional" multiparty behavior—in the first federal elections thirteen parties were represented on the ballot—but it soon acquired a decidedly more "American" feel. Increasingly, two parties, the CDU/CSU and the SPD, appealed to a wide spectrum of voters across class and geographic divisions. By the end of the 1950s West Germany had developed into a two-and-a-half party system, with the Liberals running a distant third to the two major groups. Essentially, the CDU/CSU represents the center-right; the SPD represents the left-of-center; and the Liberals (FDP) became a smaller swing party in the center that has shifted alliances several times between the CDU/CSU and the SPD. One man, Konrad Adenauer, the leader of the CDU/CSU, was largely responsible for the transformation of the West German party scene. Aided by undaunted self-confidence, considerable charisma, and the "economic miracle" of the 1950s (see pp. 277–299), Adenauer succeeded in transforming the CDU into a party that transcended religious and class boundaries. In fact, in the 1957 federal election it became the first party in German history to win more than 50 percent of the popular vote in a free election.

The Christian Democrats' success had two major consequences for West German politics. One was the disappearance of the smaller parties; the CDU simply absorbed most of them. Even more important, the CDU's strategy forced the other major parties to make programmatic and stylistic changes as well. The Liberals were the weakest in adapting to the new era. The CDU's success soon dashed the FDP's hopes of carving out a small, but safe middle-class constituency, and confronted the Liberals with a chronic dilemma. Not only was the CDU able to form governments without the FDP's cooperation, but the Christian Democrats succeeded in making major inroads into the Liberals' traditional voter reservoir.

The FDP became a party chronically fearful of not clearing the 5 percent hurdle.

During the 1950s the FDP tried to escape its dilemma by seeking refuge in the shadow of the CDU. The Liberals served in a succession of cabinets headed by Konrad Adenauer, acting as the self-proclaimed voice of Germany's upper-middle class and professionals. By the end of the decade, however, that strategy had led to voters widely lumping the FDP in with the CDU, and the Liberals' left wing demanded that the party take steps to preserve a political identity of its own.

The result was a drawing-together of FDP and SPD, a development that was made possible because the success of the CDU also forced the Social Democrats to become a "new" party. Kurt Schumacher, SPD leader, had believed that the magnitude of West Germany's economic difficulties after World War II would "proletarianize" a large majority of the population, who would then be receptive to the idea that democratic socialism alone could rebuild the country. But this SPD theory did not work out. The Social Democrats did almost as well as the CDU in the 1949 elections, but in the subsequent national contests of the 1950s the party's share of the popular vote grew only slowly above the 30 percent level, while the CDU approached and eventually exceeded the 50 percent mark. In other words, Schumacher's strategy seemed to doom the SPD to the status of a permanent minority party.

Schumacher died in 1952. His successor, Erich Ollenhauer, a "comfortably rotund, innately decent, and averagely competent" party bureaucrat, as the British journalist Terence Prittie described him, recognized the SPD's dilemma. The SPD had to transcend its traditional image and voter appeal. Ollenhauer quietly encouraged the rise of younger, more dynamic people to leadership positions in the party. Significantly, the newcomers, for the most part, had made their mark not as party functionaries, but as municipal and state government officials.

They included Ernst Reuter, the mayor of West Berlin during the blockade, Willy Brandt, Reuter's protege and successor, and Carlo Schmid, the prime minister of Baden-Württemberg who had been the principal architect of the Basic Law.

In 1958, the year after the federal election in which the CDU gained over 50 percent of the popular vote, the SPD's national convention met in Bad Godesberg and adopted a new party program. It was the first major revision of the SPD's ideology and platform since the Erfurt Program of 1891. The changes embodied in the Bad Godesberg Program were profound. In essence, the SPD cast off its Marxist mantle and became a pragmatic, issue-oriented party that attempted to appeal to a wide spectrum of voters. The SPD emphasized reform instead of revolution, cooperation instead of class struggle. The goals of centralized planning and socialization of the means of production yielded to the slogan "as much economic freedom as possible, as much economic planning as necessary."

The self-transformation of the major parties was instrumental in bringing about one of the most surprising developments in West German politics, the rapid disappearance of the splinter-party problem. In the 1949 federal election the splinter parties still attracted 28 percent of the popular vote, but by 1965 their combined total was only 3.6 percent. The trend was a surprise, since the political and especially the economic situation in the early years of the FRG seemed readymade for radical politics. Indeed, the occupation authorities were so fearful of the potential for radical politics among refugees that they refused to "license" a refugee party.

For this reason, the Union of Expellees and Dispossessed (*Bund der Heimatlosen und Entrechteten*, BHE) was not organized until 1950, when the Allied controls on party formation had been dropped. The history of the BHE quickly demonstrated, however, that fears of refugee radicalism were vastly exaggerated. The party, whose program included demands for the return of Germany's eastern territories and special benefits for refugees living in West Germany, captured more than 5 percent of the popular vote in 1953, but this figure represented less than 20 percent of those refugees who cast ballots. The party's initial success, moreover, was also the high point of its political influence. Within four years most of the refugee vote had been absorbed by the mainstream parties, primarily the CDU. In the 1957 election, the BHE was unable to clear the 5 percent hurdle, and thereafter the party rapidly disappeared from the political landscape.

Even more than by the large number of special-interest parties, Weimar democracy had been weakened by political extremism. The FRG has escaped this problem as well. Communist and neo-Nazi parties did attempt to gain a foothold, but neither has developed into a serious political force.

The failure of West German communism was closely related to the Cold War and Stalin's control of East Germany and the West German Communist Party. Between 1947 and 1951 the KPD's internal organization was seriously weakened by a purge of "Titoists," a term the party leadership used to characterize members whom the Soviets accused of deviating from Moscow's Stalinist line. During the first federal election campaign the Communists, who resolutely defended the SED's and SMAD's policies, were very much on the defensive trying to justify the Soviet blockade of West Berlin. The KPD still managed to obtain 5.7 percent of the popular vote in 1949, but thereafter its appeal declined rapidly. The party's membership dropped from 300,000 in 1945 to 60,000 in 1956. In the 1953 Bundestag election the KPD's popular vote fell to 2.2 percent. This was the party's last national campaign effort. In 1956 the Federal Constitutional Court determined that the party was attempting to destroy parliamentary democracy in West Germany and ordered its dissolution.

While domestic and foreign communism

The ideological significance of the SPD's Bad Godesberg program. Erich Ollenhauer, the leader of SPD, is throwing Marx on the rubbish heap of history. (Source: *Lachen*, p. 363.)

appeared to be the major threats at the height of the Cold War, both the Allies and the leaders of West Germany's new democracy were also concerned about the rise of neo-Nazism. The Nazi Party, of course, was prohibited, but there were fears that rightist extremism would attempt to rise under a variety of subterfuges. In fact, the neo-Nazis did become active again very quickly. The German Reich Party (*Deutsche Reichspartei,*

DRP), which had been established as a conservative group in late 1945, became increasingly extremist as ex-Nazis gained the upper hand in this organization. Fortunately, its voting appeal remained small. In the 1949 election the DRP gained only 1.8 percent of the vote nationwide, although it rose above 5 percent in the state of Lower Saxony, where many refugees and ex-Nazis lived.

Like the Communists, the neo-Nazis could not hold on to a place on the West German political landscape. In 1950 the DRP split. Its conservative elements eventually became part of the FDP and the CDU, while the radicals went on to found a new group, the Socialist Reich Party (*Sozialistische Reichspartei*, SRP). The leaders of the SRP were easily recognizable as prominent ex-Nazis (including Werner Naumann, a former state secretary in Goebbels' propaganda ministry), and the program left no doubt about the party's fascist aims. As a result, the Federal Constitutional Court outlawed the SRP before it could participate in the 1953 election. After 1953 the neo-Nazis remained an unorganized force until they reappeared in a different guise in the 1960s.

With both the splinter parties and the extremists unable to gain a significant portion of the vote, elections during the Adenauer era were dominated by shifts in popularity among the "big three," the Christian Democrats, the Social Democrats, and the Liberals. The first Bundestag election seemed to indicate that the forces would remain somewhat balanced. The CDU/CSU (31 percent) and the SPD (29.2 percent) stood at almost equal strength, while the Liberals came in a respectable third (11.9 percent). Since no party had a parliamentary majority, Konrad Adenauer put together a coalition composed of the CDU/CSU, the Liberals, and some smaller parties. In the 1953 election the voters gave the coalition a strong mandate to continue governing West Germany. The government was credited with the economic recovery (see p. 279), while the Russians' suppression of

freedom in East Germany (p. 309) and the outbreak of the Korean War seemed to show that there was no realistic alternative to the Western alliance. In 1953 the CDU/CSU's share of the popular vote exploded to 45.2 percent; the FDP dropped to 9.5 percent, and the SPD fell to 28.8 percent. It was also clear from the election statistics that the Social Democrats' decline would have been even greater had the SPD not inherited much of the earlier KPD vote.

In the "stomach election" of 1957 the CDU/CSU did even better. As noted above, for the first time in German history a single party gained a majority of the popular vote (50.2 percent) in a free election, enabling the CDU/CSU to form a cabinet on its own without coalition partners. The SPD's share also rose slightly, but this was primarily the result of the further disintegration of the KPD. Finally, the 1957 contest brought evidence that the FRG was becoming a two-party state. The Liberals' meager 7.7 percent vote share brought them dangerously close to the 5 percent barrier.

But Adenauer's 1957 triumph also began the long and in some ways sad political decline of the CDU's leader. The chancellor was now eighty-one years old and had been the unchallenged, dominant figure in West German politics for almost a decade. Adenauer remained physically and mentally fit, but he was also becoming increasingly irascible and suspicious of potential rivals. For some years now the chancellor's heir apparent had been Ludwig Erhard, the minister of economics since 1949 and the man credited with engineering West Germany's "economic miracle." Erhard was one of the CDU's most popular figures, and both he and many of the party's leaders felt that the time had come for him to take Adenauer's place. But although Adenauer respected Erhard's skill as economics minister, he was convinced his heir apparent would be a disaster as head of the government.

At the beginning of 1959 an opportunity seemed to present itself for a politic solution

One of the most famous and controversial campaign posters of the post-1945 era. In the 1953 Bundestag election, the CDU, campaigning against a still officially Marxist SPD, argued, "All Marxist roads lead to Moscow. For that reason [vote] CDU." (Source: *Anschläge*, no. 141.)

to the impasse. Since 1949 the federal president had been Theodor Heuss, a respected scholar and urbane Liberal. His second term was coming to an end, and a number of CDU leaders proposed to Adenauer that he should become federal president. After some consideration, the chancellor refused the largely honorific office. He proposed Erhard instead for the job, an offer that the economics minister regarded as an insult.

The 1959 "presidential crisis" ended with ill feeling on all sides, and the results of the 1961 federal elections provided further evidence that the voters, too, were becoming disillusioned with the Adenauer era. The campaign itself was characterized by a series of blunders and setbacks for the government. Even before the election, the Liberals had announced that they would demand Adenauer's resignation as chancellor as a precondition for reestablishing a coalition with the CDU/CSU. Adenauer's lame response to the Berlin Wall (see p. 314) antagonized many voters. The chancellor himself seemed to campaign almost as much against his heir presumptive, Ludwig Erhard, as he did against the SPD opposition. In contrast to the CDU's tried-and-true approach, the SPD presented a fresh platform in the Bad Godesberg Program, and its shadow chancellor—the forty-seven-year-old photogenic and charismatic mayor of Berlin, Willy Brandt—personified the postwar generation of political leadership.

The 1961 election results were a severe disappointment to the chancellor and the CDU. The Christian Democrats' share of the popular vote dropped to 45.3 percent, while the SPD's broke the 35 percent barrier, rising to 36.2 percent. Equally significant, the Liberals' campaign for a CDU/FDP coalition without Adenauer seemed to rescue them from political oblivion; their popular vote this time was 12.8 percent.

It was unfortunate that scandals marred Adenauer's last months in office. The most damaging of these was the *Spiegel* Affair in October 1962. *Der Spiegel* ("The Mirror"), then, as now, the leading newsmagazine of West Germany and Europe, had a well-deserved reputation for irreverence, iconoclasm and, on occasion, sensationalism. In the fall of 1962 the magazine published leaked documents demonstrating the lack of defense readiness of some West German army units. With Adenauer's approval, the minister of defense, Franz Josef Strauss (CSU), ordered the arrest of *Der Spiegel's* editors and a police search of the magazine's offices in Bonn and Hamburg. The reaction to this high-handed action was a storm of indignation from the press and public opinion over what appeared to be a clear attack on freedom of the press. The Liberals threatened to quit the coalition (which would have brought down the government) unless both Adenauer and Strauss resigned. The defense minister did so immediately, and while Adenauer lingered in office for a few months longer, his days were also numbered. In September 1963 the chancellor finally retired; he died three years later at the age of ninety-one.

Economic Prosperity

Ludwig Erhard became chancellor of the Federal Republic in September 1963. More than any other individual he personified the most dramatic success story in the FRG, the country's postwar "economic miracle." The prospects for rapid and sustained economic recovery were certainly not promising in 1949. The list of the country's economic and social needs were staggering: reconstruction of houses, apartments, and industrial plants; repair of the transportation system; resumption of industrial production; reopening of export markets; and integration of the millions of refugees and homeless into the fabric of society. These were tasks formidable enough to daunt most economic planners, but Ludwig Erhard, for one, remained optimistic. He recognized that, hidden beneath the prevailing picture of physical destruction and social misery, West Germany possessed some major assets. The influx of people brought overcrowding in many areas, but also a ready supply of workers, so that economic recovery would not be held back by a shortage of labor. Labor-management relations had been put on a new footing. The German workers were not organized in a single union, the German Labor Association (*Deutscher Gewerkschaftsbund*, DGB). The new umbrella organization embraced socialist, liberal, and Catholic unions and facilitated collective bargaining on a national level. Labor was also accorded a much larger role in the process of economic decision making. A 1952 federal co-determination law mandated that the employees of all major corporations elect at least one member of the board of directors. The result was a new era of quite harmonious labor-management relations. West Germany has experienced far fewer strikes and other forms of labor unrest than most leading industrial nations.

The very magnitude of the rebuilding effort also meant that for many years there would be a virtually limitless market for civilian goods and, provided production was sufficiently high, an almost total absence of inflationary pressures. It was, in other words, a golden opportunity for daring and innovative entrepreneurs. The same was potentially true for the international markets; after long years of war-related shortages, there was an international sellers' market for civilian goods. For a time West Germany had a serious capital problem, but the growing strength of the Deutsche Mark, which was backed by the U.S. dollar, soon made West Germany an attractive place for foreign and domestic investors.

In recent years the significance of the Marshall Plan and its aid has been questioned as a factor in the recovery of Western Europe. It now appears that American help acted more as a catalyst than as a causal agent. One researcher has estimated that only about 7 percent of the capital and materials needed for recovery was provided from U.S. sources; the remainder was generated by the Europeans themselves. At the same time, the psychological impact of U.S.

aid for the war-ravaged Continent should not be underestimated. In contrast to the situation after World War I, the Marshall Plan signified that America would not turn her back on Europe. As far as the German economy was concerned, U.S. willingness to underwrite the new West Germany currency was crucial in preventing a new "inflation mentality" from developing.

But all these factors were of the "If this . . . then that" variety, and they left unanswered two fundamental questions. One involved the best method for stimulating the productive forces of the country, and the other concerned the social implications of any economic policy adopted. In 1949 the social misery index in West Germany was very high, but it was rather evenly distributed. If the forces of a free market economy were unleashed, was there not a very real danger that prosperity would come to a few, while most remained destitute? Such a scenario—and the many poor were likely to include the millions of refugees who were already bitter about their fate—raised real fears of political destabilization and a return to the conditions of Weimar.

Erhard and the Social Democrats proposed radially different plans for West Germany's economic recovery. Both as chief administrator for economic affairs in the Bizone and later as economics minister in succession of federal cabinets, Erhard argued that relatively unfettered market forces would provide the greatest amount of prosperity for the largest number of West Germans. The minister, a former professor of economics, recognized of course, that the free enterprise system would increase the gap between rich and poor, but he was also convinced that the rapid increase in the country's GNP, made possible by freewheeling opportunities, would generate sufficient resources to reduce the misery index for all. In effect, the benefits would be highly differentiated in relative terms, but in absolute terms all would be better off.

The SPD vigorously opposed Erhard's plan for recovery, which it saw as perpetuating the rule of capitalism in West Germany and widening the gap between rich and poor. Until the middle of the 1950s the Social Democrats advocated a centrally planned economy with public ownership of basic industries and natural resources. The remaining privately owned major enterprises would be under the joint control of management and labor. Prohibitive taxation of large incomes would insure that there was an equitable system of income distribution.

As we saw, the election returns of the 1950s demonstrated that the voters in increasing numbers sided with Erhard. For almost a decade and a half Ludwig Erhard presided over the making of the West German "economic miracle." As the minister had anticipated, after some initial pump-priming by the European Recovery Program (ERP), as the Marshall Plan was formally called, the economy became self-propelled. What Erhard called a "social market economy" provided the West Germans with a level of prosperity unprecedented in German history. Pockets of poverty remained, but virtually all West Germans benefited from the spectacular expansion of most sectors of the economy.

The figures were truly impressive. Between 1951 and 1963 the West German economy expanded at an average annual rate of 7.1 percent. Disposable income of the average German household grew by 400 percent between 1950 and 1970. In 1950, 16.4 million families had to live in 10.1 million houses and apartments. Eight years later the housing shortage had been significantly eased by the construction of 4.5 million units. Unemployment dropped from 8.1 percent in 1950 to an extraordinary 0.5 percent in 1965. In economic and political terms the Erhard program was so successful that in 1954 the SPD dropped its proposals for state-directed planning and endorsed the concept of free by "socially responsible" competition.

Translating economic growth into social policy required political decisions and com-

promises. In part, the goal of social responsibility was realized by earmarking large amounts of public money for social welfare projects. Much of the housing construction, for example, was made possible with government subsidies. In addition, two major laws were instrumental in making the fruits of economic expansion available to all segments of the society. Both came in the early 1950s, that is to say, at a time when the West German economy was clearly "taking off."In May 1952 the Bundestag passed the Law for the Equalization of Burdens (*Lastenausgleichsgesetz*). Under the provisions of this legislation the government provided payments stretching over a number of years as partial compensation for war-related losses of either real property or liquid assets. By the end of 1986 over DM 130 billion ($68.4 billion) had been distributed to 57 million applicants.

The same principle of compensation was also extended to Jewish victims of Nazi persecution. The West German government negotiated an agreement with the State of Israel to give money payments to German Jews and their descendants. Between 1952 and 1966, DM 3.5 billion ($820 million) was appropriated for this purpose.

Equally important was the second piece of legislation, the Refugee Law (*Vertriebenengesetz*) of February 1953. Germany's refugee population was very unevenly distributed. Disproportionate numbers resided in the rural areas closest to the Soviet zone—Schleswig-Holstein, Lower Saxony, Hessen, Bavaria—causing severe problems for state and municipal governments and resentment among the local population. The Refugee Law determined a quota for proportional and equitable resettlement of the refugees throughout the West German *Länder* and provided federal funds for new housing and job training.

The sums involved in these two major social policy efforts were quite large. Between 1952 and 1962, DM 47 billion ($11.2 billion) were distributed under the auspices of the two laws; individual payments averaged DM 6,000 per person. But the effort was well worth it. The income redistribution policy undoubtedly removed what might have become a serious source of political radicalism—it certainly helped to undermine the strength of such groups as the BHE—while the overall rise in the standard of living mitigated the resentments against the wealth of the old and new rich that was a definite part of the "economic miracle."

Still, for all its undoubted benefits, Erhard's "social market economy" was essentially a trickle-down economy, and one that in absolute terms widened the rift between rich and poor. It became acceptable and indeed was enthusiastically endorsed by most West Germans because the trickle came fast enough and in sufficient amounts to provide major increases in the standard of living for virtually all. But these results could be achieved only by economic growth rates that have not been possible in the 1970s and 1980s.

International Recognition

Ludwig Erhard personified the "economic miracle," but there was never any doubt that Adenauer himself directed West Germany's foreign policy. Especially for the early years of the Adenauer era it is actually a misnomer to speak of West Germany's foreign policy. Under the Occupation Statute of 1949 the Allied high commissioners reserved for themselves the power to conduct West Germany's foreign policy. Not until 1954 did the FRG regain the right to conduct her own foreign relations. In his quest to have the Federal Republic rejoin the family of nations on a near-equal basis, Adenauer identified three issues as pivotal for West Germany's international standing. First, priority was given to continuing good relations with the Western Big Three, with West Germany's ties to the United States of paramount importance. Closely related was the area of political, military, and economic cooperation with the countries of Western Europe, especially France. Finally, there was

the problem of West Germany's relationship to the Soviet Union and the countries of Eastern Europe. (Incidentally, it will have been noted that relations with East Germany do not appear on this list. This was not accidental. During the Adenauer years the Federal Republic did not regard the GDR as a country, much less a foreign one. In the West German cabinet East German affairs were handled by the ministry for all-German affairs, not the foreign office.)

As far as relations with the Western Big Three were concerned, Adenauer single-mindedly set out to demonstrate to West Germany's former enemies that the Federal Republic would become and remain their loyal friend. The chancellor fully recognized the initial weakness of the FRG's position (Kurt Schumacher called him "chancellor of the Allies" during a foreign policy debate in the Bundestag in November 1949), but Adenauer was convinced that as the occupying powers recognized West Germany's support for the Western position in the Cold War, they would relinquish their remaining controls piece by piece.

In essence Adenauer was right, although the process was slow and the price high. A major breakthrough came with the General Treaty (*Generalvertrag*) of 1952. Under this arrangement the Western Allies agreed to formally abolish major parts of the Occupation Statute of 1949, although they still retained "supreme power" in Germany. They also promised to defend West Germany and West Berlin if attacked. But, in return for West Germany's inclusion in the Western defense perimeter, the Adenauer government yielded to American pressure and agreed to reestablish armed forces in West Germany. The Social Democrats severely criticized the General Treaty. They objected particularly to the remilitarization of the Federal Republic.

The fierce battles between government and opposition over West Germany's foreign policy in the early Adenauer years were reminiscent of the lack of national consensus during the Weimar years, but by the mid-

1950s the apparent success of Adenauer's strategy of slow steps to sovereignty had taken much of the steam out of the opposition. The SPD increasingly dropped its resistance to Adenauer's foreign policy. Disagreements on details remained, of course, but since about 1954 West Germany has enjoyed a large measure of bipartisan consensus on major foreign policy goals.

Adenauer's first official visit to Washington in 1954 was an important symbolic milestone in the Federal Republic's quest for recognition as an equal in the Western concert of powers, but the key development was the 1954 Germany Treaty (*Deutschlandvertrag*). Under this agreement West Germany became a formally sovereign nation, able to conduct its own foreign policy. The Western Allies also recognized the Federal Republic as the sole representative of the German people, thereby supporting the FRG's contention that there was only one legitimate German state. Allied troops remained stationed on German soil, but as allies and friends, not occupiers. A year later, West Germany became a full member of the North Atlantic Treaty Organization (NATO).

Adenauer and his supporters looked upon the Germany Treaty as a major setback to Russian efforts toward gaining international recognition for the GDR and luring West Germany to accept unification under Russian hegemony. Throughout the Adenauer years the Russians consistently argued that the only way to restore German unity was through the demilitarization of the country and mutual recognition of both German states. Adenauer as well as the two U.S. secretaries of state in the 1950s, Dean Acheson and John Foster Dulles, rejected this scenario out of hand. For a time the West German opposition seemed willing to consider the Russian proposals. The Social Democrats offered to guarantee Germany's permanent demilitarization if the Soviets consented to free elections in East and West Germany. The Russians, however, sent conflicting messages. On the one hand, in 1955 the Soviets set a precedent by agreeing to remove all foreign troops from Austria provided that this country remained permanently neutral and demilitarized. On the other hand, the Russians also forced the pace of Stalinization in East Germany making a united, democratic Germany less likely.

In 1955, after the Western Allies and Adenauer had repeatedly rejected Soviet overtures, and the Germany Treaty had been signed, the Soviets moved to assert their two-Germanys doctrine. They forced the West German government to open diplomatic relations with the Soviet Union, largely by threatening to refuse to release the thousands of German POWs and civilian internees who were still held in Russia. The Soviets became the first power to send ambassadors to East Berlin and Bonn, thereby underscoring their contention that there were two legitimate German states.

Although the agreement for mutual recognition between Bonn and Moscow did no oblige the Federal Republic to recognize the GDR, the West Germans were clearly fearful of the diplomatic precedent created by the exchange of ambassadors. The Adenauer government attempted to counter any spread of the dual-state theory with the Hallstein Doctrine. (Walter Hallstein was the state secretary of the West German foreign ministry from 1951 to 1958 and later president of the European Common Market.) Under this policy West Germany announced that it would refuse or break diplomatic relations with any nation, except for the Soviet Union, that simultaneously recognized East and West Germany. With the support of the United States, and by using its impressive economic strength to pressure Third World countries, West Germany for some years succeeded in enforcing the Hallstein Doctrine. The GDR's diplomatic ties were limited to the Communist regimes of Eastern Europe and Asia.

While the Adenauer cabinets were erecting diplomatic barriers against the East, they sought by every means possible to hasten the integration of the Federal Republic into the fabric of the Western Alliance. An important part of this effort was West Germany's willingness to supply military forces for the defense of Western Europe. This development aroused considerable controversy. The Americans endorsed a new German army early on, but the French remained understandably suspicious of a German military establishment only a few years after the end of World War II. For this reason the European Defense Community (EDC) seemed ideally suited to meet the dual objectives of rebuilding the German army, while laying to rest French fears of independent German military action. The terms of the EDC, negotiated at the same time as the General Treaty of 1952, provided for an integrated Western European army. Troops from the six major West European countries—France, Italy, West Germany, and the three Benelux countries—would be removed from the control of their national general staffs and deployed under an international command composed of officers from the six countries. In effect, then, any West German army would become a military force under international control.

The EDC was politically controversial in Germany, but the Bundestag eventually ratified the treaty and passed the necessary amendments to the Basic Law, removing the constitutional prohibitions against a West German military establishment. In August 1954, however, the French National Assembly defeated the EDC concept, ending the effort to create an integrated European military force. With the EDC jettisoned, West German troops became part of the NATO forces in 1955. Two years later conscription was reintroduced in West Germany, and by the early 1960s Germany's full contingent of 500,000 men, divided into twelve divisions, had been turned over to the NATO command.

Paralleling their talks on the abortive EDC treaty, the six countries also negotiated a series of agreements that would eventually lead to the European Economic Community (EEC). Spearheaded by the French foreign minister, Robert Schuman, "the Six" agreed to establish the European Coal and Steel Community (ECSC). (Schuman, an Alsatian, had very personal reasons for wishing to reduce Franco-German animosity: He fought on the German side during World War I, when Alsace was part of the German Reich, and for the Free French during World War II) The ECSC abolished tariffs and created a common market for coal and steel products among the six countries. Even more important, control of trade and manufacturing levels of these products was turned over to an international High Authority whose judgment superceded national decision-making bodies.

The ECSC was the forerunner of the Treaty of Rome, which in 1956 established the European Economic Community. This time "the Six" agreed to a whole series of cooperative agreements, ranging from tariff reductions to conducting joint research into the peaceful uses of atomic energy. At the heart of the Treaty of Rome was a commitment to a timetable for tariff reductions until all levies among the six countries were abolished. In addition, the partners established a Common Agricultural Policy (CAP) providing for massive subsidies to Europe's farmers. As in the case of the ECSC, the administration of the Common Market is vested in a multinational European Commission, headquartered in Brussels, Belgium.

The Treaty of Rome was a genuine compromise. West Germany benefited politically by finally being reaccepted as an equal in the European family of nations. Economically, Germany's industry, the strongest and most advanced among the six countries, was the primary beneficiary of the agreement to abolish tariffs among the six partners. The CAP, however, was most beneficial to France, the country that had the largest agricultural establishment. The FRG contributed the largest share of the EEC's fund for farm subsidies.

West Germany's accommodation on the

CAP as well as her general "good citizenship" in Europe were instrumental in putting Franco-German relations on a new footing. A major symbol of the new era of good feelings was the return of the Saar to German control. France, it will be recalled, had severed this territory, German in population and culture, from Germany and placed it under French economic and political control. As they had after World War I, in 1955 the French proposed the "Europeanization" of the Saar, which really meant establishing some sort of permanent international administration linked to French control. Although Adenauer publicly favored the scheme as part of the price Germany had to pay for better Franco-German relations, the people of the Saar overwhelmingly defeated the proposal in a plebiscite. France in turn proved a gracious loser. The French obtained some economic concessions in the Saar, but politically the territory returned to German control. On January 1, 1957, the Saar became the eleventh German *Land*.

The treaties leading to West European integration as well as the return of the Saar were negotiated with the leaders of the French Fourth Republic. An entirely new situation arose in 1958 with Charles de Gaulle's return to power in France as president of the Fifth Republic. It was a pleasant surprise to the Germans that de Gaulle was no longer the vindictive Free French leader, but anxious to continue along the road to Franco-German rapprochement. De Gaulle and Adenauer got along particularly well. The French president made a triumphant tour of West Germany, and the picture of the two leaders praying side by side in the cathedral at Reims symbolized around the world the new era of Franco-German friendship. The relationship culminated in 1963 with the signing of a mutual consultation treaty. Since then the leaders of West Germany and France have held regular summit meetings twice a year to discuss questions of mutual interest.

The balance sheet of the foreign relations during the Adenauer era is mixed. Franco-German rapprochement, the economic and political integration of Western Europe, and the Federal Republic's return as a respected member of the family of nations were obviously positive items on the ledger. These were goals that had eluded the leaders of the Weimar Republic. But there were also some significant setbacks. Most important was the failure of the strategy for German reunification. Relying on the West's strength and determination to force the Soviets out of East Germany clearly did not work. It remains an open question if the Russians would have permitted a democratic and united, although neutral and demilitarized, Germany, but neither the West Germans nor the Western Allies seriously explored this possibility. The West rejected not only Stalin's tentative overtures in this direction in the early 1950s, but also a 1958 plan for a demilitarized and nuclear free zone in Central Europe that was floated (with the obvious approval of the post-Stalin leadership in Russia) by the Polish foreign minister Adam Rapacki.

In 1963 it had also become obvious that Adenauer's policy of attempting to deny the GDR's existence was a failure. In fact, the inherent dangers of that policy were searingly obvious when at the end of 1958 the Russian leader Nikita Khrushchev initiated the Berlin crisis that was to culminate in the building of the Berlin Wall (see p. 314). By the end of the Adenauer era the existence of the GDR was secure, while the Hallstein Doctrine was becoming threadbare. The major countries of Western Europe and the United States still supported West Germany's effort to isolate the GDR, but the rapidly multiplying number of Third World governments had little interest in these *querelles allemandes*, and they saw no reason why they should not maintain diplomatic relations with both Germanies. In 1957 Egypt became the first non-Communist country to recognize East Germany. The Federal Republic immediately invoked the Hallstein Doctrine and severed diplomatic relations with Egypt, but it was clear even then that the Hallstein

Doctrine would not for long prevent other countries from following Egypt's example.

Even rapprochement with France had its negative side. The price for de Gaulle's friendship was high. To be sure, the French leader had a sincere interest in better Franco-German relations, but he was also seeking German support for his policy of freeing Western Europe from what he regarded as the excessive control by the Americans and British. The West Germans, for whom friendship with the United States was the bedrock of any foreign policy, had considerable difficulty reconciling the goal of Franco-German friendship with maintaining a special relationship to the Anglo-Saxon powers. West Germany could not, for example, prevent de Gaulle's unilateral veto in January 1963, which blocked Great Britain's application for membership in the Common Market. By the time Adenauer reluctantly resigned from office, the solidarity of the Western Alliance upon which he had built his foreign policies was showing serious cracks.

THE CHANGING OF THE GUARD, 1963–1974

When Ludwig Erhard became chancellor in September 1963 he did not anticipate troubled time ahead, although in fact Adenauer had bequeathed him a difficult legacy. The departure of the old chancellor left the CDU/CSU with a number of problems that would become magnified in the years ahead. The Christian Democrats were composed of many wings and factions. A strong leader like Adenauer had been able to prevent dissension and factionalism from getting out of hand, but Erhard did not possess these qualities. He had little interest in day-to-day party affairs, believing that his personal popularity with the voters would enable him to remain aloof from partisan politics.

Without the integrative force of a strong national leader, the Christian Democrats became a coalition of "feudal fiefs"—re-gional or interest groups led by the party's deputy chairpersons. This development in turn strengthened the position of the Bavarian CSU in the Christian Democratic camp. In the course of the 1960s the Bavarian CSU became the unchallenged political force in Bavaria, regularly obtaining more than 50 percent of the popular vote cast in Bavaria in state and national elections. Unlike the decentralized CDU, however, the Bavarian CSU was firmly controlled by its chairman, Franz Joseph Strauss. The Bavarian leader gained a strong favorite-son position, which he used effectively to influence the outcome of the power struggles in the CDU by backing one or another of the CDU's factional leaders.

Erhard's strength was also undermined by the growing power of the Social Democratic opposition. The SPD gathered the political fruits of the personnel and ideological changes that the party had introduced since the mid-1950s. The party's younger and more dynamic leadership was able to attract a significant following among intellectuals and academics. Moreover, for the first time in its century-long history the SPD, too, developed into a genuine *Volkspartei* able to attract a sizable share of the middle-class vote. Figures like Willy Brandt, who became party chairman after Erich Ollenhauer's death in 1963, and Helmut Schmidt, the party's dynamic parliamentary leader after 1966, were attractive spokespersons for the concerns of the postwar generation of German voters from virtually all economic strata. As a result, the social profile of the party's membership also changed. In 1960, 55.7 percent of the SPD's members were blue-collar workers and only 21.2 percent were salaried employees or civil servants, but at the end of the decade the blue-collar share had dropped to 39.6 percent while the white-collar proportion had risen to 33.6 percent.

True, younger and more educated members and voters presented the SPD with problems as well as votes. Many in the new generation of Social Democrats demanded far-reaching social reforms that would lead to a new "quality of life." Especially among the university-educated members, most of whom joined the party after the collapse of the student movements in 1968–1969 (see pp. 287–88) there was a resurgence of interest in Marxist ideological positions. By 1973 some 25 percent of the party's executive committee described themselves as "Leftists."

The Liberals undoubtedly experienced the most radical changes among the major parties. In fact, the FDP almost became a new party. Increasingly frustrated by their inability to secure a stable bloc of voters on the right side of the political spectrum, the Liberals sought an opening to the left. The shift did not come suddenly or without intraparty dissension. The opening to the left began in 1966 with an agreement between the FDP and the SPD to form a coalition in Germany's largest sate, North Rhine-Westphalia. Two years later, there was a change in the party's leadership. Delegates at the FDP's annual convention elected Walter Scheel, who had strongly supported FDP-SPD coalition in North Rhine-Westphalia, as the party's national chairman. Scheel replaced Erich Mende, a staunch right-wing Liberal and nationalist. (Mende liked to remind listeners that in World War II he had been awarded the Knight's Cross, the *Wehrmacht's* highest decoration for valor.) The old chairman had also been a loyal ally of Adenauer and favored continuing the CDU/CSU-FDP coalitions.

The political consequences of the Liberals' experiment were mixed. The party did gain a portion of the new *Mittelstand* vote, especially among middle-level executives and professionals. But there was a price to pay. The FDP lost most of its traditional support among the old *Mittelstand* strata, and its farm vote all but disappeared. In 1953, 15 percent of Germany's farmers voted Liberal, in 1972 that figure had sunk to 2 percent. In general, the party's own polls concluded only 25 percent of those

who had voted FDP in 1965 (when the party was still allied to the CDU) cast their ballots for the Liberals in 1969. The FDP's political shift had essentially succeeded in exchanging one set of supporters for another, rather than gaining new members and voters.

The fear of falling below the 5 percent mark remained acute. In 1970, a year after the Liberals had become the SPD's partner in a national coalition (see p. 289), the FDP's popular vote dropped to less than 5 percent in state elections in Lower Saxony and the Saar. In North Rhine-Westphalia the FDP cleared the barrier only with the help of voters "borrowed" from its new ally, the SPD. The practice of borrowing and lending votes, which is really a form of ticket-splitting, became increasingly common in elections of the 1960s and 1970s. Because delegates to the national and state legislatures are elected both from single-member districts and on the basis of proportional representation, German voters always cast two ballots: one to indicate the choice for representative in the single-member district, and a second to designate the party list from which the other half of the members of the legislatures will be chosen. In close national contests some voters developed the habit of casting their first ballot for the direct candidate of their own party, and their second ballot for the party that had indicated it would form a coalition with the first party. The political significance of "borrowing" was well illustrated in the 1972 federal elections. The FDP's share of the popular vote rose from 5.8 to 8.4 percent and later analyses showed that many SPD voters had "lent" their second ballots to the Liberals.

The 1960s brought not only changes for the major parties but also a seeming rebirth of political extremism. After the government quietly dropped its prohibition against Communist organizations, the German Communist Party (*Deutsche Kommunistische Partei*, DKP) was founded in September 1968. The DKP pays lip service to parliamentary democracy in order to stay within the bounds prescribed by the Basic Law, but the party is really a West German branch of the East German SED from whom it receives its political directives and most of its financial support. Largely because of this tie the DKP has not been very successful. In 1969 it had only 20,000 members and its share of the national vote was 0.6 percent; it has not done significantly better since then.

While the Communists remained an unimportant splinter group, the extreme right for a time appeared to present a graver threat. By 1961 neo-Nazism had sunk into political oblivion; even the "moderate" DRP polled less than 1 percent of the popular vote in the Bundestag elections. The extreme right was about to undergo a marked change, however. In 1964 a leader emerged to breathe new life into the movement. Adolf von Thadden was a member of the DRP, but he recognized the futility of the quest by its aging ex-Nazi leaders to bring back the past. Instead of attempting to resurrect the moribund DRP, Thadden and his allies dissolved the group and founded a new political organization, the National Democratic Party (*Nationaldemokratische Partei Deutschlands*, NPD).

The party was (and is) careful not to advocate the overthrow of West Germany's constitutional system, but both the NPD's program and its tactics leave little doubt that the party continues the traditions of the German extreme right. Chauvinism ("We have a right to all of Germany [including the areas east of the Oder-Neisse line]!"), xenophobia ("Throw out all foreigners!"), and attempts to whitewash Nazi crimes and criminals justify labeling the NPD as neo-Nazi, even if, largely for demographic reasons, the actual number of old Nazis in the party is small and declining.

Political extremism in Germany had always benefited from adverse economic conditions, and the NPD had the good fortune to make its appearance just as West Germany experienced its first serious postwar recession. The NPD quickly gained representation in a number of state legislatures,

receiving 8 percent of the popular vote in the 1966 state elections in Hessen and Bavaria. Two years later it reached 10 percent in Baden-Württemberg. A number of analysts were uncomfortably reminded of the earlier rise of the Nazis, particularly since the NPD's support was strongest in areas that had also been pockets of strength for the old Nazis. At the height of its popularity more than a million voters cast their ballots for the NPD in state and local elections. Thadden confidently predicted that fifty NPD delegates would sit in the Bundestag after the 1969 federal elections.

Fortunately, the NPD's leader turned out to be a poor political prophet. The party did not clear the 5 percent hurdle in 1969 but received only 4.3 percent of the national vote. The setback, along with the rapid economic recovery, deflated the acute threat of rightist extremism. The NPD fell victim to factional infighting and disintegrated rapidly. In the Bundestag election of 1983 its share of the popular vote was only 0.2 percent.

The challenges to parliamentary democracy and the recession of 1966–1967 (see pp. 290–91) formed the background for the creation of the Federal Republic's first bipartisan government, a "great coalition" composed of the CDU/CSU and the SPD. Because of the chancellor's inability to lead the CDU effectively, the Erhard government was in trouble almost from the start. Its fate was sealed when the "father of the economic miracle" was unable to cope with the recession. In the meantime, leaders of the CDU/CSU and the SPD had discussed the formation of a bipartisan government. Adenauer, who continued his public criticism of his successor during the years of his retirement, enthusiastically endorsed the concept. The new cabinet took office at the end of November 1966. Each partner had its own reasons for forming the unusual coalition. The CDU/CSU was anxious to saddle the SPD with part of the responsibility for dealing with the recession, while the SPD, which had not been part of a federal government since March 1930, wanted to show that it could govern responsibly before facing the voters in the next election.

As the stronger party, the CDU/CSU was to provide the chancellor in the bipartisan government. Two men were seriously considered: Gerhard Schröder, one of the leaders of the CDU's Protestant wing and West Germany's foreign minister since 1961, and Kurt-Georg Kiesinger, the prime minister of the state of Baden-Württemberg. The choice between the two candidates was determined to a large extent by Franz Josef Strauss, and the Bavarian leader favored Kiesinger. The post of vice-chancellor and foreign minister fell to Willy Brandt as the leader of the SPD. The Social Democrats also provided the economics minister—at least in the short run the most important member of the cabinet—Karl Schiller, a young economics professor. The "great coalition" was in many ways a watershed in the postwar development of West Germany. Its leaders personified a nation divided that had come together again. Kiesinger, as a young and ambitious career diplomat, had joined the Nazi Party in 1933. During the Third Reich, he remained a nominal party member while working in the propaganda section of the foreign ministry. Willy Brandt, on the other hand, had had to flee Nazi Germany as a teenager, and during World War II he had been active in the political campaigns against Nazism while in exile in Norway and Sweden.

The new government succeeded in bringing West Germany out of the recession, but it was by no means all smooth sailing for the great coalition. The two leaders, Kiesinger and Brandt, did not work well together. Not only did they have quite different personalities, but Brandt resented what he regarded as Kiesinger's attempt to run the foreign ministry from the chancellor's office. More important, the formation of the great coalition essentially suspended the normal processes of parliamentary democracy, which depend on the give and take

between government and a constructive but vigorous opposition. With both SPD and CDU/CSU backing the cabinet, there was virtually no opposition party in the Bundestag. The FDP, which had obtained less than 10 percent of the vote in 1965 could do little in the face of the coalition's parliamentary strength. It was particularly unfortunate that this development came at a time when a new generation of Germans born in the years immediately after World War II reached political maturity. Some of them formed what they called the "extraparliamentary opposition" (APO), a concept that had no constitutional basis in a parliamentary democracy.

It must be remembered that the 1960s were a time of worldwide turmoil. The American protest movement against the Vietnam War, French student revolts, and the activities of the West German APO were all symptoms of a vague but passionate search for a new "life style" and a fundamental change of consciousness. The age of materialism, which in the eyes of young Europeans and Americans had characterized the decade of the 1950s, was to end as a new generation of leaders took charge.

The APO, in reality a few thousand activist university students, exploded on the German scene on June 2, 1967. Students from the Free University in West Berlin had organized a large demonstration to protest a visit by the then shah of Iran to the city. The demonstration erupted into violence and, as a result of clashes between demonstrators and police, one student, Benno Ohnesorg, was killed. The tragedy polarized the country. In the next few weeks demonstrations in virtually all university towns protested against "police brutality" at home and the "fascist" American war in Vietnam. At the same time especially the right wing of the CDU/CSU called for effective measures to deal with the "young hoodlums."

The newspapers owned by West Germany's largest publisher, Axel Springer, were particularly vociferous in their editorial support of demands for the effective suppression of student protest. Springer's papers were read by millions daily (the tabloid *Bild* ["Picture"] alone has a circulation of more than 6 million) and day after day they portrayed the student activists as agents of international communism whose real aim was to extend Moscow's rule to West Germany. This was certainly not true for most of the APO, although the East Germans did subsidize some antigovernment publications. The monthly *konkret* ("concrete"), for example, a successful mixture of soft pornography and leftist politics with a large circulation among high school and university students, received some DM 2 million in laundered funds from East German sources between 1965 and 1968.

The polarization of the country escalated. In April 1968 the most popular APO leader, Rudi Dutschke, was shot and severely wounded by a self-proclaimed nationalist and anti-Communist. The immediate reaction was a new wave of demonstrations all over Germany. Some of those demonstrating attacked and burned some printing plants and editorial offices of the Springer press. Fringe groups in the APO went still further. The firebombing of a Frankfurt department store was a prelude to the terrorist activities that were to plague West Germany in the mid-1970s (see p. 299).

The cabinet of the great coalition was remarkably ineffective in dealing with the signs of unrest. Kiesinger had trouble finding the right words to communicate with the young generation of Germans, and Strauss was one of the leaders in the camp of hardliners. In May 1968, after the violent demonstrations that followed the assassination attempt on Rudi Dutschke, the Bundestag passed a package of Emergency Laws that enlarged the powers of the police in dealing with demonstrations and significantly increased the speed with which leaders of violent demonstrations could be brought to justice.

The Emergency Laws pleased the hardliners, but they did little to alleviate the malaise that had led to the demonstrations in the first place. However, the scheduled election of a new federal president in May 1969 provided an opportunity to show the APO that the establishment was mindful of the changing times. The West German federal president, who has no real power but can be effective as a spokesperson for the nation's concerns, is elected every five years. Since 1949 all of West Germany's presidents had been either Liberals or Christian Democrats. In 1969 the *Bundesversammlung*—an assembly that elects the president, composed of all members of the Bundestag and an equal number of delegates from the state legislatures—had the same political makeup as the Bundestag. The largest bloc of delegates came from the CDU/CSU, but the Social Democrats and Liberals together formed a majority.

The two candidates in 1969 were Gerhard Schröder (CDU) and Gustav Heinemann (SPD). Schröder was well known, respected, and conservative; Heinemann was a political maverick. Originally a Christian Democrat, Heinemann had served in the first Adenauer cabinet as minister of the interior. He resigned in 1950 to protest Adenauer's rearmament plans. Eventually Heinemann joined the SPD. In the great coalition cabinet he was minister of justice, a position from which he repeatedly expressed his understanding of the APO's concerns. The election of Gustav Heinemann, then, would be seen as a breath of fresh air in the rather frozen tableau of West German politics. Heinemann's election required the cooperation of the Social Democrats and the Free Democrats in the *Bundesversammlung*. Walter Scheel, the FDP's new leader, persuaded his party to cast its votes for Heinemann as part of the Liberals' opening to the left, and the Social Democratic candidate was elected.

As it happened, the 1969 Bundestag campaign was scheduled for September, only a few months after the presidential election. The CDU/CSU attempted to "pass the NPD on the right," portraying itself as the guardian of national unity and law and order. The SPD appealed to the voters as a progressive, reform-minded party whose dynamic minister of economics had been primarily responsible for bringing Germany out of the recession. The FDP, finally, sought to gain the benefits of not having participated in the government. It pictured itself as a new, young party unencumbered with the failures of the great coalition.

The results were yet more "massing at the center," although in practice the relatively minor shifts in voter sentiment had a profound impact. The CDU/CSU's share of the popular vote dropped slightly, from 47.6 to 46.1 percent. The SPD did somewhat better, increasing its share from 39.3 to 42.7 percent. The pollsters attributed the Social Democrats' success to the charismatic image of Karl Schiller and the effect of "comrade momentum," that is to say, the snowballing effect of the voters' continued enchantment with the SPD's new image. The FDP vote was a severe disappointment to its new leaders. The Liberals' share of the popular vote went from 9.5 to 5.8 percent.

Since the CDU/CSU remained the strongest party in the legislature, Kurt Georg Kiesinger confidently expected that he would lead a new government. He preferred a coalition with the FDP to a continuation of the great coalition, expecting the Liberals to be contrite and pliable after their defeat in the election. As soon as it became clear, however, in the evening of September 27, that Social Democrats and Free Democrats together would have a very small majority in the new *Bundestag* (it turned out to be a margin of 6 out of 529), Brandt called Scheel with an offer to form a coalition agreement. The Liberal leader accepted immediately.

The FDP-SPD coalition was less of a marriage of political opposites than it might appear at first. True, the two parties were far apart on most economic issues. The Liberals had traditionally taken positions in favor of free enterprise and against powerful unions, while the Social Democrats were historically the party of labor. On the other hand, the new partners agreed on the need for foreign-policy initiatives, and they favored judicial and educational reforms.

On October 21, 1969, Willy Brandt became federal chancellor—the first freely elected Social Democrat head of government since March 1930. The members of the Social-Liberal cabinet, as it was called, included some quite distinguished figures. Walter Scheel turned out to be an effective foreign minister. Karl Schiller continued as economics minister. Helmut Schmidt, another of the rising young Social Democrats, switched from chairing the SPD's Bundestag caucus to serving as the first Social Democratic minister of defense since 1920. Hans-Dietrich Genscher, the deputy chairman of the FDP, headed the interior ministry.

The impact of the Social-Liberal coalition on West Germany's political and social life was profound. Despite its narrow majority in the Bundestag the cabinet was able to push through a reform program that helped to create a more open, less tradition-bound society, while in the area of foreign policy the *Ostpolitik* succeeded in putting West Germany's relations with the Soviet Union and Eastern Europe on a new footing (see pp. 291–94).

In the 1972 election the voters gave the SPD-FDP coalition an overwhelming victory. For the first time since 1949 SPD and CDU/CSU ran almost neck to neck: 45.8 percent for the CDU/CSU, 44.8 percent for the SPD. The Liberals' gamble also paid off; their share of the popular vote rose to 8.4 percent.

The triumph came just before the fall. Less than two years later Willy Brandt left office. In April 1974 West German counterintelligence exposed one of Brandt's personal assistants, Günter Guillaume, as an East German spy. GDR agents in West Germany have long been a serious problem. It was inevitable that East Germany's State Security Service would be able to hide a number of spies among the 3 million refugees who have fled Communist East Germany since 1949. Guillaume was a "mole" of this type. The agent and his wife came to West Germany as ostensible refugees in 1956. Guillaume soon became active in Social Democratic politics and, in 1970, joined the chancellor's office. When his role as a long-time agent was revealed, Brandt felt that his own position was so compromised that he could not continue as head of the government. In May 1974 he resigned as chancellor; Helmut Schmidt became his successor.

The Weakening "Economic Miracle"

In the 1960s West Germany's economy was buffeted by challenges and problems. In 1964, Erhard's first full year in office, all signs pointed to continued growth and prosperity. Industrial production was up by 8 percent, wages and salaries increased by 8.5 percent. Inflation and unemployment were virtually nonexistent. A year later, the Federal Republic went into a serious recession.

There were a number of reasons for the downturn of 1965, not all of them German-made. The mid-1960s saw the beginnings of a worldwide inflationary wave, and the West German economy, with its high dependence on exports, was particularly sensitive to inflationary pressures in the world market. Still, some of the difficulties were undoubtedly the Germans' own responsibility. The earlier boom had stimulated overinvestment, while hiding structural dislocations, such as topical unemployment among coal miners, demographic changes, and the chronic inefficiency of West German agriculture. The sustained growth rates had enabled the country to institute massive retaining and subsidy programs in the 1950s and early 1960s, but the costs were high. In fact, increasingly large expenditures for social services and government subsidies to various interest groups were a primary cause of the recession in the mid-1960s.

When the economy began to slow down the Erhard government was faced with a dilemma. Ever since the runaway inflation of the 1920s Germans have been particularly sensitive about uncontrolled government spending. In an attempt to head off the political and economic consequences of this psychology, the government took immediate steps to slash the federal budget, but the short-term effect was to deepen the recession. For the first time since 1955 unemployment became a significant problem.

Led by the economics minister, Karl Schiller, the grand coalition attacked the recession with a bevy of neo-Keynesian measures. The 1967 budget was balanced partly by tapping the balance-of-payment reserves accumulated in the boom years of the 1950s by the German Federal Bank, but also by raising taxes. Some of these taxes came in the form of surcharges on higher incomes, but in order not to cut off private investment the bulk of the new taxes fell on consumers. Specifically, the Value Added Tax (VAT), a national sales tax whose proceeds are divided between the federal government and the states, was raised to 11 percent. To create a climate of cooperation among the major partners in the economy, Schiller organized the "concerted action," a series of summit meetings between the leaders of labor and management, presided over by Schiller himself. The government's crisis management was successful. By the fall of 1968 the unemployment rate had fallen to 1 percent, and the economy was again growing at an annual rate of 7.3 percent.

Except for the 1966–1967 recession, the economy, until 1974, faced more potential than actual dangers. Some of these would cause serious difficulties for the Social-Liberal coalition in the latter 1970s and 1980s, but until then both money and resources seemed plentiful. There was a chronic labor shortage, especially after the building of the Berlin Wall cut off the stream of refugees from the GDR, but millions of foreign "guestworkers," with Turkey supplying the largest contingent, eased the problem. The massive influx of foreigners, in turn, caused some major social problems (see p. 301), but these lay in the future. For the moment West Germany's booming export industry enabled the government to continue a broadly based social welfare program. Social Security pensions were raised repeatedly during these years, and farm subsidies, in part mandated by the Common Market's CAP, continued to take up a large portion of the federal budget.

The Brandt-Scheel government also spent massive sums on efforts to improve the infrastructure of the society. These included a vast expansion of the network of *Autobahnen*, labor retraining programs (many earmarked for the by-now chronically depressed coal-mining industry), and federal help to construct a whole series of new universities and other institutions of higher learning. Many of these projects would later be criticized as too expensive, but given the continuing growth rates and the obvious need for preparing for structural changes in the West German economy, there was some logic behind the government's decisions. The neo-Keynesians who made economic decisions in the years 1963 to 1974 were convinced that as the tertiary sector of the economy became increasingly important, the country's physical and especially its educational infrastructure had to keep pace.

Ostpolitik

The decade between Erhard and Schmidt also saw some dramatic developments in the area of foreign relations. Instead of concentrating almost exclusively on relations with the United States and Western Europe, the FRG's leaders inaugurated the *Ostpolitik* ("Eastern policy") in an effort to improve West Germany's dealings with the Soviet Union and its European satellites, including the GDR.

The contours of the Cold War confrontation softened as times and leaders changed. In the United States a new generation of leaders headed by John F. Kennedy saw Asia, and specifically Vietnam, rather than Europe and the GDR, as the pivot of East-West relations. On the other side of the Iron Curtain the post-Stalin leaders of the Soviet Union made it clear that they would not sit idly by while the United States and West Germany continued to refuse to acknowledge the "postwar realities" in Europe. Nikita Khrushchev and his successor, Leonid Brezhnev, were determined to see that West Germany acknowledged she had no claim to the areas east of the Oder-Neisse Line, and that there were now two separate and independent states on German soil. The lever was not difficult to find. Ever since 1958 the Soviet Union had periodically reminded the West Germans that Russia held a trump card in this test of wills: The Soviet Union could create a Berlin crisis any time she wished.

This background of a world in flux led to a division of views in the West German foreign-policy establishment. Since the founding of the FRG all responsible leaders in West Germany had agreed that the country is not and does not wish to be a Great Power pursuing a foreign policy independent of its allies. This consensus did not, however, prevent considerable differences of opinion over the arranging of priorities, particularly in the 1960s and 1970s. To begin with there were the "Atlanticists" who, much like Adenauer, felt German-American relations were the bedrock of West Germany's security. They argued for close support of the American positions even if this meant some cooling in Franco-German relations. A second group, the "German Gaullists," whose most prominent spokesman was Franz Josef Strauss, sharply disagreed. They argued that de Gaulle was right: European (and hence German) interests were not necessarily the same as those of the United States, Europe needed to follow its own priorities, including the development of a nuclear strike force that would be under European rather than American control.

Both the "Atlanticists" and the "German Gaullists" were minorities in the German foreign policy establishment. Most decision makers counted themselves among the "new realists." This third group, which certainly included Brandt and Scheel, the leaders of the Social-Liberal coalition, did not reject the FRG's Western orientation. On the contrary, they felt it was precisely West Germany's unquestioned allegiance to the Western camp that would enable her to test the possibility of detente with the Soviet Union and the countries of Eastern Europe. The overall objective of the *Ostpolitik* was to achieve improved East-West relations, politicoeconomic stability for West Berlin, and increased "humanitarian" contacts between East and West Germans. In return, the West Germans would be willing to give up the Hallstein Doctrine and accept Russia's position that the post-1945 boundary changes in Eastern Europe could not be altered without the Soviet Union's agreement.

The *Ostpolitik* did not come into being overnight. In the Erhard cabinet Foreign Minister Gerhard Schröder had followed a policy of "small steps" to bring about a thaw in relations between the Soviet bloc and West Germany. Schröder's initiatives were severely limited, however, since the right wing of the CDU/CSU regarded all such efforts with deep suspicion. In the FDP-SPD government these hindrances did not exist. Willy Brandt and Walter Scheel worked closely together to advance the cause of the *Ostpolitik*. In addition, a major force behind the scenes was Egon Bahr, a former Thuringian who had been Brandt's confidential advisor since the chancellor's Berlin days.

Bahr had been "thinking the unthinkable" for some years. He recognized the Soviet Union's deepseated fears of a reunited and remilitarized Germany. He felt that Russia's legitimate security demands could be met by acknowledging the existence of Russian control over Eastern Europe and East Germany. In a little-noticed speech in 1963 he suggested it was futile to expect the GDR or the Soviet Union to change their repressive character as a result of pressure from the West. "Change resulting from East and West drawing together" (*Wandel durch Annäherung*) was far more likely.

When the Social-Liberal coalition assumed office the evidence that the Soviet Union was not about to be dislodged from Central Europe had just been strengthened. In August 1968 Warsaw pact troops had invaded Czechoslovakia to oust the Communist, but independently minded, Dubček government. American inaction confirmed once again, as had the similar attitude of the United States at the time of the building of the Berlin Wall, that the leader of the West was not prepared to use force to push back the Soviet empire in Europe.

The *Ostpolitik* was a process and a goal whose concrete results were a series of bilateral agreements between West Germany, the Soviet Union, the Communist regimes of Eastern Europe, and finally the GDR. For both prestige and practical reasons, the negotiations began with the Soviet Union. In January 1970, Egon Bahr met with the Russian foreign minister Andrei Gromyko. Eight months later a treaty was signed. The actual terms were not very dramatic. West Germany recognized the "map of Europe," which meant she acknowledged the German losses in World War II, including, of course, the annexation of part of East Prussia by the Soviet Union. The West Germans also agreed to support Moscow's call for an international conference, with both Germanys participating, to legitimize the status quo in Europe. More important from West Germany's point of view, the Soviet Union agreed to put pressure on the GDR to negotiate a *modus vivendi* with the Federal Republic.

In 1970 and 1971 analogous treaties were signed with Poland and Czechoslovakia. Again, the FRG recognized the legitimacy of these countries' 1945 frontiers. In the case of Poland particularly Brandt felt a dramatic, symbolic gesture was needed to underscore the importance of the new relationship. He traveled to Warsaw to sign the treaty, and while there knelt publicly before the Warsaw Ghetto memorial.

The most difficult part of the *Ostpolitik* was the "*Grundvertrag*" (Basic Treaty) with the GDR. Under its aging dictator, Walter Ulbricht, the East German regime had deep fears about any opening to the West and attempted to hinder the progress of the *Ostpolitik* by every means possible. Prodded by the Soviets, the GDR agreed to a meeting between Willy Brandt and the East German prime minister Willy Stoph in the Thuringian town of Erfurt in March 1970, but the conference was not very productive. Embarrassed by spontaneous demonstrations of affection for Willy Brandt among the East Germans of Erfurt, the GDR delegation went out of its way to maintain a frosty atmosphere. In fact, it was not until the Russians forced Ulbricht out of office that meaningful progress could be made.

To be sure, the German-German agreement faced special difficulties. The East Germans wanted full and unequivocal recognition; the FRG was willing to acknowledge the GDR as a sovereign state with recognized boundaries, but not as a foreign nation. To press their point, the West Germans insisted that part of the instruments of ratification for the Basic Treaty include a statement issued by the Bonn government that reiterated the right of all Germans to self-determination through free elections.

The problem of West Berlin was in some ways the most complicated aspect of the *Ostpolitik*. It came up in every one of the negotiations between West Germany and the East European countries, but since the Western Allies retained rights of sovereignty over the Western sectors of the former German capital, any settlement of the Berlin problem required Four Power talks. In 1972, after months of tough negotiations, the Big Four initialed an agreement detailing Western rights of access across the GDR and the nature of the ties between West Berlin and West Germany. The Western Big Three recognized East Germany, in return for which the Russians and the GDR agreed to respect West Berlin's political, economic, and social ties to West Germany. In exchange for a diminished West German political presence in Berlin, the GDR agreed not to interfere with the land, water, and air access routes to West Berlin.

Was the *Ostpolitik* a success? World opinion certainly thought so. In 1971 Willy Brandt received the Nobel Peace Prize largely for his efforts to advance the cause of East-West detente. Brandt was the first German statesman since Stresemann to receive the prize. But the policy was also controversial. The opposition, led by the "German Gaullists," accused Brandt and Scheel of "giving away" German rights and lands, while neglecting the Western alliance in favor of chasing after *ostpolitische* illusions. The CDU/CSU brought a case before the Federal Constitutional Court to test the constitutionality of the Basic Treaty with GDR. The suit claimed recognition of the GDR violated the Basic Law, which postulated a single German nation. Ruling on very narrow grounds, the court decided that the specific terms of the treaty between the FRG and the GDR did not violate the constitution.

Brandt and Scheel countered the criticism by pointing out that Adolf Hitler, not the Social-Liberal coalition, had lost the territories east of the Oder-Neisse Line and divided the German nation. The *Ostpolitik* merely ended a sterile policy that had attempted to deny the consequences of Hitler's actions. As for neglecting the FRG's relations with Western Europe, the Liberals and Social Democrats noted that the coalition had been instrumental in smoothing the way for British membership in the European Common Market as well as enlarging the EEC to include Denmark, Ireland, and Greece.

Today, almost two decades after the *Ostpolitik* treaties were signed, it is perhaps possible to assess the impact of the opening to the East without the emotional overtones of the 1960s and early 1970s. Certainly, West Germany gave up no territories as an result of the *Ostpolitik*. World War II permanently changed the map of Europe, whether the Federal Republic acknowledged this or not. As for the Hallstein Doctrine and the policy of isolating the GDR, by 1970 that strategy had clearly failed. On the other hand, West Germany gained some concrete benefits from the *Ostpolitik*. International recognition of the GDR has led to some internal liberalization in that country. The Federal Republic's economy benefited from the increased trade with Eastern Europe and the Soviet Union that followed in the wake of the treaties with these countries. (In fact, economics played a part in the *Ostpolitik* right from the start: The path to the successful treaty with the Soviet Union was smoothed by a DM 1.2-billion credit package that a consortium of West German banks extended to the Soviet Union.) The absence of recurrent Berlin crisis certainly helped that city and contributed to a lessening of Great Power tensions in Central Europe.

Twenty years after the first *Ostpolitik* initiatives were launched, the principles of that policy have become part of the bipartisan foreign-policy consensus in West Germany.

Whatever hopes Brandt, Scheel, and especially Bahr had had for the *Ostpolitik* as harbingers of a new era of global detente were premature. The *Ostpolitik* could not be (and was not intended to be) separated from the fate of the U.S.-Russian detente, and when the latter failed, little remained of the *Ostpolitik* except a series of concrete agreements devoid of a larger spirit of understanding.

CULTURE AND SOCIETY, 1949–1985

As one would expect, West Germany's social and cultural history evolved in tandem with the profound changes in the country's political and economic life. In 1980 the Federal Republic's population profile was considerably different than it had been thirty years earlier when the FRG was founded. Not only had the population increased rapidly (from roughly 50 million to 61.5 million), but the West Germans were also getting younger. Part of the reason was a baby boom that accompanied the return of prosperity. Then, too, many of the more than 2 million East Germans who fled to the West between 1949 and 1961 were under twenty-five years of age. Finally, toward the end of the 1960s when the labor shortage again became acute, West Germany actively recruited foreign "guestworkers," and many of the 3.4 million persons who had been brought to West Germany by 1974 were also young.

When the FRG's history began, these developments still lay in the future. During the Adenauer years sociologists were more impressed with the evidence that in many ways little had changed in German society; signs of social and cultural continuity seemed to abound. Elite continuity was strong in many areas, including the leadership of both Catholic and Protestant churches, union officials, business executives, and university professors. Social mobility remained low since the educational system restricted upward mobility to a narrow stratum of the population. Throughout the decade of the 1950s only 2 percent of the eighteen-year-olds went on to institutions of higher learning, and virtually all of them came from families in which the father (but not the mother) had graduated from a university.

To be sure, this was not the whole story. As we saw earlier, young professionals who had learned their craft in Allied reduction programs moved early into leadership positions in both the print and electronic media. Equally significant was the striking absence of some traditional sociopolitical elites from the West German scene. For the first time in modern German history neither the Prussian landed aristocracy nor that state's ubiquitous bureaucracy played major roles in the society.

Socioeconomic developments during the Adenauer years created what the sociologist Helmut Schelsky has called a "leveled-off middle-class society." Portions of the traditional upper classes and underclasses were merged into a large middle class consisting of skilled blue- and white-collar workers and technicians. The rural population—and especially the number of independent farmers—declined precipitously. Along with urbanization (and "suburbanization") came secularization and increased leisure time. The average work week declined from forty-eight hours and a six-day week in 1950–1957 to forty hours and a five-day week by the end of the decade. At the same time, the increasing number of women employed outside the home (this development was, in part, a result of the war-related absence of men) affected the traditional patterns of family relations.

Cultural life during the first part of the Adenauer era was still dominated by traditional forms—the print media, radio broadcasting, live theater, concerts, and movies. Especially the last three modes of entertainment tended toward the traditional and established classics rather than avant-garde productions. Average Germans spent much of their leisure time as they always had, in organized club activities ranging from sports to "colonies" of weekend gardeners. As prosperity and leisure increased, vacations and travel became a West German obsession. Growing numbers wanted to spend "the most beautiful weeks of the year" in foreign parts, notably the sundrenched countries around the Mediterranean. The rapidly growing number of privately owned cars (by 1974 West Germany was close to the American level of "motorization") facilitated the mania for travel still further.

Television became a mass medium at the end of the 1950s. The first German TV station began broadcasting in 1952, but as late as 1958 only some 2 million West German households had TV sets. Television programming and administration remained in the hands of the existing radio broadcasting networks. In 1957 the Adenauer government attempted to create a second, commercially financed television network alongside the ARD, but the prime ministers of the *Länder* frustrated these efforts. (ARD is the abbreviation for *Arbeitsgemeinschaft der Rundfunkgesellschaften Dentschlands*, network of broadcasting stations of Germany.) The second channel finally established in 1961—it bears the pedestrian name *Zweites Deutschen Fernsehen* ("Second German Television," ZDF)—is also a publicly financed network run by a politically "balanced" board of directors. It is only in the 1980s, with the availability of cable television, that a number of commercial channels have begun operating.

Much of West German mass culture reflected a desire for material comfort and value stability. There was little concern for searching questions about either the past or the present in the 1950s. Intense concern with "conquering the past" was, for the most part, limited to intellectual circles. A particularly noteworthy and successful effort was the establishment in 1953 of the Institute for Contemporary History in Munich. Largely financed by public funds, the Institute has become a leading clearinghouse for research into the causes and consequences of modern German history, especially the Weimar and Nazi eras.

Most West Germans in the Adenauer era, however, wanted the symbols and symptoms of the *heile Welt* ("intact world")—that is, scenes of harmonious family life and uncomplicated narratives. The films of the 1950s abound with what one angry critic has called *süsser Kitsch* (sweet Kitsch). There were some popular German films, generally comedies starring established stars from the 1930s and 1940s like Heinz Rühmann and Hans Moser, but most films shown in West Germany were American imports. In fact, the Adenauer years also saw a pronounced, if superficial, "Americanization" of German society. It was then that American popular music (especially jazz), films, and fast-food outlets began to proliferate in West Germany.

There is little doubt that most Germans were facile and materialistic, but there was already evidence of a growing generation gap. This was a period of widespread, if naive, idealism among the generation born after 1930. Enthusiasm for European unification ran high, and thousands spent at least some time in youth camps with compatriots from neighboring countries. There was also a sense of atonement for Nazi crimes that expressed itself in such projects as helping to rebuild the bombed cathedral at Coventry. A wave of "philo-Semitism" surged through the generation of young Germans. Many observers noted that the philo-Semites knew as little about Jews and Judaism as the anti-Semites had earlier, but it is also true that these developments were symptoms of a sincere effort to deal with a troubled past. The youthful initiatives are all the more remarkable in that they were undertaken with little guidance from the educational establishment. It was not really until the 1960s that attempts to deal honestly with the Nazi era became part of the regular school curriculum. Until then the "time of troubles" was largely ignored.

The 1960s and 1970s were a period of transition and conflict. The "rock-and-roll generation" that came of age in the 1960s was disdainful of the materialism and self-satisfaction of their elders. Within and outside the APO young West Germans demanded increased chances for social mobility, concern for the ecology, and a greater emphasis on the "quality of life." The "revolt of the young" did not bring about a cultural revolution as some of the leaders had hoped, but especially in the area of education some important and permanent changes were introduced. Against the bitter opposition of the conservative establishment, twelve-year comprehensive schools (*Gesamtschulen*) were established in significant numbers to compete with the three-tiered system dominated by the *Gymnasien* and elite universities.

Student revolts and the vast expansion of the university system undermined the pattern of privilege that tenured professors had traditionally enjoyed in German higher education. Instead, more democratic—often hyperdemocratic—structures of collegial government were instituted. More important in the long run, the self-perpetuation of the educated elite was broken. The number of eighteen-year-olds who went on to institutions of higher learning rose from 2 percent in the 1950s to around 20 percent in the mid-1980s. But here, too, progress was not without its price. Job opportunities have not kept pace with the expectations of social mobility among increasing numbers of university-educated West Germans, and a volatile academic proletariat has been the result.

Literature is perhaps the best mirror of a society's values and problems. In their novels, plays, and films German intellectuals commented on, often critically, the values of their society and molded them as well. In the first part of the Adenauer era the trends we observed for the occupation years continued. Foreign authors, particularly American, French, and British, remained very popular. In the 1950–1951 West German theater season almost as many productions by non-German authors were produced as by German playwrights. It was also symptomatic that the most popular contemporary German-speaking authors were not German but Swiss, Max Frisch and Friedrich Dürrenmatt. Among writers of fiction and poetry there was a return to the pre-Nazi era. A survey among Munich university students in 1950 listed Hermann Hesse, Gerhard Hauptmann, and Rainer Maria Rilke as the three most popular German authors. Ernst Jünger and Gottfried Benn, both of whom had established their reputation as right-wing authors in the 1920s, experienced comebacks with depoliticized and unideological prose. But for the decade as a whole Ernest Hemingway was far and away the bestselling author; Thomas Mann ranked only ninth.

A genuine postwar literature did not

really emerge until the second half of the 1950s. A group of younger writers (that is, of the generation born after World War I) scored major successes in 1959. Virtually all were associated with a literary organization called Group 47, one of the more remarkable intellectual peer groups in German history. The Group 47 was organized in 1947, hence the name, by a number of young authors for the purpose of mutual criticism and encouragement. In 1959 three members of the organization, all previous winners of the annual prize Group 47 awarded to the most promising authors, published works that became international bestsellers.

Heinrich Böll's *Billiard um halbzehn* ("Billiards at Half Past Nine") introduced a laconic, sarcastic look at the Establishment's foibles before and during the Adenauer years. Günter Grass' *Die Blechtrommel* ("The Tin Drum") portrayed the horror and surrealism of the Nazi and early postwar years through the eyes of a child (and later man) who refuses to grow. Finally, Uwe Johnson's *Mutmassungen über Jakob* ("Speculations about Jakob") was an understated novel about the life and death of an East German railway dispatcher. The three authors illustrate well the thematic and stylistic eclecticism of the new German literature. The topics ranged from Böll's concern with the Adenauer years to Grass' obsession with the Nazi era and Johnson's attempt to portray the dilemma of life in East Germany. Stylistically Böll's "neo-verismo" contrasted with Grass' surrealism and Johnson's minimalist, Fontane-like approach.

In the 1960s and 1970s these authors continued to be recognized as major literary talents; in 1972 Heinrich Böll was awarded the Nobel Prize for Literature. Increasingly, however, their work and that of emerging new talents attempted to "conquer the past," which in Germany refers to dealing both with the horrors of Nazism and the effort by the Adenauer establishment to forget the whole experience. As Grass' *The Tin Drum* had done earlier, Heinrich Böll's *Gruppen-*

bild mit Dame ("Group Portrait with Lady," 1971) and Siegfried Lenz' *Die Deutschstunde* ("The German Lesson," 1968) contain central figures who cannot lead "normal" lives because Nazism has destroyed their moral equilibrium. Rolf Hochhuth's *Der Stellvertreter* ("The Deputy," 1963) makes the same point in dramatic form and also accuses Pope Pius XII of moral indifference in the face of his knowledge of Nazi crimes.

The Adenauer era was subjected to growing criticism in the years after the grand coalition came to power. Intellectuals contended that instead of using the opportunity to establish a new and better society, the leaders in the 1950s chose the road of exploitative capitalism, egocentrism, and materialism. Some more radical APO leaders went even further and, following the ideas of Herbert Marcuse's very influential *Der eindimensionale Mensch* ("One Dimensional Man"), whose German edition appeared in 1967, argued that real freedom was impossible under conditions of capitalist democracy. Typical of this sort of view of contemporary society was Bernward Vesper's description of the process of buying a pack of cigarettes:

> . . . the anonymous automat, which makes our subjugation obvious. Sitting there like a trap . . . . The Coins that I insert connect me to a circulatory system: An unknown corporation increases its profits, a huge bureaucracy is financed by my purchase. . . . I, myself an automation, stand before the machine carrying out orders drafted by advertising executives.

Such ideas hardly became commonplace, but it is true that they planted the seeds of the large-scale alienation which bore fruit both among the terrorists of the 1970s and such political and intellectual movements of the 1980s as the Greens.

This sense of alienation was by no means devoid of artistic merits. Critics have been particularly impressed with the series of films directed and produced in the 1970s and 1980s by Rainer Werner Fassbinder. In films like *Effi Briest* (based on the Fontane novel) and *Die Ehe der Maria Braun* ("The Marriage of Maria Braun") Fassbinder, who died in 1982, mounted attacks on the establishment that were also consummate works of art. The intellectuals' effort to confront West Germans with their past has also borne some fruit. The U.S. television production *Holocaust* was seen by 20 million people when it was shown on German television in January 1979; almost a third of the nation saw one or more of the episodes.

West German cultural developments in the post–World War II era, then, were and are dominated by two somewhat contradictory characteristics. On the one hand, West German culture is an integral part of the larger Western scene. This is particularly true for visual art, music, and architecture. Postwar German art was until fairly recently for the most part abstract—just like its American, French, or Dutch counterparts. In the last ten years, however, there has been a return to figurative art in the West. This development was to some extent spearheaded by the New Expressionism that emerged in West Germany in the late 1970s. In rebuilding Germany's cities architects turned to a sort of a neo-Bauhaus style which German refugee architects had already popularized in the United States. However, in the field of literature something of a "Pan-German tradition," to use the critic Marcel Reich-Ranicki's phrase, has continued. As we shall see, East German authors are concerned with many of the same themes as their West German colleagues.

TROUBLED 1970S AND 1980S

Willy Brandt's resignation as chancellor changed the personnel but not the political makeup of the Social-Liberal coalition. The new chancellor was Helmut Schmidt, like Brandt a Social Democrat from northern Germany. (Brandt continued as party chairman after he left the government.) Schmidt had earned a reputation as a tough admin-istrator when he served as minister of the interior in his native city-state of Hamburg during the early 1960s. Subsequently he became an effective leader of the SPD's Bundestag caucus and, after 1969—to use the words of one British observer—an "outstandingly successful" minister of defense in the Brandt-Scheel cabinet. A few months after Brandt left office, Scheel succeeded Heinemann as federal president. His place in the cabinet was taken by Hans-Dietrich Genscher, who also became the new national chairman of the FDP.

Schmidt and Genscher were a less effective team than Brandt and Scheel had been. In contrast to Scheel's bonhomie, Genscher was (and remains) a more secretive politician who guarded anxiously the FDP's "independent profile." The new chancellor, a man who liked to be his own boss, found Genscher's efforts at political autonomy increasingly irritating. In the face of growing personnel, domestic, and foreign-policy problems, it was remarkable that the coalition survived for another eight years.

The most serious domestic challenge in the mid-1970s was a wave of political terror that swept through the country. The domestic reform program enacted by the Brandt-Scheel government (especially the expansion and structural changes in the universities) persuaded most of those active in the APO to join the mainstream parties, but the failure to overthrow the government and "make the revolution" infuriated a small but volatile radical fringe. Some of these elements formed minuscule political sects, some three hundred by 1978, to which the West German Office for the Protection of the Constitution gave the collective name "K-groups" (*K* derived from *Kommunist*). The K-groups have few characteristics in common except a belief that the DKP (and the Soviet Union) have abandoned the path of true Marxism. Their activities are confined almost entirely to student politics. Lacking any real popular support, they are annoying but harmless. Unfortunately, their existence has provided an excuse for the emergence of similar sects on the extreme right.

More serious were the activities of some self-styled anarchist groups, notably the *Rote Armee Fraktion* (Red Army Fraction, RAF) and its spinoffs. The RAF, also known as the Baader-Meinhof gang, was led by an eclectic group of misfits. They included Andreas Baader, a high school dropout; Ulrike Meinhof, the former wife of the publisher of the magazine *konkret*; and Gudrun Ensslin, a sociology student. In the early 1970s these radicals determined that only acts of individual terror would succeed in destablizing West German society to the extent that it would be ripe for a revolution. Between 1974 and 1977 the RAF and its allies were responsible for a series of murders, kidnappings, and bombing attacks. Among the victims of assassination were a West Berlin judge, the head of the FRG's employers' association, and West Germany's solicitor general.

RAF terror did not succeed in destroying the political and social stability of West German society. Despite their numerous contact with various Middle Eastern and Western European terrorist groups, Baader, Meinhof, Ensslin, and most of their associates were eventually captured, tried, and sentenced to long prison terms. (There is no death penalty in West Germany.) Ulrike Meinhof committed suicide while in prison in 1976. A year later an attempt by some Middle Eastern associates to free Baader, Ensslin, and some others by highjacking a Lufthansa passenger plane failed when a special anti-terrorist unit of the Federal Republic's Border Protection Police successfully liberated both plane and passengers in Somalia. When the failure of the highjacking attempt became known, the major imprisoned RAF leaders, including Baader and Ensslin, committed suicide.

Terrorism challenged West Germany's ability to defeat internal subversion without resorting to measures that were not sanctioned by the democratic constitution. By and large, the Federal Republic met the test well, although some of the anti-terrorist legislation was controversial. Civil rights activists objected particularly to a 1977 law mandating a political litmus test for civil servants. The law attempted to exclude opponents of parliamentary democracy from entering the civil service. Some critics in Germany and abroad labeled the law a *Berufsverbot* (prohibition to enter a profession), a term the Nazis had used to exclude Jews and political opponents from public employment. It is certainly true that this sort of political-conscience examination violated at least the spirit of democracy, but it should also be noted that in practice the law was applied very sparingly. Of the 745,000 applicants for civil service jobs between 1977 and 1979, 287 were refused employment for political reasons. Since 1979 the practice of making routine inquiries about prospective civil servants has been abandoned.

The 1976 election confirmed the Schmidt-Genscher coalition in office, but its majority in parliament was cut considerably. The Social Democrats' share declined from 44.9 to 42.6 percent and that of the FDP from 8.4 to 7.9 percent, although Schmidt's personal popularity remained very high. The CDU/CSU opposition increased its popular vote from 45.8 to 48.6 percent, but the CDU had problems of its own. The opposition lacked an effective leader to compete with Helmut Schmidt's increasing popularity. The CDU/CSU's shadow chancellor in 1976, Rainer Barzel, was an experienced parliamentarian, but also a pedestrian public figure. Shortly after the 1976 election a major scandal surfaced around Hans Filbinger, the right-wing CDU prime minister of Baden-Württemberg. Published documents revealed that Filbinger, in his capacity as a *Wehrmacht* judge in Norway, had imposed wholly unnecessary death sentences in the last days of World War II. The Filbinger affair and the CDU/CSU's equivocal attitude in 1979 toward extending the statute of limitations for Nazi war crimes (it was eventually extended by a vote of the Bundestag) gave the CDU/CSU a reputation for attempting to hide Germany's Nazi past.

These developments as well as West Germany's economic difficulties (see p. 301) brought about a realignment of forces on the West German political scene. Frustrated by ten years out of power, the CDU/CSU turned to Franz-Josef Strauss and named him shadow chancellor for the 1980 campaign. It was a politically disastrous decision. The CDU/CSU's popular vote fell to 44.5 percent, while the SPD, helped by the personal popularity of Helmut Schmidt, marginally increased its vote to 42.9 percent. On paper the Liberals were the big winners; their vote share rose to 10.6 percent. However, the figures were somewhat misleading. Closer analysis showed that a significant number of FDP ballots had been "lent" by SPD voters.

Economic problems, concern over acid rain and other ecological matters, opposition to the nuclear arms race, but also Strauss' stridently right-wing campaign facilitated the growth of a new political phenomenon, the Green Party. Founded in 1978, the new group was less a party than an amalgam of local and regional organizations. The "Greens" were convinced that the mainstream parties were not addressing West Germany's most pressing problems, which the newcomers identified as the ecology and the arms race. The members of the new organization came from a wide variety of backgrounds, ranging from some K-groups to macrobiotic food sects and extreme pacifist organizations. Although they already had representation in a number of city councils and state legislatures, in 1980 the Greens' share of the national vote was only 1.5 percent.

Despite its good showing in the election, the days of the Social-Liberal coalition were numbered. Chronic economic problems and the end of detente eroded the grounds of cooperation that had supported the coalition since 1969. In 1982 Genscher and a majority of the Liberals decided to end their cooperation with the SPD and instead form a coalition with the CDU/CSU. Helmut Kohl, a former prime minister of the *Land* Rhineland-Palatinate became chancellor. In the new cabinet Genscher retained his position as foreign minister. Other major figures included Gerhard Stoltenberg (CDU), a former prime minister of Schleswig-Holstein, as finance minister; Count Otto Lambsdorff (another holdover from the old cabinet) as economic minister; and Friedrich Zimmerman, the head of the CSU caucus in the Bundestag, as minister of the interior.

The 1983 elections gave the CDU/CSU-FDP coalition a parliamentary majority, although they also revealed a growing polarization among the voters. The CDU/CSU increased its popular vote to 48.8 percent, but the Liberals suffered from their reputation as political turncoats. The FDP's vote dropped sharply from 10.6 to 7.0 percent. The SPD seemed to suffer from political burnout. Intra-party quarrels and high-handed treatment of the party's left wing lost the SPD votes. Its share of the popular vote fell to 38.2 percent. Many disgruntled, younger SPD voters had given their ballots to the Greens, enabling them to obtain 5.6 percent of the vote to become the first new party since 1953 to clear the 5 percent hurdle.

The 1983 election, like the 1957 contest, was a "stomach election"; this time, however, the issue was not continued prosperity but finding solutions to nagging structural problems. By the 1980s the bloom was off the "economic miracle"; for the first time since the 1950s West Germany's economy experienced not a brief "growth recession" but a long-term leveling off. Two "oil shocks" in 1973 and 1979 fueled inflation (6 percent annually in 1983) and disrupted world trade patterns upon which Germany's export-oriented economy depended. The German economy actually began to show "negative growth rates," that is, it was contracting. At the same time the high cost of the reforms of the 1960s and early 1970s had significantly increased the West German national debt; in 1983 it was approaching DM 55 billion. Compared to other industrialized countries the Federal Republic was still doing well, but for a country that was used to stable prices, rapid growth, and budget surpluses these were disturbing developments. The climate of cooperation between management and labor cooled; the number of strikes increased.

The Schmidt-Genscher cabinet had compounded the problems by inaction and paralysis. The Liberals and Social Democrats disagreed on fundamental policy questions. The economics minister Lambsdorff gave top priority to budgetary belt-tightening, and while Schmidt sympathized with this approach, the bulk of the Social Democrats felt achieving full employment was more important. The government took a series of half measures that satisfied neither side.

Since coming into office the new Kohl-Genscher government concentrated its efforts on deficit reduction, controlling inflation, tax reform, and stimulating private investment. Some of the results were impressive. The federal deficit was cut in half to DM 24 billion and inflation to around 2 percent annually. But growth rates remained sluggish in the mid-1980s (2.5 percent for 1984) and only increased toward the end of the decade. Moreover, despite the increased growth rates unemployment has become a chronic problem, with the jobless rate remaining fairly constant at between 7.5 and 10 percent. That in turn raised some major social issues, including the future of the millions of foreign "guest-workers," whom the country had eagerly sought in the 1960s and 1970s.

The role of the guestworkers in West German society has become the subject to increasingly heated debates. Much of this involves demagoguery and hyperbole ("they are taking away German jobs"), but there are some very real economic and social problems. When German firms began recruiting foreign workers in the 1960s and 1970s their aim was to relieve a labor shortage; little thought was given to the difficulties that the immigrants would confront in adjusting to life in a strange environment. Soon guestworker ghettoes with all their attendant problems became commonplace in many German cities. The district of Kreuzberg in West Berlin, for example, has had a majority of Turkish inhabitants for a number of years. In some inner-city schools a large percentage of students did not speak German as their first language. The difficulties are most severe in the case of the largest contingent of guestworkers, those of Turkish origin. Not only their linguistic and cultural but also their religious traditions are far different from those of Germany. So far the problems have defied solutions. The Social-Liberal coalition worked hard to facilitate the eventual integration of most foreign workers into German society, but as unemployment became a major problem in West Germany that curse of action became increasingly unpopular. The Kohl government, prodded by the energetic but controversial minister of the interior, Friedrich Zimmermann, has relied instead on a variety of monetary incentives to persuade guestworkers to return home—so far with limited success.

The nagging social problems exemplified by the guestworker issue had repercussions for West Germany's political life in the second half of the 1980s. At first all seemed to go well for the new coalition. In the 1983 election the voters gave the Christian Democrats and Free Democrats a clear mandate. The CDU/CSU obtained 48.8 percent of the popular vote, a substantial increase over the results of 1980 (44.5 percent). The Free Democrats were less successful. Their vote fell from 10.6 to 7.0 percent; a number of liberal voters were obviously unhappy with the FDP's sudden switch of coalition partners. Nevertheless, with a combined total of 55.8 percent of the popular vote, the two parties had a clear majority in the new Bundestag.

The victory of the Liberals and Conservatives in 1983 also made possible the 1984 election of a new federal president from the ranks of the CDU, Richard von Weiszäcker.

(The West German president is elected by the "Federal Assembly," a body that is composed of all members of the Bundestag and an equal number of delegates selected by the state legislatures.) In retrospect, Weiszäcker's election was a piece of singular good fortune for West Germany. He has become not only the most popular officeholder in the country but also an internationally respected statesman. Although his office is a largely ceremonial one, the president has used it very effectively to articulate democratic sentiments and the need for consensual politics. In May 1989, Weiszäcker was reelected for a second five-year term; this time he was unopposed.

The 1987 elections brought severe setbacks for the coalition parties. Despite a generally favorable economic climate, the CDU/CSU's vote fell to 44.3 percent, its worst showing since 1949. The FDP picked up a few of the votes lost by its conservative partner (they received 9.1 percent in 1987, as compared to 7 percent in 1983), a circumstance that most observers attributed to the popularity of West Germany's long-time Liberal foreign minister, Hans-Dietrich Genscher, and the corresponding lack of charisma exhibited by the Christian Democratic chancellor, Helmut Kohl.

The most important result of the 1987 election, however, was not the relatively poor showing of the coalition (with a combined vote of 53.4 percent the government remained in office), but the indications of major shifts in the overall political landscape of West Germany. The big winner in 1987 was not the largest opposition party, the SPD (its vote actually fell from 38.2 to 37 percent), but a new force in politics, the Green Party. The Greens were able to increase their popular vote from 5.6 percent in 1983 to 8.3 percent in 1987.

This trend of loosened political contours has continued since 1987, forcing the established parties to scramble for new program and new leaders. Under attack on their left flank, the Social Democrats have attempted to steal the Greens' issues by emphasizing the SPD's concern for ecological matters and the role of labor in the "postmodern" age. At the same time, talks of a possible "Red-Green" coalition after the 1990 election are in the air. There have even been informal talks between leaders of the two parties, and what might be seen as a "practice coalition" at the state level: In February 1989, the SPD and the Greens formed a coalition government in West Berlin.

The Christian Democrats faced similar challenges on the Right. In 1988 a new extreme right-wing group, the *Republikaner* (Republicans), made its appearance. The new party was led by Franz Schönhuber, a former soldier in the Nazi *Waffen-SS*, an actor, and sometime journalist, whom one pundit described as a combination of "Mr. Average and political arsonist." Like similar groups in other West European countries, the Republicans appealed to voters with real or perceived resentments: workers displaced by structural changes, farmers dissatisfied with the Common Market's agricultural policies, and anybody who disliked the "postmodern" world.

In 1988 Franz-Josef Strauss, for many years the unchallenged champion of the German Right, died. With his powerful presence removed from the political scene, the Republicans were able to gain 7.5 percent of the vote in the February 1989 West Berlin election. (For comparisons, the CDU obtained 37.8 percent, the FDP 3.9 percent the SPD 37.3 percent, and the Greens 11.8 percent in the same contest.) A few months later Schönhuber's group repeated its Berlin triumph in the elections for the European Parliament. Here the Republicans were able to obtain 7 percent of the vote, mostly at the expense of the CDU/CSU.

The CDU's and especially the chancellor's primary reaction to his party's declining fortunes (in 1987 the CDU also lost control of the state of Schleswig-Holstein) has been to make personnel changes. Insisting that his policies are correct, Kohl reshuffled his cabinet in the spring of 1989. He dismissed the unpopular minister of defense, Rupert

Scholz, and placed a number of trusted "Kohl men" in key ministries. Even more dramatic was the dismissal of Heiner Geisler, the CDU's longtime secretary general. Widely regarded as the architect of the CDU's good showing in the 1983 election, Geisler made no secret of his conviction that Kohl was increasingly becoming a liability for the Christian Democrats. Whether these personnel changes, which certainly strengthened Kohl's leadership of the party, will be effective in reversing the CDU's misfortunes at the polls, only the 1990 Bundestag election will show. Public opinion polls do not augur well for the incumbent coalition.

One reason for the government's complacency in the face of electoral setbacks is the belief that the recent good news on the economic front, as well as the dramatic changes in the GDR (see pp. 331–34 for a discussion of these events), will be reflected in voter support in upcoming elections. For much of the decade the West German economy has exhibited a lackluster performance. The Kohl-Genscher cabinet could (and did) take pride that its supply-side economic policies had halted the danger of inflation, but in many other areas the record was far less impressive. West Germany's version of the American "rust belt"—the iron- and steel-producing regions in the Saar and Ruhr valleys—languished in need of restructuring. For the nation as a whole, until 1984 the disposable income of the average German worker actually fell from a high point in the 1970s. Incomes began climbing again in 1984, but as late as 1986 they had reached only the levels of 1977. Above all, unemployment remained high; above 2 million, some 9 percent of the workforce.

Beginning in 1987, however, things began to look up. Supply-side economics produced high business profits (after adjustment for inflation, in 1985 wages and salaries rose by 2.5 percent, but capital gains and corporate profits by 7 percent), which in turn led to increased investments, especially in export-oriented industries. And

exports were indeed the "locomotive" that pulled the West German economy. Recession-free economies in the Federal Republic's largest trading partners—members of the European Community and the United States—helped West Germany to amass huge favorable trade balances. Excelerated growth of the economy (almost 4 percent in 1988) finally made a dent in the unemployment figures as well. Unemployment fell to 2.2 million (8.4 percent of the workforce) in August 1988, and a year later it dropped to 1.9 million (7.5 percent of the workforce), its lowest level since 1982.

Foreign relations, too, have grown more complicated since 1974, although both the Schmidt-Genscher cabinet and its successor stressed the continuity of West Germany's foreign-policy aims: ongoing close cooperation with the United States and the EEC, and simultaneous pursuit of improved relations with the Soviet bloc, especially the GDR. The difficulties have been in the area of implementation. Relations between Bonn and Washington especially in the early years of the Reagan era were subject to some strains. The United States has faulted the Federal Republic's backing for American positions in Vietnam and the Middle East, finding it less enthusiastic than Washington would have liked. Most serious, however, was the rift over detente. In the latter 1970s the Soviets began a massive buildup of their nuclear strike force in Europe. Responding to this threat, the members of NATO in 1979 decided on countermeasures in the form of a dual-track response. On the one hand, NATO would strengthen its nuclear capabilities. Specifically, the United States and its NATO partners agreed to station Pershing II and cruise missiles in several Western European countries, including West Germany. At the same time, the members of the alliance voted to pursue intensive negotiations with the Soviets on arms control in the hope that an agreement would make the planned military countermeasures unnecessary.

The Schmidt-Genscher government and

the Reagan administration, which came into office in 1980, attached different degrees of importance to the two parts of NATO's "double decision." The West German policymakers, taking into account the strength of public opposition to new nuclear arms on German soil, emphasized negotiations, while the Reagan administration felt that until the Western defenses had been strengthened and the missiles deployed, the Russians would not begin serious bargaining.

The relaxation of tensions between the superpowers, which made possible the 1987 treaty on the elimination of medium-range ballistic missiles in Europe, inaugurated something of a new era in West Germany's foreign relations. The Federal Republic's longtime foreign minister, Hans-Dietrich Genscher, has been in the forefront of those leaders who argue that the West should actively support the efforts of the new Soviet leader, Mikhail Gorbachev, to institute far-reaching political and economic reforms in the Soviet Union.

As a result, German -Soviet relations have been remarkably free of tensions in recent years. In the fall of 1984 a scheduled visit by the East German leader Erich Honecker to West Germany had been cancelled at the last moment—obviously as a result of Soviet pressure—but in June 1989, Gorbachev himself visited the Federal Republic. He was welcomed by enthusiastic crowds wherever he traveled, and his talks with the country's leaders went extremely well. West Germany has also been notably reluctant to accept the necessity of new short-range missiles on her soil, a stand that led to some disagreements with the new Bush administration.

Reaction to these moves has not been uniformly positive. Especially in the United States some commentators expressed fears that West Germany's continued pursuit of detente would lead to her "Finlandization," that is to say, she would opt out of the Western camp in favor of neutralism. The Russians were far more blunt in indicating

their displeasure of closer ties between West Germany and the GDR.

Both the Social-Liberal coalition until 1983 and the Christian Democratic-Liberal government of the mid-1980s tried to continue the *Ostpolitik* as best they could. Relations with the Russians cooled considerably after Brezhnev's death, but mutual acrimony between West Germany and East Germany has given way to cooperation. In 1978 the two governments signed an agreement for the construction of an *Autobahn* between Berlin and Hamburg, and five years later the Kohl government guaranteed a DM 1-billion commercial credit for the GDR in return for the prospect of further "humanitarian" concessions for the East German people.

In 1989 relations between the two countries briefly became acrimonious again. In the summer and fall tens of thousands of young East Germans took advantage of the more liberal policies in some of the East European countries to escape to West Germany. By the end of the year more than 200,000 persons had fled the German Democratic Republic and settled in West Germany. The East German government angrily protested what it called a concerted media effort by the West Germans to "lure" East German citizens to the West as an unacceptable "interference in the internal affairs of the GDR."

But the collapse of the GDR's Communist regime in the fall of 1989 virtually overnight dramatically altered the relationship between the two German states. Suddenly the borders were opened, there were discussions of agreements for large-scale economic cooperation, and unification seems a realistic possibility in the foreseeable future.

CONCLUSION

Uncertainties characterized the situation of the present-day Federal Republic. It is true, as one government publication put it, that the last forty years have been "a mandate for democracy." Consensus remains high, and political extremism is not a serious problem. The overwhelming majority of West Germans endorses close cooperation with the United States and the countries of Western Europe. The economy remains solid, especially in comparison with the lackluster performance of some of the FRG's West European trading partners.

In 1989 the Federal Republic celebrated its fortieth anniversary with a flood of self-congratulatory articles and books. Yet, in the midst of the celebration of success it was difficult to overlook a note of creeping anxiety. One major West German newspaper caught this mood well when it described the FRG as a forty-year-old "provisional entity." The country's capital, Bonn, is an urban embodiment of the sense of hovering between past and present that characterizes much of German life. Despite some present-day pretensions to international sophistication, the federal capital retains some of the flavor of a sleepy university town on the Rhine.

Moreover, a mood of pessimism or at least uncertainty about the future was spreading. Public opinion polls in the early 1980s revealed that some 8 million West Germans felt *angst* about the future, and about a third of West Germans under twenty-five were convinced the future would not be better than the past. This phenomenon of youthful alienation is undoubtedly linked to the immediate economic problems, but there is also widespread concern about less tangible issues, like the threat of ecological disaster or the possibility of reunification. Like much of Western Europe, the Federal Republic stands at a crossroad but West Germans face some peculiar problems of their own. The future remains shrouded, but it is clear that the simplistic answers of the 1950s and 1960s provide inadequate guideposts for the 1990s and beyond.

CHAPTER 11

THE GERMAN DEMOCRATIC REPUBLIC, 1949–1990

Dealing with the troubled path of German history has always been difficult for leaders of the German Democratic Republic (GDR). While West Germany sees herself as the legitimate heir of all German history, and officially continues to pursue the goal of national unification, the East German rulers have alternately (and sometimes simultaneously) proclaimed a number of contradictory self-images.

Until the late 1950s they insisted that there was a common German history and a single German nation. During these years the East German regime claimed that only the West German government and its American backers prevented Germany's reunification and evolution toward socialism.

The adoption of a new national flag in 1959 (until then both East Germany and West Germany had the same red-black-gold flag; the GDR now added a hammer-and-protractor emblem to its banner) signaled the beginnings of a new line. After the building of the Berlin Wall the regime increasingly stressed *Abgrenzung* (demarcation) between East and West Germany. In 1972 Albert Norden, the chief propagandist of East Germany's ruling Communist party, proclaimed that Germany had always been two nations, one bourgeois, the other proletarian, with no common ground between them. This view was officially sanctioned by a new East German constitution in 1974, which dropped all of the references to a single German nation that had been part of the GDR's earlier constitutional documents. Since then the regime has mounted vigorous propaganda campaigns stressing patriotic pride among its citizens with the slogan "my fatherland is the GDR."

But there is another side to the GDR's attitude toward Germany's past. In contrast to the official line, most East Germans have never looked upon West Germany as a "foreign" country, or felt that Germany's common history has no meaning for them. In recent years the GDR's rulers, who always insisted that their nation represented all progressive forces in German history, have attempted to appropriate such "all-German" historical personages as Bismarck, Frederick the Great, and Luther who, at first glance, hardly seem "progressive" in a Marxist-Leninist sense.

In 1981 Erich Honecker, until quite recently East Germany's Communist leader, all but returned to the GDR's original position. He proclaimed that "one day" the "workers of the Federal Republic would begin the socialist reconstruction of the FRG," thereby creating the basis for a reunification of the country. In the meantime Honecker acknowledged that while there are two German states, there remains a common German nationality.

There is finally the irony that East Germany, for all its pretensions to representing Germany's socialist future, has always been more like the "old" Germany than the "new" Federal Republic. The GDR's physical appearance, its authoritarian political system, and even its social relations contain vivid reminders of life in Germany and especially Prussia before 1945.

THE QUEST FOR VIABILITY

Although many of the concepts and terms used in East German official parlance—elections, democracy, progress, prosperity, people, and parliament—are familiar to Western readers, East Germany emerged from the ravages of World War II to develop into a "socialist" society in the Marxist-Leninist sense. In practice, the GDR was controlled by the Communist party and its affiliated organizations.

The contradictions between idealistic catch-phrases and actual political practice were already apparent in the GDR's first constitution, adopted in October 1949 by the Third People's Congress for Unity and

a Just Peace. On the surface this document seemed to enshrine the principles of federalism and parliamentary democracy. The country was divided into five *Länder*, Brandenburg, Mecklenburg, Saxony, Saxony-Annhalt, and Thuringia; all five had either been separate states or Prussian provinces in the Weimar era. Whole passages, especially in the section dealing with civil liberties, were lifted verbatim from the earlier Weimar constitution. The document permitted a multiple-party system and free elections. The constitution also gave workers the right to organize unions and to strike. The reality of political practice in the GDR, however, was determined not so much by the words of the constitution as by the ideology of Marxism-Leninism as interpreted by the East German Communists and their allies in Moscow. This lack of real reliance on the constitution also explained the lack of permanence for what should have been the basis of the GDR's political and social system. As the party line changed, so did the constitution. Since 1949 there have been four separate constitutions in the GDR.

The key to understanding the 1949 constitution was the concept of a people's democracy as enunciated by the Soviet leaders and the East German Communists. According to Soviet ideologists by 1949 the countries of Eastern Europe, including East Germany, had reached this level of societal development—"people's democracy"—and were but one step behind the Soviet Union, which had already achieved socialism. In a people's democracy elements of society's bourgeois-capitalist structure are thought to remain in existence (hence the Western-sounding constitution), but real power is in the hands of the class of workers and peasants. Under the guidance of its political vanguard, the Communist party, the proletarian class was to lead the GDR toward socialism.

In the case of East Germany the Socialist Unity Party (SED), in cooperation with the Communist Party of the Soviet Union, claimed the historic right and duty to "create socialism on German soil." For this reason the role of the SED was pivotal for understanding the history of the GDR, even though the party's role was not even mentioned in the country's constitutions until 1968.

The principle of the SED's societal leadership is well illustrated by elections in the GDR. The members of the People's Chamber (*Volkskammer*), the East German legislature, are elected regularly every four years, but the voters have no genuine choices in selecting their representatives. Rather, voters "elected" the entire list of candidates presented on the ballot, more than half of whom were always members of the SED, by dropping a printed ballot into a box. A "no" vote or not voting at all was considered a sign of asocial behavior. GDR statistics invariable reported "yes" votes above 99 percent for the official list of candidates.

For many years the SED slavishly followed the Communist Party of the Soviet Union in its structure and ideology. In theory, policy and programmatic decisions were made by the SED's Party Congress, which met every four years. The delegates were ostensibly elected by the membership-at-large. The congress in turn elected a Central Committee (CC), consisting of between 150 and 200 members and "candidates." (As in the Soviet Union, candidate members have a voice, but no vote on the committee.) The Central Committee acted in the name of the congress when the latter was not in session. The CC in turn elected the Politburo, a body consisting of between fifteen to twenty-five members and candidates, whose members staffed a variety of commissions that paralleled the major government ministries and offices.

All of this sounds reasonably democratic in a Western sense, but again the appearance is deceptive. In reality, the principle of democratic centralism transforms the appearance of making policy and personnel decisions from the bottom up to the reality of control from the top down. While infor-

mation did filter upward through the ranks of the membership at large, all substantive decisions were determined by the Politburo and rubberstamped by the Central Committee and the periodic congresses. The members of the Politburo had a final say on all appointments in the *nomenklatura* (the East Germans use the Russian term), the list of major positions in the party, the government, and the economy. The Politburo also selected delegates to the congresses.

The SED's congresses permitted neither free debate nor democratic decision making, but over the years they have been important as indicators of major shifts in policy, ideology, or personnel. The July 1950 congress, for example, signaled the increasingly close alignment between the SED and the Communist Party of the Soviet Union, and the victory of the "exile" Communists over the KPD and SPD members who had remained in Germany during the Nazi era. Shortly after the congress, the newly elected Politburo launched a massive purge of the SED's membership. Some 150,000 party members were expelled as sympathizers of the "Tito clique." (In 1948 Moscow broke with the Yugoslav Communist leader Josip Broz Tito. "Titoism" was therefore a form of "anti-Soviet deviationism.")

The SED, of course, did not limit its role in East German society to resolutions and doctrinal announcements. Numerous officials held party and government jobs simultaneously, providing critical links between party and government at all levels of administration. Most members of the Politburo were also ministers in the GDR's cabinet. In 1952 the federal structure of the GDR, provided for in the 1949 constitution, was abolished, and the five *Länder* were replaced by fourteen districts. After that all of the chiefs of district administration were SED functionaries. The Politburo also had direct control of the system of political repression in the GDR. In 1950 the ministry for state security (*Ministerium für Staatssicherheit*), known in the GDR as *Stasi*, was established. The minister of the *Stasi* was invariably a member of the Politburo, who reported directly to the party body rather than to his colleagues in the cabinet.

The SED's control of the major mass organizations also constituted an important aspect of its system of political and social manipulation. The concept of the people's democracy assigned mass organizations a specific role as "transmission belts" in creating and maintaining a "socialist mentality," particularly among segments of the society that had not yet achieved a "proletarian consciousness." The purpose of the mass organizations was openly political; for this reason the Communists regarded it as indispensable that members of the SED, as the most "advanced" segment of society, should occupy leading positions in the mass organizations. Among the most important of these groups were the labor unions (*Freier Deutscher Gewerkschaftsbund*, FDGB), the GDR's youth organization (*Freie Deutsche Jugend*, FDJ), the German Women's Association (*Deutscher Frauenbund*, DFB), and the Association for German-Soviet Friendship (*Gesellschaft für Deutsch-Sowjetische Freundschaft*, DSF). All of these mass organizations, as well as several others, formed institutionalized components of the East German political and social system. Their theoretical functions changed somewhat as the GDR advanced from the status of a people's democracy to that of "developed socialism," but their main task remained the installation of a "socialist mentality" among all segments of East German society.

Paralleling the "positive" controls of the mass organizations was a system of political repression. Freedom of expression in the Western sense did not exist in the GDR. Press, radio, and all other media were tightly censored to prevent the airing of views "contrary to the interests of the people." *Stasi* officials—160,000 thousand by 1988—kept their eyes on every sphere of activity. Beginning in 1950 Western countries, particularly the Federal Republic and the United States, were classified as "warmongering" states. Expressing views favorable to these "warmongers" became a criminal offense.

The leaders of the GDR regarded the development of a sophisticated, industrialized economy in East Germany as the key to building socialism in the GDR and later all of Germany. It was a formidable task. Except for some deposits of soft coal and potash, the GDR had (and has) few natural resources. On the whole, agricultural land has always been poorer east of the Elbe than on the Western side. Human decisions added to the natural difficulties. The Soviets' policy of "first charge" for reparations, which they did not abandon until 1952, massively weakened East Germany's productive capacity. Until 1952 some two hundred industrial enterprises, the SAGs, which included many of the country's largest industrial firms, produced exclusively for export to the Soviet Union.

Above all, however, the Communist regime in East Germany imposed upon the country a system of economic planning and production that maximized politicization and centralized control while minimizing individual initiative and responsibility. Following the path charted by Stalin for the Soviet Union in the 1930s, the decade of the 1950s marked the systematic advance of collective—that is to say, state and party—control of the major sectors of the economy. A key milestone in the nationalization of the GDR's economy was the restoration of the SAGs to East German control in 1952. These production facilities were not returned to their former owners, but were converted immediately into *Volkseigene Betriebe* ("people-owned enterprises," VEB) and placed under the direct control of the state. By the end of the decade privately owned companies constituted only a minor part of the East German economy. (In 1949 almost 40 percent of East Germany's productive capacity was in private hands; by 1960 that figure had sunk to 3.8 percent.)

Another plateau in the takeover of the economy came in 1959–1960 when the regime decided to collectivize East Germany's

A West German view of Stalinization in the GDR. Pieck and his dog, Ulbricht, are herding the East German people (sheep) into a barred stable with a Soviet red star over the entrance. (Source: *Lachen*, p. 337.)

agriculture. By 1963 more than 90 percent of the GDR's farmers worked on Agricultural Production Cooperatives (*Landwirtschaftliche Produktionsgenossenschaften*, LPG), or collective farms.

The East German leaders considered rapid growth rates and an accelerated pace of industrialization indispensable corollaries to nationalization for the construction of socialism. The first Five Year Plan voted at the SED's 1950 congress targeted a 100 percent increase in the GNP over the levels of 1936 and a 72 percent increase in productivity. The party also assigned absolute priority to the heavy industry sector (steel, electrification, machinery). The manufacture of consumer products was considered relatively unimportant.

Nationalization meant not only the elimination of private enterprise but also massive centralization of decision-making authority in the economy. Individual VEBs received their orders from one of eight economic ministries (heavy industry, light industry, and so on). The government directives in turn were implementations of the multi-year plans worked out by the state planning commission. Following the Soviet example, these documents were extremely detailed, determining not only what and how much was to be produced, but also wages, hours, and prices. Until 1958, when the system was changed (see pp. 316–17), the individual manager of a VEB had very little autonomy for executive decisions.

Especially in the early part of the 1950s—when the West German boom was just beginning—the centralized economic system in the GDR did not work well. Success, such as it was, came in spite of, rather than because of, the system. The lack of resources, coupled with politically determined production goals and an unwillingness to give economic managers (not to mention labor) the freedom to make decisions, led to chronic shortages and widespread public dissatisfaction. The plan fell particularly short in meeting its goals in areas not accorded top priority, that is, consumer-oriented and light industries. Agricultural production was similarly treated as an economic stepchild. The regime tried to make up for a serious shortage in investment capital by increasing work norms and sponsoring "socialist competitions" in the manner of the Stalinist *stakhanovite* campaigns of the 1930s, but ideological incentives were no compensation for a miserably low standard of living and lack of political freedoms.

The most visible result of the GDR's misguided economic policy was a development that in itself further worsened the situation in East Germany: The GDR's citizens "voted with their feet." Taking advantage of the open frontier in the city of Berlin, between 1949 and 1961, 2.5 million East Germans moved permanently to the Federal Republic. Moreover, to the consternation of the regime's leaders, almost half of the refugees were under twenty-five years of age, so that the country was steadily losing a major part of the economically most productive segment of its population.

The GDR's reaction to the massive signs of dissatisfaction (between 1950 and 1952 alone there were more than 500,000 refugees) was not to reconsider its economic course, but to intensify the pace of development and tighten the screws still further. In July 1952 the SED's Central Committee voted to "accelerate the construction of socialism." There was to be even more emphasis upon heavy industry at the expense of consumer goods. To achieve the new plan objectives, production norms and work hours were increased. Food rations, however, would remain low and unchanged.

Stalin had given his approval both to the GDR's original Five Year Plan and to the mid-1952 changes, but in March 1953 the Russian dictator died. The new Soviet leadership, confused and unstable, sent a different message to East Berlin. As early as April 1953 the Russians urged the East German authorities to reduce economic pressures and appease popular discontent. In response, on June 9, the SED's Politburo adopted a new line: It voted to introduce the "New Course." This new policy provided for an increase in the production of consumer goods, a halt to further nationalizations, and some incentives for those who had fled the West to return to the GDR. However, like Stalin's successors in the Soviet Union, the SED leaders were divided. Walter Ulbricht, the secretary general of the party since July 1950, and some other Stalinists followed the new Soviet line only reluctantly. On the other hand, Rudolf Herrnstadt, the editor of the SED's official newspaper *Neues Deutschland*, and Wilhelm Zaisser, the head of the *Stasi*, were in the forefront of those arguing for more economic reform and less political repression.

Despite its good intentions, the New Course failed to ease tensions in East Germany because it did not address the one feature of the old plan most resented by many East German workers: an additional arbitrary increase in work norms decreed at the end of May 1953. On June 17, 1953, spontaneous demonstrations and strikes erupted among East Berlin's construction workers. They were soon joined by others. At first the workers demanded only an immediate rescinding of the increased norms, but when the regime resisted agreeing to this concession, the strikes quickly became a full-scale, nationwide political uprising. The population demanded free elections, parliamentary democracy, and reunification with West Germany. In numerous localities angry demonstrators set fire to SED offices and hauled down red flags. By the afternoon of June 18, the regime had lost control of the situation; units of the *Volkspolizei* (People's Police, VP) sent out to contain the crowds often fraternized with the demonstrators. It was not until the Soviets intervened with tanks and troops that order was restored.

The reaction of the East German leadership to the June uprising was an inconsistent mix of purges and tactical concessions. Ulbricht and other Stalinists moved quickly against the reformers in the Politburo. Both Zaisser and Herrnstadt were accused of anti-party activity and expelled from the party. And the purge was not restricted to the top echelons. At least eighteen lesser functionaries were executed for their failure to contain the uprising. More than half of the SED's district party secretaries and almost two-thirds of the county secretaries were dismissed. Among rank-and-file members a large-scale purge took place as well.

The collapse of the June 1953 uprising marked the end of the first phase of the GDR's history. The unrest had demonstrated the regime's lack of popularity, but also the Soviets' determination to maintain Communist control in East Germany. Beginning in the summer of 1953 the GDR's rulers set out to repair their shaken power position. For a time the average, nonpolitical East German experienced relief from the pressures of "accelerated construction of socialism." In July 1953 priorities for the Five Year Plan were permanently readjusted. The projected annual growth rate for heavy industry dropped from 13 to 5.6 percent while the output of consumer goods was to be increased by 30 percent. The regime announced an end to arbitrary arrests, and intellectuals were promised greater artistic freedom (see p. 322). These changes were not without positive effects. The stream of refugees, until 1961 always a good barometer of public opinion in the GDR, decreased from 331,330 in 1953 to 184,198 a year later.

In retrospect, it is clear that Ulbricht and his allies never regarded the New Course as anything but a tactical and temporary maneuver. However, others among the SED's leaders demanded permanent policy changes. Encouraged by Nikita Khrush-

chev's denunciation of Stalin's errors at the 1956 Twentieth Congress of the Soviet Communist Party, they argued that the GDR needed to become a more decentralized and open society. The SED should permit greater freedom for intellectuals and more autonomy for economic managers. These leaders also advocated better relations between East and West Germany. The group included Wolfgang Harich, East Germany's leading Marxist philosopher and editor of a major ideological journal, *Deutsche Zeitschrift für Philosophie* ("German Journal for Philosophy"); Fred Oelssner, the secretary for propaganda of the party's Central Committee; and Fritz Selbmann, the head of the State Planning Commission.

For a time, the SED's old guard was put on the defensive, but in the spring and fall of 1956 the Hungarian Revolution and widespread unrest in Poland inadvertently strengthened the position of Ulbricht and the SED's conservatives. The Russians feared for the cohesion of their satellite system and hastily withdrew their support of further liberalizations. This left the East German reformers isolated and vulnerable. In November 1956 Harich was arrested on a charge of conspiracy and "revisionism." He was subsequently sentenced to ten years in prison. Selbmann and Oelssner lost their government positions and were purged from the party. The SED's July 1958 Congress gave official party sanction to the restored hard line. The congress confirmed that the GDR had now achieved "the foundations of socialism."

A superficial glance revealed some striking parallels in the foreign relations of the Federal Republic and the GDR during the decade of the 1950s. Both countries wanted to establish their international viability, and that required recognition from their sponsoring superpower and its allies. For West Germany support from the United States was of paramount importance, while the GDR needed approval from the Soviet Union. At the same time, these surface parallels should not obscure some fundamental differences in the relations of the FRG to its allies and those of the GDR to the Soviet Union and the countries of Eastern Europe. The new West German republic was an open society whose political system was supported by the overwhelming majority of the people. In sharp contrast, the GDR's leaders were dependent upon the physical presence of Russian troops to maintain themselves in power. As a result the relationship of the GDR and the Soviet Union, at least until the 1960s, was not an alliance that both partners chose freely; East Germany remained a Russian satellite.

Still, the formal steps that led to the GDR's integration into the Eastern bloc in large part paralleled the process by which the FRG joined the Western alliance. As was true for West Germany, economic ties preceded political ones. East Germany was accepted into membership in the East European Council for Mutual Economic Aid (Comecon) in 1950, although the GDR did not become a formally sovereign state until September 1955 when East Germany and the Soviet Union signed a treaty of friendship. Soviet troops remained stationed in East Germany, but since 1955 they have been there officially at the invitation of the East German regime. In the same year the East German state joined the Warsaw Pact, the Soviet bloc's equivalent of NATO.

Along with East Germany's technical sovereignty came diplomatic recognition by all of the countries of the Soviet bloc. In contrast to West Germany, the GDR did not maintain any claims to Germany's lost territories. Rather, as part of the agreements between East Germany and the other Soviet satellites, the GDR recognized the de jure legitimacy of the de facto annexations of the territories east of the Oder-Neisse Line by Poland and the Soviet Union.

Before 1961 the GDR was unsuccessful in breaking through the barrier of the Hallstein Doctrine. The West Germans, their Western Allies, and most of the countries of the Third World did not recognize East Germany. To end this isolation the Soviets

and the East German regime repeatedly proposed official talks between the East and West German governments as a prelude to a confederation of East and West Germany. What appears to have been the most serious offer came in March 1952. The Soviet Union and the GDR suggested that after a period of confederation between the GDR and the FRG, there would be free elections for an all-German government. Scholars are divided about the real aim of Stalin's initiative. Some regard it as an obvious propaganda ploy to prevent West German rearmament (this was the time of the debate over the European Defense Community [EDC] in West Germany), while others, without denying this motive, claim that the Russians were also sincerely interested in exploring the possibility of exchanging German reunification for permanent demilitarization of the entire country. In the end it did not matter, since both Adenauer and John Foster Dulles rejected the Russian proposal out of hand.

Toward the end of the decade there were increasing signs that the dream of a united Germany under Communist or neutral control had been abandoned, and that the GDR was determined to seal itself off from the West. In December 1957 a new law made *Republikflucht* (flight from the republic) a criminal offense. A year later, Khrushchev, who needed a triumph after the Hungarian and Polish disasters of 1956 to overcome the challenge of his opponents in the Soviet Central Committee, heeded the pleas of the GDR's leaders to adopt measures that would put an end to the flow of refugees and help the SED consolidate its control over the GDR. In November 1958 the Russians unilaterally abrogated the Four Power agreement on Berlin and issued an ultimatum to the Western Big Three. The Soviets set a deadline of six months for negotiations that would lead to an agreement recognizing West Berlin as a "free and independent political entity." Western troops were to be removed from the city. If the Western Allies did not agree to the proposal, the Russians threatened to turn the fate of West Berlin over to the GDR.

In their reply to the Soviet ultimatum, the Western powers enunciated three "essentials" of their Berlin policy: guaranteed access from West Germany to West Berlin, undisturbed use of the air corridors, and guarantees for the viability of the Western sectors. The "essentials" did not involve East Berlin, and they did not include a demand for continued unrestricted travel between East and West Berlin. Since it was the last which was of major concern to the Russians and the GDR, the Western reply was, from their point of view, an encouraging development.

Shortly after midnight on August 13, 1961, East Germany began the construction of the Berlin Wall. The Wall was quite literally that, a concrete barrier preventing uncontrolled travel between East and West Berlin. Travel between the two halves of the city became possible only by passing through one of four check points manned by East German guards. The barrier began in Berlin, and in the next few months it was extended along the entire boundary between East and West Germany. The physical barrier was reinforced by sophisticated electronic detection devices and heavily armed guards.

The Western Allies protested vigorously against the Wall as a violation of the Potsdam Agreements providing for Four Power control over all of Berlin, and there were some tense scenes as American tanks rumbled close to the Eastern sector. But, as the Russians had anticipated, the West took no concrete measures to force a dismantling of the barrier between East and West Germany.

The Wall was simultaneously the GDR's greatest success and its most abject failure. On the one hand, the barrier made obvious that the East German regime had been unable to win the voluntary consent of its own people. At the same time, the Wall demonstrated that the GDR's existence could no longer be ignored. The West Germans, the Western Allies, and above all the East German people could not wish the SED's regime away. After August 1961 the East Germans had no choice but to deal with the reality of their country. The flow of refugees stopped abruptly. In all of 1962, 21,356 persons succeeded in reaching West Berlin and West Germany; this was less than half of the figure for the first twelve days of August 1961. (47,433).

THE ULBRICHT ERA

The building of the Berlin Wall brought to a climax a development that had been increasingly apparent since 1958: The rise to undisputed power of the SED's first secretary, Walter Ulbricht. The party secretary's triumph over the Harich group at the party's 1958 congress also assured his own undisputed power. Ulbricht became the object of increasing public displays of adulation. It was the Wall, however, that became the real foundation for Ulbricht's unchallenged rule and ambitious plans.

The GDR's powerful and hated leader was a personally unprepossessing individual. Walter Ulbricht was the epitome of a party functionary. Born in 1893 in Leipzig as the son of a tailor, he learned a trade as a carpenter but soon became a full-time political functionary. In 1919 Ulbricht joined the newly founded KPD, and by 1921 he was the party's district leader in Thuringia. Two years later he was elected to the KPD's Central Committee, and in the last years of the Weimar Republic Ulbricht headed the party in Berlin. After the Nazis came to power Ulbricht went into exile, spending the years of the Third Reich in the Soviet Union. Throughout the Stalinist purges he never wavered in his support of the Soviet dictator's policies. (Ulbricht, for example, heaped fulsome praise on the Nazi-Soviet Pact in the years 1939–1941.) As we saw, in April 1945 the Red Army brought the Communist leader back to Germany.

For the Marxist-Leninist ideologists in the SED, reaching socialism in the GDR was of more than semantic significance. The process had important implications for the role of the Communist Party in East German society. The SED was no longer just the spokesperson for the interests of the dominant class in East Germany; it was the institution charged with the "scientific management of society." In other words, as the GDR made its leap toward socialism, the party would take an even greater direct role in influencing all aspects of social life.

A new constitution adopted in 1968 gave legal sanction to the SED's new role. Article 1 of the new constitution described the GDR as "a socialist state which under the leadership of . . . its Marxist-Leninist party is building socialism." At the end of the 1960s Ulbricht proclaimed that the GDR had reached the stage of "developed socialism."

As the SED increased its power in East German society, Ulbricht's personal stature grew as well. In September 1960 Wilhelm Pieck, the jovial president of the GDR and co-chairman of the SED, died. Instead of naming a successor, the regime replaced the office of president with a twenty-eight-member State Council; Ulbricht became its chairman. Four years later, Otto Grotewohl, East Germany's prime minister since 1949 and the GDR's most prominent former Social Democrat, also died. He was succeeded by Willy Stoph, another old-line Communist, who had been minister of defense since 1956.

During the 1950s the SED was dominated by veteran Communists of the Weimar and Nazi era and characterized by frequent factional strife. In contrast, the Ulbricht era was a period of orderly transition and rejuvenation. In 1963 the Politburo consisted of fourteen members and nine candidates. All of the full members had served on the highest party body since 1958 (ten since 1954), but the entire group of candidates was newly elected in 1963. Here, then, lay the personnel basis for what Ulbricht hoped would be his continued power. The trend

was even more noticeable in the numerically larger Central Committee. By 1963 the majority of its members were functionaries who became politically active only after World War II. The social composition of the party's rank-and-file membership was also changing rapidly. The SED was successful in attracting large numbers of blue-collar workers to the party. Between 1961 and 1971 the percentage of those who listed their occupation as "workers" increased from 33.8 to 56.6 percent. Perhaps most significant, however, the party was becoming accepted as the vehicle to power and success even by groups outside the working class. The percentage of members from the "intelligentsia" almost doubled in the same period, from 8.7 to 17.1 percent.

Ulbricht's rising personal stature ironically coincided with Khrushchev's repeated denunciations of Stalin's cult of personality. In 1956 and again in 1961 the Russian leader attacked Stalin's excessive vanity and praised Lenin's supposed adherence to the principles of collective leadership. Ulbricht gamely followed suit, but in the process he subtly enhanced his own stature. Since in the 1960s it was no longer necessary to deny the significance of the German socialist tradition in favor of praising Stalin and the Russians, Ulbricht was able to portray himself (or have others do so) as the culmination of an ongoing line of leaders that included Marx, Lenin, and Thälmann before him. At the end of the 1960s Ulbricht boldly put the GDR's status as a developed socialist state on the same level as that of the Soviet Union. He also suggested the two societies would remain parallel for some time to come—implying that the Russians would not soon push ahead to reach true communism.

The SED's enlarged role in East German society became apparent as well in the reallocation of Volkskammer seats and the redefinition of the role of the non-Communist parties in the GDR's political life. In 1963 the composition of the GDR's legislature was changed to give the Communists an even greater majority among the delegates. Until then the SED had been allotted 100 seats in the Volkskammer, and the non-Communist parties (Liberals, Christian Democrats, Conservatives, and Farmers) 45 each. The remaining 110 seats went to representatives of the mass organizations; virtually all of these were also SED members. Now the number of SED and mass-organization delegates was increased to 110 and 144, respectively, while the other parties remained at 45 each. In reality, of course, these changes were largely symbolic. All votes in the Volkskammer were unanimous in support of decisions taken earlier by the SED's leadership. At the same time the "official" function of the non-Communist parties of the GDR was redefined. Instead of acting as voices for the interests of their voters and members, they too were to serve as "transmission belts" explaining the reasons for the SED's policies to their supporters. Their role, in other words, was not essentially different from that of the mass organizations.

The attainment of "socialism" and with it the regime's ability to stay in power ultimately depended upon the performance of the GDR's economy. We have already seen that the failure of the system to satisfy the minimum needs of its people had led to the uprisings of June 1953. Since then the situation had definitely improved, largely because the GDR's leaders rearranged the planning priorities to increase the supply of consumer goods. The growth figures for the economy toward the end of the 1950s were impressive; in 1957, for example, the economy grew by 7.9 percent. At the SED's July 1958 Congress Ulbricht announced that within three years the GDR would have reached and surpassed West Germany's standard of living. In 1960 Ulbricht prophesied that within ten years the GDR would be completely independent of Western imports.

Since at the time labor productivity in the GDR was 25 percent below that of the FRG, and East Germany had a standard of living that was 40 percent lower than West Germany's, where did the first secretary and his supporters get their vastly inflated expectations for the performance of the East German economy? In part the reason was misplaced faith in the structural transformation that had been completed by the end of the 1950s. All sectors of the economy with the exception of some small businesses (mostly craftspeople doing repair work) had now been nationalized. Overall, almost 90 percent of all industrial goods were produced by VEBs, more than 90 percent of the GDR's food production came from collectivized farms, and almost 80 percent of all retail operations were transacted by state-owned stores. In addition, the GDR benefited indirectly from the West European Common Market. To emphasize its position that there was only one German nation, the FRG had insisted that the GDR be treated as part of the West German tariff area. This meant essentially that East Germany was part of an expanding free market in Western Europe.

Most important, however, the East German leaders felt they had found the solution to the problems created by the economy's cumbersome decision-making apparatus. Under the catchy label the New Economic System (NES), Erich Apel, Fritz Selbmann's successor as chairman of the State Planning Commission, attempted to apply some of the ideas of the Soviet economist Evsei Liberman to the East German situation. Liberman, who enjoyed great favor with Khrushchev, argued that real costs, profitability, and plans calculated on the basis of real productivity had a legitimate place in socialist economy. Using these ideas the East Germans hoped to increase the freedom of economic decision making for individual plant managers, without abandoning effective political control. In an effort to reduce the multiple layers of decision-making authority, the eight separate economic ministries in East Germany were abolished. The State Planning Commission took over most of their functions. The sphere of decision making of individual VEB managers was increased, and they now dealt directly with the State Planning Commission, while regional associations of VEBs exercised day-to-day supervision. For production-line workers "socialist competition" provided both material and ideological incentives to increase productivity. Simultaneously, a major curriculum reform in the public schools stressed polytechnical education and vocational training to smooth the transition from school to factory.

For some years after it was introduced in 1958, the NES appeared to be highly successful. The standard of living for the average East German increased significantly. The regime continued its traditional policy of heavily subsidizing the cost of housing and basic foodstuffs, while the NES for the first time made sophisticated consumer goods—washing machines, cars, television sets—available on a larger scale. Equally important, party officials dropped the emphasis on the "primary of politics" and facilitated rather than hindered the production process.

But there were problems as well. It required vast levels of capital investment to bring the East German economy to the level of West Germany. Since the GDR did not interact with the international investment market, the funds would have to come from the East German people. Yet massive levels of investment (estimated at around 66 billion East German marks between 1961 and 1964) could only be maintained if the economy enjoyed steady and phenomenal growth rates. That economic surge, however, was hampered by the structural problems which continued to plague major sectors of the East German economy.

Agricultural production on the collectivized farms consistently lagged behind planned projections, and the GDR had to import large amounts of foodstuffs. In addition, despite efforts at decentralization, the system of economic decision making remained cumbersome. Projected goals for future plans were routinely based upon the anticipated accomplishments of previous plans, although it was obvious that the historical plans had often fallen short of their goals. Decision makers continued to ignore production costs and the quality of products they made; quantity alone counted. Especially in the mid-1960s, when it became clear that economic liberalization was also leading to demands for more artistic and political freedom, some party functionaries had second thoughts about the benefits of economic reforms.

Finally, the GDR experienced firsthand the negative consequences of socialist internationalism. When the Soviet economy began to develop massive difficulties (one reason leading to Khrushchev's downfall in 1964), the Soviets turned to help from the satellites. In December 1965 East Germany was forced to sign a new trade treaty with the Russians that contained extremely favorable terms for the Soviet Union. There were even rumors that Erich Apel's suicide at the end of the year was a form of protest against Russia's exploitation of East Germany's economy.

And the East Germans were to mimic still further their Soviet counterparts in the years to come. In April 1967 the Seventh Congress of the SED voted to modify substantially the NES and replace it with the Economic System of Socialism (ESS). This followed the fall of Khrushchev, when the Soviets returned to a more centralized control of their economy. The GDR, too, reinstituted a centralized planning system (the ESS). A technologically advanced society remained the ultimate goal, but instead of emphasizing individual material incentives and decentralized decision making, the East German leaders now attempted to combine the concepts of developed socialism and the theory of cybernetics to create a new form of self-regulating economic structure in the GDR.

Cybernetics as a theory of system control and information has aroused much interest on both sides of the Iron Curtain, but in the GDR it did not become respectable until

1961 when Khrushchev described it as the "fundamental science of the coming age." For East German theoreticians, notably the philosopher Georg Klaus, cybernetics promised to create the "man-machine symbiosis" that they saw as the essence of socialism. They claimed that under developed socialism alienation between worker and machine had been eliminated, so that by applying the theoretical precepts of cybernetics to the work process it could be made completely controllable. It followed then that the knowledge of cybernetics and dialectical materialism would enable East Germany's leaders to create an economy that was simultaneously dynamic and ultra-stable because it would not be subject to any inherent contradictions.

All this sounded very appealing to the GDR's economic planners disappointed by the performance of the NES, but the long-range promises of the ESS remained unfulfilled as long as the regime proved incapable of solving even its short-term economic problems. Recognizing the futility of modernizing all aspects of the economy, the ESS gave priority to those sectors that promised to be competitive on the international market, primarily chemicals, precision machinery, and eventually high-technology products. The East German leaders were particularly hopeful that exports in these areas would bring in enough hard currency to pay for needed food imports (agricultural productivity increased by only 1.7 percent per annum between 1967 and 1971) and for computerized machinery from the West. The hopes proved illusionary. Concentrating on specific economic sectors meant a general neglect of those parts of the East German economic infrastructure that were not high-priority items, with the result that the hidden costs of all East German products increased substantially. The decision in 1970 to freeze all prices was a temporary solution at best.

When the Ulbricht era came to an end, the East German economy had experienced some impressive growth rates and the standard of living had increased substantially. In the 1960s there was really something of an East German "economic miracle." In both productivity and standard of living East Germany far outstripped its Communist allies in Eastern Europe, including the Soviet Union. On the other hand, productivity and the standard of living remained (as today) substantially below that of West Germany and other Western countries. Despite its boast that the GDR had reached the stage of "developed socialism," East Germany had not found a way that enabled the regime simultaneously to maintain total political control while creating an economy that could match the productivity and prosperity of the West.

The construction of the Berlin Wall in 1961 also inaugurated a new era in the country's foreign relations. Emerging from the isolation of the 1950s, the GDR went on the diplomatic offensive. East Germany's political stability, impressive economic performance, and growing military strength provided the GDR with increased self-confidence.

The beginnings of the East German armed forces, the *Nationale Volksarmee* (National People's Army, NVA) go back to the early 1950s, but the NVA was not officially established until 1956. The GDR introduced conscription in 1962, and the NVA has since grown into an impressive military force of some 170,000 soldiers. To an even greater extent than the West German *Bundeswehr* all NVA units are integrated into the multinational Eastern alliance and remain under the control of the commander-in-chief of the Warsaw Pact forces, who is always a Soviet general. The GDR's armed forces are equipped with the most sophisticated conventional weapons, but, again like the West German *Bundeswehr*, they do not have control over any nuclear arms.

In the 1960s the GDR established diplomatic relations with most of the new nations of Africa and Asia. These ties benefited both sides. The newly independent nations of Africa and Asia were as anxious for international recognition as the GDR, and they had no preconceived ideas about the "German problem." At the same time their relationship to the former Western colonial powers and the United States was often strained. In addition, the GDR's seeming ability to build a "socialist" economy in a country with few natural resources impressed many Third World nations who faced similar development problems. East Germany, for its part, gained international respectability and the goodwill of the Soviets; it is clear that in the Third World the GDR often acted as the surrogate of the Soviet Union. In 1965 Ulbricht, in his capacity as chairman of the State Council, traveled to Egypt, his first state visit to a country outside the Soviet bloc.

While international recognition was gratifying to the East German regime, success also brought problems. In the 1960s the rigid contours of the bipolar bloc system were becoming more fluid. The Sino-Soviet split destroyed the myth of the Communist monolith, and East-West detente brought further uncertainties. In the Sino-Soviet dispute the GDR never wavered in its support of the Soviet Union, but detente was a less simple matter. Precisely because the Wall had left no doubt about the GDR's viability, a number of East Germany's Communist allies were moving toward establishing diplomatic relations with both East and West Germany. In an effort to counter the danger of isolation in the Communist camp, the GDR—just at the time West Germany was abandoning the Hallstein Doctrine—invented the "Ulbricht Doctrine." Its aim was to force Communist nations to refuse recognition to West Germany as long as the FRG did not treat the GDR as an equal.

The GDR's contention that detente was dangerous for the cohesion of the Soviet bloc was given unwitting credence by the 1968 crisis in Czechoslovakia. In the spring of that year Alexander Dubček, the chair-man of the Slovak Communist Party, replaced a holdover from the Stalinist era, Klement Gottwald, as leader of Czechoslovakia. Dubček was willing to allow substantial reforms in the Czechoslovak economic system, and his promise of "socialism with a human face" was enthusiastically welcomed by the people of Czechoslovakia. Unfortunately, as spring turned to summer there were signs that the Communist Party's monopoly of political power was being threatened. Meeting at Karlovy Vary in mid-August, the leaders of the Warsaw Pact attempted to persuade Dubček that he needed to take firm measures to restore Communist control. If he failed to do so the Russians and their allies would invade the country and restore order.

When the Czechoslovak situation seemed to deteriorate further, Soviet troops, aided by units from other Warsaw Pact nations, including the GDR, invaded Czechoslovakia on August 21. Dubček was taken to Moscow, forced out of office, and replaced by the hard-liner Gustav Husak. The invasion of Czechoslovakia was justified under the Brezhnev Doctrine (Leonid Brezhnev had in the meantime replaced Khrushchev as Soviet leader), which claimed it was the duty of all socialist nations to come to the aid of any country in which socialism appeared threatened. Both at Karlovy Vary and later, Ulbricht was an enthusiastic supporter of the Brezhnev Doctrine, not only because he disapproved of Dubček's reformism, but also because it seemed a guarantee of Russian help for the East German regime in case the East German People again revolted against the Communist dictatorship.

While Ulbricht and Brezhnev saw eye-to-eye on Czechoslovakia, the GDR was far less enthusiastic about the Soviet Union's interest in West Germany's *Ostpolitik*. For the Russians the policy of intra-European detente promised long-sought recognition of the Soviet Union's preeminent position in Eastern Europe, but for the GDR it posed the danger of isolation as West Germany, the Soviet Union, and the Communist countries of Eastern Europe dealt directly with each other. Far from supporting detente, Ulbricht and his allies in the Politburo dragged their feet as much as they could. Two meetings between Willy Brandt and his East German counterpart, Willy Stoph, were near disasters. As we have seen, during the first meeting in Erfurt, cold formality on the part of the East German officials contrasted with the embarrassing and spontaneous enthusiasm by the people of Erfurt for Willy Brandt. Stoph's return visit to Kassel in May 1970 did not improve matters. The East German prime minister began the discussion by demanding that West Germany pay the GDR 100 billion Deutsche marks to compensate East Germany for "luring away its people" between 1949 and 1961.

Simultaneously Ulbricht held fast to the position that West Berlin was to become an "independent political entity," with the Western sectors of the city existing at the sufferance of the GDR. The Soviets, of course, knew that if they supported this line no *Ostpolitik* agreement would be possible. The presence of the Western Allies in West Berlin and the acknowledgment of the economic and social ties between the city and the FRG were sine qua nons for West Germany.

Foreign policy disagreements as well as Ulbricht's economic failures at home seemed to have persuaded the Russians and a majority of the members of the SED's Politburo that a change in leadership was needed. In May 1971 Walter Ulbricht was forced out of power. He resigned as first secretary of the SED, but it was not a graceful exit. In fact, Ulbricht leaked his version of the ouster to the Western press to show that his fall from power had not been voluntary. The former strong man of East Germany continued as chairman of the State Council until his death in August 1973, but his successor as first secretary, Erich Honecker, saw to it that the State Council was stripped of all real power.

CULTURE AND SOCIETY

When discussing art, literature, and education in the GDR it is important to keep in mind the special position that Marxism-Leninism assigned to all cultural endeavors. Since the GDR saw itself as a socialist state, this meant that artists, educators, and writers had the task of acting as "engineers of the soul." It was their duty to help create a "socialist mentality" among the East German people. The regime over the years has taken this self-defined goal quite seriously. To set the stage for a new era in interpersonal relations, the SED's 1958 Congress voted a set of "Ten Commandments of Socialist Morality," which stressed that the interests of the working class rather than the biblical admonitions, should guide all individual behavior.

The GDR's educational system was an integral part of the country's *Kulturpolitik*. As we saw, the structure of education in the Soviet zone had already been fundamentally changed during the years of occupation. In the 1950s reform of the school curriculum emphasized ideological indoctrination; Marxism-Leninism and Russian became required subjects. Religious instruction, traditionally a regular subject in German schools, was eliminated. The regime also attempted to use education to further the social mobility of blue-collar workers. Workers and children of workers were given preference for admission to institutions of higher learning, while it was made more difficult for children from middle-class backgrounds to attend universities. By 1954, 13 percent of all East German university students came from a blue-collar family background. The comparable figure for West Germany was less than 2 percent.

In the 1960s the curricular focus shifted toward "polytechnical" education, with an emphasis on science and technology at the expense of humanistic education. One-third of the curriculum after the primary grades was devoted to science courses and prevocational training. To prepare children for their role in the production process, pupils spent considerable time outside the school; at least one day a week was to be spent in a factory or on a collective farm. Grade school and junior high school classes "adopted" as models of behavior individual "heroes of labor." (As in Russia, this title is awarded to workers who have significantly exceeded their production norms, as well as to party functionaries.) Increasing amounts of time both in school and during extracurricular activities were given over to sport and pre-military training. The results, at least as measured by the success of GDR athletes in international competition in recent years, have been spectacular.

These trends continued under Honecker. Indeed, the emphasis on polytechnical education brought its own problems. Predictably, the regime found that science teachers had little interest in political indoctrination. Party functionaries complained that in some schools not one teacher subscribed to the SED's official newspaper. More important, the transformation of the economy did not kept pace with the changes in education. Specifically, the number of jobs requiring sophisticated skills has not been large enough to absorb the increasing number of university and technical-college graduates. As a result, many graduates have been forced to perform production-line tasks considerably below their skill level.

The GDR's attitude toward artists and writers has shifted over the years, although essentially the changes were variations of the basic line laid down by the party in 1951. Cultural life during the years of occupation from 1945 to 1949 had been relatively free, but the situation changed abruptly in March 1951. The SED's Central Committee passed a resolution "Against Formalism in Art and Literature—For a Progressive German Culture"; this resolution established socialist realism, the cultural policy which had been in effect in Russia since 1934, as the official guideline for East Germany's "cultural producers." The pure Stalinist form of socialist realism, which insisted on the superiority of all things Russian and Soviet, became diluted after the dictator's death, but the dogma that art and literature must exhibit "party-mindedness, typicality, and optimism" remained in force.

The SED used the concept of socialist realism to control the GDR's artistic life and to enable the political leadership to convert art into propaganda. Writers were admonished to picture life in the GDR "realistically as it will progress toward the future," that is to say, to describe what the party had proclaimed would be, not what was true at present. "Typicality" also had a specific political meaning. In portraying workers, for example, artists were told that in the GDR the abolition of capitalism had led to the "self-realization of man." The face of a worker in a painting or his actions in a novel should mirror that the worker was simultaneously "producer, owner, and holder of political power" in the German Democratic Republic.

The "positive" concept of socialist realism was contrasted with the "negative" term *formalism*. Formalism referred to individual artistic indulgence and introspection, which the regime identified with Western culture and U.S. imperialism. All schools of art and literature other than socialist realism were regarded as reactionary and degenerate. These included expressionism, abstractionism, and naturalism. Even Bertold Brecht, a lifelong sympathizer of communism, was criticized for his libretto for the 1951 opera *The Trial of Lucullus*. The review in the SED's newspaper, *Neues Deutschland*, complained that Brecht's text was excessively abstract and failed to put the working class at the center of the action.

In the iron grip of socialist realism, East German cultural life in the early 1950s quickly became a wasteland of hacks. Endless "production-oriented" narratives ("I love you, but my tractor is more important") saturated the market. Painters and sculptors presented idealized revolutionary and factory scenes with assembly-line monotony. Some distinguished writers, including established figures and longtime Communist sympathizers like Arnold Zweig and Anna Seghers—both of whom, like Brecht, had returned from exile in the West to live in the GDR—attempted to evade the party's censors by writing about historical topics, such as World War I and the Weimar years. Others took to writing poetry, a literary field that, because of its masked content, was less subject to control by the party's censors.

The New Course and the establishment of a ministry of culture in 1954 raised hopes of a cultural thaw. Under its editor Wolfgang Harich the *German Journal for Philosophy* became a major vehicle for attacks on the SED's Stalinist cultural policy and a forum for pleas to permit artists to experiment with new forms and new themes. Spearheaded by recognized Communists like Anna Seghers, delegates to the Fourth Writers' Congress in January 1956 demanded a return to the freedom and experimentation of the early Bolshevik years before Stalin imposed socialist realism in the Soviet Union.

The SED's culture czars remained noncommittal for a time, but when the 1956 Hungarian Revolution revealed what they perceived as the consequences of liberalization, they returned to a hard line. In 1959 a sort of modified version of socialist realism called the Bitterfeld Movement became official literary policy. A conference of writers, functionaries, and industrial workers assembled at the Bitterfeld chemical works and proclaimed the need for close contact between East German writers and the country's industrial workers. Writers were encouraged to visit factories to learn how workers lived their lives of "optimistic typicality." But the Bitterfeld Movement had another side to it as well. Under the slogan *"Greif' zur Feder, Kumpel"* ("pick up a pen, buddy") industrial workers were to become authors in addition to serving as literary models. This aspect of the Bitterfeld Movement was spearheaded by Alfred Kurella, a Communist writer who had been active in a similar venture during the 1920s.

The Bitterfeld Movement and other efforts to breathe life into "production-oriented" literature and art did not meet with great success. Few of the worker-authors turned out to be hidden literary talents; living a proletarian life did not, it appeared, mean that one could produce great proletarian literature. The intellectuals who went into the factories were profoundly affected by their experience, but not always in the way the party had hoped. Many came away from their factory experiences impressed not with the new "socialist mentality" of the workers, but with the emptiness of their lives and the conflicts between individual self-realization and the enforced ideal of artificial collectivity. "Developed socialism," that is to say, had not eliminated alienation.

Along with building the Berlin Wall the SED intensified other efforts to seal off the GDR from Western, and particularly West German, cultural influences and contacts. In December 1961 Alexander Abusch, the GDR's minister for culture, proclaimed the "two-culture" doctrine: East and West Germany belonged to two separate cultural spheres, one progressive and humanistic, the other reactionary and imperialistic. For East German writers and artists only the experiences of life in the GDR and other socialist countries formed valid bases for cultural productions. East German journals, like the leading literary forum *Sinn und Form* ("Meaning and Form"), which until 1962 frequently published contributions by West German authors, abruptly stopped the practice. To be sure, these efforts at cultural isolation failed. The common language and ready availability of West German radio and television in most parts of the GDR assured that news from the West would continue to reach East Germany.

Even without "interference" from the West the GDR was having problems in its own camp. Marxist philosophers like Robert Havemann argued that armed with the scientific insights gained from cybernetics and

Marxist dialectical materialism, neither economic planners nor artists needed the constant interpretive guidance of party functionaries and ideologues. The party took swift action against such heretical views. In 1964 Havemann was expelled from the party, although he was an old-line Communist and antifascist activist. (During the Third Reich the Nazis had imprisoned Havemann in the same jail as Honecker.)

Havemann's writings (and the regime's criticism of them) caused a major stir among the GDR's intellectuals and Marxist theorists, but the SED was even more concerned about the impact on the public at large of critical views expressed by the country's bestselling authors. A favorite theme of East German literature during the 1960s was the conflict between the individual's desire for self-realization and society's pressure for conformity. Wolf Biermann's very popular poetry accused the party functionaries of "preaching Communism by destroying men's souls." In the novel *Gedanken über Christa T.* ("Thoughts about Christa T."), Christa Wolf, an internationally respected author and candidate member of the SED's Central Committee, told the story of a young woman who commits suicide because she cannot resolve the conflicts between maintaining her individuality and yielding to the pressures of collectivity. The most popular novel in the 1960s was Erwin Strittmatter's *Ole Bienkopp* ("Old Beehead") published in 1963. Ole Bienkopp is a wily peasant who establishes his own small-scale cooperative farm, only to see it destroyed by party functionaries who insist on his joining a much larger agricultural commune. And these were only the works that got past the censor. A book like Stefan Heym's *Tag X* ("Day X"), a novel about the June 1953 uprisings, could not be published in the GDR "because it contained obvious errors." (It was published in West Germany.)

A central concern of all these writers was the problem of alienation—and particularly youthful alienation—in the German Democratic Republic. The party's functionaries claimed they did not object to treating alienation per se. And in fact in the early 1960s they made an effort particularly to accommodate youthful iconoclasm. The chairman of the East German youth organization (the FDJ) Horst Schumann, announced in 1963 that the party was not trying to raise a generation of "little Lord Fauntleroys." The FDJ's official organ even printed some early Biermann poems. In the mid-1960s, however, as Brezhnev turned against dissidents in the Soviet Union, the SED also cracked down again on cultural freedom in East Germany. The party functionaries objected particularly to portrayals of party functionaries as unfeeling bureaucrats, rather than as friends who would resolve the conflict between individual and society. In addition the party criticized the tragic outcome of many stories. Pessimism, after all, was not in accord with socialist realism. The freer treatment of sex by some East German authors also aroused the ire of the SED's puritanical censors.

Led by Erich Honecker, the former head of the FDJ and already Ulbricht's heir apparent, the Central Committee at the end of 1965 launched a broad attack on cultural revisionism. Incipient signs of rowdyism, aping of Western dress and mannerisms, and listening to "unaesthetic beat music" were condemned as evidence of the influence of Western television and radio. The party's aim was clear from its treatment of Christa Wolf. That author's *Gedanken über Christa T* was condemned as too pessimistic, but her 1963 work *Der geteilte Himmel* ("Divided Heaven") received high praise. *Der geteilte Himmel* dealt with the decision by a young East German woman to return to East Berlin after having lived for some time in the Western part of the city; despite the material advantages there, she finds life in the West empty. Strittmatter's *Ole Bienkopp*, too, fell afoul of the party's critics. The functionaries would have preferred a happy end, complaining that the party should have been portrayed as helping Ole Bienkopp win his case for smaller collective farms. (In the novel the party functionaries recognize the value of Bienkopp's proposals only after his death.)

Intellectuals, artists, and the party coexisted uneasily in the last years of the Ulbricht era. While "cultural producers" had more freedom than during the early 1950s, the party continued to insist that artists and writers conform to its political dictates. Despite some distinguished works, especially in literature, the artistic results of East Germany's *Kulturpolitik* were disappointing. Painters and architects, for example produced few works of real distinction. The GDR journal *Deutsche Architektur* ("German Architecture") editorialized in 1964 that since 1945 East German architects had produced absolutely nothing of note. The author of the article was denounced for his attempt "to escape party discipline."

CONFLICTING SIGNALS: EAST GERMANY UNDER ERICH HONECKER, 1971–1989

The choice of Erich Honecker to succeed Walter Ulbricht did not come as a surprise; for some years he had been regarded as Ulbricht's heir apparent. The new East German leader was born on August 25, 1912, in Neunkirchen, a small industrial town in the Saar region of West Germany. He came from a family of coal miners and left-wing political activists. Honecker's father was a local leader of the Communist Party during the 1920s, and Honecker himself joined the KPD's youth organization when he was only ten. As an official of the Communist youth movement, Honecker was on the Nazis' list of dangerous political opponents; he spent the years from 1935 until the end of World War II in Nazi jails.

After the war Honecker remained in East Germany, serving as chairman of the official East German youth organization, the FDJ, from March 1946 to May 1955. In 1950 at the relatively young age of thirty-eight Honecker became a full member of the SED's

Central Committee, and a candidate member of the Politburo. In the CC he was responsible for youth and security affairs. In 1956 and 1957 Honecker was in the Soviet Union, apparently for advanced training, and at the SED's Fifth Congress in 1958 he was elected a full member of the Politburo.

Unlike Ulbricht, Honecker's name had not been associated with a particular ideological school in the SED. Honecker instead personified the type of pragmatic *apparatchik* whose major aim was to preserve the Communist Party's monopoly of political power. At the same time, he was far more "GDR-oriented" than his predecessor. To the end of his life Ulbricht apparently continued to hope that he would see the victory of developed socialism in all of Germany. Honecker was content to safeguard Communist control in the GDR; the new 1974 constitution ("Honecker's constitution") was the first to contain no mention of a German nation. Honecker liked to use the phrase "real existing socialism" to characterize East German society rather than the more ambitious and finished-sounding "developed socialism."

Much as Ulbricht did, Honecker surrounded himself with personnel of his own choosing. This process involved both a generational and a functional shift among the top ranks of the GDR's leaders. Of the twenty-nine full and candidate members of the Politburo elected in 1976, nine were former FDJ functionaries. These men—the only woman to occupy a major position was Honecker's wife, Margot, who was minister of education—generally belonged to a generation of Communist leaders who became politically active at a time when both a united Germany and the old Communist movement had disappeared.

At the same time there was evidence of growing professionalization among the party bureaucracy at the middle-management level: the ranks of county, city, and district secretaries. Increasingly under Honecker these officials came from the ranks of the intelligentsia and professionals, rather than the working classes—in other words, people who had deliberately chosen the party as a management career. The dominance of the professional political managers had given the GDR in recent years a more pragmatic, less frantic, but also ideologically more flexible image than it had under Ulbricht. The East Germans and their self appointed leaders seemed to have grown accustomed to each other. The average East German neither loved nor feared the regime. The SED still ruthlessly suppressed organized opposition and dissent, but it tolerated unfocused grumbling and withdrawal into private life.

The new leaders were aware, of course, that economic difficulties at the end of the 1960s had hastened Ulbricht's fall. For this reason Honecker and his men worked hard to raise the East German standard of living. Structurally, Honecker intensified the drive for nationalization. The sectors of the economy which had retained a sizable percentage of privately owned businesses, notably independent artisans and small-scale building contractors, became part of the network of VEBs. By the end of 1972, 99.4 percent of all industrial workers in the GDR worked for a state-owned enterprise. After 1980 the industrial production was further centralized by uniting groups of related VEBs into *Kombinate* (literally, "combinations"). The new organizational forms were really vertical or horizontal cartels, although, of course, they did not have the economic power which that term implies in the West. Each of the *Kombinate* employs between twenty thousand and fourty thousand workers.

Honecker's regime modified some of the economic decision-making apparatus it inherited. Ulbricht's successor did not share his predecessor's fascination with cybernetics, and Honecker reintroduced some centralization in economic decision making. (The economics ministries abolished in 1958 were all reestablished.) Moreover, emphasis on the production of consumer goods and continuing efforts to bring certain sectors

of the economy, notably chemicals, precision machinery, and electronics, to the level where East German products can compete in the world market, characterized the GDR's planning priorities since 1971.

Despite some impressive gains in these export-oriented sectors during the 1970s, the goal of earning enough hard currency to pay for food imports and sustain a rising standard of living was not achieved. The 1976–1980 Five Year Plan fell far short of meeting its goal. The problems were not all the responsibility of the GDR's planners. As a country which has to import virtually all of its raw materials, East Germany was particularly adversely affected by the rapid rise in the cost of raw materials and energy during the 1970s and 1980s. Between 1970 and 1980 the Soviets cushioned the effect of the oil shock for their satellites. The price of Russian oil—the GDR obtains virtually all of its oil from the Soviet Union—increased by 22 percent, but this increase was modest in comparison to the staggering price of oil on the free market. Since 1980, however, the Soviets, who have their own economic problems, have ceased such subsidies to their allies and raised prices for Russian oil to world levels. In addition the GDR had to pay world market prices for the raw materials obtainable only on the "capitalist world market."

Nevertheless, some of the problems were clearly the responsibility of the GDR's economic planners. The continued absence of political freedom and the overly centralized economic decision-making apparatus certainly contributed to the difficulties. Labor productivity in East Germany is still some 30 percent lower than in West Germany. The productivity problem in the GDR has been compounded by its rapidly aging population, a problem that has intensified recently by the flight of tens of thousands of refugees—most of them under twenty-five years of age—from the GDR to West Germany.

In the late 1970s the GDR for the first time experienced the consequences of significant, albeit hidden, inflation. In the West increased costs are routinely passed on to the consumer, but in East Germany political and social reasons precluded this course of action. Basic foodstuffs, housing, and local transportation remained heavily subsidized, so that the gaping cost-price chasm had to be closed in some other manner. In part the GDR cut back on the production of nonbasic consumer goods. (As a result, used private automobiles are twice as expensive as new ones, since there is a two- to three-year waiting period for a new car.) A second strategy was to go into debt. Like other East European countries the GDR accumulated sizable obligations to Western banks. The East German debt, exclusive of money owed to West Germany, was estimated at some $11.4 billion at the end of 1981. Since then it has been reduced to around $7.5 billion.

Above all, the complicated financial ties between East and West Germany play a major role in the GDR's strategy for coping with its economic problems. In her trade relations with the FRG, East Germany, can draw upon a sizable, interest-free credit line. Millions of Deutsche Marks are paid annually by West Germany in the form of user fees for postal, railroad, and road services in connection with travel by West Germans to and from West Berlin—and until recently as "compensation" for the release of political prisoners from East German jails to West Germany. Individual East Germans were permitted to receive up to DM 500 per visit from West German friends and relatives. Since the signing of the Basic Treaty of 1972, private West German travel in East Germany has grown considerably; in 1985, 6.7 million West Germans and West Berliners made trips to the GDR. East Germany benefited directly from these visits, since visitors had to exchange twenty-five Deutsche Marks—at the official exchange rate of one to one for East German marks—for each day spent in the GDR.

The consequence of this influx of hard currency was the establishment of a dual system of marketing consumer goods in the GDR. To prevent the hard currency in private hands from generating a black market in currency speculation, the state created special hard currency stores called *Intershops*. Run by the state retail trade organization, they offered a variety of goods unobtainable in regular stores. Payment, however, had to be made in Western currencies. With the cutback in the production of many durable consumer goods, the GDR developed a problem familiar in other East European countries as well: too much money chasing too few goods. To siphon off some of the extra East German marks in the hands of its citizens, the regime set up another string of stores, the *Exquisitshops*, which sold scarce consumer goods for East German marks, but at much higher prices than those officially set.

These strategies were effective in containing popular discontent with rising prices for consumer goods (or, conversely, the lack of availability of such products at the officially set prices), but they were hardly the hallmarks of a well-functioning socialist economy. In fact, since about 1975 the East German economy had been treading water. And by the mid-1980s the regime clearly still had no ready answers for the economy's long-range structural and production problems. Honecker's hope that exports would propel the economy permanently forward proved illusionary. The East German economy remained dependent upon West German imports and financial subsidies. At the same time, the GDR's economic problems should not be exaggerated. East Germany's GNP is higher by a third than that of any other Soviet bloc country. Technologically, the economy is the most advanced among the Comecon nations, and the GDR even exported some high-technology products, such as small computers, to the West.

Under Honecker the GDR scored some remarkable foreign policy successes. The Hallstein Doctrine is simply a memory of the past, and the GDR has become a recognized member of the family of nations. East Germany maintains full diplomatic relations with most countries in the world, including the United States and other NATO members. And for both East Germany and West Germany, diplomatic milestones in the achievement of international respectability were their simultaneous acceptances as members of the United Nations in 1973, and their participation as sovereign nations in the 1975 Helsinki Conference on European Security and Cooperation.

Despite the GDR's growing international recognition, Honecker never lost sight of the real foundations of his power. Except for taking a somewhat softer line on the deployment of American missiles in West Germany in the mid-1980s, the East German leader had been a loyal and consistent supporter of the Soviets' foreign policy line. Among the USSR's East European satellites only Bulgaria and Czechoslovakia aligned themselves more closely with the Soviet Union. The GDR and the Soviet Union were particularly close in their views of the difficulties in Poland that began in 1981 with the formation of the *Solidarity* free labor-union movement. Like the USSR, East Germany showed no sympathy with the aims of the reformers inside and outside the Polish government. In Third World countries East Germany continued its role as Soviet surrogate. The GDR established sizable economic and military aid programs and sent several hundred military advisors to African and Asian countries, notably Angola, Ethiopia, Cuba, and Vietnam.

Within the context of Communist bloc politics the GDR benefited from her close alignment with the Soviet Union, but especially in recent years the relationship has involved sacrifices as well. Unlike Ulbricht, Honecker was anxious to continue the policy of detente. When it became obvious in 1980 that the world's two superpowers, the United States and the Soviet Union, were abandoning detente and returning to the politics of confrontation, both the GDR and the FRG for a time attempted to continue something like a "little entente" in their bilateral relations, but that effort quickly

aroused the Soviets' ire. The Soviets in the early 1980s launched a massive propaganda campaign against the West Germans, accusing them of planning a revanchist war to destroy the GDR. For a time the East Germans attempted to ignore the Soviet line, but in the fall of 1984 the GDR's lack of diplomatic autonomy became glaringly apparent. Honecker was forced to cancel a scheduled visit to West Germany when the Soviets made it clear that they would disapprove of such an obvious deviation from their own confrontational line toward the FRG. East Germany's foreign relations, then, remained severely constrained by the GDR's extremely close relationship to the Soviet Union. Honecker himself admitted as much when, in response to a reporter's question during an official visit to Finland in November 1984, he noted, "small nations can't do much without the approval of great powers."

Despite continuing economic problems and obvious foreign policy constraints, the GDR during the Honecker years became a "normal" and stable society. The regime held out to its citizens no promises of major political reforms, but it had also abandoned any attempt to force the East Germans to sacrifice immediate material benefits in the name of a future socialist utopia. In fact, rather the reverse was true. Honecker and his associates gave priority to improving the standard of living of the East Germans in the obvious hope that material benefits would push aside the dissatisfactions caused by the continuing lack of political freedoms. East Germany became a somewhat drab and unexciting but "real, existing"—to use favorite adjectives of the SED's propaganda machine—welfare state.

Very early on, the GDR developed into a cradle-to-the-grave welfare state with clear, ideologically determined social-policy priorities. The system was designed to benefit particularly the industrial working class. Such necessities of life as basic foodstuffs—particularly bread and potatoes—housing, and local transportation were heavily sub-

XX Jahre DDR im festen Bündnis mit der Sowjetunion

Woche der Deutsch-Sowjetischen Freundschaft 4.-10. Mai 1969

East German propaganda from 1969. A poster advertises the annual "Week of German-Soviet Friendship." A stylized "XX" formed by the flags of the GDR and the USSR illustrate the text, "XX years of firm alliance with the Soviet Union." (Source: *Anschläge*, no. 159.)

sidized by the state. For example, a mass transit ride in any East German city, including East Berlin, costs 20 East German *Pfennigs*—less than seven U.S. cents at the official rate of exchange. Housing, too, is very cheap in East Germany, but the enforced low rents have also meant that there has been little incentive for private initiative to provide additional or improved housing. The units that have been built were constructed by the state, and until the 1970s housing ranged low in the planning priorities, so that there was a chronic housing shortage. Honecker gained immediate popularity with his people when he pushed through a massive program of housing construction. Between 1971 and 1980 more than 1.3 million apartment units were newly constructed or renovated, making housing construction one of the few parts of the 1976–1980 Five Year Plan whose targets were actually exceeded.

In contrast to the basic necessities of life, items which the regime identified with a middle-class or "capitalist" life style remained very expensive, in part to make up for the low prices on subsidized consumer products. Despite the high prices, cars, color televisions, refrigerators, and washing machines have been in short supply. The average East German has had to wait months and often years before being able to buy such big-ticket items, and even then he or she pays five or six times the comparable Western price for a lower-quality product.

Toward the end of the decade the GDR's economic high-wire act became increasingly difficult to maintain. Although the country's per capita income was still the highest among the Eastern bloc nations, the East German economy was stagnating. In the 1970s East German machines and machine tools were quite competitive on world markets, but in the 1980s they faced increasing competition. As a result, the country's positive trade balance dropped from 4.5 billion marks (at the official rate of exchange about $2.25 billion to 3.9 billion marks). Moreover, the GDR's workers have to put in dispro-

portionately long hours for their relatively high standard of living. The East German standard of living is much lower than that of West Germany, but on average East German workers labor 300 hours a year more than their counterparts in the Federal Republic. Above all, the GDR's much-vaunted "perfecting of the planning mechanism" was anything but perfect. Over-centralized, staffed with aging functionaries (in 1989 the average age of the members of the SED's Politburo was sixty-seven), East Germany more and more stood as odd man out among the countries of Eastern Europe in which *glasnost* (openness) and *perestroika* (restructuring) were becoming the norm.

The faltering economy did much to explain why the GDR's leaders still failed to "win the hearts and minds" of their people. The Honecker regime had clearly hoped that the ready availability of basic necessities at low prices, improved housing, and such undoubted advantages in a socialist state as a guaranteed job, would remove the barriers of alienation between the East Germans and their Communist rulers. That, however, did not occur. Relative material well-being did not erase the negative effects of the continued intellectual and political constraints that the regime imposed on its people. Honecker's East Germany continued to be characterized by distrust between the people and their leaders.

Each year thousands of East Germans (estimates for 1985 ran as high as 400,000) applied for exit permits to leave the GDR and resettle in West Germany. They objected to the manner in which the SED administered the GDR's version of "real, existing socialism." Increasingly, the iron law of oligarchy seized hold of the party organs at all levels of administration. The process was described well by Rudolf Bahro in his book *Die Alternative* ("The Alternative"). Bahro, who was a young SED functionary at the time he wrote the work, subjected the GDR's party and state bureaucracy to stinging criticism. (East German censors prohibited publication of the work in the GDR; it was published in West Germany.) Bahro accused the East German "Politburocracy" of existing to perpetuate its own power, rather than serving the needs of society. In 1984 another work published in West Germany, *Der Rat der sozialistischen Götter* ("The Council of Socialist Gods"), made the same observation from an even better vantage point. Before emigrating to the FRG the author, Franz Loeser, had been the party secretary at East Berlin's prestigious Humboldt University, and he had frequent dealings with the highest officials of the SED's Central Committee and Politburo.

The regime's reaction to attacks by insiders like Bahro, Loeser, and others was swift, though restrained repression. Unlike Ulbricht, Honecker did not resort to massive purges in the party or wholesale terror for the population at large. Rather, the regime attempted to silence criticism by expelling its most prominent critics from the country. Leading opponents of the SED were simply deprived of their East German citizenship and deported to West Germany. Bahro has embarked on a second career in the West as a prominent spokesperson for the radical, anti-industrial wing of the West German Green Party. Loeser now teaches philosophy at the University of Kiel. In some cases, like that of Robert Havemann, the regime resorted to internal repression. The famous Marxist philosopher was not deported but placed under house arrest; he was prohibited from writing or speaking publicly until his death in March 1982.

While the regime reacted strongly to criticism from within the SED, it was even more concerned about the signs of growing alienation among the country's youth. It was this phenomenon that made the case of the popular singer and song-writer Wolf Biermann such a *cause célèbre*. Biermann had long been a thorn in the side of the party establishment. As early as 1965 Honecker had pointed to Biermann's poems, which were bitingly critical of the regime's inhumanity, as examples of the influence of

Western decadence. In November 1976 Biermann, too, was expelled from East Germany; he now lives in the Federal Republic.

Biermann was deported at a time when, ironically, there were signs that the SED was relaxing its definition of socialist realism. Although in the 1960s Honecker had acquired a well-deserved reputation as a cultural hard-liner, the party censors after 1971 seemed to work with a less heavy hand. An interesting case of liberalization came in 1980 with the first public production of Heiner Müller's play *Der Bau* ("The Construction Site"). Written in 1965, the play concerns the fate of a party secretary who succeeds in raising the productivity of the construction site for which he is responsible, but who loses his personal integrity in the process. When it originally appeared in print the play was severely criticized by party officials (among them Honecker) and not allowed to be produced until 1980.

But such evidence of liberalization was largely negated by the practice of *Ausbürgerung*. Intellectuals reacted strongly to the process of depriving some East Germans of their citizenship, a practice that was reminiscent of the Nazis depriving Jews and other opposition figures of their rights as German citizens. When Wolf Biermann was expelled from the GDR more than a hundred prominent East German artists and writers signed a Statement of Protest against the regime's measures. The list included virtually every well-known East German author. The SED reacted swiftly, mounting a massive campaign of criticism against the signatories of the Statement. Eventually some thirty members of the writers' union were expelled from the organization for their antisocial activity, a punishment that is tantamount to being blacklisted since authors who are not members of the writers' union have great difficulty being published in the GDR. World-famous writers, like Stefan Heym and Christa Wolf, were largely silenced in their own country.

The crackdown on intellectuals heightened the significance of the mass-membership institutions that had succeeded in evading direct control by the SED, the churches. In East Germany this has meant primarily the Protestant churches, since about two-thirds of those individuals who maintained church affiliation are Protestant. In the early years after the founding of the GDR, the regime pushed through a total separation of church and state, and during the Stalinist and Ulbricht phases the churches were actively persecuted as well. The Communists especially tried to discourage younger East Germans from maintaining church membership. (Being a church member was sufficient reason for being barred from attending universities and other advanced training institutes.) The regime also introduced a secular *Jugendweihe* (youth consecration) ceremony to take the place of Christian confirmation. In addition, the churches were forced to cut off all institutional connections to their counterparts in West Germany.

The uneasy accommodation between leaders and people in the GDR was shattered in the summer and fall of 1989. Tensions had been building for some time. The East German regime was clearly uncomfortable with Mikhail Gorbachev's policies in the Soviet Union, and it sought to reduce their fallout in the GDR as much as possible. East German censors prohibited the dissemination of the suddenly less controlled Soviet periodicals. Again and again, spokesmen reiterated that while changes might be needed in the Soviet Union, reforms in the GDR were not necessary.

In the summer of 1989 the GDR and the other Soviet bloc countries seemed to embark on increasingly divergent paths. Freedom of expression was the watchword in the Soviet Union, a non-Communist government took power in Poland, and Hungary permitted non-Communist parties to organize, but in the GDR there were no moves in the direction of greater freedom and pluralism. On the contrary: The regime went out of its way to praise the brutal repression of the Chinese students' move-

ment for more democracy in June. In sharp contrast to developments in Hungary, the East German authorities specifically prohibited the organization of independent political groups.

To persist in a course of action that was at odds with developments among its neighbors and unpopular with its people, the GDR needed strong and firm leadership. But precisely that was lacking. In the spring of 1989 Erich Honecker fell ill; an official announcement spoke of minor gallbladder trouble. However, his slow recovery—Honecker was not seen in public for weeks—quickly led to rumors that his health problems involved cancer, not gallstones. Whatever the actual nature of his illness, the regime's decision-making apparatus was paralyzed as Honecker's associates were unwilling to act in the absence of their leader.

This combination of paralysis at the top and dissatisfaction at the bottom began a process of dramatic change in East Germany. Taking advantage of Hungary's decision to dismantle its border fortifications with Austria, in July and August thousands of East German vacationers in Hungary decided not to return to the GDR, but to flee instead to Austria and from there to West Germany. Several thousand more took refuge in the West German embassies in Prague and Warsaw. The East German authorities eventually permitted them to travel to the West as well. By the end of the year some 400,000 East Germans—mostly young families and skilled workers—left the GDR in 1989, the largest exodus since the Berlin Wall was built in 1961.

While the flight of the refugees was an embarrassment to the East German regime, the massive anti-government demonstrations that began in October endangered the regime's very existence. In Leipzig more than 100,000 people took to the streets in what became weekly "Monday night" demonstrations. The situation was reminiscent of events in June 1953, but this time there was a fundamental difference. When Gorbachev was in East Germany for the GDR's fortieth anniversary celebrations, he made it clear to the East German leaders that the Soviet troops stationed in East Germany would not intervene in the conflict between the regime and its people. The SED was on its own.

Honecker, who had returned to work, was undaunted. Clearly taking the brutal repression of the Chinese students' movement for democracy in June as his model, the East German leader ordered the army to be prepared to break up the next antici- pated Monday night demonstration in Leip- zig on October 9—with live ammunition if necessary.

The order was countermanded by the Politburo member in charge of implement- ing it, Egon Krenz. There was more than a touch of irony in Krenz's emergence as a leader of a new generation of East German moderate leaders. Krenz had long been regarded as Erich Honecker's protegé. Moreover, it was he, who, in the name of the SED's Politburo, had congratulated the Chinese Communists in June for their force- ful repression of the "counter-revolution- aries" assembled in Bejing's Tianamen Square.

Now the old order in the GDR crumbled fast. Confronted with ever-larger popular demonstrations, increasing criticism from the leaders of the usually subservient non- Communist parties, and fast-growing new political groups like the New Forum and the Social Democratic Party, the SED has- tened to throw out old leaders and old policies. In mid-October 1989 the Politburo forced Erich Honecker and his closest as- sociates to resign. Honecker was succeeded as head of the party and chief of state by Egon Krenz.

In the manner of a Western politician, the "youthful" Krenz (he was fifty-two; Ho- necker was seventy-seven) moved energeti- cally to convince the East German people he represented a true "turn-around." (He used the word *Wende* in German, the same term Helmut Kohl had used to characterize his new course in 1982.) But the selection of a new leader was not enough, and more

profound changes soon followed. In the first week of November 1989, the entire Politburo and all members of the East Ger- man cabinet resigned. The new prime min- ister was Hans Modrow, the SED's district chief in Dresden. Modrow had long advo- cated economic and political reforms, and it was precisely for that reason that Ho- necker had kept Modrow out of the Polit- buro and the seats of national power.

The regime also announced plans to de- centralize the economy and, most impor- tant, an easing of travel restrictions. At first free travel to Western countries was to be limited to thirty days per year, but on No- vember 9 the East German authorities an- nounced that effective immediately the cit- izens of the GDR were free to travel any- where. (Again, the ironies of history: The 1918 revolution in Berlin began on Novem- ber 9, and exactly five years later in 1923, Hitler launched his abortive Beer Hall Putsch.) In effect, the new policy meant the end of the Berlin Wall. On the following weekend 2 million East Berliners and East Germans visited West Berlin and West Ger- many for the first time in twenty-eight years. The Berlin Wall had become a porous, if still ugly, concrete structure.

If the SED had anticipated that these changes would be sufficient to appease the aroused people of East Germany, its hopes were soon shattered. Revelations by the newly free press in the GDR of widespread corruption among the top leaders soon led to further personnel and policy changes. Erich Honecker and his associates had for years preached austerity in the name of egalitarian communism, but it now became clear that austerity was meant only for the people, not the party leaders. The members of the Politburo lived in a style of personal luxury more suited to Western tycoons than to self-professed leaders of the working class. The top echelons of the SED occupied a separate housing compound, had hunting preserves at their disposal, shopped in spe- cial stores well-stocked with Western goods, and some even maintained secret Swiss bank accounts.

The furor over these revelations led to the arrest of the leading members of the old guard (because of his illness Honecker was only placed under house arrest), and it swept Egon Krenz from power after only forty-six days in office. Although there was no evidence that he had personally benefited from the corruption at the top, Krenz's long years of close association with Honecker now made him a political liability. He resigned as both party leader and head of state. In the latter position he was succeeded by Manfred Gerlach, the head of the small Liberal Democratic Party. The East German liberals had long been a mere appendage of the SED, but in the fall of 1989 the party and its leader became vigorous advocates of further reforms and democratization.

Throwing Egon Krenz to the wolves of popular discontent was only the first step in the SED's desperate attempt to retain a measure of popularity among the people of East Germany. At a hastily called special party congress in mid-December, the delegates voted to rename the SED "Party of Democratic Socialism (PDS)." They also agreed to eliminate all of the familiar institutional trappings of a Marxist-Leninist party. The post of general secretary was abolished, and a democratically elected executive committee replaced the dictatorial Central Committee and Politburo. The congress also elected a new leader (who holds the title of chairman), who really was untainted by the sins of the past.

Gregor Gysi, the PDS's new chairman, is a forty-one-year-old lawyer who had never been close to, much less at home in, the corridors of power. However, what he lacked in age and experience, he seemingly made up in moral stature and personal integrity. The son of a Communist resistance fighter who was persecuted by the Nazis both for his political views and his Jewish ancestry, Gregor Gysi joined the SED at age nineteen, but he never became an *apparatchik.* Instead, he remained in private law practice, and many of his clients were dissidents and opponents of the regime.

Would the rejuvenated SED be able to lead the GDR along a path of "socialist democracy," a course that Gysi proclaimed a "third way" between Stalinism and capitalism in his inaugural address to the party congress that elected him? At the end of 1989 the party's prospects were not promising. Almost a half million members (out of a total of 2.3 million) had resigned their party membership in the course of the year, and in an interview with a West German magazine, Hans Modrow acknowledged that "our newly active sociologists" predicted the SED would get no more than 20 percent of the vote in a free election.

Modrow was overly optimistic. On March 18, 1990 East Germany held its first genuinely free elections in fifty-eight years, and the results were both surprising and decisive. Although the SED's regime had been toppled by indigenous, grass-roots political groups, the March campaign was dominated by parties that were all but sister organizations of the major West German parties. The Alliance for Germany was an amalgam of three groups closely affiliated with the West German CDU/CSU, the Social Democratic Party was linked to the SPD, and the Union of Free Democrats had the support of the FDP. Prominent West German politicians also campaigned widely throughout the GDR.

Political observers had originally expected the Social Democrats to lead in the balloting, but instead, the Alliance for Germany was the run-away victor. With 93.3 percent of the eligible voters casting their ballots, the Alliance, vigorously supported by Helmut Kohl, and campaigning on a platform of unification with West Germany as soon as possible, gained 48 percent of the popular vote. The Social Democrats were second with 21.9 percent and the former SED (now the Party of Democratic Socialism) came in a poor third with 16 percent. Hans Modrow's days as prime minister were clearly numbered. His successor, with a mandate to guide the GDR towards union with the Federal Republic, was Lothar de Maizière, the unprepossessing lawyer and musician who heads the East German CDU.

CONCLUSION

Much like the Federal Republic, but for entirely different reasons, the German Democratic Republic in the 1990s finds itself at a crossroads. In some ways East Germany was a very successful society. Starting from a poor base of natural resources and devastated by war and reparations, the GDR had given its people a standard of living that was higher than that of any other Soviet bloc country.

During the Ulbricht years, the regime had a vision of the future that, while it was utopian and unrealistic, did give the society, and especially its leaders, a goal that set the GDR apart from the "other" Germany. The Honecker regime largely abandoned ideological utopianism in favor of pragmatism and short-term economic goals, but it did not relax the political dictatorship.

But the Communist dictatorship imposed on the GDR by Stalin and his German partners and successors has never been accepted by the East German people. Neither Ulbricht's nor Honecker's version of "real existing socialism" satisfied the citizens of the GDR, most of whom wanted political and economic freedoms for their country. True, in the absence of any alternative, the citizens of the GDR in time seemed to accept, if not love, their leaders and system.

All of the GDR's accomplishments were thrown into question by the Gorbachev era. While processes of political and economic liberalization were taking place in other East European countries, the GDR remained a neo-Stalinist Communist dictatorship. But Honecker and his associates could not hold back the tide of reform. As this is written, it appears that the East German people have triumphed. The new leaders have come a long way in a short time. They have moved to expose and punish the rampant corruption among the old leaders, eliminated travel restrictions, lifted press censorship, and abandoned the constitutionally mandated "leading role" of the SED. East Germany has also disbanded the hated state security service, the *Stasi*.

Under Hans Modrow the government began decentralizing the economy and making it responsive to "market forces." The prime minister welcomed investors from the West and encouraged joint ventures with Western companies. But it was not at all clear how such changes could be accommodated in a system that continued to call for "socialism," and in fact by the spring of 1990 the GDR was well on its way toward abandoning its fiscal and economic independence. Negotiations between the central banks of East and West Germany on a currency union between the two countries resulted in an agreement, and many experts expected that the Deutsche Mark would become the East German currency on July 2, 1990. Political union between East and West Germany is likely to follow a year or two later. The GDR's history as an independent state was drawing to a close.

CHAPTER 12

CONCLUSION

The more than one hundred years of modern German history covered in this book have had a disproportionately large impact upon the history of Europe and the world. As we noted at the outset, much of modern German history is the story of the "German problem." Although recent scholarship has shown that in many ways the course of German history in the nineteenth century was not all that different from that of her neighbors in the West, the central fact of Germany's asymmetrical modernization remains. Modernization in Germany did not involve the simultaneous transformation of all aspects of society. Instead, Germany had a tendency to advance rapidly in some areas, while lagging behind in others.

The examples of asymmetry were many. Rapid economic development in the years following unification contrasted with the simultaneous preservation of what was essentially a pre-modern political system. National unification did not resolve the Reich-state problem. States' rights even in the united Reich remained strong, which meant in practice that Prussia retained its hegemonial role in German federal affairs. The political disenfranchisement of the laboring classes was a festering sore in a country that was rapidly becoming the most industrialized nation in Europe. Traditions of anti-Semitism continued alongside what, before the rise of the Nazis, had become one of the most thriving and assimilated Jewish communities in Europe. The overall results of the modernization warp were internal tensions in the society that prevented consensual pluralism from being firmly established.

The rulers of Germany were not unaware of the problems created by asymmetrical modernization but, rather than address them forthrightly, before 1945 they repeatedly tried to use victory abroad to quell dissatisfaction with the status quo at home. It was unfortunate for the country's long-range future that Bismarck's effective use of the "primacy of domestic politics" in the conduct of Germany's foreign relations seemed to endow it with the stamp of success. The widespread and enthusiastic acceptance of the Bismarck Compromise as the price and corollary for national unification following a victorious foreign war persuaded successive sets of German leaders that the gamble should be tried again and again despite increasingly higher stakes. The primacy of domestic politics meant that Germany's involvement in World War I was not only a desperate gamble to change the international balance of power permanently, but also a last-ditch attempt to keep intact the domestic balance of power. Unlike Bismarck, the rulers of Wilhelminian Germany failed in their quest. In 1918 the authoritarian social and political system that Bismarck and his successors had defended against growing opposition was defeated along with the German armies.

The political, social, and cultural pluralism which the Weimar Republic attempted to implant in place of the momentarily discredited authoritarianism had difficulty sinking its roots in German soil. Many Germans, including the old elites, associated political modernization with their own diminished status and influence, defeat in war, the loss of Germany's stature as a great power, and, perhaps most important, chronic economic and fiscal problems. In addition, the fathers of the Weimar Republic lacked the courage of their own convictions; in many spheres of public life they left the old forces in positions of real power. Consequently, despite the earnest labors of some of its leaders, real economic and social progress, and the undoubted brilliance of its cultural life, the Weimar Republic, too, fell victim to its own contradictions. In the end it provided too little too briefly to withstand the attacks from the rise of a new form of nihilism. Nazism had its roots in some long-standing German traditions, no-

tably anti-Semitism and the desire for *völkisch* integration, but it ultimately succeeded because the Depression destroyed the already frayed fabric of value consensus in Germany. Adolf Hitler and his henchmen rose to power only partly because they promised relief from the effects of the Depression to millions of Germans. In the end Hitler became chancellor because the New Conservatives were convinced—mistakenly—that in cooperation with them the Nazis would restore the greatness of the Bismarckian and Wilhelminian past.

The Third Reich represented the culmination and worst consequences of Germany's asymmetrical road to modernization. The dictator had no intention of restoring the authoritarian system of the Bismarck era; Hitler's aim was the establishment of a full-scale totalitarian society. Nazi anti-Semitism was not the relatively genteel prejudices advocated by Freytag or even the German Conservatives, but the virulently racial variety that led logically and tragically to the physical murder of more than 6 million European Jews. Similarly, while Bismarck and the leaders of Wilhelminian Germany had sought to exclude from political power groups they defined as the "enemies of the Reich," the Nazis abolished all vestiges of the *Rechtsstaat* and established a network of terror and concentration camps that meant years of incarceration, physical maltreatment, and death for thousands of Nazi opponents.

In foreign relations Hitler's interests went far beyond regaining the German boundaries of 1914 or even of attaining the war aims articulated by the military in World War I. The evidence is persuasive that the Nazi dictator's aim was the conquest of all of Europe and later the rest of the world. The result of this new and vastly more ambitious policy was World War II and its consequences. The stakes were immeasurably higher than in World War I, and so were the "fruits" of defeat. At the end of the second global conflict German national unity had been destroyed, and the country was subjected to physical destruction on a scale unprecedented since the Thirty Years' War. Some 6 million Germans had died and another 12 million became refugees. In 1918 Germany lost some 13 percent of its prewar territory; in 1945 fully one-third of what had been Germany in 1871 was irretrievably lost. The Holocaust associated the German name with some of the worst government-sponsored outrages in any historical period.

The Reich's total defeat in 1945 finally led virtually all Germans—and not just because the victorious Allied powers insisted upon it—to confront their recent past and draw some lessons from it. The result was the admission, sometimes tacit, sometimes open, that in the future the state and culture of Germany needed drastic course corrections. It was a recognition that for much of its modern history Germany had been too "inner-directed." In domestic affairs various groups in German society—the old Prusso-German establishment, but also the radical Left and Right—were excessively "inner-directed"; they insisted that unless their parochial *Weltanschauung* were imposed on Germany, regardless of the consequences for other segments of society, history would have lost its meaning. In foreign relations "inner-directedness" led the leaders of Germany to look upon the country's power and stature as ends in themselves, rather than as means to help maintain an international balance of power.

After 1945 there was an understandable tendency to replace the failed "inner-directedness" with an equally sweeping "other-directedness." Germans both east and west of the Elbe wanted to throw off the burden of German history before 1945 and attempt to start over again at the point of "Zero Hour." There was a temptation to draw the value base for the new beginning not from the failed past of German history but from the values of the "others," that is to say, the victorious Allies and especially the two new superpowers, the United States and the Soviet Union.

The vagaries of modern German history. Although the East German old lady has never moved, her address changes constantly as the street name is altered to fit political circumstances. (Adolf Hennecke was an East German *stakhanovite* in the late forties. He was celebrated as a national hero for repeatedly exceeding his work norms.) (Source: *Lachen*, p. 336.)

Fortunately, East and West Germans came to recognize as well the futility and ahistorical nature of other-directedness. The open pluralist society of West Germany led the way, and, more recently, the Communists in East Germany have also acknowledged that to establish an ongoing national identity, all Germans need to integrate the entirety of the German past. In a sense, since 1945 the components of the "other" Germany, the liberal, pluralistic, and Marxist traditions, have been freed and allowed finally to become the dominant forces in

German society. True, these traditions also reflected the Allied program for remaking Germany, but they were not just imposed from the outside. They represented indigenous German forces that all too often tend to be overshadowed by the facile identification of modern German history with Prussian militarism and Nazi totalitarianism.

The remarkable success of the two Germanys after World War II testifies to the historic vitality of the "other" Germany. For the first time in its modern history, Germany can be said to have achieved balanced modernization; the asymmetry in its societal makeup has been largely eliminated. To be sure, the process of self-realization was undoubtedly hastened by the defeat and subsequent division of the country. This development forced the Germans to recognize that the two states were no longer great powers but are inextricably linked to the larger community of European nations.

For almost forty years after the end of World War II it seemed axiomatic that the two Germanys would remain separate countries, tied to opposing power blocs. But at the end of 1989 after the dramatic events in East Germany and Eastern Europe there was suddenly talk of German reunification. The tearful scenes of East and West Germans coming together as the physical barriers between the two states crumbled seemed to indicate that there was one German people after all.

Anxious to take the initiative, West German chancellor Helmut Kohl at the end of November 1989 proposed a multistep plan for a confederation and eventual unification of the GDR and the FRG. Kohl was careful not to insist on a timetable, but even so his initiative sent up warning flags in Moscow and Washington as well as in Paris and London.

The Soviet Union and the new leaders of East Germany both reacted sharply, claiming reunification was not "on the agenda." The United States supported Kohl in principle, but also made it clear that a united Germany was not a high priority item on the American agenda, and if and when reunification came, a united Germany needed to be tied to NATO and the European Community. The reaction of West Germany's partners in the European Community was similar. At a hastily called summit conference in Strasbourg in mid-December, the leaders of the EC (including Kohl) issued a statement favoring that "the German people will regain its unity through free self-determination," but the leaders also warned that the process of unification had to take place in the context of better European and superpower relations. Moreover, they insisted that a united Germany had to be created within the territorial boundaries established in 1945.

In the face of opposition from the East and cautioning statements from the West, the Federal Republic quickly retreated. Government leaders from president von Weiszäcker on down emphasized that "there should be no effort to push it [unification] to frantic growth." Ironically, words of caution also came from some of the leaders of the East German dissident groups. They, too, noted that they needed time to "find ourselves." At the beginning of the 1990s the future of Germany (or the Germanys) remains a question mark. Perhaps the East German writer and opponent of the Communist regime in the GDR, Christoph Hein, expressed the feelings of uncertainty best: "Right now, nothing is final; guesses are futile; events are moving too fast."

But such "go slow" sentiments did not count on the true feelings of the East German people. Faced with the GDR's collapsing economy and the prospect of experiencing the prosperity and freedom of Western pluralism for the first time, the citizens of the GDR rushed headlong toward reunification with the West. As we saw, in the elections of March, 1990, the big winners were the parties that promised to bring about rapid reunification. Proponents of a revitalized East Germany that would travel along a "third way" between socialism and capitalism found little support.

SUGGESTIONS FOR FURTHER READING

Note: Space limitations make it necessary to limit the extent and nature of the bibliography that follows. As a result only English-language works have been included, and the annotations have been kept to an absolute minimum. An effort has been made, however, to include some of the most recent and historiographically significant studies.

GENERAL WORKS

BENNET, BENJAMIN. *Modern Drama and German Classicism: Renaissance from Lessing to Brecht.* Ithaca, NY: Cornell University Press, 1979.

BERGHAHN, VOLKER R., ed. *Militarism: The History of an International Debate 1861–1979.* New York: St. Martin, 1980.

CRAIG, GORDON A. *The Germans.* New York: Meridian, 1982.

———. *From Bismarck to Adenauer.* Baltimore, MD: Johns Hopkins University Press, 1965.

DEHIO, LUDWIG. *Germany and World Politics in the Twentieth Century.* New York: Norton, 1959. (Superb study of the problem of hegemony in international relations.)

DEIST, WILHELM, ed. *The German Military in the Age of Total War.* Dover, NH: Berg, 1985.

ELEY, GEOFF. *From Unification to Nazism.* London: Allen & Unwin, 1986.

EMMEL, HILDEGARD. *History of the German Novel.* Trans. by Ellen Summerfield. Detroit, MI: Wayne State University Press, 1984.

EVANS, RICHARD J., AND W. ROBERT LEE, eds. *The German Peasantry.* New York: St. Martin, 1986.

FEST, WILFRIED. *Dictionary of German History, 1806–1945.* New York: St. Martin, 1979.

HILLGRUBER, ANDREAS. *Germany and the Two World Wars.* Trans. by William C. Kirby. Cambridge, MA: Harvard University Press, 1981. (First-rate comparative analysis of Germany's political and military strategic problems in the First and Second World Wars.)

IGGERS, GEORG G. *The German Conception of History: The National Tradition of Historical Thought from*

Herder to the Present, rev. ed. Middletown, CN: Wesleyan University Press, 1983.

KRIEGER, LEONARD. *The German Idea of Freedom: History of a Political Tradition.* Boston: Beacon, 1957. (Pioneering analysis of the peculiarities of German political thought in the nineteenth and twentieth centuries.)

GATZKE, HANS W. *Germany and the United States: A Special Relationship?* Cambridge, MA: Harvard University Press, 1980.

KITCHEN, MARTIN. *A Military History of Germany from the 18th Century to the Present Day.* Bloomington: Indiana University Press, 1975.

KOHN, HANS. *The Mind of the Germans: The Education of a Nation.* New York: Harper & Row, 1960. (Pioneering study of the problems and peculiarities of German nationalist thought.

STERN, FRITZ. *Dreams and Delusions: National Socialism and the Drama of the German Past.* New York: Vintage, 1989. (Retrospective collection of essays by one of the foremost historians of modern Germany.)

CHAPTER 1: THE QUEST FOR UNITY, 1815–1871

ALSOP, SUSAN MARY. *The Congress Dances: Vienna, 1814–1815.* New York: Harper & Row, 1983.

BAUMGART, WINFRIED. *Peace of Paris, 1856: Studies in War Diplomacy and Peacemaking.* Trans. by Ann Pottinger Saab. Santa Barbara, CA: ABC-Clio, 1983.

BIGLER, ROBERT M. *The Politics of German Protestantism: The Rise of the Protestant Church Elite in Prussia, 1815–1848.* Berkeley: University of California Press, 1972.

BLACKBOURN, DAVID, AND GEOFFREY ELEY. *The Peculiarities of German History: Bourgeois Society and Politics in Nineteenth Century Germany.* Oxford: Oxford University Press, 1984.

BRAMSTED, ERNEST K. *Aristocracy and the Middle Classes in Germany: Social Types in German Literature, 1830–1900.* Chicago: University of Chicago Press, 1964. (Classic study of the image of social classes in nineteenth-century German literature.)

BRUFORD, W. H. *The German Tradition of Self-Cultivation: Bildung from Humboldt to Thomas Mann.* Cambridge: Cambridge University Press, 1975.

CRAIG, GORDON. *The Prussian Army in Politics.* Oxford: Oxford University Press, 1975. (Still unsurpassed analysis of the Prussian army's crucial role in shaping the social and political evolution of Germany's largest state.)

CRANKSHAW, EDWARD. *Bismarck.* New York: Viking, 1981. (The best one-volume biography in English.)

EYCK, FRANK. *The Frankfurt Parliament, 1848–1849.* New York: St. Martin, 1968.

FOUT, JOHN C., ed. *German Women in the Nineteenth Century: A Social History.* New York: Holmes & Meier, 1986.

GERSCHENKRON, ALEXANDER. *Bread and Democracy in Germany.* Berkeley: University of California Press, 1943. (Classic, if somewhat one-sided study of the Junkers' role in retarding the political modernization of Germany.) Reprint 1966. New Edition: Charles S. Maier, ed. Ithaca, NY: Cornell University Press, 1989.

HAGEN, WILLIAM H. *Germans, Poles and Jews: The Nationality Conflict in the Prussian East, 1722–1914.* Chicago: University of Chicago Press, 1980.

HAMEROW, THEODORE S. *The Social Foundations of German Unification, 1858–1871.* Princeton, NJ: Princeton University Press, 1972. (Still the best one-volume analysis of the causes and failures of the Revolution of 1848.)

HENDERSON, WILLIAM A. *The Rise of German Industrial Power, 1834–1914.* Berkeley: University of California Press, 1975.

HENDERSON, WILLIAM O. *The Zollverein.* Cambridge: Cambridge University Press, 1939. (A model of detailed analysis.)

IGGERS, GEORG G., ed. *The Social History of Politics: Critical Perspectives in West German Historical Writing.* New York: St. Martin, 1986.

JOERES, RUTH-ELLEN B., and MARY JO MAYNES, eds. *German Women in the Nineteenth and Twentieth Centuries.* Bloomington: Indiana University Press, 1986.

KRAEHE, ENNO E. *Metternich's German Policy: The Congress of Vienna, 1814–1815.* Princeton, NJ: Princeton University Press, 1983. (Definitive work on the post-Napoleonic settlement.)

McCLELLAND, CHARLES E. *State, Society, and University in Germany, 1700–1914.* New York: Cambridge University Press, 1980.

MOSSE, GEORGE L. *The Nationalization of the Masses: Political Symbolism and Mass Movements in Ger-*

many from the Napoleonic Wars through the Third Reich. New York: Meridian, 1975. (Controversial tour-de-force.)

MOSSE, W. E. *The European Powers and the German Question, 1848–71.* Cambridge: Cambridge University Press, 1958.

MOSSE, WERNER E. *The German-Jewish Economic Elite, 1820–1935.* New York: Oxford University Press, 1987.

PFLANZE, OTTO. *Bismarck.* Princeton, NJ: Princeton University Press, 1963. (When completed, this promises to be the definitive multivolume biography.)

REINHARZ, YEHUDA, ed. *The Jewish Response to German Culture.* Hanover, NH: University Press of New England, 1985.

SAGARRA, EDA. *A Social History of Germany, 1648–1914.* London: Methuen, 1977.

SCHROEDER, PAUL W. *Austria, Great Britain, and the Crimean War: The Destruction of the European Concert.* Ithaca, NY: Cornell University Press, 1972.

SHEEHAN, JAMES J. *German Liberalism in the Nineteenth Century.* Chicago: University of Chicago Press, 1978. (Definitive and excellent.)

SIMON, WALTER M. *The Failure of the Prussian Reform Movement, 1807–1819.* New York: Howard Fertig, 1955.

TAYLOR, A.J.P. *Bismarck: The Man and the Statesman.* New York: Alfred A. Knopf, 1955. (Controversial interpretation by the gadfly of British historians.)

VALENTIN, VEIT. *1848: Chapters of German History.* Trans. E. T. Scheffeur. London: Allen & Unwin, 1940. (One-volume English-language condensation of the author's classic two-volume study; originally published in German in 1930.)

WALKER, MACK. *German Home Towns: Community, State, and General Estate, 1648–1871.* Ithaca, NY: Cornell University Press, 1971.

CHAPTER 2: THE FOUNDERS' GENERATION, 1871–1890

ANDERSON, MARGARET LAVINIA. *Windhorst: A Political Biography.* New York: Oxford University Press, 1981.

BERLIN, ISAIAH. *Karl Marx.* 3rd. ed. New York: Oxford University Press, 1963.

BISMARCK, OTTO VON. *Reflections and Reminiscences.* Trans. by A. J. Butler. New York: Howard Fertig, 1966. (Bismarck's memoirs, unreliable but indispensable.)

CECIL, LAMAR. *The German Diplomatic Service, 1871–1914.* Princeton, NJ: Princeton University Press, 1977. (Important institutional history.)

DOMINICK, RAYMOND H., III. *Wilhelm Liebknecht and the Founding of the German Social Democratic Party.* Chapel Hill: University of North Carolina Press, 1982.

DORPALEN, ANDREAS. *Heinrich von Treitschke.* New Haven, CT: Yale University Press, 1957.

EDERER, RUPERT J. *The Social Teachings of Wilhelm Emmanuel von Ketteler: Bishop of Mainz (1811–1877).* Washington, DC: University Press of America, 1982. (Important for a Catholic perspective on German industrialization.)

EVANS, ELLEN LOVELL. *The German Center Party, 1890–1933.* Carbondale: Southern Illinois University Press, 1981.

GALL, LOTHAR. *Bismarck: The White Revolutionary.* 2 vols. Trans. by J. A. Underwood. London: Allen & Unwin, 1986.

GEISS, IMANUEL. *German Foreign Policy, 1871–1914.* London: Routledge, Kegan & Paul, 1976.

HOWARD, MICHAEL. *The Franco-Prussian War: The German Invasion of France.* New York: Macmillan, 1961. (Definitive account of this important conflict.)

LAMBI, IVO N. *Free Trade and Protection in Germany, 1868–1879.* Wiesbaden: F. Steiner, 1963.

MITCHELL, ALAN. *The German Influence in France after 1870.* Chapel Hill: University of North Carolina Press, 1979.

MOSES, JOHN A. *Trade Unionism in Germany from Bismarck to Hitler, 1869–1933.* Totowa, NJ: Barnes & Noble, 1982.

PULZER, PETER. *The Rise of Political Anti-Semitism in Germany and Austria.* New York: Wiley, 1964.

REMAK, JOACHIM. *The Gentle Critic: Theodor Fontane and German Politics, 1848–1898.* Syracuse, NY: Syracuse University Press, 1964.

SHEEHAN, JAMES J., ed. *Imperial Germany.* New York: Franklin Watts, 1976.

STEENSON, GARY P. *"Not One Man! Not One Penny!" German Social Democracy, 1863–1914.* Pittsburgh: University of Pittsburgh Press, 1981.

STERN, FRITZ. *Gold and Iron: Bismarck, Bleichröder, and the Building of the German Empire.* New York: Alfred A. Knopf, 1977.

STOLPER, GUSTAV, et al. *The Economic Development of Germany, 1870 to the Present* Trans. by Toni Stolper. New York: Harcourt Brace Jovanovich, 1967.

TAL, URIEL. *Christians and Jews in Germany: Religion, Politics, and Ideology in the Second Reich, 1870–1914.* Ithaca, NY: Cornell University Press, 1975.

WEHLER, HANS-ULRICH. *The German Empire, 1871–1918.* Trans. by Kim Traynor, Dover, NH: Berg, 1985. (First-rate "structural" analysis by one of the leading proponents of the *Sonderweg* thesis.)

WHITE, DAN S. *The Splintered Party: National Liberalism in Hessen and the Reich, 1867–1918.* Cambridge, MA: Harvard University Press, 1976.

WINDELL, GEORGE, G. *The Catholics and German Unity, 1866–1871.* Minneapolis: University of Minnesota Press, 1954.

CHAPTER 3: WILHELMINIAN GERMANY, 1890–1914

ALBERTINI, LUIGI. *The Origins of the War of 1914.* Trans. and ed. by Isabelle M. Massey. 3 vols. London: Oxford University Press, 1952.

ALLEN, ANN TAYLOR. *Satire and Society in Wilhelmine Germany: Kladderadatsch and Simplicissimus, 1890–1914.* Louisville: University Press of Kentucky, 1984. (Unusual literary-political study.)

BACH, H. I. *The German Jew.* New York: Oxford University Press, 1985.

BALFOUR, MICHAEL. *The Kaiser and his Times.* London: Cresset Press, 1964. (Probably the most satisfactory one-volume biography of William II in English.)

BARKIN, KENNETH D. *The Controversy over German Industrialization.* Chicago: University of Chicago Press, 1970.

BERGHAHN, VOLKER ROLF. *Germany and the Approach of War in 1914.* New York: St. Martin, 1973.

CECIL, LAMAR. *Albert Ballin: Business and Politics in Imperial Germany, 1888–1918.* Princeton, NJ: Princeton University Press, 1967. (Empathic biography of Germany's leading shipping magnate.)

———. *William II.* Chapel Hill: University of North Carolina Press, 1989.

CHICKERING, ROGER. *We Men Who Feel Most German: A Cultural Study of the Pan-German League, 1886–1914.* London: Allen & Unwin, 1984.

ELEY, GEOFF. *Reshaping the German Right: Radical Nationalism and Political Change After Bismarck.* New Haven, CT.: Yale University Press, 1980.

EVANS, RICHARD. *The Feminist Movement in Germany, 1894–1933.* Beverly Hills: Sage, 1976.

———. ed. *Society and Politics in Wilhelmine Germany.* London: Croom Helm, 1978.

FLETCHER, ROGER, ed. *Bernstein to Brandt: A Short History of German Social Democracy.* New York: Edward Arnold, 1987.

———. *Revisionism and Empire: Socialist Imperialism in Germany, 1897–1914.* London: Allen & Unwin, 1984.

GAY, PETER. *Freud, Jews, and Other Germans: Master and Victims in Modernist Culture.* New York: Oxford University Press, 1978. A collection of essays by a dean of cultural historians.)

GUTTSMAN, W. L. *The German Social Democratic Party, 1875–1933.* London: Allen & Unwin, 1981.

HERWIG, HOLGER H. *The German Naval Officer Corps: A Social and Political History, 1890–1918.* Oxford: Clarendon, 1973. (Superb study of the leadership of the Kaiser's favorite branch of the military.

JARAUSCH, KONRAD H. *Students, Society and Politics in Imperial Germany: The Rise of Academic Illiberalism.* Princeton, NJ: Princeton University Press, 1982.

KEHR, ECKART. *Economic Interest, Militarism, and Foreign Policy: Essays on German History.* Ed. by Gordon A. Craig; trans. by Grete Heinz. Berkeley: University of California Press, 1977. (Influential collection of essays by the foremost revisionist German historian of the early twentieth century.)

KELLY, ALFRED, ed. and trans. *The German Worker: Working-Class Autobiographies from the Age of Industrialization.* Berkeley: University of California Press, 1987.

KENNAN, GEORGE. *The Decline of Bismarck's European Order.* Princeton, NJ: Princeton University Press, 1984. (Original interpretation by a master of diplomatic theory and practice.)

KENNEDY, PAUL. *The Rise of Anglo-German Antagonism, 1860–1914*. London: Allen & Unwin, 1980.

KITCHEN, MARTIN. *The German Officer Corps, 1890–1914*. Oxford: Oxford University Press, 1968.

LAMBI, IVO N. *The Navy and German Power Politics*. London: Allen & Unwin, 1984.

LAQUEUR, WALTER. *Young Germany*. New York: Basic Books, 1962. (Places the pre-1914 youth movement within the context of the tensions of Wilhelminian society.)

LEVY, RICHARD S. *The Downfall of the Anti-Semitic Political Parties in Imperial Germany*. New Haven, CT: Yale University Press, 1975.

LIDTKE, VERNON L. *The Alternative Culture: Socialist Labour in Imperial Germany*. New York: Oxford University Press, 1985.

MOMMSEN, WOLFGANG J., ed. *Theories of Imperialism*. Trans. by P. S. Falla. New York: Random House, 1980.

MOSSE, GEORGE L. *The Crisis of German Ideology*. New York: Grosset & Dunlap, 1964. (Controversial interpretation of the nineteenth-century intellectual roots of Nazism.)

MUNCY, LYSBETH. *The Junkers in the Prussian Administration under William II, 1888–1914*. Providence, RI: Brown University, 1944. (Still the best one-volume study in English.)

NETTL, JOHN P. *Rosa Luxemburg*. 2 vols. London: Oxford University Press, 1966. (Definitive biography of the intellectual leader of the SPD's left wing.)

NICHOLLS, J. ALDEN. *Germany After Bismarck: The Caprivi Era, 1890–1894*. Cambridge, MA: Harvard University Press, 1958.

RINGER, FRITZ K. *The German Mandarins*. Cambridge, MA: Harvard University Press, 1969. (First-rate analysis of the German academic establishment.)

RÖHL, JOHN C.G. *Germany Without Bismarck*. Berkeley: University of California Press, 1967.

ROSENBERG, ARTHUR. *Imperial Germany: The Birth of the German Republic*. Trans. by Ian F. D. Marner. Boston: Beacon Press, 1964. (Influential analysis by one of the founders of the USPD.)

ROSS, RONALD J. *Beleaguered Tower: The Dilemma of Political Catholicism in Wilhelmine German*. South Bend, IN: University of Notre Dame Press, 1976.

SACKETT, ROBERT E. *Popular Entertainment, Class, and Politics in Munich, 1900–1923*. Cambridge, MA: Harvard University Press, 1982.

SCHORSKE, CARL E. *German Social Democracy, 1905–1917: The Development of the Great Schism*. Cambridge, MA: Harvard University Press, 1955. (Classic analysis of the revisionism-anti-revisionism controversy in the SPD.)

STACHURA, PETER D. *The German Youth Movement, 1900–1945*. New York: St. Martin, 1981.

STERN, FRITZ R. *The Politics of Cultural Despair: A Study in the Rise of the German Ideology*. Berkeley: University of California Press, 1961. (Classical analysis of the anti-modernist trends in Wilhelminian intellectual and political life.)

ZEENDER, JOHN K. *The German Center Party, 1890–1906*. Philadelphia: American Philosophical Society, 1976.

CHAPTER 4: THE FIRST WORLD WAR, 1914–1918

BERGHAHN, VOLKER, R., and MARTIN KITCHEN, eds. *Germany in the Age of Total War*. Totowa, NJ: Barnes & Noble, 1981.

BIRNBAUM, KARL. *Peace Moves and U-Boat Warfare*. Hamden, CT: Archon Books, 1970. (Although a specialized study, this is a superb analysis of the interaction between diplomacy and military strategy.)

CARSTEN, FRANCIS L. *War Against War: British and German Radical Movements in the First World War*. Berkeley: University of California Press, 1982.

EDWARDS, MARVIN L. *Stresemann and the Greater Germany, 1914–1918*. New York: Twayne, 1963. (Specialized study of the foreign-policy aims of the leader of the National liberals.)

FARRAR, LANCELOT L. *The Short War Illusion: German Policy, Strategy, and Domestic Affairs, August–September 1914*. Santa Barbara, CA: ABC-Clio, 1973.

FELDMAN, GERALD D. *Army, Industry, and Labor in Germany, 1914–1918*. Princeton, NJ: Princeton University Press, 1966. (First-rate analysis of the conflict and symbiotic cooperation of the country's major interest groups in wartime.)

FISCHER, FRITZ. *Germany's Aims in the First World War*. New York: Norton, 1967. (Revisionist interpretation that became a *cause celèbre* in the 1960s.)

HARDACH, GERD. *The First World War.* Berkeley: University of California Press, 1977. (Examines particularly the structural economic changes that took place as a result of the war.)

HORN, DANIEL. *The German Naval Mutinies of World War I.* Rutgers, NJ: Rutgers University Press, 1969.

HORNE, ALISTAIR. *The Price of Glory: Verdun 1916.* New York: Penguin, 1962. (Detailed analysis of one of the crucial battles on the Western front.)

JARAUSCH, KONRAD H. *The Enigmatic Chancellor: Bethmann Hollweg and the Hubris of Imperial Germany.* New Haven, CT: Yale University Press, 1973.

KITCHEN, MARTIN. *The Silent Dictatorship: The Politics of the German High Command Under Hindenburg and Ludendorff, 1916–1918.* New York: Holmes & Meier, 1976.

KOCKA, JÜRGEN. *Facing Total War: German Society, 1914–1918.* Trans. by Barbara Weinberger. Cambridge, MA: Harvard University Press, 1985.

MAYER, ARNO J. *Political Origins of the New Diplomacy, 1917–1918.* New York: Howard Fertig, 1959. (Interpretation that stresses extrapolitical, especially economic, influences in diplomatic relations.)

MORGAN, DAVID. *German Left-Wing Socialism: A History of the German Independent Social Democratic Party.* Ithaca, NY: Cornell University Press, 1975. (Definitive account of the USPD's complex ideological and organizational makeup.)

VINCENT, C. PAUL. *The Politics of Hunger: The Allied Blockade of Germany, 1915–1919.* Athens: Ohio University Press, 1985.

WHEELER-BENNET, JOHN. *Brest-Litovsk: The Forgotten Peace.* New York: 1939. Reprint, 1971. (Classic but still unsurpassed study of this important episode.)

CHAPTER 5: REVOLUTION, INFLATION, AND PUTSCHES: THE SEARCH FOR A NEW CONSENSUS, 1918–1923

ANGRESS, WERNER T. *Stillborn Revolution.* Princeton, NJ: Princeton University Press, 1963. (Still the best account of the KPD's repeated and abortive attempts to stage a second revolution in the early years of the Weimar Republic.)

BURDICK, CHARLES B., and RALPH H. LUTZ, eds. *Political Institutions of the German Revolution, 1918–1919.* Stanford, CA: Hoover Institution, 1966. (The title is misleading; the book actually contains the debates of the executive committee set up by the National Congress of Workers' and Soldiers' Councils.)

CALKINS, KENNETH R. *Hugo Haase: Democrat and Revolutionary.* Durham, NC: Duke University Press, 1979.

CARSTEN, FRANCIS L. *Fascist Movements in Austria: From Schönerer to Hitler.* Beverly Hills, CA: Sage, 1977. (Important for the Austrian background of the Nazi movement.)

———. *The Reichswehr and Politics. 1918–1933.* Oxford: Oxford University Press, 1966.

———. *Revolution in Central Europe. 1918–1919.* Berkeley: University of California Press, 1972. (Puts the German events in the context of the Europe-wide post–World War I upheavals.)

COPER, RUDOLF. *Failure of a Revolution.* Cambridge, MA: Harvard University Press, 1955. (Detailed analysis of the Spartacist uprising in January 1919.)

DIEHL, JAMES M. *Paramilitary Politics in Weimar Germany.* Bloomington: Indiana University Press, 1977. (The most comprehensive book on the subject.)

EPSTEIN, KLAUS. *Matthias Erzberger and the Dilemma of German Democracy.* Princeton, NJ: Princeton University Press, 1959. (Definitive biography of this important and controversial Center Party leader.)

EYCK, ERICH. *History of the Weimar Republic.* 2 vols. New York: Antheneum, 1970. (Well-written and engaging political history by a contemporary; the author was a DDP member of the Berlin city council.)

FELDMAN, GERALD D. *Iron and Steel in the German Inflation, 1916–1923.* Princeton, NJ: Princeton University Press, 1977. (Superbly done continuation of the author's earlier book; details the interaction of business, labor, and government in the early years of the Weimar Republic.)

———. ed. *The German Inflation Reconsidered.* New York: De Gruyter, 1982.

FISCHER, FRITZ. *From Kaiserreich to Third Reich.*

Trans. by Roger Fletcher. Boston: Allen & Unwin, 1986. (A reassessment of the "Fischer thesis" by its author 25 years after the publication of Fischer's *Germany's Aims in the First World War.*)

FRYE, BRUCE B. *Liberal Democrats in the Weimar Republic.* Carbondale: Southern Illinois University Press, 1985.

GORDON, HAROLD J., JR. *Hitler and the Beer Hall Putsch.* Princeton, NJ: Princeton University Press, 1972. (The most detailed and satisfactory book on the subject.)

GRATHWOL, ROBERT P. *Stresemann and the DNVP: Reconciliation or Revenge in German Foreign Policy, 1924–1928.* Lawrence: University of Kansas Press, 1980.

HALPERIN, S. WILLIAM. *Germany Tried Democracy.* New York: Norton, 1946. (Older, but still useful one-volume history of the Weimar Republic.)

HARDACH, KARL. *The Political Economy of Germany in the Twentieth Century.* Berkeley: University of California Press, 1980.

HERTZMAN, LEWIS J. *DNVP.* Lincoln: University of Nebraska Press, 1963. (Still the best short history in English of the post–World War I conservatives.)

HUGHES, MICHAEL L. *Paying for the German Inflation.* Chapel Hill: University of North Carolina Press, 1988.

HUNT, RICHARD N. *German Social Democracy, 1918–1933.* New Haven, CT: Yale University Press, 1964. (The best one-volume overall treatment of the SPD during the Weimar years; critical of the party's leadership.)

KAUFMANN, WALTER H. *Monarchism in the Weimar Republic.* New York: Octagon, 1973. (Together with Hertzman's book, a basic source for right-wing politics in the Weimar years.)

KESSLER, COUNT HARRY. *In the Twenties.* Trans. by Charles Kessler. New York: Holt, Rinehart & Winston, 1971. (Somewhat gossipy diaries of an aesthete who traveled widely in social and political circles.)

MAIER, CHARLES S. *Reconstructing Bourgeois Europe.* Princeton, NJ: Princeton University Press, 1975. (Well-done comparative analysis of German, Italian, and French society in the 1920s.)

MAYER, ARNO. *Politics and Diplomacy of Peacemaking: Containment and Counter-Revolution at Ver-* *sailles.* New York: Alfred A. Knopf, 1967. (Controversial interpretation that argues the Versailles settlement was motivated primarily by the Allies' fear of left-wing revolutions.)

MITCHELL, ALAN. *Revolution in Bavaria.* Princeton, NJ: Princeton University Press, 1965.

RYDER, A. J. *The German Revolution of 1918.* Cambridge, MA: Harvard University Press, 1968.

SCHWABE, KLAUS. *Woodrow Wilson, Revolutionary Germany, and Peacemaking, 1918–1919: Missionary Diplomacy and the Realities of Power.* Chapel Hill: University of North Carolina Press, 1985.

SMITH, BRADLEY F. *Adolf Hitler: His Family, Childhood, and Youth.* Stanford, CA: Hoover Institution, 1967. Reprint, 1979. (This and the next entry are superb short studies by a master of detailed analysis.)

————. *Heinrich Himmler: A Nazi in the Making, 1900–1926.* Stanford, CA: Hoover Institution, 1971.

STEVENSON, DAVID. *French War Aims Against Germany, 1914–1919.* Oxford: Oxford University Press, 1982.

TAYLOR, RONALD. *Literature and Society in Germany, 1918–1945.* Totowa, NJ: Barnes & Noble, 1980.

TRACHTENBERG, MARC. *Reparations and World Politics.* New York: Columbia University Press, 1980. (Along with the Schuker entry listed under chapter 6, one of a number of recent works arguing that contrary to what most Germans—and many historians—thought, the Versailles settlement was not particularly harsh on Germany.)

WAITE, ROBERT G. L. *Vanguard of Nazism: The Free Corps Movement in Post-war Germany, 1918–1923.* Cambridge, MA: Harvard University Press, 1952. Reprint, 1970. (Classic study emphasizing the proto-fascistic nature of the Freikorps; now somewhat eclipsed by the Diehl entry.)

WALDMANN, ERIC. *The Spartacist Uprising of 1919.* Milwaukee, WI: Marquette University Press, 1958.

CHAPTER 6: FOOL'S GOLD: THE WEIMAR REPUBLIC, 1924–1930

ALDCROFT, DEREK H. *From Versailles to Wall Street: The International Economy in the 1920's.* Berkeley: University of California Press, 1977.

BERLAU, ABRAHAM JOSEPH. *The German Social Democratic Party.* New York: Octagon, 1949.

BESSEL, RICHARD, and E. J. FEUCHTWANGER, eds. *Social Change and Political Development in the Weimar Republic.* London: Croom Helm, 1981.

BRADY, ROBERT A. *The Rationalization Movement in German Industry: A Study in the Evolution of Economic Planning.* Berkeley: University of California Press, 1933. (Classic study on the transformation of German capitalism in the second half of the Weimar years.)

BRAUNTHAL, GERARD. *Socialist Labor and Politics in Weimar Germany: The General Federation of German Trade Unions.* Hamden, CT: Archon Books, 1978.

BREITMAN, RICHARD. *German Socialism and Weimar Democracy.* Chapel Hill: University of North Carolina Press, 1981. (Especially valuable for its analysis of the confrontation of the SPD and the rising Nazis.)

BULLOCK, ALAN. *Hitler: A Study in Tyranny.* London: Odhams Press, 1952. (The first scholarly biography of Hitler to appear after World War II.)

CARR, E. H. *German-Soviet Relations Between the Two World Wars, 1919–1939.* Baltimore: Johns Hopkins University Press, 1951. Reprint, 1983.

CHILDERS, THOMAS. *The Nazi Voter: The Social Foundations of Fascism in Germany, 1919–1933.* Chapel Hill: University of North Carolina Press, 1983. (One of a number of recent works using sophisticated quantitative methods to analyze Nazi support.)

DEAK, ISTVAN. *Weimar Germany's Left-Wing Intellectuals: A Political History of the "Weltbühne" and its Circle.* Berkeley: University of California Press, 1968. (The left-wing periodical *Weltbühne* was one of the most influential publications during the Weimar years.)

EISNER, LOTTE. *The Haunted Screen: Expressionism in the German Cinema and the Influence of Max Reinhardt.* Berkeley: University of California Press, 1969.

EVANS, RICHARD J., and DICK GEARY, eds. *The German Unemployed, 1918–1936.* New York: St. Martin, 1987.

FEST, JOACHIM C. *Hitler.* New York: Harcourt Brace Jovanovich, 1973. (Probably the best of the recent crop of Hitler biographies.)

FOWKES, BEN. *Communism in Germany Under the Weimar Republic.* New York: St. Martin, 1984.

GATZKE, HANS. *Stresemann and the Rearmament of Germany.* Baltimore: Johns Hopkins University Press, 1954.

GAY, PETER. *Weimar Culture: The Outsider as Insider.* New York: Harper & Row, 1968. (Iconoclastic interpretation of Weimar intellectual life.)

HAMILTON, NIGEL. *The Brothers Mann: The Lives of Heinrich and Thomas Mann, 1871–1950, 1875–1955.* New Haven, CT: Yale University Press, 1978.

HEBERLE, RUDOLF. *From Democracy to Nazism.* Baton Rouge: Louisiana State University Press, 1945. (Pioneering study analyzing electoral support for the Nazis in the rural area of Schleswig-Holstein.)

HERF, JEFFREY. *Reactionary Modernism: Technology, Culture, and Politics in Weimar and the Third Reich.* New York: Cambridge University Press, 1984.

HESS, HANS. *George Grosz.* New Haven, CT: Yale University Press, 1974. (One of the few English-language studies of the Weimar Republic's leading caricaturist.)

JACOBSON, JON. *Locarno Diplomacy: Germany and the West, 1925–1929.* Princeton, NJ: Princeton University Press, 1972.

JÄCKEL, EBERHARD. *Hitler's World View: A Blueprint for Power.* Middletown, CT: Wesleyan University Press, 1972. (The best short analysis of Hitler's basic ideas and motivation.)

JAMES, HAROLD. *The German Slump: Politics and Economics, 1924–1936.* Oxford: Clarendon Press, 1986.

JONES, LARRY EUGENE. *German Liberalism and the Dissolution of the Weimar Party System, 1918–1933.* Chapel Hill: University of North Carolina Press, 1988.

KATER, MICHAEL H. *The Nazi Party: A Social Profile of Members and Leaders, 1919–1945.* Cambridge, MA: Harvard University Press, 1983. (Like the Childers entry, an analysis that makes use of sophisticated quantitative research methods.)

KOLB, EBERHARD. *The Weimar Republic.* Trans. by P. S. Falla. Boston: Unwin & Hyman, 1988.

KRACAUER, SIEGFRIED. *From Caligari to Hitler: A Psychological Study of the German Film.* Princeton, NJ: Princeton University Press, 1947. (Pioneering study in the sociology of the cinema.)

LAQUEUR, WALTER. *Weimar: A Cultural History.* New York: Putnam, 1974.

LEBOVICS, HERMAN E. *Social Conservatism and the Middle Classes in Germany.* Princeton, NJ: Princeton University Press, 1969. (First-rate analysis of the motivation underlying the anti-republican and anti-democratic attitudes of many middle-class Germans.)

MASON, TIM. *Social Policy in the Third Reich.* New York: Berg, 1990. (Makes available in English important writings of a British historian, most of whose work had previously appeared only in German.)

MERKL, PETER H. *The Making of a Stormtrooper.* Princeton, NJ: Princeton University Press, 1980. (Well-done sociopolitical profile of the Nazis' paramilitary organization.)

NOAKES, JEREMY, ed. *Documents on Nazism, 1919–1945.* Atlantic Highlands, NJ: Humanities Press, 1974. (The best collection of basic primary materials in English.)

ORLOW, DIETRICH. *The History of the Nazi Party, 1919–1933.* Pittsburgh: University of Pittsburgh Press, 1969.

PLUMMER, THOMAS G. et al., eds. *Film and Politics in the Weimar Republic.* New York: Holmes & Meier, 1982.

PRIDHAM, GEOFFREY. *The Nazi Movement in Bavaria, 1923–1933.* New York: Harper & Row, 1973. (Representative of a number of excellent analyses on the rise of the Nazis on the regional and local levels.)

RAUSCHNING, HERMANN. *Hitler Speaks.* London: Butterworth, 1939. (Revealing memoirs by an early Nazi supporter who later broke with the movement.)

SCHRADER, BÄRBEL, and JÜRGEN SCHEBERA. *The "Golden" Twenties: Art and Literature in the Weimar Republic.* Trans. by Katherine Vanovitch. New Haven, CT: Yale University Press, 1988.

SCHUKER, STEPHEN A. *The Financial Crisis of 1924 and the Adoption of the Dawes Plan.* Chapel Hill: University of North Carolina Press, 1976. (Like the Trachtenberg entry [in chapter 5], this work takes a revisionist view of Versailles.)

STACHURA, PETER D. *Nazi Youth in the Weimar Republic.* Santa Barbara, CA: ABC-Clio, 1975.

———. ed. *Unemployment and the Great Depression in Weimar Germany.* New York: St. Martin, 1986.

STEINBERG, MICHAEL S. *Sabres and Brown Shirts:*

The German Students' Path to National Socialism, 1918–1935. Chicago: University of Chicago Press, 1977.

TURNER, HENRY A. *Stresemann and the Politics of the Weimar Republic.* Princeton, NJ: Princeton University Press, 1963. (An important monograph that makes extensive use of the Stresemann papers.)

WILLETT, JOHN. *Theater of the Weimar Republic.* New York: Holmes & Meier, 1984.

CHAPTER 7: FROM AUTHORITARIANISM TO TOTALITARIANISM, 1930–1938

ALLEN, WILLIAM S. *The Nazi Seizure of Power: The Experience of a Single German Town, 1922–1945.* New York: Franklin Watts, 1984. (Revised edition of what has become a classic in local history.)

ANSEL, WALTER. *Hitler Confronts England.* Durham, NC: Duke University Press, 1960.

BARKAI, AVRAHAM. *The Nazi Economy: Ideology, Theory, and Policy, 1933–1945.* New York: Berg, 1989.

BENNETT, EDWARD W. *The German Rearmament and the West, 1932–1933.* Princeton, NJ: Princeton University Press, 1979.

———. *Germany and the Diplomacy of the Financial Crisis, 1931.* Cambridge, MA: Harvard University Press, 1962.

BENTLEY, JAMES. *Martin Niemöller.* New York: Free Press, 1984. (Biography of one of the founders of the Confessional church.)

BESSEL, RICHARD, ed. *Life in the Third Reich.* New York: Oxford University Press, 1987. (A good example of the genre of history of "everyday life.")

BEYERCHEN, ALAN D. *Scientists Under Hitler: Politics and the Physics Community in the Third Reich.* New Haven, CT: Yale University Press, 1977.

BINION, RUDOLPH. *Hitler Among the Germans.* New York: Elsevier, 1976. (This book and the later Waite and Stern entries are representative of efforts to analyze the Hitler and Nazi phenomena with psychohistorical methods.)

BRACHER, KARL DIETRICH. *The German Dictatorship: The Origin, Structure, and Effect of National Socialism.* Trans. by Jean Steinberg. New York: Praeger, 1970. (This and the following entry are the best one-volume histories of the Third Reich and its antecedents.)

BROSZAT, MARTIN. *Hitler and the Collapse of Weimar Germany.* Trans. and intro. by Volker R. Berghahn. New York: St. Martin, 1987.

———. *The Hitler State: The Foundation and Development of the Internal Structure of the Third Reich.* London: Longman's, 1981.

CAPLAN, JANE. *Government without Administration: State and Civil Service in Weimar and Nazi Germany.* Oxford: Clarendon Press, 1989.

CONWAY, JOHN S. *The Nazi Persecution of the Churches, 1933–1945.* New York: Basic Books, 1968.

DEIST, WILHELM. *The Wehrmacht and German Rearmament.* Toronto: University of Toronto Press, 1981.

DESCHNER, GÜNTHER. *Reinhold Heydrich.* New York: Stein & Day, 1981.

FARQUHARSON, J. E. *The Plough and the Swastika: N.S.D.A.P. and Agriculture in Germany, 1928–1945.* Bloomington: Indiana University Press, 1976.

FISCHER, CONAN. *Stormtroopers: A Social, Economic, and Ideological Analysis, 1929–1935.* London: Allen & Unwin, 1983.

FRAENKEL, ERNST. *The Dual State: A Contribution to the Theory of Dictatorship.* New York: Octagon, 1969. (Classic study emphasizing the uneasy relationship between party and state in the Nazi system.)

GILES, GEOFFREY J. *Students and National Socialism in Germany.* Princeton, NJ: Princeton University Press, 1985.

GROSSHANS, HENRY. *Hitler and the Artists.* New York: Holmes & Meier, 1983.

HAFFNER, SEBASTIAN. *The Meaning of Hitler.* Trans. by Ewald Osers. Cambridge, MA: Harvard University Press, 1983. (Thought-provoking attempt to assess the historic significance of Hitler and the Nazis.)

HAMILTON, RICHARD F. *Who Voted for Hitler?* Princeton, NJ: Princeton University Press, 1982. (Revisionist analysis which argues that contrary to what many scholars thought, the Nazis' electoral support was strongest not among the lower-middle classes, but among upper and upper-middle-class Germans.)

HAYES, PETER. *Industry and Ideology: I.G. Farben in the Nazi Era.* New York: Cambridge University Press, 1987. (Definitive history of the chemical conglomerate.)

HILDEBRAND, KLAUS. *The Foreign Policy of the Third Reich.* Trans. by Anthony Fothergill. London: Batsford, 1973. (The best short treatment of the subject.)

———. *The Third Reich.* Trans. by P. S. Falla. London: Allen & Unwin, 1984. (Especially useful for its insightful comments on the historiography of the Nazi era.)

HÖHNE, HEINZ. *The Order of the Death's Head.* New York: Coward McCann, 1969.

HOMZE, EDWARD L. *Arming the Luftwaffe: The Reich Air Ministry and the German Aircraft Industry, 1919–1939.* Lincoln: University of Nebraska Press, 1977.

HULL, DAVID S. *Film in the Third Reich: A Study of the German Cinema.* Berkeley: University of California Press, 1969.

JARAUSCH, KONRAD H. *The Unfree Professions: German Lawyers, Teachers, and Engineers, 1900–1950.* New York: Oxford University Press, 1989.

KELE, MAX. *Nazis and Workers.* Chapel Hill: University of North Carolina Press, 1972. (Argues that Nazi support among German labor was stronger than generally thought.)

KERSHAW, IAN. *The Nazi Dictatorship: Problems and Perspectives in Interpretation.* London: Edward Arnold, 1985. (Particularly important for its discussion of the historiography of Nazism.)

———. *Popular Opinion and Political Dissent in the Third Reich: Bavaria, 1933–1945.* New York: Oxford University Press, 1985. (One of a number of recent works demonstrating the limits of Nazi totalitarianism as far as life for the average German was concerned.)

KINDLEBERGER, CHARLES P. *The World in Depression, 1929–1939.* Berkeley: University of California Press, 1973.

KLEMPERER, KLEMENS VON. *Germany's New Conservatism.* Princeton, NJ: Princeton University Press, 1957. (Pioneering study of the New Right.)

KOCH, HANNSJOACHIM W. *The Hitler Youth.* London: Macdonald & Jane's, 1975.

KOONZ, CLAUDIA. *Mothers in the Fatherland.* New York: St Martin, 1987. (Important study of the Nazi women's organization.)

LEOPOLD, JOHN A. *Alfred Hugenberg: The Radical Nationalist Campaign Against the Weimar Repub-*

lic. New Haven, CT: Yale University Press, 1977.

Lewy, Günter. *The Catholic Church and Nazi Germany.* New York: McGraw-Hill, 1964.

Mosse, George L. *Nazi Culture.* New York: Schocken, 1981.

Müller, Klaus-Jürgen. *The Army, Politics, and Society in Germany, 1933–1946.* New York: St. Martin, 1987.

Overy, R. J. *The Nazi Economic Recovery, 1932–1938.* London: Macmillan, 1982.

Peterson, Edward N. *The Limits of Hitler's Power.* Princeton, NJ: Princeton University Press, 1969. (Like the Kershaw entry, one of the books that demolished the myth of Nazi totalitarianism.)

Ritchie, James M. *German Literature Under National Socialism.* Totowa, NJ: Barnes & Noble, 1983.

Smelser, Ronald. *Robert Ley.* New York: Berg, 1988. (The only English-language biography of the head of the Nazi German Labor Front.)

Schweitzer, Arthur. *Big Business and the Third Reich.* Bloomington: Indiana University Press, 1964. (Somewhat misleading title; the book is really an economic history of the early years of the Third Reich.)

Seabury, Paul. *The Wilhelmstrasse.* Berkeley: University of California Press, 1954. (Institutional analysis of the German Foreign Ministry.)

Stephenson, Jill. *Women in Nazi Society.* New York: Harper & Row, 1981.

Stachura, Peter D. *Gregor Strasser and the Rise of Nazism.* London: Allen & Unwin, 1983. (The only full-scale study in English of the man who, until his resignation from the NSDAP at the end of 1932, was regarded by many as one of the most influential men in the Nazi Party.)

Stern J. P. *Hitler: Führer and People.* Berkeley: University of California Press, 1974.

Turner, Henry A., Jr. *German Big Business and the Rise of Hitler.* New York: Oxford University Press, 1984. (Argues convincingly that financial support from the business community for the Nazis was not nearly as extensive as often claimed.)

Waite, Robert G. L. *The Psychopathic God: Adolf Hitler.* New York: Basic Books, 1977.

Wegner, Bernd. *The Waffen-SS: Ideology, Organization, and Function.* Trans. by Ronald Webster. Oxford: Basil Blackwell, 1989.

Weinberg, Gerhard L. *The Foreign Policy of Hitler's Germany: The Diplomatic Revolution in Europe, 1933–1936.* Chicago: University of Chicago Press, 1970. (Along with the volume by the same author covering the later years—cited under chapter 8—this book is the definitive treatment of the Third Reich's foreign policy.)

Welch, David. *Propaganda and the German Cinema.* New York: Oxford University Press, 1985.

Zeman, Zbyněk. *Nazi Propaganda.* New York: Oxford University Press, 1964. (Still the best treatment in English of the Nazis' and especially Joseph Goebbels' propaganda aims and methods.)

CHAPTER 8: CONQUEST, DEATH, AND DEFEAT, 1938–1945

Arendt, Hannah. *Eichmann in Jerusalem: The Banality of Evil.* Rev. ed. New York: Penguin, 1964. New ed., 1977. (Controversial interpretation of the Holocaust and Adolf Eichmann's role in it.)

Bauer, Yehuda. *A History of the Holocaust.* New York: Doubleday, 1982. (Updates to some extent the more detailed but also older Hilberg entry.)

Beck, Earl R. *Under the Bombs: The German Home Front, 1942–1945.* Lexington: University Press of Kentucky, 1986.

Black, Peter R. *Ernst Kaltenbrunner.* Princeton, NJ: Princeton University Press, 1984. (Biography of Heydrich's successor. Kaltenbrunner was the man primarily responsible for implementing the Holocaust.)

Calvocoressi, Peter, and Guy Wint. *Total War: Causes and Courses of the Second World War.* New York: Penguin, 1972. (Has been described as "the best one-volume history of the Second World War.")

Carell, Paul. *Hitler Moves East, 1941–1943.* Boston: Little, Brown, 1964.

Ciechanowski, Jan M. *The Warsaw Rising of 1944.* New York: Cambridge University Press, 1974.

Dallin, Alexander. *German Rule in Russia, 1941–1945.* 2nd ed. Boulder, CO: Westview, 1981.

(Originally published in 1957, this is still the best account of the Nazis' misguided and cruel occupation policies in the Soviet Union.)

DAWIDOWICZ, LUCY S. *The Holocaust and the Historians*. Cambridge, MA: Harvard University Press, 1981. (Argues passionately and somewhat unfairly that the historical establishment has slighted the Holocaust.)

FLEMING, GERALD. *Hitler and the Final Solution*. Berkeley: University of California Press, 1984. (Important work that convincingly lays to rest any claims that Hitler did not personally order the Holocaust.)

FLOWER, DESMOND, and JAMES REEVES, eds. *The Taste of Courage: The War, 1939–1945*. 5 vols. New York: Putnam, 1960. (Probably the best detailed history of World War II.)

GILBERT, MARTIN, and RICHARD GOTT. *The Appeasers*. Boston: Houghton, Mifflin, 1963. (The best analysis especially of the motivation of the British appeasers.)

HEINEMAN, JOHN L. *Hitler's First Foreign Minister: Constantin Freiherr von Neurath, Diplomat and Statesman*. Berkeley: University of California Press, 1979. (Definitive but also somewhat apologetic biography of a traditional conservative who served the Nazis to the end.)

HELMREICH, ERNST CHRISTIAN. *The German Churches Under Hitler: Background, Struggle, and Epilogue*. Detroit: Wayne State University Press, 1979.

HILBERG, RAUL. *The Destruction of the European Jews*. Rev. ed. New York: Holmes & Meier, 1985. (Remains the best, most reliable, and most detailed account of the Holocaust.)

HOMZE, EDWARD L. *Foreign Labor in Nazi Germany*. Princeton, NJ: Princeton University Press, 1967.

JUKES, GEOFFREY. *Hitler's Stalingrad Decisions*. Berkeley: University of California Press, 1985.

KOEHL, ROBERT L. *The Black Corps: The Structure and Power Struggles of the Nazi SS*. Madison: University of Wisconsin Press, 1983.

LIFTON, ROBERT JAY. *The Nazi Doctors: Medical Killing and the Psychology of Genocide*. New York: Harper & Row, 1986.

LUZA, RADOMIR. *Austro-German Relations in the Anschluss Era*. Princeton, NJ: Princeton University Press, 1975.

MACKSEY, KENNETH J. *The Partisans of World War II*. New York: Stein & Day, 1975.

MAYER, ARNO J. *Why did the Heavens Not Darken? The "Final Solution" in History*. New York: Pantheon, 1989. (Provocative interpretation of the Holocaust that attempts to place it in a longitudinal historical setting.)

MEINECKE, FRIEDRICH. *The German Catastrophe*. Cambridge, MA: Harvard University Press, 1950. (Historiographically important early attempt by a leading German historian to assess the significance of Hitler and the Nazis.)

MICHEL, HENRI. *The Shadow War: European Resistance, 1939–1945*. New York: Harper & Row, 1972.

MILWARD, ALAN S. *The German Economy at War*. London: Athlone Press, 1965. (The best one-volume account of the wartime economy.)

ORLOW, DIETRICH. *The History of the Nazi Party, 1933–1945*. Pittsburgh: University of Pittsburgh Press, 1973.

READ, ANTHONY, and DAVID FISHER. *The Deadly Embrace: Hitler, Stalin, and the Nazi-Soviet Pact, 1939–1941*. New York: Norton, 1988.

SCHRAMM, PERCY ERNST. *Hitler: The Man and the Military Leader*. Trans. by Donald S. Detwiler. New York: Franklin Watts, 1971. (Schramm, a leading German historian, during World War II was assigned to the *Wehrmacht* high command as war diarist.)

SCHULTE, THEO. *The German Army and Nazi Policies in the Soviet Union*. New York: Berg, 1988.

SHEPHERD, GORDON. *The Anschluss*. Philadelphia: Lippincott, 1963. (Classic account of the annexation of Austria by the Third Reich.)

SPEER, ALBERT. *Inside the Third Reich*. New York: Macmillan, 1970. (Speer has been described as the friend Hitler would have had if the dictator had been capable of forming friendships; Speer was also the only one of the defendants at Nuremberg to acknowledge the evil nature of the Nazi regime and his part in it.)

STEIN, GEORGE. *The Waffen SS*. Ithaca, NY: Cornell University Press, 1966. (First-rate analysis of the Nazis' elite fighting corps.)

TAYLOR, A.J.P. *The Origins of the Second World War*. 2nd ed. New York: Antheneum, 1961. (Argues—not very convincingly—that World War II resulted from Hitler's miscalculations, not his premeditated intent to unleash a war of conquest.)

TREVOR–ROPER, HUGH R. *The Last Days of Hitler*.

3rd ed. New York: Collier Books, 1962. (Superior piece of detective work detailing the last days of the war in Hitler's bunker.)

WEINBERG, GERHARD L. *The Foreign Policy of Hitler's Germany, 1937–1939*. Chicago: University of Chicago Press, 1980. (The second volume of what will be the definitive, multivolume history of Nazi foreign policy.)

ZIEMKE, EARL F. *Stalingrad to Berlin: The German Defeat in the East*. Washington, DC: Office of the Chief of Military History, 1968.

CHAPTER 9: "CONDOMINIUM OF THE ALLIED POWERS," 1945–1949

ALMOND, GABRIEL A. *The Struggle for Democracy in Germany*. Chapel Hill: University of North Carolina Press, 1949.

BACKER, JOHN H. *The Decision to Divide Germany*. Durham, NC: Duke University Press, 1978.

———. *Winds of History: The German Years of Lucius Dubignon Clay*. New York: van Nostrand Reinhold, 1983.

BALFOUR, MICHAEL. *Four Power Control in Germany and Austria, 1945–1946*. London: Oxford University Press, 1956.

———, and JULIAN FRISBY. *Helmuth von Moltke: A Leader Against Hitler*. New York: St. Martin, 1972. (Sympathetic biography of an important leader of the German resistance.)

CAIRNCROSS, ALEC. *The Price of War: British Policy on German Reparations, 1941–1949*. New York: Basil Blackwell, 1986.

CHILDS, DAVID. *The SPD from Schumacher to Brandt: The Story of German Socialism, 1945–1965*. New York: Pergamon, 1966. (The best short history of the postwar SPD in English.)

CLAY, LUCIUS D. *Decision in Germany*. Garden City, New York: Doubleday, 1950. (Memoirs of the American military governor who had a crucial role in determining the future fortunes of West Germany.)

CLEMENS, DIANE SHAVER. *Yalta*. New York: Oxford University Press, 1971. (First-rate account of the most controversial of the wartime Allied summit conferences.)

DAVIDSON, EUGENE. *The Trial of the Germans*. New York: Macmillan, 1966. (Detailed and fair treatment of the trial of the major Nazi war criminals before the International Tribunal at Nuremberg.)

DE PORTE, ANTON W. *The Enduring Balance Between the Super Powers*. New Haven, CT: Yale University Press, 1979. (One of a series of works—the Gaddis and Yergin entries are others—attempting to explain the emergence of the Cold War and the division of Germany as consequences of the developing global conflict among the superpowers.)

DULLES, ALLEN W. *Germany's Underground*. New York: Macmillan, 1947. (The author headed American intelligence efforts in Europe and was personally acquainted with many of the German resisters.)

EDINGER, LEWIS J. *German Exile Politics: The Social Democratic Executive Committee in the Nazi Era*. Berkeley: University of California Press, 1956.

———. *Kurt Schumacher: A Study in Personality and Political Behavior*. Stanford, CA: Stanford University Press, 1965. (A psychohistorical biography of an important and abrasive political leader.)

FARQUHARSON, JOHN E. *The Western Allies and the Politics of Food: Agrarian Management in Postwar Germany*. Dover, NH: Berg, 1985.

FEIS, HERBERT. *Between War and Peace: The Potsdam Conference*. Princeton, NJ: Princeton University Press, 1960. (Somewhat dated but still useful account of the conference that many historians feel sealed the division of Germany.)

GADDIS, JOHN. *The United States and the Origins of the Cold War*. New York: Columbia University Press, 1972.

GLASER, HERMANN. *The Rubble Years*. New York: Paragon House, 1987.

GIMBEL, JOHN. *The American Occupation of Germany: Politics and the Military, 1945–1949*. Stanford, CA: Stanford University Press, 1968.

HANSER, RICHARD. *A Noble Treason: The Revolt of the Munich Students Against Hitler*. New York: Putnam, 1979. (Background of the White Rose student resistance.)

HEARNDEN, ARTHUR, ed. *The British in Germany*. London: Hamilton, 1978. (A collection of essays especially useful on the "re-education" efforts of the British.)

HOFFMANN, PETER. *The History of the German Resistance, 1933–1945*. Cambridge, MA: MIT

Press, 1977. (The definitive work on the subject.)

KRISCH, H. *German Politics Under Soviet Occupation.* New York: Columbia University Press, 1975.

MASTNY, VOITECH. *Russia's Road to the Cold War: Diplomacy, Warfare, the Politics of Communism.* New York: Columbia University Press, 1979.

MEE, CHARLES. *Meeting at Potsdam.* New York: M. Evans, 1975. (Journalistic and somewhat superficial account.)

MILWARD, ALAN S. *The Reconstruction of Western Europe, 1945–1951.* Berkeley: University of California Press, 1984. (Revisionist interpretation that downgrades the significance of the Marshall Plan as a factor in the economic revival of West Germany and Western Europe.)

NETTL, JOHN G. *The Eastern Zone and Soviet Policy in Germany, 1945–1950.* New York: Oxford University Press, 1951.

PETERSON, EDWARD N. *The American Occupation of Germany: Retreat to Victory.* Detroit: Wayne State University Press, 1978. (Argues that U.S. occupation policies succeeded because the military government successively abandoned its original intentions and premises.)

PFANNER, HELMUT F. *Exile in New York: German and Austrian Writers After 1933.* Detroit: Wayne State University Press, 1983.

PIKE, DAVID. *German Writers in Soviet Exile.* Chapel Hill: University of North Carolina Press, 1982.

PRONAY, NICHOLAS, and KEITH WILSON, eds. *The Political Re-Education of Germany and her Allies After World War II.* Totowa, NJ: Barnes & Noble, 1985.

RÜCKERL, ADALBERT, ed. *The Investigation of Nazi Crimes, 1945–1978.: A Documentation.* Trans. by Derek Rutter. Heidelberg: C. F. Müller, 1979. (An important introduction to a subject that is not well covered in English; the author was a federal German prosecutor of war crimes.)

SANFORD, GREGORY W. *From Hitler to Ulbricht: The Communist Reconstruction of East Germany, 1945–1946.* Princeton, NJ: Princeton University Press, 1983.

SCHOLL, INGE. *Students Against Tyranny: The Resistance of the White Rose, Munich, 1942–1943.* Trans. by Arthur R. Schultz. Middletown, CT: Wesleyan University Press, 1970. (The author is the sister of Sophie Scholl, one of the leaders of the White Rose resistance group.)

SMITH, BRADLEY F. *The Road to Nuremberg.* New York: Basic Books, 1981. (The best short introduction to the International Military Tribunal trial.)

WILLIS, F. R. *The French in Germany, 1945–1949.* Stanford, CA: Stanford University Press, 1962. (Remains the only full-scale study in English of French occupation policies.)

YERGIN, DANIEL. *The Shattered Peace: The Origins of the Cold War and the National Security State.* Boston: Houghton, Mifflin, 1977.

CHAPTER 10: THE FEDERAL REPUBLIC OF GERMANY, 1949–1990

ADENAUER, KONRAD. *Memoirs.* Trans. by Beate Ruhm von Oppen. Chicago: Henry Regnery, 1966.

BALFOUR, MICHAEL. *West Germany: A Contemporary History.* New York: St. Martin, 1982. (Probably the best short history of the FRG.)

BERGHAHN, VOLKER R. *The Americanization of West German Industry, 1945–1973.* New York: Cambridge University Press, 1986.

BRAUNTHAL, GERALD. *The West German Social Democrats, 1969–1982.* Boulder, CO: Westview Press, 1983.

BURKETT, TONY. *Parties and Elections in West Germany: The Search for Stability.* New York: St. Martin, 1975.

CAPRA, FRITJOF, and CHARLENE SPETNAK. *Green Politics.* New York: Dutton, 1984. (Attempt to assess the significance of a recent political phenomenon by two authors who are sympathetic to the Greens.)

DEMETZ, PETER. *Postwar German Literature.* New York: Pegasus, 1970.

ERHARD, LUDWIG. *Germany's Comeback in the World Market.* New York: Macmillan, 1954. (Somewhat self-congratulatory account by the "father" of West Germany's "social market economy.")

FELDMAN, LILY G. *The Special Relationship Between West Germany and Israel.* London: Allen & Unwin, 1984. (An important contribution to a somewhat tabu subject.)

FISHER, STEPHAN L. *The Minor Parties of the Federal Republic.* The Hague, The Netherlands: Nijhoff, 1974.

GRIFFITH, WILLIAM C. *The Ostpolitik of the Federal*

Republic of Germany. Cambridge, MA: MIT Press, 1978.

GROSSER, ALFRED. *Germany in Our Time.* Trans. by Paul Stephenson. New York: Praeger, 1971. (Insightful and sympathetic history by a leading French political scientist.)

HANRIEDER, WOLFRAM, ed. *Helmut Schmidt: Perspectives on Politics.* Boulder, CO: Westview Press, 1982.

———. *West German Foreign Policy, 1949–1979.* Boulder, CO: Westview Press, 1980.

KATCHER, LEO. *Post Mortem: The Jews of Germany Today.* New York: Delacorte Press, 1968. (Somewhat dated account of a unique and painful subject.)

KLINEBERG, OTTO, et al. *Students, Values, and Protests: A Crosscultural Comparison.* New York: Free Press, 1979. (Deals among other topics with the role of the APO and West German terrorist groups in the 1970s.)

KOKINSKY, EVA. *Parties, Opposition, and Society in West Germany.* New York: St. Martin, 1984.

LAQUEUR, WALTER. *Germany Today: A Personal Report.* Boston: Houghton, Mifflin, 1985.

LATTIMORE, BERTRAM C. *The Assimilation of German Expellees into the West German Polity and Society Since 1945.* The Hague, The Netherlands: Nijhoff, 1974.

MAIER, CHARLES S. *The Unmasterable Past: History, Holocaust and German National Identity.* Cambridge, MA: Harvard University Press, 1988. (The best English-language treatment of the *Historikerstreit.*)

MARKOVITS, ANDREI S., ed. *The Political Economy of West Germany: Modell Deutschland.* New York: Praeger, 1982.

MENDERHAUSEN, HORST. *Two Postwar Recoveries of the German Economy.* Amsterdam: North Holland Publ. Co., 1955.

MERKL, PETER H. *German Foreign Policies: West and East.* Santa Barbara, CA: ABC-Clio, 1974.

NAGLE, JOHN D. *The National Democratic Party: Right-Radicalism in the Federal Republic of Germany.* Berkeley: University of California Press, 1970.

PAPADAKIS, ELIM. *The Green Movement in West Germany.* New York: St. Martin, 1984.

POLLOCK, JAMES K., et al. *German Democracy at Work.* Ann Arbor: University of Michigan Press, 1955. (Pollock was one of Gen. Clay's civilian political advisors.)

PRIDHAM, GEOFFREY. *Christian Democracy in Western Germany: The CDU/CSU in Government and Opposition, 1945–1976.* New York: St. Martin, 1977.

PRITTIE, TERENCE. *The Velvet Chancellors: A History of Postwar Germany.* New York: Holmes & Meier, 1979.

———. *Willy Brandt: Portrait of a Statesman.* New York: Schocken Books, 1974.

SCHICK, JACK M. *The Berlin Crisis, 1958–1962.* Philadelphia: University of Pennsylvania Press, 1971.

SIMONIAN, HAIG. *The Privileged Partnership: Franco-German Relations in the European Community, 1969–1984.* New York: Oxford University Press, 1985.

SPOTTS, FREDERIC. *The Churches and Politics in Germany.* Middletown, CT: Wesleyan University Press, 1973.

TAUBER, KURT P. *Beyond Eagle and Swastika: German Nationalism Since 1945.* Middletown, CT: Wesleyan University Press, 1967. (Interesting and detailed, but somewhat dated account written at a time when neo-Nazism was felt to be a major threat to West German democracy.)

TILTON, T. A. *Nazism, Neo-Nazism, and the Peasantry.* Bloomington: Indiana University Press, 1975. (An attempt to update the Heberle entry listed earlier [chapter 6].)

WHETTEN, LAWRENCE L. *Germany's Ostpolitik: Relations Between the Federal Republic and the Warsaw Pact Countries.* London: Oxford University Press, 1971.

CHAPTER 11: THE GERMAN DEMOCRATIC REPUBLIC, 1949–1990

BARING, ARNULF M. *Uprising in East Germany: June 17, 1953.* Ithaca, NY: Cornell University Press, 1972.

BAYLIS, THOMAS A. *The Technical Intelligentsia and the East German Elite: Legitimacy and Social Change in Mature Communism.* Berkeley: University of California Press, 1974.

CHILDS, DAVID. *The GDR: Moscow's German Ally.* London: Allen & Unwin, 1983. (Despite some superficialities, this is probably the best introduction to the GDR.)

DENNIS, MIKE. *German Democratic Republic: Politics,*

Economics, and Society. New York: Columbia University Press, 1988.

FLORES, JOHN. *Poetry in East Germany: Adjustments, Visions, and Provocations, 1945–1970.* New Haven, CT: Yale University Press, 1971. (Important analysis of a medium that in Eastern Europe is often used to express disagreements with the regime.)

HONECKER, ERICH. *From My Life.* New York: Pergamon, 1981.

HUEBENER, THEODORE. *The Literature of East Germany.* New York: Ungar, 1970.

IGGERS, GEORG, ed. *Social History in the GDR: New Orientations in Recent East European Historiography.* New York: Berg, 1989.

LEPTIN, G., and M. MELZER. *Economic Reforms in East German Industry.* Trans. by Roger A. Clarke. London: Oxford University Press, 1978.

LUDZ, PETER CHRISTIAN. *The German Democratic Republic from the Sixties to the Seventies: A Socio-Political Analysis.* Cambridge, MA: Center for International Affairs, 1970.

MCADAMS, A. JAMES. *East Germany and Detente: Building Authority After the Wall.* New York: Cambridge University Press, 1985.

MCCAULEY, MARTIN. *Marxism-Leninism in the German Democratic Republic.* Totowa, NJ: Barnes & Noble, 1979.

SONTHEIMER, KURT, and WILHELM BLEEK. *The Government and Politics of East Germany.* Trans. by Ursula Price. New York: St. Martin, 1975.

SLUSSER, ROBERT M. *The Berlin Crisis of 1961.* Baltimore: Johns Hopkins University Press, 1973.

STEELE, JONATHAN. *Inside East Germany: The State That Came in from the Cold.* New York: Urizen Books, 1977.

WALLACE, I., ed. *The GDR Under Honecker, 1971–1981.* Dundee, UK: GDR Monitor, 1981.

INDEX

K

L